PERCEPTUAL ORGANIZATION

PERCEPTUAL ORGANIZATION

Edited by

MICHAEL KUBOVY
Rutgers—The State University

JAMES R. POMERANTZ
State University of New York at Buffalo

 LAWRENCE ERLBAUM ASSOCIATES, PUBLISHERS
1981   Hillsdale, New Jersey

Lawrence Erlbaum Associates, Inc., Publishers
365 Broadway
Hillsdale, New Jersey 07642

Library of Congress Cataloging in Publication Data
Main entry under title:

Perceptual organization.

Bibliography: p.
Includes index.
1. Gestalt psychology. 2. Visual perception.
3. Auditory perception. I. Kubovy, Michael.
II. Pomerantz, James R.
BF203.P3   153.7   81-786
ISBN 0-89859-056-6   AACR2

Printed in the United States of America

Contents

Preface

Perceptual organization has been synonymous with Gestalt psychology, and Gestalt psychology has fallen into disrepute. In the heyday of Behaviorism, the few cognitive psychologists of the time pursued Gestalt phenomena. But today, Cognitive Psychology is married to Information Processing. (Some would say that it was a marriage of convenience.) After the wedding, Cognitive Psychology has come to look like a theoretically wrinkled Behaviorism; very few of the mainstream topics of Cognitive Psychology make explicit contact with Gestalt phenomena. In the background, Cognition's first love—Gestalt—is pining to regain favor.

The cognitive psychologists' desire for a phenomenological and intellectual interaction with Gestalt psychology did not manifest itself in their publications, but it did surface often enough at the Psychonomic Society meeting in 1976 for us to remark upon it in one of our conversations. We also noticed that in their talks, our colleagues mentioned Gestalt as some might praise a novel like *Lolita:* —with faint embarrassment, brought on by concern that one's audience might think one enjoyed it for the wrong reasons.

This book, then, is the product of our curiosity about the current status of ideas first proposed by Gestalt psychologists. For two days in November 1977, we held an exhilarating symposium, supported by Larry Erlbaum (to whom we and all the participants are ever so grateful), that was attended by some 20 people, not all of whom are represented in this volume. At the end of our symposium it was agreed that we would try, in our contributions to this volume, to convey the speculative and metatheoretical ground of our research in addition to the solid data and carefully wrought theories that are the figure of our research.

This is the first volume devoted to perceptual organization since Köhler's last book, *The Task of Gestalt Psychology*, was published in 1969. True, several important books in the past decade were strongly influenced by Gestalt ideas (Kahneman's *Attention and Effort*, Garner's *The Processing of Information and Structure*, Gibson's *The Ecological Approach to Visual Perception*), but each was written from a special point of view and did not provide the reader with an appreciation of the wealth of problems the Gestalt approach inspired. Nor could they show how much theoretical disagreement still surrounds the very concept of perceptual organization. Both these aims are achieved in this volume.

This is also the first time that auditory perception has played more than a minor role in discussions of perceptual organization. We wished to make demonstrations, which are such an important part of discussions of perceptual organization, as available for the *auditory* chapters as for the visual ones. Unfortunately, sounds are not as easy to reproduce as pictures. So we have prepared a cassette tape recording to accompany the book. Probably the only recording of its kind, it contains demonstrations to accompany the chapters by Bregman, Kubovy, and Shepard (as well as two by Diana Deutsch) and can be obtained from Lawrence Erlbaum Associates. It is described in the pages following this Preface. We urge all readers to obtain this tape; the extra cost will be well rewarded.

Most of the material in this book is comprehensible to any of those who have had some exposure to theories and research in perception, be they psychologists, physiologists, or students of visual arts or music. We think that it can serve well as an adjunct to teaching at both the undergraduate and graduate levels. At the same time, the book contains many findings that are new—by virtue of not having been published before, or by virtue of the new context in which they are embedded; and as such, we expect the book to be of greatest interest to our colleagues who are engaged in perceptual research.

We wish to thank Loretta Polka for preparing the reference index; and Janet Davis and Michael Muller for their cheerful assistance in reading proofs.

Michael Kubovy
James R. Pomerantz

Three chapters in this volume (by Bregman, by Kubovy, and by Shepard) refer to auditory phenomena. We are making illustrative recordings of these phenomena available on a stereo cassette. On this cassette we have also included two important demonstrations recorded by Diana Deutsch. The cassette may be obtained from Lawrence Erlbaum Associates. For the convenience of the reader who does not have the recording at hand, we have summarized the contents of this cassette (and have provided timings in parentheses).

Contents of the Cassette

SIDE 1

(monophonic, recorded on left channel)

General Introduction (*55 sec*).

ALBERT BREGMAN
  Introduction (*10 sec*).
  Illustration 1: Backwards speech (*25 sec*).
  Illustration 2: Random sounds (*28 sec*).
  Illustration 3: Warren's loop of four unrelated sounds (*48 sec*).
  Illustration 4: Bregman and Campbell's loop of three high tones alternating with three low tones, producing streaming (*36 sec*).
  Illustration 5: Dannenbring and Bregman's illustration of the effects of continuity in streaming.
    Introduction (*8 sec*).
    Part 1: Loop of alternating high and low tones connected by Pitch-glides, which tends to resist streaming (*35 sec*).
    Part 2: The same loop of tones without the pitch-glides is more likely to produce streaming (*35 sec*).
  Illustration 6: Two streams are formed by the alternation of a 1000-Hz tone and the burst of a band of white noise centered about 1000 Hz (*47 sec*).
  Illustration 7:
    Part 1: A tone repetitively glides up and down in frequency. The instants of reversal from ascending to descending glide and from descending to

Illustration 11: A pair of target tones is played once, then played again bracketed by two lower distractor tones.

Part 1: The order of the target tones is hard to judge (*42 sec*).

Part 2: The addition of a stream of tones at the same frequency as the distractor tones "strip off" the distractor tones, isolating the target tones in their own stream. The order of the target tones is easier to judge (*55 sec*).

ROGER S. SHEPARD

The decoupling of auditory pitch from sound frequency. The pitch appears to undergo a continuous ascending glide, even though the frequency of the tones is higher at the beginning of the demonstration than at the end. The demonstration is repeated three times (*1 min, 55 sec*).

SIDE 2

(some segments are stereophonic)

General introduction (*42 sec*).

MICHAEL KUBOVY

Introduction (*14 sec*).

Illustration 1 (stereophonic): Binaural pitch segregation without monaural familiarity cues.

Introduction (*14 sec*).

Part 1: Sample of the left ear input (*25 sec*).

Part 2: Sample of the right ear input (*25 sec*).

Part 3: Continuing with the right ear channel, the left ear channel is faded in. A well-known tune is heard. Then the right ear channel is faded out; the tune fades out too (*1 min, 20 sec*).

Conclusion: The name of the tune is revealed, and the cause of the clicks explained (*35 sec*).

Illustration 2 (right channel only): Intensity-change pitch segregation.

Part 1: A chord composed of six tones separated by more than a critical band (here eight semitones), is heard at all times. No new components are introduced into the chord. Nevertheless a scale is heard. Each note of the scale is played by first decreasing the intensity of that tone (by 12 dB) and then restoring it to its original intensity, .03 seconds later. The scale is played at about 3 notes per second. This effect is not easy for some to perceive at first, and should be listened to several times patiently (*1 min, 45 sec*).

Part 2: When the tones are less than a critical band apart no segregation is heard. Here the tones are two semitones apart (*52 sec*).

Part 3: Ruling out spectral splatter as the cause of the onset segregation. Every time the intensity of the target tone is changed, the intensity of all the other tones deviates from their standard level by the same number of decibels for .005 seconds. Despite the numerous abrupt changes applied to the background tones, the scale formed by the target tones can still be discerned.

Illustration 3 (right channel only): Segregation of harmonics of a complex tone by phase.

A 100 Hz buzz is played, composed of 12 pure tones ranging from 300 Hz to 1400 Hz separated by 100 Hz intervals and aligned in cosine phase. A scale is heard, as if emerging from the buzz, consisting of the components of the complex tone. The segregation is caused by shifting the phase of each component of the complex tone so that it is not aligned in cosine phase with the others, and then returning it to cosine phase at the same time the next note of the scale is shifted out of phase. At that instant the phases of all the other components of the complex tone are reset to cosine phase, causing a click to be heard at the beginning of each note of the scale (*3 min, 15 sec.*).

DIANA DEUTSCH

Illustration 1 (stereophonic): the octave illusion.

The right ear receives a loop of alternating 400 and 800 Hz tones; the left ear receives a complementary loop of alternating 800 and 400 Hz tones. Almost no one interprets this stimulus veridically. In addition to listening to this illustration as instructed by the narrator, it is illuminating to listen to each channel separately. (See Deutsch, 1975a, 1980.)

Illustration 2 (stereophonic): The scale illusion.

Notes of the ascending C-major scale are alternated between right and left ears, while concurrently notes of the descending C-major scale are alternated between the ears, so that when the right ear receives a note of the descending scale, the left ear receives a note of the ascending scale. (See Deutsch, 1975a, 1975b, 1980.)

PERCEPTUAL ORGANIZATION

1 Psychophysics of Spatial-Frequency Channels

Norma Graham
Columbia University

ABSTRACT

The concepts of spatial-frequency analysis (Fourier analysis) and of spatial-frequency channels are briefly introduced. The various kinds of psychophysical experiments providing evidence for spatial-frequency channels are discussed at some length. Tentative conclusions from these experiments about properties of the spatial-frequency channels are then described. Finally, several ways in which spatial-frequency analyses might be useful in explaining perceptual phenomena are mentioned.

INTRODUCTION

During the last decade, various investigators have suggested using spatial-frequency analyses of visual stimuli to help understand perceptual phenomena. At the very least, spatial-frequency analyses are enlightening simply as a new description of visual stimuli. In a sense, spatial-frequency descriptions and pointwise descriptions are opposites. A stimulus consisting of a single spatial frequency is completely localized on the frequency dimension but infinitely extended in space, while a stimulus consisting of a single point is completely localized in space but infinitely extended on the frequency dimension. Having two such different descriptions that emphasize different aspects of the stimulus may well suggest ideas to the human investigator who is trying to understand visual perception.

In the long run, however, spatial-frequency analyses will be most useful if they help in describing not just the stimuli themselves but the visual system's responses to the stimuli as well. A large number of psychophysical results are now being explained on the assumption that the visual system contains multiple channels, each sensitive to a different range of spatial frequencies. The ability of this concept of multiple spatial-frequency channels to account for a wide range of psychophysical evidence is quite impressive. Perhaps it will be able to account for perceptual phenomena as well.

The psychophysical evidence for the existence of spatial-frequency channels is less clear-cut, however, than some investigators seem to believe, and the probable properties of the channels are somewhat different from those frequently assumed in discussions of visual perception. The purpose of this chapter is to introduce and discuss the body of psychophysical evidence regarding spatial-frequency channels in the hope that a clearer understanding of this evidence will aid in developing and evaluating explanations of visual perception that depend on spatial-frequency analyses.

First, the concepts of spatial-frequency analysis (that is, Fourier analysis) and of spatial-frequency channels are briefly introduced. More extensive introduction can be found in a number of places (e.g., Cornsweet, 1970; Graham, 1979; Julesz, 1980a; Weisstein & Harris, 1980a). Then the various kinds of psychophysical experiments providing evidence for spatial-frequency channels are discussed at some length. After this section on psychophysical evidence, the probable properties of spatial-frequency channels in the human visual system (or the possible meanings of the phrase *spatial-frequency channels*) are described. Finally, a very brief section mentions several ways in which spatial-frequency analyses might help in explaining perceptual phenomena.

Fourier Analysis

To understand Fourier analysis as applied to visual patterns, begin by considering one simple pattern—a *sinusoidal grating*. A sinusoidal grating is a pattern that looks like a set of blurry, alternating dark and light stripes. In such a pattern, the luminance in the direction perpendicular to the stripes varies sinusoidally, whereas the luminance in the direction parallel to the stripes is constant. As this chapter is not concerned with color, we generally ignore wavelength, making the assumption that the wavelength composition of the light is approximately the same at every point of a pattern. Several parameters are used in describing sinusoidal gratings. The one of most concern here is *spatial frequency*, which is the number of cycles of sinusoid per unit distance or, in other words, the number of dark-bar–light-bar pairs per unit distance. (The usual unit of distance is a degree of visual angle.) Spatial frequency and size of bar are inversely proportional to each other; a grating of high spatial frequency has narrow bars, and a grating of low spatial frequency has wide bars. The *mean luminance* of a grating is the average of the luminances at every point across the whole spatial extent of the grating. The *contrast* of a grating is a measure of the difference between the maximum luminance and minimum luminance, usually taken to be one-half that difference divided by the mean luminance. One of the attractions of sinusoidal gratings is that the mean luminance of a grating can easily be held constant, keeping the observer in a relatively constant state of light adaptation, while the contrast and spatial frequency are varied.

Now consider any visual stimulus, the luminance of which varies along only one dimension (called a one-dimensional visual stimulus). As follows from a theorem due to the 18th-century mathematician Fourier, *any* such stimulus can be constructed by superimposing sinusoidal gratings of different spatial frequencies, contrasts, and phases (positions). Further, there is only one set of sinusoidal gratings that can be superimposed to form a particular stimulus. Thus, any one-dimensional visual stimulus can be described as containing certain spatial frequencies. The amount and phase of each spatial frequency contained in a stimulus (the contrast and phase of the component sinusoidal grating of that spatial frequency) are given by the *Fourier transform* of the stimulus.

Analysis into spatial frequencies is not restricted to one-dimensional visual stimuli. Consider an ordinary black-and-white photograph as an example of a two-dimensional visual stimulus. Any such pattern can be constructed by adding up sinusoidal gratings that differ in orientation as well as in contrast and phase. The amount and phase of each spatial frequency at each orientation is given by a *two-dimensional Fourier transform*. Fourier transforms can be computed in higher dimensions as well.

For lack of space, this chapter concentrates on one-dimensional patterns differing in spatial-frequency content but identical in orientation. Many experiments have used one-dimensional patterns differing in orientation but identical in spatial-frequency content, and some experiments have used two-dimensional patterns varying both in spatial frequency and orientation. The only discussion of these experiments on orientation occurs in the "Sensitivity Characteristics: Bandwidth" section. The third dimension, depth, is ignored entirely.

Spatial-Frequency Channels

Let's start by considering one extreme kind of spatial-frequency-channel model. Consider a set of channels, each of which is sensitive to a very narrow range of spatial frequencies, a range so narrow that the channel effectively responds to only one spatial frequency (the channel's *characteristic* spatial frequency). Suppose that in response to a visual stimulus, the output of each channel is a single number (or two numbers) proportional to the amplitude (or amplitude and phase) of the channel's characteristic spatial frequency in the stimulus. Suppose also that there exist a very large number of channels with characteristic frequencies covering the whole range of spatial frequencies responded to by the human visual system. Then, for any visual stimulus, the function relating the one output (or two outputs) of each channel to the channel's characteristic spatial frequency is a good approximation of the amplitude part (or amplitude and phase parts) of the Fourier transform of that stimulus. One might say, therefore, that such a set of channels actually performs a strict Fourier analysis. This extreme kind of spatial-frequency-channel model can be rejected easily, however, as a description of the bulk of psychophysical results.

Another extreme kind of "spatial-frequency-channel model" claims only that there are different subsystems sensitive to different ranges of spatial frequency. In this sense, spatial-frequency channels certainly do exist, for individual neurons are known to respond to different ranges of spatial frequency. (See Movshon, Thompson, & Tolhurst, 1978, for example.)

Investigators of visual psychophysics and perception, however, generally want something more of spatial-frequency channels. They want these channels to play an important role in explaining visual phenomena. Whether such interesting channels can reasonably be said to exist and, if so, what they are like are the questions of concern here.

Because the search for empirical evidence in favor of channels and the development of alternative conceptions of the channels have proceeded concurrently, further discussion of the concept of spatial-frequency channels is postponed until experimental results have been presented.

PSYCHOPHYSICAL EVIDENCE FOR SPATIAL-FREQUENCY CHANNELS

The use of spatial frequencies in describing visual stimuli is only two or three decades old, and the papers explicitly proposing spatial-frequency channels in the visual system are even more recent (Campbell & Robson, 1964, 1968; Enroth-Cugell & Robson, 1966). In the short time since then, however, a great deal of work has been done. I make no attempt, therefore, to mention all relevant work but give references to the original studies and to representative recent ones. This section of this chapter presents the major results from different kinds of psychophysical experiments and outlines the usual argument made from each kind for the existence of spatial-frequency channels. The next section describes tentative conclusions drawn from these experiments about the properties of the spatial-frequency channels.

Effect of Adaptation on Threshold Sensitivity and Suprathreshold Perceived Contrast

In these adaptation experiments, the observer inspects a suprathreshold grating (called the *adapting grating*) for several minutes and then looks at another grating (called the *test grating*). As Pantle and Sekuler (1968) and Blakemore and Campbell (1969) first showed, the contrast thresholds of test gratings close in spatial frequency to the adapting grating (and identical in all characteristics other than spatial frequency) are elevated after adaptation while the thresholds of test gratings further away in spatial frequency are unchanged. Similarly, the perceived contrast of suprathreshold test gratings close in spatial frequency to the adapting grating is reduced after adaptation, although the perceived contrast of test gratings further away in spatial frequency is unchanged (Blakemore, Muncey, & Ridley, 1971, 1973; Hertz, 1973).

These frequency-selective effects in adaptation experiments have often been explained as the result of "desensitization" (or "differential fatigue" or "adaptation") of multiple spatial-frequency channels. If an individual channel adapts (becomes less sensitive) after a period of being excited, the channels responsive to the adapting grating should be less sensitive after the observer inspects the adapting grating than they were before. The channels that are not responsive to the adapting grating should be unchanged by inspecting the adapting grating. On the assumption (1) that detection of a grating occurs whenever the response of at least one channel is big enough and (2) that perceived contrast of a grating is determined by the size of the response of the most responsive channel, this desensitization explanation qualitatively predicts the observed results. Accordingly, the properties of individual channels (in particular, absolute or relative bandwidths) have been inferred from selective adaptation results (e.g., Blakemore & Campbell, 1969; Graham, 1972). Although models of desensitization could be developed to predict quantitatively the effect, for example, of changing contrast in the adapting grating (analogous to Stiles' work on chromatic adaptation), very little theoretical work of this sort has been done (but see Dealy & Tolhurst, 1974, and Graham, 1970).

Recent explanations of selective adaptation effects have tended to invoke inhibition of one type or another rather than desensitization. Inhibition has been suggested by evidence that adapting to a combination of two frequencies produces less threshold elevation than adapting to one frequency alone (Nachmias, Sansbury, Vassilev, & Weber, 1973; Stecher, Sigel, & Lange, 1973; Tolhurst, 1972), by consideration of the minimum amount of contrast needed in the adapting grating (Dealy & Tolhurst, 1974), and by evidence that facilitation is observed when test and adapting frequencies are very far apart (DeValois, 1977; Tolhurst & Barfield, 1978).

If inhibition among channels is involved in the selective adaptation results, the properties of individual channels cannot easily be deduced from these results. It is not yet clear, however, what kind of inhibition, if any, is involved (Tolhurst & Barfield, 1978).

A few attempts have been made to extend these adaptation experiments to aperiodic stimuli like lines, edges, and random dots (Bagrash, 1973; DeValois & Switkes, 1978; Fiorentini, Sireteanu, & Spinelli, 1976; Georgeson & Sullivan, 1975; Legge, 1976; Sullivan, Georgeson, & Oatley, 1972; Williams & Wilson, 1978). If spatial-frequency channels are important, one would expect the effect of any adaptation stimulus on a subsequent test stimulus to depend on the degree to which the stimuli share spatial frequencies. To a large extent, the experimental results agree with this expectation. To compute exactly what effect one would expect, however, is complex. The aperiodic stimuli have all contained a wide range of spatial frequencies. The computation, therefore, would involve a large number of channels, and the exact mechanism of the selective adaptation effect is crucial. Little such computation has been attempted. In any case, although the experimental results are somewhat mixed, the evidence they give of the importance of spatial-frequency content seems quite good enough to encourage further exploration.

As far as one can tell at present, the results from selective adaptation experiments are consistent with the notion of spatial-frequency channels. Before taking these results as compelling evidence for the existence of such channels, however, one should ascertain that there is no other plausible explanation not involving such channels. One explanation often mentioned in this and similar contexts (Harris & Gibson, 1968) is local point-by-point adaptation. This kind of adaptation could occur as peripherally in the visual system as the retinal receptors and would not require any channels selective for spatial frequency. Results using stabilized-image techniques (Jones & Tulunay-Keesey, 1975) make this explanation unattractive, however. A second possibility is the model formulated by Wilson (1975). In this model, there is selective adaptation of the different lengths of connections between neurons. Since all the neurons have receptive fields of the same size, some people would not consider this to be a multiple-spatial-frequency-channels model. (See the section entitled "Summation at Threshold" for further discussion of receptive-field sizes and spatial-frequency channels.) This model is not a viable alternative either, however, because it cannot handle some of the experimental results described later. In short, because the available alternative explanations for spatial-frequency–selective adaptation effects can be ruled out, the adaptation effects do seem to be strong evidence for the existence of channels selectively sensitive to spatial frequency and active in psychophysical situations.

Effect of Masking on Threshold Sensitivity and Suprathreshold Perceived Contrast

In masking experiments, the detectability of one stimulus (the *test stimulus*) is measured in the presence of another (the *mask stimulus*). In some cases, the mask stimulus may precede or follow the test stimulus by a brief interval. (These cases are classified here as masking experiments rather than adaptation experiments because it seems likely, from what is known regarding the time courses of the responses of spatial-frequency channels, that the channels' responses to the mask stimulus and to the test stimulus do overlap in time.) When gratings are used in masking experiments, there is a frequency-selective effect at threshold resembling the effect in adaptation experiments; the threshold elevation is, in general, largest when the frequencies of test and mask gratings are identical. This is true whether the gratings overlap spatially (Legge, 1978; Mostafavi & Sakrison, 1976; Pantle, 1977; Sansbury, 1974; Stromeyer & Julesz, 1972; Tolhurst & Barfield, 1978) or do not overlap spatially (Rogowitz, 1977, 1978), and whether the mask grating is on continuously (e.g., Pantle, 1977) or occurs briefly at the same time as the test grating (e.g., Tolhurst & Barfield, 1978).

Masking also affects suprathreshold perceived contrast or clarity (Weisstein & Bisaha, 1972; Weisstein & Harris, 1980; Weisstein, Harris, Berbaum, Tangney, & Williams, 1977; White & Lorber, 1976). Very few frequencies of gratings have been used in these suprathreshold experiments, but the available evidence does show frequency-specific effects. Further, in Weisstein and co-workers' experiments with aperiodic stimuli, the amount of masking depends on the degree to which the spatial-frequency content of test and mask stimuli overlap.

These frequency-selective masking effects are usually interpreted as evidence for multiple spatial-frequency channels, presumably because it is difficult to think of any acceptable explanation not involving multiple channels. This prevalent interpretation seems reasonable, but how multiple channels lead to masking effects is still unclear. Masking effects, like adaptation effects, could be caused by (1) inhibition between the channels excited by the test stimulus and those exited by the mask stimulus, or (2) desensitization of channels excited by the test stimulus because these channels are also excited by the mask stimulus. Masking effects could also be a result of some kind of interference when the mask stimulus and the test stimulus excite the same channels, or of difficulty at a higher-level decision stage in discriminating between the channels' responses to the test stimulus and those to the mask. Although the clearest statements of possible mechanisms for spatial-frequency-specific masking have usually postulated inhibition among channels (Breitmeyer & Ganz, 1976; Rogowitz, 1978; Weisstein, Ozog, & Szoc, 1975), the way in which this inhibition might work has not been thoroughly specified, nor have other explanations been ruled out.

Several results that seem to challenge any multiple-channels explanation of masking are worth mentioning briefly here. Masking occurs at periodicity frequencies not actually present in the stimuli (Henning, Hertz, & Broadbent, 1975); facilitation occurs for some combinations of mask and test frequencies (Nachmias & Sansbury, 1974; Stromeyer & Klein, 1974; Tolhurst & Barfield, 1978); and there are phase-specific changes in the amount of facilitation between a frequency and its third harmonic after adaptation to a square wave containing both (Sansbury, Distelhorst, & Moore, 1978).

Effect of Adaptation and Masking on Perceived Spatial Frequency

The experiments described earlier did not investigate directly the perception of spatial frequency or of size. They investigated directly the perception of contrast—either the perceived contrast of suprathreshold stimuli or the physical contrast of threshold stimuli. When the perceived frequency of test gratings is itself measured, it too is affected by previous exposure to an adapting grating (Blakemore, Nachmias, & Sutton, 1970; Blakemore & Sutton, 1969) or by the simultaneous presence of a spatially nonoverlapping masking grating (Klein, Stromeyer, & Ganz, 1974). Test gratings of frequencies somewhat higher than the adapting or masking grating look even higher; test gratings of somewhat lower frequencies look even lower; and test gratings of the same or very different frequencies seem unchanged.

The original explanation of this shift in perceived spatial frequency (Blakemore & Sutton, 1969) borrows two of the assumptions used in the desensitization explanations for the effects on threshold sensitivity and suprathreshold perceived contrast: (1) that multiple spatial-frequency channels exist, and (2) that adaptation to a pattern depresses the sensitivity of channels responding to that pattern. A third assumption, about the determinant of perceived frequency, is also needed to explain the shift in perceived frequency. (It takes the place of the assumptions about the determinants of contrast threshold and perceived contrast that were used in the earlier explanations.) Blakemore and Sutton (1969) assumed that perceived frequency is equal to the best frequency of whichever channel is most sensitive to the test grating (or perhaps to the frequency that equals some measure of central tendency of the distribution of all responding channels). According to these assumptions, adaptation depresses the sensitivity of the channels that responded to the adapting grating. Then, if the test frequency is close to the adapting frequency, the distribution of responses to that test frequency over all the channels will be different from usual, because the adapting grating will have desensitized some of the channels. The perceived frequency, therefore, will be biased away from the adapting frequency.

Unlike the corresponding assumptions about threshold and perceived contrast, this assumption about the determinant of perceived frequency requires that the output signals from different channels *not be* completely interchangeable. Any channel at all can be made to signal a threshold response or signal any given level of perceived contrast (by adjusting the contrast of the stimuli appropriately). But there is no way, according to this assumption about perceived frequency, that channels having different best frequencies can signal the same perceived frequency. Channels having best frequencies near a low spatial frequency, for example, cannot signal the same perceived frequency as channels having best frequencies near a high spatial frequency. In other words, to explain the shift in perceived spatial frequency, the channels are assumed not only to be selectively *sensitive* to spatial frequency but also to selectively *signal* spatial frequency.

Although the foregoing explanation of shifts in perceived spatial frequency is satisfactory at a qualitative level, there is some question as to its ability to account quantitatively for both threshold elevations and perceived spatial-frequency shifts simultaneously (Klein et al., 1974). Surprisingly little work has been published about the shifts in perceived spatial frequency, however, so one cannot be sure of the data, much less of the explanation.

Contingent Aftereffects of Adaptation

After an observer has adapted alternately to a red-and-black grating of one spatial frequency and a green-and-black grating of another spatial frequency, the appearance of a test grating that looked white and black previous to adaptation depends on its spatial frequency. (All gratings are of the same orientation.) If the frequency of the test grating is the same as one of the adapting gratings (e.g., the red-and-black adapting grating), the previously white bars will now appear faintly colored with a hue roughly complementary to that in the adapting grating (e.g., a faint green). If the frequency is slightly different from the adapting frequency, the colored aftereffect will be even fainter. These colored aftereffects contingent on spatial frequency, which are analogous to the original colored aftereffects contingent on orientation demonstrated by McCollough (1965), have been demonstrated in a number of studies (Green, Corwin, & Zemon, 1976; Harris, 1970, 1971; Lovegrove & Over, 1972; May & Matteson, 1976; Stromeyer, 1972; Teft & Clark, 1968). Contingent aftereffects can also be produced using orientation and spatial frequency, with the perceived orientation contingent on the stimulus spatial frequency or vice versa (Wyatt, 1974). Colored aftereffects contingent jointly on orientation and spatial frequency have also been reported (Wyatt, 1974).

These contingent aftereffects are sometimes qualitatively explained in a fashion similar to that used for explaining the perceived shifts in spatial frequency. The explanation invokes multiple channels selectively sensitive to narrow ranges of color, orientation, and spatial frequency (see Sigel & Nachmias, 1975, or Wyatt, 1974, for example). The channels are assumed to signal values selectively along each dimension. For example, the perceived value along a given dimension might be determined by the channel responding most to the stimulus or by some measure of central tendency of the distribution of responding channels. Adaptation is assumed to desensitize the channels responding to the adapting grating. Therefore, after adaptation to a red-and-black, low-spatial-frequency grating, for example, the channels sensitive to "red" wavelengths and low spatial frequencies will be fatigued. A white-and-black, low-spatial-frequency test grating will elicit less response from those channels sensitive to "red" wavelengths and low spatial frequencies than it usually does. Thus the perceived color will be biased away from red toward the complement of red, and white bars of the test grating will look faintly green.

These contingent aftereffects have certain properties that, to some people at least, seem odd if the aftereffects come from desensitization of sensory channels (Mayhew & Anstis, 1972). For example, contingent aftereffects last for weeks or even months (Jones & Holding, 1975; Riggs, White, & Eimas, 1974), and there is a report that they can be produced by imagining the color in the adapting stimuli (Finke & Schmidt, 1977). These properties have led to the suggestion that the contingent aftereffects are examples of learning, with the frequent implication that they may not demonstrate the properties of sensory channels at all (Harris, 1979; Mayhew & Anstis, 1972; Murch, 1976; Skowbo, Timney, Gentry & Morant, 1975). There is something appealing about the suggestion that "learning" or long-term changes in the nervous system are involved, but even if the effects are examples of learning, they may well demonstrate the properties of sensory channels. In order to learn, a learner must have input of some sort, and the form of that input must place restrictions on the form of learning.

Summation at Threshold

The experiments described so far all involved adaptation or masking. The experiments described next, however, do not. Rather, with the observers in what is assumed to be a neutral state of pattern adaptation, the detectability of compound patterns containing two or more component patterns is compared to the detectability of each of the component patterns alone. Underlying these experiments is the assumption that when two components excite the same channel, the results should show substantial "summation." In other words, a compound pattern containing two or more component patterns that excite the same channel should be a good deal more detectable than either component alone (because a single channel should be responding more to the compound than to either component). When the components excite different channels, however, the compound should be little or no more detectable than the most detectable component, because no channel responds more to the compound than to one of the components. (There may be a slight increase in detectability due to "probability summation"—that is, to the fact that two or more groups of channels may each have an independent chance to detect the compound pattern, whereas only one group of channels has a chance to detect a component by itself.)

Of all the kinds of experiments on spatial-frequency channels, these experiments exploring summation at threshold are the most extensive and the most quantitative. It is impossible to describe and review them adequately here. I have elsewhere (Graham, 1979) provided an introduction to these experiments and to the models describing them. For our present purposes, the most important summation-at-threshold experiments are those using combinations of sinusoidal components. These "sine-plus-sine" experiments have provided some of the strongest support for the notion of multiple spatial-frequency channels. A compound grating containing two or three sinusoidal components of very different frequencies is only slightly more detectable than its most detectable component; further, the detectability of such a compound grating does not depend on the relative phase of its components (Campbell & Robson, 1964, 1968; Robson & Graham in Graham, 1979; Graham & Nachmias, 1971; Graham, Robson, & Nachmias, 1978; Kulikowski & King-Smith, 1973; Lange, Sigel, & Stecher, 1973; Mostafavi & Sakrison, 1976; Pantle, 1973; Quick & Reichert, 1975; Sachs, Nachmias, & Robson, 1971). Such results are inconsistent with large classes of models postulating only a single channel but are consistent with models postulating multiple channels, each sensitive to a different range of spatial frequency.

Conceptual and experimental progress is being made on the specification of the exact properties of these channels. As several multiple-channel models have been refuted by summation-at-threshold experiments, the class of acceptable models has become better defined. The model that is emerging is usually described in terms of neural receptive fields, much as Thomas (1970) did (although a commitment to particular physiology is often not implied). In this description, each spatial-frequency channel contains a collection of "neural units" (or "neurons" or "detectors"), all with receptive fields of the same size. A collection of neural units with receptive fields having large excitatory centers is part of a low-spatial-frequency channel; a collection with receptive fields having smaller excitatory centers is part of a higher-spatial-frequency channel, and so forth. In one version of this model, the response of any one neural unit to a given pattern is variable, and the variability in different neural units is uncorrelated. An observer is assumed to detect a pattern whenever the response of at least one neural unit exceeds some threshold value. With these models, the detection thresholds of a large variety of patterns (periodic, aperiodic, and combinations thereof) can be quantitatively accounted for (for example, Graham, 1977; Quick, Mullins, & Reichert, 1978; Robson & Graham, 1978; Wilson & Bergen, 1977).

It is important to remember that at best, these summation-at-threshold experiments tell us about the relative sensitivity of different channels to different stimuli. The only signaling assumption required to explain these experiments is a simple one like: "An observer detects a pattern whenever at least one channel does." For these experiments, there is no need to assume that the output signals from different channels have qualitatively different perceptual consequences (much less to specify what the perceptual consequences actually are) and, therefore, no need to assume that the observer can even tell the signals from different channels apart.

Other Kinds of Psychophysical Experiments

The results of several other kinds of psychophysical experiments have been interpreted in terms of spatial-frequency channels. If all psychophysical experiments could be arranged on a continuum from "sensory" through "perceptual" to "cognitive," the ones described next would be further from the sensory end than the ones already described. An attempt to explain perceptual phenomena with the help of spatial-frequency analyses might well begin with a careful investigation of some of the results described next.

Uncertainty Effects. An observer's ability to detect a grating seems to depend on whether or not he or she expects a grating at that spatial frequency. More specifically, it depends on whether gratings of only one frequency are presented in a block of two-alternative, forced-choice trials or whether gratings of several frequencies are presented in random order on different trials of a block. The observer will be correct more often when the frequency is presented alone in a block than when it is intermixed with others (Graham et al., 1978).

Analogous uncertainty effects in the auditory domain have been interpreted by hypothesizing that the observer can pay attention to channels tuned to the appropriate frequency and thus avoid "false alarms" due to noise in other channels (Green & Swets, 1966). When frequencies are intermixed in a block, the observer must pay attention to a greater number of channels. One form of auditory experiment used unbalanced, intermixed blocks in which stimuli of one frequency, the "primary" frequency, were much more frequent than stimuli of any other frequency (Greenberg & Larkin, 1968; Macmillan & Schwartz, 1975). During such blocks, the observer would be expected to pay most attention to the channel tuned to the primary frequency. Then, detectability of stimuli that are processed by the same channels as the primary frequency should be less affected by the uncertainty of the intermixed condition than detectability of stimuli outside those channels' range. As expected, the effect of uncertainty is frequency selective, with the effect being least (the difference between alone and intermixed blocks least) at the primary frequency and becoming greater as the stimulus frequency moves away from the primary frequency. Recently, this frequency selectivity has also been obtained with visual spatial frequency (Davis & Graham, 1979).

Summation of Suprathreshold Contrast.   In an extension of the summation-at-threshold experiments to a suprathreshold case, the perceived "overall contrast" of compound gratings containing two sinusoidal components widely separated in frequency was compared to that of the components alone (Arend & Lange, 1978; Hamerly, Quick, & Reichert, 1977; Quick, Hamerly, & Reichert, 1976). The perceived contrast of the compound was independent of the relative phase of the components and equal to the sum of the perceived contrasts of the components presented alone. Because the perceived contrast of any sinusoidal component was a very nonlinear function of physical contrast, accelerating quickly near threshold, the perceived contrast of a near-threshold compound was almost completely determined by the component with the greater perceived contrast. These results can be explained by assuming that perceived overall contrast is determined by summing the outputs of multiple spatial-frequency channels, where the output of each channel is a nonlinear function of contrast. The results of a study using gratings containing 10 sinusoidal components can also be explained this way (Abel & Quick, 1978).

Recognition Near Threshold.   Several interesting and suggestive aspects of the recognition of near-threshold grating patterns have recently been discovered. For near-threshold sinusoidal gratings, an observer can recognize which of two widely separated frequencies is being presented just as well as he can detect that any pattern is there at all (Furchner, Thomas, & Campbell, 1977; Nachmias & Weber, 1975). Further, there is a range of near-threshold contrasts for which—although the observers can easily tell that a compound grating contains two frequencies (they can discriminate the compound from either frequency alone)—he cannot tell the relative phase of the two frequencies in the compound (Nachmias & Weber, 1975).

These recognition results are easily explained by multiple spatial-frequency channels if the observer can tell which channels are responding to a stimulus but cannot tell the relative phase of frequencies responded to by different channels. It is difficult, however, to imagine a single-channel model that would account for these results, for in most such models, frequency would be recognized on the basis of the response magnitudes at different spatial positions. For example, if peak responses occurred every one-third of a degree, the frequency would be recognized as 3 cycles per degree. But if observers can keep track of response magnitudes at different positions, they could probably recognize phase as well as frequency, because changing the phase changes the pattern of response magnitudes.

If two frequencies are quite close, an observer cannot always recognize which of the two frequencies is being presented (Hirsch, 1977; Thomas & Barker, 1977). This is the expected result, as the two frequencies sometimes excite the same channel.

Masking the Recognizability of Faces.   On the basis of the masking results described earlier, one might expect that adding spatial frequencies near the frequencies in a photograph would interfere with the perception of the photograph more than adding other frequencies. Masking patterns of different spatial-frequency content were added to a photograph of Abraham Lincoln (Harmon & Julesz, 1973). Inspection of the resulting pictures shows that the recognizability of a portrait is greatly impaired by added frequencies close to the frequencies in the portrait but is much less impaired by frequencies farther away. How the perception of faces might be described in terms of outputs from spatial-frequency channels (or in any terms whatsoever) is far from clear. This demonstration is consistent, however, with the notion that channels selectively sensitive to spatial frequency are involved in the recognizability of faces.

Unstable Appearance of Compound Patterns.   The appearance of a compound grating composed of widely separated spatial frequencies fluctuates (Atkinson & Campbell, 1974; Campbell & Howell, 1972). Sometimes the observer sees one component; sometimes the other; sometimes both. If the component frequencies are close together, however, the appearance is stable. These effects are interpreted as the result of alternation between the outputs of different spatial-frequency channels.

Aftereffects Seen on Blank Fields.   Although many effects of adapting to gratings have been extensively investigated (as was described earlier), the spatial-frequency analogue of ordinary colored afterimages has not. Relatively little attention has been paid to the perceptions of an observer presented with an unpatterned field after long exposure to an adapting grating. The perceptions of this sort that have been reported and also some experienced during inspection of the adapting grating seem much more complicated than colored afterimages (Georgeson, 1976a, 1976b). Calling them "psychophysical hallucinations," Georgeson attributes them to antagonism between groups of orientation and spatial-frequency channels (but see MacKay & MacKay, 1976).

Texture Matches.   In an experiment analogous to color matching, observers were required to match the appearance of suprathreshold texture patterns with mixtures of a few "primary" sinusoidal gratings of different spatial frequencies (Richards & Polit, 1974). The observers seemed to need only four different frequencies to make these matches. By the same logic that is used in color matching, these results were interpreted as demonstrating the existence of four (or more) spatial-frequency channels. These channels are not only selectively sensitive to spatial frequency; they also selectively signal spatial frequency.

Perceived Similarity of Textures.   In a related experiment, a set of 30 texture patterns made up of combinations of seven spatial frequencies was used (Harvey & Gervais, 1977). Observers judged the perceived similarity of pairs or triplets of these patterns. Multidimensional-scaling representation of these data showed that a three- or four-dimensional space could account for the structure of the similarity judgments, as is consistent with an explanation based on three or four spatial-frequency channels.

TENTATIVE CONCLUSIONS ABOUT
THE PROPERTIES OF
SPATIAL-FREQUENCY CHANNELS

A century from now, the theory of visual perception may not even mention spatial-frequency channels. Their importance has certainly not been demonstrated conclusively or even compellingly. Further, even if the best explanation of each of the various psychophysical results already described does turn out to be spatial-frequency channels, the channels that explain one result (threshold elevation due to adaptation, for example) will not necessarily be the same as those that explain another (recognition near threshold, for example), and the interrelationship of the different channels may be quite complicated. Still worse, none of the channels may be of any significance in explaining everyday visual perception.

Keeping these cautions in mind, I would like to describe tentatively the picture of spatial-frequency channels that is beginning to emerge from psychophysical studies, with an emphasis on the aspects that seem relevant to spatial-frequency analyses of perceptual phenomena. In presenting such a picture, I do, of course, use personal judgment in weighing conflicting results. Let me point out that my bias favors summation-at-threshold experiments because those are the ones most extensively and quantitatively studied.

This description of spatial-frequency channels starts with what little is known about their signaling characteristics and the rules for combining their outputs. This is followed by a discussion of what is known about their interactions with one another. Channels' sensitivity to different stimuli (including their bandwidths and temporal properties) is then described at some length. The section ends with a brief discussion of how many channels there might be.

Signaling Characteristics and Combination Rules

If spatial-frequency channels are to explain perceptual phenomena, it is essential to answer the question of the perceptual consequences of the output from these channels. One aspect of this general question is that of signal form. Can the output of a channel (at any moment) be represented by a single number giving the magnitude of response? Or should the output be thought of as a function giving a number for each spatial position? (The number for a particular position could be the magnitude of the response of the neural unit having the receptive field that is located at that position and of the appropriate size for the channel in question.) Or does the output from a channel have some totally different set of characteristics?

Another aspect of the question of perceptual consequences is the issue of combination rules. How do the outputs from different channels combine or cooperate to determine the observer's response? What happens to the outputs of the set of spatial-frequency channels, usually conceived of as being relatively "early" in the information-processing hierarchy or relatively "peripheral" in the nervous system, as they enter into complicated perceptual and cognitive operations? (The question of combination rules is at least partially confounded with the question of direct influence from one channel on another. In most cases, it will be difficult to decide whether an observed interaction occurs at the higher level embodied in the combination rules or at the level of the channels.)

Unfortunately, very little is known about the perceptual consequences of the output signals from the spatial-frequency channels. Several points are worth making, however.

In discussion of color channels, the observer is frequently assumed to see a particular color whenever a particular channel responds. In some opponent-color theories, for example, the observer sees amounts of red (or green), blue (or yellow), and white (or black) that are proportional to the magnitudes of positive (or negative) outputs from the red–green, blue–yellow, and white–black channels respectively. In other words, any patch of color is thought to be perceptually analyzable into the component perceptions of red (or green), blue (or yellow), and black (or white), and these component perceptions correspond to the outputs of different channels (Hurvich & Jameson, 1974). In the case of spatial-frequency channels, however, it would not be reasonable to assume that a person sees a grating of a particular spatial frequency whenever a particular channel responds. Such an assumption is clearly inconsistent with everyday perceptions; the world does not, in general, look like superimposed gratings. More promising signaling assumptions are available.

The case of spatial frequency in vision may be similar to the case of frequency in audition. A compound grating consisting of two widely separated spatial frequencies can be seen as the juxtaposition of two sinusoidal gratings of different spatial frequencies, just as an auditory stimulus consisting of two widely separated frequencies can be heard as a chord of two tones of different pitches. Landscapes do not look like superimposed gratings, however; nor do spoken sentences sound like series of overlapping chords.

The example of color channels illustrates another point. In addition to the three opponent channels already referred to, there are indubitably at least three pigments serving color vision. These pigments are, of course, selectively *sensitive* to wavelength. Further, they *signal* wavelength selectively in the sense that the output signal from one pigment is not completely interchangeable with the output signal of another pigment at some point upstream (for normal observers). The output signal from any one pigment, however, does not correspond to any one of the perceptual components of color. In short, according to modern theory, there are at least two levels of color channels; both levels are selectively sensitive to wavelength and selectively signal wavelength, but only the higher level produces output signals that correspond in any simple way to perceptual components (Hurvich & Jameson, 1974). There is every reason to suspect that the processing of spatial-frequency information is at least this complicated, for we do not even have a clear idea of what the perceptual components of pattern or spatial vision might be.

Interesting answers to these questions of spatial-frequency channels' signaling characteristics and combination rules could be provided by psychophysical results that imply selective signaling of spatial frequency. The perceived spatial-frequency shift, the contingent aftereffects, and the recognition-near-threshold results are examples of such results and do suggest strongly that selective signaling exists. Unfortunately, most results of this kind have not yet been thoroughly investigated or are equivocal in the sense of being difficult to explain quantitatively within a multiple-channels framework.

Signaling characteristics are mentioned again in the section on temporal sensitivity characteristics.

Interactions Among Channels

The contrast thresholds of observers in a neutral state of pattern adaptation are consistent with channels that are independent of one another (see Graham et al., 1978, for example). This independence is of two kinds. First, there is probabilistic independence. The variability in the response of a channel to repeated presentations of the same stimulus is completely uncorrelated with the variability in every other channel's response; or, as is often said, there is probability summation among channels. Second, there is noninteraction among the average responses of different channels. That is, the average response of a channel to a stimulus (averaged over repeated presentations of the same stimulus) depends only on that channel's sensitivity to the spatial frequencies contained in the stimulus and is not influenced by how much or how little any other channel responds to that stimulus.

Several results are not easy to explain if the channels are always independent. In particular, several of the masking and adaptation results described earlier, where one of the patterns involved is suprathreshold or the observer is not in a neutral state of pattern adaptation, seem inconsistent with independent channels. Consequently, various forms of nonindependence have been proposed. Inhibitory interactions are the current favorite. The exact nature of this inhibition has not been specified, however. To put it another way, it has not yet been demonstrated that inhibition among channels could rigorously account for even one of the results it is invoked to explain, much less that one kind of inhibition could account for several of the results. Such a demonstration would handsomely repay the work necessary to attempt it.

Sensitivity Characteristics

Several types of psychophysical results imply channels that are selectively sensitive to spatial frequency without, however, implying channels that selectively signal spatial frequency. Many of these experiments (e.g., summation-at-threshold, effect of masking, and adaptation on thresholds) have been done and done carefully. They give us a good deal of information about the sensitivity of spatial-frequency channels to different stimuli.

Bandwidth. How large a range of spatial frequencies does an individual channel respond to? The very smallest estimates of bandwidth come from the original interpretations of sine-plus-sine summation-at-threshold experiments (Kulikowski & King-Smith, 1973; Quick & Reichert, 1975; Sachs, Nachmias, & Robson, 1971), but even according to these estimates, the range of frequencies responded to by an individual channel was not very narrow. Recent interpretations of sine-plus-sine experiments, which take into account independent variability in the responses of neural units at different spatial positions (Graham &

Rogowitz, 1976; Mostafavi & Sakrison, 1976; Quick et al., 1978) and also the interpretations of adaptation, masking, and near-threshold recognition experiments (see references given earlier), suggest a medium bandwidth (perhaps an octave at half amplitude).

Suppose (as was suggested in the earlier section, "Summation at Threshold") that a channel is conceived of as a collection of neural units having receptive fields that are identical in all properties except visual field location. Then one can interpret the bandwidth of a channel in terms of these receptive-field properties. Each receptive field has an excitatory center and inhibitory flanks and may have further secondary excitatory and inhibitory sections. The frequency responded to maximally by a channel is determined by the size of the receptive-field sections, with larger sections corresponding to lower frequencies. The bandwidth of a channel is determined by the number of sections in each receptive field. A channel in which each receptive field has only an excitatory center and inhibitory flanks responds to a relatively wide range of spatial frequencies. As secondary excitatory and inhibitory flanks are added to the outside of each receptive field, the range of frequencies to which the channel responds shrinks. In general, the greater the number of subsections in the receptive field, the smaller the range of frequencies; for if there are a very large number of subsections, even a small change in stimulus frequency away from the channel's best frequency produces a mismatch between the stimulus and the receptive field. (See Graham, 1979, for further explanation.) A bandwidth of about an octave corresponds to receptive fields that have an excitatory center, inhibitory flanks, and, perhaps, secondary excitatory outer flanks.

For a complete description of the sensitivity characteristics of a channel, one needs to know the orientation bandwidth as well as the spatial-frequency bandwidth; in other words, one needs to know the region in two-dimensional Fourier space to which the channel is sensitive. In terms of receptive fields, one needs to know how elongated the excitatory and inhibitory regions of the field are. If they are very long relative to their width, the receptive field will respond only to a very limited range of orientations. At the other extreme, if the excitatory and inhibitory regions are circular and concentric, the receptive field will respond equally well to all orientations. Much psychophysical evidence suggests that the channels respond only to a limited range of orientations. The narrowest orientation bandwidth estimates come from the original interpretations of summation-at-threshold experiments. More recent interpretations of these experiments and also of the results of selective adaptation and masking experiments suggest a rather broader bandwidth. (Many references are relevant here, but for lack of space, only a few representative ones can be given: Blakemore, Carpenter, & Georgeson, 1970; Blakemore, Muncey, & Ridley, 1973; Blakemore & Nachmias, 1971; Campbell & Kulikowski, 1966; Ellis, 1977; Kulikowski, Abadi, & King-Smith, 1973; Thomas & Shimamura, 1975; Tolhurst & Thompson, 1975.)

In any case, an individual channel certainly responds to more than a single spatial frequency and to more than a single orientation. The set of spatial-frequency channels is certainly not doing a strict Fourier analysis in the sense of the extreme model presented in the introduction.

Nonuniformity of the Visual Field.   The visibility of high spatial frequencies relative to low ones decreases as one goes from the center to the periphery of the visual field. To account for this, the relative sensitivities of different spatial-frequency channels must shift as one goes from the center to the periphery. The quantitative description of this inhomogeneity is beginning to be worked out (e.g., Limb & Rubinstein, 1977; Robson & Graham, 1978; Wilson & Bergen, 1977; Wilson & Giese, 1977). This nonuniformity of the visual field is not so great, however, as to separate spatially the channels sensitive to different frequencies. At each location in the visual field, there must be more than one responsive spatial-frequency channel or, in other terms, more than one size of receptive field (Graham et al., 1978).

Temporal Sensitivity Characteristics

Fast and Slow Responses.   Trade-offs between temporal and spatial visual resolution have long been noted. This spatiotemporal trade-off is evident in the different temporal characteristics of the visual system's responses to different spatial frequencies. The responses to low spatial frequencies are, in general, "faster" than the responses to high spatial frequencies. Let me distinguish among four possible ways in which responses might be "fast" or "slow" before discussing the temporal characteristics of different spatial-frequency channels.

Three of the ways concern responses to stationary stimuli. Consider the response to the onset of a stationary, long-duration stimulus. First, there may be a *delay* between the onset of the stimulus and the onset of the response. Second, there will be a *rise time* during which the response goes from zero to its peak. Third, after reaching its peak, the response may continue at the peak level, in which case we will call the response perfectly *sustained;* it may decay back to zero, in which case we will call it perfectly *transient;* or it may decay back to an intermediate level, in which case we will call it relatively sustained or relatively transient depending on whether the intermediate level is close to the peak level or to zero. In general, responses having shorter delay times, shorter rise times, or more transient time courses might be called "faster." Analogous distinctions can be made about the responses to the offsets of stationary stimuli.

If the system under consideration is linear or approximately linear, there is another way of describing the preceding three senses of "fast." Instead of describing the system's responses to stationary stimuli, one can describe its responses to stimuli flickering or drifting at different temporal frequencies. Delay time to a stationary stimulus translates into *phases* of responses to different temporal frequencies. Rise time translates into the *high-temporal-frequency cutoff*. The shorter the rise time, the higher the temporal frequencies to which the system can respond. Finally, a perfectly sustained response to a stationary stimulus corresponds to a complete absence of *low-temporal-frequency decline* (i.e., of decline in the system's sensitivity as one goes from medium to low temporal frequencies). In this case, the system responds equally well to all low frequencies. The more transient the response becomes, the more pronounced the low-frequency decline.

A fourth possible sense of "fast" depends on the responses to movement. The higher the rate of movement a channel is sensitive to, the faster the channel's responses might be said to be. If a channel is a linear system, its sensitivity to moving stimuli will be predictable from its temporal-frequency characteristics, and this fourth sense of "fast" will be closely related to the second—that is, to the rise time or high-temporal-frequency cutoff. The channel may not be linear, however, if, for example, it is truly directionally selective in the sense of responding best to one particular direction of motion, whatever the polarity of contrast in the moving stimulus. (See discussion in King-Smith & Kulikowski, 1975.) In that case, this fourth sense of fast is not equivalent to the first three.

Psychophysical Evidence for Spatiotemporal Interaction.   A priori, these four meanings of "fast" do not necessarily go together. A channel may have, for example, a fast delay time and a slow rise time. As far as can be told from the limited psychophysical evidence available, however, channels sensitive to low spatial frequencies are faster in all four ways than channels sensitive to high spatial frequencies. Let's briefly review that evidence.

Both the longer reaction times to high-spatial-frequency gratings than to low- (Breitmeyer, 1975; Lupp, Hauske, & Wolf, 1976; and Vassilev & Mitov, 1976) and the precise timing of metacontrast effects using sinusoidal gratings as stimuli (Rogowitz, 1977, 1978) suggest that the time to the peak of a channel's response (delay time plus rise time) gets longer as the characteristic frequency of the channel gets higher.

Measurements of sensitivity to sinusoidal gratings presented with various time courses indicate that as the spatial frequency gets higher, the rise time of the response becomes longer (the high-temporal-frequency cutoff moves to lower temporal frequencies), and the response becomes less transient (the low-temporal-frequency decline becomes less pronounced). Sensitivity has been measured for gratings flickering or drifting at different rates (e.g., Robson, 1966; Van Nes, Koenderink, Nas, & Bouman, 1967; Watanabe, Mori, Nagata, & Hiwatashi, 1968), for stationary gratings exposed for different amounts of time (e.g., Legge, 1978; Nachmias, 1967; Schober & Hilz, 1965; Tynan & Sekuler, 1974), for gratings exposed twice with various interstimulus intervals (Breitmeyer & Ganz, 1977; Watson & Nachmias, 1977), and for a long exposure of a grating combined with a short exposure at various onset asynchronies (Tolhurst,

1975b). Also, the varying shapes of reaction-time distributions to gratings of different spatial frequencies suggest that the response to low-spatial-frequency gratings is more transient than the response to high (Tolhurst, 1975a). A similar conclusion may be drawn from studies of stimuli with specially designed time courses (Breitmeyer & Julesz, 1975; Wilson, 1978; and Wilson & Bergen, 1977).

For a discussion of evidence relevant to the fourth sense of "fast," which depends on the responses to moving stimuli, see Sekuler and Levinson (1977) and Sekuler, Pantle, and Levinson (1978). MacLeod (1978) reviews recent physiological as well as psychophysical evidence on spatiotemporal interaction.

Are There Only Two Kinds of Temporal Channels?   As we have seen, there is an interaction between spatial and temporal visual sensitivity. Within a multiple-channels framework, this interaction can be expressed by saying that the low-spatial-frequency channels tend to be faster than the high ones. The details of this interaction are far from clear, however. Let me describe two rather different possibilities, neither of which I would be comfortable rejecting on the basis of current evidence.

One possibility is that there are only two kinds of temporal characteristics an individual channel can have. A channel's temporal characteristics can either be slow (sustained) or fast (transient). At the lowest spatial frequencies, there are only fast channels. At the highest spatial frequencies, there are only slow channels. For a wide range of intermediate spatial frequencies, there exist both slow and fast channels sensitive to each spatial frequency. As one changes spatial frequency in this range, the relative sensitivities of the slow and fast channels change dramatically (and their temporal characteristics may change a little). I am not sure that any investigators have proposed exactly this scheme, but suggestions of Kulikowski and Tolhurst (1973), Breitmeyer and Ganz (1976), Rogowitz (1977, 1978), and Watson (1977, 1978) are of this general sort.

The second possibility is that there is a continuum of kinds of temporal characteristics an individual channel can have, ranging from slowest (perfect sustained) to fastest (perfectly transient). At each spatial frequency, there is only one channel. The temporal characteristics change continuously from fastest to slowest as spatial frequency changes from lowest to highest.

Although these two possibilities seem quite different from each other, they both can account for the gradual change of temporal characteristics measured psychophysically as spatial frequency is changed. In fact, remarkably little evidence exists favoring one or the other possibility. One basic difference between the two possibilities is that the first but not the second postulates the existence of two distinct channels having the same preferred spatial frequency but different temporal characteristics. Watson (1977, 1978) found some evidence for the existence of two temporal channels at a single spatial frequency by measuring sensitivity to compound stimuli containing two flickering sinusoidal components of different temporal frequencies but the same spatial frequency. Further, some results from metacontrast experiments with pieces of sinusoidal gratings as stimuli are difficult to interpret unless there are two different temporal channels at a single spatial frequency (Rogowitz, 1977, 1978).

Another difference between the two possibilities is that the first, but not the second, divides the whole set of channels into two distinct groups on the basis of temporal characteristics and therefore suggests that these two groups serve two distinct functions. Perhaps (e.g., Breitmeyer & Ganz, 1976; Kulikowski & Tolhurst, 1973; Tolhurst, 1973) the set of faster, low-spatial-frequency channels is specialized for detecting temporal changes (as in motion perception, control of eye movements, and global processing of new scenes), whereas the set of slower, high-spatial-frequency channels is specialized for detecting spatial changes (as in pattern recognition, form perception, and local scrutiny of scenes).

If this distinction in function is valid, these two different groups of channels may have different signaling characteristics—that is, produce different perceptions. One difference between two perceptions is often taken as support for the notion of two distinct groups of channels. Observers are said to be able to distinguish between a perception of "movement" or "flicker" and a perception of "pattern," and to be able to set a threshold corresponding to either (e.g., Hood, 1973; Keesey, 1972; Van Nes et al., 1967; Watanabe et al., 1968). Assuming that these two different perceptions indicate which of the two groups of channels—fast or slow—is determining threshold, several investigators have used the two different thresholds to explore the spatiotemporal sensitivity of each group of channels (King-Smith & Kulikowski, 1975; Kulikowski & Tolhurst, 1973; Tolhurst, Sharpe, & Hart, 1973). This distinction between two different perceptions near threshold may correspond to other distinctions between perceptions of movement that have also led people to postulate two subsystems—one for handling movement irrespective of form, and one in which form is involved (Pantle & Picciano, 1976; Rashbass, 1968; Saucer, 1954).

The three pieces of evidence just summarized seem to favor the first possibility described—a dichotomy between slow and fast channels—over the second possibility—a continuum of temporal characteristics. Caution should be maintained, however, as the temporal summation effects obtained by Watson are small; the metacontrast timing effects obtained by Rogowitz are small; the phenomenological distinction between the two perceptions is not always easy for an observer to make and does not always lead to the expected results (e.g., Watson & Nachmias, 1977); and there are many other possibilities in addition to the two discussed.

Number of Spatial-Frequency Channels

The smallest number of spatial-frequency channels estimated is three or four on the basis of texture-matching and texture-similarity judgments (Harvey & Gervais, 1977; Richards & Polit, 1974). Wilson and Bergen (1977) also argue that four channels (four different sizes of receptive fields) at each location in the visual field are sufficient to account for an observer's sensitivity to a large variety of patterns. Four receptive-field sizes at each location, of course, imply many more altogether because of the nonuniformity of the visual field.

Although logically there is no necessary reciprocal relationship between bandwidth and number of channels, one might argue that the recent relatively broad estimates of bandwidth mean that relatively few channels would be sufficient to cover the range of visible spatial frequencies at any location in the visual field.

Early interpretations of selective adaptation effects suggested a rather large number of channels, because the largest threshold elevation was almost always at a test frequency identical to the adapting frequency (Blakemore & Campbell, 1969, for example). Also, early interpretations of the fact that the psychophysical contrast sensitivity function (which gives the observer's sensitivity to sinusoidal gratings as a function of spatial frequency) did not show individual bumps corresponding to individual channels suggested a rather large number of channels. When allowance is made for visual field nonuniformity and probability summation among channels, however, these two observations become consistent with a small number of receptive-field sizes at each spatial location.

On one hand, therefore, there may only be three or four spatial-frequency channels at each location. On the other hand, all the available evidence is probably also consistent with many more. Good estimates of the number of spatial-frequency channels remain remarkably elusive.

A NOTE ON SPATIAL-FREQUENCY CHANNELS AND PERCEPTION

The possible usefulness of spatial-frequency analyses in explaining visual perception has been pointed out by a number of investigators. Ginsberg (1971) concentrated on some of the patterns used to demonstrate Gestalt phenomena. He suggested that the stimulus information contained in certain ranges of spatial frequencies may be the basis for these phenomena. Many attempts have been made to explain visual illusions on the basis of spatial-frequency- and orientation-selective channels (e.g., Blakemore, Carpenter, & Georgeson, 1970; Bouma & Andriessen, 1970; Ginsburg, 1971; Oyama, 1977; Wallace, 1969). Georgeson and Sullivan (1975) suggested that spatial-frequency channels might be responsible for contrast constancy. The recognizability of visual stimuli despite changes in size and position has been attributed to encoding by spatial-frequency channels (e.g., Blakemore & Campbell, 1969). Numerous other suggestions have been made tentatively about the possible use of spatial-frequency channels in detecting Gibsonian texture gradients, in recognizing patterns (in letter confusion, for example), in encoding visual information in distributed form for memory storage (Weisstein & Harris, 1980), and so forth.

Of particular relevance to perceptual organization (e.g., Chapter 6 by Pomerantz in this volume) is the proposal that the low spatial frequencies in a pattern—which are processed by faster channels—are important for "global" processing, whereas the higher spatial frequencies—which are processed by slower channels—are important for "local" processing (e.g., Breitmeyer & Ganz, 1976; Broadbent, 1975, 1977; Kinchla, 1977).

Another application of spatial-frequency channels comes from work on "effortless texture discrimination," which is described in Julesz's Chapter 2 in the current volume. Julesz and his colleagues have studied visual textures to discover the conditions under which differences between regions of different textures become immediately and effortlessly apparent to observers. According to one form of Julesz's original conjecture, effortless texture discrimination is primarily based on the power spectra differences of textures and ignores their phase spectra. The power spectrum of a pattern is just the square of the amplitude part of a (two-dimensional) Fourier transform of the texture pattern; this amplitude part is, in turn, simply the function telling how much of each spatial frequency at each orientation is present in the pattern. Thus, two patterns differ in their power spectra if and only if differences exist between the amplitudes of corresponding sinusoidal components in the two patterns. Therefore, this form of the original conjecture can be reworded to say: If two texture regions differ sufficiently in the amplitudes of corresponding sinusoidal components in the two regions, the regions will be effortlessly seen as two separate regions. If two regions differ only in the phases of their components and not in the amplitudes, however, then the regions will blend into each other, appearing as one region of uniform texture.

Spatial-frequency channels could easily mediate the discrimination postulated by this conjecture if the channels signaled amplitude but not phase information to the higher centers. Then comparing the outputs of the channels in one region to the outputs in another region would reveal amplitude (power spectrum) differences between the two regions but not phase differences. (Because the spatial-frequency channels have greater-than-zero bandwidths, their outputs are not precisely proportional to the amplitudes of individual sinusoidal components. That is, the channels do not perform a strict Fourier analysis. They may perform one good enough to account for texture discrimination, however, for no one claims that the quoted conjecture is precisely true.)

These explanations of perceptual phenomena in terms of spatial-frequency analyses are in various states of development. Some have been investigated extensively; some barely at all. No one of the suggestions, however, has been developed enough to be compelling. This state of affairs should come as no surprise. The problems of explaining perceptual phenomena are much too difficult to permit solutions without an enormous amount of work.

The available psychophysical evidence clearly demonstrates that there are channels (or subsystems or mechanisms) in the visual system that are selectively *sensitive* to spatial frequency. Although quantitative, rigorous explanations of many of the results remain to be constructed, a very large amount of data can be organized with the help of the concept of such channels. The psychophysical evidence also suggests that there are channels that selectively *signal* spatial frequency in the sense that the output of one channel is not completely interchangeable with the output of another. What happens to these outputs from the channels, however, is still unclear. We do not know how they combine with or inhibit one another. More generally, we know very little about their perceptual consequences. It is, of course, the nature of these perceptual consequences that will largely determine how useful the channels are in explaining perceptual phenomena.

ACKNOWLEDGMENTS

The preparation of this chapter was supported in part by a grant from the National Science Foundation (BNS 76-18839). I am grateful to E. Davis, B. A. Dosher, J. E. Hochberg, D. C. Hood, P. Kramer, C. R. McCauley, J. Nachmias, J. P. Thomas, and A. B. Watson for their helpful criticisms of early drafts of this chapter.

Figure and Ground Perception in Briefly Presented Isodipole Textures

Bela Julesz[1]
Bell Laboratories

It is not the accumulation of observations which I have in mind when I speak of the growth of scientific knowledge, but the repeated overthrow of scientific theories and their replacement by better or more satisfactory ones.

—Karl Popper (1963)

INTRODUCTION

At the time of this symposium, some exciting discoveries were made in my laboratory on the texture discrimination paradigm I have been working on for 15 years (Julesz, 1962). I have been preoccupied by two other areas of research in this period—one being global stereopsis of random-dot stereograms and the other, spatial-frequency channels in monocular and binocular vision. Two long review articles have already been published—one entitled "Global stereopsis: Cooperative phenomena in stereoscopic depth perception" (Julesz, 1978a), and the other, "Spatial frequency channels in one-, two- and three-dimensional vision: Variations on an auditory theme by Bekesy" (Julesz, 1979). These articles cover in great detail the most important developments in the random-dot stereogram and the spatial-frequency-channel paradigms that took place since the publication of my book (Julesz, 1971). Therefore, in this chapter I restrict myself to reviewing briefly the history of the texture discrimination paradigm with the new

---

[1]In the winter semesters of 1977, 1978, and 1979, he was a Fairchild Distinguished Scholar at Caltech, Pasadena, California.

findings that led to a radical reevaluation of my thinking. Although this chapter is meant to be self-contained, the interested reader could consult a popular article of mine as an introduction (Julesz, 1975).

Finally, let me note that symposium proceedings are not the proper place to publish new findings, and to clutter the literature with already published material is a crime. So the only excuse for this article was the editors' guidelines to include authors' personal views, motivations, recollections, and future plans (which are almost completely suppressed in professional journal publications). Because it is my firm belief that a scientist's work cannot be fully understood through published findings alone, I adhered to these guidelines and hope that my esteemed colleagues at the symposium will follow suit.

IMMEDIATE PERCEPTION

In this article I review work on effortless texture discrimination, so the first task is to define effortless perception. My use of *effortless* refers to perceptual tasks that can be performed without scrutiny or deliberation. Operationally, it is defined as perceiving certain structures in the stimulus array when the stimulus is briefly presented—say, for less than 160 msec. Such brief exposures prevent the observer searching over the stimulus array for some complex details, because both saccadic eye movements and shifts of attention take longer than 160 msec. Thus, I define *effortless perception* operationally, and the name *immediate perception* is more appropriate. Probably this immediate perception is similar to the concept of *preattentive perception*, following the usage of Neisser (1967), and in several of my demonstrations, the reader can inspect the stimulus array for seconds if he or she is willing to refrain from scrutinizing. However, in all my research, I prevent scrutinizing by presenting the stimulus very briefly, but in most of these studies, the erasure of the afterimages is not necessary. A typical example of what is *not* effortless perception is the perception of connectivity as shown in Fig. 2.1, where one of the figures is a single connected line whereas the other consists of two unconnected lines. However, if the reader looks at these two figures for only a few seconds, it will be impossible to detect which one of these two complex figures is the connected one. On the other hand, for simpler figures, such as shown in Fig. 2.2, the connected one can be perceived in a tachistoscopic flash. This is then an example of effortless perception, which I

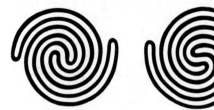

FIG. 2.1. Connectivity of a complex pattern cannot be effortlessly perceived but requires scrutiny (Minsky & Papert, 1969. Copyright 1969, MIT Press. Reprinted by permission.)

FIG. 2.2. Connectivity of a simple pattern is immediately (effortlessly) perceived (Julesz, 1975).

also called instantaneous, or immediate, perception. In this chapter I prefer the name *immediate perception*.

In my previous publications I gave many other perceptual illustrations of immediate perception (Julesz, 1975). Here it will suffice to draw an analogy to *subitising*. It is well known that a brief presentation of up to four clearly visible objects enables the observer to guess the number of objects without error, whereas with more than seven objects, the correct percentage of guesses rapidly deteriorates. So, guessing the number of items up to four (when briefly presented to avoid counting) is another example of immediate perception. Whether one should include the subitising of five or six items as immediate perception (when performance is less than 100%) is a question of definition. Because attention can wander, it is advisable to define immediate perception of a given perceptual task by giving an experimental criterion, such as being able to perceive the task 95% correctly in repeated but randomized presentations of 50-msec durations.

TEXTURE DISCRIMINATION

In 1962 I became interested in the problem of effortless texture discrimination. I generated, with the help of a computer, two random arrays of dots side by side, or one array embedded into the other, such that the statistics of the multicolored (black, gray, white, and so on) dots were determined by two different stochastic processes (Julesz, 1962). I wanted to find out whether it would be possible (mathematically) to have two stochastic processes that agreed in their nth-order statistics but differed in their $(n + 1)$th-order statistics and, more importantly, what the lowest n would be for which *no* instantaneous texture discrimination was possible (Julesz, 1962).

In order to be self-contained, let me briefly define first-order, second-order, third-order, . . . nth-order statistics as used in random geometry. In Fig. 2.3 a discriminable texture pair is shown where both the left and right fields contain the same number of black dots; the left field was generated by a Poisson process, and the right field was generated by the same Poisson process, but in the right field, no two dots could be nearer than an ϵ distance. Now first-order statistics can be obtained by randomly throwing measuring dots (confetti with infinitesimal diameters) on the texture and observing the frequency with which the confetti land on black. By performing this experiment on Fig. 2.3, one could convince oneself that the first-order statistics for both half-fields agree. The second-order

FIG. 2.3.   Texture pair with identical first-order, but different second-order (dipole), statistics (Julesz, 1975).

(or dipole) statistics are obtained by randomly throwing on the texture dipoles (needles) of any length and orientation and observing the frequency with which both end points of each dipole fall on the same color (e.g., black). The dipole statistics for the two textures in Fig. 2.3 are clearly different, since in the left half-field any dipole length will occur, whereas in the right half-field no dipole can fall on black that is shorter than ϵ. If one throws trigons (triangles) of any shape on the texture in a random fashion and collects the statistics on how often all three vertices of each triangle land on certain colors, the trigon statistics or third-order statistics are obtained. Similarly, the random throwing of n-gons on the texture and measuring the frequency with which all n vertices of each n-gon fall on certain colors gives the n-gon statistics or nth-order statistics. Of course, going from second-order to third-order statistics, the complexity of data collection increases exponentially. Furthermore, if two textures agree in their nth-order statistics, then all their lower-than-nth-order statistics must be identical, too.

MARKOV TEXTURES

In 1962 two mathematicians, Mark Rosenblatt and David Slepian, became interested in my problem and invented some special nth-order Markov processes such that their nth-order statistics were statistically independent, whereas their $(n + 1)$th-order statistics were dependent (Rosenblatt & Slepian, 1962). Such Markov processes could only exist with at least three brightness levels (black, gray, white, and so on), and their construction required very special algorithms. In the same year, I constructed many such Markov textures and found with great surprise that when these textures agreed in their second-order statistics but differed in their third- and higher-order statistics, they usually could not be discriminated (Julesz, 1962). Of course, slight differences in first-order statistics yield effortless discrimination due to an apparent change in their tonal quality. Similarly, the operation of keeping the first-order statistics identical, but generating textures with different second-order statistics, usually yields strong discrimination (as illustrated in Fig. 2.3), and one perceives this as a difference in granularity. I was surprised by the finding that Markov textures usually did not yield discrimination when their second-order statistics agreed (i.e., they were isodipole). I was convinced that differences in third-order statistics would yield discrimination, and perhaps only textures with identical trigon statistics would escape discrimination. However, in the Markov textures with isodipole statistics, the trigrams (three *adjacent* samples) had very different statistics in the corresponding texture pairs and still did not yield effortless discrimination. Even if one hemifield consisted of high-probability trigrams of WWW, BBB, or GGG, whereas three black, white, or grey dots occurred only rarely in the other, adjacent hemifield, one could not notice the presence or absence of a few dozen trigrams. Of course, one could increase the probability of identical-brightness trigrams in one texture to the extent that long stripes of BBBBBB, WWWWWW, and so forth could form, but I regarded these stripes as a degenerate case.

I do not want to discuss Markov textures further because they are inherently one-dimensional whereas vision is two-dimensional, so Markov textures are rather atypical in vision research. However, I would like to draw attention to an error committed by several authors who mixed up my (1962) observation about the impossibilities to discriminate isodipole Markov textures by confusing isodigram statistics with isodipole statistics. The interested reader might like to read a comment of mine on this error (Julesz, 1978c). Here I only note that isodipole constraints mean that in two textures, *any* two samples (end points of dipoles) have the same probability, whereas isodigrams constraints force only the identity of two *adjacent* samples; in general, two samples further apart will be very different. I also note that we generated auditory Markov textures of diatonic pitches—that is, Markov melodies—with identical second-order statistics but different third-order statistics; yet even trained musicians could not discriminate these melodies (Julesz & Guttman, 1965).

THE ISODIPOLE TEXTURE CONJECTURE

Since Markov textures are atypical for vision, we had to wait until 1973, when—with the help of two mathematicians, Edgar Gilbert and Larry Shepp, and a quantum chemist, Harry Frisch—we were able to generate isodipole textures in *two dimensions* (Julesz, Gilbert, Shepp, & Frisch, 1973). We found three methods that could generate two-dimensional textures with identical second-order, but different third- and higher-order, statistics. The first method generates textures by randomly throwing (without rotation) identical micropatterns (of any shape) without overlap. The dual texture is obtained by rotating the micropattern by a θ amount and randomly throwing it (without further rotation). Such a texture pair is shown in Fig. 2.4a. Since the dipole statistics are different, the inner square is perceived as distinctly different from the surround. However, it is easy to prove that $\theta = 180°$ rotation yields an isodipole dual texture (Julesz et al., 1973). This is shown in Fig. 2.4b, and in spite of the fact that u's and n's are very different letters (and overlearned since first grade), this isodipole texture pair cannot be discriminated without detailed scrutiny.

Our second method generates textures by throwing identical micropatterns of any shape in random orientations, and the isodipole dual texture is similarly obtained by taking the *mirror image* (reflection) of the micropattern. Such a texture pair, composed of randomly rotated R's and their mirror images, respectively, is shown in Fig. 2.5. Here again the proof of isodipole statistics is easy (Julesz et al., 1973), and no texture discrimination can be obtained until one inspects each letter one by one.

These examples shown in Figs. 2.4b and 2.5 are so convincing that one is tempted to conjecture that textures with iso-dipole statistics cannot be effortlessly discriminated. That such a conjecture—based on simple stochastic constraints—cannot be compatible with the existence of the many ad hoc feature extractors that were found in the visual cortex of the monkey (and must surely be similar in humans) is most likely. Indeed, in all my publications, I emphasized how improbable it is that dipole statistics alone could describe the combined

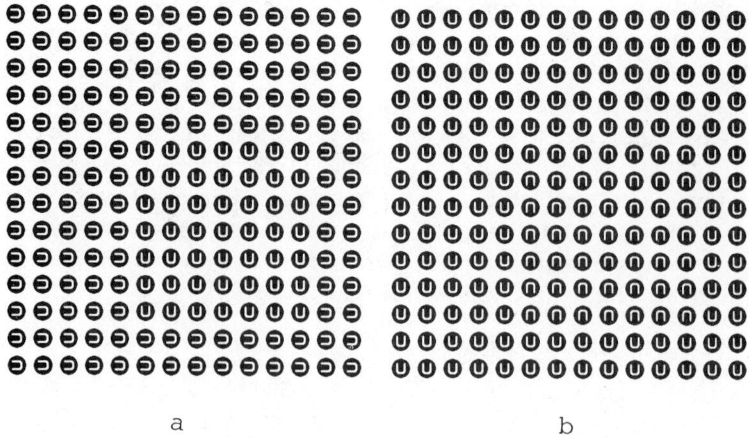

a   b

FIG. 2.4.   (a) Texture pair with different dipole statistics, which yields effortless discrimination; (b) texture pair with identical dipole statistics, which cannot be discriminated effortlessly (Julesz et al., 1973).

FIG. 2.5.   Texture pair composed of randomly thrown *R*'s and mirror-image *R*'s, which have identical dipole statistics and do not yield effortless discrimination (Julesz et al., 1973).

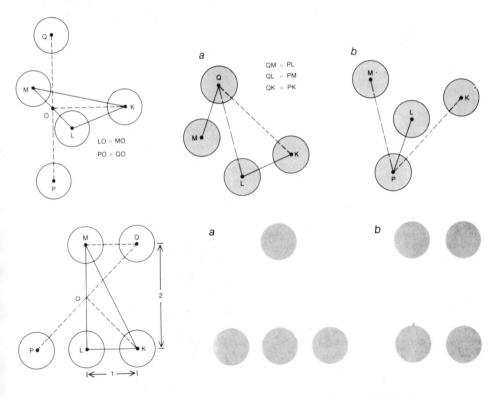

FIG. 2.6.   The "four-disk method" that generates micropatterns and dual micropatterns that, when randomly thrown, form texture pairs with identical dipole statistics (Julesz et al., 1973).

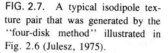

FIG. 2.7.   A typical isodipole texture pair that was generated by the "four-disk method" illustrated in Fig. 2.6 (Julesz, 1975).

action of the many simple, complex, hypercomplex cortical feature extractors (Julesz, 1962, 1965; Julesz et al., 1973). Our third method, the "four-disk method" (Julesz et al., 1973) illustrated in Fig. 2.6, nevertheless generated some isodipole textures that were nondiscriminable, even if the individual micropatterns and their duals in isolation appeared very different. One would have assumed that the T-shaped and Π-shaped micropatterns at the bottom of Fig. 2.6 were triggering very different complex or hypercomplex cortical feature detectors; yet the texture pair in Fig. 2.7 composed of these micropatterns is not discriminable.

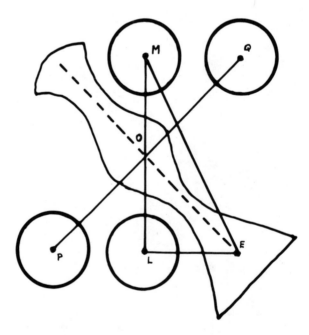

FIG. 2.8.   An extension of the "four-disk method" by substituting in place of disk A any shape E with bilateral symmetry across the EO axis, shown in Fig. 2.6 (Caelli, Julesz, & Gilbert, 1978).

Furthermore, one can extend the four-disk method by realizing that instead of disk A, any shape E with bilateral symmetry across the AO axis can generate isodipole textures, as shown in Fig. 2.8 (Caelli, Julesz, & Gilbert, 1978). And one can select E such that with the disks of B, C, and D, a micropattern of a human face with two eyes and a gnome without eyes is formed, whereas the dual micropattern consists of two faces having only one eye. Regardless of the assumed importance of a two-eyed face as a Gestalt, an inspection of Fig. 2.9 shows that in texture discrimination, Gestalt organization does not operate.

In spite of all my skepticism that a simple isodipole statistical constraint could prevent texture discrimination, all the examples reviewed thus far were so convincing that I regarded this as a worthwhile conjecture. Thus my conjecture was that texture pairs with identical dipole statistics cannot be effortlessly discriminated [Julesz et al., 1973, p. 397]. As a matter of fact, Schatz (1977) found no counterexample to this conjecture in spite of intensive search, and as we will see, a slight modification of this conjecture might have prevented its downfall. Indeed, the conjecture—that if one selects two textures from a pool of textures with identical dipole statistics they will have a very high probability to be nondiscriminable—might survive any test. However, as I will point out— agreeing with Karl Popper the philosopher—a conjecture cannot be regarded as scientific if it cannot be disproved. It is much more important to state a conjecture that is very difficult to disprove, but as a challenge generates much research

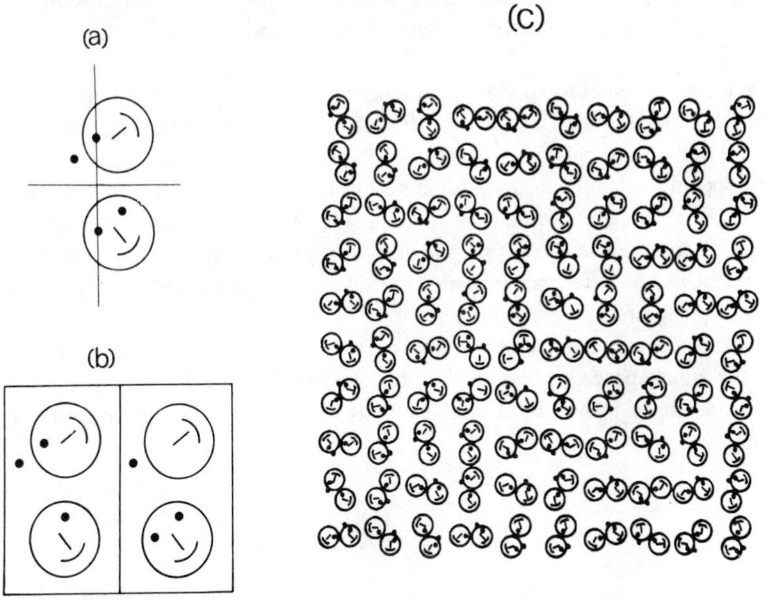

FIG. 2.9. Isodipole texture pair composed of "two-eyed" and "one-eyed" faces, where the micropattern duals are generated by the method of Fig. 2.8. No effortless discrimination is obtained (Caelli, Julesz, & Gilbert, 1978).

and leads to some unexpected counterexamples and insights, than to be a proud owner of a "true" conjecture that, by its static infallibility, is probably ignored as an empty truism. I think that the generality and unspecificity of the Gestalt "laws" of organization belong to this category. The way these laws are stated, such as "good Gestalt," "closure," "symmetry," and "proximity," have changing meaning for each application and thus remain always "true"; but of course, because they cannot be falsified, they do not challenge the mind. I return to this basic epistemological problem in the last section.

A SIMPLE THEORY BASED
ON AUTOCORRELATION

Let us note (Julesz, 1978b) that the dipole statistics uniquely determine the auto-correlation function which in turn yields the power spectrum. Thus all the non-discriminable texture pairs in Figs. 2.4b, 2.5, 2.7, and 2.9 have identical autocorrelation functions and therefore identical power spectra. One could thus reword my texture conjecture by stating: that texture discrimination is primarily based on the power spectra differences of textures and ignores their phase spectra. (Thus, visual texture perception is similar to audition where phase information has a limited role.) When scrutiny is prevented, the different parts of the texture (eyes, facial contours, and so sorth) do not form a Gestalt because their proper spatial position (i.e., their phase) is ignored by the texture perception system.

Scrutiny thus corresponds to attending to both the amplitude and phase spectra. Indeed, in all the demonstrations that are nondiscriminable, one can inspect the texture pairs with identical power spectra from such a far distance that they appear suddenly as two separate entities, although this is a rather weak effect. What happens is that we reach a size limit under which the texture pair becomes so small that it is not viewed as a texture but as two distinct figures, where the phase difference of their Fourier spectra can be perceived by the figure perception system.

In summary, the difference between the texture (ground) perception system and the figure perception system is that the latter does attend to spatial position (i.e., the phase information of the picture elements), whereas the former does not.

THE FALL OF THE TEXTURE CONJECTURE

Up to now we have shown the validity of my original texture conjecture by ignoring some of the weak counterexamples that we noted in one of our main papers in which this conjecture was revisited (Julesz et al., 1973). Indeed, in

1973 we already had a few isodipole texture pairs that were weakly discriminable. In Fig. 2.10 we show such a weakly discriminable texture pair generated by the four-disk method. What is really surprising is not the weak texture discrimination but rather how weak this is when the individual "open" and "closed" micropattern duals look so strikingly different. However, the fact that the four-disk method can generate isodipole texture pairs that fluctuate between nondiscriminability and weak discriminability made me wonder about the validity of my conjecture. Indeed, a few months ago, Terry Caelli from the University of Melbourne joined my laboratory for 1 year, and as the first project, we investigated systematically hundreds of isodipole texture pairs that were generated by a computer in rapid succession (at 10-sec intervals) and flashed for 50 msec. With the help of this Monte Carlo method, we found one—and only one—strong counterexample to my texture conjecture. Because the four-disk method has only three degrees of freedom, it is possible to search through the set of texture pairs in a random fashion and find the counterexample in reasonable time. Indeed, with the Monte Carlo method and a naive observer, it is possible to find the counterexample in a 1-hour session. However, Caelli started our project by selecting the parameters in advance such that the "open" micropattern in Fig. 2.10 would be opened still wider while keeping the "closed" one closed. As a result of this insight, we obtained the counterexample at the first few trials, and the random search stumbled upon the same counterexample over and over again. So we are confident that with the four-disk method, only one strong counterexample exists to my texture conjecture. This is shown in Fig. 2.11, where texture discrimination is based on the quasi collinearity of the disks in one texture, whereas in the dual texture this property is absent. Thus the isodipole statistical constraints cannot prevent the formation of quasi-collinear structures (Caelli & Julesz, 1978). We have probed the tuning curves of these quasi-

FIG. 2.10.   Isodipole texture pair generated by the four-disk method. Discrimination is borderline (Julesz et al., 1973).

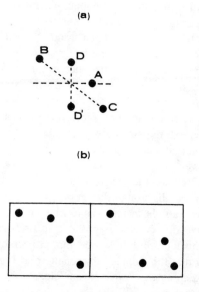

FIG. 2.11.   Isodipole texture pair generated by the four-disk method. Texture discrimination is strong, based on "quasi-collinear" strings of disks (Caelli & Julesz, 1978).

collinear detectors (QCD) or "chevron detectors," and for details, the reader is referred to Caelli and Julesz (1978). Although with the four-disk method, the only counterexample we found was based on collinearity—and we proved that the four-disk method is unique in generating isodipole micropatterns of four disks—we were unwilling to conclude that this was the only counterexample. So in this paper (Caelli & Julesz, 1978), we postulated two *classes* of detectors: Class A, for detecting differences in dipole statistics; and Class B, those detectors that can discriminate between textures with isodipole statistics. We regarded the QCD as the first example of a Class B detector. However, the search for other Class B detectors requires novel methods that can generate isodipole micropattern duals with five or more disks. Recently, Edgar Gilbert joined us in this effort, and in the next section we show how such more complex isodipole micropattern duals led us to the discovery of two additional Class B detectors.

THE SEARCH FOR "PERCEPTUAL QUARKS"

It would go too far to describe all the novel methods that were invented in the last few months in order to generate isodipole micropattern duals of five and more disks and even of nondisklike structures. For details, the reader is referred to our

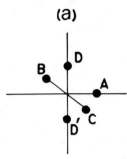

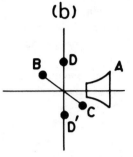

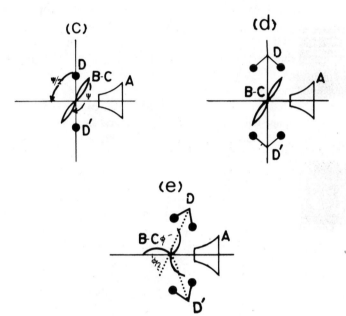

FIG. 2.12.   Generalizations of the four-disk method: (a) The four-disk method, described in Fig. 2.6; (b) first generalization of the four-disk method, described in Fig. 2.8; (c) second generalization of the four-disk method by converting the disks B, C into any shape with centric symmetry (180-degree rotation invariant); (d) third generalization converts the disks D, D' into two shapes where each shape is invariant under reflections on the Y axis and D' is the X-axis reflection of D; (e) the fourth generalization demonstrates how B–C can become a shape rotation invariant for $180/n$-degree rotations, whereas D and D' are symmetric with respect to axes determined by $360/n$-degree rotations (Caelli, Julesz, & Gilbert, 1978).

recent paper (Caelli, Julesz, & Gilbert, 1978). Here we show only a progression of ideas of how the four-disk method is further generalized by replacing some of the disks by general shapes of certain symmetries. This is shown in Fig. 2.12, and the caption describes some of the details.

These methods with five and more disks have increasingly high degrees of freedom with exponentially increasing random search times for finding new counterexamples. Therefore, it is highly desirable to think about the method to be used and, within the capabilities of the method, to try to select some prospective candidates first, and only then to search for anything else. Indeed, the two new counterexamples we found were guessed by us before trial, and we used the Monte Carlo method merely to be sure that we did not miss some others. As a matter of fact, we used random search only for the four-, five-, and six-disk methods. We tried the isodipole five-disk method in order to find new Class B detectors but could find only the QCD. With an isodipole six-disk method (illustrated in the insert of Fig. 2.13), we found a second Class B detector—and only one, after inspecting several hundred such texture pairs. This case is illustrated by Fig. 2.13 where the strong discrimination is based on the presence of "corners" in one of the textures. It is not the angle of the corners that matters (as differences in angle could be detected by the Class A detectors) but rather the presence of two quasi-collinear disk strings that end in a common point, thus becoming a "corner." Because one needs at least three disks to define "perceptual collinearity," it is obvious why a "perceptual corner" needs at least six disks.

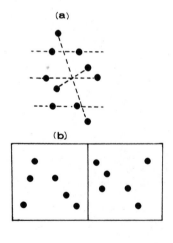

FIG. 2.13.   Isodipole texture pair generated by the six-disk method (illustrated in the insert). Effortless texture discrimination is based on the presence of "corners" (Caelli, Julesz, & Gilbert, 1978).

Similarly, with 8-to-11-disk isodipole micropattern duals, one can find the third Class B detector. In the insert of Fig. 2.14, we show the micropattern duals generated by the 11-disk method that yielded strongly discriminable textures. An inspection of Fig. 2.14 convinces us that the underlying property yielding texture discrimination is "closure." Indeed, if the same patterns are defined by 7 disks, one is under the threshold of effortless texture discrimination. At 8 or 9 disks, one reaches above threshold, and with 11 disks (shown in Fig. 2.14), discrimination is strong. Because 7 disks can define three collinear disk structures that form a triangle or three rays meeting in one point, and because these two micropattern duals do not yield texture discrimination (Caelli, Julesz, & Gilbert, 1978), it is clearly shown that for closure, the disks have to be placed rather densely, as in Fig. 2.14.

One can generate micropatterns with an increasing number of disks, but because of the isodipole constraints, more and more of the disks must be the same for the dual micropatterns. Therefore, it is very unlikely that changing a few disks (with the majority of disks being the same in the dual micropatterns) will lead to discrimination in very complex micropatterns. Thus the question of whether there are further Class B detectors beyond the QCD, corner, and closure detectors remains open.

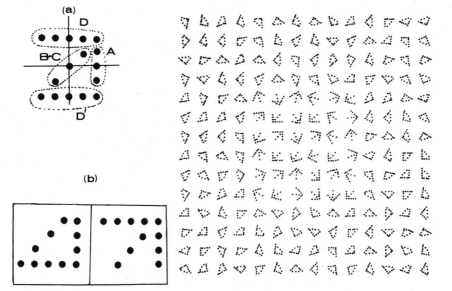

FIG. 2.14.   Isodipole texture pair generated by the method described in Fig. 2.12c, where the micropattern duals consist of 11 disks. Effortless texture discrimination is based on "closure" (Caelli, Julesz, & Gilbert, 1978).

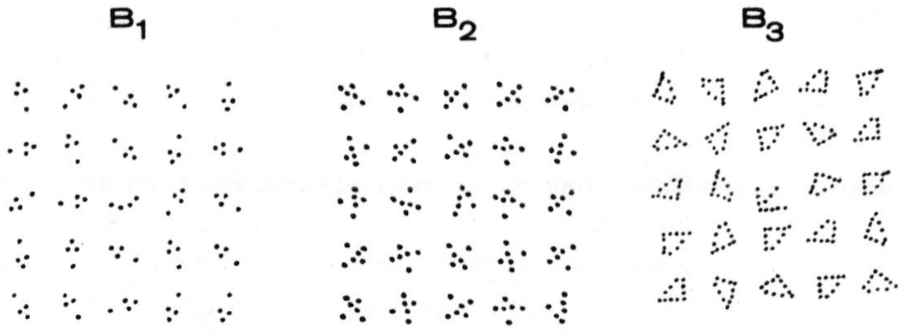

B₁   B₂   B₃

FIG. 2.15. Isolated micropattern with properties of quasi collinearity (B₁), corner (B₂), and closure (B₃), respectively, which yield effortless detection when embedded in isodipole dual textures demonstrating their figurelike properties (Caelli, Julesz, & Gilbert, 1978).

What is important, however, is that these three fundamental properties of collinearity, corner, and closure stand out by themselves as *single* features amongst a set of isodipole dual micropatterns. This surprising finding is demonstrated by Fig. 2.15. This implies that these three features are the "quarks of form," the fundamental elements of form perception, and that they resist becoming ground (texture) even in immediate perception. On the other hand, a *single* micropattern with Class A property does not stand out from a set of isodipole dual micropatterns. This is expected, because even a *set* of micropatterns with Class A property does not yield discrimination.

TOWARD A PERCEPTUAL TOPOLOGY
OF FORM

It is interesting to note that the three fundamental formlike features in immediate perception are a mixture of geometrical and topological properties. Quasi collinearity, or chevron shape with a certain curvature or shallow intersection angle range, is a "fuzzy" geometrical concept. So is the notion of a corner. The corner must be beyond a certain angle (otherwise, it will trigger the QCD), but otherwise, there is no restriction on the angle. However, it is important that the lines or curved lines that cross at the corner do not extend beyond the crossing point. Finally, the property of closure is a strictly topological notion. One could regard these B₁, B₂, and B₃ detectors (to rename QCD, corner, and closure detectors) as defining a primeval perceptual geometry or topology. For instance, projective geometry preserves collinearity, corners (but not angles), and conics. The latter means that closed ellipses can become open hyperbolas (however, for foveal-sized targets, one cannot project an ellipse on the retina of such a closed range that it appears as a hyperbola). Similarly, quasi collinearity, corner, and closure might define a "projective topology" of effortless perception. Of course, the metric properties are taken care of by the Class A detectors to a large extent. That we found such a hidden topology in immediate perception is the more interesting because in form perception (with scrutiny), topological properties are often overlooked. The definition of a topologist as "a person who cannot tell apart a doughnut from a teacup" strikes us as funny because topological properties seem so artificial in everyday life. However, we know now how fundamental topological notions are in modern mathematics. Perhaps these strange quarks of form might also tell us something of how form emerges from ground.

THE SIGNIFICANCE OF
ISODIPOLE CONSTRAINTS

It should be stressed that the B_1, B_2, and B_3 detectors were found among thousands of isodipole texture pairs that did not yield discrimination in a brief flash. (Even in this sense, there is an analogy to physical quarks, whose existence can be inferred only after inspecting thousands of traces.) Thus the Class A detectors are by far the most important detectors in texture perception. What the isodipole statistical constraint accomplishes is to render useless for discrimination all the large number of cortical feature extractors other than the three Class B detectors.

So if one avoids Class B detectors (i.e., keeps them identical in both textures) and changes slightly the dipole statistics, it is possible to study the tuning curve of Class A detectors near the equilibrium point (of isodipole statistics). Such a case is shown in Fig. 2.16 (from Caelli, Julesz, & Gilbert, 1978). Although it remains to be seen how the many Class A detectors start to show their idiosyncratic behavior when the second-order statistics greatly differ, it seems very likely

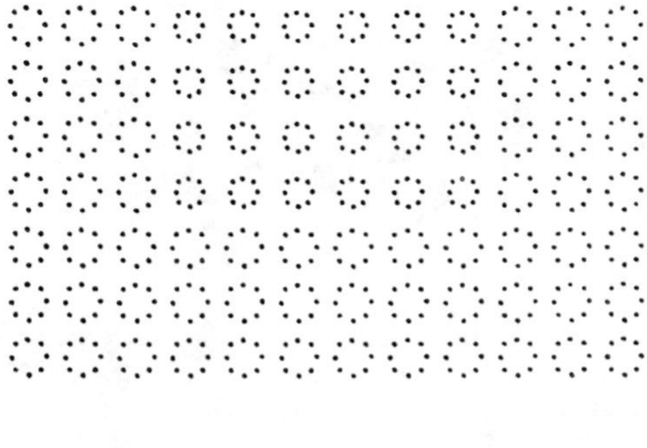

FIG. 2.16.   Texture discrimination based on dipole (length) differences, whereas the "quasi-collinear," "corner," and "closure" properties are kept identical in the two textures (Caelli, Julesz, & Gilbert, 1978).

that a small perturbation around the isodipole equilibrium will lead to a theory of Class A texture discrimination.

In summary, the visual system can be subdivided into two basic functions: attentive viewing with scrutiny (i.e., figure perception), and unattentive viewing without scrutiny (ground or texture perception). However, unattentive viewing can be regarded as an early warning system, which suddenly switches to attentive viewing if Class A or B detectors become stimulated. The only difference between Class A and Class B detectors is that the latter fire for *local* B_1, B_2, or B_3

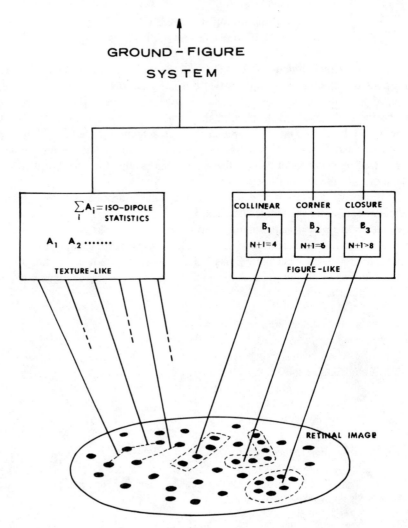

FIG. 2.17.   A model of immediate perception of textures based on Class A and Class B detectors (Caelli, Julesz, & Gilbert, 1978).

features, whereas the former fire only for *global* changes (i.e., for a larger area) involving differences in dipole statistics. This system of unattended viewing is thus the immediate perceptual system for texture discrimination, which we draw as a model in Fig. 2.17.

Because the Class A detectors with B_1 (QCD) are equivalent to an autocorrelator, they constitute a linear model (Caelli & Julesz, 1978). However, the addition of B_2 and B_3 detectors makes the model highly nonlinear.

Previously, we discussed the possibility of developing a perturbation theory of texture discrimination around equilibrium based on Class A detectors. If one determines the tuning curves for the B_1, B_2, and B_3 detectors (as Caelli & Julesz, 1978, already did for B_1), then one has to consider that small perturbations in dipole statistics can have an effect on the Class B detectors that, in turn, can be evaluated from their tuning curves. The implications of such a theory are now discussed.

IMMEDIATE PERCEPTION AS A MODEL SYSTEM FOR CHANNELS

The notion of independent perceptual channels came into vogue again with the postulation of spatial-frequency analyzers in vision (Blakemore & Campbell, 1969; Campbell & Robson, 1968; Pantle & Sekuler, 1968: for detailed review see Julesz, 1979). Problems of their interaction (e.g., probability summation) in detection and perception tasks are now intensively studied. However, these spatial-frequency channels (what I call *visual critical bands*) overlap with each other so densely (partly because they are so broad and partly because there are so many of them) that it is impossible to study the interaction between channels that are closer than one to two octaves from each other.

At this time, the "model system" for studying channels was color perception, using Stiles' (1939) increment threshold paradigm. Even these color channels are rather broadly tuned and greatly overlap, so one has to use sophisticated adaptation techniques and increment thresholds to show by psychophysical means the existence and interaction of these channels. Furthermore, the existence of the Young–Helmholtz red, green, blue primary system and the red–green, yellow–blue opponent system by Hering at the next stage makes these studies quite complex. Finally, dependence on spatial frequency and transient behavior further complicates the picture.

On the other hand, the number of isodipole textures in two dimensions is infinite, and there are only a few texture detectors found (thus far, only four—those that detect second-order statistical differences, and B_1, B_2, and B_3). So these four detectors are very remote from each other (in the feature space of isodipole textures close to equilibrium), and therefore their interactions should be easier to study. I could envisage a psychophysics of texture perception based on studying the interactions between these channels.

ON CONJECTURES AND "LAWS"
IN PSYCHOLOGY

The recent fall of the Julesz conjecture as it happened is an exciting outcome. We know from Karl Popper (1935/1968) that it must be possible for an empirical scientific system to be refuted by experience. The fact that it resisted 15 years of attempts to disprove it, and that the few counterexamples found have led to a fundamental topology of form, indicates that the conjecture was a genuine scientific theory. It generated new ideas both in mathematics and in perception in the quest to disprove it, and after the falsification of the theory, a new insight was gained into visual perception.

If I had been slightly more conservative in 1962 and had emphasized that *no iso* $-5gon$ textures can be discriminated, then I probably would have stated a psychophysical "law."

Indeed, all the counterexamples we know have different 5gon (pentagon) statistics. So, an iso -5gon constraint on the textures had suppressed the features of quasi collinearity, corner, and closure. Thus I would still be the "proud" owner of a law but of an empty law that, although it might have been respected, probably would have been ignored by workers in science. Obviously, if a constraint is so strong that it prohibits the formation of anything interesting in perception, who would have regarded it as a challenge to refute it?

The conjecture that isodipole textures are not discriminable has been in the best tradition of hypotheses in physics, and such negative hypotheses are very few in psychology. Obviously, since the null hypothesis can never be verified, only falsified, when the zero hypothesis is a negative statement, one single counterexample can discover the existence of a novel entity. If this negative statement is corroborated for many cases, then its disproof is an interesting scientific outcome by itself, but what is more—the counterexample must be significant in its own right. This explains the immediate acceptance by the scientific community of the implications of the computer-generated random-dot stereograms (Julesz, 1960). What happened was that a single demonstration of monocularly shapeless and contourless random arrays giving rise to binocular forms and contours (as shown in Fig. 2.18) refuted the prevailing belief (Ogle, 1959, pp. 362–394.) that binocularly disparate monocular contours and form cues are necessary for stereopsis. That random-dot stereograms, in addition, proved themselves a valuable tool in psychoanatomical investigations (Julesz, 1971) and in the unfakeable testing of stereoscopic depth perception (Julesz, 1964) is beside the point. I only wanted to stress here that a single counterexample that falsifies a theory is adequate, whereas a long list of experiments that corroborate a theory are not adequate "proof" of the theory.

This is in contrast with nonscientific (metascientific) theories that cannot be even falsified. Some of the "Gestalt laws" come to my mind. Here, notions of "good Gestalt," "good continuation," "proximity," and so forth are so vague-

FIG. 2.18. Simple random-dot stereogram (Julesz, 1960) that when binocularly fused, disproved the "null hypothesis" according to which stereopsis required corresponding monocular contours and shapes in the left and right images. (Copyright 1960, American Telephone and Telegraph Company, Reprinted by permission.)

ly defined that depending on their applications, one can always find some "meaning" in which they can be applied.

Let me give a concrete example of the metascientific ways one could apply Gestalt principles to random-dot stereograms. We showed (Julesz & Chang, 1976) that an ambiguous random-dot stereogram can be perceptually biased by a few unambiguous dots whose disparity is adjacent to one of the possible depth organizations. This then would corroborate "proximity" as an important property for Gestalt grouping in stereopsis. On the other hand, I pointed out in my early publications (Julesz, 1964) that the perceived vertical contours of a cyclopean square (i.e., an area hovering in vivid depth over its background in a random-dot stereogram) appear jagged. This is due to the fact that there is a 50% probability that any dot of the vertical boundary might belong to the center square or the surround. If good Gestalt prevailed, then one would perceive the contours as straight lines, contrary to the findings, because a square has a good Gestalt. Thus some aspects of random-dot stereograms agree, some disagree, with Gestalt principles.

I am sure that one could easily define the underlying parameters in random-dot stereograms such that all Gestalt rules would be obeyed. Or one could postulate that stereopsis is such an early process and that the avoidance of all form cues in random-dot stereograms is so total that no "top-down" process can operate, and thus Gestalt organization cannot prevail. My purpose with these comments is not to ridicule Gestalt psychology, which had an enormous historic signifiance half a century ago. I want only to stress that a generation later, some areas of psychology become ripe for scientific theories that can be falsified.

Let me note that my isodipole texture conjecture as a "probabilistic statement" is as valid as most "laws" of psychology. That is, I could state: "From a pool of isodipole textures, any two textures selected at random will have a very high probability to be nondiscriminable.'' However, it is my firm belief that visual perception can now avoid probabilistic theories and instead—as in mature sciences—can affort to post scientific theories of the ''all-or-none'' kind, theories that can be refuted.

PERCEPTUAL AND
NEUROPHYSIOLOGICAL ANALYZERS

Visual perception experts are polarized. In one camp belong those who regard the epoch-making discoveries of Kuffler (1953), Hubel and Wiesel (1962, 1968), Lettvin, Maturana, McCulloch, and Pitts (1959), and other researchers of neural feature extractors as a *solution* to perceptual problems. The other camp, including most of my esteemed colleagues at this symposium (as attested by their contributions printed in these proceedings), completely ignore the present state of visual neurophysiology. (As a matter of fact, at this symposium several of my colleagues stated that the greatest mistake of the Gestalt psychologists was to have taken their contemporary neurophysiologists too seriously.)

I agree with the second camp that the relationship between the *local* discipline of present neurophysiology—based on single microelectrode recordings—and the highly *global* discipline of visual perception—preoccupied with complex and enigmatic semantic problems of form perception—is too remote. On the other hand, it seems to me that the perceptual tasks of immediate texture discrimination are less global than those of form perception and therefore are more closely related to single electrode neurophysiology. Furthermore, the perceptual detectors of texture discrimination, such as the B_1, B_2, and B_3, are now adequately concrete concepts (defined by strictly psychological means) that they can be compared to the simple, complex, and hypercomplex cortical units of the neurophysiologists. For instance, the B_1 (QCD) detector could be easily modeled by a simple cortical unit of the Hubel and Wiesel type with elongated receptive field (a narrow rectangle, or an elongated ellipse), as shown in Fig. 2.19. In Fig. 2.19 we illustrate (Caelli & Julesz, 1978) that isodipole four-disk micropattern duals may or may not fall on an elongated rectangular receptive field. The B_2 (corner) detectors, however, cannot be simply explained by evoking the actions of hypercomplex cortical units found in the monkey by Hubel and Wiesel (1968). Some of the known hypercomplex units respond best to perpendicular corners, and conceptually it is not difficult to imagine ways to connect such hypercomplex units, which are tuned to different corner angles and form a general corner detector. Nevertheless, a B_2 detector is more global than any hypercomplex feature analyzer known by neurophysiologists at present. The B_3 detectors tuned to the topological property of ''closure,'' to my knowledge, have not been found by neurophysiologists yet. Furthermore, it is not clear how a gamut of simple,

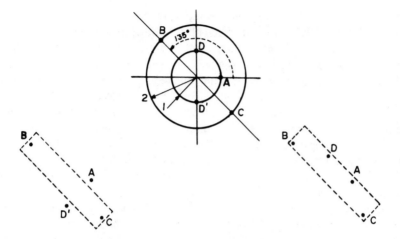

FIG. 2.19. Receptive field structure of the quasi-collinear detector and the isodipole four-disk configurations that result in texture discrimination in Fig. 2.11 (Caelli & Julesz, 1978).

complex, and hypercomplex neurophysiological analyzers together can act as Class A detectors, measuring small deviations from isodipole statistics. Nevertheless, the fact that all cortical feature analyzers in cats and monkeys are selectively tuned to orientation and many of them to specific length makes it conceptually possible to regard a subset of such neural analyzers as a dipole statistics detector.

As we see, even such a relatively simple perceptual task as immediate texture discrimination necessitates perceptual detectors that are beyond the complexity of present neurophysiological analyzers, although some come quite near to them. On the other hand, isodipole textures could serve as stimuli for neurophysiological studies, and perhaps the perceptual detectors we discovered in human texture discrimination might still be found by single microelectrodes in the monkey cortex.

CONCLUSION

We have seen how the simplification of the perceptual task by presenting the stimulus briefly (to avoid eye movements and scrutiny), by imposing stochastic constraints on the stimulus, and by restricting the task to texture discrimination can bring the study of perception to a level that can be handled by scientific methods. Particularly stressed was the importance of studying perception by posing a scientific theory (conjecture) that is adequately concrete to be disproved. The Julesz conjecture of the nondiscriminability of isodipole textures without scrutiny was reviewed, and its recent refutation was discussed. It turned out that the isodipole constraints made all the known feature extractors inoperative except for three—tuned to quasi-collinearity, corner, and closure. These perceptual features behave in a figurelike manner (i.e., they can be perceived singly within a set of isodipole dual micropatterns) and constitute a fundamental topology of form. It is my firm belief that perception is so complex that as long as the "top-down" processes are not reduced, the "bottom-up" processes cannot be studied. The immediate texture discrimination of textures with isodipole statistics is one such attempt to study "bottom-up" processes free from the enigmatic problems of memory, semantics, and the many "top-down" processes that together are often called Gestalt organization and that interfere with the "bottom-up" processes in unknown ways.

Let me conclude this essay with a philosophical note. My 1962 conjecture of texture discrimination, the 15 years of intensive research to disprove it, and the discovery of Class B detectors that falsified the conjecture serve as a further corroboration of Karl Popper's epistemology. His basic criterion of an empirical scientific statement—that it must be falsifiable—(Popper, 1935/1968) has been tested on a concrete psychological example. It is my belief that this psychological example requires less mathematical knowledge from the readers than the usual physical examples that illustrate epistemological treatises. Although generating isodipole geometrical structures—or nth-order Markov processes of the Rosenblatt–Slepian type—presents very difficult mathematical problems, *after* they are constructed, they can be easily understood and verified even by the intelligent layman. So they are conceptually much simpler than the tensors of Riemann geometry or the linear partial differential equations of quantum physics, a thorough knowledge of which is required from the reader in order to understand deeply the many relativistic and quantum physical illustrations of modern epistemological ideas. So, I claim, it is easier to comprehend the epistemological problems of science through visual perception than through the usual examples collected from modern physics.

Let me illustrate this point with an example, again from Popper's epistemology (Popper, 1935/1968). He has a long chapter with many complex examples to illustrate his thesis: "that theories of a lower dimension are more easily falsifiable than those of a higher dimension [p. 141]." My reader who understood that my second-order statistical conjecture of texture nondiscrimination could be falsified after a larger effort than disproving a similar first-order conjecture, whereas a third-order statistical conjecture of texture nondiscrimination is still corroborated and its falsification vastly more difficult, understood the essence of Popper's epistemology as well.

Popper's philosophical ideas were used only as a typical example for modern epistemology, because he had a substantial influence on many contemporary scientists and thinkers—John Eccles (1977), Manfred Eigen and Ruthild Winkler (1975), and Jacob Bronowsky (1977), to name only a few.

This emphasis on the refutation of a theory, of course, has serious limitations for probabilistic phenomena, as Popper himself realized. We all know from statistics that the *rejection* or *acceptance* of a statistical hypothesis comes from entirely *symmetrical* criteria, leading to either a Type 1 or Type 2 error, respectively (i.e., accepting a wrong hypothesis or rejecting a correct one). Because Popper developed his ideas after quantum physics had been proven *inherently* probabilistic, his asymmetric theory—based on rejection alone—was limited to macroscopic events alone, already at its birth. Because suprathreshold phenomena in visual perception are macroscopic events, I have chosen Popper's main idea as my slogan. Needless to say, the originality, generality, coherence, predictive capability, and so forth of a theory are as important as its refutability. However, in psychology, many of the "famous" theories are highly original, appeal to our aesthetic sense, have great generality, yet cannot be disproved. Therefore, I thought that an account of the rise and fall of my texture conjecture, with the resulting emergence of a primitive topology of form, might have some interest for workers in psychology.

The idea to illustrate epistemological problems in physics by perceptual examples was tried by Michael Polanyi in his essays "Tacit Knowing" and "The Unaccountable Element in Science" collected in Polanyi (1969). However, Polanyi was a physicist-philosopher, and his illustrative examples of visual perception were only phenomenological. As a matter of fact, I am writing a book in which I try to illustrate the many problems of scientific research with my own research in visual perception. This essay is a synopsis of this planned monograph. I can only hope that many ideas that were stirred by these recent developments will become clearer in the years to come.

EPILOGUE

Almost 3 years have passed since I wrote this essay, and now that it goes to the printer, I wish to comment on some important late developments. Instead of incorporating these recent findings in the manuscript and revising some statements, I felt it would better fit the general tenor of this essay to keep it intact but add this epilogue. This demonstrates the constant interaction between one's ideas and scientific facts, which in turn are collected as a result of one's prevalent ideas.

One of the most important recent developments was the discovery of a new texture class that is *isotrigon yet strongly discriminable* (Julesz, Gilbert, & Victor, 1978). What is more, discrimination is based on texture "granularity," as illustrated in Fig. 2.20. Here the first row and middle column contain randomly selected black or white picture elements, and the texture pair is generated by moving a 2 × 2 picture-element square aperture row by row to the left and right, respectively. In the left scan, the aperture must contain an *even* number of

EVEN ⟵ -- ⇓ -- ⟶ ODD

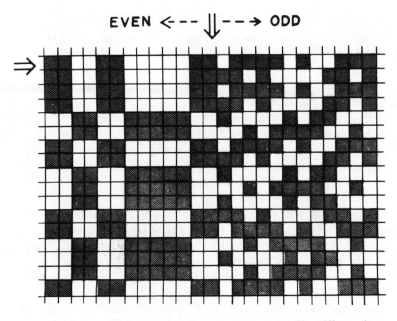

FIG. 2.20.   Strongly discriminable *isotrigon* texture pair based on difference in perceived "granularity" (Julesz, Gilbert, & Victor, 1978).

black picture elements, whereas scanning in the right direction, the number of blacks must be *odd*. Since isotrigon textures, by definition, are also isodipole, "granularity" can be regarded as a B_4 counterexample. That texture grain (granularity) is not determined by the power spectrum will surprise many experts, but that it is even beyond third-order statistical constraints is most unexpected. Furthermore, one can extend this newly discovered texture class by using non-square-shaped apertures of five or more picture elements and can find very weakly discriminable texture pairs that are iso-4gon (Julesz, Gilbert, & Schmidt, in preparation); however, iso-5gon textures seem to be nondiscriminable.

The texture class depicted by Fig. 2.20 is very different from the ones generated before, and one never knows whether an entirely new texture type might not be discovered that yields discrimination; yet the local properties could not simply be described as "closure," "granularity," etc. On the other hand, if one tries line segments and uses the geometric constraints of Fig. 2.12 to generate isodipole micropattern duals, a B_5 counterexample can be found based on "connectivity" (Julesz, 1980b). So "gaps" in a simple line drawing that are the elements of a texture are well discriminable from a dual isodipole texture formed from gapless, connected line drawings.

Recently, I showed (Julesz, 1980b) that all the local nonlinearities in isodipole textures (of the B_1, B_2, B_3, B_4, and B_5 types) could be further reduced to two fundamental perceptual units called *textons*. These two texton classes are the *elongated blobs* (and quasi-linear segments) of given orientation, width, and length and their *terminators*. The preattentive perceptual system cannot measure the exact position (phase) of these textons, only a difference in their numbers. For instance, the counterexamples based on corners and closures in Fig. 2.13 and 2.14 can be regarded as detecting the difference in terminator numbers between dual micropatterns. So B_2, B_3, and B_5 conspicuous dual elements can be regarded as differences in the number of terminator textons, whereas the B_1 and B_4 dual element differences are based on differences in the width and aspect ratio of elongated-blob textons.

These two texton classes seem to parallel the cortical units of the simple, complex, and hypercomplex types that are tuned to elongated blobs and their end points (terminators). Marr (1976), in his "primal sketch" model, was the first to postulate the importance of elongated blobs and their terminators for machine vision. Marr incorporated in his model all the known neurophysiological detectors that yielded workable algorithms. On the other hand, the findings reported here were derived by strictly psychological methods, and the investigators were often skeptical of the role of the highly local neurophysiological detectors in global perceptual phenomena. It took us 16 years to become convinced that such cortical detectors are indeed utilized in texture perception. In view of the differences between the techniques and motivations of researchers in neurophysiology, artificial intelligence, and psychology, it is most gratifying that in the area of preattentive perception, we start to witness a consensus among workers in these diverse fields.

It should be stressed that the texton class of elongated-blob detectors contains many members, each selectively tuned to a blob of given orientation, width, and aspect ratio. It remains to be seen whether the texton class of terminator detectors has more than one member. Obviously, color detectors constitute a third texton class, as suggested by the colored-dot texture studies of Julesz (1965) and by the recent work of Anne Triesman (1979). She observed that conjunctions of features (color and shape) did not yield preattentive perception whereas disjunctive features (color and shape) did. Again, the texton class of color detectors has at least three members (the red, green, and blue detectors). (It turns out that after hundreds of trials, even conjunctions of textons can be taught to yield preattentive discrimination, but only if these conjunctions of textons cover elongated blobs of different sizes and thus are textons themselves, as shown by Julesz and Burt, 1979.)

In conclusion, work with isodipole textures helped to untangle the role of local texture-element detection from that of global (statistical) computation, which appear simultaneously in the discrimination of natural textures. The existence of indistinguishable texture pairs with identical second-order statistics suggests that the preattentive texture discrimination system *cannot globally* compute statistical parameters of third or higher order! I regard this weaker version of my original conjecture as my new conjecture, since all discriminable isodipole texture pairs found so far contained locally conspicuous feature differences (i.e., textons), too. Indeed, as I recently observed, the local elements of these preattentively distinguishable isodipole texture pairs, when presented in isolation, were themselves preattentively distinguishable. That is, when a dual texture-element pair was presented in the periphery at 6 degrees of arc from the fixation point on either side for 120 msec, followed by erasure, the members of the pair could be told apart.

Thus, preattentive texture discrimination is mediated either by local texton differences or by differences in the density of similar textons. Even though focal attention to local texture elements enables detection of the positional (phase) relationship between textons, preattentive (distributed) attention during texture discrimination permits only detection of the presence (or absence) of certain textons. If we regard the global (statistical) processing as the "Gestalt organization" in texture discrimination, then the Gestaltist psychologists were most likely wrong. The wholistic percept of texture is not an indivisible entity, but rather is mediated by local perceptual elements—the textons. The fact that only the simplest first-order statistical parameters (e.g., density) of textons contribute to texture discrimination points to a basically local process. Whether my modified texture conjecture will ever be falsified—that is, whether isodipole texture pairs will ever be found that yield preattentive texture discrimination *without* their local elements being preattentively discriminable too—remains to be seen. Only then would we find an example for a Gestaltist kind of wholistic texture percept.

3

Concurrent-Pitch Segregation and the Theory of Indispensable Attributes

Michael Kubovy
Rutgers University

This chapter is divided into three parts: the first is empirical, the second is theoretical, and the third is philosophical. In the empirical part of the chapter, I describe my research on *pitch segregation*—the segregation of one tone among other concurrent tones. In describing this research, I point out that it draws upon analogies between visual and auditory perception. In the theoretical part of the chapter, I introduce an approach that may be helpful as a heuristic for drawing intermodal analogies. This approach is embodied in the *theory of indispensable attributes*. In the philosophical part of the chapter, I relate the theory of indispensable attributes to classical and contemporary ontology.

CONCURRENT-PITCH SEGREGATION

In this part of the chapter, I propose to describe several strands of research on auditory perception that have much in common with problems that Gestalt psychologists dealt with in their studies of visual perception. After presenting my initial efforts in this field, I give a general characterization of my approach to auditory perception, from which the rest of my work flows.

My work on pitch segregation began with the discovery of a way to create auditory analogues of the Julesz (1971) stereograms. Although most readers of this chapter will be familiar with the Julesz stereograms, it may be useful to review how they are generated. In Fig. 3.1, I have reproduced a schematic explanation of the way random-dot stereograms are created. The most important feature of such stereograms is that the information extracted by the two eyes together is not available, not even partially, to either eye alone. Thus, informa-

1	0	1	0	1	0	0	1	0	1
1	0	0	1	0	1	0	1	0	0
0	0	1	1	0	1	1	0	1	0
0	1	0	Y	A	A	B	B	0	1
1	1	1	X	B	A	B	A	0	1
0	0	1	X	A	A	B	A	1	0
1	1	1	Y	B	B	A	B	0	1
1	0	0	1	1	0	1	1	0	1
1	1	0	0	1	1	0	1	1	1
0	1	0	0	0	1	1	1	1	0

1	0	1	0	1	0	0	1	0	1
1	0	0	1	0	1	0	1	0	0
0	0	1	1	0	1	1	0	1	0
0	1	0	A	A	B	B	X	0	1
1	1	1	B	A	B	A	Y	0	1
0	0	1	A	A	B	A	X	1	0
1	1	1	B	B	A	B	X	0	1
1	0	0	1	1	0	1	1	0	1
1	1	0	0	1	1	0	1	1	1
0	1	0	0	0	1	1	1	1	0

FIG. 3.1.   How to create a Julesz stereogram. A typical random-dot stereogram consists of two 100 × 100 square arrays of randomly selected black and white cells. This figure illustrates how one can cause the segregation of a 4 × 4 square, using a 10 × 10 array in which cells with 0, A, or X entries are to be white, and cells with 1, B, or Y entries are to be black. The left and right images are identical wherever there are 0 or 1 entries; the regions with A or B entries are also identical. Thus the images differ in the relative position of the central (A,B) square relative to the frame (0,1). Only the cells with X or Y entries cannot in general be matched with any predetermined entries in the other image. When these images are binocularly fused, the central square will segregate and appear to float above the background. (After Julesz, 1971, Figure 2.4-3.)

tion is being synthesized, as Julesz (1971) has put it, at "the 'mind's retina'— that is, at a place where the left and right visual pathways combine [p. 3]," thus bypassing, as it were, the peripheral visual apparatus.

How can one present information to the "mind's cochlea"—information synthesized at a place where the left and right auditory pathways combine, thus bypassing, as it were, the peripheral auditory apparatus?

Consider a *chord* consisting of several (say, 7) pure tones (sinusoids) whose frequencies are drawn from the well-tempered (i.e., logarithmic frequency) scale (i.e., the scale playable on a piano). During the playing of this chord, all the tones are present concurrently, without varying in intensity. The chord sounds quite discordant, as you would expect if you simultaneously hit seven piano keys spanning no more than an octave. If we play this chord to a listener's right ear and the identical chord to the listener's left ear, the binaural sound seems to originate inside the head, midway between the ears. Now suppose the two chords differ slightly: their onset and offset times coincide, but the peaks and troughs of the tones in the right-ear chord lag (or lead) by, say, 0.6 milliseconds behind (or ahead of) the peaks of their respective counterparts in the left-ear chord. We have introduced an *ongoing interaural time disparity* between the sounds presented to the right ear and the left ear.[1] The introduction of this disparity causes the sound to seem to originate inside the head, close to the leading ear; in terms of pitch, it makes no perceptible difference.

Suppose we applied one disparity to 1 of the tones and a different disparity to all the other tones (for instance, 1 tone in the right ear leads its counterpart in the left ear by 0.6 msec, whereas all the other tones in the right ear lag behind their contralateral counterparts by 0.6 msec). Although one might expect the "odd man out" pair of tones (called the *target*) to be perceptually segregated from the remaining pairs of tones (called the *background*), a stationary sound of this type fails to segregate the target. One additional step is necessary to obtain segregation: One must successively apply the differential disparity to different pairs of tones in the chord; at any time, only 1 tone has the status of target, and the rest are background. If the frequencies of the tones in the chord are the constituents of a melody, and one makes each of these tones into a target in the appropriate order for the right duration, it is possible to play a melody that cannot be heard with either ear alone but is compelling when listened to dichotically (Kubovy, Cutting, & McGuire, 1974).[2] Figure 3.2 explains the construction of such a stimulus. I call this phenomenon (as well as other related ones) *concurrent-pitch segregation*, because at each moment, one of several concurrent pitches is segregated.

Some Characteristics of This Approach

In order to set this work in context, I now compare it to three related lines of research.

Comparison with Masking and Detection Research

The analogue of the Julesz stereogram already described is not entirely without precedent.[3] First, segregating a tone by ongoing interaural phase disparity is related to the technique of enhancing the detectability of a tone embedded in white noise by using phase differences: This is the topic of the vast literature on

---

[1]The qualifier *ongoing* emphasizes the fact that there is no onset or offset interaural time disparity between them. I refer to ongoing interaural time disparity simply as "disparity" as long as no ambiguity is likely.

[2]On the demonstration tape that accompanies this volume, you can hear a rendition of a well-known tune followed by an announcement of its name. See if you can hear anything monaurally, and then see if you can recognize the tune dichotically.

[3]Its potential was not, however, recognized before the Kubovy et al. (1974) publication. See, for example, Julesz's (1971, pp. 50–53) extensive discussion of the difficulty involved in creating an auditory analogue of the random-dot stereogram.

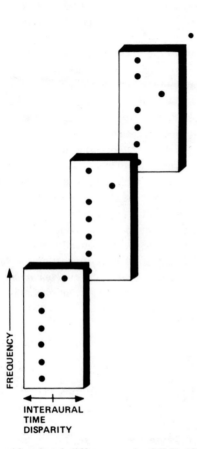

FIG. 3.2.   An auditory analogue of
the Julesz stereogram. Each slab represents a segment of sound about
300 msec long. The abscissa represents
interaural time disparity, or expected
localization in the apparent auditory
intracranial space between the ears;
the ordinate represents frequency on
a logarithmic scale. The "odd man
out" tone is the target in each segment. The stimulus is playing a descending scale.

FREQUENCY

INTERAURAL
TIME
DISPARITY

the masking-level difference, the MLD (Green, 1976, pp. 218–225).[4] Second,
the possibility of creating an impression of pitch in a dichotic stimulus in the
absence of any monaural pitch cues was discovered in 1956 by Huggins.[5]

There are several features that set the present work apart from work on the
MLD and other signal detection phenomena. First of all, in studies of signal

---

[4]A dichotic tone embedded in dichotic noise is more detectable when the tone and the noise have
different interaural time disparities (say, when the noise is in phase in both ears and the tone is 180°
out of phase in one ear relative to the other) than when the tone and the noise have the same
disparities.

[5]The right ear receives broadband white noise while the left ear receives the same noise except for
a temporal delay applied to a narrow band of frequencies. The resulting perception is of a faint signal
that sounds like the shifted narrow band of noise segregated on a background of broadband noise. The
phenomenon has been experimentally explored by Cramer and Huggins (1958), who call it the
"creation-of-pitch." Durlach (1972) calls it the "binaural-subjective-tone"; Jeffress (1972) calls it
"Huggins's pitch."

detection, the typical stimulus involves noise, usually with a continuous spectrum. In the present work, we study sets of discrete tones, well separated in frequency.[6] Second, in signal detection studies, the energy at the signal frequency is greater when the signal is present than when the signal is absent. In the present work, we study pitch segregation—that is, the perceptual enhancement of a target tone that always has the same energy as the background tones. In other words, in these stimuli, there is the same amount of energy at the signal (or target) frequency regardless of whether the signal (target) is present (segregated) or not (i.e., the signal-to-noise ratio is zero). Thirdly, MLD and other signal detection experiments often demand complicated experimental designs and data analytic techniques. In contrast, even though stimuli that give rise to pitch segregation have a signal-to-noise ratio of zero, the phenomena in question are usually so robust and compelling that they can be demonstrated easily to the naive listener.

Comparison with Visual Gestalt Phenomena

These characteristics of pitch segregation studies are reminiscent of the classic Gestalt demonstrations. Take, for instance, a matrix of 16 *o*'s arranged in 4 rows and 4 columns. One can cause grouping and segregation in such a pattern by coloring one column differently from the other columns or by replacing the *o*'s in one column with *x*'s:

    o o x o
    o o x o
    o o x o
    o o x o

The characteristics mentioned earlier apply here: (1) The stimulus consists of an array of discrete entities; (2) the column of red *o*'s or of *x*'s is not segregated because its members radiate more energy (because they do not); and (3) the segregation is compelling and does not require elaborate techniques to be demonstrated.

Comparison with Stream Segregation

It is also important to distinguish the present approach from the complementary work of Bregman (1978; Chap. 4, this volume) and van Noorden (1975). Bregman (1978) and his co-workers (Bregman & Campbell, 1971; Bregman & Dannenbring, 1973; Bregman & Rudnicky, 1975; Dannenbring & Bregman, 1976) and van Noorden (1975) have explored phenomena of organization in frequency and time. Consider an alternating sequence of tones—the lower frequency being 1 kHz, the higher being variable; each tone lasts 40 msec and is separated from its successor by a 60-msec pause. If the tones are 1 semitone

---

[6]The tones are usually separated by at least a semitone.

apart, a warbling, continuous sound is heard. This phenomenon is called *temporal coherence* (van Noorden), 1975). If the tones are 5 semitones apart, a very different organization is heard. The temporal relationship between the low and the high tones is all but lost, and an intermittent low tone is heard concurrently with an intermittent high tone. The high and the low tones have segregated into two streams, a phenomenon called *stream segregation* by Bregman and *fission* by van Noorden.

The visual analogue (noted by Bregman & Achim, 1973, and by van Noorden, 1975, p. 48) is well known. Take, for instance, two lights that flash in alternation; each flash lasts 40 msec and is separated from its successor by a 60-msec pause. If the lights are 1° of visual angle apart, an oscillating, continuous light is seen. This phenomenon is called *stroboscopic motion*. If the lights are separated further (e.g., by 3°), a very different organization is seen. The temporal relation between the right and left lights is all but lost, and an intermittent light is seen on the right concurrently with an intermittent light on the left (Kolers, 1972, p. 152). The two lights have segregated into two streams.

Stroboscopic motion is a phenomenon of space–time organization because of the parallel roles played by space and time: The smaller the distance in space, the shorter the interval required between flashes for the perception of optimal stroboscopic motion to occur. Similarly, temporal coherence is a phenomenon of pitch–time organization because of the parallel roles played by frequency and time: The smaller the distance in frequency, the shorter the interval required between tones for the perception of auditory temporal coherence (for a general theoretical framework that relates, among others, time and frequency scales, see Jones, 1976). In contrast, I am concerned in this chapter with pitch segregation phenomena in which time does not trade off with frequency in this manner. Of course, the stimuli that manifest pitch segregation are extended in time, and they must manifest *some* change; they are, however, "static" or atemporal when compared with the phenomena studied by Bregman or van Noorden.

Successive-Difference Cues versus Concurrent-Difference Cues

What causes concurrent-pitch segregation in the Kubovy et al. (1974) stimulus? On the face of it, a *concurrent-difference cue* seems to be responsible; that is, at each moment, a tone is segregated because it is the "odd man out" with respect to some property. In our case, the property in question would be interaural time disparity: A tone may be segregated because it differs in interaural time disparity from all the other tones.

If we examine Fig. 3.2 more closely, however, we will notice a second kind of potential segregation cue. Each target tone may be segregated because of a *successive-difference cue;* that is, at each moment, a tone may be segregated because it changed with respect to some property, whereas the other tones did not. In our case it would be a change in interaural time disparity: A tone would be segregated because it had changed in interaural time disparity, whereas the others had not. Thus the Kubovy et al. (1974) stimulus confounds two new types of potential segregation cues: a concurrent-difference cue and a successive-difference cue.

In order to tell which is the effective cue in this stimulus, I created two kinds of stimuli, which disentangle successive-difference segregation cues from concurrent-difference segregation cues. Figure 3.3 shows the structure of a sequence of stimuli in which the target is distinguished from the background only by concurrent-difference cues. The first chord localizes the target tone toward the subject's right and localizes all the other tones toward the left. In the second chord, 2 tones remain where they were in the first chord—the tone that is the target in the first chord (in this case, the highest-pitched tone) and the tone that is supposed to be segregated in the present chord. Thus all changes occur in what are supposed to be the background tones, and no segregation can take place because of a *change* in the target.

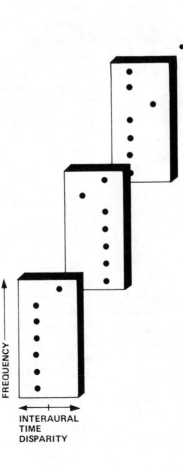

FIG. 3.3.   An auditory analogue of the Julesz stereogram that has only a concurrent-difference cue.

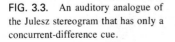

INTERAURAL
TIME
DISPARITY

Figure 3.4 shows a sequence of stimuli that contain only successive-difference cues. The first chord localizes 4 tones toward the listener's right and 3 toward the listener's left. The second chord is identical to the first except for a shift in the localization of the second-highest tone. Now there are 3 tones on the right and 4 on the left. Because each chord is almost symmetrical with respect to interaural time disparity, it is impossible for a tone in one of the clusters to be segregated by virtue of a concurrent-difference cue; whatever segregation is observed must be due to a successive-difference cue.

Six stimuli were generated—one pair of each type of stimulus (confounded, successive, and concurrent cues). Each pair consisted of one stimulus playing an ascending scale and the other playing a descending scale. Subjects were given a forced-choice task—to identify the direction of the scale.[7]

The results of this experiment show that the auditory system is extremely versatile: Subjects could hear both kinds of segregation. They could hear the pure successive-difference cue as easily as the confounded-cues stimuli (on the order of 95% correct identifications of whether the scale was ascending or descending); but they were significantly less accurate in their identifcations of the scale direction when the concurrent-difference cue was used (about 75% correct), although their performance was still significantly better than chance.

The relative weakness of the pure concurrent-difference cue can be explained as follows: In order to apply a pure concurrent-difference cue to a *target tone*, we were forced to move the *background tones* in each successive chord. In other words, we applied a successive-difference cue to the background while applying a concurrent-difference cue to the target. Thus the pure concurrent-difference cue, applied to just 1 tone, overcame the combined effects of a successive-difference cue applied to 6 tones. In conclusion, the notable finding in this experiment is not the relative weakness of the pure concurrent-difference cue, as it may seem at first blush, but rather its ability to cause any segregation at all.

Applying Successive-Difference Cues to Echoic Memory

According to the received view on the relation of perception to memory, information acquired through the senses is transferred, after various amounts of processing, to various types of memory systems, each of which has its characteristic mode of storage and time course. It is not known at what stage in the flow of processing perceptual organization takes place. (See Pomerantz & Kubovy, Chap. 13, this volume, for a discussion of the evidence in favor of bottom-up and

---

[7]In a typical experiment on pitch segregation, the procedure is this: A subject is introduced to the type of stimulus studied in that particular experiment by means of a continuous, cyclic, ascending and descending sequence of targets. When the subject gives a reasonably accurate description of the stimulus (such as "it goes up, and then it goes down"), the experimenter tells the subject that he or she will hear a cyclic sequence of ascending *or* descending scales and that it will be necessary to identify whether each scale is ascending or descending.

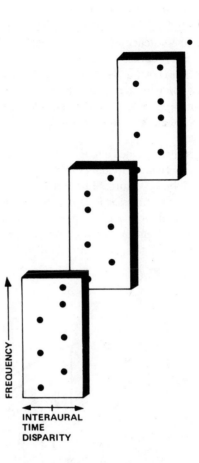

FIG. 3.4.   An auditory analogue of the Julesz stereogram that has only a successive-difference cue.

FREQUENCY

INTERAURAL
TIME
DISPARITY

top-down processes in perceptual organization.) In this section I describe an application of the concept of successive-difference cue, which shows that perceptual organization can be made dependent on a fairly central echoic memory, a finding that limits the degree to which this perceptual organization can be peripheral. At the same time, the demonstration I am about to discuss is not easy to reconcile with top-down processing.

The notion of a successive-difference cue can be generalized to sounds that are not contiguous in time. Consider two successive chords such as those shown in Fig. 3.4 but that are separated by silence. If the pause is lengthy, no segregation will occur. But if the successive-difference cue is effective in the absence of a temporal gap, then there must exist gaps so brief that they will not disrupt the effectiveness of the cue. In other words, by introducing pauses between chords related by a successive-difference cue, it is possible to measure the cue's temporal reach and thus measure the amount of time that the auditory information present in the first chord is sufficiently preserved that it can interact with the second chord. To put it yet differently, successive-difference cues enable us to measure the persistence of echoic memory. (For a review of sensory memory, see Crowder, 1978b.)

Kubovy and Howard (1976) performed such an experiment in order to obtain estimates of the persistence of echoic memory. The structure of the stimuli is illustrated in Fig. 3.5. Although the stimuli were more complex than those shown in Fig. 3.4, their structure is sufficiently similar for Fig. 3.5 to be self-explanatory.

The experiment yielded a rough estimate of 1 second for the persistence of this echoic memory (with individual subjects ranging from .5 to 1.5 sec, although one exceptional subject performed perfectly with an interburst interval of almost 10 sec), which is five times as long as estimates arrived at by Huggins (1975) in a study of the intelligibility of temporally segmented speech—that is, of continuous speech broken up by the insertion of silent intervals. Crowder (1978b) has argued that this discrepancy is not surprising, attributing it to differences in the

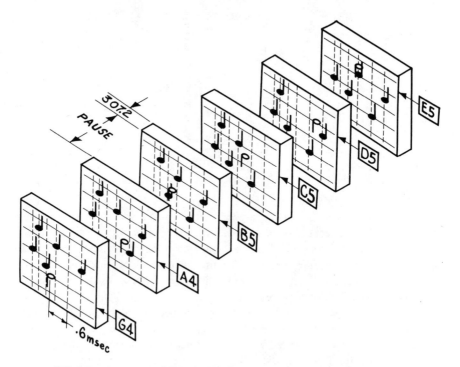

FIG. 3.5. A sequence of dichotic stimuli like the one in Fig. 3.4. There are two differences from Fig. 3.4: (1) Each tone has a different interaural time disparity. (2) A variable pause is introduced between successive chords. The sequence shown is cuing the six tones of an ascending diatonic scale. (From Kubovy & Howard, 1976.)

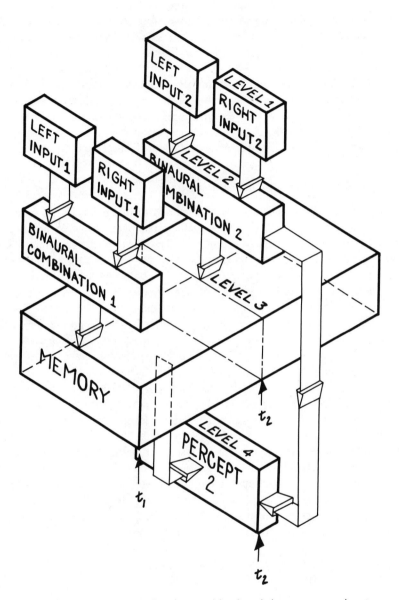

FIG. 3.6. An information flow suggested by the echoic memory experiment.
(From Kubovy & Howard, 1976.)

amount of information one is required to store in order to understand temporally segmented speech compared to the amount of information contained in the Kubovy and Howard stimuli. It remains to be seen whether the persistence of this type of memory can be manipulated by varying the complexity of the chords, as Crowder's suggestion implies.

Figure 3.6 shows an information flow suggested by the results of the Kubovy and Howard study: Information from the two ears is combined and then stored in echoic memory; when the next chord is presented, the stored information is compared to the current input. Segregation can occur if the information stored in echoic memory and the current input are related by a successive-difference cue.

A Monaural Successive-Difference Cue

The segregation phenomena we have discussed to this point are all based on dichotic processing. Because most visual Gestalt phenomena do not require binocular viewing, I turned to the problem of monaural pitch segregation. Two such effects are discussed in the remainder of this section: One is based on a successive-level-difference cue, and the other is based on a concurrent-phase-difference cue. We turn now to the first of these effects.

Consider a monaural chord of 7 nonharmonically related pure tones (whose frequencies were selected from the diatonic scale) of equal sound-pressure level. Suppose we attenuate 1 of these tones for about one-tenth of a second and then restore it to its original level. Assuming no pitch segregation, we would expect to hear the following sequence of events: (1) a click at the moment the level of the tone is reduced; (2) a chord of reduced loudness until the level of the tone is restored; (3) a click when the level of the tone is restored; and finally, (4) a chord perceptually identical to the one heard before the level of the tone was reduced. When such a demonstration is actually generated, the listener's experience is strikingly different from the one I have just described. Although the foregoing description fits the first three events, the fourth event sounds quite different. The restored chord sounds rather like a chime, whose pitch corresponds to the pitch of the restored tone, on the background of the remaining tones. If various tones are manipulated in this fashion at the rate of two or three times a second, it is possible to play a tune composed of tones whose levels never exceed the level of the other tones in the chord. I have called this effect the *onset-segregation effect* (Kubovy, 1976).[8] This effect appears to be due to a successive-difference cue: The target tone is segregated because its level *changes*.[9]

---

[8]The demonstration tape that accompanies this book contains a sample of this effect.

[9]Although this effect may appear similar to one reported by Duifhuis (1970, 1971), it is not. Duifhuis suppressed the nth harmonic of the spectrum of a periodic pulse; the present demonstration does not deal with harmonically related sounds at all.

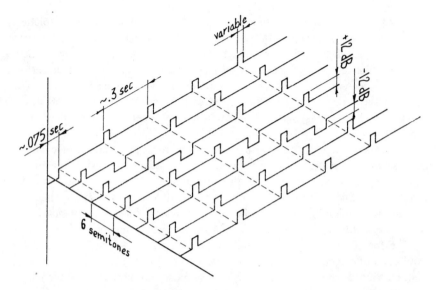

FIG. 3.7.   Schematic representation of a monaural chord used to demonstrate that onset segregation is not caused by energy splatter. The sequence shown is cuing the first five tones of an ascending scale.

Is Onset Segregation Caused by the Spread of Spectral Energy?

It might be objected that the onset-segregation effect may be due to the spread of spectral energy to frequencies other than the frequency of the target tone each time a target tone is restored to the level of the other tones (see Yost & Nielsen, 1977, pp. 134–135).

I conducted an experiment designed to disprove this hypothesis. Consider the chord shown in Fig. 3.7. It consists of 7 equal-level tones equally spaced on the well-tempered scale. They are 6 semitones apart, and their frequencies range from 311 Hz ($D_4\#$) to 3520 Hz (A_7). The level of each tone is attenuated by 12 dB for 76.8 msec and then restored. After 307.2 msec have elapsed, the next tone in the sequence is attenuated, also for 76.8 msec, and then restored.[10] Each time a target tone is restored to its canonical level, the level of all the other tones in the background chord is briefly incremented by 12 dB. As a result, energy splatter is introduced in all the tones. After a variable amount of time has elapsed, the background tones are restored to their canonical levels. If the target tone segregates despite the energy splatter caused by the masking increment in the back-

---

[10]These strange durations were chosen for convenience of interaction with our computer, which took 307.2 msec to read a track from the disk. All durations were chosen so as to be simple fractions of 307.2 msec.

ground tones, we can safely assume that segregation is not due to energy splatter. Figure 3.8 shows the results of a typical group of 11 subjects, whose task was to identify the direction of the scale played by the target tones. The independent variable is the duration of the masking increment. The data show that performance is a decreasing function of the duration of the masking increment. The data also show that the effects of the onset persist for more than 160 msec, because a 160-msec masking increment fails to reduce performance to the chance level (50% correct).

These results suggest that we are dealing with the persistence of a phasic response to the restored target. Suppose a response to the restoration of the target's amplitude consists of a burst of responding that gradually decays to its resting level. Such responses are observed in all peripheral sensory neurons (Adrian, 1928; Granit, 1955). In the auditory system, the decay of phasic responses typically extends over less than a second (see Simmons, 1970); such is the case for all units of the mammalian auditory nerve (Kiang, 1965) and for many units of the cochlear nucleus (Mast, 1970; Moushegian & Rupert, 1970; Pfeiffer, 1966; Smith & Zwislocki, 1971). Suppose, furthermore, that the masking increment applied to the background tones causes independent phasic responses that are inhibited when the tones are attenuated back to their canonical level. If segregation is the expression of the level of activity in one frequency-

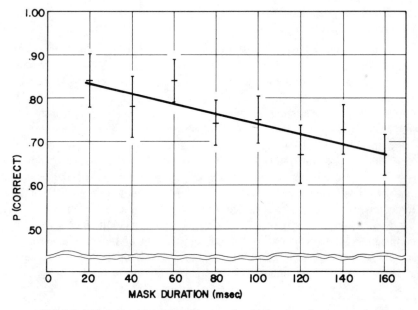

FIG. 3.8.   Proportion correct identification of scale direction of onset-segregated tones as a function of duration of the masking increment in the background tones. The vertical bars extend 1 standard error above and below the mean proportion correct.

specific subsystem relative to the levels of activity in other frequency-specific subsystems, then brief masking increments applied to the background tones at the time of the restoration of the target's intensity should allow the target to segregate, because the phasic activity caused by its restoration will not have decayed by the time the masks are removed. On the other hand, long masking increments should hinder segregation, because the phasic activity caused by the target's onset will have adapted by the time the masking increments are attenuated.

An important assumption made here is one of independence: The time course of the phasic response to 1 tone is assumed not to affect the time course of the phasic response to other tones in the chord. In order to investigate this independence, I varied the frequency intervals (FI) separating the 7 tones composing the chord and did not apply masking increments to the background tones. All tones in the chord were at their canonical level until each in turn (every 307.2 msec) was reduced by 24 dB for 76.8 msec. The values of the FI were 2 semitones (ranging from F_5 [698 Hz] to G_6 [1568 Hz]); 4 semitones—high frequency (A_4# [466 Hz] to D_7 [2349 Hz]); 4 semitones—low frequency (F_2# [93 Hz] to A_4# [466 Hz]); and 6 semitones (D_4# [311 Hz] to A_7 [3520 Hz]). These values were chosen so that two of these chords would have an FI *exceeding* the critical bandwidth (namely, the 6 semitones and the 4 semitones—high-frequency chords) and two of the chords would have an FI *less* than the critical bandwidth (namely, the 4 semitones—low frequency—and the 2-semitone chords). The subjects' task was to identify the direction of the scale (ascending or descending) played by the segregated tones.

The subjects' identification performance was significantly poorer for the chords with an FI less than the critical bandwidth (64% correct, *s.e.* = 4%) than for the chords with an FI greater than the critical bandwidth (77% correct, *s.e.* = 5%): Eighteen of the 22 subjects showed the effect. Thus, when more than 1 tone is present within a critical band but the onset cue is applied to only 1 of them, onset segregation is weaker than when there is only 1 tone in the critical band. This observation suggests that this segregation represents the phasic response of a critical band rather than the phasic response of a subsystem that processes individual tones.[11]

A Monaural Concurrent-Difference Cue

Of the segregation phenomena I have studied, the following has the greatest implications for classical theories of audition. It was discovered serendipitously as I explored variations on the auditory analogue of the Julesz stereograms. In the Kubovy et al. (1974) demonstrations, the tones in the chord are nonharmonically

---

[11]This is not the case for the segregation demonstrated in the Kubovy et al. (1974) analogue of the Julesz stereogram. In that demonstration, several tones fell within a critical band. Informal observations indicate no strengthening of the phenomenon with tones about one critical band apart.

related. That is, the ratios of their frequencies (taken two by two) are irrational numbers because they are chosen from a set of frequencies whose logarithms are equally spaced. I wanted to hear what would happen if the frequencies were harmonically related. The question is of much interest because harmonically related tones fuse perceptually to yield a pitch that is that of the fundamental frequency of the harmonic set—that is, the frequency that is the lowest common factor of all the tones in the set (provided that frequency is not too low) regardless of whether the stimulus contains energy at that frequency.[12] I modified the 1974 stimulus (Kubovy, 1978) so that its frequencies were harmonically related and discovered that the resulting segregation was perceptible both monaurally and dichotically. Although the question of dichotic segregation with harmonically related tones remains meaningful and deserves to be answered, it cannot be studied before the issue of monaural segregation by phase is better understood (lest monaural effects be confounded with the dichotic effects).

Generating the monaural phase segregation phenomenon is simple: Consider a set of harmonically related sinusoids starting all with a positive zero-crossing (i.e., in the sine phase) and having a common zero-crossing at the frequency of the fundamental. Suppose we moved one of these sinusoids out of sine phase for a few hundred milliseconds, and then another (while moving the first back into the sine phase), and so on. The out-of-phase sinusoids will segregate perceptually from the complex sound, and a melody will be heard if the stimuli were appropriately generated.[13]

This effect is a concurrent-difference cue and not a successive-difference cue: Great care was taken to reset the phases of all the components each time a new component was moved out of phase relative to the others, thereby introducing a successive-difference cue in all tones; thus a successive-difference cue cannot account for the segregation of the target.[14]

This result has great importance for theories of pitch perception because the issue of phase sensitivity is crucial to understanding the role of temporal analysis in pitch perception.

Wightman's Pattern-Transformation Model of Pitch

Consider, for example, one of the most influential current theories of pitch perception—Wightman's (1973a; Wightman & Green, 1974) pattern-transformation model. The model is based on evidence, marshaled by Wightman (1973b), against the sensitivity of the auditory system's pitch extraction

---

[12]This phenomenon is known as *the problem of the missing fundamental* (Green, 1976, pp. 175–197).

[13]I believe that the first reports of this type of phenomenon are Schroeder (1959), which is a conference-paper abstract, and Pierce (1960), who described Schroeder's work informally. Unfortunately, the theoretical importance of the phenomenon has not been reflected in the numerous recent discussions of theories of pitch.

[14]The demonstration tape that accompanies this book contains a sample of this effect.

mechanism to the relative phases of the components of a complex stimulus (Schouten, 1940, and many others after him; see Schouten, Ritsma, & Lopes Cardozo, 1962; Wightman, 1973b). Phase-sensitive theories are sometimes called *fine-structure theories of pitch*. The data Wightman (1973b) collected were pitch matches to complex sounds. In one experiment, a replication of Ritsma and Engel (1964), he was unable to discover any effects of relative phase on the pitch matches to two 3-tone harmonic complexes centered at 2000 Hz: In one complex, all 3 tones started in cosine phase, in the other complex, however, the 2 flanking tones started in cosine phase, whereas the center component started in sine phase. In a second experiment, a replication of Patterson (1973), Wightman used 12-component anharmonic complexes evenly spaced in frequency (every 200 Hz): There was no detectable difference in the pitch matches to these complexes when all the components started in cosine phase, compared to when the starting phases of these components were random.

According to Wightman's (1973a) model, pitch perception is the outcome of a series of transformations of what he calls "patterns of neural activity [p. 415]." First of all, the acoustic waveform is transformed into a "peripheral" activity pattern, which preserves the essential features of the power spectrum of the waveform. Secondly, the peripheral activity pattern undergoes a Fourier transformation, resulting in a pattern akin to the autocorrelation function of the waveform. Pitch perception is determined by the peaks in this autocorrelation-like pattern. These two transformations insure that pitch perception will be insensitive to phase. The temporal fine structure of the waveform does not affect pitch perception unless it influences the peripheral activity pattern. Thus, if pitch perception is affected by phase, an entirely different class of models would be required.[15]

Some Data and an Explanation

Ray Jordan and I have recently collected data that persuasively document the ear's sensitivity to phase (Kubovy & Jordan, 1979). The stimuli consisted of the 3rd to 14th harmonics of a 200-Hz fundamental, played in the sine phase, forming a 12-component complex (with components ranging from 600 Hz to 2800 Hz). Every 307.2 msec, the phases of all components but one were reset to 0° (i.e., a successive-difference cue was applied to all components); the phase of the remaining component (the target) was set to some other phase angle. The sequence of targets formed either an ascending or a descending scale. Fourteen values of phase shift were studied for each of eight subjects; the results are shown in Fig. 3.9. Beyond a phase shift of 40°, the accuracy of subjects' scale-direction judgments is essentially perfect.

---

[15]This theory does not claim that the ear is insensitive to all effects of phase. For instance, it does not deny that phase affects timbre.

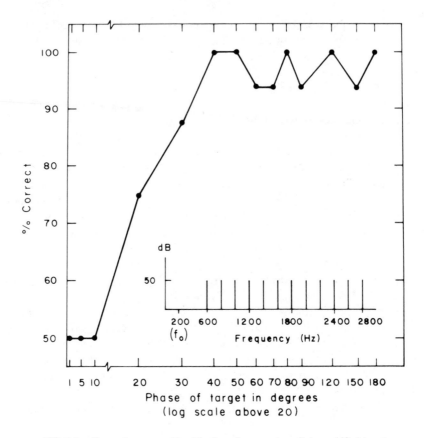

FIG. 3.9.   Proportion correct identification of progression of phase-shifted target tones as a function of phase shift in degrees. (From Kubovy & Jordan, 1979.)

Although these results seem to argue overwhelmingly against theories that maintain phase insensitivity of the single ear, we should not be too hasty to reject theories like Wightman's. For suppose that these theories were essentially correct but that at some peripheral stage of processing, the concurrent-difference cue in question (the phase disparity of the target) were transformed into some other concurrent-difference cue such as intensity. In such a case, the ear would *appear* to be phase sensitive, but the pitch perception mechanism would not be.

Such a processing stage is in fact quite likely, given the nonlinear, compressive psychophysical function. Suppose that the waveform is transformed by a compressive power function—a cubic-root transformation, for instance.[16] Then it can be shown that there exists a peak in the power spectrum of the compressed waveform *at precisely the frequency of the phase-shifted component*. Figure 3.10

---

[16]The argument I am about to develop does not hinge on the precise value of the exponent, only on its being less than 1—that is, on the nonlinear stage obeying a compressive function.

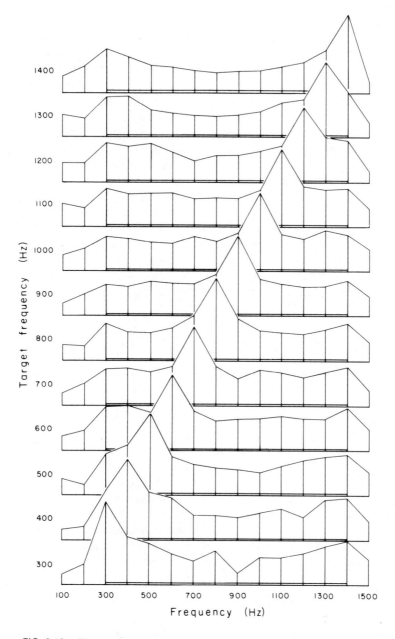

FIG. 3.10. The power spectra of 12 chords after undergoing a cubic-root transformation in the time domain. The waveforms at input to the transformation were characterized by uniform power spectra (equal power at frequencies 300, 400,..., 1300, 1400) and nonuniform phase spectra only with respect to one component in each chord. The power spectra of the output waveforms show a peak at the frequency of the "odd man out" with respect to phase in the input waveform. (From Kubovy & Jordan, 1979.)

shows 12 power spectra, each corresponding to one segment of the stimulus employed in the experiment. In each segment, 1 tone was phase-shifted by 90° relative to the other tones. The resulting waveform was submitted to a cubic-root transformation, the output of which was submitted to a Fourier analysis, from which the plotted power spectrum was calculated. It is apparent from this demonstration that simple and plausible mechanisms can transform phase differences into power differences. This observation has, of course, no more than the status of an existence proof; it does not provide direct evidence concerning the source of the ear's sensitivity to phase. But it is, from my point of view, a valuable existence proof. It demonstrates that the problem of the ear's sensitivity to phase is inextricably bound to the problem of nonlinearities in the auditory system. Until the latter problem is solved, it will not be possible to create the stimuli needed to test theories such as Wightman's—stimuli that have a phase difference in one component but present a uniform power spectrum to the pitch perception system.

On the other hand, this observation does suggest a way of determining the nature of the ear's nonlinearity and answering the question of phase sensitivity at the same time. Suppose the ear's nonlinearity can be described by a function $f(x)$. Suppose, furthermore, that we applied the inverse transformation, $f^{-1}(x)$, to the stimulus employed in the experiment with Ray Jordan. If this stimulus were presented to the ear, the nonlinear stage would take the inverse of an inverse, which is a null transformation. Thus we would effectively restore the power spectrum of the stimulus as processed by the pitch extraction stage to uniformity and its phase spectrum, to an ''odd man out'' state. If listeners could still detect the target tones in the appropriately transformed stimuli, then one could argue strongly in favor of a phase-sensitive system.

Of course, we do not know the function $f(x)$. We must therefore search for it. The procedure would be to find the nonlinear anticompressive function $g(x)$ that minimizes the strength of the segregation by phase. If one is willing to assume that $g(x)$ is the inverse of the nonlinear compressive function in the auditory system, then one can ask: Is this minimum strength of segregation after $g(x)$ is applied greater than zero? If it is, the system is phase sensitive; otherwise, the system is phase insensitive, and confidence in the current theories of pitch perception can be restored. If the system is phase sensitive, these theories will have to be replaced, probably by fine-structure theories. Until the time that such a decision is made, we must consider the issue undecided.

Coda

My goal in this part of the chapter was to convince the reader that concurrent-pitch segregation is a rich vein deserving further exploration. Aside from its intrinsic interest and the exhilaration one can experience while creating and listening to demonstrations of pitch segregation, it may be a valuable—and demanding—testing ground for psychoacoustic theories developed in other contexts. Furthermore, it is an approach that can provide answers to a long-standing problem in attention that has not traditionally been studied in auditory psychophysics: the cocktail party problem. The approach taken by students of auditory psychophysics to this issue is, I believe, well captured by the following quotation from Jeffress (1972):

> Many of the facts of binaural listening are summarized in the commonplace, "Two ears are better than one." Two ears provide a spare, they permit us to localize sound quickly and accurately, and they help us detect a signal in noise—for example, speech in a background of other speech (the "cocktail-party effect") or a tonal signal in a background of thermal noise [p. 351].

There are two problems with this approach. First of all, it overlooks the selective attention possible in a one-eared person. In other words, it focuses on that aspect of the cocktail party problem to which the masking-level-difference phenomenon can be applied. Second, it adopts a detection point of view rather than a "parsing" point of view (such as illustrated by Bregman in Chap. 4, this volume). The notion of detection presupposes that the device knows what it is looking for. That may be an appropriate model for a person scanning a radar screen or listening to sonar, but it is an extremely implausible simplification of the way human beings (and probably other animals, for that matter) deal with ambient sound. An auditory system cannot be assumed to be constantly "listening for" specific stimuli (even for those stimuli that are particularly effective triggers of behavior). Rather, one must assume that the auditory system, like the visual system, is perpetually engaged in constructing a mental representation of the acoustic environment (see Shepard, Chap. 10, this volume). A necessary condition for achieving such a representation is to group parts of the acoustic input and segregate others, in a process that creates auditory "objects" (see Bregman, Chap. 4; Julesz, Chap. 2; Kahneman & Henik, Chap. 7; and Pomerantz, Chap. 6; this volume).

Because the problem of concurrent-pitch segregation is the study of (relatively) nontemporal features of sound that cause the perceiver to group parts of the acoustic input and segregate others, solving this problem is a precondition to solving the cocktail party problem.

THE THEORY OF INDISPENSABLE ATTRIBUTES

In the first part of this chapter, I described research using the following rough-and-ready heuristic: In order to discover Gestalt phenomena that are analogous in vision and audition, map the spatial distribution of the visual stimulus into a distribution over frequency in the auditory domain, and map the temporal distribution of the visual stimulus into a temporal distribution of the auditory stimulus. Although there is no assurance that this heuristic will produce analogical phenomena (which is why I call it a heuristic and not a law), it is an extremely useful way of thinking about similarities between visual and auditory stimuli. The theory of indispensable attributes, to which our discussion presently turns, is a systematic attempt to justify this heuristic. After developing the theory, I show how it can be used as a guide to predict where one may observe phenomena of perceptual organization and as a guide to the prediction of how one can form attentional channels. But before we turn to the theory, we must deal with a traditional analogy that compares visual space to auditory space, and visual time to auditory time. (For an illuminating review of the literature on intermodal analogies, see Marks, 1978.)

The Traditional Intermodal Analogy

The traditional intermodal analogy emphasizes the assumption that all perceptual systems are designed to facilitate our commerce with a spatiotemporal environment, to allow us to orient in space and time, and to deal with three-dimensional objects and with the events in which those objects participate. Thus if perceptual systems seem to exhibit analogies, it is because they process information about the same objects and events. This is my interpretation of Gibson's (1966) view. He asks us to consider a fire "a terrestrial event with flames and fuel." A fire provides information for the ears, the nose, the skin, and the eyes. "The crackling sound, the smoky odor, the projected heat, and the projected dance of the colored flames [p. 54]" are all information about the same event, and each alone is sufficient to allow us to detect the fire. For this event, the four kinds of stimulus information are *equivalent*. Gibson (1966) continues:

> If the perception of fire were a compound of separate sensations of sound, smell, warmth, and color, they would have had to be associated in past experience in order to explain how any of them could evoke memories of all the others. But if the perception of fire is simply the pickup of information the *perception* will be the same whatever system is activated, although, of course, the conscious sensations will not be the same. If all perceptual systems are activated, the information is redundant. . . . .
>
> Different stimulus energies—acoustical, chemical, and radiant—can all carry the same stimulus information. The equivalence of different ''stimuli'' for perception has long been a puzzle, but it ceases to be puzzling if we suppose that it results from equivalent stimulus information being carried by different forms of stimulus energy [p. 54].

Another version of the same position relies on a comparison of descriptions of visual and auditory stimuli. An optical array can be described as a function of four variables $f(x,y,t,\lambda)$ where x and y are spatial coordinates, t is time, and λ represents wavelength. This function describes the amount of radiant energy passing through every point of an imaginary frontal plane before the observer, at every moment and for every wavelength. Analogously, an acoustic field can be described as a function of four variables $g(x,y,t,\omega)$ where x and y are spatial coordinates, t is time, and ω represents frequency. This function describes the distribution of vibrations at every point of an imaginary horizontal plane passing through the listener's ears. The belief that we use the information contained in the optical array and in the acoustic field in order to orient in space–time leads most naturally to analogies that map the spatiotemporal aspects of vision into the spatiotemporal aspects of audition. The tendency to create such analogies is further reinforced by the observation that the nonspatiotemporal dimensions in vision and in audition—the wavelength of light and the frequency of sound—can be conceptualized as wave phenomena.

It is, I believe, this analogy that guided Helmholtz's (1877/1954) observations about differences between the sense of sight and the sensation of tone.

> Two different kinds or grades must be distinguished in our becoming conscious of a sensation. The lower grade of this consciousness, is that where the influence of the sensations in question makes itself felt . . . without our needing or indeed being able to ascertain to what particular part of our sensations we owe this or that relation of our perceptions. In this case we will say that the impression of the sensation in question is *perceived synthetically.* The second and higher grade is when we immediately distinguish the sensation in question as an existing part of the sum of the sensations excited in us. We will say then that the sensation is *perceived analytically* [p. 62].[17]

The Theory

In the first part of this chapter I discussed similarities between auditory temporal coherence and visual stroboscopic motion. This analogy is strengthened by the observation that melodies are often likened to objects moving in pitch space (Helmholtz, 1877/1954, p. 252; Koffka, 1935, p. 435; Zuckerkandl, 1956/1969, pp. 74–148). These observations suggest a more general analogy between frequency in audition and spatial location in vision. In fact, a number of writers have discussed such an analogy. Mach (1906/1959), for instance, wrote:

> A tonal series occurs in something which is an analogue of space, but is a space of one dimension limited in both directions and exhibiting no symmetry like that, for instance, of a straight line running from right to left in a direction perpendicular to

---

[17]The terms were coined by the English translator of *On the Sensations of Tone*, A. J. Ellis; Helmholtz's terms were *appercipirt* and *percipirt*, respectively, which were borrowed from Leibniz. Similar contrasts can be found in Külpe's "doctrine of compounds" between "colligation" and "fusion" (Külpe, 1895, pp. 19–21, 300–301); in Erickson's (1968) distinction between "topographic" and "nontopographic" modalities; in Julesz's (1971, pp. 133–136) discussion of "perceptual decomposition operators"; and in Berglund, Berglund, and Lindvall's (1976, p. 434) distinction between "heterogeneous" and "homogeneous" percepts.

the median plane. It more resembles a vertical right [straight] line. . . . That the province of tone-sensation offers an analogy to space, and to a space having no symmetry, is unconsciously expressed in language. We speak of high tones and deep tones, not of right tones and left tones, although our musical instruments suggest the latter designation as a very natural one [p. 278].[18]

Pratt (1930) and Roffler and Butler (1968) have empirically confirmed Mach's phenomenological report. They have shown a correlation between the pitch of a sound and the apparent location of its source: The higher the pitch, the higher the apparent location of its source.

More recently, Attneave and Olson (1971) have elaborated on the special status of frequency in hearing and have—implicitly at least—likened it to spatial location (following upon Ehrenfels, 1890). Just as a visual object can be moved in spatial location without destroying its perceptual identity, "a melodic phrase. . . . is *transposable:* the pattern as a whole may be raised or lowered in pitch without destroying its perceptual identity. The corollary of this statement is that pitch is a *medium,* in which the same pattern may have different locations [p. 148]."[19]

The goal of the theory of indispensable attributes is to explain why visual spatial location is analogous to auditory frequency. We first develop the theory with respect to a general function with which we can describe visual stimuli, $f(x,y,t,\lambda)$, defined over two dimensions of spatial location,[20] event time,[21] and wavelength. The theory will tell us how to partition these four dimensions into two groups: (1) the indispensable attributes (event time and the two dimensions of spatial location); and (2) a dispensable attribute (wavelength).

The Thought Experiment

I have found it convenient to introduce the concept of an indispensable attribute by means of a thought experiment. Before presenting the procedure of the experiment, we must first define a special type of stimulus it requires.

Discrete Stimuli.   Consider a stimulus that consists of several compact (technically, arcwise connected) sets, each of which is isolated (technically, mutually disconnected) from all the rest, in a four-dimensional spatial location—event time—wavelength Euclidean space.[22] We will call such a stimulus a *discrete stimulus.*

---

[18]See also Mach (1906/1959), pp. 282–284.

[19]According to Attneave and Olson, spatial location and pitch are both *morphophoric* or form bearing (from the Greek *morphe*, form; and *phorein*, to bear).

[20]I use this term instead of *space* in order to distinguish it from *spatial frequency*.

[21]I use this term instead of *time* in order to distinguish it from *frequency*.

[22]A nonempty set S in Euclidean space is said to be *arcwise connected* if any two points in S can be connected by a continuous arc completely contained in S. For our purposes, a disconnected set can be thought of as a set that is not arcwise connected.

In order to visualize a discrete stimulus, consider a physical analogy in standard three-dimensional Euclidean space. Imagine a sealed aquarium filled with water and a number of viscous blobs floating in the water. Assume, for the sake of this illustration, that the blobs cannot break up or mix. The blobs are the arcwise connected sets; they are mutually disconnected because they cannot mix. As long as the blobs do not mix, the blobs can take on any shape and intertwine in complicated ways without losing their discreteness.

Returning to stimuli, consider a stimulus that consists of two well-separated patches of color—one emitting radiant energy in the red region of the spectrum, the other emitting radiant energy in the green region of the spectrum. If you represent such a stimulus as a three-dimensional plot—two axes for spatial location and one for wavelength—the plot will consist of two arcwise connected but mutually disconnected blobs; hence the stimulus will be classified as discrete. More complicated kinds of discrete stimuli are possible, of course. As an example, imagine these two patches moving and following identical spatial trajectories, with one lagging behind the other, so that each retains its connectedness and at every moment, the objects remain mutually disconnected.

Perceptual Numerosity.   Having introduced the concept of discrete stimulus, we can proceed to the thought experiment proper. In the experiment, an observer is shown a discrete stimulus and is asked to say how many *entities*[23] are visible in the stimulus—that is, to judge its *perceptual numerosity.* For instance, the stimulus described earlier—consisting of two well-separated patches of color, one red and the other green—will most likely elicit a perceptual numerosity judgment of "two." Although the number of disconnected sets in a stimulus may equal its perceptual numerosity, such an equality is not necessary. A stimulus that consists of N_m disconnected sets may elicit a smaller judged numerosity.

Indispensable Attributes.   Suppose we transformed the discrete stimulus described earlier in the wavelength domain so that its two patches were identical in wavelength. We would still expect an observer to report seeing two entities.[24] If, on the other hand, we had transformed the stimulus in the spatial domain so that the two patches were indistinguishable spatially, we would expect an observer to report seeing just one entity. In visual stimuli that vary along the two dimensions of wavelength and spatial location, variation in spatial location is necessary for these stimuli to be perceived as consisting of multiple entities. Roughly, this is what we mean when we refer to indispensable attributes: Without variation on these dimensions, accurate report of perceptual numerosity is not possible.

The example I just discussed is a bit too simple to do justice to the concepts. If

---

[23]In the visual context, the word *entity,* as I use it, will sometimes be synonymous with the word *object* and sometimes with the word *event.*

[24]With some exceptions to which we return later.

the stimulus did not consist of two temporally coexistent patches of color, but of two patches appearing both at different places and at different times, then eliminating variation with respect to spatial location would not cause an observer to see just one entity. Because the two patches would appear at the same spot at different times, the observer would still see two of them. Similarly, eliminating variation with respect to event time would not cause the observer to change the judgment of numerosity. Variation with respect to both spatial location *and* event time must be abolished for the observer to have a reduction in perceptual numerosity. In other words, spatial location and event time are jointly indispensable but individually dispensable: They are individually dispensable in the sense that either of them alone cannot invariably reduce perceptual numerosity; but they are jointly indispensable in the sense that elimination of variation on both of them together will invariably reduce perceptual numerosity.

Three Putative Counterexamples

I have already asserted that the indispensable attributes of vision are spatial location and event time. In order to help the reader assimilate the concept of an indispensable attribute, I analyze in this section three arguments that have been put forth in objection to the indispensability of spatial location. The three arguments are couched in terms of thought experiments in which the stimulus is distributed over spatial location and wavelengths but not over time.

The first argument concerns the concept of perceptual numerosity. Consider once more the stimulus that consists of two spatially separated patches of color—in this case, one appearing red and the other appearing yellow. In order to show that spatial location is indispensable, we eliminate variation with respect to spatial location and inquire whether the perceptual numerosity of the stimulus is reduced. Although the mixture will usually be called orange, suggesting that usually the numerosity of the stimulus will have been reduced from two to one, orange does look like a mixture of red and yellow, raising the possibility that the mixture might be seen as red plus yellow (see Metelli, 1974, on "color scission"). If the latter happens, how can we argue that spatial location is indispensable, since it failed to reduce the numerosity of the stimulus? In response to this point, we note that the numerosity of orange is illusory, because *all* instances of orange appear to be numerous in the sense of appearing as a mixture of red and yellow regardless of whether the experience is caused by a monochromatic 600-nanometer (orange-appearing) light, or by a mixture of a 570-nm (yellow-appearing) light and a 670-nm (red-appearing) light. In view of this example, I propose to refine somewhat the notion of perceptual numerosity: If it can be shown that the experience of numerosity for a given stimulus does not require that the stimulus be discrete, then the numerosity judgment should not be taken at face value.

The second argument concerns the necessary and sufficient conditions for being an indispensable attribute. Let us consider a chessboard as a discrete stimulus consisting of 64 regions that differ with respect to both wavelength and spatial location. A subject asked about the numerosity of this stimulus would, most likely, reply "64." Now suppose we reduced the stimulus with respect to the dimension of wavelength: If the squares on the board are not outlined in some other color, the pattern on the board will disappear, and it will be uniform; and thus its numerosity will be reduced. Why does this not constitute evidence that wavelength is an indispensable attribute? The criterion of indispensability is not that abolishing variation with respect to a dispensable attribute *never* decreases the perceptual numerosity of a stimulus, but rather that abolishing variation with respect to the indispensable attributes *always* decreases the perceptual numerosity of the stimulus. In general, as we have seen, there are two indispensable attributes in vision. Thus abolishing variation with respect to the two indispensable attributes will always reduce the perceptual numerosity of a stimulus, whereas abolishing variation with respect to any other pair of attributes will sometimes reduce perceptual numerosity and sometimes not.

The third argument concerns the breadth of the term *indispensable*. The very perceptibility of a stimulus depends on attributes other than space and time. If there were only variation with respect to space and time, only *Ganzfelden* would be possible. Some variation in brightness or color is necessary for a nontrivial stimulus to exist. Thus these attributes are, in some sense, indispensable. This point rests on the interpretation of *indispensable* in its everyday meaning rather than its technical sense as defined by our thought experiment and is not relevant to the concept of indispensable attributes developed here. The theory does not hold that dispensable attributes are unnecessary but rather that they do not play a role in determining whether or not a stimulus will be seen as perceptually numerous.

Application to Auditory Stimuli

Earlier I discussed Helmholtz's implicit analogy between visual spatial location and auditory spatial location, between visual event time and auditory event time, and between wavelength of light and frequency of sound. I then presented some grounds for an analogy between visual spatial location and auditory frequency. Actually, if we wish to draw analogies between phenomena that take place in the indispensable attributes of vision and audition, we are faced with the following problem: Because the spatial attribute of vision is two-dimensional, the indispensable attributes of vision form a three-dimensional system, whereas the two indispensable attributes of audition are unidimensional. Therefore any analogy will involve the mapping of the three indispensable attributes of vision onto the two indispensable attributes of audition. Thus there are two alternative approaches one can take: (1) Map two-dimensional spatial patterns of vision onto two-dimensional frequency-time patterns in audition, thus allowing the analogy to preserve the two-dimensionality, but mapping what is static in one modality on dynamic patterns in the other. (2) Map two-dimensional spatial patterns of vision onto one-dimensional frequency patterns, thus allowing the analogy to map what is static in one modality on static patterns in the other, but impoverishing the pattern by reducing two dimensions to one. (For a detailed discussion of these two "translation schemes," see Julesz & Hirsh, 1972.)

Arguments for the Analogy Between Spatial Location and Auditory Time

I have found three types of argument in favor of translating the spatial aspects of visual form into the temporal aspects of auditory form.

Spatial and Temporal Resolution. Julesz and Hirsh (1972) imply that it is inappropriate to map a highly sensitive attribute of one sense modality into a relatively insensitive attribute of another. Thus, because the spatial resolution of the visual system is vastly superior to the spatial resolution of the auditory system, some attribute other than auditory localization space should be used as an analogue of visual space. The visual system can resolve a sinusoidal grating (a conservative test of acuity) of 30 cycles/° (Campbell & Robson, 1968)—that is, a visual angle of at least 2'—whereas the auditory system cannot resolve more than 1° between successive pulses of tone (Mills, 1972, pp. 309–310).

The temporal resolution of the auditory system is, on the other hand, far superior to the temporal resolution of the visual system.[25] The ear can resolve 1000 interruptions per second in white noise (Miller & Taylor, 1948), whereas the eye is helpless above 50 Hz (de Lange, 1958). So, if we apply the criterion of mapping vision's most sensitive attribute into audition's most sensitive attribute, we will map visual space into auditory time.

Visual and Auditory Gestalt Phenomena. It is possible to construct auditory analogues of certain classical visual Gestalt phenomena by mapping one dimension of visual space into audio frequency and the other into audio time (e.g., Garner, 1974b, Lecture 3; Julesz & Hirsh, 1972; Kahneman, 1973, p. 76; van Noorden, 1975; Pollack, 1977). Bregman (1978) has done so in detail. He recently presented six principles of auditory stream segregation that correspond to classical principles of Gestalt in vision.

Differences Between the Objects of Vision and the Objects of Audition. Gibson (1966, pp. 86–90) and Julesz and Hirsh (1972) emphasize the visual world's stability in time compared to the auditory world's instability. As Julesz and Hirsh put it: "sounds ordinarily begin and end in time, whereas visual objects do not [p. 320]." Moreover, the important sources of sound are *emitters* of sound; that

---

[25]Disregarding the temporal aspect of visible electromagnetic radiation.

is, they are the sites of mechanical disturbances: events. On the other hand, the important sources of light are merely passive *reflectors* of light: things. It is thus quite natural to require that a sensory system be in agreement with its objects— that vision be primarily spatial and that audition be primarily temporal.

The Alternative Mapping: Space into Frequency and Time into Time

However persuasive the foregoing lines of reasoning, I have been following the second heuristic—namely, to map auditory frequency into a visual one-dimensional space in order to allow auditory time to be mapped into visual time. I now reexamine the arguments in favor of mapping visual extension into auditory duration in order to show that none of them is sufficient to rule out the alternative approach I prefer. Although my main justification for choosing this heuristic does not rely on a priori arguments but on its fruitfulness, both experimental and conceptual, this section deals with the three a priori arguments that can be brought to bear on the issue.

Event Resolution of the Visual and Auditory Senses.   Let us distinguish between a sensory system's responsiveness to high frequencies and the degree to which a temporal code is preserved throughout the levels of information processing. Another way of making this point is to distinguish between two aspects of a system's temporal modulation transfer function, one mediated by a device that loses temporal information in the process of coding it (e.g., as the tonotopic organization of the auditory cortex would suggest; see Aitkin, 1976), the other by a device designated to preserve temporal information as event information. The upper bound on the latter's temporal acuity, which we might call the device's event resolution, may be said to constitute a boundary between two subsets of the duration continuum. It is convenient to distinguish between *micro time* (covering four orders of magnitude from the order of 10 microsec to 10 msec) and *event time* (with orders of magnitude of 100 msec or more). Micro time covers the range of pitch-generating periods and interaural time (and phase) differences. When events are separated by such small time intervals, they will be perceived to be fused and not successive. Event time covers the range of times between acoustic events that are perceived as distinct, successive events. There is no fixed boundary between these two ranges, and other factors, such as those that determine stream segregation, determine where this boundary will be. (The distinction between micro time and event time is strongly supported by the work of Hirsh and his co-workers, who have extensively studied the topic of temporal order and auditory perception: Divenyi & Hirsh, 1974, 1975; Gengel & Hirsh, 1970; Hirsh, 1959, 1974, 1975, 1976; Hirsh & Fraisse, 1964.) In order to emphasize the distinction between these two ranges, I adopt the convention of specifying events occurring within the micro-time range by their frequency, and events occurring within the event-time range by their time.

The statement that the auditory system is able to process high frequencies better than vision is true only in micro time. Indeed, vision is exquisitely tuned to spatiotemporal events—as, for instance, in identifying gaits given severely impoverished information (Cutting & Kozlowski, 1977). Although the comparison with audition in this respect is difficult, there does not appear to be any evidence to suggest the superiority of audition in event resolution (Hirsh, 1976).

One-Dimensional Visual Gestalt and Auditory Gestalt in Frequency. There are two classes of visual Gestalt phenomena—those that require two spatial dimensions, and those that can be observed with only one spatial dimension. Consider a page on which vertical black bars alternate with vertical white bars. This is a luminance pattern that varies in the horizontal direction and is constant in the vertical direction. What factors can determine the organization of the display?

1. *Proximity.* Suppose all black bars were equal in thickness but that their spacing varied, as follows: ||| ||| |||. The bars that are close to each other form clusters by virtue of their proximity.

2. *Area.* Suppose that the thickness of the black bars was much smaller than the space between them. The pattern would then be seen as black stripes on a white background. If the black stripes were made much thicker than the spaces between them, the impression would be of a black field on which thin white stripes had been superimposed.

3. *Symmetry.* Szilagyi and Baird (1977) have demonstrated that subjects are sensitive to the symmetry of one-dimensional visual patterns. I do not know of a compelling demonstration of symmetry-based grouping in a one-dimensional pattern, but I believe one could be found.

4. *Similarity.* Consider the following pattern:

|||||||||||||||

The lines in this pattern tend to group according to their lightness.

5. *"Common fate."* Consider a random distribution of vertical black bars. If half of them were moved to the right and half were moved to the left, the right-moving bars would segregate from the left-moving bars.

Hochberg (1971a, pp. 433–437) lists four other determinants of figure-ground organization (orientation, closedness, good continuation, homogeneity, or simplicity), all of which require two spatial dimensions in the display.

Having shown that a fair number of Gestalt phenomena can take place when variation is possible over only one dimension, we can ask: Why not study auditory Gestalt in the frequency domain? This is what I have done and have discussed in the first part of this chapter.

Visual Time and Auditory Time.   Garner (1974b, Lecture 3) suggests that the rules of organization for temporal patterns are similar for vision and for audition. Furthermore, there appears to be an intimate connection between the perceived rate of auditory flutter and the perceived rate of concurrent visual flicker (Gebhardt & Mowbray, 1959; Knox, 1945; Shipley, 1964), an effect that does not depend on whether the auditory and visual sources have the same location (Regan & Spekreijse, 1977). Thus the heuristic that maps visual space into auditory frequency and visual time into auditory time is not unreasonable.

Frequency and Event Time as Indispensable Attributes

We discussed earlier the description of visual stimuli with reference to the function defined over a dimension of event time, a dimension of wavelength, and two dimensions of spatial location. We now discuss the description of auditory stimuli with reference to a function defined over two dimensions of spatial location, a dimension of event time, and a dimension of frequency. Also, just as we interpreted the two spatial dimensions of the visual stimulus as coordinates on a frontal plane through which all light reaching the observer's eye passes, we now interpret the two spatial dimensions of the auditory stimulus as coordinates on a horizontal plane passing through the ears. Which are the indispensable attributes here? Earlier, I pointed out that visual spatial location is in many respects analogous to auditory frequency. I also said that the goal of the theory is to explain why this should be the case. We are now in a position to reach this goal by showing that auditory frequency is an indispensable attribute of audition, just as visual spatial location is an indispensable attribute of vision. In doing so, I also show that auditory spatial location is not an indispensable attribute of audition, although event time is.

We proceed by performing a thought experiment like the one we described earlier. Consider two sources of sound (two loudspeakers, say), one to the right and one to the left of a blindfolded listener in an ideally anechoic chamber. Suppose the left-hand speaker emitted an A_4 (440 Hz) and the right-hand speaker emitted an E_5 (659.3 Hz). The listener would report hearing two tones. If both tones were played over the left-hand speaker while the right-hand speaker was silent, the listener would still report hearing two tones. If, however, both speakers emitted an A_4, the listener would report hearing only one tone originating from a point in space between the two loudspeakers. Therefore an auditory stimulus cannot be perceptually numerous if it is distributed over space alone— that is, without being distributed over frequency (and/or event time). Thus frequency and event time are the indispensable attributes of audition, whereas spatial location is not.

Event time is the second auditory indispensable attribute. The reasons why parallel those given for vision; they need not be reiterated here.

Indispensable Attributes and Perceptual Organization

Up to here, I have presented the theory of indispensable attributes as a justification for drawing analogies between vision and audition. More generally, however, the theory can be used as a guide to predict where one may observe phenomena of perceptual organization.

Configural Properties

The Gestalt psychologists spoke of perceptual organization deriving "directly from the fundamental nature of the physiological processes that are set into action by the sensory stimulation" (Hochberg, 1974b, p. 180) and not from the stimulus itself. Thus, the point of departure of Gestalt theory, as of other traditional theories of perception, was that the input itself is not organized. In contrast, the point of departure of the present account (which follows Garner, 1978a, in many respects) is that stimuli are best thought of as being organized, regardless of how they are perceived, and that they consist of *parts,* of *relations* among them, and of an *attribute* over which these parts are distributed.

We refer to the relations that hold among the parts of a stimulus as *configural properties*. Since configural properties are relations among parts of the stimulus, they cannot be changed without changing some of the parts of the stimulus. For instance, symmetry is a configural property because it is impossible to shift the axis of symmetry of a figure without moving some of its parts. Perceptual organization is the process that occurs when a configural property of a stimulus is perceived. To perceive a configural property means to perceive the parts *and* the relations among them. That is why the Gestalt psychologists spoke of the whole being different from the sum of its parts. Both the parts and the relations among them are perceptible in the whole, Presumably the notion of "the sum of the parts" referred to the enumeration of the parts with no mention of the relations among them. The experience of perceptual organization may be a grouping of subsets of stimulus parts, a figure–ground segregation, a perception of symmetry or repetition, or even the perception of the impossibility of an object represented by a drawing. Some of these experiences can be observed while looking at Fig. 3.11. A *T* can be seen segregated on a background of *x* shapes; the segregation of the *T* can also be thought of as the grouping of the *o* shapes by virtue of their similarity; and finally, the *T* is observed to possess mirror symmetry about a vertical axis.

Because configural properties are stimulus properties, they are sometimes perceived and sometimes not. The difference between those that are perceived and those that are not can be quite subtle. For instance, Julesz (1971) has shown that mirror symmetry in random-dot matrices can be most compelling when the axis of symmetry is vertical but quite difficult to see when the axis of symmetry is horizontal.

```
XXXXXXXXXXXXXXXXXXXXXXXXXXXXXX
XXXXXXXXXXXXXXXXXXXXXXXXXXXXXX
XXXOOOOOOOOOOOOOOOOOOOOOOXXX
XXXOOOOOOOOOOOOOOOOOOOOOOXXX
XXXOOOOOOOOOOOOOOOOOOOOOOXXX
XXXXXXXXXXOOOOOOXXXXXXXXXX
XXXXXXXXXXOOOOOOXXXXXXXXXX
XXXXXXXXXXOOOOOOXXXXXXXXXX
XXXXXXXXXXOOOOOOXXXXXXXXXX
XXXXXXXXXXOOOOOOXXXXXXXXXX
XXXXXXXXXXOOOOOOXXXXXXXXXX
XXXXXXXXXXOOOOOOXXXXXXXXXX
XXXXXXXXXXXXXXXXXXXXXXXXXXXXXX
XXXXXXXXXXXXXXXXXXXXXXXXXXXXXX
```

FIG. 3.11. Figure-ground segregation as an example of a configural property.

The Role of Indispensable Attributes

Consider a stimulus that has a configural property, such as the fivefold symmetric pattern shown in Fig. 3.12 (see Loeb, 1971, pp. 7–8). Three ingredients are necessary to define a configural property (rotational symmetry) displayed by this pattern: *parts*[26] (the triangle), a *relation* between parts[27] (a 72° rotation about a given center of rotation), and an *attribute*[28] (the plane).

As a second example, consider a chord, such as a major triad (G_3, B_3, D_4). The chord has parts (the 3 tones) and a relation (the distance between adjacent elements of the triad—namely, a third). The attribute of this configural property is, of course, frequency.

Now consider a third stimulus: a patch of light that contains exactly 3 wavelengths. It is possible to think of such a stimulus as having a configural property. Here too we have parts—the individual wavelengths, a relation among them—the distance between the wavelengths, and an attribute over which the stimulus is distributed—wavelength. Yet the experience we have when we perceive the stimulus is not one of perceptual organization in the sense described earlier and intended by the Gestalt psychologists. We cannot perceive any relation that holds among the parts of the stimulus, because the parts themselves are not present in our experience. I claim that this is so because the parts are not distributed over an indispensable attribute.

Similarly, consider an array of loudspeakers forming a geometric pattern in space, and suppose that each one emits a different frequency. Such stimuli have

---

[26]Sometimes called the "motif" (Loeb, 1971), the "mode" (Asch, Ceraso, & Heimer, 1960), or the "material" (Goldmeier, 1972, p. 42).

[27]Sometimes called the "form" (Asch et al., 1960) or the "over-all form" (Goldmeier, 1972).

[28]This could be thought of as a "medium" in which the parts are placed.

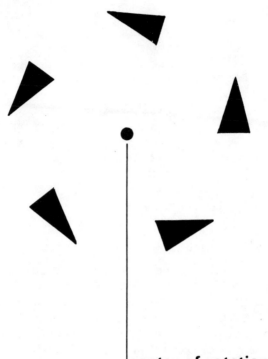

center of rotation

FIG. 3.12.   Parts (triangles) that generate a stimulus possessing a configural property (fivefold rotational symmetry) distributed over an attribute (spatial location).

been called *spatial chords* by Julesz and Levitt (1966). It is impossible to identify their geometric layout, even though it may be possible to tell the different spatial chords apart. These spatial chords have at least two configural properties: one in space, the other in frequency. Although the configuration in space may have some perceptual effects, the configural property itself cannot be perceived, whereas the configural property in frequency can usually be perceived. A relation between parts of a stimulus that are distributed over an attribute that is not indispensable cannot be perceived.

In support of this hypothesis, Deutsch (1975b; 1980) has shown that pitch takes priority over ear of presentation (which I take to be spatial location) in determining perceptual organization. The stimuli for this experiment were composed of an ascending 8-note scale—with successive tones alternating from ear to ear—played simultaneously with a descending 8-tone scale—which also alternated from ear to ear—such that when a component of the ascending scale was in one ear, a component of the descending scale was in the other, and vice versa. All the subjects grouped the tones by frequency range; that is, all of them reported hearing a rising sequence of 4 tones followed by a descending sequence of the same tones, repeated cyclically. Some reported just one stream of tones; others heard two parallel streams. No subject reported an 8-tone ascending or descending scale. The most important finding for our purposes, however, is that no subject grouped the tones by ear, suggesting that grouping by frequency is the more natural way to group auditory stimuli, as predicted by the theory of indispensable attributes.[29]

Indispensable Attributes and Attention

The Concept of a Channel

The analysis of perceptual organization proposed in the preceding section can also shed light on theories of attention. The present section is an attempt to clarify the concept of a channel. We point out the significance of this explication for information-processing theories of attention in general and for theories of dichotic listening in particular.

Following Garner (1974a), we define a channel as any property of the stimulus (or the organismic equivalent of the property) that specifies for the organism what information is relevant to the task it is to perform but is not itself part of the information-bearing aspect of the stimulus. Garner (1974a) clarifies this definition with the following examples:

It is clear that spatial location can be used to specify an information channel. The experiments on short-term memory by Sperling (1960) and Averbach and Coriell (1961) both used spatial location in specifying which items should be reported in partial-report conditions. . . . This technique of partial reporting was used more recently by von Wright (1968). His stimulus materials were either two rows of four letters or three rows of three letters, but these items differed (in addition to location) in chromatic color, brightness, size, and angular orientation. Thus for the partial-report conditions, any of these dimensions could be used to specify a ''channel'' for selective attention (the letter being the information variable) [p. 45].

Similarly, in a dichotic listening task, the right ear is often specified as the channel to be selectively shadowed, to the exclusion of information presented to the left ear.

Two Types of Channel.   Not all channels are equal, however. Let us consider the following array of words:

lamp TEN roof fish
SIX time plant ONE
soon TWO door bird

---

[29]See Deutsch (1980) for a broader context within which to consider these findings. The demonstration tape that accompanies this book contains a sample of this and other phenomena discovered by Deutsch.

Now compare the following two tasks: (1) Read the words printed in uppercase letters; (2) read the three-letter words. The correct responses in both cases are the same. Yet the first task seems much easier than the second. The first task exploits the natural tendency of capital letters to stand out as figure on ground and thus allows the reader not to process all 12 words. In the second task, the three-letter words fail to segregate from the other words, forcing the reader to scan all 12 words in order to decide whether they are "in the channel" or not.

The foregoing example suggests a distinction between two sorts of channels: (1) *Figural channels,* formed by processes of grouping and figure–ground segregation that are relatively independent from the experimenter's decision as to what will count as relevant information to be processed by the subject; and (2) *nonfigural channels,* a rubric that covers all the cases not covered by the first category.

Consider two arrays of words. The first is the one shown earlier:

    lamp TEN roof fish
    SIX time plant ONE
    soon TWO door bird

The second array contains the same words in a different order:

    soon time door bird
    ONE TWO plant lamp
    SIX TEN roof fish

Because the latter array is easier to organize spatially, the segregation of the words in capital letters should be easier with the latter stimulus, because two grouping cues are present in the latter (letter form and spatial proximity), whereas only one grouping cue is present in the former (letter form). Therefore, given a sufficiently sensitive selective attention task, it could be shown that selective attention to the words in capital letters is more thorough—that is, suffers less interference from the irrelevant words, or requires less effort—with the latter array than with the former. To generalize, I am proposing the following conjecture: Selective attention to parts of a stimulus that are concentrated in a compact region of an indispensable attribute is easier (presumably, by any measure) than selective attention to parts of a stimulus that are scattered over various regions of an indispensable attribute. Although this conjecture is straightforward when applied to scanning words distributed in space, it has a rather interesting application to dichotic listening.

In selective attention tasks using dichotic listening, the subject is asked to pay attention to the input delivered to one ear and to ignore the input delivered to the other. Is the attended ear likely to form a figural channel? To answer this question, we wish to determine the indispensable attribute over which parts of the stimulus are distributed. Suppose that lists of letter names are delivered to right and left ears and that the subject is asked to shadow the input to the right ear. Because spatial location is not an auditory indispensable attribute, the indispensable attribute over which two simultaneous letter names are distributed must be frequency. There is, admittedly, only a small difference in frequency if the letter names are spoken by the same voice, but some difference must be present if the two words are to be at all distinguishable. Furthermore, this difference is not consistent. The relevant channel is not consistently higher pitched or lower pitched than the irrelevant channel. Because the separation of relevant from irrelevant channels on the indispensable attribute is not consistent, the channels may be nonfigural. What, then, is the role of the ears? If a figural channel is formed, then the ears must play the role of segregation cue.[30]

To clarify this point, imagine an analogous visual task in which printed words are displayed successively on one line, not necessarily centered in the field, but sometimes shifted a few spaces to the right or to the left. Like this:

```
| Very        |
|     fine    |
| is          |
|     my      |
| valentine   |
|    . . . .  |
```

(In the preceding figure, I have vertically spread out successive words that appear on the same line in the display. Thus the vertical dimension in this figure represents time.) Suppose, furthermore, that simultaneously, and in the same field with each word, other words are presented, printed in red:

```
|          Was |
|    the       |
| king         |
|        or    |
| room         |
|    . . . .   |
```

(Think of the vertical lines that mark the boundaries of the field as being in register in the two examples I have just given.) The subject's task would be to read the red input. Red is the cue that tells the subject to which channel each word belongs. The words are not consistently separated over the indispensable attribute (space), and therefore the two channels may be nonfigural.

Returning to auditory selective attention, consider the following task, which is much more likely to create figural channels than is the dichotic listening task: Two streams of spoken letter names are presented to one ear at widely separated frequencies (e.g., a soprano and a bass reading the two lists). The task is to shadow the high-pitched voice. The relevant channel is likely to be figural

---

[30]It should be stressed that it is impossible to determine a priori whether a figural channel is formed or not. It may depend on the amount of experience the subject has had with dichotic listening tasks.

because the subject is instructed to direct his or her attention towards a consistent and compact region of an indispensable attribute. The visual analogue is straightforward. Two streams of words are printed in black, two-by-two on a given line. For instance:

Very   Was

fine   the

is   king

my   or

valentine   room

. . . .

The subject's task is to shadow the words on the right or the left. Here, too, the relevant channel is likely to be figural because the subject's attention is directed toward a compact and consistent region of an indispensable attribute.

Having suggested that the distribution of relevant and irrelevant items over an indispensable attribute is likely to affect processing, let us consider evidence in favor of this conjecture from the work of Pastore and his co-workers.

The Case of Dichotic Listening: Pastore's Data

Recently, Pastore and his co-workers (Ahroon & Pastore, 1977; Friedman & Pastore, 1977; Puleo & Pastore, 1978) have provided strong evidence against the definition of channels in dichotic listening in terms of ears.

Consider, for instance, the study by Puleo and Pastore (1978). There are three basic conditions in their experiment: a monaural condition, a selective attention condition, and a divided attention condition. The typical *monaural condition* in this study consisted of a traditional yes–no signal detection task: Continuous background white noise was presented to (say) the left ear, and during well-specified observation intervals, a brief 1500-Hz tone was embedded in the noise with a probability of .5. After each observation interval, the subject was to decide whether or not it contained a signal. The remaining two conditions were dichotic: In addition to the input to one ear, the subject's contralateral ear received, during the same observation intervals, an independent series of 1565-Hz signals (with a priori probability of .5) embedded in noise (which was uncorrelated with the noise in the other ear). In the *selective attention* task, the subject was instructed to ignore the input to one ear, whereas in the *divided attention* task, the subject was instructed to respond yes or no to the inputs to both ears.

The results showed a performance deficit in both dichotic conditions relative to the monaural condition, and furthermore these deficits were not significantly different between the two conditions. The crucial data for the interpretation of these results comes from an analysis of the trials into four types: (1) signal in both ears (SS); (2) signal in neither (NN); (3) signal in relevant ear (SN); (4) signal in irrelevant ear (NS). The concepts of relevant and irrelevant ears apply to both the selective and divided attention tasks, as follows: In the selective attention task, "relevant" refers to the attended ear, and "irrelevant" refers to the unattended ear. In the divided attention task, each block of trials is analyzed twice—once with one ear as the relevant ear, and once with the contralateral ear as the relevant ear. That is, in divided attention blocks, an SN trial for one ear is an NS trial for the contralateral ear.

Using these definitions, we can calculate several values of d': The first index of interest is d', which is calculated for the monaural condition. The second index of interest is d'_n, which is calculated in both dichotic conditions by considering the SN trials as signal trials and the NN trials as noise trials. The third index of interest is d'_s, which is calculated by considering SS trials as signal trials and the NS trials as noise trials. Puleo and Pastore found a much greater deficit in d'_s relative to d' than in d'_n, both in the selective attention task and in the divided attention task. Since the stimulus in the relevant ear is the same for both indices, the difference in performance deficit must be due to the presence or absence of a signal in the irrelevant ear. These data suggest that "observers could detect the presence of a signal but had difficulty identifying its source" (Puleo & Pastore, 1978, p. 8).

Puleo and Pastore also studied performance with widely separated stimuli: a 1500-Hz signal and a 3065-Hz signal. With these stimuli, they found no significant deficit in the selective attention task; nor did they obtain a difference between d'_s and d'_n. In contrast, they did find a strong deficit in the divided attention tasks for d'_s but not for d'_n. These findings suggest that the frequency separation of the signals enabled the subjects to identify the source of the signal (because there was a consistent and perfect correlation between ear of input and frequency of signal). They also suggest that subjects were able to divide their attention over the two channels, but that the presence of a signal in both channels overloaded the subjects' capacity and caused a decrement in their ability to process either signal.

In the terminology already developed, this evidence compellingly suggests that the ears are not figural channels whereas frequency bands are likely to be. Such a conclusion also implies that the experiments on selective attention in dichotic listening may have been motivated by and interpreted with the misleading heuristic notion of the ears as figural channels (beginning with Broadbent's, 1958, filter model of attention).

Coda

My goal in the second part of this chapter was to show how a heuristic developed for the purpose of creating analogies between vision and audition can yield more general insights. The first insight concerns perceptual organization: Indispensable attributes are like media within which perceptual organization takes place. If parts of a stimulus are not distributed over an indispensable attribute, configural properties of the stimulus will not be perceptible. In the light of this analysis, it is possible to interpret the Gestalt psychologists' dictum: "The whole is different from the sum of its parts." Figure 3.13 presents this interpretation schematically.

The second insight concerns the relation of perceptual organization to attention. This theme has been developed by Kahneman and Henik (Chap. 7) and by Pomerantz (Chap. 6). Assuming that there is an intimate relation between percep-

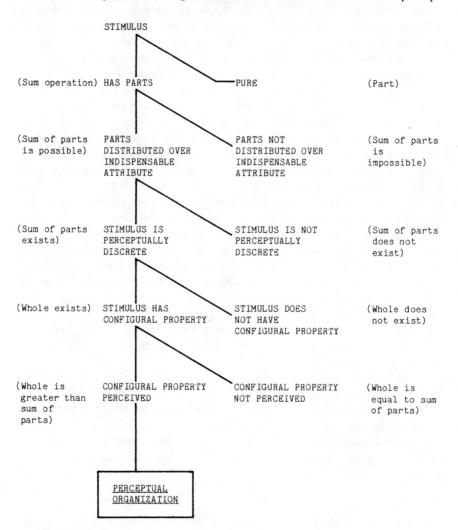

FIG. 3.13.   An interpretation of the Gestalt dictum, "The whole is more than the sum of its parts." The term *sum of parts* is interpreted as the perception of the parts of a perceptually discrete stimulus *without* perceiving a configural property that the stimulus may have. The term *whole* is interpreted as the perception of the parts of a perceptually discrete stimulus while perceiving a configural property of that stimulus.

tual organization and attention, and armed with the knowledge that perceptual organization can occur only when parts of a stimulus are distributed over an indispensable attribute, it follows that not all selective attention is alike. In particular, I have suggested that experimenters cannot arbitrarily define channels for selective attention experiments and expect to develop theories that apply equally to all types of channels. For instance, the two ears (which are not distributed over an indispensable attribute) are unlikely to yield selective attention data similar to two spatial locations in vision (which are distributed over an indispensable attribute).

A Conceptual Hierarchy of Attributes

Consider once more Fig. 3.11. Suppose the *o* shapes were replaced by red *x* shapes, so that the relation that defines the configural property is not form but color. Let's assume that perceptual grouping occurs. Shall we describe this phenomenon as grouping *by* color *in* space or as grouping *by* spatial location *in* color? The former is a more acceptable expression because it captures our intuition of indispensable attributes as "media" in which perceptual organization takes place, whereas the relation in the configural property is most commonly thought of as a "cue" that causes the parts of the stimulus to become organized.[31]

At a more general level, I contend that the notion of indispensable attributes can account for a hierarchy of attributes described by Navon (1978). Navon argues that humans conceive of attributes as if they formed a hierarchy of dimensions in which time dominates space and space dominates every other dimension.

> Consider, for example, a line of circles of various diameters uncorrelated with their positions on the horizontal axis. If someone were to describe in everyday terms an array like this one, we would accept a statement like "The size of the circles is random" or "The circles are not ordered according to size" as intelligible though not fully precise. In contrast, we would probably have a hard time understanding a statement such as "The position of the circles is random" or the like. . . . The size dimension is blamed exclusively for the apparent "disorder." This suggests that horizontal position precedes size in the hierarchy of dimensions, at least in the sense discussed here [p. 224].

By a similar argument, Navon shows that time precedes spatial position in this hierarchy. In other words, "If the order of stimuli covarying on two dimensions is attributed to just one dimension, this dimension is regarded as dominated by

---

[31]Sometimes it is difficult to distinguish the "cue" from the "medium." Consider, for instance, a pattern such as Fig. 3.11, in which the *T* figure is segregated by proximity rather than form. Specifically, all the parts are alike (all *x* or all *o*), but the spacing between the parts forming the *T* is smaller than the spacing between the remaining parts. In such a case, the grouping and segregation cue is a relation of spatial locations, whereas the indispensable attribute is spatial location. The same is true of a chord: The relation is a spacing in frequency; the indispensable attribute is frequency.

the other one [p. 227]." He proposes two further types of criteria for organizing attributes in a hierarchy. The first is: "If objects are said to undergo change of one dimension over a second one but not vice versa, the first is viewed as dominated by the other one [p. 227]." The second is: "If objects are said to assume values of one dimension *at* a given value of a second one but not vice versa, the first one is viewed as dominated by the second [p. 227]."

Navon may be wrong about spatial location dominating all attributes other than time. Consider, for example, a row of loudspeakers, each emitting a different frequency of a different loudness. By Navon's criterion, pitch dominates loudness because it makes sense to say "The loudness of the tones is random" but not "The pitch of the tones is random." When it comes to pitting spatial location against pitch, we can say "The pitches at these locations are random" but also "The locations of these pitches are random." Thus neither spatial location nor frequency dominates the other. Both, however, are dominated by time: If a loudspeaker emits a series of tones varying in loudness or pitch, we will find "The loudnesses (or pitches) at these instants are random" acceptable, but we will reject "The times of these loudnesses (or pitches) are random."

This analysis suggests an extension of Navon's conceptual hierarchy of attributes: Time, the indispensable attribute common to vision and hearing, dominates all visual and auditory attributes. Within each sense modality, the nontemporal indispensable attribute dominates all other attributes. These indispensable attributes are of the same rank in the hierarchy.

We turn now to the final part of this chapter, in which I relate the concepts developed in this part to traditional and modern philosophical concepts.

PRECURSORS OF THE CONCEPT OF INDISPENSABLE ATTRIBUTES

The concept of perceptual numerosity is related to the long-standing philosophical problem of the relation of individuals to universals; namely, what permits us to say that two things, two individuals that are alike in all respects (i.e., belong to the same universal), are in fact two entities? Lucas (1973) formulated the problem as follows:

Tweedledum and Tweedledee were alike in all respects. There was nothing that could not be truthfully said of Tweedledum that could not be truthfully said of Tweedledee. Tweedledum was fat: so was Tweedledee. Tweedledee wore a schoolboy cap: so did Tweedledum. Tweedledum was quarrelsome, but timid in the face of ornithological monstrosities: exactly the same could be said of Tweedledee. Yet, although one in corpulence, in dress sense, and in temperament, they were two people. They were the same in respect of any quality we cared to consider, but different when we came to count them. We express this technically by saying that Tweedledum and Tweedledee were qualitatively identical (the same in all respects) but numerically distinct (counting as different when being counted) [p. 112].

This problem, known in medieval philosophy as the *problem of individuality* (Windelband, 1901/1958, pp. 337–347), led various philosophers to propose their version of the *principle of individuality* (*principium individuationis*), which I have recast as the concept of indispensable attributes.

Thomas Aquinas (13th Century) was one of the earliest to argue that space and time were the principles of individuality. The problem has remained a central one in philosophy, one that preoccupied Leibniz (who wrote *De Principio Individui*) in the 17th Century, Schopenhauer (*Die Welt als Wille und Vorstellung,* Book 2, 23) in the 19th Century, and such contemporary philosophers as Bergmann (1967, p. 23), Carnap (1928/1967, §§ 91, 118, 158), and Lucas (1973, §§ 25–26). The latter four philosophers (but not the former; see Leibniz's *New Essays Concerning Human Understanding,* Book 2, Chap. xxvii) are all agreed with Thomas that space and time are the principles of individuation. In this paper I have replaced the ontological[32] question of individuals with the psychological question of perceptual numerosity, and a solution based on a general principle of individuation that characterizes "the world," with one based on a different set of indispensable attributes for each sensory modality.

A second line of thought to which my analysis is related is Kant's *Critique of Pure Reason.* Kant argues that although "we can never represent to ourselves the absence of space [p. A23/B38],"[33] "we can quite well think of it as empty of objects [pp. A24/B38–39]." Here Kant is inviting us to perform a thought experiment akin to the construction of perceptually numerous stimuli and their reduction with respect to the attribute of space. Kant's conclusion that space and time are the forms of perception (what I have been calling indispensable attributes) is explained by Körner (1955) thus: "To use a very crude analogy, space and time are the spectacles through which our eyes are affected by objects.[34] The spectacles are irremovable. Objects can only be seen through them [p. 37]." According to the theory of indispensable attributes, objects can be perceived only if they are distributed over an indispensable attribute or over indispensable attributes. In the case of vision, these attributes are the same as Kant's forms— namely, space and time.

Recently, students of Kant have argued that Kant's conclusions rely excessively on one sensory modality. Bennett (1966), for instance, writes: "There is . . . no reason for letting eyesight dominate our inquiries into spatial concepts; but I shall argue further that such a domination, in the form which it usually takes in philosophical writing, is positively dangerous [p. 30]." Indeed, Bennett proceeds to examine hearing (following Strawson, 1959) and concludes that frequency is "spatial" for hearing.

Lucas (1973, § 27) also developed Strawson's argument, with the minor difference that his nonvisual world is couched as a "wireless world" in which

---

[32]Ontology is the branch of philosophy that deals with being, with what exists.
[33]It is customary to refer to the two editions of the *Critique* as A and B.
[34]*Critique of Pure Reason,* pp. A50/B34.

"each listener can 'move' in . . . 'frequency space' [p. 125]." He comes very close to the method I am proposing to define indispensable attributes in the following passage:

> Although one station can occupy different positions in [frequency] space at different times, and different stations can occupy the same position at different times, different stations cannot occupy the same position in [frequency] space at the same time. For if they came to occupy the same position at the same time there would be no way of telling them apart, or identifying them thereafter [p. 130].

More important, however, is the recognition that there cannot be universal principles of individuation. From the philosopher's point of view, each "possible world" has its own principle of individuation. From the psychologist's point of view, that means that each sense modality has its own indispensable attributes.

ACKNOWLEDGMENTS

The work reported in this chapter was supported by USPHS Grant 1 RO3 28531 and NSF Grant BNS76-21018. An early draft was written while I was Senior Associate at the Department of Psychology, Melbourne University, Victoria, Australia, in June and July 1977. I am grateful to P. Ellsworth, L. E. Marks, L. Kaufman, A. Koriat, J. Pomerantz, and A. J. Wearing for their detailed critiques; and to N. Graham, F. P. Howard, D. Irvine, R. Jordan, D. Kahneman, D. H. Krantz, P. Podgorny, M. Posner, R. Tourangeau, T. S. Wallsten, and the Apocalyptic Determinists for their comments.

4 Asking the "What For" Question in Auditory Perception

Albert S. Bregman
McGill University

The theme of this conference is "organization in perception." I would like to discuss an approach to organization that allows us to gain a great deal of leverage in studying it and that generates a large number of new questions. It involves asking the question, "what is the role of this organization in the larger system of perception and cognition?" Rather than treating organization as a subject in its own right and trying to establish finer and finer details about how it works, one moves up a level and tries to see the organization as serving some useful end. This involves thinking about the problems that the whole person faces in using the information available to his or her sense organs in trying to understand an environment. We have been sensitized to a number of these problems from two directions recently. One is the forceful advocacy by James J. Gibson (e.g., 1966) of an ecological approach to perception, one in which the researcher is constantly aware of the structure of the environment, of how the person moves about in it, and of what sorts of information the interaction with the environment makes available to the person. A second recent influence is research on perception in the field of artificial intelligence (e.g., Winston, 1975). Because intelligent machines are required actually to work and to achieve a useful result, their designers have been forced to adopt an approach that always sees a smaller perceptual function in terms of its contribution to the overall achievement of forming a coherent and useful description of the environment. To know how to design the smaller perceptual functions, the designer must be very clear about the overall design of the perceptual system, and to do this, they must have a good understanding of the difficult problems involved in interpreting sensory input. The lesson to be drawn for students of perception is that we should follow a phenomenon upward, to the level of the overall functional system. In this way the phenomenon can be placed in a context and will often be seen as an oblique glimpse of an adaptive activity. With a hypothesis in hand concerning the role of the phenomenon in an overall system, one can move back down again with new questions.

Having developed in the midst of these ideas, my recent research on auditory streams demonstrates their influence. I am going to present some of this research, therefore, in the form of a story, in which the process of trying to understand perceptual phenomena by moving upward is made explicit. You may be convinced by the end that I have moved too far upward and that it is hard to come back down to the perceptual laboratory, but I am convinced that this is not so and that I have been rewarded for this upward search by the discovery of new empirical questions.

The Integration of Auditory Sequences

A number of years ago, I was interested in the process of the learning of words by infants, particularly in how they could know where the word boundaries were in connected discourse. The problem, it seemed, would disappear after the words were known as units. With a template for each word, the infant listener could slide these templates along the input. A match to a particular template could then define both the position of that word in the input as well as the boundaries of adjacent words. However, how could the bounded word have been discovered in the first place in a stream of continuous speech? There are no acoustic properties in continuous speech that signal the beginnings or ends of words. For a possible answer, I turned to the Associationists' account of the formation of complex ideas. These are similar to what Hebb (1949) has called phase sequences and what George Miller (1956) has referred to as chunks. According to this view, simple ideas, if repeatedly encountered in contiguity, would become associated with one another and form a complex idea. It is possible that if, as infants, we were equipped with innate perceptual analyses for acoustic segments that were much shorter than a word, and that if we frequently encountered a fixed sequence of these in our experience, we would come to treat the sequence as a unit. This would be the origin of the template for a word.

I set up an experiment on myself to verify this theory. I selected 10 words and created a long sequence of these, counterbalanced for pairwise adjacencies. Then I intoned these in a continuous manner into a tape recorder, being careful not to leave breaks between the words. I then played the tape backward to myself repeatedly and hoped that eventually I would recover the word units. The backward presentation was used because it destroyed the familiarity of the words and even many of the phonemes. (A recording of this backward sequence is given in Tape Illustration 1.) Gradually, in about an hour of listening, I had recovered all but the shortest words. This seemed to support the Associationists' theory. Then I began to reconsider. Perhaps there are special features of speech that assist grouping, and perhaps it was these, and not the contiguities alone, that had done the job. A similar experiment without speech sounds had to be created. I took 26 continuous, natural, nonspeech sounds, like water splashing in a sink, a doorbell, a dentist's drill, and the like, and used them as if they were phonemes. I took about a .1-second segment of each sound and spliced these segments together to make the analogues of 10 words. Then I put these 10 words into a long, counterbalanced sequence and again listened repeatedly to this sequence, trying to recover the fixed subsequences. (This sequence appears in Tape Illustration 2.) This time I found it impossible. I could hear groupings that jumped out at me, but they happened too irregularly to be the sequences I was listening for. Clearly there was something in speech that was different from an arbitrary sequence of sounds. Real speech contained glides in frequency, alternations of consonant and vowel, and so on. In listening again to the sequence of random sounds, I noticed that the groupings that jumped out at me were ones in which the component sounds strongly resembled one another. This brought to mind the Gestalt law of groupings by similarity. The problem with the random sounds now became clear. Accidental groupings of sounds in adjacent words had become unitized by similarity, and these chance units had bridged the boundaries between the arbitrary units that I had constructed randomly. Clearly, a perceptually based unit took precedence over one defined by a fixed sequence of arbitrary sounds.

Perception of Order in Repeating Cycles

About a year later, I heard of an experiment done by Richard Warren and his colleagues (Warren, Obusek, Farmer, & Warren, 1969). They had spliced four sounds into a repeating loop and asked listeners to judge the order of the sounds. The listeners could easily do so when the four sounds were spoken digits but found it extremely difficult when the sounds were a hiss, a buzz, the phoneme *ee*, and a whistle. (Tape Illustration 3 is a copy of Warren's stimulus.) For many subjects, the sequence had to be slowed down to over 700 msec per sound before they could correctly judge the order. It occurred to me that Gestalt principles were again involved. It seemed likely that some of the sounds were grouping together and overriding the physical proximities, as had happened in my artificial word experiment. So an analogue of Warren et al.'s experiment was put together using sounds whose similarities could be known in advance: three high-pitched sine tones of different frequencies and three low-pitched ones (Bregman & Campbell, 1971). The high and low tones were alternated, and the sequence was played to subjects at 100 msec per tone in a repeating cycle. In order to prevent the use of the onset and offset of the cycle as boundaries, the cycle was faded in, played for a while, then faded out. (An example is given in Tape Illustration 4.) We found that many of the subjects, presented with alternating high and low tones, believed that the three high tones had been adjacent in the sequence and that the three low ones had formed another group. Using a pattern recognition task, we found that if a pattern involved both high and low elements, it could not be picked out of the sequence. Listening to the stimulus, we had the experience of two independent streams of sound—one involving high tones and the other one, low tones. This "streaming" effect destroyed the true sequence of sounds.

Auditory "Descriptions"

The phenomenon was intriguing, and the problem of how to pursue it immediately arose. Should it be traced downward to the level of fine detail or upward to its role in the general process of perception? The upward route seemed more interesting. Precision of detail could always be pursued later if necessary. To follow a phenomenon upward in a system means to ask what it is for: What does the auditory system do in general, and how does streaming fit into this activity?

Hearing is a way of knowing things by their effects on the vibration of a medium, usually air. "To know something" means to form a description of it that can be used in calculating expectations and actions (Bregman, 1977). Hearing helps us to form descriptions of the objects and events that surround us. It can tell us their locations, their directions of motion, and the changes in their activity levels, and it can supply information about the types of objects and events they are.

If an object or event has audible effects on the vibration of air or another medium, we can call it an acoustic source. We can call our experience of that source an auditory description. Hearing, then, is the mapping of acoustic sources into auditory descriptions. In any system that uses descriptions, each description, though new, is built out of old aspects. For example, if we see a green pencil lying on the surface of a brown table, the constituents *green, brown, table,* and *pencil* are old aspects; so are the notions *lying on* and *surface of.* However, the particular arrangement of these aspects is new. It is not the table that is green but the pencil. The pencil is lying on the table and not vice versa. Therefore it is not sufficient to detect and represent the old features in a new situation; we must also represent the particular way in which they go together now. We can refer to this as the structure of the situation. The stock of old notions that we use to build descriptions of new situations arises from two sources: Some of them, like *surface,* are probably innate; others, like *pencil,* are learned.

Besides having a set of notions out of which descriptions of world situations may be built, a description system using evidence drawn from the senses has to contain tacit knowledge about how the various aspects of the world manifest themselves in the sensory evidence. It turns out that this is not a simple matter, because a particular feature of the world—the shape of a familiar object, for example—does not always manifest itself in the sensory evidence in the same way. This arises for two reasons—differences in context and differences in the viewpoint of the observer. The context is the set of other objects or aspects of the world that accompany the object of our interest, and the viewpoint of the observer (in vision) is his or her viewing position. Certain aspects of the sensory input change in different contexts and with different viewpoints. For example, in a particular context and from a particular point of view, the outline of a flat, square object may be long and thin on the retina and interrupted in the middle by the outline of another object standing between the square and the observer. In order to recover descriptions of both the square and the occluding object, the visual system must contain knowledge about occlusion—about what happens to the outline form of an object when another lies between it and the observer. It has to know when to group discontinuous regions as part of the same object—that is, how to detect whether or not the discontinuity is caused by the overlap by another object. This is a central problem in visual scene analysis in artificial intelligence (Winston, 1975). Only when the scene is parsed into components correctly can pattern recognition be successful. An example of this can be seen in Fig. 4.1, where the first string of letters makes no sense. However, when we have evidence that this string is formed by two strings overlapping, both are readable.

A schematic view of the process of perception is shown in Fig. 4.2. Here an A, B, and C, though distinct in the world, are superimposed on the retina of the observer due to the angle of view. Perception processes must use this sensory evidence and form a description in which the object concepts composed together by relational concepts will adequately account for the patterns in the sensory projection. To do so, relational factors such as occlusion must be understood (at some level).

There are analogous problems in hearing. In most natural situations, there is more than one source of sound, and the influences of all sources are summed in the pressure wave that reaches the ear of the listener. Because we are interested in recognizing individual sources, we must recover from the input separate descriptions of the sources that, in combination, have created the input. This process of

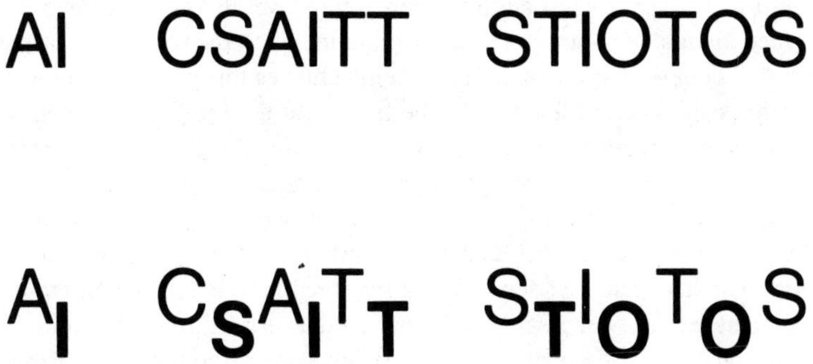

AI   CSAITT   STIOTOS

A_I   C_SA_IT_T   S_TI_OT_OS

FIG. 4.1.   The top string of letters makes no sense because it is a mixture of two messages whose words can be recognized only when the letters are visually segregated as shown below.

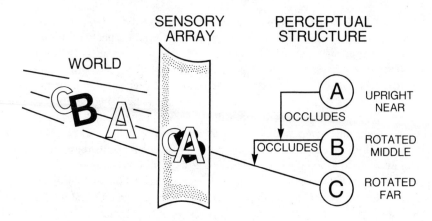

FIG. 4.2. A schematic view of perception. The letters A, B, and C, though distinct in the world, are superimposed and distorted on the observer's retina due to the angle of view. Information on the sensory surface is used by processes of scene analysis to create a structure in which the A, B, and C are seen as whole and normal in shape but as yielding the obtained sensory input due to occlusions and rotations.

undoing combinations is analogous to the problem in language of recovering a deep-structural description of a sentence from its surface structure. To solve the problem in language, knowledge of individual linguistic patterns (such as the verb–adverb pattern) is not sufficient. We must also understand the rules of composition, or how a particular linguistic form combines with others to make a sentence. In the process of combining, a component linguistic pattern may undergo a transformation. Because this transformation is related to the role that the pattern is now playing, it helps us to recover a deep-structural description of the sentence, in which the underlying linguistic patterns are made available to computational processes. In auditory perception, we also want to recover from the surface input a deep-structural description in which the sources are separately described. I believe that the auditory system achieves this goal by using heuristic rules which capitalize on features of the input that tend to be true whenever the input has been formed by the composition of a number of distinct sources.

We can go back, then, and look at the streaming effect as the auditory system's description of the input as a mixture of two sources—one high in pitch and the other low. This is the system's best bet as to the deep structure of the situation. The heuristic that seems to be involved here is this: Temporally adjacent segments are not necessarily to be grouped as arising from the same source, especially when the segments themselves have sharp boundaries. (Remember that the streaming effect was produced with distinct tones with definite onsets and offsets.) In such cases, the events are to be grouped according to similarity.

Gestalt Principles or Scene Analysis?

The mention of similarity immediately brings to mind the Gestalt principles. A few years ago Julesz and Hirsh (1972) described how a number of Gestalt organizational principles applied both to vision and hearing. I accept their analysis and can add more examples. However, what I want to emphasize here is that if we follow the Gestalt principles upward and ask what function they serve, we arrive at the idea that these principles have probably been evolved by our perceptual systems as heuristic rules to solve the problem of finding the deep structure when the effects arising from a particular visual object or auditory source are present in the sensory input mixed with the effects of other objects or sources and with the point of view of the observer.

The notion that the Gestalt processes are specialized for dealing with mixtures, or what we can call scenes, is supported by the fact that some Gestalt processes of grouping "come alive," as it were, only in complex situations. Let us take, as an example, the familiar Gestalt notion of closure. No matter how long you stare at the circle on the left in Fig. 4.3, it does not close. It seems incomplete; yet the same interrupted circle on the right does not seem incomplete, because the shape of its incompleteness is accounted for by the shape of another form that stands between the viewer and the circle. Because the visual system understands how occlusion modifies the image, the circle is described as

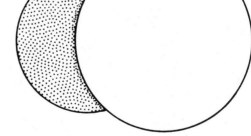

FIG. 4.3.   An incomplete circle: (a) Without information for occlusion, it does not "complete" itself; (b) with incompleteness "explained" by occlusion, the circle seems whole.

whole but as occluded by another form. One can create examples where the grouping of forms changes dramatically with overlap; in Fig. 4.4 the fragments do not show any pronounced tendency to close, whereas in Fig. 4.5, a letter of the alphabet can be clearly seen. The only difference is that in Fig. 4.5, some of the spaces are occluded by an overlaid form, which "accounts for" parts of the letters being absent.

Examples are just as easy to find in audition. If we record a continuous sound on a tape and erase a bit of it cleanly, we will hear a sound with a gap in it. Gestalt processes of closure never close the gap, even though the part of the sound that precedes the gap is in good continuation with the part that follows the gap. An example is a sine wave repeatedly gliding up and down in pitch with a brief portion cut out of each glide (Dannenbring, 1976). When we listen to it, we can clearly hear the breaks. But if we insert in each gap a loud noise burst, the glides sound continuous. You can hear the sound gliding right through the noise.

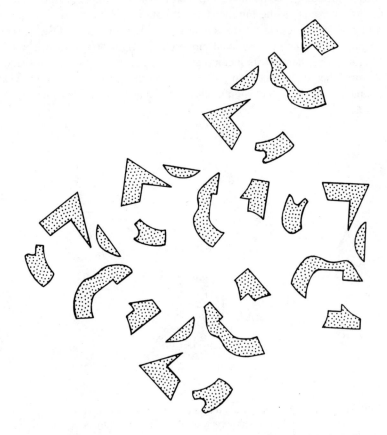

FIG. 4.4. Fragments do not organize themselves strongly when there is no information for occlusion.

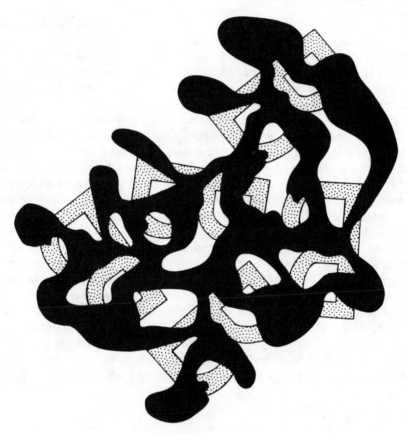

FIG. 4.5.   The same fragments as shown in Fig. 4.4 except that information for occlusion has been added, causing the fragments on the boundaries of the occluding form to be grouped.

(We hear Dannenbring's glides, first without noise bursts and then with noise bursts in the breaks, in Tape Illustration 7.) We can infer that the Gestalt property of closure in audition is a heuristic for decomposing an input in which one source of sound has been masked by another (Warren, Obusek, & Ackroff, 1972); we draw this conclusion because the continuity only occurs when the acoustic evidence strongly suggests that the absence of the missing part can be fully accounted for by an interruption and masking by a louder sound. The requirements are quite precise. If the louder sound is not loud enough to have masked the missing part if it were there, or if it is not of the right frequency to mask it, we will hear a gap (Warren et al., 1972). The placement of the occluding noise in the gap must also be precise. Unless the occluding noise fully fills the gap, we tend to hear the tone as discontinuous. Furthermore, if the absence of tone in the gap could be attributed, not to the gap, but to a change in the amplitude of the tone itself, the gap will tend to reappear even though it is completely filled by the noise. We can produce evidence for the auditory system that something is happening to the tone itself by smoothly changing its amplitude up or down by as little as 10 db in the 100 msec just preceding the gap. In this case, we reduce the tendency of the tone to be heard as continuing through the noise (Bregman & Dannenbring, 1977).

It is interesting to note the similar fact that in the visual case, the circle is likely to be seen as incomplete if the interrupting form cannot fully account for why we cannot see all the parts of the circle. For example, if the interrupting form can be made to seem hollow, as in Fig. 4.6, then the missing part of the circle is not accounted for by the overlap, and there is an increased tendency to see the circle as incomplete. In this example we seem to observe a case of visual description that exhibits a series of dependencies that resemble an inferential process: If the triangle is not occluded, then the big ring is hollow; if the big ring is hollow, it cannot occlude; if it cannot occlude, then the disk is not occluded; if the disk is not occluded, then it is incomplete. It is as if a set of possible descriptions is generated for each region of the figure, and then requirements for consistency select out a single description for each region. This process could resemble the so-called relaxation methods proposed for computer vision (e.g., Zucker, 1976). The role of consistency in visual perception is illustrated by a recent paper by Gilchrist (1977), which showed that the brightness of a visual surface is perceived so as to be consistent with its perceived illumination. A bounded region of a fixed physical luminance can be made to seem much darker

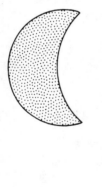
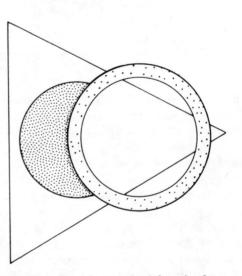

FIG. 4.6.   The same shapes as shown in Fig. 4.3 except that information for hollowness of the big ring has been added. Now the circle no longer seems closed.

if cues are introduced to suggest that it is located on a surface which is brightly illuminated. The received luminance is then interpreted as the result of seeing a region of dark color under high illumination. We can view Gilchrist's demonstration as showing that the light reflected from a surface is inherently ambiguous in conveying surface color but that consistency requirements among perceived color, position, and illumination can, in an actual scene, disambiguate the color.

Ideals and Descriptions

The consistency requirements seem to employ rules that relate to ideal forms and ideal relations. For example, an ideal circle is round and has no parts missing. An ideal visual object is either transparent or not transparent. The ideal relation, *in front of,* specifies a relation between two ideal objects, A and B, such that A is either in front of B or not in front of B. These ideal objects or relations do not always occur exactly in reality. Yet our perceptual systems seem to employ these ideals to encode natural sensory inputs. When a region of input like the incomplete disk form cannot be encoded by one ideal taken alone, then other ideals are added into a composition. In other words, the fact of being composed with a second ideal serves as an "excuse" for the alteration of the first ideal. The composition of ideal forms and relations is used as a whole to encode the input. This can work because any ideal relation (e.g., occlusion) implies a transformation of the sensory input arising from the ideal forms involved in the relationship. For example, let us take the relation *in front of.* When object A is in front of object B, this implies that a region will be missing from the visible outline of B and that the remaining part of B will have a contour that is exactly the shape of the outer contour of A. Furthermore, as the eye of the observer moves, the visible part of B will expand or contract at the boundary of A. This is what is implied by occlusion. If any of these requirements are not met, the ideal relation of occlusion is weakened, and other ideal relationships are favored. Sometimes, in order to account for a scene, ideal forms have to be modified by the assignment to them of certain ideal properties. In our visual example, the occluding ring in Fig. 4.6 was made hollow by a manipulation on the right-hand side of the ring, not on the left-hand side where the "occluded" disk is. However, when ideal properties combine with visual regions, they tend to combine ideally: If part of a region is background seen through a hollow object, then all of the region tends to be background. We do not get little parts of it not being background just because there is no local evidence for its being so. Nor do we get bits of hollowness floating around unconnected with the object. Hollowness is always hollowness *of* something.

   These ideal relationships are bets about the world. We bet that if evidence of "being behind" is found locally at an edge of a region, it applies to the whole region bounded by certain contours. We bet on this so strongly that it influences our interpretation of other features of the scene.

At this point I would like to examine the question of whether audition also works by encoding an input as a composition of ideal forms with ideal properties united in ideal relationships. What, for example, is the auditory version of an object? I would propose that it is a stream. Just as visual features—like color, glossiness, and transparency—are seen as features of objects, auditory features—like pitch, timbre, onset edge, offset edge, rhythmic modulation, component part, and so on—are heard as features of streams.

The auditory description of an acoustic environment is built up out of descriptions of separate streams and of relations between them. The acoustic input must be analyzed for evidence that justifies a particular description. An ideal stream is one that has homogeneous features. It tends to continue over time with a relatively constant pitch; when it has any changes, they are smooth; when one of its frequency components changes, the others change in a parallel fashion. The auditory description process accounts for the input in terms of the co-occurrence of a number of such ideal streams interacting in ideal ways. The properties of ideal streams can be used as heuristic guides for the interpretation of the acoustic input. For example, when a set of acoustic features that might possibly be a coherent stream fails to have the ideal property of staying in the same pitch region, this serves as evidence that a second stream with another pitch center is possibly being mixed with it. (*Mixture* is an ideal relationship in audition.) If two sets of components can be found, each of which has properties nearer to that of an ideal stream, and if a mixture of these better streams will account for the input, the incoming signal will be represented in this form. This is the streaming effect that I discussed earlier.

The laboratory findings about streams are consistent with this view. Streams are broken into substreams if they change too suddenly and too far in frequency and do so repeatedly so as to occupy two separate frequency ranges (Bregman, 1978; Bregman & Campbell, 1971; Dannenbring & Bregman, 1976; Miller & Heise, 1950). When streams change in frequency, they are more likely to remain integrated when the changes are smooth trajectories (Bregman & Dannenbring, 1973; Heise & Miller, 1951). These principles apply not only to pure tones but also to vocal sounds (Cole & Scott, 1973; Dorman, Cutting, & Raphael, 1975; Lackner & Goldstein, 1974) and to alternations of tones with noises or of noises with one another (Dannenbring & Bregman, 1976).

Some of these principles are demonstrated in the tape illustrations. Tape Illustration 8 presents tones of high and low pitch alternating in a galloping rhythm. As the speed gets faster, the experience changes from a single stream with a galloping rhythm to a percept involving two streams, a high and a low one, each with a regular meter (cf. van Noorden, 1975).

Tape Illustration 5 gives examples of alternations of high and low tones. In the first example, each tone is joined to the next one by a frequency glide. In the second case, there is an abrupt frequency shift from one tone to the next. In the latter case, there is a greater tendency for the high and low tones to form separate streams.

Tape Illustration 6 shows that spectral differences affect stream segregation. A 1000-Hz pure tone segregates from sharply filtered band-passed noise centered at 1000 Hz.

In following the streaming phenomenon upward, so as to consider its position in a larger view of the perceptual process, we have been led to a consideration of how the senses deal with complex scenes. They seem to cope with such situations by having an a priori expectation of ideal objects related to one another consistently by means of ideal relations. In order for this not to be merely a philosophical exercise, this view of the description process should lead us to new empirical investigations. I should like to show how it can.

Assigning Co-occurring Components to Streams

The stream segregation studies led upward to the idea that these effects were due to heuristic processes of scene analysis. It then became evident that in studying simple alternating patterns of high and low tones, we were not dealing with a very frequently encountered situation in our acoustic environments. More commonly, sounds from different sources mix haphazardly, and the frequency components are superimposed for varying periods of time. The auditory system cannot simply treat each temporal segment as arising from one definite source or another. The signal at each moment could be a superimposition of several sources. With this in mind, we began to study acoustic mixtures and the assumptions made by the auditory system in order to decompose them.

The realization that we frequently hear sounds as parts of mixtures brings up problems related to the perception of timbre. The auditory system seems to exhibit something that we can call timbre constancy. For example, a friend's voice has the same perceived timbre in a quiet room or at a cocktail party. At the party, however, the many frequency components arising from the friend's voice are mixed at the listener's ear with frequency components from other sources. Yet if the frequency components in a voice are responsible for its unique timbre, those components have to be isolated from their acoustic context. A wrong choice for the friend's voice from among the frequency components present at the ear would change the timbre of that voice. The existence of timbre constancy implies that we regularly choose the right frequency components regardless of context.

In a simple case, if we present two pure tones overlapping in time, then the choice of whether or not to group them as pure-tone components of a single sound ought to determine the perceived timbre. If they are grouped into one stream, they generate a single rich timbre, but if they are treated as two separate streams that are merely co-occurring, they generate two sounds of pure-tone quality. Recent experiments in our laboratory have looked at whether two overlapping pure tones will fuse. The method involves using an observation of van Noorden (1975)—namely, that if a pure tone of frequency f is rapidly alternated with a complex tone containing f as a component, the pure tone will pull frequency *f* out of the complex tone into a serial organization. The listener can hear a series of pure tones of frequency *f* at a rate that is fast enough to imply that every second one has come from the complex tone. What we see here is a competition between sequential and simultaneous grouping.

We have used this effect in a simple experimental setup involving three pure tones as shown in Fig. 4.7. A pure tone A is closely followed by a more or less simultaneous pair of pure tones B and C in a repeating cycle (Bregman & Pinker, 1978). If B is grouped with its temporal partner C, a rich timbre is heard with a pitch determined by C. If, however, B is grouped with A, then a pure-tone stream containing ABAB and so forth is heard, and this seems to be accompanied by a pure-tone stream of repetitions of C. We have found that we can do things to influence the grouping. If we move the frequency of the pure tone A near that of B, then A and B will be more likely to form a sequential stream together. Thus, in a series of pure-tone components, the closeness of the frequencies of these components will influence their grouping.

Another factor that affects the organization is the synchrony between the onsets of the temporal partners B and C. If their onset is synchronous, B and C tend to remain bound together, whereas when they are asynchronous in onset, they are more easily pulled apart by competing organizations. (Tape Illustration 9 presents two examples: (a) because B and C are synchronous in their onsets and A is far from B in frequency, B and C fuse and generate a rich timbre; (b) the onsets of B and C differ by 58 msec, and A is brought closer in frequency to B. In

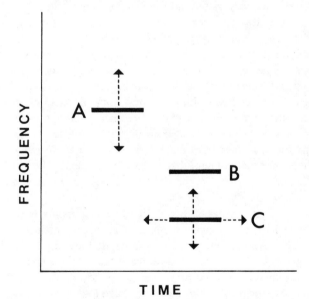

TIME

FIG. 4.7.   Diagram of an auditory experiment in which a pure tone A is alternated with a pair of pure tones, B and C.

this case, B groups with A and not with C. The tones all sound like pure sine tones.)

This experiment suggests that the auditory system fuses or decomposes the set of simultaneously present frequency components, using information distributed over time. A frequency component is pulled out of the set by good relations with previously occurring components. It is pulled into the set by good relations with co-occurring components. What defines a good relation? For sequential components, it is undoubtedly the same factors as we have investigated with nonoverlapping pure tones. These include nearness in frequency and slowness and continuity of change in frequency. Some recent experiments (McAdams, 1977) also show that a pair of simultaneous tones that modulate together over time, maintaining a constant ratio of frequencies, will tend to form a sequential stream.

As for co-occurring components, the good relations, which fuse them into a timbre structure, seem to include synchronous onsets and offsets. It also promotes fusion if higher-frequency components (e.g., the component B in Fig. 4.7) have lower amplitudes (Dannenbring & Bregman, 1978). In addition, there is evidence that when simultaneous components go up and down in frequency together, they tend to fuse and pull away from other co-occurring components that are not being modulated in the same way (Halpern, 1977). (In Tape Illustration 10, two streams are created in this way. A set of three pure-tone components glides up and down in frequency together, maintaining the ratios 3:4:5 and forming one stream. A single pure-tone component that glides up and down out of step with the others is rejected into a separate stream.)

This last factor reminds one of the Gestalt principle of "common fate." This principle means that parts of a sensory field will be grouped together when they undergo synchronous and similar changes. An example of it is the finding by Johansson (1964, 1973) that when the motions of two dots of light in a complex display are correlated, the dots are seen as parts of a rigid object in motion.

It is, however, possible to view any principle of grouping as a principle of segregation. In the case of auditory streams, the principles of grouping make some acoustic features go together, but they also make them segregate from other parcels of features. Common fate can therefore be viewed as a principle of decomposition that says that parts of a sensory field that undergo nonparallel or nonsynchronous changes will be segregated from one another. This way of looking at it suggests that a phenomenon employed by Kubovy and Howard (1976) to study acoustic memory works by the principle of common fate (see also Julesz & Levitt, 1966). Kubovy and Howard sent a chord into one ear of a listener with all tones synchronous in onset. At the same time, they sent the same chord into the other ear with each frequency component advanced or delayed by a slightly different amount. This had the effect of causing the different frequencies to be localized at different spatial locations. This manipulation constituted what we can call one frame of sound. Kubovy and Howard sent a sequence of such frames to the listener in such a way that in each frame, one selected tone was localized at a slightly different spatial position than it had been in the previous frame. All the remaining tones of the chord remained at the spatial location that they had occupied in the previous frame. They "moved" a different tone in each successive frame. This procedure caused the moved tones to stand out perceptually from the remainder of the chord and, in a series of frames, to play a tune. This can be seen as an example of common fate. To see it this way, we must consider that being stationary is a type of movement. All the tones with non-changed positions from one frame to the next had a common type of motion, and the single tone whose position had been changed had a different type of motion. The two types of motion might well have led to a decomposition of the display that caused the moved tone to be perceptually isolated. If this interpretation is true, the isolation effect could be obtained even if the motion of the background tones from frame to frame was nonstationary, as long as it was uniform and fairly continuous.

I have discussed a number of good relations between components of sound that cause one component to be integrated with other components or segregated from them. All these good relations can be viewed as properties of an ideal stream of sound. Such a stream changes its frequencies slowly and continuously over time, and all its pure-tone components go up and down in frequency together, maintaining a constant frequency ratio. All its frequency components tend to come on and go off together, and its higher frequencies are softer than its lower ones (Dannenbring & Bregman, 1978). It seems reasonable that all frequency components of the ideal stream should have simple harmonic relations to one another. A reported computer program, for example, that can disentangle two superimposed voices does so by grouping all the components that could be harmonics of the same fundamental frequency (Parsons, 1976). Recent unpublished research in our laboratory has provided evidence that human audition also binds components together by this principle. (It would be interesting to synthesize two artificial voices with nonharmonic components and to see whether the human ear has any trouble segregating the two voices when they are superimposed.)

Belongingness

There are also ideal relations *between* streams; these include the "mixing" of streams and the "occlusion" of a softer one by a louder one. The auditory system tries to hear the input as a minimal set of ideal streams composed by these ideal relations. To see how this is accomplished, let us look at the relation of "occlusion." The Gestalt psychologists made frequent use of the principle of "belongingness." It refers to the fact that in drawings like that of the partially occluded circle (Fig. 4.3), the common edge is assigned to one form or the other but not to both. We can interpret this process of assignment as a necessary part of a perceptual process that interprets a sensory input as having been generated by objects that can occlude one another. Many of the boundaries that surround a visual surface belonging to an object are not actually generated by the shape of that object, but by the shape of other objects standing between the viewer and the surface in question. It is a very rare case in normal sensory experience where two objects are touching and their outer contours exactly match so that only one boundary is seen. Therefore a good heuristic processor should be biased in favor of assigning the boundary as an edge of one object and representing its edge as occluding a part of the other object.

Belongingness, by this reasoning, occurs as a consequence of the attempt to detect disjoint objects or events and to deal with mixture. We should therefore not be surprised to find it in audition. We have observed it in a case where the order of a rapidly presented pair of tones, A and B, is to be judged (see Fig. 4.8). If the target pair, A and B, is bracketed between a pair of tones, X_1 and X_2, such that X_1 and X_2 have identical frequencies but are somewhat lower than the frequency of A and B, the AB pair becomes absorbed into a four-tone sequence that begins and ends on the same pitch (Bregman & Rudnicky, 1975). The sequence XABX is hard to discriminate from the sequence XBAX. However, if a stream of tones at the frequency of the Xs is added to the sequence to absorb the Xs only, the pair AB is released from the effects of the Xs, and the order of A and B becomes easy to determine. (In Tape Illustration 11 we hear first the target tones and then their occurrence in the sequence XABX. Then we hear the target tones again and their occurrence in XABX when the Xs are stripped off by a capturing stream of tones.) It is the belongingness of X_1 and X_2 that is in question

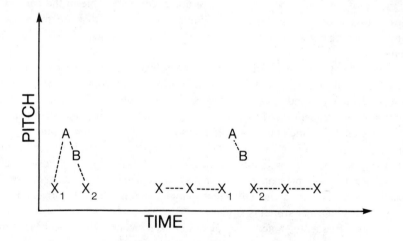

FIG. 4.8.   (a) Diagram of an auditory experiment where a pair of bracketing tones, X_1 and X_2, are assigned to the same stream as A and B, camouflaging the order of A and B; (b) if an added tone stream captures the Xs, the order of A and B is easily judged. The dotted lines indicate the perceptual streams formed in the two cases.

in this experiment. When they are made to belong with other Xs, they no longer are involved in a stream with the AB pair. Tones seem not to be able to belong in more than one stream at a time, and streams compete for tones. Belongingness is a necessary outcome of any process that decomposes mixtures, because any sensory effect must be assigned to some particular source.

Timbre, for example, must be the timbre *of* some sound. When a partially synchronous pair of tones (as in Fig. 4.7) is made to segregate into two separate streams by our capturing one into a sequential organization, what becomes of the timbre of the mixture? The two tones are still physically co-occurring, and the physical interactions that are responsible for timbre still exist. In fact, you can still hear timbre if you listen for it. But it is not the timbre *of* anything, and therefore, in ordinary listening it is lost. It would not affect the recognition of either of the overlapped tones because it is not assigned to either one. It seems that accidental interactions, such as the timbre arising when two unrelated sounds occur at the same time, are not assigned to either source. This would provide a constancy of acoustic features for sources, independent of context, because it is only the assigned properties that affect the perceptual representation of the source.

The same reasoning can account for another finding: When recycling sequences of alternating high and low tones split into two substreams, temporal relations between elements of different streams are lost (Bregman & Campbell, 1971; Dannenbring & Bregman, 1976). Because these temporal relations are interpreted as arising from an accidental mixture of streams, they are not assigned to either one. They are therefore not directly available in the perceptual description and must be created by inference processes that are too slow to operate accurately in a situation where a short tonal sequence is repeating rapidly.

Assignment processes are probably also involved in Deutsch's illusions (1975a, 1975b) where continuity of spatial position and continuity of frequency are placed into contradictory relations. An ideal stream should maintain both its continuity in frequency and its continuity of spatial position, and when listeners receive signals in which these two requirements are in contradiction, they synthesize a percept that minimizes the contradiction according to the heuristics of their auditory systems. The assignment process is most striking here because it takes properties that were presented at one spatial position and assigns them to a stream that is represented as having a different spatial position. This, of course, happens only in very unusual stimulus situations.

A more frequently noted case of assignment occurs when we hear a tone continue through a noise of sufficient intensity to mask it (as in Tape Illustraion 7). There is an acoustic boundary at the onset of the noise, but this is assigned as a boundary of the noise, not of the tone, and hence there is no evidence for the discontinuity of the tone. This resembles the case in vision, illustrated in Fig.

4.3, where the boundary common to two regions was assigned as a shape-defining edge to only one form, the one seen as nearer the observer. In audition, when two homogeneous sounds are temporally adjacent, the louder sound may be the one privileged to be assigned the acoustic "edge," just as in vision, the nearer region is so privileged (Bregman & Dannenbring, 1977).

The key to the notion of "assignment" processes is our use of the preposition *of* in describing features of sound. Onsets must be onsets *of* a sound; timbre must be timbre *of* a sound; sounds need to be sounds *of* a stream; and features will be reconnected and even moved around in perceptual time and space to satisfy these requirements. Because the belongingness of features to objects or events is true about the world, it also has to be a fact represented in our perceptual descriptions of the world. A critic of such a view, however, might argue that there is no particular *of* in our actual perceptual representations; this is only a way of talking about percepts. The syntax is in our verbal descriptions; neither the world itself nor our perceptions of it have a syntax. I believe such a criticism can be answered as follows: If there were no actual assignment processes, there could be no misassignment. Yet a number of illusions seem to be interpretable as errors of assignment or, if you like, as syntactic errors. So far as I know, the world never makes syntactic errors about timbre or edges; so I do not attribute any assignment processes to the world. But perception does make such errors, and so I do attribute such processes to perception. The perceptual effects that I have described are not typically cases where the individual, raw perceptual features have been picked up incorrectly. They have just been put together the wrong way.

The last thing I want to say about assignment processes is that they, too, may be governed by ideals. An ideal sound has timbre, beginnings and ends, shape (in time-frequency space), parts, loudness, and perhaps other obligatory features. Our processes of perceptual description may be governed by the attempt to create such ideals. I think I am saying the same thing as Minsky (1975) when he proposes that scene analysis processes in computers can be guided by "frames," which consist of a description of the general types of parts and relationships that can be expected in a certain kind of scene.

I hope, now, that I have shown how pursuing the inappropriate grouping of sounds upward by considering the role of grouping in the overall hearing process has led back downward to questions that would otherwise not have been asked. It has allowed us to see a number of phenomena as closely related ones. The process that I have been advocating is not merely one of going from data to theory and back again. There are all kinds of theories, from factor analytic models of the similarities among judgments to tight mathematical models of the relations between two layers of neurons. The kind of theory I have found most useful in generating new questions is one that tries to describe the role of smaller perceptual phenomena in the larger process of perceiving and understanding a natural environment. In other words, it asks the question: "What for?"

ACKNOWLEDGMENTS

The author's research has been supported by grants from the National Research Council of Canada, the Quebec Ministry of Education, and the McGill Faculty of Graduate Studies and Research. Much of the research used the facilities of the Computer-Based Laboratory of the McGill University Department of Psychology. The author would like to express his gratitude to the following research collaborators: Jock Campbell, Gary Dannenbring, Gary Bernstein, Alex Rudnicky, Steven Pinker, Stephen McAdams, Lynn Halpern, and Jack Torobin.

5 The Analysis of Unanalyzed Perceptions

W. R. Garner
Yale University

"We can take it for granted that a visual form is a unitary whole [p. 253]." There can be no better way for me to open my paper than with this statement, which is an actual quotation from E. G. Boring's *Sensation and Perception in the History of Experimental Psychology* (1942). Since I know all of the participants in this conference, at least by publication, if not personally, I know that this is a statement you would subscribe to if you took no more than a quick look. But on further examination, we would be less willing just to take it for granted. We might want to qualify the statement by saying that *some* perceptions are of unitary wholes, or are processed in an unanalyzed way. But in this day of process models that depend so heavily on the assumption of feature or other attribute processing, it is less clear that we want to buy the idea of a unitary whole quite so quickly. At least speaking solely for myself, I think there are some very real metascientific issues involved in the idea that forms or other types of stimuli are perceived or processed as wholes.

One problem that I have always had with the idea of holistic perception, or unanalyzed percepts, is that I consider the essence of scientific behavior to be that of analysis. When we want to understand a phenomenon, we must somehow analyze it, take it apart, see what its components are, and otherwise subdue the holistic percept into analyzed components. And by analysis, I want to make clear that I am not arguing for a reductionist position of metascience. In fact, I have rather a distaste for the reductionist position, since it doesn't really seem to have worked all that well over the years. But reductionism is simply one form of analytic behavior on the part of the scientist, and I even want to agree with Kenneth Spence (1948) that an argument for an analytic posture in science is not an argument for reduction. The analytic approach only demands that we do much more than simply catalog the various phenomena that we psychologists encounter, and that we try to find underlying attributes or constructs that allow us to say things such as that four phenomena are composed of an orthogonal combination of two dichotomized constructs. Thus the phenomena A, B, C, and D are to be understood as w_1x_1, w_2x_1, w_1x_2, and w_2x_2 where w and x are the dichotomized constructs or variables.

Dual Epistemology

There has always been for me—and for other psychologists as well, I believe—this problem of how to consider there to be unanalyzed perceptions while at the same time as a scientist considering it my function to analyze the perceptions in as many ways as possible. The answer lies in the acceptance of a dual epistemology—one for the subjects (the ordinary persons) who are the objects of our study, and the other for ourselves. I shall call the epistemology that is appropriate to our objects of study a *primary epistemology* and that of the scientist a *scientific epistemology* or, even as the commonly used term, a *meta-science*.

Epistemology is, of course, a long-standing discipline concerned with the nature of knowing. Quite why that particular term remained in the taxonomy of philosophers but ceased being used by the psychologists who broke away from their philosophical forebears, I do not know. We psychologists have come to use terms such as *cognition* (which my dictionary defines as the act or process of knowing and even uses *perception* as a synonym) for the actual phenomena we study, so perhaps we don't feel the need for a term that itself refers to the study of knowing. Nevertheless, *epistemology* is a term of considerable use to those of us who study knowing, but we do have to distinguish ways in which the ordinary person comes to know and ways in which the nonordinary person called a scientist comes to know.

I have argued elsewhere (Garner, 1974b) that although a dual epistemological position can certainly be defended, I did not choose to do so. My reason was that I wanted to argue for the epistemological position of critical realism as appropriate for both primary and scientific epistemology. I still want to argue that critical realism is the appropriate epistemological position for both forms of epistemology, but I think that the difference in types of measuring and analytic mechanisms available to us as scientists is so great that the dual epistemology is called for. Thus I want to accept the fact that a great deal of perception involves a complete lack of analysis by the perceiving organism, that forms are perceived as unitary wholes, that attributes may be perceived as integral under some circumstances, and that such stimulus properties as good figure, symmetry, rhythm, and even motion are perceived in a totally nonanalytic way. At the same time I want to argue that for us as scientists, each of these holistic or unanalyzed phenomena is capable of the kind of careful and constructive analysis that allows us to come to understand the true nature of the phenomena under study.

In both primary and scientific epistemology, I feel that critical realism is the correct position. In arguing for realism for both the ordinary observing organism and for the scientist observing the observing organism, I completely accept the fact that there is a real world to be perceived. Perception does not occur as a subjective creation for the ordinary perceiver and, I most certainly hope, not for the scientist as perceiver and knower. In fact, I suppose my acceptance of the position of realism for the scientist is almost a statement of faith. I do not understand how we scientists can justify our activities without the assumption that there is a real world, a real knowledge, even a truth to be understood. I do not mean to imply that there are not subjective (i.e., intraorganismic) activities that we, as the particular breed of scientist called psychologist, want to understand. Indeed there are such, but these are primarily representations of a reality, not creations of it. Even when we use imagery to recombine things to form a novel composition, we are combining things that are representations of reality, and the ultimate composition can be checked against reality and known to be imaginary if it does not agree with some (at least possible) reality.

But at the same time, I argue for critical realism, because I do feel that the organism is a very active participant in the process of coming to learn about the real world and that this activity is of the form that acquires, cross-checks, and seeks missing information if necessary to arrive at a correct percept. People are not direct or naive realists in just accepting simple input as indicative of reality. Reality can be more complicated than information obtainable from simple inputs can tell us, so we seek more information to clarify the nature of that more complex reality.

But if the primary epistemology appropriate to the ordinary perceiver is the same as the scientific epistemology appropriate for the perceptual psychologist, why is there a need for a dual epistemology? The answer lies in the degree of sophistication available in the critical aspect of critical realism. Although an ordinary perceiver may seek more information to provide more accurate knowledge of the world, the techniques readily available to that perceiver are indeed limited. And at times, the perceiver will engage in totally nonanalytic perception because he or she is unable to engage in analytic perception. That is, at times the critical part of critical realism will fail for the ordinary perceiver. Yet we as scientists do not have to be as limited. Just as scientists have more precise methods of observation than the ordinary perceiver, so do we also have statistical, mathematical, computer, and even logical tools available to us to analyze phenomena that are not analytic in ordinary perception. Thus because a phenomenon is nonanalytic to the ordinary perceiver does not mean that we scientists are allowed to try to understand the phenomenon in a nonanalytic way. We have a considerably greater responsibility than that.

Dual Behaviorism

This distinction between primary epistemology and scientific methodology is not unlike that which has been made by many writers (see, e.g., Turner, 1968) between two forms of behaviorism. The first of these, *metaphysical behaviorism,* is that applied to the ordinary object of the psychologist's study—be it rat, monkey, or human. It is a theory about the organism itself, and it argues that the essence of the organism is its behavior—the connections between stimuli and responses and even between subresponses if necessary to maintain the basic behaviorist position. In its more extreme form, it argues that there is no thought, only subvocalizations; no perception, only responses to stimuli; and no knowledge or cognition at all, because these do not require responses. You are all more than familiar with the basic theories of such men as Hull, Spence, and Skinner, which subscribe to a clear metaphysical behaviorism.

Probably most people at this conference do not subscribe to a metaphysical behaviorism; nor do most psychologists who label themselves *cognitive,* although the many dimensions of meaning for the term *cognitive* as used currently make one question whether it has any single meaning or even cluster of meanings. But whatever others here or elsewhere feel about metaphysical behaviorism, for myself, I do not accept it as a good theory of organismic function.

The second form of behaviorism is commonly called *methodological behaviorism,* and I accept this form of behaviorism completely. It states that although there may or may not be such things as cognitions, images, dreams, and other nonbehavioral phenomena, in order to study these phenomena, the scientist has to study the behavior of organisms, because that is the only means of communication between us scientists and the organism we study. However, in accepting methodological behaviorism, we are not accepting that the behavior (in our case, usually responses to stimuli) is the phenomenon to be understood: The response is simply an indicant of the phenomenon, not the phenomenon itself. Osgood (1953) made this point some time ago, but it might be useful to reemphasize it now.

So we have two kinds of behaviorism—one for the ordinary object of our study, and one for the scientist. And just as it is logically permissible to subscribe to a different epistemology for the scientist and for the perceiving and knowing organism, so also it is logically permissible to accept methodological behaviorism while rejecting metaphysical behaviorism. Incidentally, my acceptance of methodological behaviorism is as much a statement of faith as is my acceptance of critical realism as the correct position for scientific epistemology. I do not know how to study the organism without communicating with it. So I must study behavior in my role as scientist, even though I come to know in nonbehavioristic ways.

Now the important point of this discussion is this: We psychologists must use behavior as our object of direct study; at the same time, we must remember that the behavior is only an indicant of the phenomenon to be understood, and it must not be confused with that phenomenon. The way to cope with this situation is to deal with the information we obtain from our experiments and our observations as critical realists; we must engage in all kinds of analytic activities that can be described generally as providing the critical part of critical realism. And with these skills we can as scientists analyze the nature of phenomena that we as ordinary persons do not perceive analytically.

MODES OF ANALYSIS

If we can (in our scientific roles) be analytic about unanalyzed perceptions, what are the ways in which we can do so? There are three basic analytic functions that can and need to be carried out: specification of our fundamental constructs, specification of stimulus properties appropriate to possible holistic perceptions, and specification of task or processing variables that can serve to differentiate the nature and function of holistic perception. I discuss each of these in turn.

Types of Unanalyzed Perception

One problem that has plagued perceptual psychologists is the lack of a clear definition of what we mean by either analyzed or unanalyzed perception. Words such as *features, dimensions, cues, attributes, components, aspects,* and *parts* are all used to refer to the stimulus properties that are (at least potentially) perceived analytically, but little formal distinction between the terms has been made. And words such as *template, whole, gestalt,* and *configuration* have been used for stimulus properties that are not perceived analytically, and again little formal distinction between the terms has been attempted. Still further, holistic perception is often defined by default: If we can find no specific evidence of analyzed perception or processing (i.e., evidence that features, dimensions, or whatnots have been used), we then conclude that a particular stimulus or set of stimuli has been processed holistically. But I think we can do better than that, and I have recently attempted some hopefully useful definitions (Garner, 1978a).

First, let us distinguish between the two basic classes of stimulus property appropriate to our concerns. I shall call the component properties *attributes,* and the alternative I shall simply call *holistic properties.* Attributes in turn are usefully differentiated into at least two major types: A *dimension* is a variable attribute of a stimulus such that if the dimension exists for a set of stimuli, it exists at some positive level for every stimulus in the set, and these levels are mutually exclusive. A *feature* is an attribute that either exists or does not exist for each stimulus in a set; but if it exists, it has only a single level, the alternative level being absence of the feature. Thus features are always dichotomous, whereas dimensions may or may not be. And in an information-processing sense, one would interrogate about dimensions by asking at what level the dimension exists for a particular stimulus in a set, whereas one would interrogate about features by asking whether the particular stimulus has the feature.

Although my primary concern here is with holistic properties, it is of some interest to consider whether the distinction between features and dimensions may not enter into what we call holistic processing. When a set of stimuli is generated from alternative positive levels of dimensions, each stimulus has equivalent status; and though different stimuli within the set may differ in their holistic properties, these have to emerge from the particular dimensional combinations. With a set of stimuli generated solely from features, however, there are two very special stimuli in the set—the *null* stimulus, in which all features are missing; and the *complete* stimulus, in which all features are present. To illustrate, consider the following stimuli: -,)-, -),)-). (I have, incidentally, used the hyphen as a "handle" on which to add the two features on the left or the right in order to avoid having to illustrate or use a stimulus that is literally nothing.) From some research I discuss later (Garner, 1978b), I know that the complete stimulus will be a very good stimulus in a focusing task in which one stimulus is sought or classified against all alternatives only if, in itself, it is configurally good; the null stimulus, however, seems to act like a good stimulus regardless of the configural properties of the other stimuli in the set. It seems to be an anchor with many of the nice information-processing consequences that we normally expect to be provided only by configurally good stimuli.

However, to return to the question of types of unanalyzed perception, I have distinguished between three major constructs that have been used: simple wholes, templates, and configurations.

Simple Wholes.   Any stimulus can be described in terms of its components, and if in fact we describe all the components of a stimulus, then in some sense we have described or defined a whole. Such a description, however, in no way implies or asserts that this whole is in any way different from the sum of its components, and even less does it imply or assert that the whole is more than the sum of the components. Truly, the concept of a simple whole is a very minimal concept, and it is a concept that best illustrates my earlier comment that holistic properties, at least in terms of their processing consequences, are frequently defined by default.

The concept of a simple whole is closely tied to the distinction between serial and parallel processing. If we have a series of items, or a set of items each of which can be defined by its component properties, and if an experimental outcome shows that there is no increase in processing time as we increase the number of items or component properties, then we conclude that processing has been parallel rather than serial. Such a conclusion is that the stimulus is processed as a whole. But there is never a positive definition of what it means to process as a whole, and there may in fact never have been a percept of a whole.

To say that we can do two things at once as fast as we can do each separately is certainly saying that we are doing two things in parallel. But it is a long way from such a statement to stating that the things we do simultaneously have become holistic, or have even interacted. In fact, there is an almost ironic note here: Ordinarily we would say that if two processes can be carried out as fast as either alone, then the two processes are independent (see, e.g., Garner & Morton, 1969). Yet if we want to consider parallel processing to provide a definition of holistic processing, we really want to state that the different components are processed in an interactive way. So we seem to want parallel processing to provide evidence of both independence and interaction. Something is wrong when we find ourselves coming and going at the same time.

To summarize, although the idea of a simple whole may be useful in differentiating the concept of simple component summation from other types of holistic property, it is really not very useful in trying to understand unanalyzed perception or processing. Nor is it clear that the distinction between parallel and serial processing is useful for distinguishing analyzed and unanalyzed perception.

Templates.   In the vastly increasing literature on information processing, *template processing* is the term most often used to contrast with *component* (usually feature) *processing;* yet it has never had a really satisfactory definition. Furthermore, its definition often is by default, as with that of a simple whole.

However, it seems to me that Neisser (1967) has used the term with a kind of definition that can be positive and useful. He refers to templates as "prototypes" or "canonical forms," and in either case, the information-processing idea is that identification occurs by coincidence or congruence with a basic model. This idea is very much like that of a schema and clearly lets in the necessary corollary idea that there are both relevant and irrelevant attributes. One of the problems with the use of the idea of a template has always been that it is simply impossible to mean that a stimulus is matched as a template in every conceivable respect. The internal representation cannot possibly have been stored with respect to every property of the stimulus—properties such as size, slant, location, and so forth. If the relevant property, however, is form, then it does seem conceivable that the properties of the stimulus relevant to form are stored, and that these properties may interact to provide a meaningful template that is processed holistically. But until we accept the idea that a template cannot mean whole in the sense of everything, but can only mean whole in the sense of some part of everything, it cannot be very useful. Given the distinction between relevant and irrelevant properties, however, the idea of a template as schema, as canonical form, or as prototype can be very useful.

Configurations.   The only construct concerning holistic properties with a clearly positive definition is that of configuration. For a configuration, the whole of the stimulus is indeed more than, or certainly other than, the sum of its parts. Furthermore, the properties of the whole that are different from the sum of the parts can in most instances be expressed without a psychological experimental outcome. In other words, the circularity or negativism involved with the concept of whole as simple whole is avoided, and the limited definition of template is also avoided.

A configuration has properties that have to be expressed as some form of interaction or interrelation between the components, be they features or dimensions. Thus, to illustrate, to state that a figure is a square is to state not only that the figure is a quadrilateral but also that the four sides bear a certain relationship to one another. It is not at all necessary, please note, that in any particular processing task, the property of squareness be the processed property. A discrimination task could be carried out on the basis of presence or absence of verticle lines in figures, with the fact of squareness in a particular figure being totally irrelevant to the processing task.

This particular example illustrates what is to me the important aspect of a configurational property: It exists in addition to, not instead of, other properties such as features and dimensions. In fact, the configural properties can only be described as relations between component properties. So configural properties coexist with other properties, a fact meaning that there is indeed an experimental question of which properties are used—the configural or the component properties. But with the idea of configuration as a specifiable relation between component properties, we do have a construct appropriate to unanalyzed or unanalyzable perception that does not beg the question; nor does it exclude the possibility of coexistence of configural and other nonconfigural properties. Or to turn the statement around, the same stimulus has components that may be used in analyzed perception and configural properties that may be used in unanalyzed perception.

Specification of Configural Properties

I have been arguing, of course, that before we can investigate the nature of unanalyzed perception, we need a construct appropriate to the question, and I have also argued that the idea of a configuration, in which the specified properties involve relations or interactions between stimulus components, is the best construct available. Simply to state that configural properties are appropriate to holistic processing, however, is not enough; indeed, we could very quickly fall into the same circular trap that has plagued this field for so long, that of defining as configural that which leads to nonanalytic processing or perception.

In order to avoid this circularity, we must be able to express configural properties of the stimulus that are truly independent of the experimental outcome of whatever experiments we choose to do. Without this independent definition, we cannot determine when unanalyzed perception does and does not occur. And most important is to remember that any stimulus that has configural properties also has component properties, the component properties providing relations to define the configural properties. But what are some possible configural properties?

The one that will most readily come to mind is, of course, symmetry. It can easily be specified as a property of the stimulus without any known experimental outcome. And it does involve relations between component properties. Next in line comes repetition, in which two or more stimulus components simply are identical except for location in space or in time. These are the two that Eleanor Gibson (1969) called redundancy in describing properties of letters, although she described repetition as cyclic change. But certainly there are others to add to the list, properties that involve interaction or relations between component properties. I would consider intersection to be one such property. Two lines can exist; but if they touch or intersect, an additional property exists—a property that can easily form the basis of classification, discrimination, and other such standard laboratory tasks. Possibly the conjoining of two lines at their ends is a separate configural property, or it may be just a subcategory subsumed under intersection. But the angular separation between lines, even when the lines themselves are curved, is a configural property, and the lines do not have to intersect or conjoin for them to have an angular relation. Possibly more general configural properties exist and are useful, such as Attneave's (1954) use of redundancy in its information-theoretic sense as a configural property—pertinent to goodness of pattern—or even my own narrower use of rotation and reflection subsets of equivalent stimuli as a configural property also pertinent to goodness (e.g., Garner, 1974b).

The Role of Converging Operations.   But I do not want to continue listing possible configural properties, because I want to emphasize the role of such stimulus definitions in our perceptual and information-processing research. Basically, the use of strictly stimulus definitions of configural properties is only a starting point in the analytic process for the perceptual psychologist. Given the starting point, it then becomes necessary to validate the role of any particular specification of configural properties as pertinent to any organismic outcome. The general tactic involved is what might be called bootstrapping, because essentially the perceptual activities of the organism validate the original configural definition at the same time that the stimulus definitions validate the differentiation of alternative perceptual and processing activities. Of course, in polite psychological society, we refer to this process as the use of converging operations, a term with which I have been associated for some time (Garner, Hake, & Eriksen, 1956) and a process that I consider to be essential in the research enterprise.

This business of using converging operations is at times quite a sophisticated and elusive thing, because it is necessary not only to show that there are performance differences due to the defined differences in stimulus properties but also to show that the performance differences validate the differences in stimulus properties as having something to do with their configural nature. To use James Gibson's (1966) ideas to illustrate, suppose we want to validate his idea of an *invariance* as a configural property (and I might add that he uses the term in such a way that it can only be a relational, i.e., configural, property). So we start by defining something like a texture gradient, and we can easily enough generate stimuli that differ systematically in the density of whatever elements there are over a visual field. Thus, we find that people can, say, differentiate gradients. But that is not enough, because the gradients are themselves defined as a relation between components; thus, the components also exist in the stimuli and could have been used as the basis for the discrimination. You all can recognize the kinds of controls that one would need in such an experimental venture to demonstrate that it is the configural rather than the component properties that are being discriminated.

But let me use an even more complicated example. I recently read with great pleasure a book by Vurpillot that had been translated into English (1976). Her work is concerned with developmental aspects of visual perception, and in one series of researches she reported, she used the concept of primary structure in an investigation of the perception of embedded figures. She provides one of the best entirely objective definitions of a Gestalt property of stimuli that I have come across, and I briefly outline her criteria for primary structure:

1. All lines are involved in the primary structure.
2. No line can belong to more than one primary structure.
3. A line belongs in its entirety to a single primary structure.
4. The primary contour structures are preferably symmetrical or at least regular.
5. The number of primary structures must be the fewest possible.

In all of these criteria except the fourth, I felt quite able to determine what a primary structure was for a stimulus with no circularity of judgment. So the first part of the problem, that of providing an independent specification of the configural properties of the stimuli, was accomplished quite well.

Then she generated a series of embedded figure problems that differed in the role of the primary structure and tested children of different ages with these graded problems. The results showed the expected improvement with age and the expected differentiation of task difficulty. But I would now argue that that is not enough to validate the basic stimulus definition of the configural property, because the result simply showed that some problems were more difficult than others and that some people were better with the problems than others. In other words, the subjects and the problems formed a Guttman scale (see, e.g.. Torgerson, 1958). There was nothing in the experimental design to validate that the reason for the difference in difficulty level was truly the configural property. Her results were certainly persuasive that the kinds of stimulus property she was dealing with were of developmental importance, but they simply did not go that last step of guaranteeing that relational or configural properties were important. Configural properties always coexist with component properties because they are relational, and this fact makes the proof of the role of configural properties very difficult to provide.

The Gestalt Tradition.   I would like to make just a comment or two about the attitude of most if not all of the early Gestalt psychologists toward this question of an objective definition of configural properties that is independent of an experimental outcome. Gestalt psychology, tradition has it, was founded on the basis of the early work of Wertheimer and others on phi movement. This phenomenon, described in almost any text on experimental psychology, occurs when two lights are spatially separated and are lit in rapid succession. Under the right set of circumstances, movement is seen even though, of course, there is no actual physical movement of the lights. At this early stage of Gestalt psychology, an extremely thorough analysis of stimulus properties was engaged in, leading finally to the well-known laws of motion worked out by Korte (see Boring, 1942) specifying the relations between time, intensity, and distance necessary for phi motion. Thus the beginning of Gestalt psychology was based on a thoroughly analytic approach to stimulus properties.

Yet the particular phenomenon investigated (movement) had no parallel in the stimulus, because the lights did not actually move. So the movement was quite properly attributed to neural properties of the organism and not to the stimulus. Gestalt psychologists seemed to forget that the phenomenon was clearly a restricted function of stimulus properties and only to remember and emphasize that the particular percept had no stimulus counterpart. Thus Köhler (1947) can say that the view that *Gestalten* exist outside the organism is entirely erroneous and, even further, that "there is no organization among these stimuli [p. 160]." This is a view to which, of course, I take strong exception, and it is the view that has led, in my opinion, to the failure of Gestalt psychologists to progress in an understanding of some truly fascinating facts of perception—facts that emphasize the role of structure, organization, and configuration.

Instead, Gestalt psychologists undertook simply to catalog phenomena that were more or less holistic but ceased utterly to be analytic about their phenomena. The justification for this approach was that the phenomena had no stimulus counterpart, so why should one seek it? But I am arguing that one must still be analytic about the nature of the stimulus, whether or not the perception has an exact counterpart, just as the Gestalt psychologists had themselves done earlier. This nonanalytic approach led ultimately to the famous paper by Helson (1933) in which he lists 114 different laws of *Gestalten*. Few if any of these laws have any analytic basis, and most of them can be communicated only by demonstration. As some examples, consider: (Boring, 1942, pp. 253–254) "A field tends to become organized and to take on form." Or: "A strong form coheres and resists disintegration." Or still: "A form tends to preserve its proper shape." None of these laws has terms of any sort, much less stimulus terms, that can be defined objectively and independently of the phenomena presumably to be understood.

I am personally sorry that this tradition came to dominate Gestalt psychology, because I have long been interested in Gestalt phenomena and believe that they are very important in perception. But along with this interest is a desire to maintain what I consider to be a fruitful scientific approach to the problem; thus I suppose I am an analytic Gestalt psychologist.

Specification of Task

I have been arguing for the importance of specifying stimulus properties in our attempt to be analytic about unanalyzed perceptions. Now I want to argue that an equally important type of analytic approach is that of specifying and using many different tasks in our experiments on perception and information processing. The use of tasks with different demands on the organism will have two primary consequences: the differentiation of process, and a set of converging operations that help clarify the nature of the configural properties themselves.

Process differentiation. To state that a percept is holistic is—in today's world of information-processing approaches to perception—simply not enough. This search for process differences is now taken so for granted that I do not want to go into too much detail about it, but just enough to provide the evidence that we can profitably be very analytic about the processing of percepts that are themselves unanalyzed.

To use an illustration from research with which I myself have been involved, consider the discrimination of patterns (configurations) as some function of the goodness (in the Gestalt sense) of these patterns. Urged by some fairly conclusive evidence (summarized in Garner, 1974b), a graduate student and I (Garner & Sutliff, 1974) did a direct test of the idea that in a task requiring discrimination between two patterns and in which speed of reaction to each pattern is measured, the pattern with good Gestalt will be responded to faster than the pattern with poor Gestalt when a good and a poor pattern are paired for discrimination. We in fact obtained exactly that result, using the measure of number of rotations and reflections that produce a different pattern as our stimulus definition of pattern goodness: Good patterns have few alternatives; poor patterns have many.

At first glance, such a result should simply be explained on the basis of faster encoding for the good pattern. But Pomerantz (1977) had other ideas and ran a series of experiments for his dissertation having the general characteristic of requiring classification of one pattern against several other patterns. His reasoning was that if the advantage for good patterns was in an encoding stage, then the advantage should appear with the response made to many patterns as well as with the response made to just one pattern, because encoding would be required for all patterns. On the other hand, if the advantage for the good patterns was in a memory stage, it would appear only with the response made to the single pattern, because presumably in a one-versus-many classification task, the subject holds the single item in memory and then engages in a go–no-go strategy of simply deciding whether the particular pattern was or was not the one held in memory. His results completely justified the position that the effect is in memory, not in encoding.

Further experiments by Ruth (1976) and an experiment by Sebrechts and me (Sebrechts & Garner, 1980) have elaborated this conception. Sebrechts and I, for example, were able to show with a sequential same–different task—with reaction time measured—that differences in the goodness of the first item, presumably held in memory, had much more effect on the reaction times than the goodness of the second item, presumably encoded immediately prior to the decision. So far, this result simply confirms what Pomerantz (1977) had argued. However, our particular pattern of results suggested that although good patterns are easier to hold in memory—even for a short time—than are poor patterns, the function of the better memory item is to facilitate encoding of items like or similar to that held in memory.

These are enough examples to illustrate what I mean by saying that we can be analytic about the nature of processing of a holistic percept. We have plenty of evidence that the configurations are perceived as a whole, but such a fact should not lead us then to shrug our shoulders and say that there is little further we can do about it as perceptual scientists. Just as we can and should ask important analytic questions about the configural properties of stimuli, we can and should ask about how configured stimuli are processed. Not only do such questions allow us to differentiate between stages of processing; they also allow us to determine how various stages interact to determine the final processing outcome. And in the process, we have also validated the particular measure of a configural property of the stimuli—in this case, the number of alternatives produced by rotation and/or reflection of the patterns. This kind of mutual result, call it bootstrapping or call it the use of converging operations, is the outcome of an analytic approach to a holistic phenomenon.

Tasks as Converging Operations. As I have just noted, different tasks designed primarily to elucidate differences between processing stages have as well the general value of providing convergence to the constructs we are trying to discover and understand. If tasks differ enough, they will nearly always lead to some differentiation of processing stages or functions, but the primary purpose of the differences in task may actually be to provide the convergence about the definition and function of configural properties of the stimuli. And that is the second major reason for using different experimental tasks.

Once again, let me use my own research to illustrate, with the stimuli and tasks shown in Table 5.1. These stimuli, like those used earlier by Pomerantz and me (Pomerantz & Garner, 1973), consist of a right and a left parenthesis as the dimensions, with a right and left curvature as the two levels on each dimension. The whole set of four possible stimuli (labeled A, B, C, and D) is generated from the orthogonal combinations of the two levels of the two dimensions, and it provides a range of different configurations varying in goodness.

Each of 13 tasks requires the subject to sort a deck of 36 cards into two piles. The letters for each task state which particular stimuli are used, and the slash indicates how the stimuli are to be dichotomized in the sorting. There are three basic types of task used: *Discrimination* tasks require sorting of decks of just two cards. The A/B and C/D tasks require discrimination of the first parenthesis; the A/C and B/D tasks require discrimination of the second parenthesis; and the B/C and A/D tasks require discrimination when the two dimensions are correlated. *Focusing* tasks involve decks in which all four stimuli are used and sorting is one stimulus against the other three. There are four such tasks, one for each stimulus as the focus. *Classification* tasks again involve decks in which all four stimuli are used, but now sorting is two against two. Two of the tasks require filtering, in which the two pairs of stimuli differ from each other on a single relevant attribute and the two stimuli within each pair differ on the irrelevant attribute. The last task requires sorting when each pair of stimuli differs on both attributes. Such a task is variously called condensation or biconditional classification.

The task descriptions are in terms of the dimensions used by the experimenter to define the set of four stimuli. The experimental question is whether these component properties are those in fact used by the subjects or whether the configurational properties are used. The data displayed in Table 5.1 show that configural properties are used and, even further, that the discrimination task is carried out as a focusing task in which the better configuration is held in memory

TABLE 5.1
Sorting Times (sec) for 13 Tasks with Four Stimuli Formed
from Homogeneous Dimensions (Data from Garner, 1978b)[a]

[a] *Stimuli:*

A:	(−(	B:	)−(
C:	(−)	D:	)−)

Discrimination		Focusing		Classification	
A/B	19.6	A/BCD	21.0	AB/CD	24.4
C/D	19.1	B/ACD	20.9	AC/BD	23.3
A/C	19.2	C/ABD	18.5	AD/BC	21.8
B/D	19.9	D/ABC	20.6		
B/C	18.7				
A/D	20.5				

and the decision is then a go–no-go process. First, consider the focusing task. The C stimulus is sorted much more rapidly than the other three, and this is the stimulus that has the best figural goodness. Furthermore, the three fastest discrimination tasks are those in which the C stimulus is one of the pair of stimuli. This is the result that suggests that the same focusing procedure is used in discriminating a pair of stimuli as in sorting one stimulus against the other three. It further suggests that the configurally better stimulus is focused on and is handled in memory more efficiently than the configurally poorer stimuli. And notice that there is no evidence that the pairs of stimuli with redundant dimensions are discriminated faster than other pairs, a result arguing still further that it is the configurations and not the components that are used with these stimuli. The classification data show that the biconditional task is easier than the two filtering tasks, a result that once again argues for the role of configuration, because the biconditional task demands processing of both dimensions (if dimensions are used) whereas the filtering tasks can be processed with a single dimension. If the dimensions had been used for processing, the biconditional classification would have been more difficult than the filtering tasks requiring selective attention of dimensions.

This same pattern of results is obtained if brackets are used to generate the stimuli rather than parentheses. Table 5.2, however, shows what happens if brackets are combined with parentheses to produce stimuli generated by heterogeneous dimensions. These data differ from those shown in Table 5.1 in two important respects: First, none of the focusing tasks is as easy as any of the discrimination tasks; nor is any one especially better than the others. Second, in the classification tasks, the biconditional classification is very difficult compared to the two filtering tasks. This pattern of results suggests that the component dimensions are the processing properties rather than the configural properties, and I call such dimensions separable. Thus we have seen that by changing the

TABLE 5.2
Sorting Times (sec) for 13 Tasks with Four Stimuli Formed
from Heterogeneous Dimensions (Data from Garner, 1978b)[a]

[a] Stimuli:

A:	(−[	B:	)−[
C:	(−]	D:	)−]

Discrimination		Focusing		Classification	
A/B	20.5	A/BCD	22.6	AB/CD	21.7
C/D	20.7	B/ACD	22.8	AC/BD	21.4
A/C	20.6	C/ABD	21.6	AD/BC	26.6
B/D	21.2	D/ABC	22.6		
B/C	20.3				
A/D	20.3				

stimulus components from homogeneous to heterogeneous, processing is changed from configural property to component property.

This result, especially that contrasting the filtering and the biconditional classification tasks, is similar to one that Gottwald and I (Gottwald & Garner, 1975) had shown between two different pairs of dimensions. We generated stimuli from dimensions of Munsell value and chroma (which I shall call integral) and dimensions of value and size (which I shall call separable). Each of the dimensions in each pair of dimensions gave the same discrimination sorting time. But when the task was filtering, requiring selective attention to a dimension, the integral dimensions gave much slower times than the separable dimensions. When, however, the task was biconditional classification requiring processing of both dimensions, the separable set of dimensions gave slower sorting times than the integral set. Thus the pair of dimensions that gave best performance reversed when the task was changed from selective attention to biconditional classification.

Table 5.3 shows some results I have obtained with the same set of tasks but in which the stimuli are words formed from orthogonal combinations of the letters *s* and *r* at the beginning and *m* and *n* at the end, with the letter *u* as a constant vowel in the middle. I was interested in whether these words would be processed as separate letters, as a visual configuration, or even as an encoded word. The pattern of results is very similar to that obtained with the heterogeneous dimensions in Table 5.2 except that on the average, focusing performance with the words was better than it was with the mixed parentheses and brackets. However, of critical importance is the fact that the biconditional classification was much more difficult than the filtering classification, indicating that the subjects found it easy to attend selectively the first or last letter but found it very difficult to deal with the whole word as a single unit. Thus we would have to conclude that the component letters were the processing units—not the word, either *qua* word or as

TABLE 5.3
Sorting Times (sec) for 13 Tasks with Four Word Stimuli
Having Minimum Configuration[a]

[a] *Stimuli:*

A:	*sum*	B:	*rum*
C:	*sun*	D:	*run*

Discrimination		Focusing		Classification	
A/B	18.3	A/BCD	19.3	AB/CD	19.3
C/D	18.3	B/ACD	18.6	AC/BD	19.0
A/C	19.5	C/ABD	19.0	AD/BC	28.0
B/D	19.2	D/ABC	18.7		
B/C	18.5				
A/D	18.0				

a visual configuration. Further evidence that wordness is not important was obtained by using the same stimuli but with the letter positions reversed. Four nonwords are thus formed. The pattern of results was in no way changed from that shown in Table 5.3. Nor was the pattern changed when uppercase letters were used rather than the lowercase, either as words or as nonwords. This same lack of effect of wordness was found by Chang and Shepard (1964) in the learning of classifications or identifications of 8 three-letter words or nonwords.

To push still further the possibility that words are sometimes processed as configurations (and Silverman, 1976, had shown some evidence in favor of word processing), I used the word stimuli shown in Table 5.4. The logic of their generation is exactly the same as for the words in Table 5.3, even to the extent that these words when reversed become nonwords. These stimuli, however, have letters that go both up and down and in their various combinations, provide substantially different configurations. Once again the results with the biconditional classification show that the subjects have great difficulty using the word as a single unit, and this result is confirmed by the quite fast sorting times when selective attention to the letter positions was required. However, with the focusing task, there is indeed evidence that configuration can be used to some extent, because the two stimuli that had a rising or a falling configuration were classified faster than the other two, in fact nearly as fast as the equivalent discrimination and filtering tasks. Because this same result was obtained when the letters were reversed to form nonwords, the result is that some processing of the visual configuration was being carried out, although no word processing as such. As an overall summary, however, there is little evidence for the processing of configural properties with these word stimuli.

At this point I need to digress a bit to emphasize a point that I feel is very important about such stimuli and experiments—namely, that both component and configural properties coexist in the stimuli and that the experimental task is

TABLE 5.4
Sorting Times (sec) for 13 Tasks with Four Word Stimuli
Having Maximum Configuration[a]

	[a] Stimuli:	
A: beg	B: peg	
C: bet	D: pet	

Discrimination		Focusing		Classification	
A/B	19.7	A/BCD	19.4	AB/CD	18.8
C/D	19.1	B/ACD	20.2	AC/BD	19.9
A/C	18.7	C/ABD	20.2	AD/BC	28.0
B/D	18.7	D/ABC	19.2		
B/C	18.2				
A/D	18.7				

to determine which properties are used or processed. Some time when I have the leisure, I plan to write a book on all that we know from the experiments we know better than to do. We usually know so much about the perceptual process that we only run our experiments to clarify what we don't know. But what we don't know is then often the small or subtle part of the broader question.

The relevance to the immediate question is this: After I had finished collecting these data on words, I read a paper by Purcell, Stanovich, and Spector (1978). These authors argued quite convincingly that the word–letter effect (in which letters are perceived more accurately within words than within nonwords) occurs only with very small visual stimuli—in this case, with words subtending less than one degree of visual angle. My own interest in doing the research with these tasks, but with words rather than more abstract material, was an interest in the word–letter effect, because I was bothered about the general idea that selective attention was somehow better within units that were perceived as perceptual wholes. So I noted this article with considerable interest. My own stimuli were somewhat greater than one degree, but the question I asked myself was why I had in fact chosen that particular size. It was not an accident of the size of the typewriter available, because the stimuli had actually been slightly enlarged from typewriter size.

The answer is this: At very large sizes, it is obvious that the component letters will be easier to use than the entire word configuration; in fact, if the letters are spread over a large enough area, the subject can't even see more than one letter at a time. On the other hand, if the stimuli are so small that the individual letters can't be seen, it is still possible to perceive an overall visual configuration. So I already knew that there were both the component and the configural properties, that only configural properties could be used with very small stimuli, and that only component letters could be used with very large stimuli. I had chosen a size (with a little help in judgment from available graduate students) that seemed to offer the possibility that either a configural or a component outcome could occur. And that is the way we do most of our experiments, by choosing a set of conditions in which either of at least two experimental outcomes can occur. But we usually have very good reason from our own knowledge, scientific or commonsense, not to choose other conditions, namely, because we know what the experimental outcome would be.

This problem of whether we know more from the experiments we don't do or from the ones we actually carry out is not limited to the dual property issue I am discussing. Consider, to digress a bit longer, the experiments on iconic memory, such as those originally done by Sperling (1960) and by Averbach and Coriell (1961). The primary purpose of those experiments was to demonstrate that more information is available in a brief visual display than can be reported by a subject, and this fact is shown by using a partial report procedure, in which the subject is only required to report part of the total display. But some means must be used to inform the subject about which parts are to be reported. This is nearly always done by indicating a row, a column, or even the individual target item. The point is that what is to be reported is communicated to the subject by a spatial indicator, and that is a very natural thing to do. But this preeminence of the spatial domain in vision is quite possibly a far more important fact about vision than is the iconic memory itself. This preeminence of the spatial domain in vision is, of course, exactly what Kubovy (Chap. 3, this volume) has been arguing for in this conference. He quite probably is correct, but his evidence will come more from the experiments we knew better than to do than from the experiments we have done.

But let me return to the problem of convergence and the very special issue that concerns the fact of coexistence of both component and configural properties, and to our experimental need to show which property is used in any particular instance. I want to refer to an experiment done by Pomerantz and Sager (1975). It used card sorting again—with the discrimination tasks and also the selective attention tasks, one for each of two dimensions as relevant. The two dimensions were the actual individual element of figures and the configuration itself. For example, two configurations would be used—an X and a cross—but in one pair of stimuli the elements were X's and in the other O's. Thus discrimination or selective attention could be required for either the element forming the configuration or for the configuration itself. The results of importance right now are that in seven different comparisons, selective attention was easier to the element than to the configuration. Or, to reverse the statement, irrelevant variation in the elements produced more interference in discrimination of the configuration than did irrelevant variation in the configuration produce interference in discrimination of the elements. To summarize briefly, this experiment showed that both the configural and the component properties of stimuli can be used and that at least under these experimental conditions, the component properties could be selectively attended more effectively.

Primary and Secondary Process.   Before leaving this general topic of the use of task differences in the analysis of holistic phenomena, I want to refer again to a distinction I have made before (Garner, 1974b) between primary and secondary process. And the reason I want to concerns this matter of whether configural or component properties of stimuli dominate perception. In the experiment just described, it would appear that the component property was more salient or at least more useful. But other research (e.g., Clement & Weiman, 1970) has shown the opposite to be true.

In a more general vein, we have to consider the possibility that human performance is not an either–or matter with respect to processing of configural properties rather than component properties. In many cases it is clear that humans can use either property under the right task demands. To illustrate with the issue that first forced me to differentiate between primary and secondary process, consider the Munsell dimensions of colors: hue, value, and chroma. Various researchers (once again summarized in Garner, 1974b) have shown these dimensions to be unanalyzed and even mandatorily unanalyzable. The apparent mandatory nature of the relation between these integral dimensions appears primarily with the speeded discrimination and classification tasks because of the failure of subjects to attend selectively to a single dimension even though the task requires such selective attention, and even though subjects can do so easily with other stimulus dimensions.

However, we have to pause when we realize that these Munsell dimensions were in fact scaled by people. So if the dimensions are unanalyzable, why were humans able to carry out a scaling procedure that required the dimensions to be analyzed before they could be scaled? The answer has to be that the dimensions are integral in a primary sense and thus unanalyzable, but that they are also analyzable in a secondary sense. Thus we have to assume that the dimensions are both analyzable and unanalyzable, depending on the task constraints. I have called those processes that occur under time constraint primary and those that occur with greater time for analysis, secondary. (Just possibly we should also consider what I have called scientific epistemology to be secondary, in the same contrast to the primary epistemology. We as scientists enjoy more time to engage in the secondary processes.)

Another example of the fact that stimuli may be both analyzed and unanalyzed occurs with configural stimuli such as the parentheses that we have used in our research. We know that these stimuli are perceived primarily in terms of their configural properties, at least when there is a time constraint. But I also know that when I am generating such stimuli, I do not use their configural properties by, to illustrate, generating a basic form and then rotating it to produce others. Quite the contrary, I use the dimensional or attribute structure to generate them; and I suspect that in a free-recall experiment, the attribute structure would be more important than the configural property, even though the configural property is certainly more important in discrimination or recognition tasks. This difference is easily illustrated by a conversation I had with the illustrator who was drawing some 16 figures for me, figures that could be generated in terms of four dichotomous dimensions, but that could alternatively be perceived in terms of their rotation and reflection possibilities. The illustrator asked me why I wanted the figures. I explained to her, at which point she noticed for the first time, with an exclamation of surprise, that indeed many of the figures were exactly the same except that they were rotated with respect to each other. Yet these are the kinds of figures that many subjects, in the right experimental context, would never notice as being composed of attributes. Recognition, or other tasks passive with respect to the patterns, probably use configural properties; active generation, either originally or in free recall, probably uses the attribute properties.

But my point is, hopefully, clear. Not only must we be analytic about the stimulus properties and about the task; we must also be fully able to accept that different properties are appropriate to different tasks. Any set of stimuli, of course, has many different properties, and I have here especially emphasized that component and holistic properties necessarily coexist in a set of stimuli. So in particular, each of these properties may be used at different times, and it would be a mistake to assume that a set of stimuli has just component or just configural properties, or that just one type of property can be used by our human subject.

CONCLUSION

My conclusions are simply a summary of what I have been saying: There are perceptual phenomena that are ordinarily perceived and processed in an unanalyzed way. Furthermore, such phenomena are very important in perception and will frequently be found as the primary process for the subjects in our experiments. However, this lack of analysis in the perceptual process of the ordinary subject does not mean that we as scientists should not be as analytic about the phenomena as we are about any other phenomena we investigate. We should be analytic in developing constructs appropriate to holistic perception, about the stimulus properties that may influence holistic perception, and about the tasks we require of our experimental subjects. And with sufficient ingenuity in our analyses of stimulus and task, we will find convergences that clarify both the nature of the stimulus properties and the nature of the processes that we engage in as human perceivers.

ACKNOWLEDGMENT

This research was supported by Grant MH14229 from the National Institute of Mental Health to Yale University.

6 Perceptual Organization in Information Processing

James R. Pomerantz
State University of New York at Buffalo

ABSTRACT

This chapter summarizes a growing body of literature on organizational effects in vision. Although they are readily experienced phenomenally, these effects also surface in the performance of information-processing tasks requiring selective attention, discrimination, or search. Primary emphasis is given to perceptual *grouping* and to how it can be measured, what causes it, and what its consequences may be. Following concepts proposed by Garner and by Kahneman, grouping of parts into unitary shapes or configurations is operationally defined as a failure of *selective attention* to individual parts. Using selective attention measures, it is possible to demonstrate objectively the role of various stimulus factors, such as element proximity and similarity, in causing grouping to occur. A major consequence of grouping is the creation of *emergent features* via interaction of parts in the perceptual process. Emergent features are not identified by prior recognition of parts but instead are *recognized directly*. Nor is the speed of their recognition predictable from the speed of recognizing their constituent parts: Wholes may be recognized either more quickly or slowly than their parts. *Configural superiority* effects, wherein wholes are perceived faster than their component parts presented in isolation, arise from the direct recognition of the emergent features of these wholes. Similarly, configural *inferiority* effects arise when the whole's emergent features are recognized more slowly than its constituent parts. Two types of configuration may be distinguished—one that depends primarily on just the location of the component parts, and one that depends as well on the identity of those parts. The relationship between perception of parts and wholes is different for these two types of configuration, which may help resolve some otherwise curious discrepancies in the literature. Placing a part within a whole may create (in addition to emergent features) masking effects on that part, destruction of the part's features, or other changes in the part's appearance (e.g., its perceived orientation), all of which may impede the perception of the part but leave perception of the whole unimpaired.

INTRODUCTION

One of the hardest steps in solving any complex problem, from designing a piece of equipment to writing a scientific paper, is deciding where to begin. The task continually confronting the perceptual system in deciphering incoming sensory input is no exception. Consider the job of the visual system, for example, as seen by an outside observer. The retina of each eye contains over 125 million receptors, each of which responds over time in a complex way to the quantity and quality of light falling upon it. The task of the visual system is to create from this mass of raw data a useful, veridical representation of the outside world. I begin this chapter by asking the question: Where does the visual system begin in making sense out of the bewildering array of information given it?

The task of organizing sensory input appears, at first glance, to be awesome. Given the ambiguities of the signals reaching our receptors, given the noise in our sensory channels, and given the apparent capacity limitations of our information-processing network, it is not surprising that some have concluded (privately, if not in public) that perception must be impossible. But like the physicists who some time ago showed that in theory, it was impossible for a bumblebee to fly, we are confronted by the obvious fact that perception is not only possible—it is overwhelmingly successful. Human perception works quite well even under the worst of circumstances. I know of no better illustration of this fact than the work of Johansson (1975), who has shown that when we view movies that show only moving spots that have been filmed by attaching light sources to the actors' joints and limbs, we have little trouble perceiving the actors and their actions correctly. Demonstrations such as these remind us that in the normal environment, the perceptual system is given an embarrassment of riches, much more information than it needs. Perception is not only possible; it seems also to be overdetermined by the stimulus.

An initial goal of the perceptual system is to achieve, at a coarse level, a general outline or map of the environment, including the major objects and surfaces with their respective positions and patterns of motion. Concurrently, at a finer level, the system works toward the identity of and more detailed information about these initially segregated objects and events. At both levels, the system is working toward a representation of things more global than the local, punctate information it must start with at the receptor level. How should a perceptual system begin the task of synthesizing global representations from local information?

A seemingly necessary early step in this process would be determining which local points go with which others. That is, which points in the retinal mosaic are, so to speak, looking at identical objects in the environment? The necessity of this preliminary step in perception seems straightforward enough, because if we tried, for example, to recognize faces in a crowd without first establishing which eyes go with which noses, which noses with which mouths, and so forth, we could never begin to achieve sensible percepts of our world. I am not claiming here that, say, eyes, noses, and mouths must be recognized as such before a face as a whole can be recognized; that is a separate question that I address later. My point is that the contours and blobs that make up a face must be linked perceptually before the face can be recognized. In the context of visual pattern recognition, this is, in my opinion, the principal problem of perceptual organization.

The Gestalt psychologists attacked this problem with their well-known laws of grouping and of figure–ground segregation. The distinction between these two sets of laws, which is often ignored, is important for present purposes, because my immediate concern is where visual processing begins. As grouping is the perceptual linking of regions into unified objects and surfaces, it would seem to be logically prior to figure–ground segregation, which is essentially a matter of choosing which of the already unified objects will hold the focus of attention and which will be relegated to the background. If we look at perceptual organization from the perspective of sequential stages of information processing, grouping would seem to be localized in a stage earlier than figure–ground segregation. So let me turn first to the question of grouping.

Grouping. The classical approach to the study of grouping has been based on the phenomenological method or, as Attneave (1950) has called it, the "look-at-the-figure-and-see-for-yourself" method. The virtues and the drawbacks of this method are clear. Its main virtue is that demonstrations allow one to see the phenomenon of grouping directly, rather than having to infer it from abstract data. The drawbacks are quite serious, however. First, the procedure is wholly subjective, so technically it cannot be used to study those other than oneself without going through troublesome and potentially distorting perceptual reports. Second, the procedure is, scientifically speaking, a cul-de-sac, since it is useful more for establishing the existence of a phenomenon than for analyzing it or for localizing it somewhere in the chain of events that constitutes perception.

The research I report is based instead upon *performance* measures of grouping. The assumption here is that grouping, like other mental processes, is an operation performed on incoming stimuli, and so its effects should surface in performance on information-processing tasks, just as any other mental operation would. Further, by using performance measures of grouping, we possibly can get a clearer idea of what grouping means in information-processing terms and how it affects the flow of information through the organism; and perhaps we can eventually determine the stage (or stages) where grouping takes place in the processing stream. This would be particularly important for understanding Gestalt phenomena, because traditionally they have been described in the loosest of terms and have been explained mostly with ill-defined mechanisms.

Organization of Chapter.   I begin by showing how grouping can be operationalized in information-processing terms. Then I discuss the factors that cause or contribute to grouping and, finally, I consider some of the consequences of grouping that arise in information processing.

A DEFINITION OF GROUPING

The purpose of grouping is to divide the perceptual field into units, but what exactly is a *unit*? The term unfortunately is, like so many others in psychology, an ambiguous one. Atoms and molecules are units of matter; centimeters and kilometers are units of distance. These two kinds of units have little in common, because the units of distance are arbitrary and are chosen by convention, whereas the atoms and molecules are ''natural'' units that have physical reality (cf. Gibson, 1979, p. 12). When we talk about psychological units in visual perception, we presumably are referring to natural units with some psychological reality (cf. Fromkin, 1973).

Any natural unit is defined by its indivisibility. Seldom is this indivisibility absolute, as the unending search for the absolute, fundamental particle in physics well attests. Nonetheless, when a complex structure is broken down into parts, some breakpoints are more likely than others, and these serve to demarcate natural units. For example, a mechanic, given the usual hand tools, is likely to dissect a bicycle into certain common parts that we would call natural units and for which we have common names, such as seat, chain, handlebars, pedals, and so on. We can use this example as a model to see how the visual system, when presented with a visual object, is able to dissect it. It must be kept in mind, however, that the tools we are given to work with can determine the kinds of units we ultimately carve out. If we give our bicycle mechanic a hacksaw rather than a wrench, we may expect to see quite a different set of parts!

Selective Attention Measures

When it comes to analyzing percepts, it would be convenient if we could drop them on the floor and watch them shatter into natural pieces. The stabilized image technique is probably the closest we have come to this so far. In the absence of such a direct technique, more indirect alternatives must suffice. When Garner and I (Pomerantz & Garner, 1973) first approached the problem of grouping and configuration in vision, the dissecting tool we chose was the selective attention task. As this paradigm (and the logic behind it) is so well

known from Garner's papers on stimulus integrality and perceptual independence, I describe it only briefly. The subject is presented with stimuli that vary in
two of their component parts or dimensions. The task is to classify those objects
according to one part while ignoring the other part. The logic of this procedure is
that if the two parts in question are dissected into separate perceptual units, then
selective attention to just one part should be possible. But if the two parts are
parsed into the same perceptual unit or group, then the two should not split, and
so selective attention to just one part should be difficult or impossible. In this
manner, the success or failure of selective attention becomes an operational
measure of perceptual grouping. (See Kahneman, 1973, Chapter 5, for an enlightening presentation of this approach.)

The particular stimuli we first used to test this idea are shown in Fig. 6.1. Set
A shows four stimuli, each composed of two curved line segments (actually,
parentheses). Phenomenologically, the two parentheses of each stimulus appear
to group so that each stimulus has its own definite shape. The stimuli in Set B are
the same as those in Set A except that one of the two parentheses in each pair has
been rotated 90 degrees. Here, phenomenologically speaking, the stimuli as
wholes lack any unified shape or configuration that distinguishes among them.

The specific task the subject was given was to classify stimuli, using a card-
sorting procedure, on the basis of one of the two elements—say, the left one. The
dependent variable was the time needed to perform 32 such classifications. The
irrelevant parenthesis either remained the same for all 32 stimuli or varied randomly from stimulus to stimulus. In the first case (the control condition), the
subject might, for example, have to discriminate between the top left and the top
right stimulus. Note that here, it is the left parenthesis that is relevant because the
right-hand one is the same for both stimuli. In the second case (the filtering or
selective attention condition), the subject might have to discriminate the two

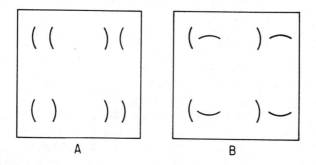

A   B

FIG. 6.1. (A) Four stimuli created by combining two possible curved elements
on the left with two on the right. These stimuli show perceptual grouping, as
defined by the inability to attend selectively to individual elements. (B) The same
four stimuli as in Panel A but with the right-hand element rotated 90 degrees.
These stimuli do not show perceptual grouping. (From Pomerantz & Garner,
1973.)

stimuli in the left-hand column from the two in the right. Again it is the left-hand element of each stimulus that is relevant, but note that the right element is now variable. If the two parentheses of each pattern did not group and so could be attended to selectively, then the two conditions should produce equal performance. The reason for this is that the two differ only with respect to the irrelevant parenthesis, and that parenthesis would not be attended to. But if selective attention were not possible and the stimuli had to be processed as wholes, then the selective attention condition should be harder than the control, if only because there are four alternative stimuli to be classified in the former and only two in the latter.

The RTs for Set A showed that this irrelevant variation interfered substantially with performance. Our interpretation of this outcome was that the pairs of parentheses in Set A could not be broken apart perceptually but had to be processed as wholes. Subjects could not *avoid* attending to the irrelevant element, and so performance suffered. With the stimuli in Set B, however, variation in the irrelevant element had no effect, indicating that selective attention was possible here. Thus, subjects seem to perceive these stimuli as two separate entities.

Stimuli that *do* configure, such as those in Set A, are not, strictly speaking, "integral" stimuli, because—among other things—they fail to show the redundancy gains that are a defining characteristic of integrality. Let me also add that our specific interpretation of the origin of RT differences between the two conditions is not critical and that other interpretations are possible. In particular, it may be that the stimuli in Set A—that is, those that show grouping—are treated as perceptual wholes, not because selective attention is literally impossible, but because wholistic processing is just easier or faster than analytic processing. In other words, it is an open question *why* selective attention fails when grouping occurs. For the moment, however, it is enough to note that a processing difference exists between Sets A and B that would not exist if selective attention were at work in both sets.

Divided Attention Measures

The notion that perceptual grouping of parts implies a failure of (or at least the absence of) selective attention to those parts suggests an immediate corollary. This corollary states that if two parts belong to the same perceptual unit, then divided attention between the two parts should be easy, whereas if they do not, then divided attention should be difficult. Although this corollary might seem straightforward, it is nonetheless important to test. Recall that in the case of the bicycle mechanic, the units into which the bicycle was parsed depended on the tools the mechanic used. The same might be true of parsing procedures in human visual perception; so it would not be prudent to rely on a single tool, the selective attention task. Divided or distributed attention tasks require that subjects pay attention to at least two aspects of a stimulus and base their responses on both aspects.

This corollary has been tested in two separate laboratories. Working with integral and separable stimulus dimensions, Gottwald and Garner (1975) showed that attention is more easily divided over integral than over separable dimensions. Working with configural dimensions, Schwaitzberg and I (Pomerantz & Schwaitzberg, 1975) have shown similarly that attention is more readily divided over elements that group than over elements that do not. Moreover, we have shown that for elements that group, divided attention is easier than selective attention.

The divided attention task we used is called a condensation task (Posner, 1964). Look again at the four stimuli of Set A; the subject's task is to classify the upper left and lower right stimuli into one response category and the two remaining stimuli—those on the upper right and the lower left—into the other. To perform this task properly, one must look at both parts of each stimulus. There-

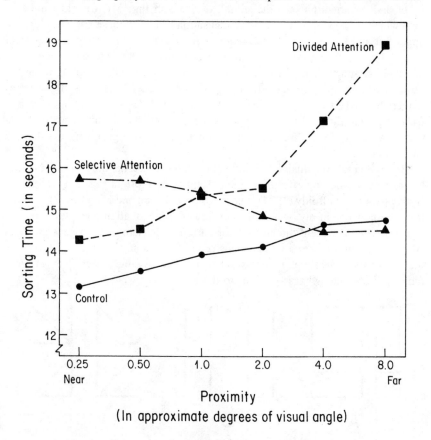

FIG. 6.2.   Reaction-time data showing how—when the elements of Fig. 6.1A are moved apart—grouping weakens, as indexed by improved selective attention and worsened divided attention. (Adapted from Pomerantz & Schwaitzberg, 1975.)

fore, the processing requirements of this task are opposite those in the selective attention task, where only one part need be attended.

The results of this experiment are shown in Fig. 6.2. When the parentheses were spaced closely so that there was a failure of selective attention (more on this later), divided attention proved quite easy. In fact, the condensation task was easier than the selective attention task, which (stated in other terms) means that it was easier to pay attention to two things simultaneously than to just one! On the other hand, when the parentheses were spaced farther apart, selective attention became quite easy, whereas divided attention became enormously difficult. So this is one piece of evidence supporting the corollary.

The second piece of evidence comes from an experiment I have never reported; in fact, I have never performed the formal experiment because the effect it demonstrates is so obvious that it needs no experiment. It concerns the possibility of divided attention with the stimuli of Set B in Fig. 6.1. Consider the ease with which you could perform the condensation task with these stimuli. Here the upper left and lower right stimuli require one response, whereas the upper right and the lower left require the other response. I have tried this task with a number of subjects, and their performance reminds me of subjects attempting to do the Stroop test. By my estimate, RTs with Set B average more than three times longer than when the stimuli in Set A of Fig. 6.1 are used. In short, it is a frustrating and difficult task, despite its overt simplicity. So again we find that parts that group by the selective attention measure also group by the divided attention measure.

Before I create the misimpression that parentheses are the only stimuli one can use to obtain grouping effects, let me present some more in Fig. 6.3. One set is from a paper by Felfoldy (1974), one is from Lockhead and King (1977), and the third is a new one of my own. What is noteworthy about all of these stimulus sets is that two independent dimensions (or parts), which are used to generate each stimulus, group to form a global shape or configuration; and in the process, the identity of the separate parts seems to become lost. Again, objective experimentation corroborates what is obvious to the eye.

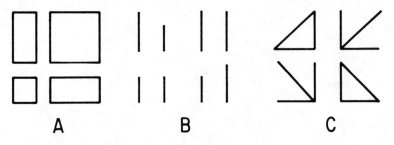

FIG. 6.3.   Three sets of stimuli constructed in a manner similar to those in Fig. 6.1, all showing configural effects.

Divisibility of Perceptual Units

The preceding experiments show that we may define a perceptual group as a set of parts that are processed as an all-or-none unit even when we try to attend selectively to a single part. But exactly how indivisible are perceptual units? It seems clear that most perceptual groups can be broken up into parts, given a conscious effort to do so. For example, the stimuli of Fig. 6.1 can be seen as individual parentheses, just as pointillistic paintings or newspaper photographs can be seen as isolated dots. (There are, however, limits to our analytic abilities, for with certain integral dimensions—such as the hue, brightness, and saturation of colors—independent attention to separate dimensions is difficult or impossible regardless of how much effort is applied to the task.)

In the case of the parenthesis stimuli (which, again, are not integral stimuli by Garner's criterion because they do not show redundancy gains), subjects may analyze the stimulus into component parts in the selective attention task, but this process requires time and effort. The evidence that this is the case comes from an unpublished experiment I performed with a student, Lawrence Sager. The stimuli used in this experiment appear in Fig. 6.4. These stimuli each have 4 parts, instead of only 2 with the parentheses patterns; so a total of 16 different patterns are possible instead of only 4. In our control condition, subjects had to discriminate between 2 patterns that differed in only 1 part (e.g., the upper left element); the other 3 parts remained constant. In the first of three selective attention conditions, 1 of the irrelevant parts also varied, resulting in a total of 4 different stimuli to be classified. In a second selective attention condition, 2 of the 3 irrelevant parts varied, resulting in 8 stimuli. In the final selective attention condition, all 3 irrelevant parts varied, resulting in 16 stimuli. Note that if

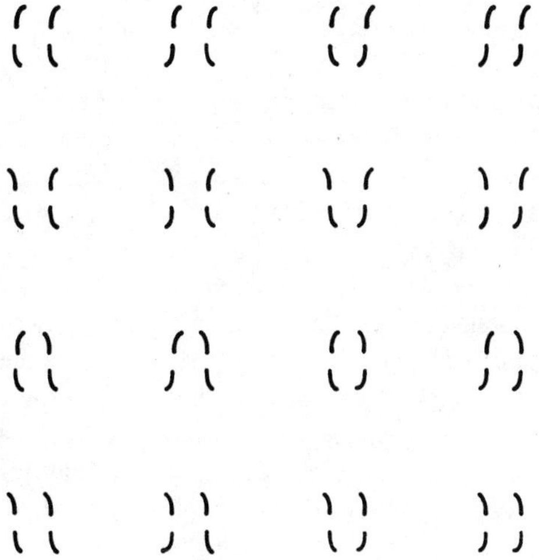

FIG. 6.4. A set of 16 stimuli created from all possible combinations of four elements, each having two alternative orientations. These stimuli show strong configural effects.

subjects did not attend only to the relevant part of the stimulus, these tasks would become progressively harder, because there would be more stimulus alternatives to process or, put another way, because there would be progressively more irrelevant information to filter. The results from our experiment were as follows: In the control condition, reaction time averaged 433 msec. In the selective attention conditions, RTs averaged 497, 509, and 511 msec with 4, 8, and 16 alternative stimuli, respectively. The small differences among these three conditions were neither systematic nor significant. So although performance was worse in the selective attention conditions than in the control conditions, it did not continue to deteriorate significantly with more irrelevant information, as would be predicted if these stimulus patterns were perceived wholistically and could not be processed as separate parts.

On the basis of this evidence and also on phenomenological grounds, it appears that it is indeed possible to break up perceptual units into smaller parts. This is an important inference, for it shows that grouping is not the result of an automatic, nonstrategic, and innate process (such as that suggested by the electromagnetic field theories of the Gestalt psychologists). But before we can claim that perceptual grouping comes under conscious control, we must rule out the possibility that the control is mediated by peripheral sensory adjustments. As noted earlier, it is possible to destroy the global organization of a pointillistic painting simply by standing too close to it. Similarly, changes in visual fixation can influence perceptual reversal of a Necker cube. The important issue here is whether grouping or other aspects of perceptual organization can be brought under *central* cognitive control.

Preattentive Processing.   Cognitive psychology has not invested much time in analyzing perceptual organization in information-processing terms. Models of pattern recognition, for example, usually bypass the problem. They assume that the input to the pattern recognizer has been cleaned up, as it were, and that there is no ambiguity in the signal as to where the stimulus is located in the field. Grouping and figure–ground segregation are assumed to have been taken care of already by some early, "preattentive" stage of processing, to use Neisser's term (1967). The characteristics of preattention are that it works at high speed, spatially in parallel, and that it is automatic. The term *automatic* is intended to mean that the preattentive processes are invoked by the stimulus without a conscious decision being made to do so, and that these processes are carried out without guidance from later, so-called "attentive" or "focal attentive" processes, which by contrast are slow, serial, conscious, and have a limited capacity for processing information. According to Neisser's analysis, the purpose of the preattentive stage is to parse the perceptual field into units upon which attention may operate, and to direct attention toward certain units in the perceptual input that seem particularly salient to the preattentive system, based on its crude analysis of the signal.

This sort of two-stage system has a great appeal on a priori grounds. Because conscious processing is slow and limited, and given that our sensory receptors are constantly bombarded by incoming information, one can hardly imagine a more useful device than a gatekeeper that sorts the input into crude categories, that filters out low-level redundancies, and that sets priorities. This would be especially true if the gatekeeper could be left on its own, without any monitoring or supervision.

One trouble with such a gatekeeper, upon further analysis, is that it might use inappropriate or obsolete rules. If the virtue of the gatekeeper is its simplicity, this same simplicity could prove an enormous liability in a changing environment. Therefore, it would be most advantageous if the gatekeeper could be sent new instructions from time to time telling it how to change its procedures.

Several theorists (e.g., James, 1890; Kahneman, 1973) have discussed this problem and have suggested that conscious control may override preattention. Examples are not difficult to find in skilled motor behavior. For instance, when an easy task (such as driving down a straight road) becomes difficult (when an unexpected turn in the road is encountered), we switch off our ''automatic pilot'' and turn to ''manual control.'' Another and perhaps better example is breathing; normally, we breathe without any conscious awareness or effort, but when we wish to, we may inhibit or induce breathing freely (within certain limits, of course).

The gatekeeper analogy and the breathing analogy imply different processing mechanisms. In the breathing analogy, conscious, attentive processes override preattentive processes, whereas in the gatekeeper analogy, consciousness merely instructs preattention how to behave. In terms of stage models for information processing, the issue is whether information bypasses the preattentive stages of processing when conscious control is exerted or whether it does not.

I do not believe we can make a firm choice between these two models on the present evidence, but my own thinking leans toward the gatekeeper analogy. My reason is based mainly on the sometimes stubborn nature of our organizational processes, as witnessed by certain hysteresis effects in perception and by spontaneous perceptual reversals or multistability phenomena (Attneave, 1971). If conscious control could simply override or displace preattention, such autonomous and independent behavior should not appear. Rather, it seems as though the gatekeeper is on duty at all times but that it has some very firmly rooted habits that it is unwilling to change at a moment's notice. In any event, regardless of which analogy is more appropriate, it is not sufficient merely to ask whether perceptual organization is automatic or is strategic, for it clearly has properties of both.

SOME CAUSES OF GROUPING

Given a satisfactory working definition of grouping, it becomes possible to isolate those factors that produce it. The classical Gestalt work on grouping identified two kinds of factors at work. The first kind was associated with certain laws of grouping, including similarity, proximity, and common fate. What these have in common is that they are all at least potentially measurable aspects of the stimulus. The second kind of factor is associated with the concepts of good figure, good continuation, and, in general, Prägnanz. The upshot of this second set of grouping principles is that the visual field will group so as to yield the "best," most stable organization.

Is the distinction between these two kinds of factors equivalent to the distinction between "bottom-up" and "top-down" processing? Essentially, bottom-up or "data-driven" processing begins with the raw stimulus and works its way toward some conceptual structure; top-down or "conceptually driven" processing works oppositely, beginning with some conceptual structure and working toward some particular stimulus (Lindsay & Norman, 1977; Rumelhart, 1977). In recognizing patterns, for example, one may sample enough aspects of the stimulus to infer the identity of the object; or one may begin with a hypothesis about the stimulus and proceed by checking this hypothesis against sensory data (Hockberg, 1970).

Grouping by proximity, similarity, and common fate could readily be accomplished by bottom-up processing (given that these three concepts were tightly defined within the processing system). However, grouping based on good figure, good continuation or Prägnanz could be based on top-down processing. If grouping proceeds so as to yield the "best" figure, then processing begins with the goal of grouping, and the task is to find some organization most consistent with that goal. Thus, this type of grouping would seem to be conceptually driven. A processing strategy consistent with Prägnanz would have the perceptual system begin processing an unknown input by making parsimonious hypotheses about how it might be structured. In other words, it would begin with a bias toward simple, or good, figures.

Local Factors

Proximity. Grouping by proximity is quite easy to demonstrate by the phenomenological method. However, as the emphasis in this chapter is on information-processing analyses of grouping, let me briefly summarize an experiment by Pomerantz and Schwaitzberg (1975) that I mentioned earlier, which demonstrates proximity grouping with performance measures. The experiment was similar to that of Pomerantz and Garner (1973) in that it required subjects to perform several types of classification tasks using the parenthesis stimuli. The new variable introduced in this study was the spatial separation between the two parentheses of each stimulus. The results, shown in Fig. 6.2, fall into a simple pattern. When the elements were spaced closely (within about 2 degrees), grouping occurred, as witnessed by the failure of selective attention and the success of divided attention. When the elements were farther apart (beyond about 4 degrees), grouping disappeared, as you can see from the convergence of the selective attention and control functions. No special importance should be assigned to the region between 2 and 4 degrees, where grouping began to break down in this experiment. Where grouping is concerned, it is almost certainly relative proximity and not absolute proximity that matters. After all, except in extreme cases where constancies break down, the grouping structure our perceptual system gives us does not change much as we manipulate visual angles. It is likely that proximity of elements in the distal stimulus, not the proximal, influences grouping (see Rock & Brosgole, 1964, for a demonstration of this effect).

Another information-processing demonstration of grouping by proximity comes from an ingenious experiment by Banks and Prinzmetal (1976; see also Prinzmetal & Banks, 1977a). They presented subjects with arrays of letterlike stimuli, all of which were the same except one. This discrepant stimulus was either a *T* or an *F,* and the task was to decide which one of these two was present as quickly as possible. The number of background stimuli—which were drawn to resemble a combination of a *T* and an *F*—was varied, as was the spatial arrangement of these background stimuli. Figure 6.5 shows some of the arrays they tested. Because the target letter could appear in any of the four corner positions of these arrays, the task was basically one of search.

Normally in search tasks, increasing the number of background stimuli to be searched through increases reaction time. This is what makes Banks and Prinzmetal's result so striking: They found that reaction times to detect the target were consistently shorter with arrays like the one in Panel B (which contains six background elements) than in Panel A (which contains only four). In other arrays, like the one shown in Panel C, reaction times were longer than in Panel A. The point is that if background (or ''noise'') elements are added in the proper way, they can actually improve performance.

The best explanation of Banks and Prinzmetal's finding may be that in Panel B, the background elements all group together because of their proximity (and, of course, their physical identity). This leaves the target item perceptually iso-

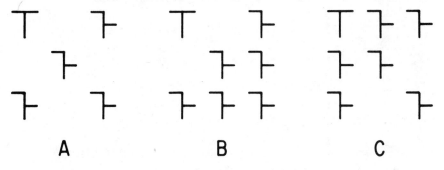

FIG. 6.5.   The *T* is detected fastest in Panel B and slowest in Panel C. (Adapted from Banks & Prinzmetal, 1976.) This contradicts the usual finding from detection tasks wherein reaction time is shortest for the display with the fewest elements (Panel A).

lated and standing out as a figure on ground. In Panel A, the target is not as likely to be isolated, because it is no farther removed from the rest of the stimuli in the array than any other corner element. Finally, in Panel C, the item that stands out as figure is not the target; but because, as figure, it captures attention, this delays the process of detecting the real target.

Similarity.   No major attempt has been made to demonstrate grouping by similarity using the selective attention paradigm, although a study by Garner, which was concerned primarily with other matters, shows that this would be easy. Garner (1978b, Chap. 5, this volume) showed that although stimuli created by parentheses, such as (), or created by brackets, such as [], do group, stimuli created by mixing a parenthesis and a bracket, such as [) or)[, do not group. Assuming that parentheses are more similar to each other than they are to brackets, similarity-based grouping can explain this outcome.

The most systematic look at grouping by similarity using performance measures comes from the studies of Beck (1966, 1967) and his associates and from the work of Olson and Attneave (1970). An example of this work is shown in Fig. 6.6. The subject is presented with a circular field containing many elements. One sector of the circle contains elements different from those comprising the remainder of the array. The task is to locate this disparate sector. Reaction-time measures and phenomenological impressions tell the same story here: The task is much easier with some arrays than with others. In particular, differences in line slope between the disparate sector and the rest of the array make for easy discrimination. Of course, other kinds of disparities are helpful, too, such as color or brightness differences (Julesz, Chap. 2, this volume), but with respect to dimensions of shape or form, slope differences are critical. Thus, slope similarity seems to be a critical factor in perceptual grouping. These results, incidentally, can be obtained with other kinds of information-processing tasks; for example, Beck (1972) has shown that when the task is to count the number of disparate

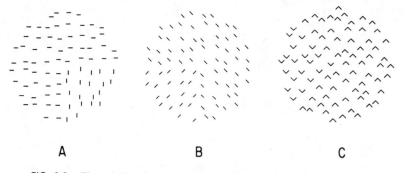

A   B   C

FIG. 6.6.   The task is to locate the region of the field containing the disparate elements. These panels show how elements group on the basis of similar line slope to make the task easy in Panels A and B but difficult in Panel C. (Adapted from Olson & Attneave, 1970.)

elements in an array, slope differences between the disparate or target items and the background items are crucial.

What makes these kinds of procedures different from ordinary, garden-variety measures of stimulus discriminability is that they tap special features of the perceptual grouping process that are not shared by other processes. In other words, these results do much more than just demonstrate that elements that differ in line slope are more dissimilar than those that do not. In fact, Beck's later work has shown that grouping by similarity has little in common with "ordinary" similarity. To illustrate, Beck and Ambler (1972) showed that in a field of several upright Ts, a tilted T is much easier to detect than is an L. The tilted T differs in line slope from an upright T, whereas an L does not. Thus, this result corroborates the preceding ones. Interestingly, however, by conventional measures such as similarity ratings (Beck, 1967), T and tilted T are no more dissimilar than are T and L. Moreover, the superiority of tilted T over L in the detection tasks above only held up when there were two or more upright Ts present as background elements in the array; otherwise, the superiority vanished.

These results show that the pairwise similarity of two elements taken in isolation does not predict whether they will group in a structured or cluttered visual field. Different stages of the perceptual system apparently use different criteria for similarity. Olson and Attneave (1970) suggested that grouping in a complex, multielement field proceeds along principles analogous to analysis of variance in statistics; if the variance (or dissimilarity of elements) *between* two regions of the visual field does not exceed the variance *within* the regions by a sufficient margin, the perceptual system concludes that they are not different; the two regions are grouped together as one, and discrimination is difficult. If the between-regions variance is larger than the within, a difference is noted perceptually, and the two regions of the field are segregated into distinct units. This between–within variance analogy is a particularly fitting one, because it explains why discriminability of elements presented in isolation may be different from that in a multielement field, for in the former case, there is no within-group variance to estimate. It also predicts that grouping can be manipulated by altering the within-group variance only—that is, while holding the between-group variance (which is normally thought of as similarity) constant. Although I know of no direct test of this prediction, there is some favorable evidence from visual search tasks. When the background elements through which the subject must search are heterogeneous, search is much slower than when they are homogeneous (i.e., are all the same, so there is no within-group variance). In fact, when they are homogeneous, reaction time is often independent of the number of background elements, suggesting that the target pops out as a figure on ground.

Another factor of potential importance for perceptual grouping has been demonstrated by Julesz (1975). Figures 2.4 through 2.10 of Julesz's Chapter 2 (this volume) show some of his effects. As with the method of Olson and Attneave, the field contains large numbers of elements; in this case, they are miniature dot configurations called micropatterns. The task again is to spot the disparate region of the array. Julesz finds that this task is quite simple for some arrays and so can be performed "perceptually," whereas other arrays are quite difficult and so require "scrutiny." In other words, some discriminations are preattentive, and others are not. Furthermore, like Beck, Julesz finds that the ease of discrimination is not at all related to the similarity of the micropatterns viewed individually. If you look closely at the individual micropatterns in Fig. 2.10 of Julesz's chapter, you will see that those in the disparate region are not really at all similar to those in the rest of the array; but despite this dissimilarity, the field does not split into two groups.

The critical variable producing similarity grouping in these arrays is, according to Julesz (1975), the absence of second-order statistical differences between different regions of the array. If second-order (or first-order) differences exist between two regions, they will be seen as separate textures; otherwise, they appear as one and can be told apart only with close scrutiny.

The definition of order statistics is complex, and the reader should refer to Julesz (Chapter 2, this volume) for details. Briefly, the first-order statistics of a texture refer to its overall density or brightness and are assessed by the probability that a randomly thrown point will land on a dark part of the texture (e.g., on a micropattern dot). Second-order statistics refer to the "clumpiness" of a texture or, more formally, to constraints on the spatial distribution of the dark regions or dots of the texture. They are assessed by the probability that pairs of randomly thrown points (at a given separation and orientation) will both land on dark parts. Third-order statistics are assessed using randomly thrown triplets of points. These have no perceptual correlate because, as Julesz argues, textures differing only in their third-order (or higher) statistics are not often distinguishable perceptually (but see Chapter 2 in this volume).

The work of Beck, of Olson and Attneave, and of Julesz has contributed much to our understanding of grouping by similarity. Still, there remain a number of unresolved questions. My research on grouping, for example, has produced results suggesting that qualifications may be needed on the foregoing conclusions about line-slope differences and second-order statistical differences in grouping. Figure 6.7 demonstrates some problems with the line-slope hypothesis. Panel A shows an array like the one shown in Fig. 6.6B, where a difference in line slope presumably makes discrimination of the disparate sector easy. Panel B shows a case where despite the absence of line-slope differences, the disparate sector is still quite readily perceptible or is at least as easy to spot as in Panel C, where line-slope differences *do* exist. Panel D shows a case where despite the *presence* of line-slope differences, discrimination is difficult, so in this case, the prediction fails in a different way than in Panel B. Thus, line-slope differences are neither necessary nor sufficient for discrimination, but just what the missing factor might be is far from clear (see Julesz, Chap. 2; Pomerantz & Sager, 1976; Sager, 1978).

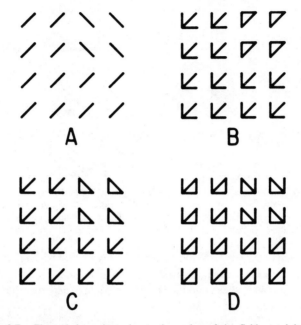

FIG. 6.7. The task is again to locate the region of the field containing the disparate elements. (A) Line-slope differences are present, and the task is easy. (B) Line-slope differences are absent, and the task is easy. (C) Line-slope differences are present, and the task is easy but no easier than in Panel B. (D) Line-slope differences are present, but the task is hard. Taken together, these panels show that differences in line slope are neither necessary nor sufficient for grouping (cf. Julesz's Figs. 2.14 and 2.15, this volume).

A second difficulty for the line-slope hypothesis is illustrated in Fig. 6.8. Panel A shows a blowup of the center four elements of Panel A in Fig. 6.7. Here there are only four diagonal line segments, with one segment having a slope opposite that of the other three. Sager and I have found that it is extremely difficult to identify the disparate element in this array, even though Fig. 6.7A suggests that it should be easy. The problem is that subjects consistently select the wrong element as the disparate one. In this particular stimulus, they see the lower left element as odd, although a little scrutiny shows that in reality, the odd one is hiding in the upper right. The likely basis of this illusion is (once again) perceptual grouping but not grouping by similarity. Rather, the four diagonals in Panel A appear to group into a unitary shape, looking like an open box with a stick popping out. The three lines forming the box are perceptually grouped into a single unit, and subjects perceive the solitary stick as the disparate element. (I return to this phenomenon later.) Panel B of Fig. 6.8 shows a set of elements where the odd element is easy to detect. Here there is no tendency for the entire array to be perceived as a global unit, as was the case in Panel A. A problem for theory is to explain why grouping works so differently in these two cases.

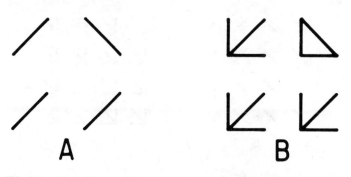

FIG. 6.8.   (A) A blowup of the four centermost elements of Fig. 6.7A, but in contrast to Fig. 6.7A, the task of locating the disparate element here is difficult. (B) A blowup of the four centermost elements of Fig. 6.7C, but the task remains easy. It is argued that in Fig. 6.8A, the four elements group to form a unitary configuration, whereas in Fig. 6.8B, the elements remain as four separate stimuli.

Some difficulties I see with the order-statistics hypothesis are shown in Fig. 6.9. Panels A and B are adapted from Olson and Attneave (1970). Although it may not look that way, these two panels are identical except that they are rotated with respect to each other. Olson and Attneave found that the discrimination in Panel B was much simpler than in Panel A. As rotating an array does not change the magnitude of differences in its internal order statistics, this rotational effect requires another explanation. It should be noted that the line-slope hypothesis also needs elaboration to handle this effect (see Olson & Attneave, 1970). Panels C and D show what appear to be further counterexamples to the order-statistics hypothesis. These stimuli came from a series of experiments performed by Randi Martin and me (Martin & Pomerantz, 1978). Panel C contains two regions that *agree* in second-order statistics, whereas Panel D contains two regions that *differ*. Despite this, the disparate region is much easier to detect in Panel C than in Panel D.

These and other counterexamples make it clear that some other factors are at work in the grouping and segregation of similar textures. Both the line-slope differences and order-statistics differences are strong predictors of grouping by similarity, but neither is sufficient to explain grouping. Along these lines, Julesz (this volume) has addressed himself to a set of strong counterexamples to the original order-statistics hypothesis and has augmented his theory of texture discrimination to include devices such as quasicollinearity detectors to supplement dipole-statistics detectors.

Global Factors

Although some of the factors influencing grouping can be identified with stimulus properties such as proximity, similarity, and good continuation, other factors are more closely tied to global or conceptual properties. Gestalt demon-

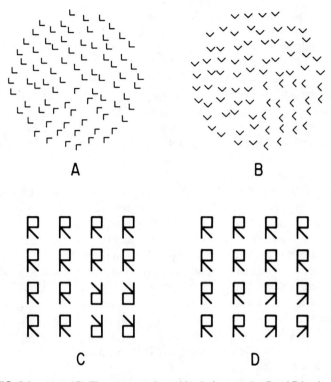

FIG. 6.9.   (A and B) These two panels are identical except that Panel B has been rotated 45 degrees counterclockwise with respect to Panel A. Despite identical degrees of second-order statistical differences in these two panels, the disparate region is easier to detect in Panel B. (Adapted from Olson & Attneave, 1970.) (C and D) Despite greater second-order statistical differences in Panel D than in Panel C, the disparate region is easier to detect in Panel C. (Adapted from Martin & Pomerantz, 1978.)

strations have shown that the role played by any one part of a configuration may be dictated by the configuration as a whole. A simple curved line, for instance, can be processed as the letter *C* when embedded in text but can be coded as a nose when embedded in a cartoon face. Thus, some local and perhaps minor perturbation in the perceptual field can have consequences for organization throughout the entire field (see Bregman, Chap. 4, this volume). If this claim is correct, it would imply that the probability that any two elements in the field will group depends on what other elements are simultaneously present. Pomerantz and Schwaitzberg (1975) demonstrated this in a performance task by showing that the grouping that exists between two normally oriented parentheses—such as)(—can be destroyed when a third parenthesis is added—such as)(). In this example, the first and second elements no longer appear to group; rather, the second and third group together and leave the first perceptually isolated (see also

Banks & Prinzmetal, 1976). It is reassuring that a standard textbook phenomenological demonstration of perceptual reorganization can be demonstrated objectively as well.

Prägnanz. The law of Prägnanz (or the minimum principle) states that the visual field will be organized in the simplest or best way possible. Phenomenological demonstrations of Prägnanz abound (Hochberg, 1974a). If we accept Prägnanz as a fact, the question becomes: *How* does the perceptual field come to be organized in the best possible way? (Let us ignore for the moment the longstanding problem of defining what is "best" without circularity.) Three alternatives suggest themselves.

The first is that organization is achieved in a purely top-down fashion. That is, the perceptual system begins with a simple organizational scheme and sees if it will work. If the elements of the field will fit this best organization, the organization is accepted, and no further schemes are tried (cf. Gregory, 1966, 1974). If not, the next best organization is attempted, and so forth. This is a pure top-down approach, because the starting point is an organizational scheme, to which one tries to fit the sensory data.

A second logical possibility is that the perceptual system rapidly attempts a large number of organizations in no particular order, and after a critical number of organizations have been attempted, or after a critical amount of time has elapsed, the best organization is accepted. This inelegant, brute-force approach is also top-down in spirit.

The third alternative, and the one that I believe comes closest to the original Gestalt theory, holds that Prägnanz works from the bottom up. Recall that according to Gestalt theory, organization worked automatically without influence from learned or strategic processing. Just as a soap bubble achieves the simplest possible configuration (e.g., the most symmetrical) without the need for goals or purposes, so does perception work automatically toward the good figure. For some, it may seem odd to link Gestalt phenomena—which are so global in nature—with bottom-up processing—with its frequent emphasis on local constraints; but this is, I believe, the correct way to classify original Gestalt theorizing in terms of current information-processing concepts.

Let me illustrate how local processing can lead to the best figure by describing a study Joseph Psotka and I performed in 1974. Subjects were presented with dot patterns of the type Garner has used in his studies of pattern goodness. Their job was to indicate how they saw each pattern to be organized by drawing lines between the elements, as in the children's game of connect-the-dots. The idea was that people organize these collections of dots as they organize clusters of stars into constellations resembling simple or familiar figures. Figure 6.10 shows some of these organizations.

For certain stimuli, subjects were in virtually unanimous agreement about how the pattern should be organized. Not surprisingly, these were, for the most

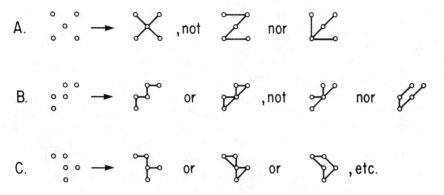

FIG. 6.10.   The task is to connect the dots of each pattern with lines so as to reflect its perceived organization. The better the dot pattern, the more agreement there is across subjects as to how it is seen to be organized. Some sample organizations that were given, and some that were not, are shown.

part, Garner's "good" patterns. For the "poor" patterns, however, there were almost as many different perceived organizations as there were subjects in the experiment. Thus, we have another way of demonstrating Garner's rule that good patterns have few alternatives (Garner, 1970b), one that can be applied to individual stimuli (and not just to reflection and rotation subsets).

Both the particular organizations with which these stimuli were perceived as well as the generally greater intersubject agreement for good patterns may be explained by bottom-up principles alone. Consider first, Pattern A in Fig. 6.10. This pattern is most often organized as an X-shaped configuration. Of all the possible ways in which this pattern could have been organized, this particular organization minimizes both the total length of the path connecting the dots and the total number of straight lines used in the path. No other organization would connect the dots so efficiently with respect to path length (i.e., proximity) or number of lines used (good continuation). Note that it also preserves the symmetry inherent in the original dot pattern; of the other logically possible connecting schemes, many would violate this symmetry. Next, look at Pattern B. This pattern is of intermediate goodness according to both Garner's objective measure (size of the rotation–reflection equivalence set) and goodness ratings. The most popular organization selected by our subjects is the "staircase" shown. This organization is optimal as it is the only one that minimizes total path length; also, it preserves fully the symmetry inherent in the unconnected dot pattern (although there are other organizations that do this equally well). But the most popular organization does not minimize the number of straight lines used in the connecting path; it employs four line segments, although only three are required. So in this case, the rules of proximity and of symmetry point toward one set of organizations, and the role of good continuation points toward a different set. Two organizations that minimize the number of straight line segments used are also shown in the figure. Note that one of these two (the third from the left) preserves the symmetry of the dot pattern, but it requires a greater path length. This organization was never selected by our subjects. So for this particular pattern, two rules of organization—proximity and good continuation—are in conflict, and proximity seems to have dominated.

Psotka and I collected perceived organizations on large numbers of dot patterns from dozens of subjects, and two general principles seem to hold. First, one can predict perceived organizations with remarkable success on the basis of a few objective, measurable properties of the stimulus. For example, for 14 of the 17 dot patterns tested in one experiment, the most popular organization was also one with the shortest path length. Second, the "good" patterns are the ones for which the *various rules of grouping all point to a single, unique organization.* These are the patterns that the subjects rate as good and for which different subjects tend to select identical organizational schemes. For the poor patterns, the story is quite different. First, the different organization rules come into conflict with one another; and second, each rule does not point toward a single solution but rather to several equally good solutions.

In conclusion, one need not appeal to hypothesis testing or similar top-down processing strategies to account for perceived organization of simple dot patterns. The best possible organization of a dot pattern can be achieved from the bottom up through the application of low-level rules. The most appropriate model would be one in which separate subsystems of preattention struggle independently to achieve a stable organization of a figure based on one grouping rule or another. If enough of these subsystems "vote" for the same organization, then the pattern will be organized quickly and predictably, and it will be seen as a good configuration. If the voting is split, then compromises will be necessary, the final organization will be slow in coming, it will be unpredictable, and the result will be seen as a poor configuration. (For evidence bearing on faster encoding of good versus poor patterns, see Bell & Handel, 1976; Checkosky & Whitlock, 1973; Garner & Sutliff, 1974; and Pomerantz, 1977.)

Pattern Recognition Models. The distinction between top-down and bottom-up processing is most often raised in the context of models for pattern recognition and object recognition. A widely held belief (Lindsay & Norman, 1977; Rumelhart, 1977) is that bottom-up models of recognition are inadequate. These models state that the identity of an object, say, is inferred from the set of features detected. The biggest stumbling block for bottom-up theories has proved to be certain Gestalt phenomena—particularly those that demonstrate that by rearranging the same features, different objects may be perceived. The whole is more than the sum of its parts, because the parts do not uniquely determine the whole.

Top-down models are relatively immune from such criticism, because they do not claim that stimuli are recognized from their features alone. In these models, the perceptual system starts with a hypothesis and then samples sensory data to see if they fit the hypothesis. Where does the original hypothesis come from? Many sources are possible, but the most important one is context. A secondary source of hypotheses is a crude (preattentive) bottom-up analysis of the input signal (which would imply a mixture of top-down and bottom-up processing.) Given an unknown object, a rough estimate of its size, color, shape, and the like can go a long way toward eliminating alternative hypotheses. When a hypothesis is matched by the sensory data, recognition takes place regardless of whether other hypotheses would fit the data as well or even better.

I stated a moment ago that the Gestalt notion of pattern perception came closer in spirit to bottom-up than to top-down processing. I wish to qualify and elaborate this point. The Gestalt position is clearly not top-down in nature, since perception is guided by innate and automatic forces. But neither is it bottom-up in the usual sense of the word, as that customarily implies that wholes are recognized by detecting combinations of elementary features. Gestalt psychology maintained that primitive elements were meaningless and played no role and that the perception of wholes was a primary and unmediated experience. If the Gestalt position on pattern recognition is neither top-down nor bottom-up, then what *is* it?

Three Routes to the Top.   Consider the case of motion detection. First, motion of an object could be detected in a bottom-up way by noting the presence of a particular object in two adjacent locations at two different times. Here motion is an inference (although it may be an unconscious one). Second, one could hypothesize motion and go looking for evidence confirming it. For instance, an eye-movement pattern could be generated and checked against a moving target by noting how well the pattern stabilized the retinal image of the target. But there is a third way to detect motion that involves neither hypotheses or component parts, and that is by direct detection of motion. Direct detection may sound mysterious, but it need not be. Gregory (1966) distinguished between a speedometer on one hand and an odometer plus a clock on the other. With the odometer and clock, motion is an inference based upon the clocked interval separating two mileage readings. Motion is detected indirectly from two separable and discrete measurements. The speedometer, however, has no clock or yardstick and so detects motion directly without making prior and independent estimates of place and time (see Lappin, Bell, Harm, & Kottas, 1975).

The example of motion detection is particularly fitting because it was the phenomenon of apparent motion that began Wertheimer's investigations. Wertheimer's interest was with "phi" motion, which is a type of apparent motion quite distinct from ordinary "beta" motion. In phi motion, one does not see any *object* moving. One sees only pure motion—a whoosh or a blur. This observation is important, because it is evidence that motion is a pure sensation, not a derived one. After all, how could motion be an inference based on seeing the same object in two places at two times if one did not see an object or discrete places?

Demonstrating the existence of phi motion is important for Gestalt theory. Ultimately, however, the existence of phi motion must be based on evidence from phenomenological report. Phi motion is a delicate phenomenon; I am not sure if I have ever seen it, despite many efforts. Later I present some more objective evidence in favor of direct detection of complex configurations, derived from experiments on the so-called word and object superiority effects. For the moment, however, let me conclude that there are at least three routes to the top—that is, to the recognition of an object or event: from information about component parts, from externally generated hypotheses, and through direct detection. Original Gestalt theory, with its postulation of innate and autochthonous forces, comes closest in spirit to the last.

SOME CONSEQUENCES OF GROUPING

Wholistic Processing

Following Neisser (1967), Kahneman (1973), and others, the ostensible function of grouping is to create the segmented and coherent units upon which later stages may operate. Thus, there should be detectable consequences of grouping on these later processes. The major consequence of unit formation is that the units so formed should be relatively indivisible. Independent processing of the components forming a unit should be difficult, whereas processing of the unit as a whole should be easy. I have already summarized a good deal of evidence from selective and divided attention tasks suggesting that this notion is correct. Let me now present corroborating evidence from two other paradigms. The first is a matching task used in an experiment by Sekuler and Abrams (1968). Subjects were presented with two dot patterns, which were created by filling in cells in a four-by-four matrix. Subjects had to decide, under time pressure, whether the two patterns were same or different. One group of subjects was told to respond "same" if and only if the two dot patterns were identical in every respect; if any cell did not correspond between the two patterns, they should respond "different." A second group was told to respond "same" so long as at least one cell corresponded between the two matrices; only if the two patterns were different in *every* respect were they to respond "different."

If dot patterns are organized preattentively into unitary configurations, then we should not expect that subjects could process them dot by dot; rather, wholistic processing should be mandatory or at least primary. This is just what Sekuler and Abrams found. Subjects were much faster in responding under the first set of instructions (which called for total identity of the two patterns) than under the second (which did not). In fact, when two patterns were identical, subjects were faster to respond that they matched in all their cells than to respond that they matched in at least one cell! This is a remarkably powerful demonstration of wholistic processing. (See Lindsay & Lindsay, 1966, for another noteworthy demonstration of this sort.)

A second piece of evidence comes from a study of Clement and Weiman (1970). They asked subjects to classify tachistoscopically presented dot patterns. Patterns were presented one at a time, but only two alternative patterns were possible in any block of trials. As in the Sekuler and Abrams study, the dot patterns were constructed by filling in cells of an imaginary matrix. In some of the conditions, the stimuli were "good" dot patterns, following Garner and Clement's (1963) criterion; whereas in others, they were "poor." In order to classify two of these dot patterns, it is necessary only to find a single cell of the matrix that differentiates between the two and to decide, on each trial, whether a dot is present or absent in that cell. Clement and Weiman reasoned that if subjects employed this simple strategy, they would not be processing entire patterns, and so there should be no effect on performance of the goodness of the whole patterns.

The results showed that subjects processed the good patterns much faster than the poor ones. Clement and Weiman next wondered whether subjects simply did not realize that they could use the strategy of attending to a single cell, and so the experimenters pointed out this possibility to them; but the superiority of good over poor patterns still held. In subsequent experiments, progressively more pressure was placed on subjects to process dots rather than patterns, but it was not until whole-pattern processing was made virtually impossible that the difference between good and poor patterns vanished. Thus, if wholistic processing is not absolutely mandatory, it surely is the natural or primary mode of processing, and experimenters must go to pains to induce subjects to process part by part.

So in two more types of task—"same"–"different" and two-alternative discrimination—wholistic processing of dot patterns appears to be the norm. What is more, as far as the "same"–"different" task is concerned, wholistic processing may be the norm regardless of what kinds of stimuli are used. It is a common finding that when subjects must match complex, multidimensional stimuli, the "same" response is faster than the "different" response (Bamber, 1969; Egeth, 1966; Nickerson, 1965, 1967). This finding poses a problem for feature analytic models of processing. In order to respond "same," it must be determined that the two stimuli match with respect to every feature or component part; but to respond "different," only one featural difference need be detected. Accordingly, "different" should be at least as fast as "same" and usually faster. Despite this straightforward logic, "same" is often faster than "different," even when the features or dimensions of the stimuli are separable in Garner's sense of the word (Egeth, 1966).

Global Superiority

In discussing the consequences of grouping, my emphasis so far has been on the indivisibility of perceptual units in processing. I hope to have established that wholes are not perceived by independent processing of parts. But how *are* they perceived? In approaching this question, a useful starting point is the fact that organized wholes can be recognized faster and better than can the parts from which the wholes are constructed. This is perhaps a counterintuitive assertion; so let me review the evidence that substantiates it.

Object Superiority Effects. Consider an experiment by Weisstein and Harris (1974). They presented subjects with visual arrays containing one of four possible diagonal line segments. The arrays were flashed tachistoscopically and were followed by a mask. The task was to decide which of the four diagonals was present in the array. The diagonal lines were presented either alone or in the context of vertical and horizontal lines. In one condition, the vertical and horizontal lines were configured so as to suggest three-dimensional cubelike shapes; in another condition, the lines were arranged to appear as a flat, two-dimensional array lacking any figural unity. But in no condition could the subject predict from the vertical and horizontal context lines (if any were present) which diagonal target line was present. That is, the context lines carried no task-relevant information in the technical sense. (Certain of Weisstein and Harris' stimuli are shown in Fig. 6.18.)

The results showed that despite their lack of relevance, the context lines made quite a difference. The diagonal lines were recognized much more accurately in the context of the cubelike configurations than in the flat context. Weisstein and Harris dubbed this the "object superiority effect," in recognition of its (at least superficial) resemblance to the "word superiority effect," in which letters are recognized better in the context of words than of strings of unrelated letters (Johnston & McClelland, 1973, 1974; Massaro, 1975; Reicher, 1969; Wheeler, 1970). However, performance was best when no context was present at all. In this respect, the object superiority effect may differ from the word superiority effect, where letters may be recognized better when embedded in words than when presented alone (but see Williams & Weisstein, 1978).

Although this study did not demonstrate that wholes are perceived better than their component parts, it led to studies that did. Schendel and Shaw (1976) compared the recognizability of whole letters and of letter fragments (i.e., small segments from which letters may be constructed). For example, subjects in one condition had to decide if a briefly flashed letter was an *H* or an *N*. In another condition, they had to decide if the flash contained just a short horizontal line or a negatively sloped diagonal line; these, of course, are the segments that distinguish *H* from *N*. In many comparisons of this nature, Schendel and Shaw found that subjects were more accurate and faster when processing entire letters than when processing parts alone.

Configural Superiority Effects. Pomerantz, Sager, and Stoever (1977) examined a large number of discriminations between simple visual elements, such as a positive versus a negative diagonal line; a horizontal versus a vertical line; a left- versus a right-curving line; and a short versus a long line. Take as an illustration the curved-line discrimination, which uses as stimuli ordinary parentheses. We know from the selective attention studies described earlier (Pomerantz & Garner, 1973; Pomerantz & Schwaitzberg, 1975) that the parentheses group. The immediate question is whether such a group can be processed faster than a single parenthesis presented by itself.

Figure 6.11 shows the paradigm used to answer this question. Subjects were presented with four stimuli arranged in a square. Three of these stimuli were always identical to one another, whereas the fourth—located at random at one of the four corners—was always different. The task was to locate this odd stimulus, and the measure was reaction time.

Figure 6.12 shows the results when the parentheses were used as stimuli. When the stimulus in each corner of the array was a single parenthesis, reaction time to locate the odd one was about 2.4 sec. When a second parenthesis was added to each corner so as to create groups, reaction time dropped to 1.5 sec,

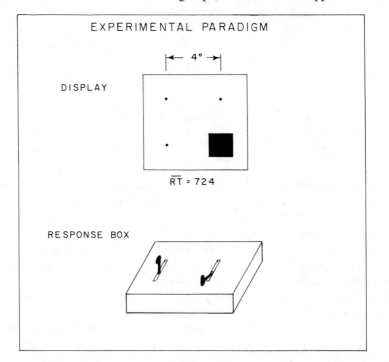

FIG. 6.11. The reaction-time task used by Pomerantz, Sager, and Stoever (1977). Three of four stimuli, arranged in a square, are identical; the task is to indicate the location of the fourth disparate stimulus by pressing the appropriate lever in the correct direction. In this example, the time to indicate that the odd stimulus (a large solid square) was in the lower right-hand corner averaged 724 msec.

DISCRIMINATION: DIRECTION OF CURVATURE

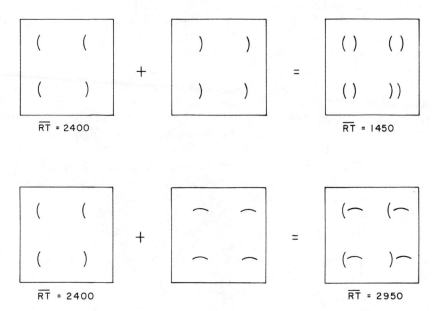

FIG. 6.12.   Reaction times to locate the disparate stimulus with no context elements averaged 2400 msec. In the context of elements that create perceptual
groups (top row), reaction time drops to 1450 msec. In the context of elements that
do not group, reaction time rises to 2950 msec. Note that the context elements do
not differ from one another in either the top center or bottom center panels.

which represents a 40% reduction. Note that the parenthesis added to each corner
was the same, so the context *by itself* contained no useful cues to aid discrimination. This result demonstrates that perceptual wholes can be processed faster than
the component parts that differentiate them. The bottom row of the figure shows
the effects of adding a horizontally oriented parenthesis. Recall that the resulting
stimuli do not group by selective attention measures and so do not form perceptual wholes. Reaction time to locate the odd stimulus in this case jumped to 3.0
sec, which represents a 23% increase. Thus the context elements acted like noise
and interfered with processing.

Figure 6.13 shows two more examples of context either facilitating or imped-
ing performance. Here the basic discrimination is between a positively and a
negatively sloped diagonal line. Reaction time to detect the oppositely sloped
line averaged 1.9 sec. When we added a context that converted the stimuli into
triangles and arrows, reaction time dropped to .75 sec, for a 60% reduction.
When a slightly different context was added, which created stimuli appearing
less wholistic, reaction time increased by 7% to about 2 sec. Finally, Fig. 6.14
shows two more cases where adding a context that appears to create good figures
improves perception. The first case involves discriminating the position of a line

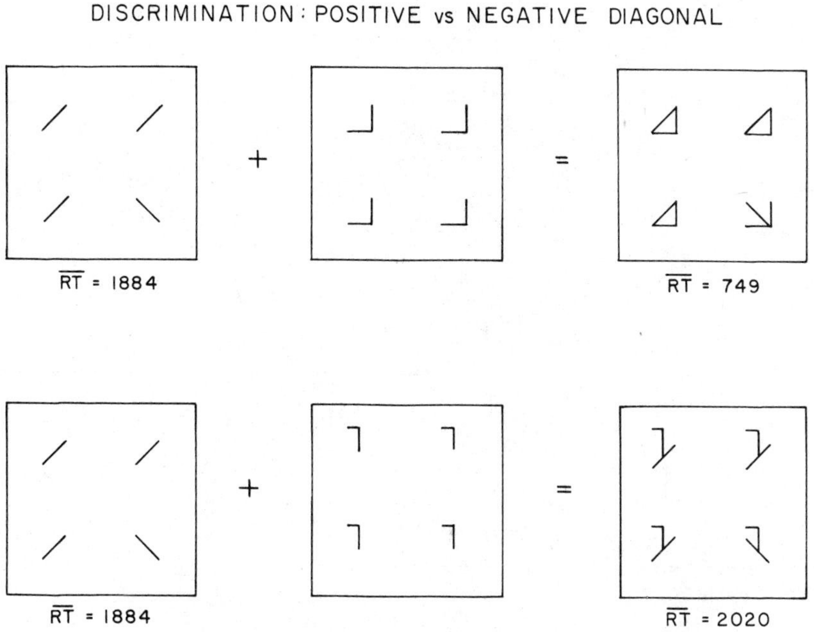

DISCRIMINATION: POSITIVE vs NEGATIVE DIAGONAL

FIG. 6.13.   The task is to discriminate the line whose slope is different from the rest. The top context helps, whereas the bottom context impedes performance compared to having no explicit context present (cf. Julesz's Figs. 2.14 and 2.15, this volume).

relative to a fixed point, whereas the second involves discriminating horizontal from vertical lines. In both cases, contexts are added that create triangle versus arrow discriminations. Reaction times to locate the odd stimulus are reduced by 65% and 34%, respectively, by the addition of context.

The point of these examples is to show that context can either *improve* or *impede* performance, depending on what kind of configuration results when context is added. The improvement, which I have called a "configural superiority effect," is the more interesting phenomenon, because it implies that wholes are not recognized by way of their component parts or at least not by way of those parts the experimenter identifies. Here context does not aid perception by way of a redundancy gain (a "horse race"), because the context by itself contained no clues or information useful to the task. Instead, context aids perception by creating *emergent features*—that is, features that are possessed by perceptual wholes but not by the parts of which these wholes are constructed (see Garner, Chap. 5, this volume).

Emergent Features.   As an example, consider the arrow-versus-triangle discrimination in Fig. 6.14. These figures possess features not shared by the line segments that comprise them. One *local* emergent feature distinguishing a

DISCRIMINATION : RELATIVE POSITION OF A LINE

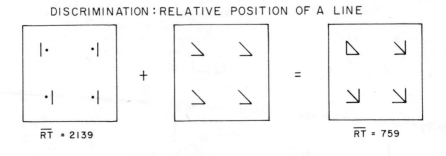

RT = 2139   RT = 759

DISCRIMINATION: HORIZONTAL vs VERTICAL

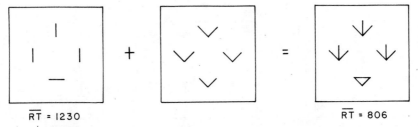

RT = 1230   RT = 806

FIG. 6.14.   Two more discriminations that are markedly improved by the addition of context.

triangle from an arrow is the fork-shaped intersection possessed by the arrow but not by the triangle. One *global* feature is the property of closedness possessed by the triangle but not by the arrow. I would contend that the arrow and triangle are more discriminable than are the lines comprising them because these emergent features are more salient to the perceptual system than are those features that the line segments along may have. In this regard, I am in agreement with Julesz's argument (Chap. 2, this volume) for the existence of Class B detectors for higher-order features such as closure and corners, although it is not clear to me how Julesz envisions Class A and Class B detectors to interact.

Emergent features are not simply defined on simpler features; they are more than the sum of their parts. Certain theories of shape recognition, such as Milner's (1974), claim that angles are derived from lines in the visual system. The support for this claim comes not only from a priori plausibility but also from the arguments of the neurophysiologists Hubel and Wiesel (1962, 1965) that simple, complex, and hypercomplex cells in the visual cortex are interconnected in a serial, hierarchical fashion. If figures such as triangles and arrows were recognized by their component angles and intersections, and if these angles and intersections were in turn recognized from their constituent line segments, then one would not predict the configural superiority effects I have been describing. If the sloped line segment were the ''natural'' unit of shape perception, then these line segments should be processed faster than, or at least as fast as, more complex features constructed from line segments. (This argument assumes that the output from line detectors would be available for response purposes; see Pomerantz, 1978, for a different assumption, called the "sealed channel hypothesis," which might allow part-to-whole theories to accommodate configural superiority effects.)

Accordingly, the most plausible interpretation of configural superiority is that the emergent features possessed by perceptual wholes are detected directly by the visual system and are not derived from the output of line detectors. Like phi motion, they are a pure or unmediated perceptual experience.

In previous discussions (Pomerantz, 1978; Pomerantz, Sager, & Stoever, 1977), I have distinguished between emergent feature processing and ordinary relative judgments. Although anyone who accepts the existence of perceptual Gestalts acknowledges that a whole is not just the sum of its parts, some of us believe that the whole is equal to its parts *plus the relations* among them (see Kubovy, Chap. 3, this volume), whereas others believe that a whole is just *different from* the sum of its parts and not necessarily *more than* the sum (and could, in fact, be less than the sum). This is essentially the distinction I present.

Return for a moment to Fig. 6.12, which shows the parenthesis discrimination task. When performance is improved by adding context, one could claim that this is because an absolute judgment has been converted into a relative one; in short, the context *adds* an anchor. Discriminating a left from a right parenthesis may be an absolute judgment of direction of curvature. By providing a second parenthesis, an anchor is established that the subject can use to calibrate decisions. According to this explanation, the subject is still judging direction of curvature, but this judgment has been made easier. The difficulty with this approach is that it fails to explain why some contexts help whereas others do not help at all. Why does adding a vertically oriented parenthesis help whereas adding a horizontal one hurts?

According to the emergent feature hypothesis, context does not serve to add an anchor. Instead, it serves to create—via the grouping process—a novel perceptual whole possessing emergent features that are detected directly. In the case of parenthesis pairs, the emergent features might include symmetry (either axial or translational), closedness, and others less readily describable. In recognizing these perceptual wholes, the visual system is detecting the presence or absence of emergent features and is no longer making judgments of direction of curvature.

To summarize, the emergent feature hypothesis claims that processing stimuli like ( ) and) (is *qualitatively* different from processing) and (. Context does not speed up a fixed process but instead induces a different process.

During the course of our research, Sager and I noticed that when processing individual parentheses, subjects showed strong stimulus–response compatibility effects. When classifying these stimuli by means of button presses or by sorting cards into piles, subjects had strong preferences about whether they should classify the stimulus (to the left and) to the right or vice versa. This kind of directional preference makes sense given that the discrimination is of direction of curvature. But with parenthesis pairs such as () and)), directional preference declined or disappeared. This supports my claim that the basis for discrimination shifts qualitatively to detection of emergent features with these two-element stimuli.

Forests Before, After, During, or Instead of Trees?

In the preceding section, I contrasted the processing of wholes with processing of components parts presented *in isolation*. The data reviewed there suggest that the processing of wholes cannot be predicted well from the processing of isolated parts. But how are parts processed when they are presented within a context? We can usually recognize parts when they are contained within larger configurations; we can perceive both the forest and the trees. How does this processing of local and global (part and whole) information proceed? I have already argued that wholes are not recognized by way of recognizing component parts, but I have not addressed any differences that may exist between part and whole processing. Let us consider the relative *speeds* of local and global perception. Which do we see first—the forest or the trees?

This question is a complex one, which must be asked correctly to get a sensible answer. Let me review some of the evidence on the matter and show where problems of interpretation may arise. This evidence comes from three sources: first, from research on configural superiority effects; second, from studies on the speed of processing of global configurations versus local details; and third, from experiments on embedded figures.

Superiority Effects. First of all, we have the word, object, and configural superiority effects I have already elaborated upon. If a complex stimulus can be perceived faster than any of its component parts presented in isolation, this might be taken as compelling evidence that we see the forest before the trees. But there are at least three reasons to question this conclusion. First, this experimental outcome does not occur much more often than does its opposite; recall the several configural *inferiority* effects I presented earlier. Given this state of affairs, it is impossible to generalize about the relative speed of perceiving forests versus trees. Second, superiority effects do not speak directly to the question as it has been phrased. The issue is whether, when presented with a forest, one sees the forest first or the trees first. Because the superiority effect experiments compare perception of a forest with perception of a solitary tree, the comparison misses the mark. Third, as I have argued earlier, when we are presented with a forest, often we may not process the trees at all, either before or after the forest. We may process emergent features of the forest (such as its density, texture, and so forth) instead. Under these circumstances, the question of before versus after is inappropriate.

Global Configurations Versus Local Details.   A second line of evidence on this question comes from experiments that use stimuli where part and whole information can be manipulated independently. Figure 6.15 gives some concrete examples from an experiment I did with Sager (Pomerantz & Sager, 1975). The idea is to construct large configurations from small ones (Kinchla, 1974). The question is whether the larger configuration or its component elements are recognized first following the onset of the entire array.

Sager and I attacked this problem by using the familiar integrality paradigm. Subjects were presented with arrays that varied in two dimensions—the global configuration portrayed and the local elements used to construct them. They had to classify the patterns using one of these dimensions and ignore the other dimension. We wished to find whether it is easier to ignore the elements or the

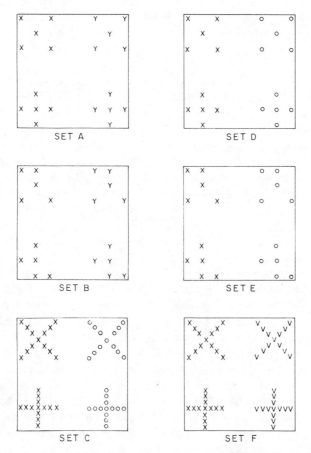

FIG. 6.15.   Large (global) configurations made up from small (local) ones. The data indicate that neither the local nor the global configurations enjoy an inherent advantage in perception; which is processed faster depends on sensory factors such as visual angle and masking effects. (From Pomerantz & Sager, 1975.)

global configuration. We reasoned that if part information became available before whole information, as a structuralist theory might hold, then it should be easier to attend to the local elements and ignore the global configuration than vice versa. But if wholistic processing was primary, as a Gestaltist theory might hold, then the opposite outcome would be predicted.

Before the proper experiment could be conducted, it was necessary to find stimuli for which the global dimension and the local dimension possess equal discriminability, because all other things being equal, the dimension having the greater discriminability will clearly be the harder one to ignore (Morgan & Alluisi, 1967). Although this might be an interesting effect, it was not the one we were looking for. The results from our experiment, in which the baseline discriminability of the two dimensions *was* matched, showed that neither dimension could be ignored completely. Thus, the dimensions appear to be integral. But the global dimension proved to be consistently easier to ignore than the local one, even in conditions where the global dimension was more discriminable than the local one. This outcome is therefore closer to a structuralist prediction than to a Gestalt one.

Recently, Navon (1977a) has reported an experiment quite similar to ours but that apparently leads to the opposite conclusion. In his patterns, the global configurations formed the same stimuli as the local elements used to construct them. For example, a big letter *H* could be constructed from little *H*s or a big *S* from little *S*s; alternatively, a big *H* could be made from little *S*s or a big *S* from little *H*s. These latter stimuli produce a conflict between global and local information much like the conflict found in the Stroop color–word test. Navon required his subjects to identify either the local or the global pattern of such stimuli. His main finding was that Stroop-type interference obtained when local elements were the relevant dimension but not when global configuration was relevant. This outcome suggests that the forest comes before the trees in classic Gestalt-like fashion.

Navon was concerned (as were Sager and I) with the problem of the relative salience or discriminability of the forest versus the trees. In particular, small letters may simply be harder to see than larger ones. Navon tried to rule out this explanation by showing that a small letter presented in isolation could be identified as well as a large, globally constructed letter. Although this provides a partial answer to the discriminability issue, perception of isolated letters may not constitute a sufficient control condition. Just as in the superiority effect experiments, what should be compared is a forest with its trees, not a forest with a solitary tree. It is quite likely that when elements are bunched together to form a larger configuration, they may inhibit one another through lateral masking. This would weaken the perceptibility of individual letters and so create the superiority of global over local processing.

Navon (1977b) believes that his conclusion is valid: Global processing necessarily precedes local processing. He points out that it is simply a fact of nature that local parts have many local neighbors and thus run greater risks of lateral masking than global configurations. Similarly, local parts are naturally smaller than global ones and thus are harder to see. My view is that if forests are seen before trees simply because of size and masking differences, then the observed effect tells us more about the effects of discriminability on perception than about any natural order of processing. My experiment with Sager showed that when the relative discriminabilities of forests and trees are matched, trees are processed faster (if anything) than forests. A recent experiment by Kinchla and Wolfe (1979), using stimuli like Navon's, showed that as the overall visual angle of the stimulus was increased, the processing advantage enjoyed by the global configuration shifted to an advantage for the local elements. This result, too, indicates that neither global nor local information is necessarily processed first. (See also Hoffman, 1980.)

Two Types of Configurations.   Part of the apparent confusion that arises from experiments on global versus local processing may be due to the existence of two distinct types of stimulus configurations that may be constructed from local elements. Figure 6.16 illustrates this distinction. Panel A of this figure shows stimuli similar to the ones used in the experiments just described. Four elements are arranged into a square configuration, and this configuration remains the same regardless of what elements are employed. Panel B shows a structurally equivalent set of stimuli that produces a greatly different perceptual effect, because changing any single element here changes the global configuration. That is, the whole is *not* independent of the identity of the parts, as it was in Panel A.

These two types of configurations may have little to do with one another, and if we do not distinguish between the two in our experiments and our theorizing,

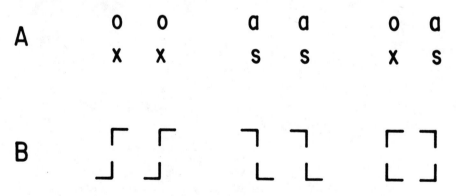

FIG. 6.16.   Two types of configurations. In Panel A, identity of the local elements does not affect the identity of the global configuration. As in Fig. 6.15, the elements serve only as placeholders. In Panel B, where a different set of local elements is used, each set of elements creates a different global configuration. Note that in other respects, the sets in Panel A and in Panel B are equivalent.

we will end up attempting to make generalizations over unrelated phenomena. With the stimuli in Panel A, the elements serve mainly as "placeholders" for the global configurations. The identity of the elements is of no consequence for the larger configuration (save for indicating texturelike information), and there is no reason why information about these elements would have to precede information about the wholes in the processing stream. In Panel B, however, the elements delineate the contours that define the configuration; so extracting the identity of the elements could, at least in principle, be of great value in recognizing the global stimulus.

Figure 6.17 shows another example of this distinction. The two arrays in Panel A are similar to the ones I presented earlier in describing Olson and Attneave's (1970) research. In these arrays, the elements serve to define different textures. The two arrays in Panel B show the four centermost elements of the arrays in Panel A. Here the elements do not serve to define different textures but rather to define shapes. For example, one of the stimuli looks like a box with a stick protruding from it, whereas the other resembles a tilted ground symbol from an electrical circuit diagram. Once again, the elements play vastly different roles in these two cases. In Panel A, they serve to mark out surfaces and their boundaries; in Panel B, they serve to define shapes.

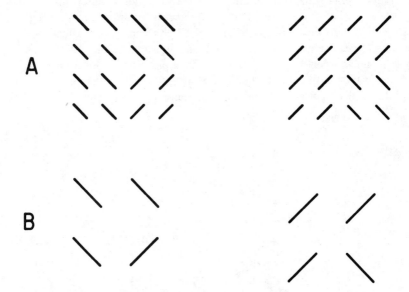

FIG. 6.17.   In Panel A, the local elements define textures (or surfaces) rather than configurations, as happened also in Figs. 6.6 and 6.7. In Panel B, only the four centermost elements of the stimuli in Panel A are shown. Here the elements group to form shapes, and the identity of the shape is determined by which elements it includes.

What does this distinction gain us? For one thing, it helps resolve apparently anomalous results in the literature. For example, as I have indicated earlier, it is quite easy to locate the disparate regions in the arrays in Panel A, but it is quite difficult to locate the odd element in Panel B. Given that in one case, subjects are processing textured surfaces but are processing unitary shapes in the other, there is no reason to expect similar performance on the two kinds of arrays. For another example, this contrast may help resolve inconsistencies in the ''forest-before-trees'' studies. With the stimuli used by Schendel and Shaw (1976) and by Pomerantz, Sager, and Stoever (1977), the elements serve to define the overall configuration, and global stimuli are perceived better than component parts. But with the multielement stimuli used by Pomerantz and Sager (1975) and by Navon (1977a), the global configurations are independent of the elements, and the evidence for superior global processing is quite weak.

Embedded Figures.   The final line of evidence bearing on the forest-before-trees question comes from studies on embedded figures (Gottschaldt, 1926). The impression one gets from viewing certain configurations is that the whole masks the parts, or that the forest hides the trees. For example, one does not normally perceive the numeral 3 embedded in the shape of the numeral 8 or the numeral 4 in the capital letter *H*. It is not difficult to ''see'' embedded figures, because their contours are clearly visible. The problem is that the embedded figure does not stand out as a discrete unit. In theoretical terms, the embedded figure—or target—groups perceptually with the context, and this grouping prevents selective attention to the target. Typically, figures are hidden by capitalizing on the laws of good continuation and symmetry, as in the case of the 3 embedded within the 8. One might argue that in cases like this, the context does not merely hide the target but actually eliminates it by eliminating its component features. For instance, if one feature of the numeral 3 were the *termination* of a line segment, then context would have destroyed the target, not hidden it. If so, such stimuli would tell us little about the relative speed of processing parts and wholes.

There are cases, however, where the target figure remains virtually intact despite the addition of context. Consider, for example, the stimuli used by Weisstein and Harris (1974), some of which are shown in Fig. 6.18. In their paradigm, the targets are the diagonal line segments, whereas the context is provided by the horizontal and vertical lines. Even in the case where the targets group with the context to form cubelike figures, the target lines are still quite apparent to the eye. Nevertheless, their appearance is altered by the context; in particular, the target lines may not appear diagonal. Instead, the stimulus is seen as a cubelike structure, drawn in perspective, containing only 90-degree angles. If the target the subjects are searching for is a diagonal line, the cube context could impede performance by hiding the target.

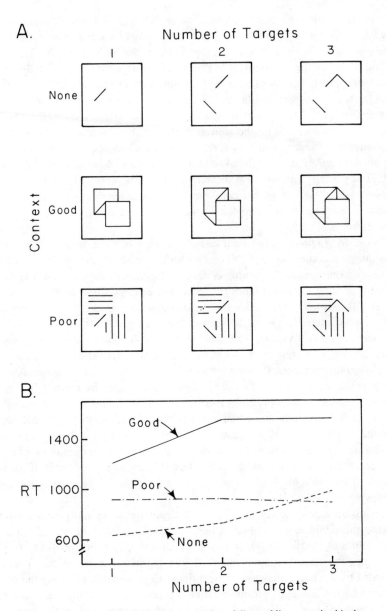

FIG. 6.18. (A) The task is to count the number of diagonal lines contained in the array (1, 2, or 3). The horizontal and vertical context lines are not to be counted. (B) Reaction times for counting. The "good", cubelike context impeded performance the most; the "poor," sticks context interfered little if at all.

In an unpublished study, Lawrence Sager and I tested this possibility. To do this, it was necessary to devise a task that forced subjects to process the target lines individually, instead of processing unitary wholes. The task we chose was *counting* (Beck, 1972), where the subject had to indicate the number of target lines present in an array. The stimuli we used are shown in Panel A of Fig. 6.18. Target lines were presented either by themselves or in one of two different contexts, which consisted of horizontal or vertical lines. Each stimulus contained one, two, or three (diagonal) target lines, and the subject indicated how many targets were present by pressing one of three response keys.

Panel B of Fig. 6.18 shows the results. For the three types of stimulus arrays, counting was by far the slowest with the cubelike configurations. So it appears, in this case, that the forest actually does hide the trees. Recall that the cubelike context *improves* performance relative to the flat "sticks" context in the superiority effects experiments, but it *hinders* performance here. This result provides an insight into the mechanism behind the object superiority effect of Weisstein and Harris (1974): Context does not improve the perceptibility *of component parts*. That is, the cubelike surround does not improve the detectability of the diagonal target lines, which is one possible interpretation of this particular superiority effect. Instead, the context makes the targets *harder* to perceive. The explanation for the superior perception of the cube stimuli in comparison to the sticks stimuli (or perhaps even in comparison to the targets presented by themselves; see McClelland, 1978; and Williams & Weisstein, 1978) is that with the cubes, subjects are processing salient emergent features that the other stimulus configurations lack. One task of future research will be to determine what those emergent features may be.

CONCLUSION

I began by asking the question: Where does the perceptual process begin when faced with a barrage of sensory information? How is it organized so that it can be processed sensibly and efficiently? This chapter presents the argument that one of the earliest steps in perception must be grouping, whereby as yet unidentified parts, or blobs of sensory input, are perceptually linked into potential objects to be recognized by later processing mechanisms. This grouping (or parsing) process creates relatively indivisible units of perception and so prevents selective attention to the parts that are so grouped. Groups of parts may contain emergent features that can be recognized directly. In this way, higher-order units are perceived without prior recognition of their components. Consequently, when these wholes contain emergent features, they can be recognized faster than their constituent parts presented alone. When placed in the context of larger configurations, parts may be more difficult to perceive than when presented alone because of masking effects, because features are destroyed, or because certain other characteristics—such as apparent orientation—are altered. Since parts are perceived differently from wholes (wholes are perceived via emergent features), the speed of perceiving wholes cannot be predicted from the speed of perceiving parts. The two processes are only partially related, and generalizations that wholes are perceived more quickly (or more slowly) than their component parts cannot be supported.

ACKNOWLEDGMENTS

This research was supported in part by NSF Grant BNS76-01227 to the author and in part by Biomedical Sciences Support Grants from Johns Hopkins University and S.U.N.Y. at Buffalo. I thank Irving Biederman, Howard Egeth, Wendell Garner, David Goldberg, Michael Kubovy, and David Navon for their many discussions that helped shape the ideas presented here. Thanks also go to all my collaborators who have shared in this work.

7 Perceptual Organization and Attention

Daniel Kahneman
University of British Columbia

Avishai Henik
University of the Negev, Beer-Sheva, Israel

ABSTRACT

The chapter develops the theme that the concept of perceptual object and the rules of grouping and organization are essential to describe the abilities and limitations of selective attention. Attention can only be directed to preattentively defined perceptual objects, and it facilitates all the responses associated with properties or elements of the selected object. Evidence is presented from studies of the Stroop task, effects of visual grouping on recall, search and selective attention in tachistoscopic displays, and the visual and auditory suffix effects. A theoretical analysis of perceptual objects is outlined, in which perceptual identity is distinguished from the process of identification.

INTRODUCTION

The thesis of the present chapter is that considerations of perceptual organization are indispensable to a theory of attention. To support this claim, several research paradigms are described, where the notion that attention is allocated to preattentively organized perceptual units provides a parsimonious account of the facts. Indeed, some of the results that are discussed could be viewed as obvious, perhaps trivial manifestations of perceptual organization. Our review of alternative treatments of these results suggests, however, that the concept of perceptual organization is rather consistently avoided in the current theories of cognitive psychology. One object of this chapter is to raise two questions in our readers' minds: Why are Gestalt-inspired notions neglected? What is the cost of this neglect? Before we turn to these questions, however, it is necessary to introduce the approach to attention within which they arise.

The variety of paradigms that are employed to study attention is large and rapidly increasing. The multiplicity of research designs is almost matched by the multiplicity of meanings for the term *attention* (Moray, 1969; Treisman, 1969). Consider, for example, the following instructions to a subject: "In each of a series of trials, you will be shown an array of numbers, printed in various colors. You are to find the red number, add 1 to this number, and report the result as quickly as you can. The red number will most frequently be shown directly to the right or left of the fixation mark, but it could also appear in other locations. On 60% of the trials, the number will be 2. You should of course say 3 whenever this occurs." Attention is involved in several ways in these instructions. First, we assume that the subject is generally set to focus on the task and to exclude other concerns. In different senses of the same word, the subject is also set to expect numbers as stimuli and to produce numbers as responses. In particular, the instructions "prime" the stimulus "2" and the response "3." They lead the subject to attend preferentially to locations in which the target is most likely to appear, and they assign a special role to the attribute of color, which defines the relevant object, and to the attribute of shape, which controls the response.

Most of the current experimental paradigms for the study of attention can be generated by selecting appropriate subsets of our sample instructions. The selected subsets may have little in common, but all are viewed as studies of attention, providing a legitimate basis for inferences about this process. Indeed, influential theories of attention have evolved in paradigms that share few significant features. For example, the priming paradigm used by LaBerge (1973, 1975) and Posner (1978; Posner & Snyder, 1975a, 1975b) does not require the subject to find the relevant stimulus, because the stimuli that are presented on a trial are all relevant to the task. The search paradigm of Schneider and Shiffrin (1977), in contrast, focuses exclusively on the task of finding a target in a display. Perhaps the only feature that is shared by the two paradigms is the priming of the specific nodes or pathways that correspond to an expected target. This feature is absent, however, in the filtering paradigms (Broadbent, 1958; Treisman, 1969): The instructions to "shadow the message on the right ear" or to "report the digits in the middle row" require the subject to select the stimuli that are relevant to the task. They prepare the subject neither for a particular stimulus nor for a particular response.

The filtering paradigm, once dominant, has lost much of its popularity in recent years, and the priming and search paradigms have gained ascendancy. Coincidentally, the most natural theoretical treatment of both these paradigms allows one to evade the uncomfortably mysterious process of stimulus selection, and to emphasize a process that is somewhat better understood—the access of stimuli to responses. The well-established idea that stimulus–response connections vary in strength is readily applied to the process by which stimuli activate their representations in long-term memory. In this light, prolonged overtraining and momentary expectancies can be seen as alternative ways of easing the access of a stimulus to its trace. The activation of overlearned associations is said to require no attention (LaBerge, 1973; Shiffrin & Schneider, 1977), whereas other associations can be facilitated by specific expectancies. Selective attention is often explained by the joint operation of such expectancies and of decision processes that control the production of task-relevant responses.

The main weakness of an expectancy theory of attention is that it contributes nothing to an explanation of filtering. The ability to shadow a message of random words presented to the right ear and to ignore a concurrent message on the left ear cannot be mediated by preactivation of specific nodes in memory, because any word in the language is equally likely to appear in either message. To explain filtering without invoking stimulus selection, one is forced to assume that tests of task relevance are applied to activated units in long-term memory in order to determine which of these units will be allowed to control behavior (Deutsch & Deutsch, 1963; Keele & Neill, 1979; Norman, 1968). However, this model runs into severe difficulties. It cannot explain, for example, why monitoring two simultaneous auditory messages for occasional animal names is easy, while responding selectively to animal names in one of these messages is difficult (Ninio & Kahneman, 1974). If the animal names on the unattended message are identified, the selective focusing task appears to demand an extra operation of testing for (spatial origin), which is not required in divided listening, but the latter task is nevertheless much harder than the former. Furthermore, the notion of relevance tests on activated nodes fails to explain a very general rule of selective attention: Stimulus set is easier than response set (Broadbent, 1970). With the notable exception of the digit–letter distinction (Jonides & Gleitman, 1972), it is generally much easier to find a relevant stimulus by physical properties such as color, pitch, or location than by properties of semantic content. There is no obvious reason why the rule should hold if attention comes into play only after all stimuli make contact with their traces. For these reasons and others that have been described elsewhere (Kahneman, 1973), it appears necessary to retain the view that attention can be selectively allocated to stimuli before they are identified, and that the process of selective attention cannot be reduced to a combination of expectancy effects and tests of task relevance.

If attention selects a stimulus, what is the stimulus that it selects? The main hypothesis of the present study is that attention operates on perceptual units, or objects, that are organized by a prior (preattentive) process. Attention can be focused narrowly on a single unit, or else it can be shared among several objects. To the degree that an object is attended, however, all its aspects and distinctive elements receive attention. An irrelevant element of an attended object will therefore attract—and waste—its share of attention. The effect of attending to an object is to facilitate all the responses that are associated with aspects or elements of that object. Sometimes, as in the Stroop task, an irrelevant response will be facilitated to the point of interfering with the performance of the task. In these ways, the efficacy of selective attention is determined by the characteristics of the preattentive mechanism that defines perceptual objects. In Chapter 6 of this volume, Pomerantz develops a similar theme.

THE STROOP EFFECT

Stroop (1935) originally reported that subjects encounter severe difficulties in the task of successively naming the colors of the inks in which a series of incompatible color names are printed. This robust finding has evoked a vast experimental literature (see reviews by Dyer, 1973a, Jensen & Rohwer, 1966). The surprising aspect of the Stroop effect is its extreme resistance to prolonged practice. The task is feasible, because careful subjects make few mistakes even on the very first trial. It never becomes easy, however, and the response to critical Stroop items always remains slower than the response to neutral items that do not elicit conflicting response tendencies. Subjects are evidently capable of ensuring that the correct answer will prevail in the conflict, but they are quite unable to prevent the conflict from occurring. Thus, the Stroop effect is one of the best-documented failures of selective attention.

A series of studies from Posner's laboratory (Conrad, 1974; Warren, 1972, 1974) has demonstrated that naming the color of a word can be slowed by any manipulation that "primes" the word (e.g., by the prior presentation of a related word). The priming of color words, which is induced by the color-naming task, explains interference in the standard Stroop situation (Posner, 1978).

The Stroop effect has often been cited in support of the theoretical position that any stimulus of sufficient intensity automatically activates its representation in long-term memory, regardless of whether or not that stimulus is attended (e.g., Keele, 1973; Keele & Neill, 1979; Posner, 1978). Even in theories that assume that the activation of a mental representation sometimes requires attention (e.g., LaBerge, 1975), the printed representation of a familiar word is the prime example of a stimulus that requires no attention to activate its trace in memory.

If the activation of a trace by a word is automatic, and if Stroop interference results from such activation, should it matter whether the relevant color and the irrelevant word belong together as a single object? In most current theories of attention, the answer could well be negative. The attribute of spatial location has no special distinction in these theories. It is merely one of many attributes by which a relevant response can be selected. A perfectly valid attribute is already available for that purpose in the Stroop situation—the tagging of an activated color name by the stimulus property that elicited it. Why, then, should the spatial attribute be involved in the selection of the response? The approach adopted in this chapter, however, distinguishes the spatial attribute of a visual stimulus from all other attributes, because space is the medium that visual objects occupy (Kubovy, Chap. 3, this volume). We assume that attention is allocated to objects and that this allocation facilitates all the responses associated with the selected object—"automatic" as well as unfamiliar, irrelevant as well as relevant. This position, of course, predicts much greater interference when the relevant color and the irrelevant word are conjoined than when they are separated.

Experiment 1

A simple test of these alternative positions is possible. Present a subject with a brief exposure of a card containing a circle and a square, on either side of the fixation point, with a colored word printed in each. Instruct the subject to report the color of the word in the circle. Vary the position of square and circle around the fixation point, randomly over trials. On each trial, one of the printed words is the name of the relevant color; one is another color name. Will the color-naming latency be affected by the arrangement of the color names in the circle and in the square? Note that the experimental design precludes any role of eye movements, so that the chances for automatic activation of pathways are precisely equal for both words.

Conducting such an experiment is somewhat embarrassing, because its outcome is intuitively obvious. The embarrassment was overcome, and six subjects were run. Four colors were used: red, green, yellow, blue. The centers of the circle and the square containing the words were horizontally separated by 8.8°; the diameter of the circle and the side of the square subtended 6.6°; the words were centered in the square and circle and subtended on average 3.9° in length and 1.3° in height. The obvious result was obtained. Color naming was much slower when the word in the circle was incompatible with the correct response than when it was compatible. The effect ranged, for different subjects, between 134 msec and 262 msec.

Experiment 2

A more elaborate experiment was then conducted, in which the printed words were either the names of the four colors used (*red, green, blue,* or *brown*) or four neutral words (*most, cute, shoe,* and *long*). The stimulus conditions were otherwise as described earlier. The experiment consisted of 144 trials. On 48 control trials, both words were neutral. On all other trials, one of the words was neutral and the other was a color name. The color name was compatible with the correct response on half the trials, incompatible on the other half. It appeared in the circle on half the trials and in the square on the other half. Comparisons of the four experimental conditions to the control condition show how the interference or facilitation produced by a color word depends on its relation to the correct response and on its position. A total of 16 subjects participated, each for one session. Half the subjects reported the color of the word contained in the square, and half reported the color of the word contained in the circle.

The results of the experiment are given below. The conditions are identified by italicizing the word to whose color the subjects were to respond. The words in the display could be neutral, compatible with the correct response, or conflicting. The results shown are mean correct reaction times (RTs) in milliseconds (msec) and percent errors.

A. *Neutral*-Neutral	906	(3%)
B. *Neutral*-Compatible	944	(4%)
C. *Neutral*-Conflicting	956	(2%)
D. *Compatible*-Neutral	858	(1%)
E. *Conflicting*-Neutral	1108	(15%)

The results are much as expected. Comparisons of the various conditions with the basic control (Condition A) indicate significant interference from both the unattended word (50 msec; $t(15) = 3.51$, $p < .01$) and the attended word (202 msec; $t = 8.69$). The latter effect is much larger, $t = 4.45$, $p < .01$. An attended compatible word causes significant facilitation, $t = 2.73$, $p < .05$. Surprisingly, an unattended compatible color name causes significant interference, $t = 2.88$.

Studies of similar design have been reported by Dyer (1973b) and by Gatti and Egeth (1978). Dyer presented a vertical color strip and a vertical printed color name randomly on either side of the fixation point. He reported significant interference from an incompatible color name and significant facilitation from a compatible name. The aim of the Gatti and Egeth study was to demonstrate a failure of spatial selectivity in visual attention. They presented a color patch at the fixation point, with words above and below it. They found that interference from an incompatible color name decreased from a value of about 90 msec, when the distance of the word from the patch was 1°, to a value of about 40 msec for a distance of 5°. Interference was still highly significant at the larger distance.

There is of course no conflict between the results of the present experiment and the findings of earlier studies. Taken together, they indicate that when an irrelevant object is presented along with a relevant one, the distracting object is processed sufficiently to cause measurable interference. Some interference occurs even when the subject is allowed to focus both gaze and attention in advance on the relevant object, as in the Gatti–Egeth study. A number of experiments in different paradigms support this conclusion (e.g., Eriksen & Eriksen, 1974; Eriksen & Hoffman, 1972, 1974; Keren, O'Hara, & Skelton, 1977). These studies allow us to reject the null hypothesis that the selectivity of attention is perfect. The purpose of the present experiment was to test a different null hypothesis, which appears to be entailed by the concept of automatic activation: that the location of the interfering stimulus should have no effect on the severity of interference. Contrary to this prediction, the activation of the incompatible color response was strongly dependent on the direction of attention.

Experiment 3

The hypothesis that attention to an object facilitates all responses to that object led to a further experiment in this series. The subjects were again exposed to a pair of words on either side of the fixation point. One of these words was always printed in black. On half the cards, the critical word to which subjects were to respond was printed in color (red, pink, blue, or green). On half the cards, only one letter of the word was colored, whereas the others were black. The possible positions of the colored letter are identified by italics in the following list: *red*, *pink*, *blue*, *green*, *cute*, *most*, *shoe*, *long*. When a color word was shown, it was always different from the correct response for that trial. The two types of cards were presented in random order to the subject, who was instructed as before to report the color of the critical word or letter. Exposure time was 200 msec. Ten subjects participated.

This study had two objectives. The first was to replicate the results of the preceding experiment with a different display. The present display provides a sharp test of the role of the spatial attribute in selective attention, because this attribute is not involved, even indirectly, in the definition of the correct response. It could be argued that the property that defined the required response in the previous experiment (inclusion in a specified figure) required a spatial choice and thereby caused attention to be directed toward the specified location. In the present study, however, the problem of response selection can be solved by a nonspatial rule: "Report the (nonblack) color response that is elicited by a color, not by a word-shape." If both words are identified, there seems to be no reason for the system to use the (irrelevant) attribute of the location of the colored material as a basis for selection.

The second aim of the study was to provide a sharper test of the hypothesis that the focusing of attention on a relevant object affects the activation of irrelevant responses. The relevant object is a single letter in the colored-letter condition, and no incompatible response is associated with that object. Consequently, it was expected that the colored-letter condition would elicit less interference than the colored-word condition.

Mean correct RT (in msec) and percent errors are given next, for the six types of stimulus cards. The word containing the color stimulus is italicized:

Colored Word:	A. *Neutral*–Neutral	858	(3%)
	B. *Neutral*–Conflicting	858	(3%)
	C. *Conflicting*–Neutral	1017	(5%)
Colored Letter:	D. *Neutral*–Neutral	905	(5%)
	E. *Neutral*–Conflicting	926	(6%)
	F. *Conflicting*–Neutral	999	(9%)

In the absence of conflict, as might be expected, the color-naming task is easier with a colored word than with a single colored letter in a word, $t(9) = 4.67$, $p < .01$ between Conditions A and D. However, a color name that is entirely in color causes more interference than a color name of which only one letter is colored (159 msec vs. 94 msec; $t = 2.28$, $p < .05$).

The hypothesis that the spatial attribute might be ignored is conclusively rejected, as the presentation of a color name in the irrelevant location caused little or no interference. However, the results are also inconsistent with the hypothesis that attention can be restricted exclusively to the relevant object, because there was considerable interference when a single letter of a conflicting word was colored. There appears to be a spread of attention, with the selected object as its focus.

Conclusions

The results of Exps. 1 through 3 are consistent with a model of attention in which preattentive processing and stimulus selection both play a central role. We propose that an early stage of processing parses the field into tentative objects. Perhaps simultaneously with this stage, the functional equivalent of a parallel search occurs, which may result in a conspicuous target calling attention to itself. If this search fails, a controlled search may follow (Schneider & Shiffrin, 1977; Treisman & Gelade, 1979). Attention is briefly directed to the objects that are scanned in this search (Keren, 1976a). It is eventually focused on the target object when that object is found. The allocation of attention to a perceptual object facilitates all the responses that are associated to its properties, but facilitation also spills over to neighboring locations. A final stage of processing is concerned with a task-directed choice among the responses that have been evoked.

It may be noted that the application of this model to Exp. 3 assumes that color information is used at two different stages—to find the relevant stimulus and to control the color-naming response. Under the exceptional conditions of prolonged and consistent practice investigated by Schneider and Shiffrin, the two stages apparently collapse, and a simple overt response is associated directly to finding the target.

One of the essential facts that any theory of attention must consider is the contrast between the ease with which attention is directed to objects and the inability to restrict attention to the relevant properties of a selected object. As Treisman (1969) noted, the Stroop effect demonstrates our inability to select a perceptual analyzer. As the present experiments illustrate, however, the efficacy of object selection is such that it greatly reduces the elicitation of conflicting responses by objects in unattended locations.

The Stroop task is unusually difficult because it prevents the operation of the mechanism that normally functions to select the relevant response among those evoked by an attended object—the prior priming of an ensemble of possible responses or of an ensemble of nodes in long-term memory. This mechanism of set is usually adequate to guarantee the speedy execution of the correct response, but it fails in the Stroop task because the same ensemble is activated by both the relevant and irrelevant attributes of the object.

Unattended objects lose most or all of their ability to evoke instrumental responses. Whether this is achieved by attenuating the processing of such stimuli or by some other means has been the subject of lively debate for the past 20 years (Broadbent, 1958; Corteen & Wood, 1972; Deutsch & Deutsch, 1963; Kahneman, 1973; Keele, 1973; Keren, 1976b; Posner, 1978; Treisman & Geffen, 1967). The present results appear to pose some difficulties for theories that explain selective attention as a process of response selection (in the Deutsch & Deutsch tradition) and for theories that reduce attention to set and explain its effects by selective preactivation of internal structures (e.g., LaBerge, 1975; Shiffrin & Schneider, 1977). It is relatively difficult to accommodate within these views the notion that the attribute of space plays a privileged role in selective attention.

FILTERING, SEARCH, AND PREATTENTIVE PROCESSES

We have proposed that attention selects among the objects or things that are made available by a preattentive process of perceptual organization. The standard formulation of filtering in selective attention, originally proposed by Broadbent (1958), is slightly but significantly different: It states that attention selects a channel or, more precisely, that it selects the information arriving on a particular channel. Broadbent initially proposed that a channel can be defined by any physical property that distinguishes relevant from irrelevant items (e.g., color in vision, voice quality in audition, or location in either modality).

In the context of visual attention, the essential difference between the two formulations lies, once again, in the treatment of the attribute of spatial location and of the integrity of visual objects. The notion that we select by channels, and that an attribute such as "red" can define a channel, suggests that we should be able to attend selectively to red elements in a complex field regardless of the spatial configuration of these elements. A similar suggestion is implied by a more recent interpretation of filtering (LaBerge, 1975) according to which the instruction to select red items preactivates a "red" node and thereby facilitates the processing of all red items. Here again, there is no reason to predict that it should make any difference whether the red items constitute a single visual object or many distinct objects.

Several recent experiments provide relevant evidence (Fryklund, 1975; Kahneman & Henik, 1977; Keren, 1976b). The starting point for these experiments was a demonstration by von Wright (1968, 1970) that subjects have some ability to attend selectively to items of a specified color in a tachistoscopic display, as indicated by a substantial partial-report advantage. The spatial configuration of relevant and irrelevant items was allowed to vary randomly in von Wright's experiments. The results of subsequent work demonstrate that this variable has a large effect on performance.

Experiment 4

Our experiment (Kahneman & Henik, 1977) was conducted in a group setting, with a display presented for 200 msec following a half second after a brief warning tone. There were two main conditions, which were alternated on successive blocks of trials. In the blue-only condition, six uppercase consonants were presented, and the subjects were instructed to report as many of these letters as they could, in any order. In the blue–red condition, the display consisted of two rows of six letters each, including six blue letters and six red letters. Six configurations were used, each in two complementary variants in which the positions of red and blue letters were interchanged. The capital letters in the display of Table 7.1 indicate the location of blue letters in one of the variants and of red letters in the other. The spatial arrangements were the same in the blue-only condition, with vacant spaces instead of red letters.

The major results of the experiment are shown in Table 7.1. Wherever the results can be compared, all findings agree closely with those of Fryklund (1975). The effects of configuration in Keren's study (Keren, 1976b) were similar in direction but rather less impressive, perhaps because he used adjacency in a circular display of widely separated letters to control grouping. In our study as well as in Fryklund's, configuration has little effect on the total number of letters reported in the absence of distractors. However, the spatial arrangement of the array has a very large effect on performance when the display contains irrelevant and potentially distracting red letters. The interference in the line and triad structures is relatively slight, although highly significant. The checkerboard configuration, in contrast, shows little partial-report advantage. Thus, the amount of

TABLE 7.1
Interference in the Recall of Letters[a]

	Blue/Only	Blue/Red	Difference	Intrusions
A B C D E F a b c d e f	3.51	2.99	0.52	0.29
A B C d e f a b c D E F	3.20	2.63	0.57	0.28
A B c d E F a b C D e f	3.61	2.38	1.33	0.39
A a C c E e B b C d F f	3.52	2.16	1.36	0.39
A b c D E f a B C d e F	3.39	2.29	1.10	0.36
A b C d E f a B c D e F	3.58	2.01	1.57	0.40

[a] Mean number of blue letters recalled. Upper- and lowercase letters are used to distinguish red from blue letters.

interference appears to increase directly with the number of discrete relevant perceptual units.

Because the same letters were never repeated in red and blue in the same array, it was possible to count the number of intrusions—that is, instances in which a letter that had been shown in red ink was included in the subject's report. The effect of configuration on this intrusion measure is highly significant, but there is a striking discrepancy between the two measures of interference—the number of relevant items lost from the report and the number of intrusions. The intrusion rate varies by only 35% between the easiest and the hardest conditions, but the omission measure varies by 300%. The discrepancy strongly suggests that subjects did not perform the task by storing items of both colors and discarding red items from their report, because such a strategy would have caused proportional effects on both measures. The possibility of selection occurring after verbal encoding can therefore be dismissed, but the mechanism by which the presence of distractors affects the processing of relevant items is not well understood. The data suggest that the relevant items are selected as groups, and that the total number of items recalled is inversely related to the number of discrete groups that must be found. A plausible hypothesis is that the presence of irrelevant material forces the subjects into a serial mode of processing, where they deal with groups one at a time. In the absence of distractors, the spatial organization of the display has little effect on total recall.

The finding that perceptual organization is relevant to visual selective attention is not easily explained by current theories of attention. As we have seen, this finding would not be expected on the assumption that color defines a channel that the subject can select. It is even more puzzling for late-selection theories of attention, which assume that all items automatically activate their representations in long-term memory and that the selection is mediated by additional tests of task relevance. The attribute of position in space is not in itself relevant to the task, and it cannot be used independently of the color attribute to distinguish relevant from irrelevant items. It is therefore quite mysterious, in terms of a late-selection theory, why this attribute should have such potent effects on performance.

The assumption of preattentive perceptual organization has implications for other tasks of selective attention, as discussed by Pomerantz (Chap. 6) in this volume. A particularly interesting application of this idea to tasks of search and detection has been reported by Banks and his colleagues (Banks, Bodinger, & Illige, 1974; Banks & Prinzmetal, 1976; Prinzmetal & Banks, 1977b). They found that increasing the number of distractors in a search display can actually improve search performance if it improves the grouping of distractor items, and that search is affected by manipulations of the perceptual embedding of the target in the field of distractors. Their predictions were based on the hypothesis of a preliminary parsing of the field according to Gestalt rules. The predictions from this hypothesis were carefully contrasted to an alternative model (Estes, 1972b,

1974), which explains the effects of similarity and proximity on search in terms of mutual inhibition at the feature detection level and confusion at the decision level. The attempt to ascribe the effects of Gestalt factors to peripheral interactions and to decision problems does not presently appear to have succeeded.

Experiment 5

Another implication of the notion of preattentive parsing can be tested by requiring subjects to search for a target that consists of several elements. It then becomes possible to arrange the display so that the target group corresponds to a natural perceptual unit or to arrange it so that the target elements belong to different units. If the initial visual grouping constrains subsequent processing, the latter condition should be more difficult.

The experiment was conducted in a group setting. On each trial, a row of eight digits was exposed on a screen for 150 msec. Four of the digits were red; the other four were blue. Four different arrangements of color were used: RRBBRRBB, BBRRBBRR, RBBRRBBR, and BRRBBRRB. An individual response sheet provided to each subject designated a pair of digits as the target for each trial. Other subjects were searching for different targets on the same trial, as no two response sheets were identical. The response sheets were designed so that both elements of the target pair were in fact shown, in adjacent positions and in the indicated order, on 50% of trials. On the remaining trials, only one of the target elements was presented. The position of the target elements in the display was varied systematically. A total of 112 trials were given. Immediately after the trial, the subjects reported whether they believed that the target pair had appeared, using a 4-point scale (0–3), where the higher value indicated high confidence that the target had been shown and the lower indicated confidence that it had not.

The main variable of interest was the effect of presenting the two target elements in the same color or in different colors. The hypothesis of the study was that correspondence of the target to the natural grouping structure induced by color similarity would facilitate detection. Consider, for example, the following sample display, where the two types represent the two colors that were used: 9*43*71862. The hypothesis entails that the target 43 should be easier to detect in this display than the target 37 (in the experiment, of course, the factor of retinal position was controlled). This expectation was confirmed: Confidence ratings were higher on positive trials when the two elements of the target were shown in the same color than when they differed in color. The mean confidence ratings were, respectively, 2.17 and 1.83, $t(24) = 3.83$, $p < .01$.

The responses on negative trials also indicated a bias toward matching the target to perceptual groups of homogeneous color. Negative trials were classified into two types, according to whether the position of the presented target element in its color group matched its position in the specification of the target pair. For the sample display just shown, the target 42 would be a matching target, because the target element that is included in the display (4) has the same position in the definition of the target and in a homogeneous color group. The target 24 would be nonmatching. Subjects were more confident that a target had *not* been shown on matching than on nonmatching negative trials, $t(24) = 3.87$, $p < .01$. The mean ratings for the two cases were, respectively, 0.62 and 0.79.

These results indicate that perceptual organization has a substantial effect on the process of comparing a memorized target to a display. Pairs of adjacent items of the same color are apparently more available to this comparison process than are heterogeneous pairs.

Experiment 6

An additional experiment was then conducted to find out whether similar results could be obtained with a different grouping factor: the letter–digit distinction. There is some evidence that this distinction is available to preattentive processing, at least by one criterion: The detection of a letter in digits, or of a digit in letters, may not require serial search (see, e.g., Egeth, Jonides, & Wall, 1972; Gleitman & Jonides, 1978). This observation raised the possibility that the letter–digit distinction could serve to organize a line of symbols into units, just as the blue–red distinction had done in the previous experiment.

The design of this study was identical to that of its predecessor. Subjects were shown rows of eight items, of which four were digits and four were consonants (e.g., 7TF94BN8). There were 112 trials, and different subjects were assigned different targets for each trial. The targets were chosen to represent equally the four possible arrangements of letters and digits. A significant difference between the two studies should be noted: With the letter–digit targets, of course, the subjects knew in advance whether the target would be homogeneous or heterogeneous in the display. They were not given equivalent information in Exp. 5.

In spite of this difference, the results of the two studies were quite similar. Homogeneous pairs were again easier to detect than heterogeneous pairs. The mean ratings were, respectively, 2.19 and 1.91, $t(18) = 4.36$, $p < .01$. There was also a slight trend toward more confident negative responses on negative trials when the target was homogeneous (.64 vs. .70 for heterogeneous targets), but this result was not statistically significant, $t = 1.59$, NS.

The Boundaries of Preattentive Processing

The similarity of the results of the two studies is intriguing, although it would be premature to draw extreme conclusions from it. We cannot confidently exclude the possibility that the effect of category identity in the second experiment arose from more efficient processing of the target in memory rather than from grouping effects in the display. In a modest Bayesian sense, however, these admittedly inconclusive findings raise the probability of the hypothesis that preattentive processes of perceptual organization are endowed with some degree of literacy. The confirmation of this hypothesis, of course, would have far-reaching implications for our understanding of the perceptual process.

In the context of the present chapter, another question is at stake: What are the capacities and limitations of preattentive processing? Following the lead of Broadbent (1958) and Neisser (1967), it appears appropriate to define preattentive operations by two characteristics: (1) They are performed in parallel over the field of stimulation; and (2) their output can be used to control attention. Accordingly, we would attribute the detection of a target to preattentive processes if there is no display-size effect—that is, if subjects can find the target equally fast regardless of the number of nontargets in the display (e.g., Schneider & Shiffrin, 1977). We would also label as preattentive the texture-forming and unit-forming operations, which utilize information from a wide area and can be completed at a glance (Julesz, Chap. 2, this volume). The reason for the preattentive label is that efficient selective attention in filtering requires both operations: The relevant object must be segregated from its background, and it must also be found. The capabilities of preattentive processes are defined by the discriminations that they can use to perform these operations.

A natural conjecture is that the same preattentive abilities are used in parallel search and in texture formation, and that the same limitations apply to the two processes. There is some support for this conjecture. On the side of capabilities, the same physical distinctions that cause a single target item to "stand out" from a field of background items also cause the formation of strong perceptual boundaries between homogeneous regions. On the side of limitations, Treisman and Gelade (1979) have shown that subjects cannot search in parallel for a target that is defined by a conjunction of attributes (e.g., the target "red O" in a field of red Ns and blue Os). Similarly, it is extremely difficult to detect a boundary that is defined by conjunctions (e.g., with red Os and blue Ns on one side, red Ns and blue Os on the other). The detection of conjunction targets requires a strictly serial and rather slow search, and the detection of conjunction boundaries involves a nonperceptual exercise in problem solving. The convergence of these operations raises the hope of developing a unique description for what the preattentive mechanisms can and cannot do. One of the many questions that are raised by the category effect in visual search is whether a corresponding effect can be found in other measures of preattentive processing.

GROUP PROCESSING

This section takes up a question that arises naturally from the notion that attention is allocated to preattentively organized perceptual units: How does the mechanism operate when the perceptual units consist of distinct elements and when familiar responses are associated to each element separately, rather than to the unit as a whole?

Experiment 7

Several of our studies have explored the effect of visual grouping on the recall of tachistoscopically presented arrays of letters or digits. Most of these experiments were conducted in a group setting, in a dimly illuminated classroom. Subjects faced a screen on which a frame was constantly in view. The sequence of events on a typical trial was as follows: An oral warning by the experimenter; a 200-msec warning tone; a delay of 500 msec; a 200-msec exposure of the stimulus material in the area indicated by the frame on the screen. The subjects were instructed to write their answer immediately after each exposure. No feedback was given. The main independent variable was the spatial organization of the items in the display. Representative results of that type of study are shown in Table 7.2, which presents the percentage of items correctly reported for each position, in six of the patterns used in one experiment, with 41 subjects (Kahneman & Henik, 1977). The subjects were shown, in separate blocks of trials, arrays of six or seven digits. Some of the six-digit arrays also contained the letter *k* in the terminal position. The subjects were instructed to ignore this visual suffix.

The most striking results in Table 7.2 are the relative homogeneity of performance within groups and the sharp discontinuities at group boundaries. The effect can be appreciated by comparing performance on adjacent items when these belong to the same group or to different groups. Thus, the mean difference in probability of recall between the third and fourth items is 52% when they belong to different groups and 2% when both belong to the first group. Similarly, the mean difference between the fourth and fifth digits is 70% when these digits belong to different groups but only 8% when both are included in the second group. The homogeneity of performance within groups and the discontinuities between groups are highly robust observations, which we have obtained in many different experiments, using a variety of grouping arrangements and different

TABLE 7.2
Percent Recall of Digits in Various Patterns

			Serial Position				
Example	*1*	*2*	*3*	*4*	*5*	*6*	*7*
1234 56	93	83	86	86	29	39	—
123 456	94	89	88	48	43	45	—
1234 56k	97	90	91	94	14	12	—
123 456k	96	95	92	36	27	17	—
1234 567	94	88	89	92	18	15	27
123 4567	96	94	92	32	23	17	29

ways of inducing grouping. Spatial separation of the groups is not a necessary condition for the effect. For example, grouping can be induced by printing the items in different colors, so that the distance between adjacent members is the same within and between groups. The same pattern of results, only slightly attenuated, is found with this arrangement (Kahneman & Henik, 1977, p. 314). The only substantial violation of within-group similarity of performance that we have observed is the occasional occurrence of a pronounced end-effect: The very last item in the array is sometimes recalled much more frequently than its neighbors. We do not know the boundary conditions for this effect.

Consider now the consequences of adding an extra item to the basic six-letter array. The significant observation is that an added digit and an irrelevant suffix have identical effects. The addition of an item interferes markedly with the recall of other members of the second group, but the only effect on the first group is a small improvement. The total number of items reported from arrays of six or seven digits is approximately the same. The addition of a suffix to the string causes a slight decrement of performance, because the subjects are not given an opportunity to report that item.

Table 7.3 displays a further analysis of the results of the same experiment. A contingency coefficient was computed within the data of each subject for the recall of items in different positions. The N for the computation of an individual coefficient was the number of trials on which each structure was repeated in the experiment. Table 7.3 presents the averages of the individual coefficients of contingency for pairs of items that belong to the same group in some patterns and to different groups in others. Correlations for items that belong to the same group are identified by parentheses.

The correlational results are strikingly consistent. All 12 within-group correlations are positive, and 11 of 12 between-group correlations are negative. A similar pattern was observed in a different, mathematically independent analysis of individual differences in the shape of the serial position curve. When the individual differences in overall performance are removed, it is observed that

TABLE 7.3
Average Within-Subject Correlations in Recall[a]

	Pairs			
Example	3–4	4–5	2–4	4–6
1234 56	(75)	−25	(52)	04
123 456	−27	(27)	−28	(25)
1234 56k	(50)	−27	(31)	−36
123 456k	−16	(18)	−20	(16)
1234 567	(59)	−32	(36)	−32
123 4567	−28	(25)	−31	(12)

[a] Correlations for pairs of items that belong to the same group are identified by parentheses.

subjects who recall an item in a particular position especially well tend also to do well on other members of the same group and poorly on members of the other group. The correlational results support the conclusion that the members of each group tend to share the same fate in the test of recall, and that the two groups compete as teams for access to the subject's report.

A Model of Group Processing

The model that we developed to account for this pattern of results, labeled group processing, invoked the notion that resources (or attention) are allocated to groups (or perceptual units) that are formed by an early preattentive process. We assumed that these resources are limited and that they are allocated hierarchically—first to groups, then to individual items within a group. The model can be made concrete by imagining two customers (the groups) shopping in a depleted store that does not stock enough goods for their needs. Each customer is a family head who must ration the purchases among the members of his or her family. Our recall data are well described by assuming that the allocation to the customers is made according to a priority rule: The first customer gets most of what he or she needs, and the second gets what is left. The application of the rule is imperfect, however, and the second customer sometimes acquires goods that the first could have used. The allocation within the families is assumed to follow a rule of equal sharing.

The homogeneity of performance that we observed is explained by the equal sharing of resources within each group. The pattern of correlations is explained by assuming some random variation in the division of goods between the customers on successive trials. Within-group correlations are positive because these fluctuations have similar effects on the rations obtained by all the members of a family. Between-group correlations are negative because any increase in the amount consumed by one family can only be at the expense of the other. Finally, we assume that the allocation of goods within a family does not discriminate between a useful citizen (i.e., a relevant item) and a useless drone (e.g., a suffix). This is a natural assumption to make if attention is allocated before the identity of the competing items is determined. It explains why a suffix and a relevant item have similar effects on the recall of other items.

Theoretical Alternatives

The diverse elements that comprise the pattern of performance that we called group processing have all been reported earlier, in a variety of experimental contexts, and they have been explained in these contexts by several unrelated theoretical notions.

Discontinuities of performance at group boundaries have been reported by Shaw (1969) in a detection task, where the subjects were compelled to process a string of items in left-to-right order. The probability of detection was much higher for the last member of the first group than for its nearest neighbor in the second group. Similar discontinuities have also been reported in a tachistoscopic whole-report task (Estes & Wolford, 1971; Wolford & Hollingsworth, 1974b). A model proposed by Wolford (1975) explains this result in terms of asymmetric lateral interference among neighboring letters. An item is assumed to suffer greater interference from neighbors farther in the periphery than from neighbors that are nearer the fixation point. The supporting evidence is that acuity at a given retinal position is affected more adversely by the presence of added peripheral elements than by more central elements (e.g., Estes, Allmeyer, & Reder, 1976). Banks, Bachrach, and Larson (1977) have suggested a different interpretation of this observation. They propose that acuity depends on the retinal position of the center of gravity of the entire configuration that the subject must resolve. The location of the center of gravity varies with the position of the masking element in a manner that could explain the observed asymmetry of masking.

Considerations of acuity could be invoked to explain why the fourth item is more easily perceived in the pattern 1234 56 than in the pattern 123 456. The fourth item has a peripheral neighbor in the latter case but not in the former. It is very unlikely, however, that acuity factors played an important role in our results. The projected letters were large, the visual conditions generally favorable, and we repeatedly observed that large variations in the distance of the subjects from the display had little effect on performance. Furthermore, the lateral masking model fails to explain a salient feature of the results shown in Table 7.2: Performance on Item 5 is better when Item 4 is adjacent to it than when the two items are separated by a space, although lateral interference can only be worse in the former case. The theory proposed by Banks et al. (1977) yields no predictions for this situation, because the number of masking elements and the location of the center of gravity both vary. The attention allocation model specifically predicts the observed result, because the resources that are left for the second customer are more abundant when the first customer shops for a small family than for a large one.

A pattern of correlations similar to that in Table 7.3 has been described by Bower (1970a) and Johnson (1972) in standard tasks of short-term memory. It has been interpreted as an effect of chunking or coding (Estes, 1972a; Johnson, 1970, 1972). It is assumed that the subject produces a unitary code for each chunk, stores these codes, and performs a decoding operation at the time of retrieval. It is easy to apply this model to cases in which a unitary code is available in advance, such as a word code for the sequence of letters *CAT*. In these situations, the chunking notion entails positive correlations among the elements of a chunk, because they are all recalled together if the chunk code is retrieved and all lost together if it is forgotten. Chunking also entails a large effect of recoding on the number of elements that can be recalled (Miller, 1956; Simon, 1975). However, this concept of chunking is not readily applied to our experimental situation, where unitary codes for the chunks are not normally used and where the total number of items retrieved is essentially independent of grouping structure.

Finally, the observation that an irrelevant suffix and a relevant extra item have similar effects on the recall of earlier items was reported by Dallett (1965) for auditory lists. This observation eventually led to a vast number of studies of precategorical acoustic storage (PAS), starting with a seminal paper by Crowder and Morton (1969). The interpretation was that the terminal item of an auditory list normally benefits from persistence in an echoic store, from which it can be retrieved at the appropriate time. The suffix or added item interferes with recall of previous material by eliminating the echoic trace. We concern ourselves with the auditory suffix effect later in this chapter. Meanwhile, it is evident that the concept of precategorical acoustic storage does not contribute to our understanding of interference by a visual suffix, although the visual and auditory effects are strikingly similar.

Experiment 8

It seems fair to conclude that the most obvious alternatives to an analysis of group processing in terms of attention cannot easily account for the data. The group-processing model, however, still remains too vague for comfort. In order to provide a better understanding of the manner in which attention affects performance in tachistoscopic perception, we decided to study possible effects of group processing in a search task. To ensure the continuity of the investigation, a dual-task design was used. On any trial, the subject was presented with an array of six digits, centered in a frame that remained permanently in view. Two grouping structures were used: 123 456 (the 3–3 grouping) and 1234 56 (the 4–2 grouping). In the dual-task condition, a target digit was indicated before each trial. The subject's task was to press a key if he or she detected the target. If not, the subject was to report orally the content of the array, in left-to-right order. A recall-only condition was also included, in which the detection task was eliminated. There were two conditions of exposure: The array was presented for 200 msec in all trials; on half the trials, it was immediately followed by a pattern mask of line fragments. The mask and no-mask conditions were alternated in successive blocks of 18 trials. Each block included 12 trials on which the target actually appeared (once in every position of the two types of array), 4 trials in which a target was designated but not shown, and 2 recall-only trials. Subjects participated in three sessions, for a total of 648 trials.

The pattern mask did not affect the results to any great extent, and the results shown in Table 7.4 are pooled over the two conditions. Table 7.4 includes recall data for two types of trials—the recall-only condition, and dual-task trials on which the target was not shown. The table also presents the percentage of correct detections and mean RT for each position, in the two types of array.

TABLE 7.4
Percent Recall, Percent Detection, and Reaction Times (Msec)

	Serial Position					
	1	2	3	4	5	6
Recall, recall-only						
4–2	98	98	95	96	44	78
3–3	99	99	96	61	64	79
Recall, no-target						
4–2	97	85	81	89	58	76
3–3	97	88	83	75	72	83
Detection						
4–2	98	90	94	99	73	88
3–3	97	90	90	84	85	92
RT						
4–2	562	596	557	529	542	542
3–3	547	581	534	541	560	545

We had anticipated that the usual priority of the first group in recall might be disrupted by the concurrent search task. A priority strategy is inappropriate in search, because the target is equally likely to appear in all positions. The recall data shown in Table 7.4 indicate that this concern was well founded. The discontinuity at the group boundaries is much attenuated in the dual-task condition, where the subjects apparently allocated attention more equitably to the two groups. Indeed, there is no significant discontinuity in the 3–3 array. Nevertheless, the characteristic signature of group processing is still detectable in the recall data of the dual-task condition: Performance on Item 4 is better in the 4–2 array than in the 3–3 array, whereas the reverse pattern holds for Item 5, $F(1,9)$ = 11.52, $p < .01$.

The main purpose of the experiment was to find out if the characteristic effect of grouping structure also holds in detection performance. The answer is positive. The same interaction of position with display is significant, $F(1,9)$ = 14.26, $p < .01$: Detection of Item 4 is much more likely in the 4–2 array, whereas detection of Item 5 is better in the 3–3 array. As was said earlier, the latter result provides the clearest test of the attention allocation model. The difference is highly consistent: Nine of 10 subjects detected Item 5 more often in the 3–3 array than in the 4–2 array, and the remaining subject showed no difference, $t(9) = 3.54$, $p < .01$.

The instruction to speed the detection response had a double purpose in the present experiment. It was intended to discourage the subject from any attempt to encode the whole array and to detect the target in the encoded representation. It was also designed to explore the possibility that the processing of the two groups is serial. The reaction times indicate that the first objective was achieved, for they appear too fast to allow for the possibility that the detection was made from a verbal representation of the entire array. With respect to the second objective, we found that the values of RT varied systematically as a function of position in the array, but the variations were inconsistent with the hypothesis of serial processing. Slow RTs were obtained for items in the middle of the first group, but the RT to the last item was quite fast. We have no ready interpretation for the different patterns of serial position effects observed in the detection and RT data.

The results of this experiment provide further support for the attention allocation model. In particular, the RT results make it very unlikely that the group-processing pattern originates at a stage where groups are sequentially "read" into some type of storage for subsequent recall. The most parsimonious account of the results is that attention was allocated to items in the hierarchical manner described earlier, and that the amount of attention allocated to an item affected the probability of its being detected, as well as the probability of its being recalled. The results also indicate that the strategy of allocation is quite flexible. The effect of the search task on recall performance suggests that the subjects adopted a compromise between the emphasis on the first group that is characteristic of the set to recall, and a more even distribution of attention that could be optimal for search. This indication of strategic control supports the view that performance in our experiments was resource limited (Norman & Bobrow, 1975), rather than constrained by peripheral factors.

THE AUDITORY SUFFIX EFFECT

The enduring fascination with the problem of attention can perhaps be traced to the nature of selective attention as a pure act of will, which controls experience (James, 1890). By merely willing to do so, we are sometimes able to think and act as if a potentially distracting stimulus had been physically removed from the scene. We can focus on a conversation at a cocktail party, exclude neighboring lines from awareness when reading, or write a letter in a busy coffeehouse. The limitations of selective attention, the stimuli we cannot ignore, define frustrating boundaries of what we can will ourselves to do.

The well-known suffix effect provides a striking instance of these limitations. The experiment is run as follows (Crowder, 1971; 1978a; Crowder & Morton, 1969; Morton & Chambers, 1976; Morton, Crowder, & Prussin, 1971). A series of digits or other words is presented to subjects for immediate recall. On some or all trials, an irrelevant item is added at the end of the list. The item can be any speech sound; the syllable "bah" is as effective as any meaningful suffix. The subject is forewarned of the identity of the suffix and of its irrelevance. Nevertheless, the presentation of the suffix has a dramatic effect on the recall of the immediately preceding relevant items. The common recency advantage of the last relevant item is completely eliminated, and the recall probability for that item may drop from a normal value of about 90% to a value of less than 50% when a suffix is presented. To a good first approximation, the effect of a redundant suffix is the same as that of adding an extra item to the list (Dallett, 1965).

The striking and robust suffix effect has been the subject of many experiments. Most pertinent to our theme were studies that attempted to map the boundaries of the effect and to identify circumstances in which an irrelevant stimulus, presented immediately after a list, does not eliminate the recency advantage. Morton, Crowder, and Prussin (1971) reported a fascinating series of experiments in which seemingly minor variations of conditions had a dramatic effect on the magnitude of the suffix effect, and several subsequent studies have been concerned with this problem. The most important condition for the occurrence of the suffix effect is that the suffix must be a speech sound. Noises and tones that follow a list do not interfere with the recall of verbal material. Morton and Chambers (1976) have described subtle physical alterations of the sound of a spoken "ah," which cause it to appear more or less speechlike and simultaneously cause large variations of suffix interference. The suffix effect can be reduced by consistently presenting the suffix in a different voice from the list or in a different location (Morton, Crowder, & Prussin, 1971). To be effective, the suffix must follow the last item: A "suffix" that is presented simultaneously with the last item causes much less interference than a suffix that is presented later (Crowder, 1978a). A suffix that is repeated three times has slightly less effect than a single suffix (Crowder, 1978a; Morton, 1976).

Theoretical treatments of the suffix effect (Crowder, 1971, 1978a; Crowder & Morton, 1969; Morton, 1970) have developed the hypothesis that traces of auditory items usually persist for a short time in an echo-box, which was labeled the precategorical acoustic store, or PAS. The PAS operates by a push-down rule, and it holds the last item presented, perhaps with faint traces of its immediate predecessors. The terminal item in an auditory list is recalled better than its predecessors because information about it is available in PAS. The suffix overwrites the last item in PAS and thereby eliminates the recency advantage.

To account for the conditions that enable a listener to resist suffix interference, Morton (1970; Morton & Chambers, 1975; Morton, Crowder, & Prussin, 1971) proposed that access to PAS is controlled by a filter, which can be preset to exclude items by such characteristics as location or voice quality. The filter was said to select a channel, as in classical filter theory (Broadbent, 1958), but Morton located the filter just prior to PAS, whereas Broadbent had placed it immediately downstream of the S-system of sensory storage. The well-known results of the split-span experiment appear to favor Broadbent's view: When pairs of items are simultaneously presented to the two ears, subjects normally report all the items heard on one ear before turning to the items presented to the other. To explain this observation, Broadbent (1958) proposed that the filter originally selects items from one ear (channel) and that other items are later retrieved from echoic storage in the S-system. Subjects' ability to perform in the split-span experiment is difficult to explain if the filter excludes items from echoic storage. Morton (1976) identified another difficulty for the original model of the suffix effect: It fails to explain the fact that the suffix effect is reduced, slightly but consistently, by repetitions of the suffix.

An alternative account has been offered by Crowder (1978a). Crowder proposes that the mechanism of interference in PAS follows the rules of recurrent inhibition (Ratliff, 1965). The suffix inhibits the traces of items that immediately preceded it, but the inhibition is reduced when the inhibiting stimulus is itself weakened by others that follow it. Thus, the repetition of a suffix improves recall by a process of disinhibition. To explain why interference is reduced when the suffix differs from the list in some physical characteristic, Crowder proposes that mutual inhibition in PAS is most severe for stimuli that are presented on the same channel. This interpretation dispenses with the notion of a filter, which had been used to explain the same results. Crowder's ingenious treatment of the suffix effect is a good illustration of the common preference for psychological explanations that rely on mechanisms that are close to the periphery, either on the sensory side or on the side of response selection, avoiding wherever possible more "central" and vaguer concepts such as perceptual grouping or selective attention.

The approach that has been developed in this chapter suggests yet another interpretation of the suffix effect, based on the following assumptions: (1) The relevant list is treated as a perceptual unit; (2) the terminal member of an auditory unit or stream (Bregman, 1978, Chap. 4, this volume) often has a special advantage in recall, perhaps because it is held in an echoic store as Crowder and Morton have suggested; and (3) suffix interference arises when an irrelevant item preempts the privileged terminal position in the relevant group. Consequently, the interference can be reduced or prevented if the potentially interfering item is perceptually segregated from the relevant list.

Unlike Morton, we do not believe that ineffective suffixes, such as tones, are excluded from echoic storage by a filter; they are merely assigned to a distinct perceptual unit. Unlike Crowder, we do not believe that the interaction between items in storage can be adequately described as a process of lateral inhibition.

Experiment 9

The alternative models of suffix interference suggest different ways of reducing this effect. Crowder's (1978a) theory implies that suffix interference can be reduced by repeating the suffix, through a process of disinhibition. In contrast, the grouping model suggests that suffix interference is more likely to be reduced by presenting additional items *before* the suffix, to provide an alternative perceptual unit in which the suffix may be embedded. This idea is difficult to implement, however, because the added items must be presented concurrently with the relevant list or interleaved with the members of that list, but they cannot be allowed to cause massive interference (Hitch, 1975).

In order to minimize this problem, we ran an experiment in which the suffix and the list were heard from different locations. The material was presented over two speakers separated by 5.4 m. On each trial, a list of nine digits was presented on the right-hand speaker at a rate of 1/1.5 sec. On half the trials, the list items were interleaved with a sequence of ''bah's'' presented on the left-hand speaker. The irrelevant series always started after the presentation of the first digit. It ended either just before or just after the last digit. The latter case is labeled the embedded-suffix condition. Finally, there were trials on which a single ''bah'' was presented on the left-hand speaker, 750 msec after the terminal digit (the suffix condition) and control trials on which no irrelevant material was heard. To eliminate intonation differences, the same series of nine ''bah's'' was used repeatedly in the recording. The first eight ''bah's'' or the last ''bah'' was eliminated by a gating circuit whenever appropriate. The four types of trials were presented in random sequence.

Subjects were instructed to write their answers in order, from left to right, indicating forgotten items by dashes. The main dependent variable was the proportion of trials on which the last digit was recalled in its correct position. These proportions were:

A. No suffix–control   94%
B. Single suffix   87%
C. No suffix–interleaved ''bahs''   92%
D. Embedded suffix   94%

As might be expected from the results of Morton, Crowder, and Prussin (1971), the effect of the isolated suffix was small, although significant, $t(14) = 2.30$, $p < .05$, between Conditions B and A. The interleaved series had no significant effect, demonstrating subjects' good ability to select the relevant stream by its location ($t = 1.08$, NS, for the comparison of Conditions C and A). The interaction of the two manipulations was significant $F(1,14) = 7.73$, $p < .02$. Suffix interference was completely eliminated when the suffix was embedded in a series of similar sounds presented at the same location.

Experiment 10

The results of Exp. 9 confirmed the effectiveness of an embedding manipulation, but the suffix effect was too small for comfort. We went on to study a situation in which the suffix effect could be expected to be more substantial. The relevant message consisted of a list of eight names of consonants, presented on the right-hand speaker at a rate of one item per 750 msec. The irrelevant material on the left-hand speaker also consisted of random sequences of consonants, presented at the same rate and synchronized with the relevant items. A consonant could not appear in both messages on the same trial. The four conditions were the same as in Exp. 9. The recording of the left-hand speaker messages was again carefully designed to avoid intonation differences among the experimental conditions. A string of nine consonants was recorded for each trial in Conditions B, C, and D; a gating circuit was used to eliminate the first eight items for Condition B and the last item for Condition C.

The subjects were exposed to a total of 64 trials, with the various conditions randomly mixed. The recall of the terminal consonant was scored for the last 40 trials:

A. No suffix–control   84%
B. Single suffix   47%
C. No suffix–concurrent string   76%
D. Embedded suffix   60%

The difference between Conditions A and B indicates almost as large a suffix effect as is commonly obtained when suffix and list are presented in the same location. This result contrasts with the small magnitude of the suffix effect in Exp. 9, and with the observations of Morton, Crowder, and Prussin (1971) on the effects of spatial separation. We have learned from subsequent experiments that the rapid rate of presentation and the use of nonredundant suffixes both contribute to our subjects' inability to resist the interference. The semantic category of the suffix appears unimportant. The statement that subjects can use a channel distinction to avoid the suffix effect is clearly an oversimplification. A number of factors act jointly to determine whether the suffix is segregated from the list.

The major result of the experiment concerns the effect of embedding the suffix in a string of consonants presented on the same speaker. Embedding reduces the effect of the suffix on the last item from 37% to 16%, $F(1,22) = 10.24, p < .01$. Indeed, the recall of the last item is significantly better when that item is both accompanied and followed by irrelevant consonants than when a single suffix is presented; $t(22) = 2.56, p < .05$ for the comparison of Conditions B and D.

The improvement that embedding causes in this study appears to be substantially larger than the marginal reduction of interference that is produced by repetition of the suffix (Crowder, 1978a; Morton, 1976). To explain the superiority of embedding over repetition, an inhibition model must include the unlikely assumption that the suffix is inhibited more strongly by items that precede it than by items that follow it. In contrast, the superiority of prior embedding follows naturally from considerations of perceptual organization: The assignment of an item (e.g., the suffix) to an ongoing stream (the list) is likely to be made almost immediately when the item is heard and is unlikely to be much altered by subsequent stimulation. Prior embedding causes the item to be heard initially as a member of an alternative stream, whereas the repetition of the suffix, in our terms, is an attempt to separate the suffix from a perceptual unit to which it has already been assigned. At best, such a manipulation can endow the suffix with the dual character of marking the end of one string and the beginning of another.

THE VISUAL SUFFIX EFFECT

The concepts of preattentive processing and perceptual organization that have guided our studies are equally applicable to the visual and auditory modalities. Indeed, the strategy of searching for rules that transfer the laws of form from one modality to the other has been pursued with considerable success in recent years (see, e.g., Bregman, 1978, Chap. 4, this volume; Deutsch, 1978; Kubovy, Chap. 3, this volume). We appear to be recovering, albeit slowly, from the damage that was done by the lack of tape recorders in the laboratories of the early Gestalt psychologists, and by the almost exclusive use of that instrument in the early studies of selective attention of the 1950s. Some analogies between auditory and visual phenomena are exceptionally striking, as in the case of the cocktail party effect and the visual superposition effects (Neisser & Becklen, 1975; Rock, Schauer, & Halper, 1976). Others are rather less surprising, as in the case of the auditory and visual suffix effects that we discuss in these sections. The deliberate search for intermodality analogies appears to be a useful heuristic for the study of perceptual organization in information processing.

The visual analogue to the auditory suffix effect is obtained by appending an irrelevant element to a briefly presented display of items that the subject is instructed to store for immediate recall. The common hypothesis for both modalities is that the added element will cause interference to the degree that it is embedded in the relevant group, and is therefore processed as if it were one of its members. We saw earlier, in the context of group processing, that a redundant suffix k, when added to an array of digits, caused precisely as much interference as an extra relevant digit in the same position.

Experiment 11

The effect of a visual suffix was originally investigated in an experiment designed in collaboration with U. Neisser (Kahneman, 1973, pp. 133–135). The results obtained with different types of suffixes are illustrated in Fig. 7.1, from Kahneman and Henik (1977). The experiment was carried out in the standard design that we have employed in most of our work: group presentation ($N = 24$); a 500-msec warning period; and a 200-msec exposure of a projected array of six digits, which sometimes also included a suffix element next to the sixth digit. The various kinds of suffix and no-suffix control arrays were presented in random sequence. Subjects were familiarized in advance with all suffixes. In particular, they were aware that the digit 0 was never relevant and could appear only as a suffix. The main dependent variable was the percentage of items correctly reported from the sixth position. This value is given in parentheses next to each type of suffix. Comparison with the control Pattern A provides a measure of the severity of interference caused by each type of suffix.

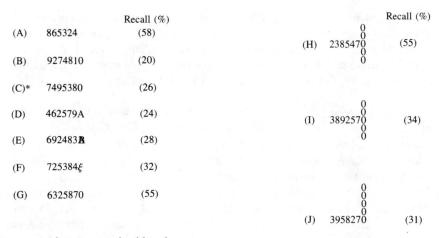

		Recall (%)			Recall (%)
(A)	865324	(58)			
			(H)	2385470	(55)
(B)	9274810	(20)			
(C)*	7495380	(26)			
(D)	462579A	(24)			
			(I)	3892570	(34)
(E)	692483**B**	(28)			
(F)	725384ξ	(32)			
(G)	6325870	(55)			
			(J)	3958270	(31)

*the zero was printed in red.

FIG. NO. 7.1   Probability of recall of sixth digit for various suffixes.

Highly significant interference occurred with all suffixes, with Conditions G and H as the only exceptions. These results confirm the original observations of Kahneman and Neisser. We now turn to a discussion of their implications.

Sperling's classic analyses of the tachistoscopic span (Sperling, 1963, 1967) implicated a definite capacity limit in the whole-report span, because the number of items recalled was independent of the number presented. A mechanism of mutual interference or competition is implied in which the successful processing of one item reduces the chances that other items will be processed with similar success. The analysis of the visual suffix effect could shed light on this mechanism because of the finding reported earlier—that a visual suffix sometimes reduces the recall of relevant items just as much as an additional relevant element would do in its place (see Table 7.2). Four hypotheses have been advanced to explain the tachistoscopic span.

Limited Capacity of a Recognition Buffer (Sperling, 1967).   A storage system is assumed, which can hold programs for the rehearsal and production of up to four items. The observation that verbally uncoded items (an unfamiliar Greek letter or an overlay of the letters *A* and *B*) cause nearly as much interference as codable items appears to be inconsistent with this interpretation of the span. It seems unlikely that such items interfere with others because they are being prepared for rehearsal.

A Limit on the Number of Visual Codes (Coltheart, 1972).   The hypothesis that the span is limited by the capacity of visual memory is consistent with our finding that verbal coding is unimportant in the suffix effect, because a visual code could be set up even for an item that cannot be verbally coded. However, an observation arguing against this hypothesis is that suffixes that cause little interference (e.g., the zero in Pattern G) are typically available to recall. If a visual code can be set up even for such ineffective suffixes, the interpretation of the tachistoscopic span in terms of visual codes becomes unlikely.

Lateral Masking (Wolford & Hollingsworth, 1974a; Wolford, 1975).   An interaction among neighboring items, at the level of feature detectors, causes a loss of information about the location of features and thereby prevents the identification of some elements. It is of interest that the reduced effectiveness of embedded suffixes (Patterns H, I, J) could perhaps be explained by adding to an interactive channel model (Estes, 1972b; Estes, Allmeyer, & Reder, 1976) an assumption of recurrent inhibition of the kind invoked by Crowder (1978a) to explain the effect of repeating an auditory suffix. If repeated suffix elements inhibit one another, a neighboring relevant item could be released from interference. This hypothesis would correctly predict that recall of the terminal item is better in Pattern H than in Patterns I and J. Pattern I involves greater distance and therefore less inhibition among the zeros. In Pattern J, the zero that is nearest the relevant items is a terminal element in the line and therefore is subject to little inhibition from other zeros. However, the lateral masking hypothesis completely fails to explain why the suffix effect was virtually eliminated in Pattern G, where the distance of the zero from its nearest relevant neighbor was only slightly larger than in Pattern B. This result is more readily interpreted as a breakdown of good continuation than as a manifestation of weakened interaction at a peripheral level (Prinzmetal & Banks, 1977b). We have also noted that the severity of suffix interference is essentially independent of viewing distance, a general feature of our results that is incompatible with the attribution of either the suffix effect or the tachistoscopic span to peripheral interactions.

Preattentive Grouping and Limited Resources   (Kahneman & Henik, 1977).   The approach that we have developed in this chapter suggests that performance in the tachistoscopic task, under favorable conditions of exposure, is jointly limited by the availability of attentional resources and by the ability to control how these resources are allocated. We have proposed that the allocation of attention facilitates all the instrumental responses that are associated to the attended object, although we have refrained from asserting that attention is *necessary* to the elicitation of responses. In this view (Kahneman, 1973), the activation of nodes in long-term memory by sensory stimuli depends on three factors: (1) the quality of the sensory information; (2) the priming of the relevant memory node by set or expectancy; and (3) the availability of an added enabling or facilitating input—attention—that is allocated to the perceptual objects into which the field has been analyzed. Under adequate conditions, it is the latter factor that limits recall from tachistoscopic exposure displays.

Our hypothesis, then, is that the suffix interferes with the recall of other items by withdrawing resources that could have facilitated their processing. The ability to resist suffix interference depends on the availability of a perceptual organization in which the suffix is segregated from relevant items. With one instructive exception, the results of Fig. 7.1 fit this hypothesis very well. The apparent exception is Pattern C, where the presentation of the suffix in a distinctive color did not enable our subjects to resist the interference. This result is reminiscent of Exp. 10, where an auditory suffix presented in a distinctive location nevertheless caused severe interference. In both experiments, the availability of a distinctive cue did not suffice to overcome potent grouping effects—rapid rhythm and temporal continuity in audition, proximity and good continuation in the case of the visual suffix. As in the case of the auditory suffix, the reduced effect of an embedded suffix most directly implicates perceptual organization in the control of selective attention. The embedding of the suffix was fully effective in Pattern H and somewhat weaker in Conditions I and J. The embedding configuration is less tight in Pattern I than in Pattern H, and the suffix in Pattern J is a corner element, which can readily be seen as belonging to either the horizontal or the vertical lines. In general, the results of Fig. 7.1 demonstrate the heuristic and predictive value of considerations of perceptual organization, in a context of selective attention.

CONCLUDING REMARKS

The main theme of this chapter has been that the concept of perceptual unit, or object, must be assigned a central role in a theory of attention. It may be useful to comment briefly on the origin of this concept and on its implications for a theory of information processing.

The concept of a perceptual object is inherited from the Gestalt tradition. Like many other Gestalt concepts, it is vague, elusive, and rooted in a compelling intuition—that there is an essential distinction between objects (things) and their properties, and that there is a sense in which the object is prior to its properties and independent of them. To appreciate the strength of this intuition, imagine a collection of random shapes of various colors, scattered in space. Now imagine that each of these shapes are set in motion, and subjected to gradual distortions and changes of hue. Such a scene will be described as a set of objects that change as they move. The phenomenal impression will be that each object retains its identity over reasonably smooth transformations of any of its properties. There is an obvious distinction between changes and transformations that are identity preserving and others that destroy the original object. We surmise that this primitive notion of identity is the core of the intuitive notion of a perceptual object.

There are no prohibitions in current psychological doctrine that bar an investigator from using an intuitive notion such as that of a perceptual object in theorizing—provided that it appears only in the role of a dependent variable that is to be explained. However, the use of such concepts in an explanatory role is strongly discouraged. Explanations that rely on intuitive or mentalistic terms are not as respectable as explanations that avoid such terms. Why is that so? One reason may be that mentalistic concepts appear to provide a license for circular explanation. We have encountered this difficulty in the discussion of the suffix effect: In the absence of independent operations for the measurement of perceptual embedding, it seems futile to assert that a suffix interferes with the retention of a list if it is perceptually embedded in that list. Another cost is the apparent appeal to a homunculus, as in the statement that attention selects an object: The selected object is in the mind, but the characteristics that are attributed to the mental representation closely resemble the characteristics of real objects, whereas the properties of attention mimic those of a physical eye that focuses on the object.

Perhaps for these reasons, or perhaps because of the strong behavioristic legacy in modern cognitive psychology, Gestalt-inspired concepts are rare in current theories. Theoretical terms in cognitive psychology commonly suggest metaphors from the world of computers (e.g., "storage"), from sensory phenomena (e.g., "lateral inhibition in PAS"), or from properties of overt responses: The "identification" of a stimulus, for example, is treated as the elicitation of an internal response through a well-practiced S–R bond. These metaphors have the aura of scientific respectability that mentalistic concepts sorely lack.

The neglect of intuitive notions, such as that of perceptual objects, is sometimes costly. It can lead to a failure to predict large effects (e.g., the difference between a checkerboard structure and a line structure in selective attention by color). We were struck by the fact that some experimental outcomes that appear self-evident to naive subjects are not implied by sophisticated theories of selective attention and actually represent an embarrassment for these theories. There is reason for concern when we observe that theories that predict subtle effects within restricted paradigms fail to predict the intuitively obvious outcomes of our studies of the Stroop effect and of selective attention by color, or when we note that the currently dominant theories of attention do not easily explain the well-known facts of selective listening. On this background, intuitive concepts can have considerable predictive power. Models that are based on such concepts are likely to be high in heuristic value—one of the important criteria by which theories are evaluated. Admittedly, however, they fare less well on the criterion of refutability. A latent dispute about the relative importance of the two criteria has been simmering in psychology at least since the days of Tolman and Hull.

The theoretical treatment of the notion of perceptual object need not be restricted to the intuitive approach that has been adopted in this chapter. The phenomenon of identity preservation that was described earlier could provide the starting point for a more formal analysis. Such an analysis might begin by specifying the abilities that a system must possess in order to maintain object identity. It is evident that the identity that is preserved in our example is not the kind of identity that is established in the process of identification, where a permanent representation in long-term memory is activated by a fixed set of stimulus properties. To maintain the identities of a set of unfamiliar and rapidly changing objects, the visual system must be able, when an object appears, to set up the functional equivalent of a temporary file, which is kept alive as long as the object is perceptually present. The file is updated, perhaps continuously, with information about the current state of the object. The file remains assigned for a while to an object that has disappeared, for the "same" object can sometimes be seen to reappear (Michotte, 1963). The maintenance of object identity in the system that we have sketched will not depend on the maintenance of a consistent identification or of any consistent properties: The red circle on the right can become a blue square on the left while remaining the "same" object.

The concept of attention selecting an object loses much of its mystery if we incorporate in our model of information processing an ability to address such perceptual objects. The evidence of perceptual studies suggests that this ability indeed exists, and the evidence of attention studies suggests that it plays a central role in the control of attention. There is reason to question the current practice of building theories of attention on a truncated and oversimplified view of perceptual processing.

8 On the Semantics of a Glance at a Scene

Irving Biederman
State University of New York at Buffalo

ABSTRACT

This chapter is concerned with the perception and comprehension of real-world scenes. Comprehension requires not only that the creatures and objects comprising the scene be identified but also that the relations among these entities be specified. No more than five classes of relations may be needed to characterize the difference in organization between a well-formed scene and an array of unrelated objects. The first two, *support* and *interposition,* reflect the general physical constraints—that most objects do not float in air and that an opaque object will occlude the contours of an object behind it. The third, *probability,* refers to the likelihood of a given object (e.g., a bassinet) being in a given scene (e.g., a service station). Fourth, objects that are likely to occur in a given scene (e.g., a gas pump in a service station) often occupy specific *positions* (e.g., not on a car). Fifth is the familiar *size* of objects. Thus, cups are not bigger than stoves. Although support and interposition can be specified without knowing what the object is, the other relations require access to the referential meaning or semantics of the object and its context.

A schema of a scene is taken to be the overall internal representation of the scene that integrates the scene's entities and relations and allows access to semantic information. Effects attributable to the semantic relations are taken as an operational definition of schema activation. Several accounts of perception hold that a schema is activated only after the physical relations are specified and the objects identified. Seven experiments exploring this issue are described. The experimental technique employed stimuli in which an object in a scene was displaced to another part of the scene or put in another scene so as to violate one to three of the five relations. Such objects appear to be floating, passing through the background unlikely to be in the scene, unlikely to be in a given position in the scene, or too large or too small for the scene. The experiments measured the effects of these violations on the speed and accuracy of (1) detecting an object undergoing a violation, or (2) detecting the presence of the violation itself.

Contrary to the physical-then-semantic-relations view of scene perception, the results indicate that semantic relations are accessed at least as fast as physical relations—fast enough, in fact, for violations of the semantic relations to affect the perception of objects. Extensive semantic processing of a scene can be readily achieved from a single fixation. It is thus unnecessary to postulate eye-fixation sequences or motion to explain scene perception. Routes to the initial elicitation of a schema through scene-emergent features and the probabilistic relations among objects are discussed. The mechanisms for gaining semantic access to a real-world scene can be triggered so quickly and efficiently that conditions can readily be found in which an expectancy for a scene or familiarity with it are neither necessary nor even helpful toward its perception.

INTRODUCTION

In the real world, meaningful auditory information comes to us in the form of sentences; meaningful visual information comes to us in the form of scenes. The past two decades have witnessed an intensive study of sentence perception and comprehension on the part of psycholinguists, who have thus transcended the study of the processing of individual sounds, words, or unrelated verbal units. Our concern is with the perception and comprehension of scenes rather than with the processing of individual elements, objects, or a display of unrelated items. We seem to be able to perceive and understand sentences almost as rapidly as they are spoken. In much the same way, when we glance at the world, even at a scene rich with detail that we have never seen before, our subjective impression is one of effortlessly and rapidly achieving a clear, integrated perception and *comprehension* of what we are viewing. It is this remarkable capacity, which in many respects exceeds our capacity for understanding sentences as they are spoken, that is the subject of this chapter.

At least two characteristics distinguish the perception of a scene from the perception of an individual object or a display of unrelated objects. One, the relations among the various entities—the creatures and objects—must be specified in much the same way that the perception of a sentence is determined by the semantic and syntactic relations among the words. Thus, to comprehend a scene with a bench, a man, and a harp requires not only that we identify these entities but that we know, for example, that the man is sitting *on* the bench and *playing* the harp. Second, at some point during the viewing of a scene, the perceiver achieves an overall representation that integrates the various entities and relations and allows access to world knowledge about such settings; so, for example, the perceiver knows that he or she is looking at a concert, a restaurant, or a parking lot. I use the term *schema* (of a scene) to refer to that representation. The *schema* specifies both the items appropriate to a given scene and the physical and semantic relations that should hold among them. This can serve as a *theoretical definition* of a schema. Although some spatial relations—for example, those describable by *on, above, in front of*—can be specified without reference to semantic information, knowledge about other relations is clearly dependent on access to meaning (e.g., that a fire hydrant is more likely to be found in a street scene than in a kitchen, more likely on the sidewalk than on top of a mailbox or in the middle of a street, and smaller than a truck but larger than a cup).

These semantic relations, which are described in more detail later, provide the basis of an *operational* definition of *schema activation,* which is extensively explored in this chapter. A schema will be said to be activated when effects attributable to the semantic relations—or their violations—are found. For example, when the identification of a hydrant on a mailbox is impaired relative to its depiction in a normal position on a sidewalk, then it will be assummed that a schema for that street scene has been elicited. That hydrants are to be found on sidewalks but not on mailboxes clearly reflects our learned knowledge about the relations of streets, hydrants, and mailboxes. In studying schema activation, we are studying how this knowledge is brought to bear on the comprehension of a scene.

The term *schema* gained widespread currency in experimental psychology with the publication of F. C. Bartlett's *Remembering* in 1932. The subsequent half-century has witnessed near unanimity in expressions of support for such a concept (e.g., Biederman, 1972; Bruner, 1957; Miller, Galanter, & Pribram, 1960; Minsky, 1975). But such expressions of support have resulted, for the most part, in little more than recoinings (e.g., *frames*) of a fuzzy concept. Testable empirical consequences or interesting theoretical insights have been rare. In fact, it may not be too risky to say that the primary usage of *schema* has been to provide a euphemism for our ignorance of the molar levels of semantic representation of pictures and stories. In retrospect, this should not be too surprising, because issues of representation are difficult to decide apart from issues of processing. The critical failing in most of this research is the absence of an adequate operational definition of the activation of a schema. A major objective of the research reported here is to evaluate the operational definition of schema activation presented in the preceding paragraph.

Methodologically, the challenge has been to develop techniques for assessing what it is that can be perceived from a scene at a single glance. Because (1) we can see so much more than we can remember, (2) our response systems are slow in comparison with the rate at which information from a single glance is lost, and (3) we do not possess a response system that allows for the direct representation of a scene, it was necessary for our techniques to be relatively uncontaminated by limitations of memory span, drawing ability, and verbal fluency in describing pictorial information. It is for this reason that our experiments primarily employ a discrete, forced-choice, information reduction methodology. We study a single glance because we've found that that's all that is required to comprehend most scenes.

THE PERCEPTION OF COHERENT
VERSUS JUMBLED SCENES

In our first investigations of scene processing, we studied the perception of pictures of scenes that had been cut up into six sections and rearranged. Because these studies have been published elsewhere (Biederman, 1972, 1977; Biederman, Glass, & Stacy, 1973; Biederman, Rabinowitz, Glass, & Stacy, 1974), only their implications for our current concerns are briefly summarized here. In all these studies, the speed or accuracy in processing information from a coherent scene was compared to the processing from its jumbled counterpart.

We found that jumbling the scene reduced the accuracy of identifying objects that had remained intact in their original position (Biederman, 1972; Biederman et al., 1974). This result parallels the observations of Miller, Heise, and Lichten (1951) on the intelligibility of words in noise: A word presented in the context of a well-formed sentence is more intelligible than that same word presented in a random-appearing string of words. Even though most objects were left intact in the jumbled versions of our scenes (i.e., they were not severed by the jumbling process), subjects were slower at inferring the "topic" of the scene (Biederman et al., 1973, 1974). Again, the result is parallel to what would be expected from the jumbling of the words of a sentence. Finally, Biederman et al. (1974) demonstrated that jumbling affected performance at exposure durations of 50 and 100 msec—durations far too brief for a second eye fixation to be made on the scene. That is, the relations among the creatures and objects that comprised a scene were affecting the information extracted from a single glance at that scene.

When psycholinguists showed that a sentence could not be profitably analyzed as the sum of individual words, they found it necessary to devise theories of the processing of the relations among words and experimental techniques for the study of the effects of variations of specific relations. We found ourselves in a similar position when we were faced with the following two questions. What are the relations that distinguish a well-formed scene from a display of randomly located objects? How might the effects of these relations be studied?

THE RELATIONS AMONG OBJECTS
IN A WELL-FORMED SCENE

No more than five relations may be needed to characterize much of the difference between a well-formed scene and an array of unrelated objects. These are listed in Table 8.1 and illustrated by *violations* of the relations in a manner similar to the way "The *angry* napkin" illustrates a semantic violation (a selectional re-

TABLE 8.1
List of Relational Violations and Examples for a Single Object

1. *Support* (e.g., a floating fire hydrant). The object does not appear to be resting on a surface.
2. *Interposition* (e.g., the background appearing through the hydrant). The objects undergoing this violation appear to be transparent or passing through another object.
3. *Probability* (e.g., the hydrant in a kitchen). The object is unlikely to appear in the scene.
4. *Position* (e.g., the fire hydrant on top of a mailbox in a street scene). The object is likely to occur in that scene, but it is unlikely to be in that particular position.
5. *Size* (e.g., the fire hydrant appearing larger than a building). The object appears to be too large or too small relative to the other objects in the scene.

striction in Chomsky's 1965 theory) or "He *smiled* the baby" results in a syntactic violation (strict subcategorication because the intransitive verb *smiled* requires a preposition *at*) (cf. Moore, 1972; Moore & Biederman, 1979).

The first two relations, *support* and *interposition,* reflect the general physical constraints that: (1) most objects do not fly or float, and (2) an opaque object will occlude the contours of an object behind it. The third relation, *probability,* refers to the likelihood of a given object being in a given scene. Fire hydrants are rarely found in kitchens. Fourth, objects that are likely to occur in a given scene often occupy specific *positions.* Although a fire hydrant is likely in a street scene, it is unlikely that it would be on top of a mailbox or a car. Last is the familiar *size* of objects. Cups are not bigger than people, nor are fire hydrants bigger than trucks. The latter three constraints—probability, position, and size—are consequences of the referential meaning (or *semantics*) of the object. Similarly, if *visual syntax* consists of visual constraints that are independent of referential meaning, then *support* and *interposition* may be thought of as *syntactic* constraints.

It should be noted that when an object that has the background continuing through it is designated as an instance of a physical *violation* of interposition, or when an object floating in the air is designated as an instance of a physical *violation* of support, then this designation of relations as *violations* is ultimately based on semantic inappropriateness. Obviously some objects can be normally transparent (e.g., glasses, windows) or normally floating in the air (e.g., birds, balloons). The point is that the origin of the *incongruity* for the interposition and support relations for those objects that normally are opaque and supported would be in an inappropriate assignment of surfaces to bodies during physical parsing in perception. It is also possible that objects that are transparent or floating in the air may be more difficult to process, independent of the semantic appropriateness of these relations. Some computer vision models (e.g., Guzman, 1968a) cannot correctly parse a scene with transparent objects. The difficulty of isolating semantic from nonsemantic effects is, of course, not without a parallel in linguistics. (Fortunately, the problems may be tractable. An experiment comparing the processing of target objects that did not inappropriately appear transparent or floating in the air [e.g., glasses and birds] could determine whether there was an effect of these relations independent of their semantic appropriateness.) The

FIG. 8.1.   An example of a position violation.

linguistic distinction between semantic and syntactic constraints merely furnishes a convenient analogy. None of the foregoing discussion is critically dependent on possible linguistic parallels to these visual relations.

To study the effects of the five relations listed in Table 8.1, we have employed scenes such as those shown in Figs. 8.1, 8.2, and 8.3. These scenes were composed by superimposing clear acetate overlays with objects drawn on them over a background scene. The background and overlay were then Xeroxed together to produce a scene with the object in it, and a slide was made of the Xerox. Objects were displaced to various sections of the scene or imported to other scenes to violate one or several of the five constraints. Figure 8.1 is an example of a position violation; Fig. 8.2 is an example of an interposition violation; and Fig. 8.3, an example of a triple violation of size, probability, and support. Note that in Fig. 8.3, the fire hydrant is in a base—or normal—position. Comparison of the violation conditions to the base conditions provided a control for specific object characteristics.

It seems to me that violations of the five relations can characterize the transformation of a well-formed scene into a display of unrelated objects. Consider Fig. 8.4, which shows sample stimuli from a recognition memory experiment reported by Hock, Romanski, Galie, and Williams (1978). Type I is a well-formed scene; Type IV is a display of unrelated objects. A display of unrelated objects is usually described by a list, at best connected with *and*s; by contrast, the objects in scenes tend to be connected with verbs (e.g., *playing*) or spatial prepositions (*on*) (Bower, 1970b). The man in the Type II picture can be regarded as undergoing a position violation; the bench and the man undergo support violations in Type III; and Type IV illustrates a probability, support, and size violation for the flowerpot and a size and support violation for the man. It is still an open question as to how rapidly a scene will lose its integrity (as in Type IV) so that its objects appear unrelated as the number (or proportion) of the objects undergoing violations increases. I suspect that there is no simple answer to this question. Violations applied to large, important, or central objects will probably disrupt a scene more than violations applied to less prominent objects. When a single object undergoes violations, as in our stimuli (Figs. 8.1, 8.2, and 8.3) and as in Hock et al.'s Type II stimuli, the appearance is one of a well-formed scene with a describable anomaly. These scenes become visual metaphors: One can readily describe Hock's Type II example as a man "riding" a harp or Fig. 8.3 as the "Goodrich sofa."

Do some of the relations listed in Table 8.1 have processing priority over the others? Research in the artificial intelligence of scene analysis (Guzman, 1968a; Winston, 1970) has shown that it is possible to parse physically a line drawing

FIG. 8.2.   An example of an interposition violation.

FIG. 8.3.   An example of a triple violation. The sofa is violating the probability, support, and size relations. The fire hydrant, which is shown in a position violation in Fig. 8.1, would be an innocent bystander in this scene. If the sofa were not present, then the hydrant would be in a base condition.

such as the one shown in Fig. 8.5. By "physically parse," I mean that the various surfaces, labeled by numbers in Fig. 8.5, are assigned to the blocks in a manner identical to the way in which a human observer would assign the surfaces to the blocks. Thus the program determines that 4, 5, 24, and 21 all belong to the same object but that 37, 38, and 39 belong to another. This is achieved through a classification of the vertices formed by the intersection of adjacent rectilinear surfaces as shown in Fig. 8.6. The arrow vertex, for example, provides evidence that the two regions along the shaft are part of the same object. The Ts are important for determining when one object is occluding another. Specifically, if a pair of matched Ts is found such that the shafts are collinear, then it is taken as evidence that the shafts are an edge of the same body. In Fig. 8.5, regions 30 and 34 produce matched Ts with regions 19 and 20 to suggest that they are the same body.

Winston (1970) demonstrated that relations such as *support* (e.g., that the body with surfaces 37, 38, and 39 supports the body with surfaces 4, 5, 21, and 24) and *interposition* (e.g., that the body with surfaces 4, 5, 21, and 24 is in front

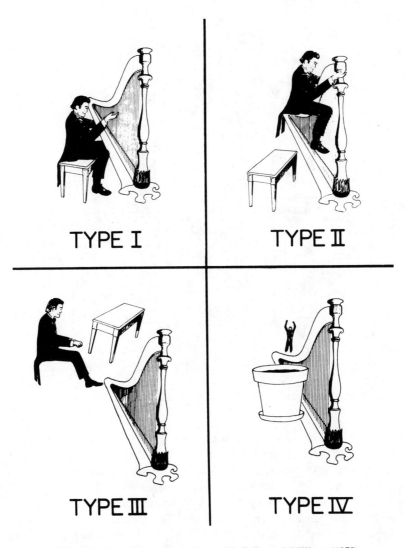

FIG. 8.4.   Stimuli from Hock, Romanski, Galie, and Williams (1978).

of the body with surfaces 19, 20, 30, 34, and 29) can be derived from the kinds of information extracted by Guzman's program. The impressive feature about this result is the claim (Guzman, 1968a) that ''SEE [the name of Guzman's program] does not require a preconceived idea of the form of the object which could appear in the scenes. It assumes only that they will be solid objects formed by rectilinear surfaces [p. 58].''

Because the work of Guzman and Winston shows that it is possible to determine physical relations such as support and interposition without identifying the

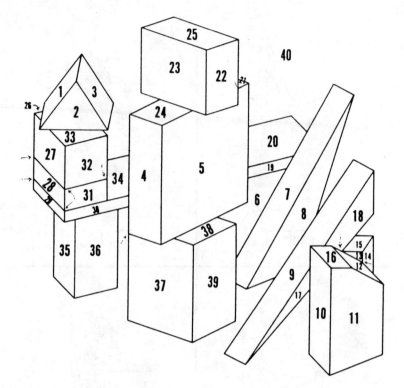

FIG. 8.5.   "MOMO," an aggregate of blocks that Guzman's SEE program can correctly parse. (From Guzman, 1968a, p. 177).

bodies, it is tempting to conjecture that in human perception, this information is extracted before relations dependent on object identity.

This "bottom-up," physical-then-semantic view may be cast as the flowchart model shown in Fig. 8.7, where bottom-up is presented left to right. The initial processing of the stimulus by the visual system is here presented as the detection of features f_f from different parts of the scene. This stage is meant to be theoretically neutral, and other characterizations (e.g., spatial-frequency components) could probably serve as well. The information extracted by the visual system—whatever it is—is used both for the physical parsing of the scene as well as for the identification of objects. It may also be necessary to draw an arrow from the physical parsing stage to the object identification stage, because when objects overlap, the routines for physical parsing may be needed to distinguish one object from another and thus facilitate object identification. The physically parsed scene is then served up to higher levels, where the semantic relations among the already identified objects are then specified. As mentioned previously, effects attributable to violations of the semantic relations are taken as an operational definition of schema elicitation. Thus the stage affected by semantic violations qualifies as a

'L'.- Vertex where two
lines meet.

'FORK'.- Three lines forming angles
smaller than 180 degrees.

'ARROW'.- Three lines meeting at
a point, with one of
the angles bigger than
180 degrees.

'T'.- Three concurrent lines, two
of them collinear.

'K'.- Two of the lines are
collinear, and the other
two fall on the same side
of such lines.

'X'.- Two of the lines are collinear,
and the other two fall on
opposite sides of such lines.

'PEAK'.- Formed by four or more
lines, when there is an
angle bigger than 180°.

'MULTI'.- Vertices formed by four or
more lines, and not falling
in any of the preceding types.

FIG. 8.6. Set of rectilinear vertices. (From Guzman, 1968a, p. 69).

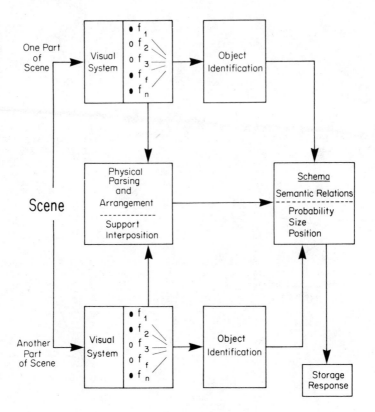

FIG. 8.7.   "Bottom-up," here shown as left-to-right, model of scene perception; f_n's represent various feature tests. The outcome of the feature testing is used both for physical parsing and object identification. The schema is elicited only after physical parsing and object identification are completed. Responses are shown, for simplification, as following schema elicitation, but it is presumed that a response could be initiated from the outcome of processing at any prior stage.

schema. The model in Fig. 8.7 proposes that the schema follows, indeed is a result of, physical parsing and object identification, so that physical parsing proceeds independently of the semantic relations. The research that I describe in the next section shows that this view is incorrect. Semantic relations are accessed at least as fast as those achievable through physical parsing—fast enough, in fact, for violations of the semantic relations to affect the identification of objects. Not only are physical and semantic relations available simultaneously; these relations also do not appear to be processed independently. This lack of independence suggests that a schema is an *integrated* representation of the relations.

EXPERIMENTAL STUDIES OF
RELATIONAL VIOLATIONS

We have run two kinds of reaction-time experiments with the scenes illustrated in Figs. 8.1 to 8.3—an object detection task and a violation detection task. In the object detection task, our primary interest was in the effect of the relational violations on the detection of objects. The violation detection task is analogous to a grammaticality judgment task (e.g., Moore, 1972). Here one must judge whether the relation between the target and the scene violates one or some of the relations listed in Table 8.1.

Experiment 1: The Effect of Relational Violations
on Object Detection

The primary purpose of this experiment, which I ran with Robert Mezzanotte and Jan Rabinowitz, was to determine if objects would be harder to detect if they violated one or more of the relations than if they did not. We were particularly interested in a comparison of the potency of violations of the semantic versus the physical relations. A violation of interposition would be severely disruptive to the processing of a scene, according to the physical-then-semantic proposals of, for example, Gibson (1966) or Winston (1970). None of the cited "bottom-up" accounts of scene perception have been developed to the point of yielding specific predictions of behavior. An assumption that an incorrect parsing made early in the processing of a scene would require more time for "backtracking" for its correction than one made relatively late in processing would yield a prediction of a greater disruptive effect from violations of physical relations. Such an analysis has been offered by Rumelhart (1977) of why "garden path" sentences ("The old man the boats") require more pauses in their reading than syntactically disambiguated sentences ("The merchants ship their wares").

Experiment 1 also allowed us to determine if the detection of normally positioned objects would be affected by the presence of violations from other objects. For example, in Fig. 8.3, would the sofa, undergoing violations of three relations, affect the detectability of an "innocent bystander" such as the hydrant? The object detection task is illustrated in Fig. 8.8. The subject first read the name of the target object and, when ready, initiated the trial by pressing a switch. A fixation point was then presented on a screen for 500 msec, immediately followed by a 150-msec flash of a slide of the scene. The 150-msec presentation duration of the scene was selected to be long enough to allow as much processing as possible within a single fixation but brief enough that we could be confident that the subject could not make a second eye fixation at the scene. The scene was, in turn, immediately followed by a cue (a dot) embedded in a mask. The position of the cue varied from trial to trial, but it always appeared at a position at which

Object Detection: Post-Stimulus Cueing

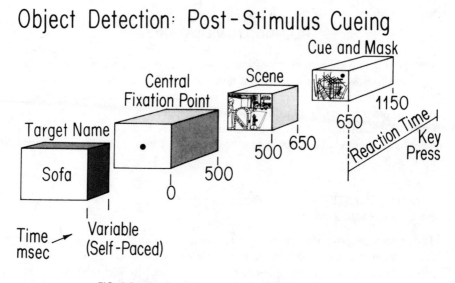

FIG. 8.8.   Sequence of events in the object detection task.

an object had been centered in the scene. On half the trials, the cue pointed to the object that corresponded to the target name. For example, if the subject was given the target name *fire hydrant,* then the cue on such a trial pointed to a position on the screen at which there had been a fire hydrant in the scene. The fire hydrant could be in a normal (base condition) position or undergoing one or more of the violations (violation conditions). On such a trial, the subject was to say "yes" into a voice key. On the other half of the trials, the cue pointed to a position at which a different object had occurred in the scene (e.g., a mailbox). On such a trial, the subject was to say "no." (In all the subsequent experiments, responses were made by depression of microswitch finger-keys.)

Ninety-six subjects each viewed 247 different scenes selected from 17 backgrounds and 42 object overlays. The cued object in each scene was either in a base condition (no violations) or was undergoing one of 10 violation conditions: 5 where the target violated only a single relation, 4 where two relations were violated, and 1 where three relations were violated. The target objects averaged approximately 2° in height and 1.6° in width. The scenes were 14° in width and 11° in height.

The number of scenes in each of the 10 violation conditions ranged between 14 and 27. A panel of three judges had previously rated the degree to which a given target violated the various relations—from "extremely obvious" (rating of 10) to "not present" (rating of 1). Scenes were selected for the various violation conditions to produce obvious (mean rating of 8.9) and subjectively equivalent degrees of violation. The 10 violation conditions and 1 base condition (42 scenes, one for each object) were also approximately equivalent with respect to their targets' degree of camouflage (rated masking of a target's critical features by the adjacent contours) and distance from fixation. The one exception to this was a higher camouflage rating for those targets violating the interposition relation. (However, this exception served to reinforce our finding of the absence of an effect of violating the interposition relation.)

Results: Object Detection.   The overall error rate of 31.2% was composed of a miss rate (responding no when the target was cued) of 43.3% and a false-alarm rate (responding yes when the target was not cued) of 19.2% (Fig. 8.9). In this task, subjects tended to respond no unless they could confidently make a positive identification. Because many of the targets were small, camouflaged, and in the periphery, a high overall miss rate resulted. Mean correct RT was 999 msec.

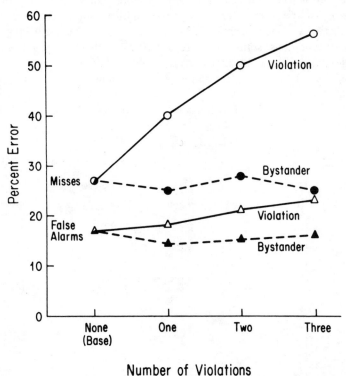

FIG. 8.9.   Mean percent misses (responding no when the cued object was the target) and false alarms (responding yes when the cued object was not the target) as a function of the number of violations in the scene and the condition of the cued object. The functions labeled "violation" are the data for cued objects undergoing violations; the functions labeled "bystander" are the data when the cued object was in a normal position but some other object in the scene was undergoing a violation.

Innocent bystanders were unaffected by the violations, but targets that violated a relation were identified with considerably lower accuracy than when in a base condition. The miss rate for the 10 violation conditions was 45.0% as compared to a 24.9% miss rate in the base condition. False-alarm rates were also higher by 2.6% in the violation conditions. The reaction times for correctly detecting a cued target in the base condition were, on the average, 31 msec faster than when the targets were undergoing a violation. I refer to this disruptive effect of the violations on detection of a target as a *violation cost*.

Figure 8.10 shows the miss rates for the individual violation conditions. More detailed comparisons of the various violation conditions will be discussed in another report, but it is apparent that despite considerable variability within conditions, violations of physical relations (support and interposition) did not interfere with object identification noticeably more than did violations of probability, size, and position. There was also a significant increase in error rates as the number of violations increased. Mean miss rates for the size, support, and probability conditions (solid line) increased 10.2% with an increase from one to three violations. It should be specifically noted that if size and probability violations, which are dependent on referential meaning, were added to the sup-

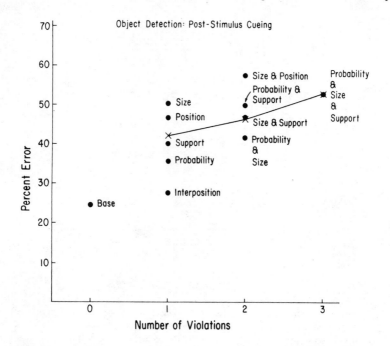

FIG. 8.10.   Mean percentage misses in detecting a cued target as a function of the number and kind of violated relations. The *X*s and the line connecting them are the mean miss rates for the size, support, and probability conditions. These conditions were run under all three levels of violation.

port violation, then the accuracy of detecting a target was reduced. As shown in Fig. 8.9, the false-alarm rates also increased with the number of violations.

The reaction times (Fig. 8.11) provided a picture similar to that supplied by the error data. Although the high error rates require that caution be exercised in interpreting RTs, a general speed-for-accuracy trade-off was ruled out by the longer RTs for the violation conditions. The one exception may be those scenes with both size and position violations. These scenes had the highest error rates— higher even than the triple-violation condition—but the RTs for this condition were the shortest. Thus, a speed-for-accuracy trade-off would have brought this condition more in line with the other two-violation conditions.

The violation cost cannot be attributed to a confounding of physical variables with the various violation conditions. When we composed the scenes, the 11 conditions (10 violation conditions and 1 base condition) had approximately equivalent specifications for: (1) distance of the target from the fixation point, (2) degree of (rated) camouflage of the target, and (3) size of the cued object. All three variables were significantly correlated with miss rates over the 247 scenes. The multiple correlation coefficient between these three variables and miss rates was .605; between them and RT, it was .399 ($p < .001$ in both cases). A multiple regression analysis was performed in which the effects of these variables were partialed out. Difference scores—between the residuals for a given set of targets

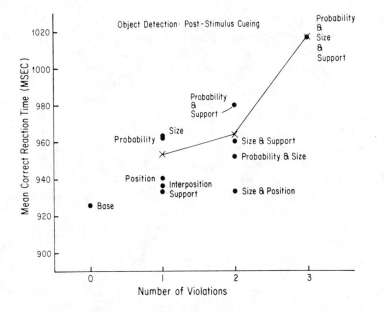

FIG. 8.11.   Mean correct reaction times for detecting a cued target (i.e., RTs for hits) as a function of the number and kind of violated relations. The solid line connecting the Xs represents the mean RTs for the size, support, and probability conditions only.

when those targets were undergoing a given violation and the residuals for that same set of targets when those targets were in base positions—were calculated. These difference scores were free of effects of the perceptibility of the individual targets included in a given violation condition. This analysis yielded results that were substantially the same as those shown in Figs. 8.10 and 8.11. The one exception was that violations of interposition showed no violation cost.

Discussion of the Violation Cost.   Objects undergoing a violation were harder to perceive than objects in a base position. The higher miss *and* false-alarm rates for such objects rule out "guessing" or "response bias" explanations of the miss rates. Such explanations would hold that subjects simply guessed "no" when they couldn't detect a target but did detect a violation. That is, they would respond no when they realized that a given unidentified blob, if it was a fire hydrant, would not belong in the scene they were looking at, or that it would be floating, and so on. Such a strategy would, indeed, increase the miss rate of targets undergoing a violation. Moreover, with this strategy, the miss rate would increase directly as a function of the number of violations. (The next experiment shows that the detection of incongruity is facilitated by an increase in the violations.) But this guessing explanation would also predict that a violation should *reduce* the false-alarm rate. However, as mentioned previously, false alarms were slightly more frequent and also slower (by 13 msec) for objects undergoing a violation than for objects in the base position.

The effects of familiarity are discussed in more detail later, but it should be noted that the violation cost was present throughout the experiment—on the very first trial that a background was presented as well as after several repetitions of the background.

The reduced perceptibility of targets undergoing a violation does not necessarily stand in contradiction to those studies showing earlier eye fixations during free scanning of pictures to targets placed in low-probability contexts (Loftus & Mackworth, 1978) or areas of high informativeness (e.g., Buswell, 1935; Mackworth & Morandi, 1967). Targets undergoing violations are harder to perceive, but once perceived, they are likely to be what is interesting about a scene.

The lack of an innocent-bystander effect should be contrasted with the deleterious effect on target detection of jumbling a scene (Biederman, 1972; Biederman et al., 1974). As was discussed with Hock et al.'s (1978) stimuli, it is possible that the difference between the two types of operations largely reflects a quantitative variation in the number (or proportion) of objects in a scene that are undergoing violations.

In another (control) experiment, the objects that were cued in Experiment 1 were shown to be readily identifiable in the absence of any context. (The presence of camouflage, and thus lateral inhibition, in the base scenes did not permit a useful comparison of the net effect of a base context compared to the absence of a context.) Because the cued objects in the present experiment (1) were often undergoing violations, it might have been in the subject's best interest simply to ignore the context. That under these conditions, a violation cost was obtained underscores the rapid, perhaps obligatory accessing of a schema. In terms of the model presented in Fig. 8.7, the effects of the semantic relations on object identification suggest that a top-down (right-to-left) arrow is needed from the schema to object identification. It also raises the possibility that the semantic relations may be accessed directly from feature tests, bypassing both the object identification stage and the physical relations. This route to a schema is discussed later.

Experiment 2: The Detection of Incongruity

What are the relative detection speeds of the violations themselves? The bottom-up model presented in Fig. 8.7 implies that violations of interposition and support would be detected more rapidly than violations of probability, position, or size. Furthermore, the addition of a semantic violation to a physical violation should not render the combined violation detectable any faster than the physical violation by itself. Thus, for example, the detection of the incongruity of a fire hydrant floating in a kitchen would not be any faster than the detection of that same hydrant when it was floating in a street. The sequence of events in a trial in the violation detection task (Fig. 8.12) was similar to that in the object detection task except that the positional cue preceded the scene and the object cued *always* corresponded to the name. So if the name was *fire hydrant*, the object that was cued would always be a fire hydrant. Thus the subject knew where to look and what object was to be judged before the scene was presented.

The subject responded with one key ("normal") if the target object was in a base setting and with another key ("violation") if it was violating any or several

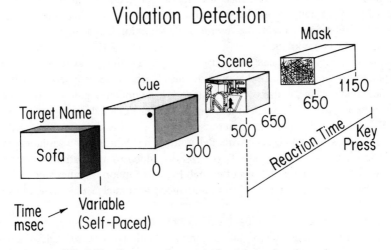

FIG. 8.12.   Sequence of events in the violation detection rask.

of the five relations. Subjects were instructed as to the nature of the relational violations and were shown several examples of each type. No subject ever complained of not understanding the task. I take the ease and naturalness of these judgments as evidence that these relations are involved in the normal perception of scenes.

Results and Discussion.   With the exception of the interposition violation, subjects were able to detect the violations within a single glance. (We have recently completed a study in which above-chance detection accuracy of semantic violations was obtained with masked presentations as brief as 37 msec.) The overall hit rate (detecting the presence of a violation) was 88%. The false-alarm rate (responses with the "violation" key when no violation was present) was 10.3%. Correct RTs averaged 851 msec. The fact that subjects can do this task so well, given only a 150-msec presentation of a picture of a scene, clearly demonstrates our notion that a schema can be achieved from a single glance at a scene. This result has important implications for theories stressing ecological validity that have placed a major explanatory status on eye-fixation sequences, or movement by the observer or the object. The perception of a scene requires neither. (Of course, one needs additional fixations for better acuity, and the perception of motion is of interest in its own right and, under some conditions, provides critical information for the recognition of the scene. But the point is that under most conditions, fixation sequences and motion are not necessary for scene perception.)

Figure 8.13 shows the RTs and Fig. 8.14 the miss rates for the base condition and the 10 violation conditions. As the number of violations increased from 1 to 2 to 3, a "redundancy gain" (Biederman & Checkosky, 1970) was apparent in that the speed (and accuracy) of violation detection increased. As in the object detection experiment, no evidence was found for a consistent priority in the processing of the support and interposition relations over the size, position, and probability relations. In fact, the interposition violation had a much higher miss rate than the other violations.

Redundancy gains can be used in determining whether several components—violations, in the present case—are processed sequentially or simultaneously ("in parallel"). For instance, a redundancy gain can rule out a sequential fixed-order model—the type of model depicted in Fig. 8.7. That model holds that support and interposition are processed before probability, position, and size. Thus, such a model implies no gain when a violation of a semantic relation—say, probability or size—is added to a violation of support. But our data show that violations of probability and support together and size and support together are detected faster (and more accurately) than violations of support alone.

A redundancy gain is compatible with both varying-order sequential detection and parallel detection of the different violations. The sequential model

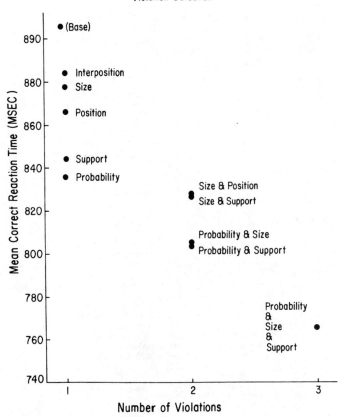

FIG. 8.13.   Mean correct reaction times for detecting the presence of any violation as a function of the number and kind of violated relations. The "base" condition is for the correct responses when a target object did not violate any relations.

predicts a redundancy gain by holding that the greater the number of relational violations in a scene, the more likely it is that one of those would be processed first (or earlier) in the sequence. The parallel model predicts a redundancy gain under the assumption that the different relations are processed concurrently, with times that are not perfectly correlated. If there is overlap in the distribution of times, then the greater the number of violations actually present, the more likely it is that on a given trial, a single one would be quickly detected. This parallel model can be likened to a horse race in which all the components (horses) start simultaneously, but the greater the number of horses, the more likely it is by chance alone that one will have a fast race. This experiment was not designed to distinguish between these models, but it should be noted that neither of them

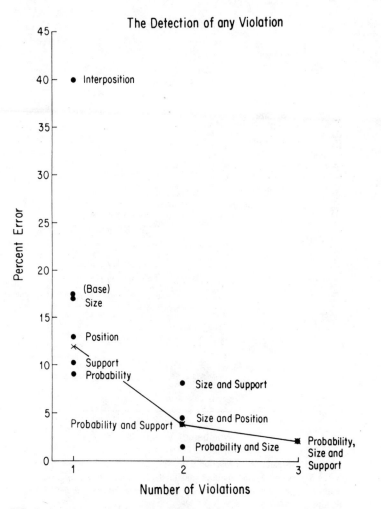

FIG. 8.14.   Mean percent error for detecting the presence of any violation as a function of the number and kind of violated relations. The "base" condition is for the errors when a target object did not violate any relations. The solid line connecting the Xs represents the means for the size, support, and probability conditions only.

posits a priority of the physical over the semantic relations. Priority, according to the varying-order sequential model, would be the earlier processing of a relation. If support was always processed prior to the semantic relations, then the varying-order sequential model reduces to the fixed-order sequential model, and no redundancy gain is predicted. Priority in the parallel model would result from one of the components being faster than the others. But if support always won the race, then no redundancy gain would have resulted.

Other aspects of the data from this experiment and the results of the next experiment lead us to favor the concurrent accessing of the physical and semantic relations as in the horse race model—with one important proviso. The horse race model stipulates that the processing of one component is independent of the processing of other components. The results of a selective attention experiment in which subjects were unable to ignore irrelevant violations cast doubt on the independence assumption.

Experiment 3: The Detection of Selected Violations

In this experiment, which I ran with Jan Rabinowitz, different groups of subjects were instructed to make a positive (yes) response to only one selected violation. One group of 12 subjects responded yes only if support was violated—that is, if the object appeared to be floating. Another group was instructed to respond only to violations of probability, and a third group was instructed to respond only to violations of size. What is the effect of irrelevant violations on the reaction times for detecting the relevant violation? When, for example, a subject attempts to judge whether an object is floating, is that judgment slowed when the object is unlikely to occur in the scene? Does it take longer to determine that a fire hydrant is floating in a street than floating in a kitchen? If so, then semantic information about probability is available when subjects are judging support. In a similar manner, when the object is *not* floating and the no response should be made, would the RTs be longer when the object is unlikely to occur in that scene?

Other than the instructions to detect only a single violation, the method and procedure were identical to the previous experiment where a subject was to detect *any* violation.

The results for the three conditions, which are labeled according to their relevant violations, are shown in Figs. 8.15, 8.16, and 8.17. These figures show the difference between the RT to an object undergoing a violation and the RT to that same object in a base condition. Because the different conditions did not have identical target sets, difference scores were used to control for target characteristics. The left panels in Figs. 8.15, 8.16, and 8.17 show the data for the yes responses—when the target did violate the instructed relation (relevant violation). The rightmost points in that panel are for scenes where irrelevant violation(s) were present as well. In Fig. 8.15, for example, these conditions are labeled ''Probability & Other Violations.'' That these RTs were longer (relative to their base RTs) than when only the relevant relation was being violated means that these irrelevant violations were interfering with the judgments. For example, Fig. 8.15 shows that RTs for the detection of a probability violation were approximately 70 msec longer when size was violated (in the probability and size condition) compared to when only probability was violated. A similar interference effect is apparent in the right panel, which shows the effects of the

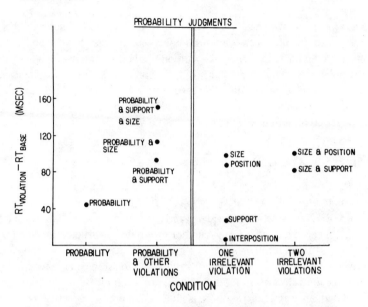

FIG. 8.15.   The effect of the presence of irrelevant violations (of size, support, position, and interposition) on the speed of correctly detecting the presence of a violation of probability in the selected violation detection task. The left panel shows the relative RTs for when violations of probability were present. The increase in RTs from probability to probability and other violations indicates an interference effect on detecting a violation of probability in the presence of other, irrelevant violations. For example, when the probability relation was violated, RTs were 45 msec longer than when those targets were not undergoing a violation (base condition). When, in addition to the violation of probability, size was also violated (in the probability and size condition) RTs were 115 msec longer than when those targets were in the base condition. The 70-msec increase as a function of the presence of a violation of size is the interference effect. The subtraction of the base RTs "corrects" the violation detection times for effects due to differences in target characteristics. This was necessary because the various violation conditions were composed of different sets of target objects. The right panel shows the correct "no" RTs when the probability relation was not violated and either one or two irrelevant violations were present. The positive differences here indicate that the irrelevant violations interfered with RTs for a no response. (The absolute height of the functions in the left panel cannot be directly interpreted because they include time differences between responding yes and responding no independent of the perceptual processing.)

number of violations for the no RTs—that is, when the instructed violation was not present. Thus, in Fig. 8.15, for example, when a target underwent a size violation—and only a size violation—approximately 100 msec more time was required to judge that probability was not violated compared to when that object was in a base condition. The sign, positive or negative, of the differences in the left panels in Figs. 8.15, 8.16, and 8.17 (when the relevant violation was present) cannot be directly interpreted, because the base scenes required a different

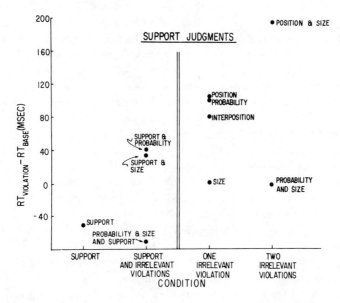

FIG. 8.16.   The effect of the presence of irrelevant violations (of probability, size, position, and interposition) on the speed of detecting the presence of a violation of support in the selected violation detection task. Refer to the caption for Fig. 8.15 for details of interpretation.

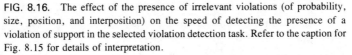
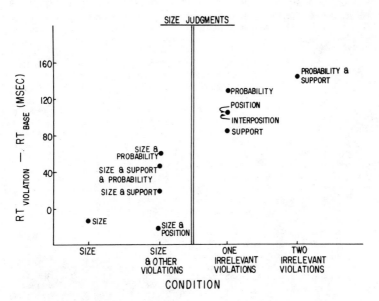

FIG. 8.17.   The effect of the presence of irrelevant violations (of probability, support, position, and interposition) on the speed of detecting the presence of a violation of size in the selected violation detection task. Refer to the caption for Fig. 8.15 for details of interpretation.

response (no) than the responses made when the relevant violation was present (yes). If there was a response bias favoring the yes response in this task, then negative difference scores (RT violation minus RT base), as were present in Fig. 8.16, could merely be a function of response bias. However, in the right panel, the same no response was made to both base scenes and irrelevant violations. Thus, the differences for these no responses are not confounded with response differences. The values are positive for every no condition for all three groups, giving clear indication of an interference effect from irrelevant violations.

In Figs. 8.15, 8.16, and 8.17, only two points depart from the picture of interference effects for the yes response. In Fig. 8.16, in judging whether support was violated, the triple violation of probability and size and support was faster than any of the other three yes conditions. Yet the triple-violation condition should have been at least as slow as the slowest of the other three conditions. Post hoc analysis of this experiment revealed that this group of subjects were using the *height of the cue* on the screen as a clue to the likelihood of support being violated. In this triple-violation condition, a large number of the targets were, in fact, high on the screen compared to the other conditions, and the strategy was successful. The targets in the other conditions with violations of support were not as high. The other condition that failed to yield an interference effect was the size and position condition for the size-judgment group shown in Fig. 8.17. We could find no satisfactory reason for this result other than sampling error.

The combined results from this experiment are shown in Fig. 8.18. The increase in the RT difference scores in the left panel (from relevant to relevant

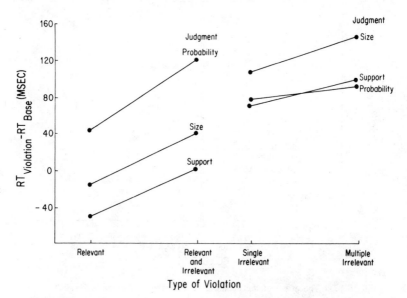

FIG. 8.18.   Combined data for the selected violation detection task as a function of the relevant violation. Refer to the caption for Fig. 8.15 for details of interpretation.

and irrelevant) and the positive values of the right panel all confirm an inter-ference effect.

The interference from irrelevant violations—the failure of selective attention—suggests not only that information about the different relations is available simultaneously but also that the relations are not accessed independently. This is what would be expected if the relations were accessed from an integrated representation—a schema. The failure of selective attention also suggests that the processing of these relations is obligatory (cf. Garner, 1974b): We can't help but see the object as floating or too large or unlikely to be in the scene.

HOW DO WE EVER GET TO THE TOP
IN TOP-DOWN PROCESSING?

Throughout this chapter I have used schemata in *deus ex machina* fashion whenever the effects of semantic relations were to be explained. Given that the scene is not exhaustively processed through all the levels of Fig. 8.7, how is a schema first achieved from that single glance? Although the final answer to this question is not at hand, we can outline three possible routes toward the construc-tion of a schema. These routes can be described in terms of the skipping of stages (short-circuiting) in Fig. 8.7 and various top-down effects in that same flowchart. Importantly, the routes are experimentally tractable.

Route 1: From Object Identification to Schema
(Exp. 4)

One route to a schema is through an initial identification of one (or more) of the more discriminable objects in a scene. This processing of the first object(s) would be independent of the processing of other objects. The implication of this route is that once an object is identified in a scene, we may quickly know the kind of company it keeps. It is as if a schema (or at least its top levels) could be directly accessed from object identification without processing the relations among the objects.

Richard Teitelbaum, Robert Mezzanotte, Gary Klatsky, and I tested the exis-tence of this route in an experiment designed to determine if information about an object's real-world setting is so accessible as to cause a "pop-out" category effect in visual detection even when the objects do not form a scene. Such effects were described by Egeth, Jonides, and Wall (1972) in a task in which the detectability of a digit was unrelated to the number of letters in the display but was directly related to the number of nontarget digits. Phenomenally, the digit appeared to "pop out" from a field of letters. Would this phenomenon occur with an object that was not likely to be found in the same setting as other objects in the field? Rapid accessing of probabilistic or setting information would not necessarily result in a "pop-out" effect. In the experiment on object identification (Exp. 1), low-probability objects were detected *less* accurately than objects that were probable in the scene. What we were primarily interested in was whether there would be *any* effect of the relation between the setting of the target and the setting of the field.

A design similar to the one employed by Egeth et al. (1972) was used: Subjects attempted to detect a target object (specified by name) in a 100-msec display of from one to six pictures of objects arranged around an imaginary clock-face. (Sometimes the "object" would actually be a small scene or compound of objects—e.g., a soldier carrying a gun.) As in the Egeth et al. (1972) experiments, a key variable was the relation between the target and field objects. In the *high-probability* display-set condition, the items in the display would be from a setting that could have contained the target. For example, the target could be "bassinet," and a display with three objects might contain a baby bottle, a rattle, and a bassinet (on a present trial) as shown in Fig. 8.19. On a trial when the target was not in the display (absent trial), a baby might be shown instead of the bassinet. All these objects could have come from a nursery. In the *low-probability* display condition, the field objects would all be likely to come from one kind of scene—just as in the first type. However, here the field items would be from a scene other than one that would include the target. For example, as Fig. 8.20 shows, with "bassinet" as the target, the other objects could be a hand grenade, a soldier, a tank, a helicopter, or a bazooka. There were 12 settings from which the objects were sampled: battlefield, kitchen, baseball field, living room, office, city street, child's nursery, backyard, campsite, farm, bathroom, and orchestra.

The relation between target and field setting did affect processing. Fig. 8.21 shows the error rates and Fig. 8.22 shows the RTs. The most striking feature

FIG. 8.19.   An example of a display with three objects in Exp. 4. If "bassinet" were the target, then this display would be a high-probability, target-present trial. If "crib" were the target, then this display would be a high-probability, target-absent trial. If "bazooka" were the target, then this display would be for a low-probability, target-absent trial.

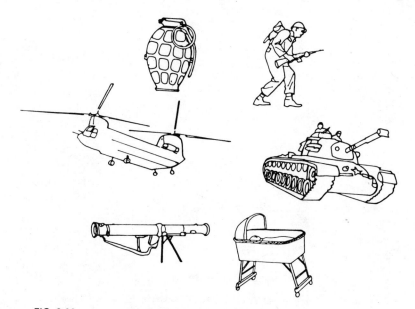

FIG. 8.20.   An example of a display with six objects in Exp. 4. With "bassinet" as the target, this display would be for a low-probability, target-present trial.

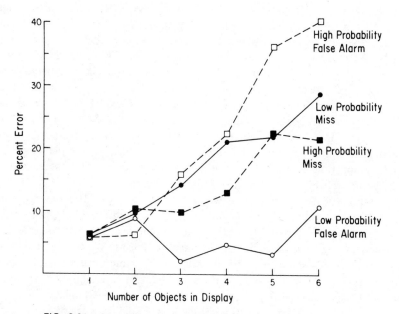

FIG. 8.21.   Mean miss and false-alarm rates in Exp. 4 as a function of the number of objects in the display and probability of the target object coming from a setting with the other objects in the display.

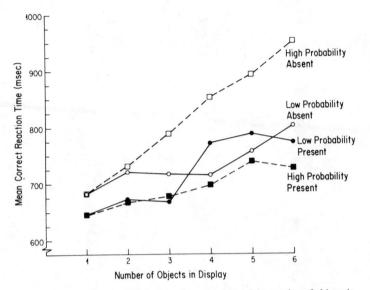

FIG. 8.22.   Mean correct RTs in Exp. 4 as a function of the number of objects in the display, the probability of the target, and whether the target was present or absent.

about these data is the interaction between probability and trial type (presence versus absence). High-probability targets were less likely to be missed than low-probability targets but high-probability targets, when not present in the display, yielded dramatically higher false alarm rates than low-probability targets. When a target was present in the display, the RT for its detection was shorter when it was of high probability than of low probability. When absent, however, high-probability targets were responded to more slowly than low-probability targets. The ordering of conditions can be explained by a model in which there is a bias to judge a target as being present when it is probable and absent when it is improbable. However, quantitatively, subjects were more accurate (higher d's) with low probability targets than high probability targets, a result incompatible with the data from Experiment 1. In that experiment, targets undergoing probability violations were harder to *see*, in that the violations resulted in higher false-alarm rates as well as higher miss rates. Part of our current experimental effort is designed toward resolving these differences. Specifically, we are exploring the possibility that improbable objects are only more difficult to see when they are in a scene-like arrangement of objects. We are also exploring why results consistent with a pop out effect (i.e., more accurate performance with low probability items) were obtained only with the false-alarm rates—where they would be least expected. Typically, if processing is found to be independent of display size, it is when subjects are responding to the presence of a target, not to its absence (Egeth, *et al.*, 1972; Neisser, 1963).

Prior to the actual experimental trials, subjects were familiarized with the names and pictures of all the objects. In this familiarization phase, each object was shown for 3 seconds along with its name. For half the subjects during this phase, the targets were grouped according to their setting, and the name for the setting (e.g., *battlefield*) was provided along with the target name. The other half of the subjects viewed the objects (and their names) in a random-appearing order without any labels for the settings. There was no effect of this variation in the familiarization phase. Thus, not only was there an effect of variations in the probability of a target to the other objects in the field, but as in previous experiments (e.g., Biederman et al., 1973), the employment of the probabilistic relations was spontaneous.

In terms of the flowchart of Fig. 8.7, the rapid utilization of probabilistic relations implies that such information can be accessed directly from object identification without any requirements from the physical parsing stage. Route 1 seems viable.

Route 2: Scene-Emergent Features

A second route to a schema might be via features that are not those of individual objects but "emerge" as objects are brought into relation to each other to form a scene. The form of such features is not known. Some possibilities have been suggested by Palmer (1975) in a discussion of what remains when a picture is defocused and by Pomerantz, Sager, and Stoever (1977) in a discussion of characteristic contours that emerge from interacting line segments. But does one need to posit scene-emergent features at all?

An answer to this question could be obtained from an experiment in which the features of the objects comprising a scene were so degraded that they were individually unrecognizable (at some specified exposure duration). Can conditions be discovered under which these objects become identifiable when placed together to form a scene? If such conditions are discovered, then it implies that individual features from different parts of the visual field can combine to elicit a schema for a group of objects that, in turn, can exert a top-down effect to influence identification. By this account, the object identification stage shown in Fig. 8.7 would be short-circuited. Whether features could directly activate semantic relations without passing through a physical parsing stage could be tested by determining whether a violation of a physical relation in a degraded scene prevents the target from being identified.

We are currently exploring various techniques to produce the desired degradation. By converting various objects to basic cylindrical or rectilinear bodies, Robert Mezzanotte has produced Figs. 8.23 and 8.24. These scenes meet the criteria of having bodies that are individually unidentifiable (in terms of their referent when placed in the scene) but, when placed together, can be semantically interpretable. Figure 8.25, drawn by Sheldon Tetewsky, illustrates another

FIG. 8.23. *Downtown Buffalo*. Drawn by Robert Mezzanotte by converting objects in a photograph to basic rectilinear or cylindrical bodies.

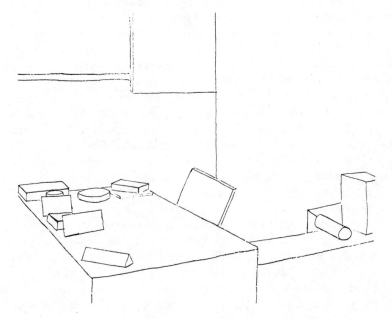

FIG. 8.24. *Office*, drawn by Robert Mezzanotte.

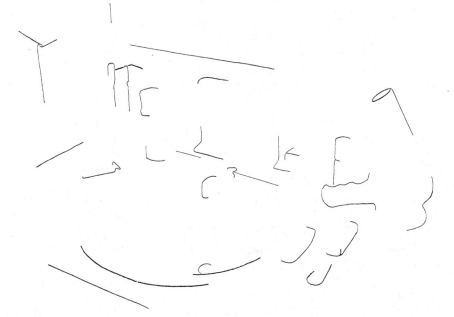

FIG. 8.25. Sample degraded scene drawn by Sheldon Tetewsky to test for the existence of scene-emergent features. Scene is that of a bathroom sink. (Look hard.)

way in which scenes can be constructed by the deletion of critical contours where even the physical parsing (present in Figs. 8.23 and 8.24) might be defeated. Route 2 looks promising, but much more study is needed.

Route 3: From Spatial Integration (Exp. 5)

Experiment 4 established that object identification could be affected by semantic information in displays where the objects did not comprise a spatially integrated scene. Would a spatial integration of semantically unrelated objects be sufficient to facilitate identification? Phenomenologically, a spatial integration can be achieved by superimposing a display of unrelated objects (as in Fig. 8.26a) onto a depthlike background (as in Fig. 8.26b). Would the scenelike arrangement of Fig. 8.26b be sufficient to facilitate the identification of the objects?

The results of our first tests of this issue suggest that a spatial integration is insufficient for the facilitation of identification. In this study, each subject viewed 63 scenes composed of six unrelated objects superimposed over one of three backgrounds: (1) a *blank* background (Fig. 8.26a); (2) a *depth* background, which resembled a path (as in Fig. 8.26b), a corridor, or tracks and which conferred a depth effect; (3) a nondepth *grid* that contained approximately the same number and types of lines as the corresponding depth background. Figure 8.26c shows the grid background corresponding to the path. The grid provided a

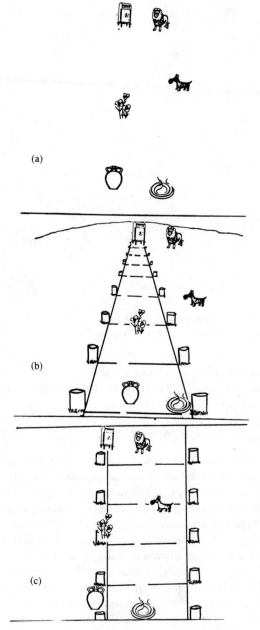

(a)

(b)

(c)

FIG. 8.26. Sample stimuli from the experiment on the effect of background gradients on object identification. (a) Blank control background. (b) Depth background. (c) Nondepth control grid background.

rough control for physical confusion or lateral inhibitory effects for the depth backgrounds. The scenes subtended a visual angle of approximately 13° horizontally and 8° vertically. Targets were all less than 1°. The poststimulus cuing technique was used with a 200-msec scene presentation duration. The subject was to respond yes if the cue designated the target object named prior to viewing the display.

Surprisingly, the depth background resulted in the *highest* error rate—49% compared to the 39% error rates for both the grid and blank backgrounds. Physical confusion or lateral inhibition effects are ruled out by the equivalence of the blank and grid conditions. The results are compatible with the idea that a consistent perspective in depth will not have a beneficial effect unless the depth can aid in the achievement (or is a consequence) of some unitary semantic representation of the scene. For example, if the objects could comprise a kitchen scene, then the perspective information could aid in the achievement of a schema for the kitchen that, in turn, might facilitate the recognition of some of the objects. With the present depth stimuli, however, no such schematic representation could readily be achieved. In fact, the depth background may have served as some large, distracting object in that subjects tried to integrate the unrelated items to it. In terms of the flowchart presented in Fig. 8.7, this result implies that Route 3 is unlikely—that we do not need to draw an arrow from the physical relations stage to object identification. However, caveats are in order. This was not a sensitive experiment. Obviously, more work is needed on this problem.

EXPECTANCY AND FAMILIARITY:
SOME NULL RESULTS

Two more routes to schema elicitation that have been conspicuously missing from consideration in this chapter are those of prior expectancy and familiarity. Because the experiments discussed up to this point have employed procedures in which the subject was uncertain as to the scene that was to be presented on a given trial and have yielded results that were not dependent on repetition of the scenes, it was unnecessary to appeal to expectancy or familiarity to account for the schematic effects that were observed in these experiments. But could expectancy and familiarity offer alternative routes toward schema elicitation?

There is typically a degree of predictability (or expectancy) from one glance to the next in our visual world. We might expect to see a living room when we entered a house for the first time—not a Burger King. Richard Teitelbaum, Robert Mezzanotte, and I experimentally tested whether such predictability could affect the processing of a scene in our task situations. Prior to viewing a scene, a subject was primed by being told that the scene would be, for example, a kitchen. Would the perception of a kitchen be faster and more accurate if such a prime were provided? The specific theoretical issue under scrutiny here is whether generic routes to a schema exist that, if activated in advance, could facilitate perception.

With respect to familiarity, it is the case that often—but not always—we have previously experienced the scenes that we encounter in our day-to-day lives. Can our perception capitalize on this experience? Again, we posed this question in the context of our experimental paradigms by determining if subjects could capitalize upon the residue of up to four fixations of a scene background presented at varying intervals. To be more specific, suppose that a scene was viewed for 100 msec (thus allowing only a single fixation) on Trial 10. Now if that scene were presented again on Trial 26, (16 scenes and a few minutes later), and again on Trial 56, and again on Trial 80, would its perceptibility be increased as a consequence of its prior presentations? An affirmative answer to this question would require not only a system with a remarkably large storage capacity but also one in which the prior exposure of specific scenes could be accessed rapidly enough to affect the time course of perception.

We have run both the object detection and the violation detection tasks in exploring these issues. The procedure for the object detection task (Exp. 6) corresponded to that of Exp. 1 (Fig. 8.8) except that on half of the trials (viz., the *primed* trials), a verbal description of the scene would appear on a video terminal along with the name of the target (e.g., "Scene: City street corner, Target: Sofa"). On an *unprimed* trial, the word *blank* would follow the word *scene*. This experiment also differed from Exp. 1 in using a briefer scene exposure duration (100 msec).

Each of the 64 subjects viewed 208 scenes. Each scene background was repeated four times (nonconsecutively) with a mean lag of 26 scenes. That is, on the average, 26 scenes would intervene between one exposure of a scene's background and the next. The purpose of the repetition variable was to study the effects of repeating the scene background as was typically done in the previous experiments. Thus, when a given background scene was repeated, the subject would typically attempt to detect an object different from the one that was the target previously for that scene and with a 50–50 chance of making a different response. And if targets were undergoing violations on successive repetitions of a scene, the violations generally would differ. The positions of the cues would also differ. Thus on Trial 20, a city street corner scene might be presented with the fire hydrant on top of the mailbox as a target, but when presented 30 trials later, the hydrant would be gone; the target object might be a truck, and the truck might be in a normal position (cued in the street), or it might be of inappropriate size.

The experimental scenes were split into two sets of 14 backgrounds each. A given subject would view the scenes from one set of 14 backgrounds, each presented four times, over the first half of the experiment. To distinguish general learning effects—for example, learning the assignment of responses to keys— from effects attributable to the accessing of the specific backgrounds, the subject would view the other set of 14 backgrounds only in the second half of the experiment. Given that learning did occur over the four presentations in the first half, if what was learned was not specific to the scene but general to the task, then this learning should have transferred to performance with the second set of scenes. If, however, what was learned with the first set was faster or better accessing of the specific scene backgrounds, then the gains in performance over the first half should not show complete transfer to the second half.

Figures 8.27 and 8.28 show that learning during the first half of the experiment did occur as evidenced by the decline in errors and mean correct reaction times (RTs) with exposures of a scene's background. However, little if any of this learning could be attributable to faster or better accessing of the specific scene backgrounds, because the reduction in RTs and errors that occurred over the four exposures in the first half of the experiment showed almost complete transfer to the first exposure (of the new scenes) in the second half.

There was no beneficial effect of priming. (If anything, presentation of the prime interfered with the first presentation or two of a scene.) This suggests: (1) that the most generic levels of a schema cannot be activated (to influence perception) by a verbal descriptor; or (2) that the other routes to schema activation work so well that no help from a prime is needed. Although the primes were ineffec-

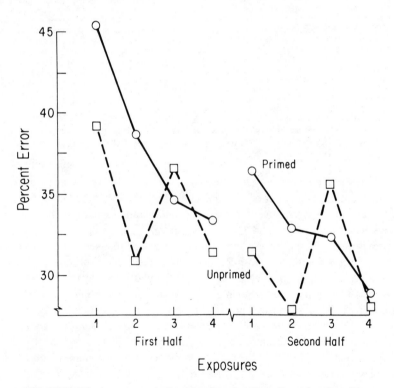

FIG. 8.27.   Mean percent errors for object detection (Exp. 6) as a function of the number of exposures of the scene background and priming condition. Different sets of backgrounds were used for the first and second halves.

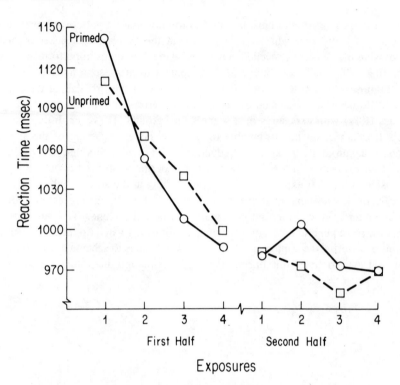

FIG. 8.28.   Mean correct reaction times for object detection (Exp. 6) as a function of the number of exposures of the scene background and priming conditions. Different sets of backgrounds were used for the first and second halves.

tive, schemata for these scenes *were* activated as evidenced by an effect of the violations of semantic relations. Targets undergoing such violations (viz., probability, position, and size) were missed at a significantly higher rate than targets in a base condition—36.7% and 31.4%, respectively. This violation cost was stable over exposures. That is, these scenes were processed to a semantic level but did not leave a residue that could influence performance on a subsequent trial.

The lack of any appreciable scene (background) specific transfer effects in Exp. 6 could be partly attributable to the nature of the object detection task. Although the background was processed perceptually, as evidenced by the violation cost, performance on an object detection task does not *require* accessing the background. Thus a violation detection experiment (7) was run with a design similar to that used for Exp. 2 (Fig. 8.12). Violation detection does require use of the background. Experiment 7 differed from Exp. 2 in that only the single violations of size, support, and position as well as size and support and size and position double violations were included. (The interposition violation was omitted because its detection was so difficult, and the probability violation was omitted because subjects could have inferred the correct response from the target name and scene descriptor.) As in Exp. 6 on object detection, on half the trials the name of the background scene was presented along with the target name. Also, as in Exp. 6, the scenes were presented for 100 msec, and the scenes were divided into two sets to evaluate transfer between first and second halves of the experiment. Finally, there were five exposures of each background.

Figures 8.29 and 8.30 show the mean error rates and RTs for this experiment. As in Exp. 6, there was no facilitation from priming (but, again, some early interference) and no appreciable transfer of specific background effects from the first to the second halves of the experiments.

What are the limits to the generalizability of our finding that verbal priming and familiarity effects are lacking? With long prior exposures (e.g., 5 minutes) of the scenes, wouldn't performance on these tasks improve? Indeed, those of us who run these experiments can often do extremely well on the violation detection task if we are given a prime. Once we know where the fixation point is, we can recall the scene and make a fairly accurate judgment as to whether the target

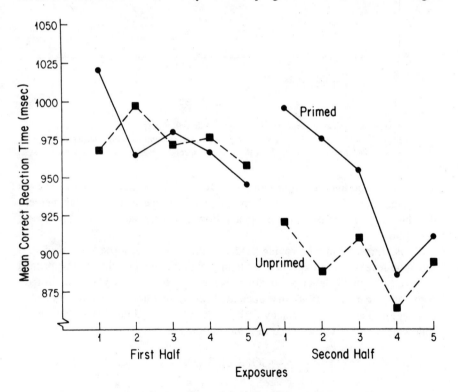

FIG. 8.29.   Mean correct reaction times for violation detection (Exp. 7) as a function of the number of exposures of the scene background and priming conditions. Different sets of backgrounds were used for the first and second halves.

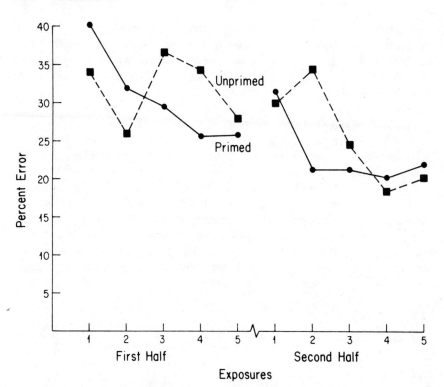

FIG. 8.30.   Mean percent errors for violation detection (Exp. 7) as a function of
the number of exposures of the scene background and priming condition. Different
sets of backgrounds were used for the first and second halves.

object would be undergoing a violation. But we can do this without ever even
seeing the scene! That is, the memory for specific scenes may not affect perception but some inferential process that follows, or proceeds in the absence of,
perception.

Thus, Exps. 6 and 7 provide evidence that a scene can be processed to a
semantic level on four exposures without yielding a memory that can be primed
or accessed quickly enough to affect perception or inference on the fifth. A
common perceptual activity that documents our contention that we don't need to
rely on familiarity or expectancy is the apparent ease and rapidity of perception
following a cut to a new scene in a motion picture.

CONCLUSION

From a single fixation at a picture of a novel scene, a viewer can often extract
sufficient information to comprehend that scene—if we use the effects of violating semantic relations as measures of comprehension. Neither a sequence of eye

movements nor motion in the scene or the observer is necessary for this process-ing. Semantic relations are accessed at least as rapidly as relations reflecting the pervasive physical constraints of interposition and support that are not dependent on referential meaning. The semantic relations appear to come integrated with the physical relations. It is convenient to talk about scene schemata in trying to describe this rapid accessing of semantic information. The schema itself may be elicited through scene-emergent features and the probabilistic relations among objects. The mechanisms for perceiving and interpreting real-world scenes can be triggered so quickly and efficiently that conditions can readily be found in which an expectancy for a scene or familiarity with it is neither necessary nor even helpful toward its perception.

ACKNOWLEDGMENTS

This research was supported by National Institutes of Mental Health Grant MH33283 and by U.S. Army Institute of Behavioral and Social Sciences Grant MDA903-A-G-0003. I have been fortunate to have had a number of excellent students who have provided invaluable assistance to this work: Arnold L. Glass, Jan C. Rabinowitz, Robert J. Mez-zanotte, Richard C. Teitelbaum, Lawrence Malcus, Elizabeth J. Gajewski, Gary J. Klatsky, Carl M. Francolini, and Dana Plude. James R. Pomerantz, Michael Kubovy, and Howard Hock made a number of helpful comments and suggestions on an earlier draft.

9 Levels of Perceptual Organization

Julian Hochberg
Columbia University

ABSTRACT

Perceptual organization refers to constraints on what is perceived (e.g., with visual angle held constant, apparent size and apparent distance covary; apparent figural quality varies with apparent simplicity of configuration). Three major classes of organizational phenomena (space, shape/form, and movement) have been important to perceptual theory. Theories of organization differ in the roles assigned to *stimulus structure* (intrastimulus constraints) and to *mental structure* (interresponse constraints) and on the degree of *wholism* posited (i.e., the size of the structure within which constraints are strong). The major perceptual theories are analyzed in these terms. Phenomena are reviewed that very sharply limit the tenability of any theory to which spatial or temporal wholism is important and that clearly demonstrate mental structure in the absence of stimulus structure.

The class of theory proposed by J. S. Mill and Helmholtz—that we perceive by fitting the most likely or expected (global) object or event to the sampled (local) sensory components—remains the one best suited to the widest range of organizational phenomena (including the Gestalt phenomena). Mental structure does not simply reflect physical (stimulus) structure, however, and the different levels of organization must be separated before such theories can be seriously considered and developed.

INTRODUCTION

Organization has meant very different things to different theorists and to the same theorists at different times. In the first part of this chapter, I try to classify the major ways in which organization has been used in the study of perception and to place the major theories in the appropriate cells of this classification scheme. In the second part, I review a body of recent data that, to my mind, rule out some of the cells and strongly support others (mostly the one that I have come to occupy, along with other right-thinking psychologists.) Two points in preview:

1. The phenomena of perceptual organization cannot be encompassed by a single rubric, for a nontrivial reason: The interactions that are responsible for organization occur at different levels and involve different processes. To try to fit a single function to the disorderly mixture and interaction of these different kinds of organization can only be done by ruling out every exception to that function on increasingly ad hoc grounds. The domains within which relatively compact explanatory systems can be applied must first be isolated by experiment, not by definition.

2. Many of the sources of organization contribute only indirectly, accidentally, or even serve as impediments to what I consider to be the most important subject matter of "visual" perception—namely *schematic maps* (which are contingent expectations of what one will see if one looks here or there) and *schematic events* (contingent expectations of what one will see *when,* in a changing visual world). Even so, we must try to identify such sources, because their contribution contaminates what we take to be the data of perceptual organization, and because they offer opportunities to rule out some classes of theory.

CLASSIFICATION OF THEORIES
OF ORGANIZATION

First, we consider classes of phenomena to which theories of organization have addressed themselves.

Classes of Organizational Phenomena

Historically, there have been three main classes of organizational phenomena in visual perception: organization of space, of shape/form, and of movement. In each, the organization consists of constraints on what will most likely be perceived—that is, on what the appearance of one aspect of a perceived object or event implies about the appearance of other aspects. I sketch them very briefly in turn.

Space.   The major constraints in spatial perception are those of size/distance, slant/shape, and distance/velocity. That is, for a given retinal image, when cues to size or distance, shape or slant, and distance or velocity are varied, apparent size is found to vary with apparent distance, apparent shape varies with apparent slant, and apparent velocity varies with apparent distance. It is usually assumed that these constraints are exhibited by proximal stimulation. That is, in the normal physical environment, the proximal stimulation specifies invariants between its terms (e.g., for an object that subtends a given visual angle, the ratio of the distal object's size to the object's distance is a constant). Note that *all theories, from at least Berkeley's on, assume that the proximal stimulus pattern normally contains enough information to account for the adult viewer's response.* That is, no clairvoyance or other ESP is invoked by any theory. The theories differ only in their predilections about how that information is used.

According to some of the theories discussed, responses like perceived size and perceived distance vary together because they are subject to constraints internal to the organism that comprise a mental structure, so that the responses covary even when the constraints are not given in the stimulus pattern. For example, if the viewer is led somehow to perceive an object as changing its distance although the stimulus pattern itself remains unchanged, the object's apparent size then changes as well.

From the point of view of theories that propose and deal with mental structure (which means the interresponse constraints already described), it is necessary to introduce abnormally impoverished stimulus patterns if we are to show the existence and nature of mental structure, because in normal circumstances there is enough information in stimulation to make it theoretically uneconomical to introduce such constraints as mental structures. To rule out of consideration either impoverished (ecologically unrepresentative) stimulus situations or abnormal perceptions (e.g., illusions) makes mental structure (i.e., organism-furnished organization) unstudiable. That is, it prejudges the question of whether mental structures exist and precludes their study if they do exist.

Shape/Form.   By a shape, I mean a silhouette or projected pattern; by a form, I mean a solid or volume. Both are classifications of some set of spatial points or regions into one class (object, group, and so forth) rather than another. Not all possible classifications that are permitted by the physical stimulus are equally available as perceptions. First, for example, there are the flip-flop figure–ground phenomena, in which it is partially true that only one object will be given shape by a contour at one time or place: That is, at any point on the contour of Fig. 9.1A, we see a vase or faces, but usually not both. Second, there are the similar ''grouping'' phenomena that occur when subjects are asked which

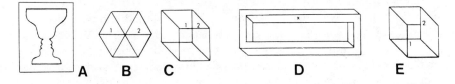

FIG. 9.1.   Organization, impossible figures and local depth cues.

dots belong together. In both cases, the relative strengths of the alternative perceptual outcomes appear to be affected by the configuration of the stimulus pattern. How wholistic the constraints exerted by such an overall configuration of object or scene may be and which rubric best summarizes these phenomena of organization are empirical questions. They are not questions to be answered either by fiat or by definition.

Movement. I mentioned under "Space" earlier, that there are distance/velocity constraints. In addition to these constraints, there is a set of problems that arise from the fact that depending on what the viewer takes to be stationary, the same pattern of retinal motions can be perceived in quite different ways. In normal viewing conditions, we usually perceive the invariant world as in fact invariant under a transformation that is provided by our own head or eye movements. In abnormal (impoverished) conditions, hierarchical vector-extraction principles have been offered (Johansson, 1950, 1977) that seem to subsume the normal case under a single organizational rubric. Whether there is a single domain of phenomena to be fit under such a rubric (rather than multiple determinants of different levels of processing that happen to produce perceptual phenomena that approximate vector extraction under Johansson's conditions and that may combine very differently under more normal conditions) is still very much an empirical question. If the Gibsonian position is that we should not study artificial situations, it is hard to see how the Johansson experiments are to be exempted from that injunction.

The three kinds of organization I have sketched are those of spatial organization (e.g., size/distance), Gestalt organization (e.g., shape/form constraints), and Johansson's hierarchical movement organization. The list is surely not exhaustive (e.g., it does not include color, to which it could easily be extended), but it suffices to show that there is a large area of phenomena and relationships to which the major theories were intended to apply. In the next section, I remind you how each was tried.

Theories of Organization

I distinguish three attributes of an organizational theory—whether it is: (1) a *stimulus structure theory,* (2) a *mental structure theory,* and/or (3) a *wholistic theory.* (I myself have been +, +, and − on this checklist for the past decade; Hochberg, 1968). Note that in general any theory will fall into more than one classification and will be + on more than one attribute.

The term *stimulus structure,* as I use it, refers to the intrastimulus constraints in the stimulation that are normally provided to our sense organs by the world. For example, an approaching object projects an expanding retinal image, so that cues in the stimulation as to the object's distance are correlated with the visual angle that the object subtends at the eye; for another example, apples are roughly spheroidal, so that the shape of a portion of one that is partially hidden from view can be predicted better than chance.

The term *mental structure,* as I use it, refers to the interresponse (or intraperceptual) constraints that can be attributed neither to structure in the present stimulation nor to the characteristics of sensory response to that stimulation (Hochberg, 1956, 1974a). Thus, mental structure involving size/distance constraints would (as already noted) be manifested if an object's perceived size and perceived distance are found to covary even when the entire retinal image remains unchanged in any way.

The term *wholistic,* as I use it, refers to the size of the structure within which constraints are strong. In Helmholtz's infamously "atomistic" sensory theory, each fundamental point sensation was taken to be independent of its neighbors; in Gestalt theory, the whole form of a configuration constrains the appearance of the parts, so that those appearances were not thought to be free to vary independently. In Gibson's theory, the constraints over a spatially and temporally extended stimulus structure (e.g., the gradient of texture density over a sector of the optic array) comprise a unitary source of stimulus information about the layout of surfaces in the world. In general, the bounds over which wholistic theories extend their analyses have not been well defined.

Stimulus Structure Theories.   The physical nature of the distal objects that we are likely to encounter and the probabilistic "laws" of environmental or ecological physics place constraints on the patterns of proximal stimulation that we are likely to receive under normal conditions.

1. The theories of Helmholtz, Brunswik, and Hebb (in principle, though not in practice) represent variations of the *classical approach to perception* (Hochberg, 1979). According to this approach, we perceive those objects or events that would, under normal conditions, most likely produce the sensory stimulation we receive. With normal seeing conditions, therefore, and an ecologically representative sample of the world, the viewer's sensory systems are "transparent" to the physical world. To Helmholtz and Hebb, who were also concerned with what the organism contributes to structure, it is important to know what structure is contained in the proximal stimulation and to know, too, the constraints imposed by our sensory limitations, inasmuch as these are the starting point of whatever contribution the organism may make. Helmholtz therefore placed great emphasis on the dynamic, movement-based information about objects and scenes that is available to active perceivers in the proximal stimulus distributions that they receive over time. Cassirer (1944) showed that Helmholtz's notions, when expressed in group theory, concern invariance under transformation; and Hebb (in his phase sequences argument, 1949) attempted to devise neural schemes for dealing with such transformations over time.

Because the perceiver would normally learn to perceive as veridically as possible, Brunswik considered proximal stimulation and neural mechanisms as "merely mediating variables"; if our perceptions are normally so distally focused (1956), what need is there to study the proximal stimulus except when perceptual achievement is poor? The psychologist's first task evidently is to survey the world and to find out, by experiments that are ecologically representative of conditions in that world, how good perception is in what circumstances. By contrast, Gibson, in his "global psychophysics" days (1950), proposed to turn the problem around and ask what stimulus information might exist in the light at the eye that would permit the organism to achieve perfect veridical perception; the answers to that question would provide the starting point for more adequate theories of perceptual processing. I discuss that proposal shortly; I do not address the neo-Gibsonian position on this matter because I have not yet grasped why "direct realists" are concerned with proximal stimulus information in the first place. That is, unless they undertake to explain the mechanisms that achieve distal focus from proximal stimulation, I cannot see why they do not, with Brunswik, concern themselves primarily with distal focus and ecological achievement.

To Helmholtz, Brunswik, and Hebb, the physical organization of stimulation is reflected in mental structure. For example, corresponding to the physical size/distance constraints in stimulation, the perceiver has acquired (through perceptual learning) internal constraints that link perceived size and perceived distance. These internal constraints are in turn evidenced in our perceptions, so that our perceptions are in this sense—the sense that intervening mechanisms are involved—"indirect." The constraints in space perception, shape perception, and movement perception reflect and reveal the structure that the perceiver brings to each stimulus pattern, by these theories. All of these theories are +, +, − on my checklist.

Note that there are two distinct components to this approach: First, there is *local sensory input*. Helmholtz's (forgivable) first assumption was that punctiform sensory input would be the simplest basis for the system to work upon, but that assumption is not viable today; nor do Hebb and later protagonists of this type of approach rely on such small receptive channels. (Read almost any issue of *Vision Research* to find retina-wide schemes for processing "local" input.) Second, there is *integrative mental structure*. Helmholtz's theory of space and motion perception, empiricist though it is, should be read with Kant's "schemata" in mind (Helmholtz's teacher Müller and his father were both Kantians); perceivers perform unconscious calculations or inferences upon their sensory data, with the constraints of size/distance, distance/velocity, and so on as their premises.

2. The Gestalt psychologists announced that the major phenomena of shape/form perception were completely beyond any possible Helmholtzian account, but we will see shortly that this claim was a premature, self-proclaimed victory. In

fact, Brunswik countered that the Gestalt laws were merely aspects of stimulus organization, reflecting the probability that any parts of the visual field belonged to the same object. We see later that this Helmholtzian argument becomes more plausible, the more we learn about Gestalt organization. Gestalt theory is +, +, + on my checklist.

3. To Gibson, the information in the proximal pattern (or optic array) potentially supplies the perceiver with a direct basis for any attribute of the physical world he or she can perceive. The organization of the stimulus information is therefore sufficient to account for perception.

This approach has come to be called a *direct theory* of perception, because its proponents often claim that our sensory systems respond directly to the information about the permanent properties of objects and layouts that is offered by the flux of stimulation that the active perceiver receives from the world. It is asserted that we pick up the size, shape, and more evolutionarily important characteristics afforded by the objects in our environment as directly as Helmholtz thought we picked up brightness or hue. (In fairness to Helmholtz, however, and to some degree depriving subsequent theoreticians of a straw man, we should note that Helmholtz did not believe that the basic sensations of brightness and hue were directly consciously experienced; indeed, with most philosophers and psychologists since James Mill, Helmholtz argued that it is the invariant properties of objects that are important to our survival and that comprise our conscious experience [cf. Hochberg, 1979], so that the issue seems to me to reduce to questions of specific receptive mechanisms, which the direct theorists have not yet provided.)

The viewer must be active in order to perceive, as in Helmholtz's theory, and the kinds of stimulus structure described by the theory are those presaged by Cassirer and Helmholtz. Because for Gibson there is no room for mental structure—indeed, what is unique to him is his rejection of mental structure—we need not consider impoverished, abnormal stimulus situations. In fact, there are positive injunctions to avoid such ecologically unrepresentative traps. Analyses of stimulus "information" compatible with this approach have been carried out for space perception, for those aspects of movement perception that meet these requirements of loosely defined ecological representativeness, and (largely by Johansson, whose views are somewhat similar to Gibson's) for those aspects of movement organization that fit easily under an invariance/transformation or vector-extraction treatment. Figure–ground, grouping, the Gestalt laws, and the illusions, however, are not only not addressed—they are ruled out of court.

To anticipate, Gibson is +, −, + on my checklist.

Mental Structure Theories.   Helmholtz and his successors (e.g., Brunswik and Hebb) assume mental structure to exist and to be important *in addition to* physical stimulus structure. This means that they assume that size/distance, shape/slant, and distance/velocity invariances are manifested in perception even when they are not given directly in the stimulus information.

Let me define this by contrast. To Gibson, for example, apparent size and apparent distance covary because the information that specifies each of them will normally covary in the proximal stimulus pattern. To mental structure theorists, on the other hand, the appearances will covary even if there is no stimulus basis for either apparent size, apparent distance, or both. Let us note here that such mental structure has been demonstrated to occur in impoverished situations, in which stimulus information cannot account for the coupling (e.g., the coupling of perceived size and distance) between appearances. Because the situations are impoverished, and perhaps are neither commonplace nor ecologically valid, the direct theorist can therefore question whether such structure plays an important role when stimulus information *is* present. The mental structure theorist's rebuttal is this: Although it is true that we can only study mental structures in their pure state in such impoverished situations (and in others that we discuss later), we can show mental structure at work even in cases in which there is good stimulus information to contradict the organization that is in fact perceived. For example, in the Ames trapezoid, the purely presumptive relative size cue or the viewer's assumptions about the rectangular shape of the rotating object overcome the information about the invariant trapezoid undergoing the transformation that should specify its true shape and rotation, and so we perceive a rectangle oscillating. This, of course, is an illusion, and like most of the illusions, it is readily accounted for in terms of Helmholtzian mental structure (cf. Gregory & Harris, 1975). It is hard to see how this phenomenon can be dismissed or ignored. One might say that the movement information lies below the thresholds required by a "direct" or Gibsonian theory. That rebuttal opens a wide range of problems, however, because as we will see, the question of limits is in fact a vital one to any such direct theory and a question that has not been seriously addressed.

Helmholtzian mental structure is (at least qualitatively) well designed to deal with perception in the impoverished and abnormal (e.g., illusory) situations that the direct theories (e.g., Gibson's) cannot handle. There has been little thought devoted by Helmholtzians to the organizational phenomena in shape/form and in movement perception, although Helmholtz does have an interesting discussion of the cue of *interposition* that reads very much like a Gestaltist description of the factor of *good continuation* and to which we return later.

Gestalt theorists also invoke mental structure in the form of a *Prägnanz* or *minimum principle:* We perceive just that organization (shape, scene, or movement) that is simplest (according to some specification). The internal relationships that must be taken into account to decide what is simplest are not a feature of the proximal stimulation but of the alternative imaginary objects that might be fitted to the proximal pattern. Gestalt principles, couched either in terms of simplicity or in terms of the specific "laws of organization," can be used to explain all of the depth cues (except for *familiar size,* which by definition must be learned), as I have demonstrated elsewhere (Hochberg, 1978a, pp. 139–140);

they can explain most of the shape/form phenomena (except for the figure-ground phenomenon itself; see the later subsection entitled "Evidence of Mental Structure"); and they can explain many of the phenomena of movement organization. The notion of slant/shape, size/distance, and distance/velocity invariances, however, are not explained but are merely taken over from the Cassirer–Helmholtz formulation.

Let us contrast these two rubrics of mental structure, *likelihood* and *simplicity*. To Helmholtz and his successors, the major rule runs something like this: *We perceive whatever object or scene would, under normal conditions, most likely fit the sensory pattern we receive.* In principle, likelihood can be measured by the objective frequency with which particular aspects of stimulation occur in the course of our interacting with the world. Nothing was said about how large a piece we try to fit at one time or about what practical methods might be found to measure "likelihood" and so forth, however.

To Gestalt theorists (and to their diverse successors), *we perceive whatever object or scene would most simply or economically fit the sensory pattern.* Note that this rubric has great difficulty in specifying simplicity or economy. Even without that difficulty, there is what I now consider to be a fatal problem to this approach. There is a specific implication that *some* overall measure of simplicity can be found and that it is to be applied to some *overall* unit (e.g., an object); otherwise, there is no proposal at all. Either the "whole determines the appearance of the parts," or there is no Gestalt theory. And I believe that this judgment applies as well to Gestalt theory's successors (e.g., Attneave, 1954, 1959; Attneave & Frost, 1969; Garner, 1962, 1970a; Hochberg & Brooks, 1960; Hochberg & McAlister, 1953).

In other respects, we would expect the Helmholtzian and the Gestalt rubrics to be roughly similar, because the constraints in the ecology are subject to the same laws of thermodynamics as are used to model a Gestaltist nervous system. The size of the unit—the "grain size" as Attneave has put it—is central to any attempt to apply either rubric, but it is crucially important to the theoretical viability of the Gestalt position. I do not know of any serious and successful attempts to specify a size of unit (details, objects, or scenes) within which the Gestalt principles apply, and I do not now believe that any such attempt could work. Grain size is also important to any "global psychophysics" of "higher-order variables." Let us consider the matter of grain size next.

Wholistic Theories. Here we complete the round. Gestalt theory and Gibsonian direct theory occupy this niche. We consider them in turn and contrast them with Helmholtz and Hebb in this regard.

It is often stated that a shape remains perceptually unchanged despite transposition (rotation, translation) on the retina. This "fact," sometimes called *the* Gestalt problem, was "explained" by saying that the form itself remains unchanged after transposition—for example, after an eye movement has moved the object to a new part of the retina—so there is presumably no problem about why the form can be perceived despite its being transferred to a totally new set of receptors. Studies of inversion, reversal, rotation, and so on have made this argument a very weak one today: Transposition is simply not immediate or instantaneous, wholistic, or complete.

As to Gibson's approach, there is nothing inherent in "global psychophysics" that requires us to assume that the viewer responds to large-scale and extended variables of stimulation, but the specific variables that Gibson has in fact considered require that the user have access to information over a relatively wide expanse of the field of view, if not over the entire optic array. A texture-density gradient, for example, or an optical flow pattern is by its nature an extended source. If we remember that acuity outside of foveal vision is very poor for small details, we can see why the variable of texture-density gradient (for example) as it is stated is a wholistic one: Depending on the size of the texture grain and the slope of the gradient, the eye may need several fixations to determine the gradient. Gibson is not concerned with such acuity questions, because he takes the entire array as the stimulus, and the movement of the fovea over the array as a form of active exploration, like that of a moving hand exploring a form: The stimulus is the invariant under transformation (in this case, the transformation that unites the successive views of the moving eye). Until (or unless) explicit provision is made for bridging successive partial glimpses, Gibson's theory is wholistic in nature.

Helmholtz, of course, assumed very small units (cones) as the first level of peripheral sensory organization, but we should note that he allowed for something like larger units or substructures to be built up by learning. In Hebb's theory, in fact, there is nothing to limit the spatial extent of a cell assembly; it might include a pattern of light over most of the retina plus a touch on the back of the knee and an efferent command to wiggle the left ear, all as a single unit. Although the line of thought that descends from Helmholtz is surely not wholistic, it can tolerate the demonstration of wholistic phenomena.

In the next section, I describe research and demonstrations in each of the three classes of organizational phenomena (space, shape/form, and movement) that argue strongly against any theory that rests on wholistic stimulus structure or wholistic mental structure. These put quietus to any form of Gestalt theory and make it necessary to consider alternative explanations of the Gestalt phenomena, of which at least one explanation appears to be viable. Strong limits are placed on a stimulus organization theory (i.e., one that denies the need for mental structure), and it is shown that mental structure can, under proper circumstances, contribute to perceptual organization, although we have not proved that such mental structure contributes to perception under conditions in which full stimulus information is available.

RESEARCH, THEORY, AND DEMONSTRATIONS

Gestalt Explanations of Form and Why They Must Be Rejected

Figures 9.1B and 9.1C provide good examples of how Gestalt theories explained perceived solidity without recourse to past experience or depth cues: Fig. 9.1B appears flat because one would have to break the good continuation between 1 and 2 in order to see those lines as the rear and front corners of a cube, whereas in Fig. 9.1C, 1 and 2 form a continuous edge of a cube—an edge that would have to be broken in order for the figure to appear flat. Alternatively, in terms of a minimum principle, Fig. 9.1B is simpler as a flat object than Fig. 9.1C, whereas the two are equally simple as cubes, so that Fig. 9.1B appears the more two-dimensional (for a discussion of this, see Hochberg & Brooks, 1960). The impossible picture in Fig. 9.1D is disturbing to this viewpoint because (as I argued in 1968) both good continuation and simplicity should cause us to perceive it as a flat pattern, whereas we quite obviously do not. When the distances between the right and left corners is reduced, such figures look flat, whereas consistent figures continue to look tridimensional under such conditions (Hochberg, 1968), strongly suggesting that the corners fail to conflict in Fig. 9.1D only because of their separation.

Figure 9.1D is an "impossible" figure and for that reason—or others—may represent a special case. Figure 9.1E, however, is perfectly possible and is of precisely the same size and kind as those in Figs. 9.1B and 9.1C, with which the Gestalt case has been made. It differs from Fig. 9.1C only in that it is made unambiguous in orientation at point 2. As long as you fixate point 2, the orientation is indeed relatively unambiguous. When you fixate point 1, however, the horizontal line does not remain in front of the vertical line as it must in order to be consistent with point 2; after a moment or two, the orientation will reverse, and the horizontal line will appear behind the vertical line in an organization that is inconsistent with the good continuation at point 2.

I think this clearly shows the operation of local depth cues and that the whole does not in any simple sense determine the appearance of its parts. Where one looks in figures like 9.1B, 9.1C, and 9.1E determines what one sees; it is simply the consistency or homogeneity of the first two that have concealed this important fact. This demonstration is important because spontaneous appearances of the organization in which the horizontal line appears to lie behind the vertical line are incompatible with any object-wide definition of simplicity that I know of, and because it argues very strongly that the figures that the Gestaltists chose to study (e.g., 9.1B and 9.1C) appear unified only because they provide consistent local depth cues to the successive glances that one executes in looking at them. So we have to take into account the differential effect of foveal and peripheral vision and of the storage of information from glance to glance—that is, the laws that govern the integration of successive views—in any attempt to describe and explain the phenomena of organization.

There really is very little of the Gestalt theory, as proposed by Wertheimer, Köhler, and Koffka, that survives the facts shown by these demonstrations: I cannot see how either a brain-field theory (no matter how metaphorical), parallel processes, or "laws of organization" much larger in scope than a couple of degrees in extent can accommodate these particularistic or neoatomistic implications.

The Gestalt phenomena themselves—figure and ground, the demonstrations of the so-called laws of organization, the purported demonstrations that the whole organization determines the appearance of the parts, and so on—remain to be explained; and I try to do this later in terms of the perceptuomotor expectancies that the peculiarities of the human gaze, taken together with the ecological probabilities of objects' characteristics, provide in the way of integrative mental structure. Note that any such explanation is more than the Gestaltists ever got around to offering (i.e., their brain fields never did explain either the figure–ground phenomenon or the laws of organization that presumably constrained figure formation—they only promised to do so).

A Direct Stimulus Organization Theory and Why It Must Be Strongly Circumscribed

What Figs. 9.1D and 9.1E tell us is that for line drawings, we must take into account the limitations of the momentary glance. Line drawings are surely not the best examples of the normal objects of perception. Can we show similar limits in the pickup or processing of the information available to the moving observer in the real world?

The two kinds of information discussed by Gibson and his colleagues are the *optical flow pattern* (Gibson, Olum, & Rosenblatt, 1955; Lee, 1974; Purdy, 1958) and the occlusion of texture that occurs in the optic array when one textured surface moves behind another surface's edge (Kaplan, 1969)—that is, *kinetic occlusion*. The Ames trapezoid, discussed earlier, is strong evidence that acuity factors limit the effects of the optical flow pattern. We will now see that differences between foveal and peripheral vision limit the effectiveness of kinetic occlusion information within the momentary glance as well. Figure 9.2 represents the stimuli and data of a study by Hochberg, Green, and Virostek (1978). A textured surface moves behind a window cut in a similarly textured surface. No brightness difference betrays the edges of the window, which is therefore defined only by the relative motion gradients of the two sets of dots. The leftmost column of dots on the rear surface disappears when the surface moves to the left and reappears when the surface moves to the right. As Kaplan (1969) has shown, this

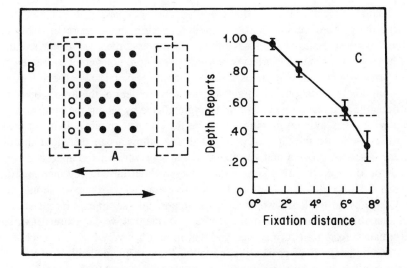

FIG. 9.2.   Kinetic occlusion as a function of fixation distance (after Hochberg, Green and Virostek, 1978).

elicits the perception that the enclosed moving surface is behind the stationary enclosing surface. When subjects fixate points at progressively greater distances from the critical leftmost column of the rear surface, however, their ratings of the rear surface's depth are progressively less affected by the kinetic occlusion of that column (as shown by the graph at right).

This experiment does not, of course, show that peripheral information about spatial layout is, in general, useless. For one thing, we would expect that with larger texture elements, the effects of kinetic occlusion would be manifest at greater distances from the fovea; for another, we as yet have no direct evidence about the importance of fixation to other forms of kinetic depth information (e.g., motion perspective). These data do tell us that the momentary gaze shows limits for kinetic, as well as for static, depth information and that therefore it is of general importance (not merely of importance in explaining the perception of drawings) to deal explicitly with the problems of how we combine the information from successive glances, or the *integration of successive views.*

Gestalt theory, which held that the form per se, regardless of its retinal location, is "the" stimulus to which we respond "directly," never really confronted the problem of how we combine the momentary glances except to introduce the terminology of *invariance* to the problem (Koffka, 1935). Gibson (1966) and Johansson (1977) have somewhat similar theoretical ways of handling this problem—essentially by denying that it exists (cf. Turvey, 1977). Their formulation is as follows: An eye movement consists of a translation. Our perceptual systems somehow extract the invariant undergoing that translation and relegate the transformation itself to information about a change in viewpoint.

Information indicating the fact that the object has not changed its place in space during the eye movement—and perhaps information about the relationship between successive partial glimpses of the object—is directly given as stimulus information. (In Johansson's terms, we extract the common vector as framework and perceive only those stimulus motions that are residual to such extraction.)

With this formulation, we might sidestep the problem of the limitation of the information that can be picked up in a single glance by taking the optic array as sampled by the actively moving eye to be the unitary stimulus. It is not clear, however, whether this approach would in fact allow us to disregard the differences between foveal and peripheral vision, nor whether the approach could really be fleshed out into a systematic theory without introducing mental structure in the form of the integration of successive glances. Further, we should note that there is no evidence whatsoever to support this argument: Its plausibility depends solely on that of the more general doctrine that we can extract invariant information from transformations, and that in turn has very little empirical support. Good analyses of proximal stimulation show mathematically that the "information" may, under some conditions, be there to extract (Gibson et al., 1955; Hay, 1966; Lee, 1974; Purdy, 1958), but there is practically no evidence to show if it is used or, if so, how it is used. Warren (1977), it is true, attempted to demonstrate that two successive views must be "ecologically transformable" into each other if they are to be seen as a single object in apparent motion; this demonstration would, if generalizable, comprise evidence very much to the point, but counterexamples are extremely easy to demonstrate (Hochberg & Brooks, 1974; Kolers & Pomerantz, 1971; Navon, 1976; Orlansky, 1940; Ullman, 1977).

In any case, however, the formulation faces a much more serious problem when it is applied to the processing of information from discrete, successive views: Regardless of the fact that the perceptual psychologist may discern "mathematical information" that relates two views to each other, the perceptual system of the viewer does not appear to be capable of using this information (unless perhaps it is packaged in ways that have not yet been specified). As we will see, the immediate perceptual response to such a sequence does not in fact use the correlated information in the two views that relates them to each other, and the immediate response may well be incorrect in consequence of that fact. Slower or more delayed responses that are in fact based on seeking information that relates the views can be executed and used to judge the views' relationship. But these responses do not use the information from the brief interval of time that includes the transition itself, and they necessarily take us out of discussions about the invariant information in the stimulus transformation and into discussions about how that interval is bridged—that is, into questions of identification, "landmarks" (Hochberg & Gellman, 1977; Lynch, 1960), and so forth. This point is spelled out in the following discussion.

The primary problem in applying a direct theory to the transition between two views is occasioned by a "low-level" phenomenon of apparent motion, which is as likely as not to result in the incorrect perception of the relationship between two views if the displacement between them is at all large relative to the appropriate units (e.g., local features) or "grain size" of the scene (a factor that is at present entirely missing from the vocabulary of the direct theory), if the field of view is at all cluttered, and if there is no extraretinal (e.g., proprioceptive) information about the relationship. The following two examples make that point.

Figures 9.3A, 9.3B, and 9.3C are successive views of a scene composed of five geometric objects, the views being related by discontinuous transformations to the right (i.e., like saccadic traverses to the left). Because the places at which objects fall in successive views are displaced slightly in the direction opposite to that in which the objects themselves are being displaced, there are *two* transformations to consider—the actual transformation, which the viewer can identify only by correctly identifying the objects in each view, and an illusory transformation, occurring between two different objects that lie near each other's places in successive views. At moderate to high rates of presentations (stimulus onset asynchronies, or SOAs, of 1000 milliseconds or less), the wrong translation is perceived (translation to the left), and after viewing the sequence, subjects' descriptions of the layout of the objects are incorrect. At very slow rates (SOAs of 1500 to 3000 milliseconds or more) and with the viewer's active effort to

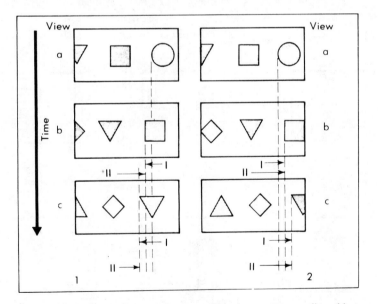

FIG. 9.3. Anomalous apparent movement between noncorresponding objects (after Hochberg and Brooks, 1974; reproduced from Hochberg, 1978a).

identify and label corresponding objects in successive views, the correct translation and layout are reported (Hochberg & Brooks, 1974). Kolers (1972) describes a similar case in which subjects completely fail to perceive the lateral displacement of an entire set of shapes from one view to the next, and instead each shape appears to change smoothly into the figure that replaces it on the same place on the screen. Navon (1976) also describes similar phenomena. A direct theorist might argue that the artificiality of the situation produces transients, which are normally masked by saccadic eye movements, and that once the transients die down, the actual transformations will prevail. (That is, one might suppose that it is the information in the transformation that provides for correct identification of motion and layout at the slow rates, rather than any process of purposive identification of specific objects.) The following experiment argues against that possibility.

In Fig. 9.4A is a set of views of a maze, with 50% overlap between successive views. Sequences of views were shown with different amounts of overlap between views, moving in one or the other direction. At the smallest displacement between successive views (85% overlap), the correct translation is perceived; at larger displacements, performance drops to chance. The stimulus information is there, but the viewer cannot use it. Note that it is not the amount of overlap that is important but its relation to "grain size": If we remove some of the maze to reduce the clutter and produce "large grains," "low-frequency information," and "large or global features" that are visible at some distance into peripheral vision and/or are processed faster, and (we have not separated these possibilities) if we remove the local features that should clutter up a succession of views like

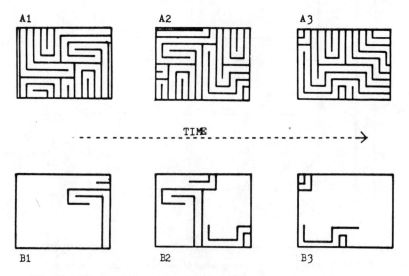

FIG. 9.4.   Translatory view sequence of cluttered (A) and uncluttered (B) mazes (after Hochberg, Brooks and Roule, 1977).

those at Fig. 9.4A with spurious local apparent movements, we get sequences like those in Fig. 9.4B. Such sequences are correctly perceived at all the displacements tested.

Demonstrations of the kind described in connection with Figs. 9.1 through 9.4 convince me that Gestalt-like approaches to the organization of shape and form must be abandoned in favor of some enlightened (more or less Hebbian) kind of atomism. But the examples in Figs. 9.2 through 9.4 show as well that a Gibsonian approach to the organization of space will have to attend to matters of threshold, time limits, parafoveal visibility, and the distinctions between high- and low-frequency information. Alternatively, Gibson's approach might go the whole route toward Brunswik's position, at which point it must both confront the horrendous problem of defining ecological representativeness in precise and quantitative terms and explain why it is studying proximal stimuli at all. If one is interested in predicting the appearance of some object or scene under representative circumstances, and if the perceptions of the world are generally correct under those circumstances, then the proximal stimuli are an unnecessary diversion. On the other hand, if the proximal stimulation is of interest because the information it contains is the first stage of processing, then sensory limitations on the pickup of such information become critically important.

We have one class of theory of organization left to consider. We have (I maintain) ruled out Gestalt-like approaches by demonstrating the efficacies of parts versus those of wholes. We have yet to explain the Gestalt phenomena and the apparent importance of wholes, and we must still decide whether stimulus structure alone suffices to account for organization or whether mental structure is also needed. Research to that point appears in the next section.

Evidence of Mental Structure

The myriad examples of figural completion, of which the Bradley, Dumais, and Petry figures (1976) and Kanisza's subjective contour patterns (1955) are the most dramatic instances, are clearly cases of "something contributed by the viewer" that is not in the stimulus, but they do not necessarily demand explanation in terms of mental structures. Sensory factors might be responsible: The fact that the fragments to be connected in such patterns are simultaneously present in the field of view makes some kind of low-level explanation at least conceivable (if farfetched; e.g., lateral inhibitory networks of greater complexity and extent than have yet been seriously considered or investigated). The following two examples, representative of research and demonstrations I have described elsewhere (Hochberg, 1968, 1978b), seem to me to be unassailable instances of "mental structure" in form perception, and they allow us to study processes of fitting and testing a global schematic map or other mental structure to a set of local features presented over time.

The first example is the kind of aperture-viewing situation I have been belaboring for the last 10 years: A series of what look like unrelated right angles are all presented at the same place in space (Fig. 9.5). Two such series, which differ only in the orientation of one of the angles in the middle of the series, will not be reliably detected as being different if the series length exceeds memory span (i.e., about 8 to 10 angles), regardless of the rate of presentation. (Suitable precautions must be taken, of course, to use enough different series that the viewer cannot learn them ''by rote''.) If, however, the viewer is first shown an entire geometrical figure of which one corner is the angle viewed through the aperture (e.g., a cross whose upper right-hand corner is the first view in the series), it then is easy for that individual to detect whether the rest of the series of angles is ''correct'' or ''incorrect,'' as long as the presentation rate allows an SOA of more than 375 milliseconds: The schematic map into which he or she fits each successive view permits the adult viewer to determine whether or not each view belongs to the sequence of views of that figure and, therefore, to judge whether or not two sequences (one of which may be ''incorrect'') are the same.

The second example addresses what Gestaltists and non-Gestaltists alike have long taken as a fundamental property of shape or form perception: figure–ground differentiation.

Note first that no satisfactory Gestalt-theoretical explanation was suggested, much less established, for either the figure–ground phenomenon itself or for the phenomena illustrating the laws of organization. (Köhler offered ''steady-state'' direct-current speculations in 1920 and 1958(b) and in his papers with Wallach (Köhler & Wallach, 1944) and Emery (Köhler & Emery, 1947), in which a denser DC current was thought to flow through the cortex in a region that corresponds isomorphically to figure as opposed to ground. That theory seems to me only an embodiment of what Helmholtz proposed as a parody or *reductio ad absurdum* of the nativist position [1856/1962, p. 23]. In any case, it is totally inapplicable to a world in which viewers are free to move their eyes four times each second.) Let us note also that the aperture-viewing task that I have described

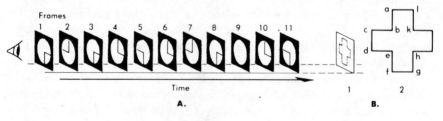

FIG. 9.5.   Successive views of the corners of a cross. If the viewer is first shown a ''long shot'' of the cross (B1), and is shown or told that the first frame (A1) is the corner marked *a* in B2, the sequence of views is comprehensible, and the viewer recognizes that the sequence has taken a shortcut from *h* to *k* on the cross. (After Hochberg, 1968; reproduced from Hochberg, 1978a).

requires a series of piecemeal decisions about figure and ground if the viewer is to treat a 90-degree outside corner and a 270-degree inside corner appropriately. I have found in discussions of this kind of experiment and its implications that the involvement of figure and ground in piecemeal shape perception is by no means self-evident; the following experiment may make that involvement and its implications more clear.

Each frame of the motion picture schematically shown in Fig. 9.6A contained two subviews, thus providing an upper and a lower visual channel. Each channel showed a segment of a Rubin vase–faces pattern. The same segment was shown in each channel. The sequence of views in each channel was essentially what would have been given by moving the outline of the figure systematically behind the aperture, circumnavigating the entire contour. Although the same section of contour was shown in each channel, a stationary black disc (stationary with respect to the aperture) was partially occluded by the ''faces'' side of the contour in the upper channel and by the ''vase'' side of the contour in the lower channel. Both channels together subtended less than two degrees of visual angle. The spacing between channels and the size of the represented pattern were such that the contents of the two channels were in conflict in this sense: If there really were an object moving behind the two apertures, the top of the object would be showing in one channel at the same time the bottom would show in the other.

When asked to attend the upper channel in such a display, all viewers report seeing the faces aspect of the Rubin figure; when attending the lower channel, they see the vase aspect. This is true even though the instructions were to fixate

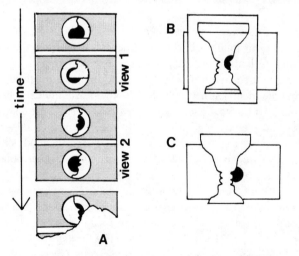

FIG. 9.6.   (A) Two-channel piecemeal presentation of Rubin faces and vase. (B) Visualization of what is perceived when attending the top channel; (C) visualization of what is perceived when attending the bottom channel (Hochberg, 1978b).

the line between the channels, and the entire display is so small that both channels surely fall in foveal vision.

This demonstration is, of course, just the figure–ground relationship that Gestalt theory took as its starting point, and with effort the viewer can temporarily reverse it. (For example, the upper channel can be perceived as a moving vase, with a changing portion of a black disc moving over its surface at a rate that keeps the disc steady within the aperture.) This demonstration makes several points:

1. It illustrates with a familiar example that the figure–ground phenomenon is implicated in the perception of shape under piecemeal aperture viewing.

2. Because of the piecemeal presentation procedure, with all parts presented in the same (foveal) region, we can be sure that *this figure–ground phenomenon (if that is what it is) does not depend on the overall configuration of the stimulus as a source of parallel processing* (i.e., no "brain-field organization" of the sort proposed by Köhler and his colleagues, nor anything remotely like it, can be invoked in an explanation of these findings).

3. Neither can we say that the stimulus information in the sequence over time *specifies* vase or faces (as the direct theory might have it); although both channels are simultaneously present and near the fovea, only the object "specified" by the attended channel is perceived. (Note that because of the size of the represented objects and the proximity of the two channels, no single object could be specified by the display.) Only when the viewer undertakes to fit a coherent object to the sequence of views given in one channel or the other does a percept result.

Such experiments show us that when the task requires viewers to draw on mental structure to fit their successive fragmentary views together, they can do so. I would like to believe that this is so because they normally draw on such structure in the course of fitting their saccadic glances together. Can we say anything about the mental structure that is fitted to the stimulus sequence in such demonstrations? As I have argued elsewhere (1962, 1970), the characteristics of the structure—the phenomenal properties of figure and ground—are those of objects' edges as fitted to the momentary glance. There are good perceptuomotor reasons for the viewer to make such "decisions" about what points lie in the same plane before executing any eye and head movements (e.g., saccadic response times are long—around 200 milliseconds—and the parallax produced by head movements will change the location of, or even occlude, the points that lie on the further plane before a planned move to fixate them can be consummated; see Hochberg, 1971a, 1971b, 1974a, 1978b). The Gestalt laws, in fact, are very easy to think of as cues on which to base that decision. For example, the "law of good continuation" is probably only an aspect of the depth cue of interposition: It is very unlikely that the eye should be (and stay) at just that place in space that will bring into precise alignment the edges of two objects that lie at different distances. A continuous line most likely identifies the edge of a single object (Helmholtz, 1856/1962; Hochberg, 1971a, 1971b, 1974b).

The mental structures of the Gestalt phenomena are therefore better subsumed under the general Helmholtzian rubric than they were explained by Gestalt theory. But it is not the physical world per se that is reflected by such mental structure; it is the constraints on perceptuomotor expectancies, not the constraints on the physical world itself. *Ecological validity (Brunswik, 1956), will not do: We cannot ignore the "merely mediating variables" of eyeball and oculomotor apparatus, of acuity differences and saccadic response times. These contribute to the characteristics of mental structure as much as do the properties of the world they mediate.*

Levels of Mental Representation: Mental Structures Simply Do Not Reflect Proximal or Distal Physical Organization

This seems to me to be an extremely important point and a very difficult problem. Most of the major perceptual theories, from unconscious inference through Gestalt organization, Brunswik's probabilistic problem solving, and Gibsonian direct theory, have been designed to avoid confronting it. But there are, I think, no shortcuts. We cannot disregard mental structures, but we cannot encompass them within a single explanatory principle, either, nor consider them within one causal domain.

Take the figure–ground example (although we could pursue this point just as well with distance, color, or movement): The properties of figure and ground surely can be attributed neither to the present proximal stimulus distribution nor (because the stimuli are lines on paper and not usually object's edges) to the present distal layout. Figures comprise structures that are evidently mental. Demonstrations like those in Figs. 9.1 through 9.6 show that the properties of figure–ground organization do not fit the wholistic prescriptions of Gestalt organization, but neither do they reflect the constraints of objects in the physical world. In fact, these demonstrations show that we can separate at least two levels of mental structure. Each intersection in Figs. 9.1D and 9.1E acts as a local depth cue. I have previously (1968) given my reasons for considering such local depth cues to be irreducible, organized, elementary features not subject to further subdivision nor to piecemeal presentation. The structures into which they fit, however, appear to have different characteristics entirely: As the aperture-viewing experiments that I already described show, piecemeal presentation is no obstacle for constructing these larger structures. In Figs. 9.1C and 9.1D, moreover, we see that such larger structures do not impose strong constraints on the local features and, as the other side of that coin, are not constrained to be consistent with them.

In short, some aspects of mental organization (mainly local regions that correspond to what central vision can grasp in a single glance, I believe) are closely constrained; others (mainly the larger layouts into which we must place them) are not. The way I have separated them is of course consonant with Hebb's speculations about cell assemblies (local, closely constrained) versus phase sequences (more extended in time and space and less closely constrained). This approach is close to Neisser's (1964, 1967). It is even closer to the classical proposals of J. S. Mill and Helmholtz that I discussed in earlier parts of this chapter—that is, that we perceive by fitting the most likely or expected (global) object or event to the sampled (local) sensory components. The process of fitting the more global and elective structures to the more local and obligatory ones must offer major opportunities for the effects of perceptual learning (Hochberg, 1968) and of set or attitude (Hochberg, 1970) to emerge, with such contextual structures to some degree determining the role or function of the part in the whole but not the part's purely local appearance. I am afraid that I cannot do much to sharpen these speculations at present, nor offer a more specific model as yet, although I have been fumbling at the task for some years. In any case, we must separate these levels of mental organization from each other and from the effects of lower-level organizational processes (cf. Figs. 9.3 and 9.4) and examine separately the rules that govern each before any concept of organization can be useful. Organization is not *a* thing.

CONCLUSIONS

If we agree to consider the Gestalt phenomena to be part of the mental structure of space and object perception, it seems to me that the neo-Helmholtzian position, with its intrinsic notions about mental structure, becomes by far the most economical position. Mental structure is not only manifested in such serial tasks as aperture viewing; it can be demonstrated (albeit not in so readily measurable a form) in connection with the perception of both spatial organization and movement. As to spatial organization, there are several compelling examples in which size and distance, or slant and shape, are coupled in an invariant relationship even when there is no information in the stimulus array to specify either. The most striking of these is probably the Ames ''window,'' in which such a mental slant–shape relationship (or interresponse constraint) not only can be obtained in the absence of any stimulus information; it is obtained *against* the information given by the differential optical flow pattern that is given in the optic array. This robust phenomenon makes it clear that the pickup of such higher-order stimulus information is subject to threshold considerations. That is, when viewed from nearby, the trapezoidal shape and rotary motion of the object are correctly perceived. As viewing distance increases to a few yards, however, the information in the flow pattern clearly falls below threshold, inasmuch as the object is very strongly perceived as an oscillating rectangle. The fact that oscillation is just what one should perceive, given that one perceives the trapezoid as a rectangle, is a strong argument for mental structure. (But an even more important fact is the demonstration that the optical flow pattern information can easily fall below threshold, and if it does so in this case, it surely must do so in others as well. The question of the nature and distribution of thresholds for the higher-order informative variables of the direct theory offers a central challenge—a challenge that has not yet been taken up, to my knowledge, by either Gestalt theorists or "direct theorists," central though it would appear to the application of the former and to any real meaning of the latter.) In the case of movement, similar couplings have been shown; a particularly striking phenomenon recently reported by Farber and McConkie (1977) shows a strong coupling between apparent distance and apparent velocity, using planes of random dots that offer no stimulus information to support such coupling. In the constancies, in the illusions, and in the Gestalt organizational phenomena, therefore, as well as in the new field of research on the integration of successive views, the same sort of Helmholtzian mental structure provides at least a qualitative description of most of the findings.

When full stimulus information is present for the observer to use "directly," it is possible of course that mental structure is not in fact activated or used. I know of no evidence one way or the other to this point. But the position so closely approaches special pleading that it seems completely unwarranted to argue that one should only study situations in which full stimulus information is indeed available, in order to avoid "unnatural" perceptual tasks. In a similar vein, one might hold that when no inconsistencies exist between parts of objects or scenes, and when all the parts are harmonious in some sense *yet to be defined* that is violated by Fig. 9.1E, then wholistic determination prevails. But again, the same caution about arbitrary exclusion of subject matter must be raised. Of the three systems into which I forced my classification of organizational explanations, some variety of Helmholtzianism comes off best by far. Overall, it takes some kind of tunnel vision to maintain that mental structure is unnecessary or even an unparsimonious construct, and the Gestalt alternative—a wholistic mental structure—appears to be untenable as a general proposition.

This does not mean that all is well with Helmholtz, despite a significant upswing in his popularity (cf. Rock, 1977). Punctiform receptors as the sole basis of visual analysis look pretty silly today, of course, and a great deal of organization clearly takes place in the peripheral reaches of the nervous system. That organization (which encompasses opponent processes, feature detectors, frequency channels, and so forth) is not the product of a single cognitive arena to which Helmholtz's rubric might be applied—the rubric that holds that we perceive what would be most likely to cause any given sensory excitation under normal conditions. Before we could hope to apply that rule, we would have to be able to identify the more peripheral and noncognitive contributions to organization. Even after that, it is hard to see, in fact, how that rubric can be used to either theoretical or practical profit without specifying what the "given sensory excitation'' refers to (i.e., what is the grain size; is it scene-wide, object-wide, or intersection-wide?) and without some way of knowing what is "likely." That is, to apply Helmholtz's rule we must first discover the relevant structure of the world as it is filtered through the proximal stimulus information and the characteristics of the sensorimotor apparatus. I know of no shortcuts. *To talk about perception as probabilistic problem solving is not much use unless we know the "premises" and the "inference rules." We do know that they are not merely the rules of physics; that much is guaranteed by Figs. 9.1D and 9.1E.*

Let me stress that point: Both Helmholtzians and Gibsonians agree that perception should and does (at least to some degree) reflect the structure of the environment, but neither offers us a method for determining what the relevant structure actually is. For example, although a convincing case can be made that the Gestalt phenomena, as well as the geometrical illusions (Gregory & Harris, 1975), comprise a set of expectations about the structure of the world, as already mentioned, we should note that neither Helmholtz nor anyone else deduced either the Gestalt phenomena or the illusions from the nature of the world. These explanations arose only after the puzzling phenomena themselves had been explored and worried over, and the explanations are still far from established. And only after such explanations are devised do we know what to look for in our studies of the perceptual ecology.

In short, I think that the study of stimulus organization is indeed essential, but that in order to know what aspect of stimulation we should be studying, we must first investigate precisely those perceptual phenomena that do not, at first glance, appear to be veridical. They set the problems to which a direct theory must be addressed. They provide the occasion for rendering unto physiology and anatomy what is rightfully theirs and what is not the consequence of either "stimulus information" or "constructive cognitive processes." Most interesting to me are those cases in which neither stimulus organization nor peripheral processes can possibly account for perceptual organization (most notably in the combination of successive glances); those cases provide windows through which the central processes of psychology—the cognitive workings, or their cast shadows—can occasionally be glimpsed.

Mental structures do contribute to perceptual organization. They seem to me to comprise the most important problems that the student of organization can confront, whether or not the circumstances in which they are manifest are ecologically representative. They are best observed in experimental circumstances that require the viewer to fill out partial presentations, like those that study how we integrate successive piecemeal glimpses of objects and scenes. They do not simply reflect the regularities of the physical world. They cannot be summarized by a single organizational rubric, because there appears to be more than one level of mental structure. Those levels must be separated empirically before general principles can be fitted to them.

10 Psychophysical Complementarity

Roger N. Shepard
Stanford University

ABSTRACT

Through biological evolution, the most pervasive and enduring constraints governing the external world and our coupling to it are the ones that must have become most deeply incorporated into our innate perceptual machinery. Especially basic are constraints conditioned by such facts as that space is locally Euclidean and three-dimensional and that significant objects, including our own bodies: (1) are bound by two-dimensional surfaces; (2) tend to conserve semirigid shape; (3) have exactly six degrees of freedom of overall position in space; and (4) tend, over time, to move between nearby positions according to a principle of least action. Because our commerce with the world necessarily takes place through the spatially very different medium of a two-dimensional boundary, internal representations need not literally resemble their corresponding external objects and events. The internal and the external must nevertheless approximate a kind of complementary mesh.

INTRODUCTION

In this chapter I attempt, from a broadly evolutionary perspective, a reconsideration of the internal processes by which we represent external objects and events and, particularly, the relation that these internal processes bear to their external referents. I find major difficulties facing conceptions of this relation either as one of literal resemblance or as one of merely causal dependence. I suggest, instead, that this relation might more successfully be regarded as one of *complementarity*.

279

I also develop the ideas (1) that an understanding of the nature of internal representations must take account of rules according to which these representations are internally transformed, and (2) that these rules of transformation are themselves complementary to corresponding regularities governing transformations in the external world.

Philosophical and Terminological Preliminaries

Before proceeding, I need to clarify the ways in which I am, for the purposes of this chapter, using certain terms—particularly the terms *internal* and *external, mental* and *physical*. Confusion might otherwise arise as to which two of the three following things are being related: (1) the physical object or event *external* to the physical body of the perceiving organism; (2) the physical process *internal* to that perceiver's body (and largely, I presume, to that perceiver's physical brain) that somehow represents the external object or event; and (3) the perceiver's subjective or phenomenal experience of the object or event. Unlike the first two of these things, the third—the *experience*—is supposed to be nonphysical and, indeed, to differ from any physical things—whether internal or external (in the specified sense)—in that the perceiver has uniquely privileged and infallible access to it.

The psychophysical complementarity with the greatest philosophical depth is the irreducible subjective–objective complementarity between what (necessarily speaking here in the first person) *I* directly and consciously experience, and the physical processes in my brain that I presume to correspond in some way to my conscious experience but that can only be studied from without, by behavioral or physiological methods. If I start with my subjective experience, the physical world (including my physical brain) becomes a construction based on invariances in my own experience—somewhat along the lines of methodological solipsism as articulated by Bridgman (1940) or, formally, by Carnap (1928/1967). If I start with the physical world, subjective experience, to the extent that it is dealt with at all, becomes a construction based on invariances in physical events—especially neurophysiological and behavioral events (including verbal reports). The two starting points are thus fundamentally complementary in the sense of Bohr (1958).

However, it is not this epistemological complementarity between phenomenalistic and physicalistic starting points with which I am concerned in this chapter. Rather, it is a different complementarity that, as I try to argue, may hold between an internal process and the object or event that it represents in the external world, where both the internal representation and its external referent are treated as having the same epistemological status. That is, whether they are taken as physical things that can in principle be studied by a third party or as constructions based on immediate experience, they are regarded as alike in this respect.

Thus, if I take the scientifically more standard "objective" starting point, the internal representation—like its external object—is in part a theoretical construction established by converging operations (Garner, Hake, & Eriksen, 1956) based on interpersonally shared procedures of physical measurement and recording—whether of stimulus properties or of organismic responses, both physiological and behavioral. And if I take the phenomenalistic or "subjective" starting point, the converging operations used to establish both of these (internal or external) types of physical entities must be based alike on regularities in my own immediate experience.

The fact that epistemologists and philosophers of science have generally abandoned the phenomenalistic starting point in favor of other, more physicalistic, behavioristic, or linguistic starting points has not weakened my own long-standing conviction that the most epistemologically defensible basis for the only knowledge I can have must be my own immediate experience. I believe that the discrediting of phenomenalistic epistemology has been a premature consequence of improper formulations by proponents and critics alike. However, the intent of this chapter is scientific, not philosophical. Accordingly, and to avoid taxing the patience of my psychological colleagues, whose orientations I judge to be more behavioristic than phenomenalistic, I adopt forthwith the scientifically more standard "objective" starting point. I leave, for some other occasion, any further consideration of the epistemological issues—including the issue of how the things presupposed by this starting point (including the physical world and my colleagues who are a part of it!) might first be constructed on the basis of regularities in immediate experience.

I shall nevertheless have occasion to speak of mental events and subjective experiences. To preserve consistency with the "objective" epistemological starting point adopted here, such terms should be interpreted to refer to the internal mediational processes that are inferred to occur in others on the basis of behavioral or neurophysiological evidence. These inferred processes are thus regarded as physical processes that are, at least in principle, susceptible to detection, measurement, and characterization by converging physical operations (see Shepard, 1978d). When I refer to a mental, subjective, or experiential event, process, or representation instead of to a specific pattern of neural activity, it is usually because I am still ignorant of the neural mechanism that I nevertheless suppose to underlie the observed behavior from which the mental event is inferred.

What we must recognize here is that there are many possible levels of description, and although they may appear very different in character, the various levels all pertain to the same underlying system. In this respect, the internal representation is no different from the external object. The very same external object, say a block of wood, can be described in terms of more and more microscopic constituents (fibers, cells, molecules, atoms, baryons, leptons, quarks) or in terms of more and more global structures (textures, corners, edges, faces, and color, size, weight, density, and overall cubical shape). Likewise, the internal representation of the block could be described, if we but knew how, in terms of its microscopic constituents (patterns of activity in specific neural circuits, individual neurons, excitatory and inhibitory synapses, and so on) or in terms of the more global functional organization suggested, primarily, by behavioral evidence.

The relationship that is of primary interest to me here is the relationship between the global properties of the external object and the corresponding functional organization of the internal process. I proceed on the working assumption that at a suitable level of abstraction, some progress toward the understanding of this relationship can be made in the absence of a detailed knowledge of the internal or external substrata alike—whether atomic or neuronal. So at this level of abstraction, I use *internal* or *mental,* quite interchangeably, to refer to certain unobserved processes in the brain that are inferred on the basis of observed behavior and that presumably have a physical (neural) embodiment, though we as yet have little information about its concrete character.

In addition to having internal representations of external objects and events, individuals can of course have internal representations of objects and events that are internal in the sense used here. Indeed the achievement of appropriate internal representations of our own internal representations would take us a long way toward the goal of understanding the relationship between internal representations and their external objects. However, from the standpoint adopted here, such reflexive representation does not appear to raise any special problem. I presume that my representation of events in my own brain would be much the same as my representation of functionally similar events in the brain of another person, though in the former, reflexive case, the internal representation is not strictly of an "external" event in the particular sense specified here. (This sense is, of course, entirely different from that of the phenomenalist who, when speaking of the construction of the "external world," means to include his or her own brain as a part of that external world.)

So, in this chapter, anyway, in speaking of "psychophysical complementarity," I am not using *psychophysical* as it has been used in earlier philosophical theories of psychophysical parallelism, interactionism, and the like—to relate a physical process to a purely nonphysical experience. Rather, I am using *psychophysical* in the specific sense in which it seems to be used by contemporary psychophysicists—to relate external stimuli to internal responses that are also presumed to have a physical embodiment, however abstractly it may be specified.

My use of the most central term that remains to be clarified, *complementarity,* is somewhat metaphorical (if not, indeed, ill chosen). Roughly, the idea is that what we know about the relationship between an internal representation and its external referent is not that it is one of physical resemblance but, rather, that it is one of a functional, complementary mesh at the boundary between the exterior and interior of the organism. It is, thus, a complementarity only in the rather extended sense in which the relation between a lock and its key is one of complementarity. I can only hope that whether *complementarity,* the term itself, seems more or less apt after reading this chapter, the notion that I have tried to capture by that term will at least be more clear.

The Central Problem of Perception

Actually, whether I am trying to account for objective behavior or subjective experience, I find that the problem of internal representation looms as *the* central problem of perception.

The occurrence of the appropriate internal processes appears to be necessary and sufficient for a perceptual experience. This is true whether those processes are externally caused by the corresponding external objects or events—as in normal veridical perception—or whether those processes are purely internally generated in the absence of the corresponding external objects or events—as in dreaming or hallucination. And conversely, even when the external objects or events are fully stimulating the appropriate sensory surfaces, if the corresponding internal processes fail to occur—whether for reasons of physical disruption of the afferent neural pathway, cortical damage, an altered state of consciousness, or merely temporary inattention—there will ensue no corresponding perceptual experience.

And, clearly, behavior is mediated by internal representational processes. Any intervention that modifies the internal representational process—whether by means of perceptual-motor relearning with displacing prisms, surgical alteration of neural pathways, or drugs—changes the ensuing behavior with respect to the very same external objects and events. Moreover, as all attempts to build explicit and detailed models capable of simulating significant sorts of perceptually guided behavior have made clear, there is much to be gained in the way of economy and power by controlling behavior in relation to an internally reconstructed representation that captures the invariant properties of size, shape, and reflectance of the external object extracted from the ever-shifting patterns projected on the sensory surfaces.

I argue that a complementary relation between perceptual processes and their external referents has been shaped by its great value for survival. I also suggest that this complementarity has evolved in parallel with powerful internal constraints that themselves represent a kind of complementary counterpart of pervasive constraints governing the projections and transformations of objects in the external world. Before sketching out this approach and some of the specific experimental results to which it has led, however, I want briefly to indicate what I currently see as the major limitations of each of several alternative approaches that have been advocated by others.

Some Previous Approaches and Their Limitations

Gestalt psychologists were the first to place what I consider proper stress on the role of internal organizational processes in perception. However, their most valuable contribution consisted in the illustration of some of the principles of organization through demonstrations that could be directly experienced rather than in the advancement of a satisfactory theory of the internal processes underlying such organizational principles. Köhler's postulation of an isomorphism between brain states and perceptual experience evidently grew out of his interest in explaining the character of perception as experienced (Köhler, 1929), but the weakness of such a postulation may have stemmed from his relative lack of concern with the role of perception in the control of behavior. Hence Skinner (1963) could subsequently remark that even if we were to discover a part of the brain in which the physical pattern of the neural activity had the very same shape as the corresponding external object—say, a square—we would not in this way have made any progress in explaining how the subject is able to recognize that object as a square, to learn to associate to it a unique verbal response "square," and so on. The conveyance of the physical shape of the external object into the subject's physical brain does not itself solve the difficult problems of pattern analysis and response selection; it only puts them off. Viewed from the outside, the train of internal processes that mediates between an external stimulus and the ensuing observable behavior with respect to that stimulus must be connected at both ends.

A more subtle issue concerns the origin and specific nature of the organizational principles to which the Gestalt psychologists have properly called our attention. Koffka (1935) and Köhler (1929, 1940) explained the organizational tendencies of the brain by analogy with minimization principles inherent in homogeneous, dynamic physical systems such as soap bubbles, which—in the absence of external constraints—tend toward certain regular forms such as the circular or spherical. Again, perhaps, by neglecting the role of perception in ensuring that behavior will be adaptive, the Gestalt psychologists failed to appreciate that the brain is not a simple, homogeneous medium but a complex system whose organizational principles have been specifically selected to achieve an appropriate match with the external world. Because the brain is itself a part of that world, it would not be surprising if the organizational tendencies of the brain were found to have something in common with minimization tendencies manifested by other physical systems; but the world has itself evolved many complexities, and a simple system modeled on the soap bubble—unless it has been reshaped and refined by repeated interactions with that world—is not likely to survive much longer than the bubble.

Behaviorists recognized that whatever internal processes go on must be inferred from the overt responses to which they give rise. But although they diligently investigated how individual organisms adapt to arbitrarily imposed environmental contingencies, they took no more cognizance than did the Gestaltists of the innate predispositions shaped by the eons and eons of evolution in a particular ecological niche. The behaviorists, unlike the Gestaltists, focused on the response end of the internal process but, in doing so, neglected the stimulus end and its inborn organizational principles that determine which aspects of a stimulus will be perceptually registered by a member of a given species and, hence, which aspects will become the condition for a particular reinforced response. Hull (1943), as Skinner, treated the stimulus as an unanalyzed entity, "S." In effect, Hull evaded the whole problem of innate perceptual organization in his single, unexplicated postulate of "afferent neural interaction."

The adaptive behavior of higher organisms depends on perceptual machinery that, to a good approximation, extracts information about properties of inherent reflectance, size, three-dimensional shape, and relative location of the distal object from a shifting proximal pattern of energy that necessarily depends on accidental circumstances of lighting, distance, orientation, and momentary direction of gaze.

Students of ecological optics, following Gibson (1966), have been emphasizing a fact of utmost importance in this regard—namely, that the space–time pattern of the incident stimulation (as exemplified, particularly, by the transformational flow of the "optic array") "affords" information that, under normal conditions, is sufficient for the accurate guidance of behavior with respect to the external three-dimensional world. The program articulated by Gibson of identifying the "higher-order" variables of the flow of the optic array that correspond to the important invariants in the external world provides an essential foundation for any attempt to explicate perception. Whereas I have been critical of the programs of the Gestalt psychologists and of the S–R behaviorists, I find no fault with the Gibsonian program, as far as it goes. I find, however, that it does not go far enough. To say that there is sufficient information in the proximal stimulus and even to point to some of the higher-order variables in which the requisite information resides is not to describe the mechanism that extracts that information and uses it to control appropriate behavior or additional cognitive processing.

That the perceptual system is governed by internalized rules becomes evident under those "impoverished" circumstances in which the proximal stimulation fails to contain sufficient information for the unique determination of the three-dimensional scene—circumstances in which the level of illumination or duration of exposure is drastically reduced or in which observation is constrained to a stationary, monocular, and specially selected viewpoint or to a merely pictorial, schematic, or ambiguous portrayal. As is most dramatically revealed by demonstrations such as those of Ames (Ittelson, 1968; Gregory, 1970), subjects uniformly use quite definite, though unconscious, rules to select (from the infinite variety of three-dimensional worlds consistent with a given retinal projection) the one that is most regular in some way—the one in which, for example, as many as possible of the lines are straight and parallel, the corners are right-angled, and the overall structures are symmetrical (see, e.g., Attneave, 1955; Attneave & Frost, 1969; Hochberg & Brooks, 1960; Hochberg & McAlister, 1953; Leeuwenberg, 1971; Metzler & Shepard, 1974; Perkins, 1972).

The perceptual system is not simply transparent to the incident stimulation. The inner machinery that underlies its selectivity in the face of greatly reduced external information does not simply go away when the conditions of observation improve. The fact that we are unaware of this machinery under favorable conditions can be regarded, instead, as an indication of how successful we have, through evolution, internalized the rules governing the projections and transformations that normally occur in a three-dimensional world. The very same world viewed through a channel of scrambled fiber optics no longer engages our innate interpretive machinery and hence remains totally unintelligible to us. Under normal circumstances, our perceptual system—in creating an internal representation that mirrors the structure of the external world, by means of rules that mirror the rules governing projections and transformations in that world—gives rise to the illusion of transparency (thereby motivating the postulation of some principle of isomorphism); but it is only an illusion. It is this insight into perception as a kind of *resonance* phenomenon that I (probably among others) have tried to capture in the metaphorical characterization of perception as "externally guided hallucination."

Physiological reductionists sometimes seem to hold that we will grasp the essential nature of the internal machinery that so effectively underlies this illusion of transparency only when we have pinned down the moment-by-moment interactions of each of the billion or so intricately interconnected neurons making up this machinery. This is a discouraging prospect for any but the most preliminary sensory stages of perceptual processing. However, this extreme form of the reductionistic claim may also be wrong.

Even if it were possible to have a concrete specification of how every neuron was interacting with every other, such a specification would only be more accessible—not more intelligible—than the brain itself. What *I* want to know, rather, is something about the *organizational principles* governing these neural interactions. And there is every reason to believe that these organizational principles could be understood—perhaps even understood best—at a more abstract level. As I believe others have noted, we may not need to refer to the concrete properties of individual neurons any more, in understanding a computation such as matrix inversion, than we need to know about the concrete physical details of electric circuits and semiconductors that underlie the computation in any particular computing machine.

Findings concerning neural interactions will undoubtedly be relevant to the formulation of the desired principles of perceptual organization. But it is unlikely that we could make sense of such a body of concrete and specific data in the absence of a more abstract and general notion of the kind of pattern for which we should be looking. This more abstract and general notion cannot itself come, I think, from the physiological details. Rather, it must come from an examination of behavioral and introspective evidence together with a general consideration of the constraints inherent in the three-dimensional world in which we live and of what these constraints imply concerning the kinds of perceptual mechanisms that are likely to be most adaptive in such a world (cf. Shepard, 1978e).

Information-processing theorists might seem to have taken exactly the approach toward which my preceding remarks have been pointing. These theorists have been striving for a specification of mechanisms sufficient to explain both objective behavior and, in some cases, subjective report. And they have been trying to do this at a level of abstraction and generality that allows for the natural formulation of organizational principles while leaving open the possibility of the eventual establishment of connections with findings at the lower, neurophysiological level. Moreover, I am in agreement with those working in the field of artificial intelligence who hold that the design of just one mechanism that is capable of duplicating significant human perceptual performances is a major achievement. Even though that mechanism may not operate in exactly the same way as the human nervous system, it provides at least a promising guess as to how that system may in some part function.

In fact, I do not entertain strong reservations about these general goals of the information-processing theorists. However, as I indicate in the following section, I suspect that the heavy dependence of their modeling, in practice, on the discrete symbol-manipulating character of present-day digital computers and on the discrete propositional formalisms of logic and linguistic theory has effectively blinded them to the possibility that analogical functions, which are fundamental throughout biology (Shepard & Podgorny, 1978, p. 227), may also underlie the correspondence between representational processes and their external referents.

Logical Versus Analogical Forms of Representation

In a particularly sustained and articulate advocacy of the "propositional" viewpoint, Pylyshyn (e.g., see 1973, 1978) argues for a single, discrete, propositional format for all internal representations, whether derived from visual or auditory, or from verbal or nonverbal, input. He bases his argument on the grounds that the postulation of a single format is most parsimonious and that if such a single format is to possess sufficient power to represent everything that might need representing, it must be propositional in character. Although his arguments have an initial appeal, I find that some of this appeal evaporates on closer consideration.

The very flexibility and generality of the propositional format, which appeared to be such an asset at first glance, turns out (as Kosslyn & Pomerantz, 1977, have also noted) to have the implication that Pylyshyn's proposal is without empirical content. True, at one time or another Pylyshyn and other propositional theorists have seemed to offer testable predictions—for example, that the times to compare visual objects varying in complexity or angular orientation should increase with complexity. Yet when empirical results have been obtained that contradict these predictions (as in the case of the results reported by Cooper, 1975; Cooper & Podgorny, 1976; and Nielsen & Smith, 1973), the same propositional theorists are quick to point out that their "semantic networks" or "articulated symbol systems" (Pylyshyn, 1978) can readily be adjusted to account for those results, too! It appears, then, that what is being proposed is not a particular testable *theory* of cognitive processing but, rather, only a general purpose *language* in which a researcher can formulate *any* such theory.

An analog process, according to the quite specific definition that my associates and I have advocated (Cooper & Shepard, 1973a; Shepard, 1975, 1978d, and later sections of the present chapter), is not inherently incompatible with a propositional format and could, if desired, be recast in terms of some such articulated symbol system. If, in recasting an analog mechanism in terms of the language of symbol manipulation, we thereby place severe constraints on the symbolic processes, I take this as an advantage rather than as a disadvantage of the imposition of an analog mechanism.

So, when Pylyshyn (1978) and Minsky (1975) ask why we should suppose that a human or other higher organism uses an analog system when a propositional system is so much less constraining—is, in fact, capable of any specifiable sort of computation whatever—I answer: "That's why!" By definition, a completely unconstrained system cannot be more competent at any one kind of thing than any other. As a result, it cannot excel at any one. Being a "jack of all trades," it necessarily is a master of none. In particular, such a general-purpose system will not be suited to the rapid prediction of and preparation for external developments in a three-dimensional, Euclidean world any more than a Turing machine will provide for the safe and efficient control of air traffic. The more nearly the constraints prevailing in the world have been "hard-wired" into the system, the greater will be the effectiveness of the system in that particular world. In the words of the poet Wallace Stevens (1945):

> "I am a native in this world
> And think in it as a native thinks [p. 30]."

Note, too, that the period during which we have evolved in a three-dimensional world vastly exceeds the period during which we have developed the linguistic competency that is primarily responsible for suggesting a propositional form of representation.

To bring out a related point, let us concede to Pylyshyn that an articulated symbol system could be devised to account for all observed forms of human performance and competence—including the types that we commonly distinguish as verbal, logical, abstract, spatial, and perceptual. I, for one, would still want to know something about the particular character of the structures and processes that, within this general system, turn out to be uniquely effective in dealing, say, with problems of a spatial or perceptual nature as opposed to problems of a verbal or logical nature. The point here is related to the point raised against physiological reductionism. To propose a monistic system in which all processes are reduced to the same elemental components, whether these be at the level of interconnected neurons or at the level of articulated symbols, is not in itself to provide any clarification of the *organizational principles* that distinguish, within that same system, one general type of processing from another.

We can perhaps *conceive* that at some sufficiently abstract level, our cognitive processes are totally unconstrained, that we can (to complete the recursion) *conceive* of any possibility—of any possible world. It would, however, be ironic if the propositional viewpoint led to this conclusion, because it derives so directly from the linguistic contributions of Chomsky, who has repeatedly stressed the importance of innate constraining schematisms in the operation of the human mind (Chomsky, 1968, 1975). Still, whatever may be the case with respect to our most abstract cognitive processes, concrete perceptual cognitions are clearly subject to powerful internal constraints. To give just one example, we perceive a rigid rotation in the two-dimensional flow of a swarm of points projected from a tumbling three-dimensional system but not from a tumbling four-dimensional one (Braunstein, 1976; Green, 1961; Noll, 1965). What are the organizational principles that tune our perceptual competencies to the three-dimensional world in which we live as opposed to some other possible world? It is by no means clear that these organizational principles are formally identical to the principles that Chomsky takes to underlie our linguistic competency. And even if they are formally related, it is still more emphatically not clear that these principles arose in connection with the evolution of language *before* they arose in the service of perception (Shepard, 1975).

Finally, the proposal that all representation is propositional in format appears to leave a curious gap between unprocessed sensation and cognitive interpretation. Pylyshyn (1978) is silent concerning the mechanisms whereby "precategorical" sensations give rise to propositional encodings. Would propositional theorists admit the existence of a middle ground in which properties of various levels of abstraction are detected, scenes are segmented into objects, and objects and their spatial relations are analyzed and encoded? If so, this middle ground is, by hypothesis, neither purely propositional nor purely precategorical, and the possibility remains that it is precisely in this middle ground that the true work of perception goes on. Or would such theorists hold that these perceptual processes of abstraction, segmentation, and relational analysis are all carried on within the propositional system itself? If so, the particular part of this system that carries out these processes and that interfaces with the raw sensory input must have some particular properties dictated by the spatial character of those processes and those inputs. Whichever question is answered in the affirmative, I feel the need of a specification of the form in which the constraints characteristic of our particular world have become internalized as an essential, though effectively invisible, part of ourselves.

COMPLEMENTARITY AT TWO LEVELS

Complementarity of Representation and Object

I have taken as fundamental to an understanding of perception the idea that an organism's construction of a mental representation of the essential properties of an external object serves an important adaptive purpose. I hope I have made clear that despite what some Gibsonian critics of constructivist theories of perception might lead one to suspect, I am *not* thereby suggesting that the construction is ordinarily based on peripheral sensory cues that are, at best, only weakly, transiently, or uncertainly indicative of what is "out there." Even when, under favorable conditions, the peripherally available information is itself sufficient, the question remains as to the form and method of generation of that representation. And this is none other than what I have taken to be the *central* question of perception.

From the same standpoint, the objection raised by Skinner (1963) to the construction of an internal likeness of an external object, though valid up to a point, goes too far. Even though the internal reconstruction of such a likeness does not in itself solve the problems of pattern recognition and response selection, to the extent that the internal representation is a likeness of the *distal* object as opposed to its proximal projection, it could serve an extremely valuable function. For, clearly, the shifting two-dimensional retinal pattern provides a much less useful basis for the control of motor acts than would a stable internal model of the three-dimensional world and, of course, of one's relation to that world.

But in order to serve this adaptive function, must the internally constructed invariant model be a likeness? Must it literally be similar to or resemble its external referent? No, not literally.

No more so, I have argued, than a lock must resemble its key (Shepard, 1978d). Just as the essential thing about a lock and its key is the unique functional relation between them whereby the lock is normally (i.e., from the outside) operated only by its corresponding key, the essential thing about a perceptual representation and its object is the unique functional relation between them whereby the percept is normally (except while dreaming or hallucinating) elicited only by its corresponding distal object.

Does this, then, mean that the relation is merely one of causal dependency and that the internal representation can be a structureless, unitary event whose functional significance is conferred on it wholly by the external object that ordinarily elicits it? No, again—not generally. True, in the special case of what I have elsewhere referred to as "unanalyzable" or "unitary" stimuli, of which homogeneous colors are perhaps the purest example, each internal representation may well be structureless in this sense (Shephard, 1964a, 1975). Any isomorphism between such internal representations and their corresponding referents can then be encoded only at what I have termed the "second-order" level—that is, the level of the functional relations (principally of mutual substitutability) between those internal representations (Shepard, 1975; Shepard & Chipman, 1970; Shepard, Kilpatric, & Cunningham, 1975).

However, most objects and scenes, unlike homogeneous colors, are quite analyzable in that one can readily attend to and thus perceive a subset of the parts or features while ignoring the rest. This fact alone demonstrates that the internal representation corresponding to such an object or scene has its own internal structure with subparts that can be selectively emphasized or dropped from moment to moment. The internal constraints that govern the ways in which these representations transform into each other and that govern skilled manipulative acts, whether overt or covert, also require that such representations possess a rich internal structure. Thus, just as a lock has a hidden structure that is to some extent complementary to the visible contour of the key, the internal structure that is uniquely activated by a given object must have a structure that somehow meshes with the pattern manifested by its object. Moreover, it is by the internal manipulation of this inner structure, presumably, that one selectively attends to or prepares for a particular stimulus or, by "reading" this structure, guides a mental or motor manipulation.

The presence of such an internal structure implies some degree of at least an "abstract first-order isomorphism" between a representation and its object (Shepard, 1975). And in this case, the presence of such a first-order isomorphism underlies and explains the "second-order isomorphism" that seems to hold so widely in human perceptual and cognitive processes (see Shepard & Podgorny, 1978, for a recent review). But in the case of the percept, as in the case of the lock, this abstract isomorphism is more one of complementarity than of similarity or resemblance. A mechanism based on this kind of complementarity is not, however, unprecedented in biological evolution. At a much lower level, the mechanism whereby an enzyme "recognizes" a particular molecule is of essentially this same complementary, lock-and-key character (Shepard & Podgorny, 1978, p. 227).

I suppose, in short, that the selective pressures of biological evolution in a common three-dimensional world have shaped, in higher organisms, a perceptual mechanism whereby objects are represented in a way that preserves the information most essential for survival—information about the inherent properties of objects and about the organism's spatial relations to them—whereas information corresponding to accidental circumstances is largely suppressed. Although the requirement that internal representations be efficient in permitting the organism to recognize, to prepare for, and to respond to significant events dictates that the essential information about the external object be preserved in the internal representation, this requirement does not prescribe that the form in which the information is preserved be one strictly of likeness or resemblance.

In fact, because the representation and its object are necessarily confined to inherently disjoint domains, they cannot be compared for resemblance or similarity. The question we can answer is not one concerning a literal resemblance between the internal and external counterparts; rather, it is a question concerning a kind of complementary "meshing" between these counterparts. The success of a hungry cat waiting at a hole for the reemergence of a mouse depends on the speed and accuracy with which the cat is prepared to perceive and to respond to that emergence when and if it occurs. But the readying of the appropriate perceptual representation and the control of the appropriate motor response, alike, take place in the internal, rather than in the external, domain of the cat. The representation that will serve the necessary recognizing and controlling function need not physically resemble the external object in order to provide for a rapid and precise mesh with it.

At this point some commentators on my position raise the objection that the complementarity between a lock and a key, like that between a photographic positive and a negative, is also in part a relation of concrete physical resemblance. Although the two objects, when brought into a mesh with each other, fill complementary regions of space, they also share a boundary having a similar physical shape. This objection does indeed bring out an inadequacy of such concrete metaphors as the lock and key or the positive and negative. But we should not take these metaphors literally. Because a representation and its object cannot literally be brought together, the "mesh" in this case is a more abstract, functional one mediated by sensory transformations more analogous, perhaps, to the Fourier transforms, which have played a central role in theories of auditory processing since Helmholtz (1877/1954) but in visual processing only recently (see Graham, Chap. 1, this volume). Such transformations preserve structural information only in a very abstractly isomorphic or "paramorphic" form (to use the less restrictive term suggested to me by Amos Tversky, 1978); they certainly do not preserve it in any concretely isomorphic form.

We need to be especially careful in considering the role of resemblance in the internal representation of three-dimensional objects. On one hand, there are many kinds of evidence that such an internal representation is a closer model of the external three-dimensional object than of the two-dimensional retinal image. (See the demonstration presented here in Fig. 10.2 and, especially, the various empirical results reported in Metzler & Shepard, 1974.) On the other hand, the now well-established fact that the time to compare two such objects in different orientations increases linearly with the angular magnitude of their orientational difference conclusively shows that the internal representation is not of the inherent three-dimensional structure of the object itself but only of that structure *as seen from a particular direction* (Metzler & Shepard, 1974, p. 196). Clearly, then, the internal representation does not achieve a strict resemblance either to the proximal stimulus or to the distal object, considered in itself. What it does achieve—via the intervening sensory (and motor) systems—is an effective "mesh" with the external object in the particular spatial relation that object currently bears to the subject.

A variant of the lock-and-key metaphor, suggested to me by Robert Shaw (1977), may have some advantages for illustrating this particular point. When we speak of "cupping" a hand to receive a physically presented cup, we do not mean that the hand as a whole is made to resemble the structure of the cup as a whole. We mean only that a portion of the hand is made complementary to a certain portion of the cup so that a fit will be achieved when the cup and the hand come together in a certain relative orientation. The mental preparation for the appearance of a certain three-dimensional object in a certain orientation has something of the same character. Whatever the detailed nature of the internal process as a whole, we might say that it "shapes" the outward-directed part of itself in anticipation of the "impression" that the object in that orientation would leave upon it.

Complementarity of Internal and External Transformation

As a number of recent discussions of internal representation have emphasized, one cannot deal with mental representations without at the same time considering the nature of the internal processes that give rise to and that in turn operate upon these representations (Anderson, 1976, Chap. 1, 1978; Pylyshyn, 1973; Shepard, 1975; 1978e; Shepard & Podgorny, 1978). The reason is, of course, that behavioral evidence does not give us direct access to mental representations. It gives us access only through the processes that mediate between that representation and the external world. We can always propose a different form for an internal representation as long as we are willing to propose, also, a compensating change in the mediational process.

In addition to considering the processes that lead from a stimulus to an internal representation and back out to an overt response, moreover, we need to take cognizance of processes that transform one internal representation into another. Indeed, beginning with our first study of "mental rotation" (Shepard & Metzler, 1971), transformations that correspond to spatial transformations in the external world have been the primary focus of much of the experimental work that I have carried out in collaboration, particularly, with Cooper and Metzler and various of our associates (including Bassman, Farrell, Glushko, Judd, Koto, Podgorny, and Robins).

Even though these transformations are purely internal, they are of direct relevance to perception for several related reasons: (1) Sometimes it is by means of such transformations that we are able to recognize an object even when it appears in a different orientation (Cooper, 1975; Cooper & Shepard, 1973a, 1978). (2) Often it is by means of such transformations that we are able to prepare for the appearance of an object expected in a particular position or orientation (Cooper, 1975; Cooper & Shepard, 1973a, 1975; Metzler & Shepard, 1974). (3) The processes underlying such voluntary mental transformations have much in common with the processes that are involuntarily driven by the corre- sponding physical transformations (Cooper, 1976; Shepard, 1975). (4) And in particular, the transformations of apparent movement, which *are* experienced perceptually, seem to obey the same constraints as the corresponding purely mental transformations (Robins & Shepard, 1977; Shepard, 1978a; Shepard & Judd, 1976). Moreover, as I suggest in a later section, there is reason to suppose that such transformational possibilities may play a role in the three-dimensional interpretation of static objects, and may even be at the basis of the perception of the shapes and symmetries of objects in general.

Figure 10.1 schematically diagrams the roles of these two general types of transformations—namely, those that mediate between an internal representation and the outside world, and those that carry one internal representation into another. A three-dimensional external object A gives rise to a proximal stimulus—say, a two-dimensional retinal image A'—by means of an external physical transformation—in this case, an optical projection p. On the basis of this projected two-dimensional surface-structure A', an internal representation or "deep-structure" A* is then constructed by some transformation f*. (I use upper- and lowercase letters for objects and transformations, respectively, and I attach asterisks to distinguish those that are internal from those that are external.) The transformation f* can be thought of as a *rule of formation* for constructing a deep-structure representation on the basis of the surface-structure information available at the periphery. In addition, however, there must be *rules of transformation* t* governing the mapping of one deep structure into another. Our exper- iments on mental transformations have provided information concerning rules of both types, f* and t*.

With respect to rules of transformation, these experiments have established that subjects prepare for or respond to a spatially transformed presentation C of an object A either by performing an internal transformation t*, which maps A* into C*, or else by performing its inverse transformation t^{*-1}, where C* is the internal representation corresponding to the externally transformed object C. Moreover, this internal transformation t* is an analog of the corresponding external transformation t in the sense that in the course of the internal transforma- tion t*, the representational process passes through intermediate states, such as B*, with a demonstrable one-to-one correspondence to what would be inter- mediate states B in the external world. Speaking abstractly, we say that the scheme depicted in Fig. 10.1 commutes: The sequence of transformations t, p, f* has the same internal result as the sequence of transformations p, f*, t*, and this holds for all such external–internal pairs (t,t*), (t_1,t_1^*), (t_2,t_2^*), and so on. Furthermore, the times required to complete the component transformations t_1^* and t_2^*, to map A* into B* and then B* into C*, are additive. (See Cooper & Shepard, 1978, for a recent overview of the relevant empirical results.)

With respect to the rules of formation, our experiments have also established that the formational mapping f* is analogous to an inverse of the optical projec-

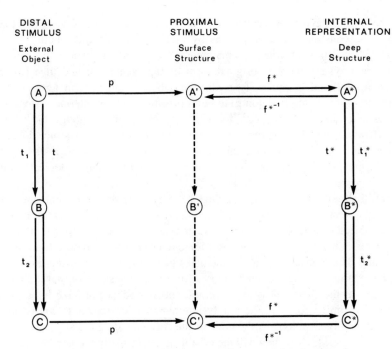

FIG. 10.1.   Schema of the projective, formational, and transformational mappings between distal objects, proximal stimuli, and internal representations.

tion p. The times required to carry out the internal transformations t^*, t_1^*, t_2^* are directly related to natural parameters of the three-dimensional distal objects A, B, C, such as the angular differences in their orientations in depth, and not to any immediately available parameters of their two-dimensional retinal images A', B', C' (Metzler & Shepard, 1974). Thus an internal representation A*, though constructed on the basis of a two-dimensional projection A', extracts and preserves the essential properties of, and thus achieves a kind of "regression" to, the three-dimensional external object A, as is required for survival.

The same evolutionary perspective leads to considerations concerning efficiency that weigh, it seems to me, against Anderson's (1976, Chap. 1; 1978) highly skeptical conclusions about the possibility of inferring the form of internal representations from behavioral data. Drawing on the theory of recursive functions, Anderson offers a proof that for any information-preserving change, from A* to g(A*), in the proposed form of all internal representations, one can construct altered mapping functions—of both the formational and transformational types f* and t*—that will exactly compensate for the proposed change in representation and, so, predict the same observable behavior. However, in our joint examination of a prepublication version of Anderson's proof, my associates Wes Hutchinson (1978), Carol Krumhansl (1978), and I reached the conclusion that the formal device he uses to establish the altered functions is artificial. In essence he constructs these functions by including within them both: (1) the inverse of the original formational mapping f_1^{*-1}, in order to back entirely out of the internal system with its original form of representation; and then (2) the altered formational mapping, f_2^*, which has been contrived (in terms of the information-preserving function g) to permit reentry into the internal system in a manner consistent with the new form of representation. Although the formal proof demonstrates that the required altered functions can be constructed in this roundabout way, it does not establish the existence of equivalent direct and efficient mappings of the sort that would have arisen through biological evolution.

Presumably the formational mappings have evolved so that matching against the distal object is optimally (1) rapid, and (2) tailored to the relevant properties of that object (cf. Shepard, 1978e). Otherwise, too much computation would remain for our hungry cat, as well as for our tasty mouse, before their actual encounter. The transformation that mediates between the internal representation and the external world, f^*, can be most efficient in this sense only if the representation has the closest possible structural correspondence or "mesh" with its object. For similar reasons, the purely internal transformations t^* can be most useful to the organism only if they mirror the corresponding transformations t in the external world. Only then will the organism be optimally prepared to respond to an ongoing event at any point in its course—an ability that is inherent in an analog representational process as my collaborators and I have defined it here and elsewhere (Cooper, 1976; Cooper & Shepard, 1973a; Metzler & Shepard, 1974; Robins & Shepard, 1977; Shepard, 1975, 1978d).

The internal transformations, like the representations transformed, need have no concrete resemblance to their external counterparts. As I have been at pains to emphasize, to speak of "mental rotation" is not to imply that there is anything that literally rotates within the subject's physical brain. Those who, in commenting on our work, sometimes use the shortcut of speaking as though we believe that subjects literally do "rotate a mental image" (e.g., Kosslyn & Pomerantz, 1977, p. 68; Pylyshyn, 1978, p. 21) must be presumed to be speaking either rather loosely or metaphorically. The only thing that we claim actually rotates is something that is rather abstract or hypothetical *and* that is defined in relation to the external world—namely, the orientation in which the external object would be most rapidly discriminated *if* it were to be physically presented at that moment. Just as I have been proposing that the relation between an internal representation and its external object is one of complementarity, not resemblance, I am now suggesting that the mental operations that transform one representation into another are complementary, not strictly similar, to the corresponding operations on the external objects.

There is a metatheoretical implication of the general approach that I am advocating, with its stress on evolutionary plausibility and its formalization in terms of internal representations and rules of formation and transformation as schematized in Fig. 10.1. A theory of perceptual processing need not be developed exclusively by gradually fitting together the bits and pieces of information gleaned from blind empirical probings, whether behavioral or neurophysiological. Since the internal representations and their rules of formation and transformation are all presumed to be complementary to corresponding external objects and their rules of projection and transformation in three-dimensional space, a consideration of the invariants of these projections and transformations should provide guidance both in the erection of tentative theories and in the design of our experiments. It is from this methodological standpoint that I find so much of value in ecologically oriented approaches such as that of Gibson (1966).

This is not, however, to say that our experimental designs should impose the same ecological structure. On the contrary, we can most effectively reveal the inner machinery of the perceptual system with external probes only if those probes are contrived to depart sufficiently from the naturally occurring environmental events to which that system has already become so well adapted as to be virtually transparent—that is, invisible. So, just as the physicist—in probing the inner constitution of matter—is driven to the construction of very special (i.e., unnatural) machines, we—in probing the inner workings of mind—may be driven to the presentation of very special (i.e., unnatural) spatiotemporal events.

EXPLORATIONS OF FORMATIONAL MAPPINGS

Obligatory Rules of Formation

The processes by means of which we transform one internal representation into another are often optional. For example, one can choose whether or not to imagine an object in some different orientation. By contrast, formational processes have been evolutionarily shaped to become so involuntary, automatic, and efficient as to give rise to the already noted illusion of transparency. Because we are largely unaware of the complex but efficient processes that underlie this illusion, we fail to appreciate the ubiquity and power of our internalized rules of formation. And even when we do achieve some intellectual understanding of these rules, this understanding has little or no effect on the perceptual experience itself.

Let me illustrate with a previously unpubished example (taken from my 1971 grant proposal to the National Science Foundation). In Fig. 10.2 I have drawn three rectangular boxes A, B, C with shaded tops. Try to override the tendency to interpret these line drawings as portrayals of three-dimensional objects. Try to see them as purely two-dimensional designs. If you think you can experience the surface structure of the stimulus free of any deep-structural interpretation, compare the sizes and shapes of the shaded parallelograms in these three patterns to see whether the shaded parallelogram in B, taken as a purely two-dimensional pattern, is more like that in A or in C. People are surprised to learn that the parallelogram in B is, in fact, identical to that in A but much longer and thinner than the shaded parallelogram in C. Just how much longer and thinner is indicated by the dashed outline superimposed over the shaded parallelogram in C. (The most effective way to demonstrate the congruence of parallelograms in A and B and the disparity in B and C is by means of a movable transparency on which the outline of the shaded parallelogram in B has been copied.)

The lesson is that the interpretive rules underlying shape constancy are largely obligatory and cannot be suppressed by an act of volition. These rules predispose us to prefer an interpretation in which all the angles are right angles in three-dimensional space over an interpretation in which the angles all fall in the same plane but vary widely in size. This, in turn, predisposes us to perceive the long axis of the parallelogram in B (now interpreted as more nearly rectangular) as more nearly orthogonal to the line of sight than the parallelogram in A. According to the knowledge of projective geometry that has been incorporated into our perceptual machinery, then, the parallelogram in A must be subject to much more foreshortening than the parallelogram in B. Because the two parallelograms as such are in actuality the very same length, the foreshortened parallelogram A must represent a rectangle, sloping back in depth, that is appreciably longer than the orthogonal one portrayed in B. Presumably the very same considerations explain why subjects have difficulty in detecting the surface features of the two-dimensional drawings of three-dimensional objects introduced by Weisstein and Harris (1974) and further discussed by Pomerantz (Chap. 6, this volume).

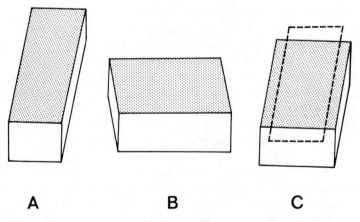

A   B   C

FIG. 10.2.   Visual illusion demonstrating the obligatory character of formational mappings. (The shaded parallelogram in B is congruent to that in A and to the dashed outline in C.)

In order to obtain some more specific empirical evidence concerning internalized rules of formation, my students and I have been investigating two-dimensional patterns that can be generated by continuous variation in a low-dimensional parameter space, some regions of which correspond to projections of three-dimensional objects (see Gauthier, 1977; Shepard, 1979; Shepard & Cermak, 1973). In experiments of this type, we ask whether the patterns that subjects recognize as correct portrayals of some specified object also define a sharply delimited region and, if so, to what extent that region coincides with the objectively correct region. From the shape of the subject-defined region, we may be able to infer the implicit rules of formation of internal representations of three-dimensional objects, whether or not these correspond to the objectively correct rules of projection. The two following subsections illustrate the two principal techniques we have tried—namely, continuous parametric variation under the subjects' control, and classification of individual stimuli exhaustively selected from a regular grid covering the parameter space.

Reconstruction of a Cube

Many people experience difficulty in attempting to draw a perspective view of a cube. Apparently, their difficulty is attributable to deficiencies in schemata of production rather than of perception: These same people will readily choose a correct perspective projection over their own drawing. In setting pencil to a blank sheet of paper, one is confronted with an unlimited number of degrees of freedom—an infinite-dimensional parameter space. To operate effectively in such an externally unconstrained situation requires highly constraining internal productive schemata that are well developed only in the artist. In order to circumvent this problem, we have built some special devices that reduce the degrees of freedom needed to reconstruct the cube to one, two, or three variable parameters. It then becomes possible for the subject to search the resulting low-dimensional parameter space to find a configuration that elicits a perceptual recognition of a proper cube.

Each such device consists of a fixed circular platform overlaid with a movable circular sheet of transparent plastic. Identical parallelograms are constructed with black lines on the fixed platform and on the movable sheet so that by sliding the transparent sheet over the opaque white platform, one can bring the one parallelogram into exact visual superposition on the other. From each corner of the movable parallelogram, a black thread passes through a hole at the corresponding corner of the fixed parallelogram and is held straight between these two corners by a weight attached to the free end out of sight beneath the opaque platform. Thus, no matter how the subject slides the plastic sheet over the fixed platform, a continuously variable two-dimensional figure results that is composed of 12 straight black lines forming six overlapping quadrilaterals, two of which are fixed parallelograms and four of which vary continuously in shape with the

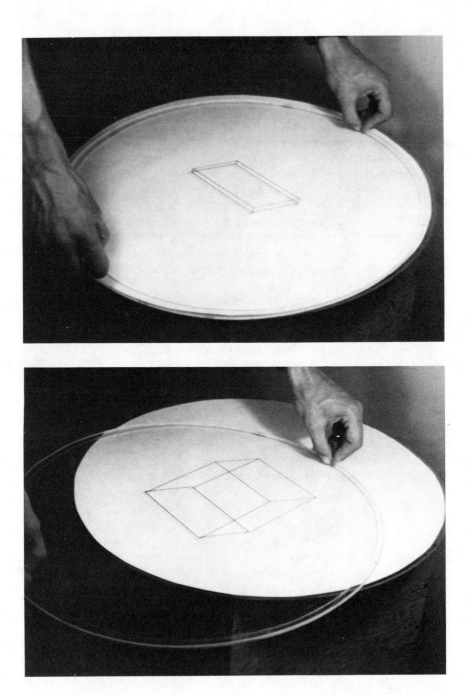

FIG. 10.3 Photographs of a device for reconstructing the two-dimensional projection of a cube (before and after a subject has slid the movable sheet).

position of the movable plate. The photographs in Fig. 10.3 show just one of these devices before and after a subject has slid the movable sheet in an attempt to achieve the appearance of a cube.

Unless additional constraints are imposed, the subject has three degrees of freedom in positioning the sheet—two of translation (the planar coordinates of, say, the center of the movable parallelogram of fixed shape), and one of rotation (the angle of the longest diagonal of that parallelogram, say, about its center point). These coordinates are determined, after the subject has finished adjusting the position of the movable sheet, by turning on a light under the platform and thus displaying the grid of a large sheet of graph paper fixed just beneath the otherwise opaque surface. The third, rotational, degree of freedom is not of particular interest here. Subjects uniformly converge to the correct rotational orientation with great accuracy on the basis, apparently, of the very simple rule that the four variable lines (the black threads) should all be parallel to each other or, equivalently, that all six of the overlapping quadrilaterals should be strict parallelograms.

The remaining two, the translational degrees of freedom, are of considerable interest, though, because there is no simple rule governing how the transparent sheet should be positioned on the two-dimensional surface. Because the device does not permit the realization of perspective convergence, there are only two (symmetrically disposed) positions that correspond to a correct projection of a cube for any given fixed parallelogram. These are the so-called parallel projections, which yield the same retinal image as does a cube viewed from a great distance. Given the fixed parallelogram defined by the lengths of two adjacent sides, r_1, and r_2, and the angle (in the two-dimensional plane) between them, Θ_{12}, the subject must determine the length r_3 and either of the two angles, Θ_{13} or Θ_{23}, as illustrated in Fig. 10.4. That this is nontrivial is indicated by the complexity of the trigonometric equations relating these three unknowns to the three givens, as shown at the right in the figure.

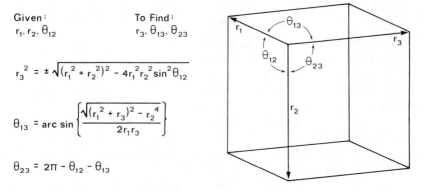

Given:
r_1, r_2, Θ_{12}

To Find:
$r_3, \Theta_{13}, \Theta_{23}$

$$r_3^2 = \pm \sqrt{(r_1^2 + r_2^2)^2 - 4r_1^2 r_2^2 \sin^2 \Theta_{12}}$$

$$\Theta_{13} = \arcsin \left[\frac{\sqrt{(r_1^2 + r_3)^2 - r_2^4}}{2r_1 r_3} \right]$$

$$\Theta_{23} = 2\pi - \Theta_{12} - \Theta_{13}$$

FIG. 10.4. Equations governing the correct positioning of the movable sheet in a device of the sort illustrated in Fig. 10.3.

Figure 10.5 shows the settings that subjects made in one condition of an unpublished experiment first outlined in my 1971 grant proposal to the National Science Foundation and subsequently carried out with the assistance of Dan Kilpatric. With respect to the fixed parallelogram, drawn at the left, the small round dots display the various positions to which subjects displaced the center of the movable parallelogram (all reflected onto the same side of the fixed parallelogram). Notice that relative to the extent of these displacements, the settings mostly fell within a quite tightly circumscribed region indicated by the dashed curve. And although there appears to be a systematic tendency of the displacements to fall to one side of the objectively correct displacement, indicated by the dashed arrow, this bias is relatively quite small.

Similar plots have also been obtained with different shapes for the given, fixed parallelogram. In later work, not presented here, we have also restricted the subjects to one degree of freedom by constraining the movable sheet to slide along a one-dimensional track. Preliminary results suggest that this permits still more accurate settings. (So perhaps even a two-dimensional parameter space is apt to lead to suboptimum solutions.) This same sort of technique would also lend itself to the systematic study of the effects, if any, of constraining the subjects to view the two-dimensional picture surface from some nonorthogonal angle. As Pirenne (1970) has argued concerning the three-dimensional interpreta-

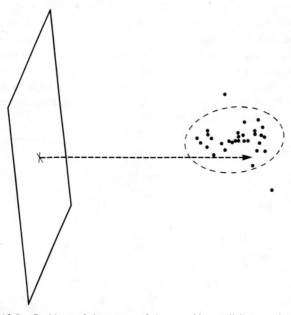

FIG. 10.5. Positions of the center of the movable parallelogram chosen by participants in an unpublished experiment by Shepard and Kilpatric. The arrow indicates the projectively correct displacement.

tion of two-dimensional perspective pictures in general, the slant of the picture surface should have a marked influence on the subject's settings only when the cues as to the slant of that surface are eliminated—for example, in a dark room with luminescent lines.

Recognition of Regular Corners

I have suggested that when it is consistent with a given two-dimensional projection, subjects prefer a three-dimensional interpretation in which all the corners of the three-dimensional object are right-angled. Accordingly, with the assistance of Elizabeth Smith and before the publication of a paper by Perkins (1972) called our attention to his closely related line of work, I undertook an investigation of the extent to which subjects have internalized the rules governing whether or not a two-dimensional projection corresponds to a rectangular corner. Although our results are consonant with those already reported by Perkins (1971, 1972), I briefly describe our somewhat different approach here in order to illustrate the use of systematic sampling from a parametric array and because our experiment, unlike that of Perkins, permits a comparison of judgments about right-angled corners with other, obtuse or acute, corners.

In this work, subjects viewed three radial lines meeting at the center of the white field exposed behind a circular aperture. On each trial they were asked to specify, in turn, whether the three lines could be seen as forming the vertex of each of three regular figures—namely, the cube, the regular tetrahedron, and the equiangular plane figure familiar to many people as the "Mercedes-Benz symbol," viewed from some angle in space. That is, they were to judge whether they were looking at a possible projection of a regular solid angle in which the three angles between the three edges were all 90°, all 60°, or all 120°, respectively. By remote control, they were free to rotate the disk containing the three lines in any way they wished, in its own plane, before making each final judgment.

If we disregard rotational differences, there are only two degrees of freedom (Θ_1 and Θ_2) for the possible two-dimensional patterns, as the three angles necessarily sum to 360°. If, further, we combine data for patterns that differ only by a reflection, we can confine our attention to just one-half of this parameter space. The reduced two-dimensional space of possible patterns that results from these simplifications is illustrated in 15° steps of the two smaller angles Θ_1 and Θ_2 in Fig. 10.6. With respect to surface features, which become relevant later, I have subdivided this triangular space into a two-dimensional region of "forks" (upper right) in which the largest angle between adjacent lines, Θ_3, is less than 180°, a two-dimensional region of "arrows" (lower left) in which this largest angle is greater than 180°, and a one-dimensional bounding set of "tees" in which this angle is exactly 180°. (Along the bottom there is also a one-dimensional bounding set of "ells" in which the smallest angle is 0° and the three lines reduce to two.)

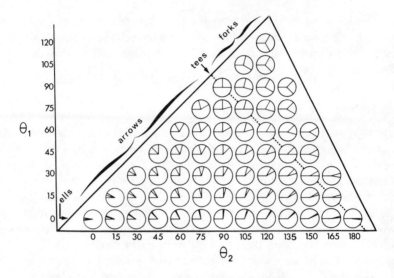

FIG. 10.6.   Two-dimensional parameter space of configurations of three lines meeting at a point, disregarding rigid rotations and reflections.

The regions of this parameter space that correspond to legitimate projections of the 120°, 90°, and 60° regular vertex (i.e., to the flat design, the corner of the cube, and the vertex of the tetrahedron, respectively) are indicated (to within the 15° grain of the sampling of the stimuli) by the dashed lines enclosing most of the larger of the black circles in Fig. 10.7. Note that the regions are quite different for the three cases and, moreover, that they break into two separate regions in the cases of the two solid objects—an upper region within which all three faces of the solid corner are "visible," and a lower region within which only two of the faces are "visible." In both cases the two regions are joined at a singular point corresponding to the unique pattern through which the surface projection must pass as any face rotates into or out of view.

The percentage of the subjects classifying each pattern as a corner of each of the three indicated types is indicated, proportionally, by the size of the corresponding black circle in Fig. 10.7, where the largest circle represents 100%. In the case of the cube, the subjective judgments were in very good accord with projective geometry. In fact, the division of the parameter space according to whether or not 50% or more of the subjects reported achievement of the cubical interpretation coincides exactly (within the 15° grain of the sampling) with the division into those regions that do and do not correspond to correct perspective projections of a right-angled corner. Apparently, human adults have internalized a good approximation to the rules that govern how 90° corners in the three-dimensional space project onto the two-dimensional retina. The agreement with projective geometry was somewhat less in the case of the plane figure and considerably less in the case of the tetrahedral corner, even though the subjects were given considerable familiarization with cardboard models of both types of structures before beginning their series of judgments of the planar projections.

There may be both structural and ecological bases for our superior accuracy in recognizing right-angled corners. Structurally, the rules for discriminating permissible from nonpermissible surface projections are somewhat simpler for the 90° than for the 60° corners (though for the 120° flat "corners," the rules become simplest of all—"forks and tees versus arrows and ells"). Ecologically, because we live in a "carpentered" environment, we have also had greater opportunity to learn the projection rules for rectangular corners. The structural and ecological considerations are not independent, however. For any given type of corner, structure determines that certain projections are ecologically less probable. Consequently there may have been less opportunity, and less reason, for the internalized rules to become sharply tuned in these regions of parameter space. This could explain why subjects tended to avoid the lower diagonal boundary of the permissible region for 120° design. For this bounding set of tee junctions represents the limiting singularity in which the plane of this flat configuration is viewed exactly edge on. The same consideration may explain the subjects' relative avoidance of the lower portion of the large upper triangular region for the 60° corner. As the angle defining the solid corner becomes smaller, that upper region (for three faces visible) becomes larger and larger while corresponding as a whole to the less and less probable circumstance in which the more and more sharply pointed corner is viewed almost "point on."

Finally, the fact that the presented stimuli are ambiguous brings out an intimate connection between perception and mental imagery. Any point within those regions in Fig. 10.7 where there is overlap of the permissible regions corresponding to the different types of corners represents a pattern that can be seen as at least two different types of corners. But the seeing of an ambiguous pattern "as" something falls somewhere between ordinary perception of an unambiguous object and the entirely imaginal picturing of an object in the absence of any external support. It is a kind of "externally guided imagery" (cf. Podgorny & Shepard, 1978; Shepard, 1978d; Shepard & Cermak, 1973). Perhaps significantly, the subjects in the present experiment reported that their responses, particularly in the case of the cubical corner, were not based upon an abstract intellectual judgment but upon a very concrete perceptual experience of actually seeing the pattern, for example, as the corner of a cube oriented in a certain position in space (cf. Attneave & Frost, 1969). Thus, it would appear that the implicit "rules of formation" that we are seeking to render explicit are the rules that underlie perception and imagery alike.

Optimization Under Projective Constraint

The results I have just described, together with the related results by others such as Attneave and Frost (1969) and Perkins (1972), imply that the rules of formation include some approximation to an inverse of the rules governing the optical

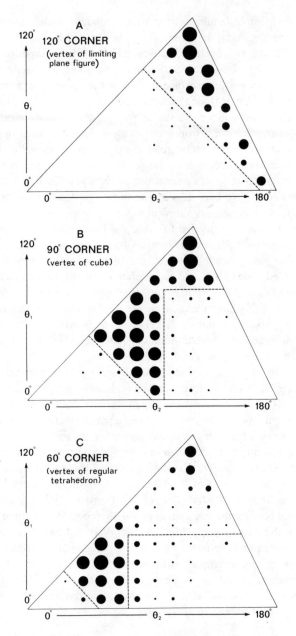

FIG. 10.7.   Percentage of choices of each of the patterns in Fig. 10.6 as possible projections of the plane figure (A), cube (B), or regular tetrahedron (C) in an unpublished experiment by Shepard and Smith. The size of each black circle is proportional to the percentage of choices of the corresponding pattern, and the dashed lines enclose the projectively correct patterns.

projection of three-dimensional objects onto a two-dimensional surface. However, this can not be the whole story. The mapping from three dimensions down into two is necessarily singular, and so—as the Ames demonstrations so dramatically attest (Ittelson, 1968)—that input mapping does not possess a unique inverse. The rules of formation must therefore incorporate some principles for selecting one out of the infinite set of inverse transformations that will, as we might put it, "retroject" any given two-dimensional projection back out into the three-dimensional world. The perceptual system may select a three-dimensional interpretation that optimizes simplicity, regularity, or symmetry. This proposal is in the spirit of the Gestalt idea that brain processes are governed by organizational principles of Prägnanz, which cause that process to tend toward a good figure. The more recent proposals by Attneave, Hochberg, and others (see Sober, 1975, Chap. 4) can be regarded as modern descendants of that original idea.

From the evolutionary perspective, however, the principles of simplicity, regularity, or symmetry that seem to explain observed phenomena of perception may not be fundamental. As I noted earlier, we can not gain a full understanding of perception by simply guessing at the form and level of organizational principles without recognizing their role in the adaptation of the species to its environment. Simplicity, for example, can be defined in various ways, and rather different conclusions might be reached depending on whether it is defined in terms of a deep-structure or surface-structure representation. It is only when we bring in considerations of the survival value of alternative schemes that we see that the optimization must be at the level where an approximate complementarity with the external world is to be achieved—that is, at the level of deep structure.

Structural Stability Under Transformation

As an illustration of how ecology may determine organizational principles, I would like to reconsider some rather old observations concerning the interpretation of visual scenes on the basis of the two-dimensional projections of the edges of simple objects. As Koffka (1935, p. 159), Hochberg and McAlister (1953), and others have noted, whereas the diagram on the left in Fig. 10.8A is invariably interpreted as a three-dimensional cube, the diagram next to it on the right—though also interpretable as a cube—is very often quite differently interpreted as a two-dimensional hexagon with intersecting diagonals. Invoking principles of symmetry or regularity, one might point out that the angles and edges in the diagram on the left become equal only when they are interpreted in three dimensions, whereas the angles and edges in the diagram on the right are already equal in the two-dimensional diagram. But from the evolutionary perspective advocated here, we should look behind such a symmetry principle for its ecological basis.

Notice, then, that under a three-dimensional interpretation, the two-dimensional projection on the left but not the two-dimensional projection on the

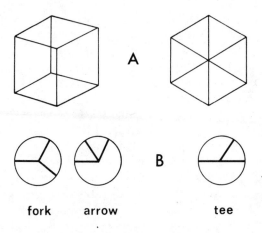

FIG. 10.8. Two-dimensional projections that (on the left) are structurally stable and (on the right) are structurally unstable under certain three-dimensional interpretations.

right is structurally stable in the sense of Thom (1975). That is, if either the three-dimensional cube or its two-dimensional diagram on the left is subjected to any suitably small rigid rotation in three-dimensional space, no topological discontinuities will be induced in the retinal projection. (An appreciable rotation of the cube is required before two lines will cross each other in the retinal projection.) By contrast, the two-dimensional projection on the right is not structurally stable under the three-dimensional interpretation. Whereas small rotations of the two-dimensional diagram again will not induce topological discontinuities, the smallest possible rotation of the three-dimensional cube (around any axis except the line of sight) will produce such a discontinuity at the center of the two-dimensional projection.

Remembering that the central problem of the organism is to infer the true structure of the external object giving rise to the current pattern of proximal stimulation, we can see the utility of the following principle of structural stability: Adopt, as the preferred three-dimensional interpretation, one for which any small perturbation of the interpretation that corresponds to a small rigid transformation in the external world leaves the projected image topologically invariant. Because the orientations of three-dimensional objects that give rise to structurally unstable projections are improbable, it is a poor perceptual policy under natural conditions, and in the long run, to infer such orientations when faced with such projections.

This idea can be traced back to Mach's (1906/1959) complementary principles of "probability" and "economy" and to a discussion, noted by Hochberg (1977), in which Helmholtz (1856/1962, Vol. 3) pointed to a connection between the visual system's heavy reliance on vernier acuity and the ecological improbability of being positioned just so that retinal projections of the contour of one object will, by accident, be aligned with the retinal projection of the contour of a second object. More recently, this idea has resurfaced in the inferential uses so effectively made of the retinally available "fork," "arrow," and "tee" junctions of the projected contours in computer-based methods of scene analysis (Guzman, 1968b; Thomas, 1978; Winston, 1975).

Thus the tendency to interpret either a fork or an arrow junction (shown on the left in Fig. 10.8B) as the corner of a single three-dimensional object derives from the improbability that for two independent objects, the edge of one would just happen to project in exact coincidence with the corner of the second. And the opposite tendency to interpret the tee junction (shown on the right in Fig. 10.8B) as the edges of two distinct objects, one behind the other, derives from the improbability that two intersecting edges of a single object would just happen to project in exact collinearity with each other. In accordance with the principle of structural stability, the favored interpretation in either case is the one for which small rigid transformations in the structure as interpreted leave the proximal pattern topologically invariant, whereas the nonpreferred interpretation leads to discontinuities under such perturbations.

The same principle sheds further light on the tendency—illustrated in Fig. 10.7—of subjects to avoid certain boundaries of the permissible regions, for (as I noted) some of these boundaries correspond to such singularities as the tee junction, for which structural stability is attained only by reinterpreting the presented pattern as two nonintersecting edges instead of three edges intersecting at the vertex of a single object.

This view of the role of structural stability in perceptual interpretation leads to the conjecture that the rules of formation of the percept of a static object depend, at least in part, on the rules governing the possible transformations of that object, for the determination of structural stability depends on internal explorations of rigid perturbations that, by my previous arguments, can be done only at the level of deep structure. Before amplifying on the possibly fundamental role of rules of transformation in perception generally, however, I need to review what we have so far learned about the nature of these internal transformations.

EXPLORATIONS OF TRANSFORMATIONAL MAPPINGS

Analog Transformations

Earlier I argued that the obligatory character of rules of formation has been favored by the greater efficiency possible with automatic processes (see Shiffrin & Schneider, 1977). I have just suggested that the representation of at least the *possibilities* of the alternative spatial transformations of an object may often have the efficient, obligatory character of formational mappings and may sometimes even determine the result of those mappings. Clearly, though, the actual performance of an internal transformation is often optional. Presumably, the reason for the difference between formational and transformational mappings in this regard is that whereas the appropriate formational mapping is relatively constrained by the requirement that it be the approximate inverse of the optical projection, the most appropriate internal transformation of the resulting internal representation is dependent on contingent knowledge gained by the particular individual about the most likely behavior of the object as well as on the momentary purposes of the individual.

In any case, when I speak of rules of internal transformation as optional, I do not mean that they have an arbitrary relation to transformations in the external world. I mean that which, if any, internal transformation is *applied* may be decided at other (e.g., "higher") levels of the system, independently of the obligatory perceptual representation. Once a particular transformation has been selected, I submit that the transformation is carried out in accordance with rules that embody constraints governing corresponding transformations on rigid physical objects.

Much of the work on mental rotation that my co-workers and I have been reporting during the last few years (see Cooper & Shepard, 1978) was, in fact, undertaken to discover the extent to which such constraints have been incorporated into mental operations. Evidence for the incorporation of such constraints is provided by the additivity of transformation times, and even more directly by the commutativity of physical and mental transformations: A match between an internal representation and a rotated stimulus can be achieved equally well by physically rotating the external stimulus into a mesh with the internal representation or by mentally transforming the internal representation into a mesh with the external stimulus. The speed and accuracy of the ensuing comparison in both cases indicates that the internal representation, even when it has been transformed, preserves the structural features of the object represented.

Our results suggest, further, that these features are preserved over the whole transformation by preserving them over each intermediate step along the way. That is, as indicated in Fig. 10.1, the transformation is carried out over a well-defined *trajectory,* each point of which is complementary to a corresponding intermediate stage of transformation of the external object. It is in this sense that the internal process is said to be a complementary *analog* of the corresponding external process. The computation of a rotated orientation by some alternative methods, such as a matrix multiplication, would not have this analog property (Shepard, 1978d).

Although the spatial transformation that my associates and I have investigated most intensively is pure rotation (Cooper, 1975, 1976; Cooper & Podgorny, 1976; Cooper & Shepard, 1973a, 1973b; Just & Carpenter, 1976; Metzler & Shepard, 1974; Robins & Shepard, 1977; Shepard & Judd, 1976; Shepard & Metzler, 1971), similar results for other types of spatial transformations suggest the analog character of other operations such as size scaling, alone or in combination with rigid rotations (Bundesen & Larsen, 1975; Larsen & Bundesen, 1978), and yet more complex sequences of reflections, rotations, foldings, joinings, and the like (Bassman, 1979; Cooper & Shepard, 1975, 1978; Shepard, 1975; Shepard & Feng, 1972).

Visual Illusion of Apparent Movement

Contrary to one current view (Gibson, 1966; Neisser, 1976), a recognition of the ecological foundations of perception need not entail experiments that mirror the spatiotemporal properties of the natural environment. I have already suggested just the opposite—that the internalized constraints of this system are most clearly revealed when our experimental probings systematically depart from the patterns to which the system has evolved a complementary fit, for only then does the system lose its "transparency" and so reveal its own inner structure. Thus, I find good reason to continue the laboratory study of perception under those artificial conditions of degraded, incomplete, or tachistoscopic presentation in which the internal constructive or filling-in tendency of the mind asserts itself.

The illusion of "apparent" motion, which arises under discrete or stroboscopic presentation, is especially illuminating for just this reason. It is no accident that Gestalt psychology got underway with Wertheimer's (1912) studies of apparent motion. The continuous impletion that is experienced between two discrete and isolated presentations reveals with special clarity the autonomous, synthetic tendencies of the underlying perceptual machinery. The research in which some students and I are currently engaged is motivated by the hope that the systematic study of apparent movement can go beyond the mere demonstration of mental impletion—to the determination of the form of the transformational principles governing such impletion.

Our first experiments on apparent motion, following our earlier studies of mental rotation, have focused on apparent *rotation*. We immediately noticed that the transformations we studied under the earlier paradigm of mental rotation were both more obligatory and (experientially) more compelling when stroboscopically driven in accordance with the paradigm of apparent movement. If we display two objects side by side, subjects can choose whether to imagine one of the objects rotated into the other in order to compare their shapes, as they apparently did in our first experiment on mental rotation (Shepard & Metzler, 1971). If pictures of the same two objects are alternately flashed in the same location, the perceptual system makes an involuntary identification between these two successive views and so has no choice but to "see" the two pictures as of one object transforming back and forth. Moreover, under appropriate circumstances, if the two objects are identical in shape and the rate of alternation is not too rapid, the subject experiences the transformation, with compelling vividness, as a rigid rotation.

As we have evolved in a three-dimensional world populated with enduring, movable, and often animated semirigid objects, it is perhaps remarkable but not entirely incomprehensible that the brain should have acquired the tendency to interpret the superficially different figural units in two successive glimpses as representing the same enduring object, or that it should try to construct—as the most probable representation of the intervening existence of that object—the most direct or minimum possible rigid transformation between the two successive views. However, such a process of mental impletion, like any mental process, must take time; and the larger the gap—that is, the larger the discrepancy between the two orientations—the more time will be required to construct an appropriate bridge.

Accordingly, in this work we have determined the critical rate of alternation at which there is a shift from the appearance of rigid to the appearance of nonrigid transformation. We have been heartened by the reliable and systematic relation between the minimum onset-to-onset interval for apparent rigid transformation and the extent of that transformation, by certain similarities between our approach and independently developed mathematical approaches to apparent movement (which subsequently came to our attention) by Foster (1978) and by Caelli, Hoffman, and Lindman (1978a), and also by the recent developmental evidence of Eleanor Gibson and her co-workers that the visual differentiation between rigid and nonrigid transformation is sufficiently basic to human perception to be demonstrable in the 5-month-old infant (Gibson, Owsley, & Johnston, 1978).

As might be expected from the more obligatory, perceptual character of rigid apparent motion, the breakdown times that we have measured have consistently been much shorter than the times estimated to carry out the corresponding mental transformations voluntarily. In the pattern of their dependence on stimulus variables, however, the estimated times for the imagined transformations of mental rotation and for the perceptually experienced transformations of apparent motion have been strikingly similar. In both cases, these times increase linearly with angular difference and at the same slope for differences corresponding to rotations in the picture plane and in depth (compare Shepard & Judd, 1976, with Shepard & Metzler, 1971). Moreover, the one-to-one correspondence between intermediate states of the internal process and intermediate orientations in the external world, which established the analog character of mental rotation, has now been provisionally established in the case of apparent motion, also (Robins & Shepard, 1977).

Impleted Trajectories of Transformation

The evidence from these two types of studies suggest a general hypothesis that can be stated in the following geometrical form: Corresponding imagined and apparent transformations take place over trajectories that tend (1) to be the same, and (2) to be the shortest or *geodesic* paths in the curved manifolds satisfying certain constraints—namely, the constraints corresponding to the maintenance of the structural rigidity of the external object. (Particularly similar in spirit to the notion of mental impletion of shortest trajectories of rigid motion proposed here and in Shepard, 1977, 1978a, is the idea of impletion of "least energy" paths of apparent motion that David Foster, unbeknown to me, had independently been developing during the last few years at the University of Keele in the U.K.; see Foster, 1978.) Although a detailed report of our own further work along this line must await the completion of several experiments now underway, the guiding ideas can be sketched as follows:

A rigid object in three-dimensional space has six degrees of freedom—three, which are rectilinear, of translation; and three, which are circular, of rotation. Disregarding translations, we are left with a three-dimensional parameter space of possible orientations of any object that—because of the cyclic nature of rotations—is of finite volume but unbounded. This parameter space, which is topologically equivalent to so-called projective space, can be modeled by the interior of a sphere in which diametrically opposite points of the surface are identified, and in which the intrinsic metric of any circular section passing through the center of the sphere is more like that of a hemisphere than like that of a flat disc. A complete 360° rotation of the object about any axis is abstractly represented by the motion of the point representing the object along a geodesic or great-circle path between two antipodal points (Shepard, 1978a).

All of this is strictly true only for asymmetric objects. If the object has a rotational symmetry, it will map into itself with some rotation short of 360°; hence, points in addition to diametrically opposite ones must be identified. Psychologically, a related consideration comes into play even for an object that is not strictly symmetric as long as the object, like most real objects, possesses some at least approximate symmetries (see Palmer & Hemenway, 1978). Then the object will, under certain rotations, become more similar to itself than under other, lesser rotations. Continuing my long-standing strategy of modeling similarity in terms of spatial proximity (Shepard, 1955, 1962, 1974), I seek a continuous deformation of the already curved three-dimensional manifold of possible orientations such that points corresponding to pairs of orientations whose similarities have been augmented by partial symmetries are brought closer together. The required deformation can be considered as carried out in some higher-dimensional embedding space.

The geometrical representation must be consistent with our findings concerning apparent motion. In addition to the already cited quantitative finding of a linear increase in the minimum time required for apparent rigid rotation as a function of the angle of that rotation, these include the following qualitative observations: (1) For any but extremely fast rates of alternation (exceeding, say, 20 cycles per second, at which apparent motion is replaced by the appearance of static but flickering superposition), subjects generally experience a single object transforming back and forth rather than two different objects appearing in alternation. (2) If the rate is slow enough and the two alternately presented objects are identical except for a rigid transformation, the apparent transformation will be perceived as rigid. (3) If the rate is increased, however, a point will be reached at which the appearance of rigid rotation breaks down (as has been noted, also, by Kolers and Pomerantz, 1971). Following this breakdown, the object often appears to undergo a smaller global transformation, whereas local features of the object exhibit nonrigid deformations or independent motions. (4) When the object possesses some approximation to symmetry such that in the particular relative orientations presented, the two objects have an augmented similarity to each other, the breakdown occurs for slower rates of alternation. (5) For views differing by a small rigid transformation of the object, the perceived motion always takes the same apparently minimum path. Thus in a collaborative study just completed by my associates Bundesen, Larsen, and Farrell (in press), the alternation between two presentations of the same shape differing both in orientation and in size leads to the perception of the minimum, helical or screwlike rigid motion in depth. (6) For views differing by a large transformation such as 180° rotation, however, there may be several equivalent paths, and the very same physical stimulus will give rise to distinctly different perceived motions on different occasions.

In the proposed geometrical model, the three-dimensional closed manifold can be thought of as a constraint surface in a higher-dimensional embedding space with these properties: (1) Motion of a point within the three-dimensional surface represents the abstract essence of a transformation of the object that preserves its rigid structure. (2) Motion along a geodesic path within that surface represents the minimum such transformation. Accordingly, when two orientations of an object are displayed in slow alternation, the brain is assumed to find, in effect, a shortest path between the two corresponding points within the constraint surface—possibly by some process of diffusion or spread of activation (cf. Anderson, 1976, Chap. 8; Shepard 1958). And having found such a path, the alternation need no longer be represented, at this abstract level, by the appearance and disappearance of the two separated points. In accordance with the principles of object conservation and least action, the same alternation can now be represented by a single, enduring point moving back and forth over the shortest connecting path.

However, when the rate of alternation is sufficiently increased, the brain will not have time to complete the connecting path during each cycle. (The required rate of completion exceeds, say, the rate of propagation of "spreading activation" within the constraint surface.) In this case, the identity of the two successively displayed objects can no longer be concretely instantiated in the strongest, and therefore most preferred, form of an identity of rigid structure. Instead, because most objects that do not conserve strictly rigid structure at least conserve semirigid structure, because most objects that do not conserve even semirigid structure at least conserve number (or volume), and so on, the brain takes recourse to successively weaker stations in a hierarchy of criteria of object identity. It relinquishes only in extremity the root hypothesis that the two objects, however transmogrified, are nevertheless the same.

By definition, a breakdown in perceived rigid rotation is represented by a motion of the point outside the constraint surface. As I have noted, the approximate symmetries characteristic of most natural objects induce convolutions in the constraint surface that bring otherwise remote regions of the surface into closer proximity in the embedding space. Accordingly, breakdowns or short circuits (produced, say, by a weaker spreading activation outside the constraint surface) are likely to occur via a shorter path through the embedding space. A transformation of the object is still seen, but it is nonrigid.

Illustration of the Role of Symmetry

The approximations to symmetry possessed by natural objects are both pervasive and complex. The proposed propagation of excitation within curved constraint surfaces might underlie the detection of these approximations to symmetry and, thus, the internal representation of shape in general. In the spirit of current Fourier analytic or "holographic" approaches to visual perception (Graham, Chap. 1, this volume; Pribram, Nuwer, & Baron, 1974), the structure of an object can be specified in terms of a generalized autocorrelation function (Uttal, 1975) giving the self-similarity of the object under every possible rigid transformation. Unfortunately, these varied and complex approximations to symmetry induce equally varied and complex convolutions of the already curved manifold of possible orientations. The differential geometry of the general case has not been worked out. However, even special cases are of some interest and at least suffice to illustrate how the geometrical approach can be brought into relation with empirical data.

In an experiment that we shall soon be reporting more fully, Joyce Farrell and I investigated a special case in which we: (1) reduced the dimensionality of the manifold of possible orientations from three to one by using random polygons that differed only by rotations in the picture plane; and (2) varied the approximation to just one specific sort of symmetry—namely, symmetry under 180° rotation (Shepard, 1977). To obtain a polygon with complete symmetry of this type, we simply cut a polygon through the center, discarded one half, duplicated the other half, and, after rotating the duplicated half 180°, attached it to the original half. (The original random polygons and the cuts were constrained to avoid undesirable discontinuities at the junction.) The resulting polygon had the desired property that the only rotation short of 360° that yielded self-congruence was the 180° rotation. Polygons of intermediate degrees of symmetry were generated by a linear interpolation between each of the original random polygons and the derived, rotationally symmetric polygons. On a given trial, a computer-driven graphical display alternately presented two different orientations of one such polygon, and by tapping a right- or left-hand key, the subject increased or decreased the rate of alternation until the point of breakdown of apparent rigid rotation in the picture plane had been determined.

Of course, any one random polygon, even one without any experimentally added rotational symmetry, will necessarily have some (albeit "random") structure. That is, unlike a circle, which is unique in having a completely flat autocorrelation function under rotation, the polygon will by chance resemble itself more at certain angular departures than at others. On the average over a number of different randomly generated polygons, however, the effects of only the experimentally imposed 180° symmetry should prevail.

Within the manifold of possible orientations, then, the geodesic path corresponding to the 360° rotation of an (asymmetric) random polygon will, on the average, approximate the great circle illustrated below the example of one such polygon on the left in Fig. 10.9. However, for the completely symmetric variant of that polygon, shown on the right, orientations 180° apart are identified, and as the polygon undergoes a 360° rotation, the trajectory in the now convoluted constraint surface completes two excursions around a geodesic curve that, on the average, approximates the smaller circle shown below the symmetric polygon on the right. For an approximately symmetric interpolated polygon, shown in the middle, the resulting trajectory takes a form in which all pairs of points corresponding to 180° disparities in orientation are close together, but not coincident, in the higher-dimensional embedding space. The two-dimensional drawing below the partially symmetric polygon in the middle provides no more than a qualitative idea of the average true structure of the resulting convoluted trajectory, which can only be isometrically embedded in a Euclidean space of four dimensions. In that drawing, the straight dashed-line segments connect points separated by 180° and are therefore all of the same length in the four-dimensional embedding space (where they in fact sweep out the nonorientable or "one-sided" band of Möbius).

The structure can be more precisely specified by means of parametric equations giving the dependence of each of the four-dimensional coordinates x_1, x_2, x_3, x_4 of the trajectory on the angular orientation Θ of the partially symmetric polygon, as follows:

$$x_1 = (\sqrt{1 - s^2}/\pi) \cos \Theta, \quad x_3 = (s/2\pi) \cos 2\Theta,$$

$$x_2 = (\sqrt{1 - s^2}/\pi) \sin \Theta, \quad x_4 = (s/2\pi) \sin 2\Theta.$$

In these equations, s (which can vary between 0 and 1) is the degree of experimentally imposed rotational symmetry of the polygon. As s approaches 0 or 1, respectively, the resulting closed curve approaches the limiting forms (embeddable in two dimensions) of the single larger circle shown in A or the doubled smaller circle shown in C.

The three plots at the bottom of Fig. 10.9 show how distance between points corresponding to different orientations of the two alternately presented polygons

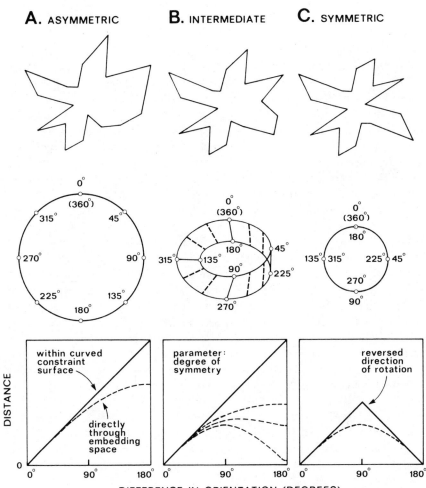

FIG. 10.9.   Representation of the set of orientations of a two-dimensional shape that is asymmetric (A), symmetric under 180° rotation (C), or intermediate between these (B). The plots at the bottom show how distance of transformation depends on angular difference for transformations that are rigid (solid lines) or nonrigid (dashed curves). (The illustrative polygons at the top are from an experiment to be reported by Farrell & Shepard, in press.)

depends on their angular disparity ϕ for each of two kinds of distance: geodesic distance within the constraint surface (indicated by the solid lines), and direct distance through the embedding space (indicated by the dashed curves). Formally, by substituting the already given parametric equations into the four-dimensional Euclidean distance formula, we can express the latter distance as the following function of the angular difference ϕ between the two orientations Θ_1 and Θ_2:

$$d = \sqrt{(2/\pi \sqrt{1 - s^2} \sin \phi/2)^2 + (s/\pi \sin \phi)^2},$$

which itself combines the single- and double-loop distances according to a two-component Euclidean rule.

The data (to be reported more fully by Farrell & Shepard, in press) are consonant with what the ideas proposed here would lead us to expect on the basis of these curves. For asymmetric polygons, the critical onset-to-onset time increases as an approximately linear function of angular disparity, as it did in the earlier experiment of Shepard and Judd (1976), and as it should if the motion is perceived as conserving rigid structure. For completely symmetric polygons, the critical time increases in a similar manner to 90° but then decreases with apparently the same slope toward 180° (where, of course, no motion is seen). For symmetric polygons differing by an angle ϕ exceeding 90°, the motion is perceived in the opposite direction through a smaller angle, 180° − ϕ.

For polygons (like the middle one in Fig. 10.9) that are linearly interpolated between the asymmetric and completely symmetric polygons, the critical times beyond 90° become more variable and increase more rapidly than for the asymmetric polygons. Usually at 180° and sometimes at 150°, subjects are not able to see a rigid motion no matter how much the alternation is slowed. As suggested by the disparity between the solid and dashed curves in the bottom middle of Fig. 10.9, the pull toward the similarly shaped and similarly oriented alternative is too strong to permit the completion of the path connecting to the identically shaped but very dissimilarly oriented alternative. The trajectory then tends to "short-circuit" through the embedding space instead of following the constraint surface.

Stated in general terms, the fact that constructive processes necessarily take time forces a trading relation between the level in the hierarchy of criteria of object identity at which two successive sensory events can be connected, on one hand, and the extent of the mental transformation required for the achievement of that connection on the other.

Apparent Movement in Auditory Pitch

Although phenomena of visual perception provide the most convenient access to internalized rules of formation and spatial transformation, considerations of ecological adaptation indicate that the representation of relations and transformations in space must be largely amodal and should manifest itself, coordinately, through other spatially oriented modalities such as those of touch, kinesthesis, and audition. Moreover, there is reason to believe that the spatial apparatus of the brain, acquired through protracted interaction with concrete physical space (and aided, possibly, by the circumstance that the brain is itself a three-dimensional spatial structure), has come—by extension or by preemption—to represent relations and transformations in spaces that are more abstract or metaphorical—

spaces of color, tone, or even (as I argue later) semantics. For the moment, the case of perceived motion in auditory pitch serves to illustrate the general point.

As Kubovy persuasively argues (Chap. 3, this volume), in the auditory domain, it is in fact pitch rather than literal space that is the "indispensable attribute" analogous to the indispensable attribute of literal space in the visual domain. On first consideration, the existence of a comparable illusion of apparent movement in pitch may seem doubtful. Certainly, two discrete notes played in alternation are never mistaken for a continuous glissando up and down between them. But the appropriate criterion for apparent motion is not that it cannot be discriminated from a real motion. The essential criterion, consonant with my definition of an analog transformation, is that the process can be shown to pass through a *path* between the two end points.

Our relative obliviousness to the connecting path of apparent movement in the case of pitch may stem from the more one-dimensional character of pitch and the consequent absence of alternative paths. In visual apparent rotation, by contrast, the phenomenon forces itself upon us by taking one of two or more equivalent paths. Thus when we alternately present a vertical and horizontal bar, as in the experiment by Robins and Shepard (1977), subjects either experience the connecting motion in the northeast and southwest or in the northwest and southeast quadrants, and the two experiences are distinctly different. But when a lower tone and a higher tone are alternated, we take it for granted that the alternation was between "lower" and "higher." Because there is no alternative path, we are not ordinarily aware that there was a "motion" over this path.

That there was, in fact, such a motion is readily demonstrated, however, by using tones that I specially contrived to be circular rather than rectilinear in pitch (Shepard, 1964b; and the example of this illusion on the audio tape accompanying this volume). When two such tones a half octave apart are played in succession, subjects hear the second tone as shifting through the musical interval of a tritone—but sometimes upward and sometimes downward in pitch. Because the two experienced shifts subjectively are entirely distinct, the fact that the shift occurred over a definite path (one way or the other around the "chroma circle") becomes obvious.

In fact, in work now underway, I am finding that something very much like the linear dependence of minimum onset–onset time for rigid motion in vision (which can be regarded as the modern quantitative equivalent of Korte's Third Law; Attneave & Block, 1973; Shepard & Judd, 1976) may hold also in the domain of pitch. As the rate of alternation of two tones is increased, there comes a point at which there is a definite subjective shift from hearing one tone moving up and down to hearing two separate tones going on and off more or less independently. And as the separation of the tones is increased in pitch (from a semitone to a half octave, say), the maintenance of the former "illusion" of motion requires longer and longer cycle durations.

Having only just now had the important paper by Jones (1976) called to my attention, I find that my notions here, as well as at several other points in this chapter, are quite parallel to hers (though she does not relate this auditory phenomenon to its long-known visual counterpart, Korte's Third Law). In agreement with Jones, I see the simple relationship of proportionality between time and distance as the basis of the phenomena of auditory stream segregation discussed by Bregman (Chap. 4, this volume). To perceive a sequence of tones as a melody is, in a sense, to perceive the sequence as a single tone moving in pitch. Whether two pitch sequences whose tones are played in temporal alternation are heard as a single melody or as two depends on the separation between the successive tones in pitch relative to their separation in time. The next tone to be identified with a given tone of one melody is the one closest to it in an abstract two-dimensional space of pitch–time. If the two component sequences are widely separated in pitch, the closest tone will always be one from the same sequence, and two separate paths will be simultaneously traced out in time. If the sequences are brought close enough together in pitch, the closest tone will always be the next one from the other sequence, and only one path threading through the two sequences will be experienced.

Current studies of the perception of musical intervals by Carol Krumhansl and myself (and initially inspired by a brilliant group-theoretic derivation of the structure of the diatonic scale by a recent Stanford Ph.D., Gerald Balzano) are revealing that in a musical context, pitch takes on a more complex structure than either the rectilinear or circular schemes just considered (Balzano, 1978; Krumhansl & Shepard, 1979; Shepard, 1978b). My own geometrical formulation brings out the relationship of these developments to the geometrical structures that I have been claiming underlie the visual representation of spatial transformations.

Much as the symmetries of a visual object induce deformations of the space of its possible orientations into a higher-dimensional embedding space, the symmetries inherent in the context of a musical key induce a deformation of the one-dimensional continuum of pitch into a double helical structure requiring an embedding space of at least five dimensions—two for a circular component corresponding to "tone chroma," two for another circular component corresponding to the "cycle of fifths," and one for a rectilinear component corresponding to simple "pitch height" (Shepard, 1978b). Moreover, much as the structure of a three-dimensional object is internally represented in a particular orientation, with differently oriented objects requiring mental rotation before comparison, the tendency of musical subjects to interpret tones relative to a particular (diatonic) key corresponds to a particular "projection" of the double helical structure, with the projections for more closely related keys obtainable by smaller angles of rotation of the underlying invariant structure. In addition, the two-dimensional (toroidal) submanifold in which this helical structure is also contained can be "unwrapped" into an infinitely repeating, flat two-dimensional lattice in which the common musical scales (including the major and minor diatonics, the pentatonic, the whole tone, and the chromatic) all form particularly simple spatial configurations. And finally, this same two-dimensional scheme turns out to be equivalent, under an affine transformation, to a two-dimensional lattice in which Balzano (1978) and Attneave (in his role as discussant at the same symposium) independently discovered that the most common chords, both augmented and diminished (including the major and minor triads, sixths, and sevenths), form maximally compact spatial configurations.

We can perhaps begin to discern some formal justification for a sentiment long ago expressed by Johannes Kepler, the man who "without predecessor" first articulated a single geometrical principle according to which all heavenly bodies advance eternally in their syncopated orbits in the manner of some stupendous "clockwork" (Holton, 1956). I refer to Kepler's statement that the "sublime" rules governing the audible harmonies of human multipart music mirror the even more sublime rules governing the rational harmonies of celestial mechanics and thus "conjure up in a short part of an hour the vision of the world's total perpetuity in time" (Popper, 1976, p. 59; also see Rodgers & Ruff, 1979; Walker, 1967).

General Principles of Impletion

I was at first surprised to find that what I had supposed to be two entirely unrelated lines of work—namely, those of visual apparent motion and the perception of musical intervals—had led me to geometrical representations that turned out to have essentially the same abstract structure. Now, however, I see this as a reflection of the accommodation of the necessarily rate-limited perceptual system, in all modalities, to very general principles of conservation, symmetry, and minimization operating in the external world. I mean, particularly, the hierarchy of principles of preservation of the structure of objects and of "least action" of their movement. These external principles have, I claim, engendered a set of internal principles for the rate-limited perceptual system that might be abstractly formulated in the proposed geometrical terms somewhat as follows:

Principle of Proximity.   Each object in a second (visual, auditory, or tactual) display tends to be perceptually identified with the object in the preceding display that is closest to it according to an abstract metric based on both literal proximity with respect to location and orientation and metaphorical proximity with respect to perceptual resemblance or similarity.

Principle of Least Path.   Each such identification is instantiated in a form corresponding, abstractly, to a shortest connecting path in the space defined by this metric.

Principle of Exclusion.   In ambiguous cases for which alternative stimuli are approximately equal in proximity or for which alternative connecting paths are approximately equal in length, the internal system exhibits a multistability such that one alternative preemptively captures ascendancy on any given occasion, temporarily suppressing all other alternatives.

Principle of Induction.   In ambiguous cases, the path constructed in one region of space tends to be the one most "parallel" or "coherent" with other paths already completed in neighboring regions of space.

It is my hope that when fully articulated, the exclusion principle, working in concert with the other principles, will suffice to explain various observations that we, following Kolers (1972) and Attneave (1974a), have been making— including the following: When two different displays consisting of the same number of dots are alternately exposed, each dot in one display tends to move back and forth into the position of one and only one dot in the other, even though two dots in one display may be the closest neighbors of the same dot in the other.

In the application of the exclusion principle, the fact that a particular path has just been traversed may be more important than the direction of that traversal, for, as I already noted, alternate presentation of a vertical and horizontal bar gives rise almost always to the experience of a 90° oscillation—almost never to the experience of a continuing 360° rotation. Apparently, the effect of the internal simulation of a motion in one direction through a particular pair of opposite quadrants leaves a sufficiently long-lasting suppression of the path through the other pair of quadrants that when the first bar is again presented, the internal simulation returns in the reverse direction over the already used trajectory rather than continuing in the same direction over the still suppressed alternative trajectory.

The principle of exclusion obviously suggests the operation of a neural mechanism akin to lateral inhibition. The principle of proximity as well as the principles of induction and least path (which might be regarded as higher-order principles of proximity) point, instead, toward some sort of excitatory mechanism. Indeed, if the neural substrate possesses the requisite metric of neural connectivity, then all three of these principles might be explainable in terms of one unitary mechanism sharing properties of the "trace-diffusion" model that I long ago proposed to account for phenomena of stimulus generalization (Shepard, 1958) and recognition memory (Shepard, 1961), the more recent "spreading-activation" models of memory search (Anderson, 1976, Chap. 8; Collins & Loftus, 1975; King & Anderson, 1976; Quillian, 1966), and a still more recent and pertinent mathematical model for the induction of apparent movement by "retarded neuronal flows" (Caelli, Hoffman, & Lindman, 1978a). Basically, the firing of one neural structure would be said to prime a host of other more or less closely related structures (with corresponding forces and delays) by triggering a wave of excitation that decays as it propagates through the underlying neural network.

Clearly, in this view the neural substrate is not the homogeneous, structureless medium seemingly envisioned by the Gestalt field theorists (Köhler, 1929,

1940). Rather, the evolutionarily shaped metric of connectivity of this substrate should probably be regarded as embodying more of our detailed knowledge about what Tolman and Brunswik (1935) called the "causal texture of the environment" than the relatively structureless principles that govern the spread of excitation and inhibition within this substrate.

Of course, what little structure has been specified for these principles is still incomplete and, even so, may be wrong. In the principle of induction, for example, exactly what motions qualify as "parallel" or "coherent" must be elaborated. About all we have to go on so far are qualitative observations that concurrent motions tend, where possible, to be experienced as taking place in parallel directions or in rotation about parallel or, still better, about coincident axes in perceived three-dimensional space.

Presumably, it is the principle of induction that underlies the well-known phenomenon of kinetic depth wherein the three-dimensional rotation of a system of points is compellingly experienced as rigid on the basis of the nonrigid swarming of those points in a merely two-dimensional projection (Braunstein, 1976; Green, 1961). Again, as demonstrated by the earlier results on mental rotation (Shepard & Metzler, 1971) and apparent movement (Attneave & Block, 1973; Corbin, 1942; Ogasawara, 1936; Shepard & Judd, 1976), the spatial component of the metric of proximity underlying the induction principle, as well as the other principles, is a deep-structure metric that models distances in the external three-dimensional world rather than distances at the sensory surface.

Connections Between Formational and Transformational Mappings

The phenomenon of kinetic depth provides striking confirmation of the hypothesis that I introduced in connection with my earlier discussion of structural stability—namely, the hypothesis that rules of formation depend on rules of transformation, and vice versa. In the context of kinetic depth, the principle of induction can be seen as extending—from a single object to a system of many objects—the pervasive preference of the interpretative machinery for transformations that are rigid or otherwise coherent. Thus, in accordance with the Gestalt principle of "common fate," we can say that as soon as the motion of a subset of objects is perceived as a rigid motion, the subset itself comes thereby to be represented as a unitary, higher-order object. We then have the extreme case in which the perception of an object depends entirely on the perception of its transformation (or on what Kubovy, Chap. 3, this volume, calls the "pure successive-difference cue"): Following cessation of its coherent motion, the subset of (lower-order) component objects loses its identity as figure and rapidly fades back into the ground of remaining objects.

In less extreme form, a similar dependence holds for objects quite generally. In apparent rotational motion, for example, the appearance of an object itself depends on the representation of its current mode of transformation. When the rate of alternation is sufficiently slow, both the motion and the object are perceived as rigid. When, under a faster rate of alternation, the apparent motion becomes nonrigid, the object appears nonrigid—that is, flexible, rubbery, hinged, or jointed. (Again, for the auditory analog, see Jones, 1976.)

The influence of the perception of the transformation on the perception of the object evidently operates in the opposite direction as well. As part of one unpublished experiment on apparent movement, Mary Koto and I alternately exposed the two patterns in Fig. 10.10A. Subjects usually reported seeing the black square at the top as stationary and the two black squares at the bottom as sliding back and forth as a rectangular unit. When, however, a single connecting square was also blackened as shown in Fig. 10.10B, subjects usually reported seeing the resulting set of four black squares as a rigid L-shaped unit. Preservation of the rigidity of this object required that the two black squares at the bottom no longer be seen as sliding back and forth. Instead, the entire structure was now seen as rigidly rotating 180° out into depth about the axis defined by the common vertical column of three black squares.

Similarly, when Sherryl Judd and I, in another as yet unpublished experiment, alternately presented a random polygon and the same polygon compressed by 50% in the horizontal direction, subjects reported seeing the polygon undergo a rigid (presumably 60°) rotation into depth rather than seeing it undergo a nonrigid compression within the picture plane. Most dramatic was the limiting case: When we alternated the polygon with nothing more than a vertical line segment of the same vertical extent, subjects saw the polygon as rigidly rotating 90° in depth between the completely flat and directly edge-on orientation. In both cases, moreover, the critical onset–onset times were in approximate agreement with

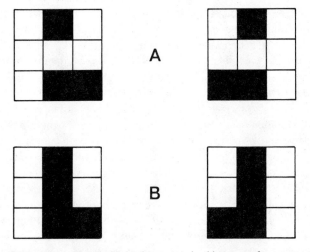

FIG. 10.10.   Two pairs of alternately presented grid patterns from an unpublished experiment on apparent motion by Shepard and Koto.

corresponding times for apparent rotation of the same polygon in the picture plane.

The angularity of these random polygons, as well as those that Farrell and I used for our study of symmetry in apparent rotation, evidently favored the interpretation of those figures as rigid objects and, thence, the perceptual experience of their rigid rotation. Curved free forms are more apt to appear three-dimensional (see Shepard & Cermak, 1973). In preliminary experiments, subjects were more likely to see forms of this type as moving in depth; hence, they were less able to achieve or to maintain the illusion of a strictly rigid rotation over large angles in the picture plane.

Furthermore, much as some figures (like the hexagon with intersecting diagonals in Fig. 10.8A) can be seen as two- or three-dimensional objects, some can be interpreted as either rigid or deformable objects. An ellipse, for example, can be seen as a foreshortened circle or as a deformable rubber band or three-dimensional balloon. And as is strikingly demonstrated by one of Gunnar Johansson's films, two luminous dots can be seen as two objects capable of independent movement or as the ends of a rigid rod. Morever, the initial perceptual interpretation of the static display influences whether or not its ensuing motion is perceived as rigid. In the case of such displays, the alternative perceptual interpretations of the display cannot be adequately represented by the same point in a constraint manifold. Instead, corresponding to each level in the hierarchy of criteria of object identity, there may be a different constraint subspace—with weaker criteria corresponding to weaker constraints and, hence, to higher-dimensional and more inclusive subspaces. Whether a certain point in the geometrical manifold represents an object as hard and rigid, as hinged and jointed, or as soft and pliable cannot, of course, be encoded in the structureless point itself; it might, however, be encoded in the degree to which each submanifold containing that point has been primed by the currently operative context.

Suppose that the metric of proximity underlying the stated principles of impletion varies from one occasion or context to the next and thereby influences the choice of connecting paths and, hence, the form and quality of the perceived identity of objects. Such a variation in metric is easiest to achieve through a variation in the differential weighting of the component metrics of the underlying submanifolds. This proposal is an extension of my much earlier notion that the momentary state of attention influences the relative contribution of orthogonal dimensions in the perception of similarity (Shepard, 1964a). The same idea is fundamental to Carroll's model for "individual-differences" analysis of similarity data collected from different subjects, conditions, or contexts. The widespread success of the INDSCAL program that Carroll and Chang (1970) based on that model attests further to the power of this idea (Wish & Carroll, 1973; and for recent applications relevant to the present paper, Shepard, 1978b; Shepard & Cooper, 1975).

In any case, the parametric investigation of apparent motion can provide information about the formation as well as the transformation of internal representations. The slower rate of alternation needed to produce the illusion of a rigid transformation stems from two sources: (1) The impletion of a geodesic path for a rigid transformation is longer than the path for a nonrigid one because it is confined to the curved constraint surface. (2) The microgenesis of the perception of an object as rigid requires the elaboration of the deep structure of the object at a more exacting level in the hierarchy of criteria of object identity. In the next section I suggest that these two sources may at basis be the same.

Toward a Transformational Theory of Perception and Judgment

In concluding my explorations of transformational mappings, I would like to develop further a possibility toward which various of the preceding lines of thought have been tending—namely, that the perception of even a static object depends heavily, perhaps entirely, on the implicit representation of the possible transformations of that object. I refer particularly to the observation made earlier in this chapter that in the manner of a generalized autocorrelator, the perceptual system might represent the rigid shape of an object in terms of the functional dependence of self-similarity on rigid transformation as reflected in the contortion of the relevant constraint submanifold. As just noted, the perceived structure of an object will not then be internally represented by the corresponding internal point itself, which is necessarily structureless. Instead, the perceived structure will be represented by the effective geometries and momentary weights of the various submanifolds in which that point resides. Such a generalization of my earlier notion of "second-order isomorphism" might provide a potentially useful formalism. And it seems in some ways to go beyond the notion of "abstract first-order isomorphism" (Shepard, 1975) that I once introduced to deal with such phenomena as selective attention and cognitive manipulation.

As radical as it might seem to say that the perception of a static object should depend on the representation of its possible transformations, it is consonant with these significant views of the perceptual process: Cassirer's (1944) early insights into the role of transformational groups in perception; Garner's (1974b) definition of the goodness of a figure in terms of the size of the class of figures that are equivalent to it under rigid spatial transformations such as reflections and rotations; and Gibson's (1966) emphasis on the free mobility of the perceiver and on the correlated transformations induced in the optic array, as well as his general notion of "affordances" (Gibson, 1977). The idea receives support, also, from Franks and Bransford's (1971) demonstrations of the psychological effectiveness of transformationally defined distance between stimuli; from the already noted demonstrations of kinetic depth; and from such more or less related demonstrations of "event perception" as those of Johansson (1950, 1976), Cutting,

Proffitt, and Kozlowski (1978), and Shaw and Pittenger (1977). I would add only two further observations—one evolutionary, the other introspective.

First, with regard to the evolution of the perceptual system, whereas an object possesses virtually unlimited degrees of freedom of shape (as well as of texture and coloration), its global movements are restricted to just three degrees of freedom of location and three of orientation. Moreover, although the objects relevant to organisms at different levels of the evolutionary tree differ widely in shape and other properties, their global movements are, and always have been, describable in terms of the same six dimensions of position. If, as I suppose, the most ubiquitous and simply described (that is, low-dimensional) constraints in the world are the ones that have been most deeply and thoroughly internalized during evolutionary history, then the representation of spatial transformations may have come to serve as the basis for representing the complexities of the intrinsic shapes of objects, rather than the other way around.

Second, having conjectured that the representation of transformations underlies the perception of objects on the basis of experimental evidence and theoretical considerations, I now find the priority of possible transformations so evident in my own visual, tactual, and kinesthetic experience that I can only conclude that it was precisely because I had always relied on my sense of positional freedom so implicitly that I had failed ever to take proper note of it. I now find that an essential part of the experience of any object is a clear, if unarticulated, recognition of the possible spatial perturbations of that object—precisely the three degrees of freedom of location (movements left or right, up or down, nearer or farther) and three of orientation (attitude, pitch, and yaw). Moreover, these are immediately and fully given as part of the experience of an object in space, even when the identity of the object and the representation of its shape are not fully established. I know how to grasp the object, turn it around, or brush it aside before I even know what the object is.

Very roughly, the lines along which I am currently seeking a theoretical account of the perception of objects now run somewhat as follows: The internal process as it first arises from a given proximal stimulus can be represented abstractly (that is, without concrete neurophysiological specification) by a point in a nested hierarchy of differentially weighted and curved submanifolds of transformationally related points. (Although more than one point might have been activated, all but one have been suppressed in accordance with the principle of exclusion.) A wave of decaying excitation propagates outward within each submanifold at a fixed rate and with a strength determined by the weight for that submanifold. Although the weights may be influenced by preceding context, submanifolds corresponding to stronger criteria of object identity, such as the preservation of rigid structure, have higher weights and hence intensities of propagation. However, as we have seen, they have more convoluted structures.

Proportionally to the excitation converging on it through the different submanifolds, any other point in the manifold (or "node" of the underlying network—to avoid the implication of continuity) becomes itself more ready to preempt control upon subsequent stimulation and, in the meantime, may serve as a representation of a possible transformation of the object useful for the guidance of either physical or mental manipulation. Then, when a subsequent stimulus does arrive, identification of objects and interpolation of paths proceed along the lines outlined in the four principles of impletion. The metric of proximity required by these principles is determined by the geometries and current weights of the component submanifolds in a manner analogous to the standard n-dimensional Euclidean rule of combination (cf. Carroll & Chang, 1970; Shepard, 1978a).

The representation of possible spatial perturbations of an object, which underlies both the formational principle of structural stability and our ability to make fast spatially oriented responses to that object, is immediately available in the local three degrees of freedom of the constraint surface of possible orientations of that object. The comparison of objects differing widely in orientation takes appreciable time, however, because a least path must be found in the appropriate constraint surface (as in apparent motion) and may then have to be traversed, step by step (as in mental rotation).

In the case of a symmetrical object, the submanifold of rigid transformations is effectively convoluted back into itself so that the spreading excitation strongly returns to the originally activated point within that constraint surface. Such a return signals the presence of a strict symmetry. Moreover, because the point of arrival is already activated, we might suppose that it acts as a second stimulus for the principles of impletion. In any case, to the extent that the path of return is instantiated, that path represents, further, the *type* of the symmetry—for example, its axis of rotation or reflection.

In the case of a general object, the various partial symmetries might be signaled similarly but more weakly, because the propagated wave must in this case return through less heavily weighted submanifolds. The total set of strengths of signals from the alternative paths of return might thus provide the basis for an autocorrelation function defining the shape of the object relative to the particular point of view corresponding to the originally activated point.

I may well regret having committed to print ideas that have yet to be worked out, that (when they are worked out) will probably prove to be wrong in detail, and that (to the extent that they are not wrong) may advance us but little beyond earlier formulations of apparent motion such as, particularly, the conceptual schema outlined by Attneave (1974a). Still, in assigning the central role to transformational constraints, the *kind* of theory that I have sketched out here does seem to offer some potential advantages: It brings a variety of perceptual phenomena into relation with one conceptual framework. It explains why symmetries are so readily appreciated by the human eye and, indeed, why they are a prominent aspect of some spontaneous visual phenomena (Shepard, 1978c). It suggests that transformations, which since Chomsky (1957) have been so much emphasized in linguistics, may possess a comparably rich structure in perception. And, however uncertainly, it at least points toward a possible neurophysiological mechanism based on the propagation of neural excitation and inhibition.

Allowing myself one further flight of unbridled speculation, I begin to discern some suggestive analogies between implications of the theoretical notions considered here and certain ideas basic to theoretical physics. At the most general level, these concern the central roles, in both cases, of transformation groups, symmetries, and of course the principle of least action (which has evolved through the successive formulations of Fermat, Leibnitz, Maupertius, Euler, Hamilton, Lagrange, and Einstein until it has come to afford, in the modern formalisms of Schwinger and Tomonaga, a possible basis for the whole of physics, from quantum mechanics to relativity). At more specific levels, there are the suggestive parallelisms between the selection and exclusion rules sketched out here and those of quantum mechanics; between the damped wavelike structures of receptive fields (which are basic to Fourier analytic theories of visual processing) and Schrödinger's wave equations; between the fixed rate of spreading excitation and the limiting velocity of electromagnetic propagation, with the implication, in both cases, that transformations conform to the Lorentz group of special relativity (see Caelli, Hoffman, & Lindman, 1978b; Hoffman, 1966); and, possibly, between least paths in curved constraint manifolds and geodesic trajectories in the gravitationally curved space–time of general relativity.

Finally, although I have been arguing that the spatial competencies of the mind must have evolved, originally, from the brain's commerce with physical space, I have also suggested that these competencies have since been extended to other, more metaphorical spaces. Certainly, the principles that determine the way in which a path is impleted between two successive stimuli are not specific to any particular modality. Apparently, they are much the same for stimuli that are visual, auditory, kinesthetic, or even tactual (see Békésy, 1957, concerning the parallelisms between hearing and touch). In fact, just as many of us have found that the time to compare two objects increases linearly with the extent of a spatial transformation that is "irrelevant" to the comparison (Larsen & Bundesen, 1978; Shepard, 1978a). Dixon and Just have recently been finding that such comparison times increase in a similarly linear manner with other, not literally spatial disparities such as those of color (Dixon, 1978; Dixon & Just, 1978). On the basis of these new results, Dixon and Just advance the promising idea that all such results reflect the operation of mental "normalizing" transformations that quite generally precede mental comparisons. Such preparatory normalizations cannot, in the case of discrepancies in color, be regarded as carried out over a path in the internal representation of concrete physical space, of course. They must be regarded as taking place in a more abstract semantic space.

Ideas recently advanced by Lockhead and his students point toward a similar conceptualization (e.g., Hutchinson & Lockhead, 1977; Lockhead, Gaylord, &

Evans, 1977). They propose that attention travels, in the manner of a "spaceship," from one location in semantic space to another, and that wherever attention is located at a given moment, discrimination between alternative stimuli in that vicinity will be especially fast and accurate. Thus, stimuli used to prime the subject have their facilitative effect through bringing attention to the approximate region of semantic space prior to the discriminative test. Consonant with my own general emphasis on fixed rates of traversal of shortest paths, and also with Dixon and Just's (1978) evidence for general "normalizing" operations, is the possibility that such shifts of attention can be shown to have the analog characteristic of passing, at a definite rate, through an ordered set of intermediate points in the same semantic space.

CONCLUSIONS AND IMPLICATIONS

Recapitulation

I have permitted myself a long and sometimes speculative consideration of the nature of the constraints on the internal representation of spatial transformations and, possibly through those transformations, on the internal representation of the objects subject to such transformations. It is time to return to the central issue of the evolutionarily induced complementarity between representational processes and their external referents. I can succinctly summarize the ideas that I have taken to be most fundamental as follows:

1. During the 3 billion years of biological evolution, the most pervasive and enduring constraints governing external objects and scenes as well as their projections and transformations must have come to be mirrored in the internal machinery of the intricately interconnected 12-billion-neuron system that, in humans, mediates between the sensory surfaces and the effector organs. Thus we have, in the words of J. Z. Young (1962), "the paradox that each creature is able to maintain its difference from the environment [i.e., its independent viability] only because it 'mirrors' or 'represents' the same environment [p. 8]."

2. The most pervasive and enduring of these constraints are thus conditioned by a world: (a) in which space is locally three-dimensional and Euclidean; (b) in which there exists a relatively stationary global frame with a gravitationally conferred upright orientation; (c) in which the most consequential local features are compact, rigid or semirigid objects that possess various enduring symmetries or approximations to symmetry; (d) in which these objects are subject to spatial transformations, relative to the global frame, of exactly three degrees of freedom of rigid translation and three of rigid rotation; (e) in which such spatial transformations tend locally to approximate (smooth) trajectories of least action; and (f) in which the individual organism, being itself such a semirigid, partially symmet-

ric object, is related by the same six degrees of spatial freedom to the global frame as well as to any other individual object.

3. Although the brain is itself a partially rigid and symmetric structure in three-dimensional space, it necessarily interacts with the external three-dimensional world only through a two-dimensional bounding surface that in the living organism constitutes an essentially unbreachable partition between the internal and the external. As a direct comparison between corresponding internal and external structures is thus normally precluded, we have no valid basis for assuming—and no currently feasible way of establishing—the existence of a literal resemblance or concrete isomorphism between such internal and external structures.

4. An internal structure must nevertheless be capable of achieving a very rapid and accurate mesh with its external three-dimensional counterpart through the interface whose two-dimensional (surface) structure is necessarily very different from the (deep) structure of either the internal representation or its external referent. The designation of the relation between corresponding internal and external structures as one of "complementarity" attempts to capture these two aspects of that relation—namely: (a) that the two structures, existing in necessarily disjoint domains, cannot be directly compared; and (b) that they must nevertheless be capable of a very precise and efficient mesh at the lower-dimensional common boundary.

5. Just as the basic six degrees of freedom of rigid motion are inherent in any solid object, the possibility of the set of such motions is implicit in its perception (or other internal representation). Indeed, the internal representation of the manifold of such possible motions may not only underlie our ability to manipulate the object either physically or mentally; it may also underlie our perception of the structure of the object itself—that is, our perception of its approximate symmetries and, via a principle of structural stability, its conformation in depth. Relevant to this conclusion are the further observations that subjects have to perform a mental rotation in order to determine that two differently oriented objects are nevertheless of the same intrinsic shape, and that there is a connection between the time required to perceive a rigid motion and the time required to perceive the full structure of a static object.

6. That mental transformations take time proportional to the extent of the transformation may be attributable to the fact that the brain is itself a three-dimensional system in which physical disturbances propagate, as in any physical system, at a limited rate. The evidence indicates that the internal system within which this propagation takes place, far from being a simple homogeneous medium, possesses a functionally rich, hierarchically nested structure that can be represented geometrically. Such a structure can only have been shaped by biological evolution in which, possibly, propagation has been potentiated within submanifolds corresponding to the satisfaction of certain ecological constraints, such as the maintenance of rigid structure.

Roots and Ramifications of Complementarity

Complementarity, in the sense considered here, plays two somewhat different roles. There is, first, the complementary relation between an internal representation and its object. And there is, second, the perhaps deeper, evolutionarily shaped complementary relation that the principles of organization of the internal system (including its rules of formation and of transformation) bear to the corresponding invariances characteristic of our three-dimensional world (including, especially, its invariances of optical projection and of rigid motion).

The Gestalt psychologists addressed a basic question, which I take the liberty of paraphrasing from Koffka (1935, p. 76) as follows: Does the world appear the way it does because the world is the way it is, or because we are the way we are? My answer can now be stated in two parts: (1) The world appears the way it does because we are the way we are; and (2) we are the way we are because we have evolved in a world that is the way it is. In short, we "project" our own inner structure back into the world, but because that structure has evolved a complementary relation to the structure in the world, the projection mostly fits. We become fully aware of the extent of the "projection" only under contrived laboratory conditions of altered spatiotemporal presentation.

It is not perhaps surprising that Bohr's celebrated introduction of the concept of complementarity into physics in 1927 (see Bohr, 1934) and, thereby, his achievement of a new intelligibility of the antinomies of quantum mechanics has been traced back, in part, to earlier influences from psychology. I am indebted to James Cutting (1978) for calling my attention to Holton's (1970) study of "the roots of complementarity" in which I find especially suggestive the evidence of important influences upon Bohr by: (1) his older friend and mentor, the Danish philosopher Harald Høffding, who is known in perception for the "Høffding step," according to which a stimulus must establish a precise mesh with an internal representation despite variations in retinal location and orientation (Høffding, 1891); (2) his fellow student, the Danish phenomenological psychologist Edgar Rubin, who had originated the well-known reversible figures in which, for example, complementary silhouettes of a vase and two faces alternate as figure and ground (Boring, 1950); and (3) William James, whose *Principles of Psychology* (1890), which emphasized a subject-object complementarity, affected Bohr, Høffding, and Rubin, and who had even stated the very thesis of this chapter: "Mental facts cannot be properly studied apart from the physical environment of which they take cognizance. . . . Mind and world in short have evolved together, and in consequence are something of a mutual fit [James, 1893, p. 4]." Later in life, Bohr came to see the principle of complementarity as extending far beyond physics (Bohr, 1958). With regard to perception, I am not sure that we have yet adequately explored the ramifications of this principle into psychology, into biology, and, as I indicated at the beginning of this chapter, into philosophy.

Implications for a General Theory of
Human and Animal Behavior

Since I entered the field, psychological theorizing has been dominated, first, by a preoccupation with functional relations between observable stimuli and responses, as in the behavioral systems of Hull and of Skinner, and then by a preoccupation with structural relations among unobservable cognitions, as in current information-processing models inspired by the discrete symbol-manipulating systems of Chomsky (from linguistics) and of Newell, Simon, and others (from computer science). I have tried here to sketch out a different approach more akin to that of the Gestalt psychologists: Principles of perceptual organization are taken to be more basic than either the regularities of observed behavior or the syntactic rules of language and symbol manipulation. This approach is not merely a retreat to the earlier approach of Gestalt psychology, however. In seeking the evolutionary origin and form of the innate organizing principles in the ecological invariances characteristic of the external world and of the organism's relation to that world, rather than in some simple minimization or field property presumed to be characteristic of nervous tissue as such, I follow Gibson more than Wertheimer, Koffka, or Köhler.

Central to behaviorism was the notion that a particular response is made because that very same response, when previously emitted in the presence of a "sufficiently similar" stimulus, was followed by a reinforcing event. But as the "stimulus" varies from one occasion to the next in relative position and orientation, the organism must solve the "Høffding problem" in order to determine whether the stimulus is "sufficiently similar." And even if it is sufficiently similar, the organism must modulate its response in complex ways appropriate to that particular position and orientation. What is invariant from occasion to occasion cannot be the proximal stimulus or the muscular response; it can only be something in the internally constructed representation.

The goal-oriented nature of human and animal behavior and its analogy with the theory of servomechanisms suggests a formulation that differs fundamentally from the usual behavioristic one in that an invariant internal representation is taken as the fixed point around which behavior is organized. Responses, according to this view, are not reemitted as preformed units; they are specifically tailored on each occasion to reduce perceived discrepancies between the prevailing external situation and an internally represented reference or goal situation (Attneave, 1974b; MacKay, 1955; Miller, Galanter, & Pribram, 1960; Newell & Simon, 1971; Powers, 1973; Tolman, 1932; Wiener, 1948). Innate organizing principles determine both the formation of the imaged goal and—as my discussions of rules of transformation suggested—the construction of a suitably direct mental path that can then guide the execution of motor acts likely to transform the perceived state of the external world into a match with the already imaged goal state. Notice that the goal, the construction of an efficient path to the goal, and the final match all take place in a representational medium that is perceptual or imagistic in character.

That behavior is guided by internal representations of perceptual-spatial relations and their transformations throughout much of the animal kingdom is suggested by the ability of primates to take a shortest route in recovering objects that they previously witnessed being hidden in a random order (Menzel, 1973), as well as by related abilities reported long before in animals as lowly as the rat (Maier, 1929) and even the wasp (Thorpe, 1950). These and other demonstrations of the role of images and cognitive maps in the control of animal behavior have recently been reviewed by Gallistel (1980), Griffin (1976), and Mason (1976). In addition, ingenious experiments in which nocturnally migrating songbirds were released inside a planetarium after the pattern and rotation of the simulated stars had been systematically altered have not only verified the use of celestial navigation in such birds (Emlen, 1975; Sauer, 1958); they have also provided evidence that some of these species establish the directions of the compass on the basis of a comparison of the rotational differences in the pattern of the celestial sphere at different times during the night (Emlen, 1970; also see Emlen, 1971; Sauer, 1971).

Indeed, mental rotation does not seem to be an exclusively human function. I recently observed the following noteworthy behavior on the part of a German shepherd who was returning a long stick that had been hurled over a high fence. Plunging toward a narrow opening where a vertical board was missing from the fence, the dog suddenly stopped short, paused for just a moment, rotated its head and thus the stick in one smooth 90° movement, and immediately proceeded on through the opening. The covert transformation that I suppose to have preceded and guided the overt rotation was not dictated by either the visual stimulus of the vertical opening or the tactual stimulus of the horizontal stick. It was dictated by a non-modality-specific representation of the discrepancy between these two angular orientations and of the incompatibility of that discrepancy with the momentary goal (also spatial) of returning the stick to the master's side of the fence.

Implications for the Origins of Conceptual and Linguistic Competencies

In the course of biological evolution, complex neural mechanisms could not have sprung discontinuously into full existence. The mechanisms required for conceptual thought and linguistic competence, in particular, must have evolved by gradual modification of existing mechanisms already capable of constructing complex, semantically interpretable deep structures and of transforming these into each other and back into surface structures.

The most highly developed cognitive system of this kind to arise during the vast history of evolution, prior to the emergence of language, may have been the spatial system that enables us to anticipate events and to plan complex coordinated acts in the three-dimensional world. Young (1962) has argued that the bilaterally symmetric structure of the brain itself evolved as "a necessity for nervous systems that operate by means of a map-like analogue system [p. 7]." In any case, this bilateral symmetry, whatever the reasons for its emergence, now has the consequence that a portion of one hemisphere, not directly tied to any highly specific and peripheral sensory or motor function, can be recommitted to a new high-level function while the corresponding portion of the other hemisphere continues to serve its original function without serious impairment in performance. Indeed, clinical evidence, including studies of the effects of localized injuries to the cortex, indicates that the very same neural tissues in corresponding right and left hemispheres can, prior to adolescence, come to subserve either the spatial or the linguistic functions (Lenneberg, 1967; Penfield, 1966).

There is, moreover, much evidence suggesting that deixis is pervasive in language (Fillmore, 1971), and that spatial gestures have played a fundamental role in: (1) the development of language (Hewes, 1973); (2) the learning of such language by individual human infants (Condon & Sander, 1974; Meltzoff & Moore, 1977; Neisser, 1976, p. 164); and (3) the varied devices of anaphora in sign language (Bellugi & Fischer, 1972) and of "place keeping" in oral communication generally. Certainly the representation of spatial relations appears to be ubiquitous in human thought, memory retrieval, problem solving, and behavior. (Think, for example, how much easier and more natural it often seems, than retrieving a verbal statement written on the blackboard or made by a participant in a seminar, simply to point to the appropriate location on the blackboard or around the table—even long after the statement has been erased or the participant has left the room!)

Is it not reasonable to suppose that the conceptual apparatus underlying the use of language, if not underlying language itself, was erected upon a system that previously evolved to deal with the representation of objects and their transformations in space? If so, a close scrutiny of structural constraints governing the deepest level of our conceptual-linguistic competencies may reveal their spatial origin (Shepard, 1975).

The first intimations of this possibility came to me when, in connection with my work on multidimensional scaling (Shepard, 1962), I was struck by the fact that in talking about relations of similarity among seemingly nonspatial objects such as colors, tones, faces, voices, and the like, people quite automatically employ a spatial metaphor. Thus they speak of one color as being "close to" or "far from" another, or of one color being "between" two others, and so on (Cunningham & Shepard, 1974). This is not, I think, an insignificant observation. The precision with which ordinal judgments of similarity relations conform to the metric constraints of distance relations in a low-dimensional Euclidean space points to the implicit carry-over of powerful spatial intuitions. True, it is only in the psychological laboratories that we engage in systematic elicitation of judgments of similarity. Still, because we are rarely confronted twice with exactly the same stimulus in everyday life, the implicit recognition of just such relations of similarity must govern virtually every response we make (Shepard & Chipman, 1970).

More recently, I have come to suspect that we should give serious considera-tion to the so-called localistic theories of language, which are among the oldest known linguistic theories (Hjelmslev, 1935–37) and which—after a long period of neglect while the leading linguists were largely preoccupied with the purely syntactic aspects of language—have been revived through the efforts of a number of linguists and psycholinguists (including Anderson, 1971; E. Clark, 1970, 1974; H. Clark, 1973; Fillmore, 1968, 1971; Gruber, 1965, 1967; Jackendoff, 1976, 1978; Traugott, 1978). Purely syntactic approaches have had to face the insufficiency of the constraints of transformational grammars, which have been shown by Peters and Ritchie to be generatively equivalent to unrestricted Turing machines (see Bach, 1974, pp. 263–265; Peters, 1972). From the psychological standpoint, there are many indications that the mastery of syntactic rules strongly depends on the availability of a semantic interpretation (e.g., see Moeser & Bregman, 1972, 1973; Neisser, 1976, p. 164). And from the standpoint that I have taken here, the transformations that I suppose to underlie perception, im-agination, and perhaps even thinking and language are subject to very strong semantically determined constraints corresponding, for example, to the con-straints of projection and rigid motion in three-dimensional space. I thus find myself agreeing with Jackendoff (1976) when he concludes that "contrary to current fashion," insight into the semantics of natural language is to be found "in the study of the innate conceptions of the physical world and in the way in which conceptual structures generalize to ever wider, more abstract domains [p. 149]."

Localistic theories are closely connected with the linguistic notion of *case* and—as developed particularly by Fillmore (1968)—with the further idea that case—far from being a merely surface phenomenon varying widely from lan-guage to language—should be regarded as a universal feature of the very deepest levels of language. In his view, the tenseless proposition underlying a sentence in any language consists of a deep-structure verb to which are attached various deep-structure noun phrases, each by its own labeled relation of case: agentive, instrumental, benefactive, locative, and so on. At the surface level, of course, these case relations are indexed very differently in different languages by such devices as inflections, prepositions, postpositions, and word order (also see Blake, 1930).

In English, which relies most heavily on prepositions for this purpose, Fillmore (1968) points out that the usual signal for the agentive is *by*, for the instrumental is *with,* for the benefactive is *for,* and for the locative is a preposition that is semantically determined by the noun phrase (thus: "*in* the room," "*at* the door," "*on* the rug"). However, following Bennett (1974), I would add that the choice of the locative preposition is determined by the spatial *interpretation* accompanying the noun phrase more than by the noun phrase itself. And perhaps, as Bennett at several points suggests, this spatial interpretation is in the form of some sort of "image." As he instructively notes, we speak of individuals living "*in* Coventry," stopping "*at* Coventry," or dropping bombs "*on* Coventry" in accordance with our momentary spatial conception of that very same town as a bounded region, a point on a map, or a horizontal surface.

As I observed concerning the way we talk about relations of similarity, the locative uses of prepositions are quite automatically carried over to merely metaphorical spaces. Just as we say, "The members of the band were playing something *between* Third and Fourth Streets," we say they were playing something "*between* two and four in the afternoon," or even "*between* jazz and folk music." Likewise, just as we say, they were playing something "*in* the nearby woods," we say they were playing something "*in* the key of F" or "*in* very poor taste." Just as we say they were playing something "*at* the end of the road," we say they were playing something "*at* a barely audible level" or "*at* the president's request." And just as we say they were playing something "*on* the opposite hillside," we say they were playing something "*on* a variety of instruments" or "*on* a theme by Handel." Notice that in the metaphorical extensions, as much as in the examples referring to concrete physical space, we do not generally accept interchanges between the simple locative *at,* the interior locative *in,* or the surface locative *on.*

These and other types of examples, such as the particularly instructive ones put forward by Jackendoff (1976, 1978) and by Eve Clark (1970, 1974), suggest to me that the uses of prepositions to signal other, "nonlocative" cases may in part be understandable as extensions of a deeply underlying locative or spatial intuition to more distant and metaphorical domains. Surely it is suggestive that the same prepositions (such as the agentive *by,* instrumental *with,* or benefactive *for*) that, in English, play the primary role in indexing the case relations that Fillmore (1968) takes to be at the very basis of all languages also have, for the most part, so transparently a spatial significance as well. Indeed, some of the cases that do not on first consideration seem to have anyting to do with physical space turn out, under further consideration, to be understandable in terms of some at least metaphorical transaction in space. Thus, in the benefactive case, a transfer of something, however intangible, may be abstractly conceived to take place from the "place" of the benefactor to the different "place" of the benefactee.

Additional evidence for the fundamental role of spatial intuition in language use comes from a consideration of verbs, which correspond to the pivotal elements in the underlying representation of sentences in all human languages, according to Fillmore (1968). Thus, for a large and varied set of English verbs, many of which do not on the surface appear to deal with space or with motion, Jackendoff (1976) found reason to postulate a small number of underlying semantic components, several of which clearly represent, however abstractly, relations or motions in space. And Gruber (1967), in an illuminating comparison of just the two verbs *look* and *see*, found compelling linguistic reasons to take ''a sentence such as 'John sees a cat' to be a metaphorical extension of 'John goes to a cat' [p. 941].''

In view of my earlier emphasis on the mental construction of connecting paths in perception and hence in the guidance of behavior generally, I am inclined to suppose, with Bennett (1974) and Jackendoff (1978), that the comprehension of sentences, too, may often require an implicit impletion of a connecting mental path—in this last example, between John and the cat or, in the earlier example, between the benefactor and benefactee. Likewise, Bennett (1974) has explicitly argued that a mental path must be constructed in order to understand such a sentence as ''The post office is over the hill.'' Here, the preposition *over* is not understood as a relation in which one of the two objects mentioned is literally above the other in physical space (as it might be in ''The helicopter is over the hill''); it is strictly only the implied connecting path between the present location of the interlocutors and the location of the post office that has a spatially superior relationship to the hill. And, if a student says, ''It's clear that old Professor Shepard is over the hill,'' even the space in which this implied relationship holds is metaphorical.

Mental rotation also may play a role in the comprehension of some sorts of sentences. To elaborate on an example suggested by Herbert Clark (1973), the statement ''There is a fly above her knee'' can be ambiguous if the person referred to is not in the canonical upright position but, say, is lying flat upon the beach. The fly can then be interpreted as hovering in the air ''above'' the knee with respect to the global coordinate framework of the external world (as in the example of the helicopter above the hill), or it can be interpreted as crawling on the leg ''above'' the knee with respect to the very different local coordinate framework of the recumbent person or even of her possibly upraised leg. The latter interpretation may, however, require a mental rotation between the canonical and the currently appropriate coordinate systems. A student and I are beginning to explore this sort of possibility by measuring the times required to verify the truth or falsity of suitable sentences following different kinds of advance information.

Implications for the Sources of Creative Thought

In reviewing the statement that a number of exceptionally creative scientists, inventors, and writers have made about their own mental processes (Shepard, 1978c), I was struck with the crucial role that so many ascribed to the formation of visual images or "mental pictures" (Maxwell) that rise up before the mind "as real objects" (Cardan, Tesla) or "as things" (Coleridge, Faraday); or that in some more "cloudy" way capture relations of inclusion, exclusion, or order as well as the "physiognomy" of the whole problem (Hadamard); that are suddenly "arranged in the mind" (Watt); that most perfectly represent "the shape, position, and relations of objects in space" (Galton); that can be viewed in perspective "from this or that side" (Helmholtz); that "can be 'voluntarily' reproduced and combined" (Einstein); that possess "perfect symmetry, and geometrical regularity" (Herschel); that undergo spontaneous "motion" (Kekulé), "change in the point of view" (Herschel), or "rotation" (Tesla, Watson); and that even "dictate" the syntax of sentences down to the specification of "how to arrange the words" (Didion).

Since compiling these statements (more fully presented, with citations of sources, in my earlier papers; Shepard, 1978c, 1978d), I have had occasion to question a number of contemporary physical scientists about the role of spatial imagery in their own creative processes. Admittedly, my sample has so far been a rather small and haphazard one, but it does include professors, directors of laboratories, and members of the National Academy of Sciences who have distinguished themselves in a variety of fields, including physics, geophysics, mathematics, applied mathematics, and engineering. It is at least suggestive, then, that all of these have affirmed that their dominant mode of scientific thinking is, without question, geometrical. Certainly I would describe my own case in this way. In fact, as I have previously reported in some detail (Shepard, 1978c), many of my most successful ideas have not only first appeared in the form of a spatially structured image but also have done so quite spontaneously, typically as I was emerging from a hypnopompic state (just upon awakening). Similarly spontaneous or state-dependent visualizations were also reported by many of the thinkers just mentioned—including, particularly, Cardan, Coleridge, Didion, Hadamard, Helmholtz, Herschel, Kekulé, Tesla, and Watt.

Why should this be? Well, the creative productions of a brain presumably stem from whatever intuitive wisdom, whatever deep organizing principles have been built into that brain as a result of the immense evolutionary journey that has issued in the formation of that brain. If the arguments sketched out in this chapter have any merit, the most basic and powerful innate intuitions and principles underlying verbal and nonverbal thought, alike, may well be those governing the relations, projections, symmetries, and transformations of objects in space.

Moreover, if much of this wisdom is most concretely and efficiently embodied, as I suppose, in the implicit, automatic, and normally "transparent" machinery of the perceptual system, it reveals its own internalized structure most clearly only when it is decoupled from the external world that normally, through a kind of complementary resonance, drives it. Transitional states, as from sleep to wakefulness, may be particularly productive because they permit a two-way engagement between: (1) the internalized perceptual machinery freed, as in dreaming, from the preemptive control of external stimulation; and (2) the more recently evolved linguistic apparatus needed both to establish abstract goals for the underlying concrete machinery and to translate the results into an externalizable and communicable form. Without some such access to the analog mechanisms of the autonomous perceptual system, the linguistic apparatus, though more abstract and versatile perhaps, would lose the powerful benefit of the internalized rules governing objects and their transformations in space—special-purpose rules indeed but, in this three-dimensional world, rules of very general service nonetheless.

In the brief philosophical introduction to this chapter, I expressed my preference for a phenomenalistic epistemology according to which knowledge of the physical world is regarded as a mental construction based on the regularities and invariances of subjective experience. It is a part of this mental construction, then, that these experienced regularities reflect regularities currently operating in a physical world outside the physical body and, also, regularities currently operating in the physical brain as a genetically conferred reflection of similar regularities that have long operated in that same external world. Because all knowledge is necessarily *mental* knowledge, in this view, the science of the operation of the mind must ultimately encompass every other science. In a paper that has already made so many of the points I have tried to develop here, Attneave (1974b) said "I have got to be at least as complex as the world as I know it [p. 493]." Elsewhere, the immediate corollary has been stated by Chomsky (1975): "Investigation of human cognitive capacity might give us some insight into the class of humanly accessible sciences [p. 25]"; and long before by the physicist Sir Arthur Eddington (1920): "It is even possible that laws which have not their origin in the mind may be irrational, and we can never succeed in formulating them" so that, in a sense, "where science has progressed the farthest, the mind has but regained from nature that which the mind put into nature [p. 200]."

I take inspiration from the thought that the goals to which the cognitive scientist can aspire, though more remote, are no less lofty than those of the physical scientist. Whatever is conceived—from the quantum electrodynamics of subatomic interactions to the general relativity of black holes and cosmological space-time—is thereby represented in the human mind. Should we expect the representation of the principles whereby the mind itself achieves and, indeed, *creates* such representations to possess any less awesome a beauty? The words of the ill-fated Captain Ahab seem to provide a fitting close (Melville, 1850):

"O Nature, and O soul of Man! how far beyond all utterance are your linked analogies! not the smallest atom stirs or lives in matter, but has its cunning duplicate in mind [p. 295]."

ACKNOWLEDGMENTS

The preparation of this chapter and the completion of most of the experimental and theoretical work on which it is based was made possible by Research Grant BNS-75-02806 from the National Science Foundation. I wish to acknowledge that the chapter has benefited from the expert graphical assistance of Tomasa Ramirez; from the helpful suggestions of many colleagues, including Fred Attneave, Eve Clark, Jim Cutting, Randy Gallistel, Christa Hansen, Kathy Hemenway, Carol Krumhansl, and Amos Tversky; and especially from the thoughtful editorial work of Michael Kubovy. Even so, I remain painfully aware of the very preliminary form in which I have had to leave some of the ideas sketched out here.

11 Coalitions as models for Ecosystems: A Realist Perspective on Perceptual Organization

Robert Shaw
University of Connecticut
M. T. Turvey
University of Connecticut
and
Haskins Laboratories

ABSTRACT

Gestalt theory essentially claims that perceptual organization is dictated by the organization of the central nervous system (Wertheimer's principle of isomorphism). this is shown to be a phenomenalist's account of knowing, where the objects of perception are treated as distinct from the objects of the environment. Such a view encounters many logical and empirical difficulties that are avoided by an alternative style of scientific inquiry based on pragmatic realism offered by the American pragmatists Peirce, Dewey, and Bentley. In the realist's view, the objects of perceptual knowing are functionally ascribed directly to objects in the knower's environment. The realist's account offered by the pragmatists derives from the observation that successful scientific theories (e.g., Einstein's) necessarily go beyond explanations in terms of (causal) *interactions* to explanations in terms of (acausal) *transactions,* defined as a reciprocity of mutual constraint existing between phenomena and their contexts. Although the transactional approach is an improvement over traditional interactional ones, it nevertheless fails to avoid "run on" explanations that regress toward ever-more-encompassing contexts of hidden constraint. Still a further improvement is the ecological style of scientific inquiry originally proposed by J. J. Gibson and extended by the authors; although in many ways consonant with the transactional approach, it avoids the context regress problem by introduction of the concept of "coalition" to model the organization of perceptual systems. A *coalition* is a superordinate system (relational structure) consisting of eight pairs of subsystems (with 1024 states) nested at four exclusive "grains" of analysis (bases, relations, orders, values) and closed at each grain under a (duality) operation that specifies how the two complementary subsystems act as reciprocal context of mutual constraint. Finally, a coalitional model is applied informally to express the symmetry of constraints in an (epistemic) ecosystem that necessarily exists between animals and their environments. In this formulation, the organization that perception takes co-implicates the organization that action takes and is not defined at the scale of animals (i.e., is not an achievement of the nervous system) but only at the scale of ecosystems.

INTRODUCTION

Can the objects of perception and the manner of their organization be identified with objects and an organization that exists when no perceiving is going on? From the point of view of a commitment to realism, the answer must be that they can; in general, however, and almost without exception, students of perception over the centuries have made certain assumptions and pursued particular forms of argument that have led to the negative answer—precisely, that what is perceived and how it is organized is, by and large, a product of mental or neural processes. But to answer the foregoing question thusly, in the negative, is more than a little curious; it is surely not in the best interests of science to distinguish ontologically between the subject matter of inquiries into perception and the subject matter of other inquiries into nature.

In several recent papers we have sought a clarification of the conceptual barriers to perceptual realism and an identification of the reconceptualization needed to dismantle them (Shaw & Bransford, 1977; Shaw, Turvey, & Mace, 1981; Turvey, 1977; Turvey & Shaw, 1979; Turvey, Shaw, & Mace, 1978). The contribution of the present chapter to a realist program is that nonrealist (phenomenalist) theories of perception are nurtured by styles of scientific inquiry that are too narrow in their conception of the logical and causal support for perception. We motivate and describe a style of inquiry—referred to as coalitional—in which the focus is the animal-environment system described in full. This style of inquiry was anticipated to a degree by American pragmatists and inheres in the ecological approach to knowing that has been championed by Gibson (e.g., Gibson, 1966). Gestalt psychology claimed that perceptual organization is an achievement of the nervous system; we claim that perceptual organization is an activity of the ecosystem—of which the animal and its environment comprise dually complementing parts.

GESTALT THEORY AS A PHENOMENALISM

Phenomenalism and Subjective Idealism

The attempt to resolve epistemological puzzles in the half century from 1690 to 1740 was both vigorous and creative, but the predicaments it gave rise to were settled in a most unsatisfactory manner from the point of view of a committed realist. Locke had sought to found an epistemology on the dictum that "there is nothing in the intellect which was not previously in the senses." He was compelled to distinguish among (1) the physical object, (2) the simple ideas or sense data that the physical object gave rise to, and (3) the complex of ideas that constituted the object of experience. Locke's perspective was that of a dualist, distinguishing as he did between two kinds of objects: the physical or real object to which perception was indirectly in reference, and the mental object—or representation—of which perception was directly an experience. Locke, in brief, accepted the Cartesian approach to the problem of perception by assuming the doctrine of representative ideas.

The doctrine invited (and continues to invite) skepticism about perception as a means of knowing reality. On Locke's theory, the perceiver is not in direct epistemic contact with the existence of physical objects; and the sense data from which the object of experience is manufactured could have arisen from sources other than external physical things (e.g., from perceivers themselves or, as some argued, from God). Ideas or impressions (i.e., putative representations) may correspond to reality, but one has no way of knowing that to be so if all that one knows directly are ideas or impressions.

Berkeley's response to the predicament of Locke's theory was to deny the assumption that sense data or the ideas derived from them were a representation of any reality. In short, Berkeley retained mind and its ideas but dispensed with external objects and thus the notion of ideas as representation. (Indeed, insofar as Locke had already proposed that the specific sense qualities represent nothing external, the representative doctrine had been undercut.) The subjective idealism implicit in Locke was made explicit in Berkeley; and where Locke had looked to the regularity of orderliness of the environment as the reason for the regularity and orderliness of ideas, Berkeley looked to God.

But Berkeley's appeal to God was not appealing to Hume, whose focus, in the long run, was more disturbing; it was, straightforwardly, the skepticism implicit in Locke—a skepticism regarding the possibility of certainty in one's knowledge of the natural world. The world erected within Hume's skeptical framework begins and ends with impressions and ideas linked in accordance with the laws of association. For Hume, experience is of phenomena only, and as to what exists other than phenomena, no one can say. In Hume's scheme of things, orderliness of experience is due neither to the external world nor to God but to the laws of association of ideas.

The contrasting perspectives of Locke, Berkeley, and Hume have left a deep impress on the development of perceptual theory but fundamentally through that aspect that is common to all three—namely, phenomenalism. By way of a brief overview, and skipping over variations on the theme, phenomenalism holds that direct knowledge of one's environment is not possible and that that which is known is constituted solely by the fact that it *is* known. Taken to its extreme, phenomenalism is skeptical about one's awareness of the environment; all that is directly knowable are phenomena—impressions, sense data, or, more generally, mental states. Some forms of phenomenalism recognize that mental states are in reference to external objects. With regard to these forms of phenomenalism, an external reality independent of mental states is assumed, and to mental states are ascribed the role of providing indirect knowledge of external reality or, at least, a basis for constructing a theory of external reality. These forms of phenomenalism that assume a reality and, therefore, might be referred to as indirect realisms are susceptible to two problems: The problem of reference—that is, how the object of experience, or the intentional object as it is often called, and the object of reference, the physical object in the environment, are coordinated; and the problem of intentionality—that is, how the intentional object should be described (see Shaw, Turvey, & Mace, 1981).

A profoundly influential perceptual theory from the last century is that of Helmholtz, and its phenomenalism is manifestly plain. In accepting Johannes Müller's theory of specific nerve energies, Helmholtz assumed that the percipient was aware of a phenomenon or representation as contrasted with the physical reference object that was the source of stimulation. And we are reminded that the phenomenal object of experience was, for Helmholtz, rarely the bare-bones sensory impression, distinguished by the term *Perzeption*, but rather those impressions elaborated by memories, a totality distinguished by the term *Anschauung*.

In the two sections that follow, we consider a profoundly influential perceptual theory from the present century—namely, the Gestalt theory that is of special concern to the present volume. The thrust of our consideration is the continuity (rather than the contrast) between the Gestalt orientation to knowing and the orientation handed down over the centuries and already given brief overview here: The continuity lies, of course, with the fact that Gestalt theory is a phenomenalist theory.

Why Do Things Look as They Do?

This question was raised and discussed most eloquently by Koffka (1935) in his celebrated *Principles of Gestalt Psychology*. He gave three answers: (1) Distal objects look as they do because they are what they are; (2) distal objects look as they do because the proximal stimuli are what they are; (3) distal objects look as they do because of the field organization of the brain to which the proximal stimulus gives rise. In rejecting the first two answers and defending the third, Koffka firmly identified Gestalt theory as a phenomenalist theory. To reject the first two answers is a clear repulse of realism, for to reject them is to introduce unbridgeable gaps between the perceiver and the world. And to promote the third answer is to focus attention on brain processes to account for perceptual organization. That is to say, given the question: Why is perception organized as it is? Koffka replied, essentially: Because the processes of the brain are organized as they are. This appeal to brain processes serves the same function as Berkeley's appeal to God and Hume's appeal to the laws of association in lieu of a reality— an animal's environment (or more precisely, as we argue, the ecosystem of which the animal is a part)—to account for the organization of an animal's perceptual experience.

Let us consider Koffka's reasons for rejecting Answers 1 and 2. Our focus is the first answer, because our rejoinder to Koffka's reasons for rejecting it generalizes to the second. One reason for rejecting the first answer rests with being able to show that for a particular perceptual experience (as distinct, presumably, for a hallucination or a dream) of type x, the existence of a physical object of type x is neither necessary nor sufficient. For example, Koffka (1935) argues that if it were necessary, then for a particular experience of type x, there ought to be a physical object of the same type to which the experience corresponds. A typical illustration of the nonnecessity of a physical object of type x is provided through a consideration of Fig. 11.1.

Koffka (1935, p. 79) and Köhler (1947) would claim that Fig. 11.1 appears to an observer as a single unit, a cross, whereas *in reality* it is nothing but a number of points in a certain arrangement. The reference object is not of the same type as the experienced object because in the absence of a line connecting the points, the points do not collectively define a single physical, crosslike unit—or so runs the argument. But it would seem that the latter contains an arbitrary definition of

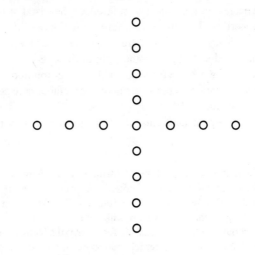

FIG. 11.1.   A cross of points.

figural unity, an arbitrary choice of a geometrical language for describing environmental objects. One could just as easily and arbitrarily conclude that the points *do,* in fact, comprise a single unit because some relation among the points does not change under a number of spatial transformations—for example, moving or rotating the page. At all events, the argument for a nonnecessary relation between the type of the object of reference and the type of the object of experience rests with there being an incompatibility between the descriptors of the two objects. It would follow that if one were committed to realism and adverse to phenomenalism, then one would seek a language in which to describe the object of reference and the object of experience so that they were one and the same. The tolerance for, or unquestioning acceptance of, inequitable or incommensurate descriptors marks the path to phenomenalism, and it is no more evident than in Koffka's second reason for denying that things look as they do because they are what they are.

The second reason is the one that is more commonly touted and has to do with the relation said to hold between the distal stimulus and the proximal stimulus. To quote Koffka (1935): "for each distant stimulus there exists a practically infinite number of proximal stimuli; thus the 'same stimulus' in the distant sense may not be the same stimulus in the proximal sense; as a matter of fact it seldom is [p. 80]." And to quote Köhler (1974):

> Thus in the reflected light no trace is left of the units which actually exist in the physical world.... Thus in countless instances sensory organization means a reconstruction of such aspects of physical situations as are lost in the wave messages which impinge upon the retina [pp. 161, 163].

We see, in short, that the function that maps distal stimuli into proximal stimuli is construed as one-to-many and destructive: The proximal stimulus equivocates on the object of reference (the distal stimulus) and fails to preserve its properties. Therefore, in reference to Answer 1 earlier, things *cannot* look as they do just because they are what they are; the means by which we visually "contact" distal objects—the light at the eye—is not specific to their structure. Elsewhere, we have referred to this time-honored understanding of the distal/proximal relation as the doctrine of intractable nonspecificity (Shaw et al., 1981; Turvey & Shaw, 1979).

The acceptance of this doctrine gives rise to a paradox, as Koffka (1935) noted:

> And that raises at once the problem: how the enormous richness and variety of our visual behavioral environment can be aroused by such a mere mosaic of light and shade and color. I think, when formulated in these terms, the problem must appear thrilling by the very paradox which it seems to involve. How can such rich effects arise out of such poor causes, for clearly the "dimensions" of our environmental field are far more numerous than those of the mosaic of the stimulation [p. 75]?

We have quoted this passage primarily because it underscores the inequity or incommensurability of descriptors theme: The descriptors of the light at the eye and the descriptors of the environment are assumed to be different numerically, in grain size, in degree of variety, and in type. And it is perhaps now evident why this assumed and received inequity of descriptors poses such an insurmountable barrier to realism and mandates phenomenalism. As scientists drawn to evolutionary theory as an account of species, we speak of the evolution of an adaptive relation holding between animal and environment. Less generally, we would say of a seeing creature that an adaptive relation holds between the animal's visual system and its environment. Here, of course, we must mean that an adaptive relation holds between the animal's visual system and the light reflected from the environment of the animal, because it is by means of the reflected light that the enviroment is seen. But if the descriptors of the light to an animal's visual system are not commensurate with the descriptors of the environment—as Koffka and most other perceptual theorists have long assumed—then an adaptive relation holding between visual systems and reflected light is not an adaptive relation holding between visual systems and environments. Insofar as consistency demands that the same story of intractable nonspecificity holds for the energy media of all senses (see Koffka, 1935, p. 75), we should be skeptical about the possibility of an adaptive relation evolving between an animal's perceptual capabilities and the reality with respect to which it lives its hours, days, or years. We might continue to speak of the evolution of such relations, but we cannot with any confidence assume that reality is one of the terms in such relations. On this line of reasoning, realism is denied, and phenomenalism is ascendant.

We have earmarked the inequity or incommensurability of descriptors theme (see Fowler & Turvey, in press) as a barrier to realism and we have pinpointed its role in determining the phenomenalist tenor of Gestalt theory. It is one of several barriers to realism (see Shaw et al., in press), but it has received special emphasis in the present section because it was, ironically, a theme to which Gestalt psychology was passionately sensitive. In the section that follows, we try to show that Gestalt theory was acutely, though myopically, aware of the scientific conundra that are heir to an inequity of descriptors.

Let us conclude the present section by noting what a commitment to realism would advocate with respect to the relation between distal and proximal stimuli: It would advocate that a description of proximal stimuli be sought such that its descriptors were commensurate numerically, in grain size, in degree of variety, and in type with the descriptors of the environment at the scale of ecology. The phenomenalist's doctrine of intractable nonspecificity is opposed by the realist's doctrine of necessary specificity—precisely, that the properties of a structured energy medium are specific (within the modulatable limits of the medium) to environmental properties (Turvey & Shaw, 1979). The latter doctrine spawns a scientific endeavor that would be referred to as ecological optics with regard to light, as ecological acoustics with regard to sound, and as ecological physics with regard to environmentally structured energy in general (Gibson, 1961, 1966).

The Issue of Geographical and Behavioral Environments

Behavior, Koffka (1935) argued, takes as its framework the behavioral (or phenomenal) environment rather than the geographical (or noumenal) environment. That is, behavior takes as its reference the environment as it appears to an observer rather than the environment as it would be described by physics. It is of course true that behavior takes place in the geographical environment and that the laws of physics cannot be compromised. Koffka's (1935) point is that the behavioral, or phenomenal, environment mediates the geographical environment and behavior. Thus we may conceive of two distinct stages: In one there is a transition from the geographical environment to the behavioral environment and in the other, a transition from the behavioral environment to behavior. It is a relatively straightforward matter to recognize, but significant nevertheless, that the first of these two stages entails a shift from a physical description of the environment, which is animal-neutral and meaningless, to a mental description, which is animal-referential and meaningful. The objects and types under the latter description are qualitatively different from the objects and types under the former description. Thus the distinction that is drawn by Koffka expresses not only Gestalt psychology's phenomenalism but also its dualism; for whatever else we might mean by dualism, it is, on the bottom line, an argument for speaking about the objects of reference and of experience in separate and irreducible languages.

Curiously, however, the feature of Gestalt theory that we wish to underscore in this section derives from the theory's *distaste* for dualism. We proceed to consider the conceptual steps taken by Gestalt psychology to avoid dualism and how and why these steps failed.

As is well known, Wertheimer, Koffka, and Köhler were adamant in their goal to work out the facts of psychology so that these facts would be continuous with those of physics and biology. Why, then, should a concept such as "behavioral environment," which would seem to introduce descriptors that have no parallel in physics, find a place in their theorizing? To Koffka (1935) and Köhler (1947), the stimulus–response analysis of behavior circa the 1930s and 1940s was unpalatable. They were adverse to the idea that the variety in molar behavior could be encompassed by combinations of a single type of molecular behavior— the stimulus–response link. They saw as unbridgeable the distinction between molar behavior that takes place in an environment and molecular behavior that takes place within an organism. But most of all, they were disturbed by the fact that meaning and significance, intrinsic as they are to molar behavior, have no place in the fine-grained stimulus–response description of behavior. For Gestalt psychology, theory building had to take *molar,* rather than molecular, behavior as its point of departure. It follows that the environment in which such behavior occurs must similarly be molar; that is, its descriptors have to be coarse grained. But more than that, the descriptors of the behaviorally relevant environment must be animal-referential; behavior is meaningful and significant because it is performed in reference to objects and events that have meaning and significance for the animal. Thus runs the rationalization for the concept of behavioral environment.

Nevertheless, Koffka (1935) argued that the behavioral environment could not be advanced as a basic category of explanation, for in order to do so, the behavioral environment would have to be ascribed special ontological status. Such ascription would be a capitulation to dualism, a denial of a single mode or universe of discourse for natural events. In a similar vein, Koffka (1935) noted that the behavioral environment must be related to the geographical environment, but if the two environments identify separate modes of discourse, then the relationship between them cannot be causal, because causal laws hold only *within* a mode of discourse; a failure to recognize this fact is to make what Ryle (1949) called a categorical error.

A simple resolution to these problems, problems bespeaking separate realms of existence, would be—as Koffka (1935) duly noted—to substitute the physical reality of the animal's physiology for the concept of behavioral environment. But if the descriptive language of physiology is continuous with the descriptive language of physics and the latter is presumed to be fine grained, then the molar descriptors captured in the concept of behavioral environment, and held to be so important to the account of behavior, would be irretrievably lost. How, then, might a theorist preserve a single universe of discourse for describing natural events, on one hand, and molar descriptors on the other? The solution, Gestalt psychology opined, lay in discarding the claim that the descriptors of physics and, therefore, of physiology are merely fine grained. To assume that they are fine grained leads any proponent of a single universe of discourse to a fine-grained, molecular description of behavior and consciousness that, Gestalt psychology argued, was contrary to fact; or it leads to the claim for no relation, or a completely mysterious relation, between physiological processes and behavioral or conscious processes. In the light of these remarks (Koffka, 1935) lies both the motivation for and the significance of Wertheimer's isomorphism principle:

> Let us think of the physiological process not as molecular, but as molar phenomena. If we do that, all the difficulties of the old theory disappear. For if they are molar, their molar properties will be the same as those of the conscious processes which they are supposed to underlie. And if that is so, our two realms, instead of being separated by an impassable gulf, are brought as closely together as possible with the consequence that we can use our observations of the behavioral environment and of behavior as data for the concrete elaboration of physiological hypotheses. Then, instead of having one kind of such processes only, we must deal with as many as there are different psychological processes, the variety of the two classes must be the same [p. 56].

Let us pause at this juncture to assess what the foregoing strategy achieved. Noting that the descriptors of physics, contrary to a more popular interpretation, were fundamentally coarse grained (Gestalt psychology, we are reminded, highlighted the role of field concepts in physics) made possible the claim that the descriptors of physiology were more aptly construed as molar rather than as molecular. Thus, Gestalt theory was able to avoid a marked discontinuity in the grain size of descriptors across the domains of physics, biology, and psychology; for it was self-evident that the descriptors of the behavioral environment were coarse grained or, at least, that they had to be if psychology were to be of any value to, say, the historians and artists with their interests in molar behavior (Koffka, 1935).

But is it the case that the discontinuity-in-descriptors problem is resolved by demonstrating a common and coarse grain size of descriptors? In the sentence of the foregoing quote that reads: "For if they are molar, their molar properties will be the same as those of the conscious processes which they are supposed to underlie," Koffka seems to answer yes. But this affirmation is illusory; for although the steps taken to demonstrate coarse-grained or molar descriptors across the different domains *may*, in principle, relate to the issue of why the experienced object has the structural appearance that it has, they do not, in principle, relate to the issue of why the experienced object has the meaning that it has.

Gestalt theory sought a thoroughgoing physicalism, but its thrust, we argue, was not epistemological problems—the problems of animals as knowing agents—as much as it was a desire to preserve a uniformity in mode of discourse across the *disciplines* of physics, biology, and psychology construed as the investigations of three different phases of matter. Consider how Gestalt theory chose to explain the characteristics of objects to which behavior is referenced, characteristics that Koffka (1935) said invited or demanded behavior. Seeing an object is to know what can be done with it or about it; and the immediacy of his knowing impressed Gestalt theorists. But what is the status of these characteristics that invite specific behaviors? At odds with its thoroughgoing physicalism, Gestalt theory ascribed to them phenomenal, rather than real, status. These characteristics that invite behavior are not ordinary physical characteristics, for they owe their very existence to a perceiver in the sense that they are inexistent outside of perception. Thus, it is argued, the mailbox has the characteristic of inviting letter posting only where one has the need to mail a letter (Koffka, 1935). In like vein, it would be argued that a particular arrangement of surfaces is a place to hide for an animal only when the animal needs to hide; another arrangement of surfaces is a brink in the terrain that demands leaping over only when the animal has a need to leap, and so on. In sum, by this kind of analysis, physical (qua real) dimensions are ordinarily neutral with respect to an animal and its capacity for activity; thus those dimensions or characteristics of the world that the animal-referential and activity-relevant must be extraordinary, nonphysical (qua nonreal) dimensions.

We see, in short, that the dualistic distinction with which we began this section—that of the geographical environment with its animal-neutral, meaningless descriptors and the behavioral environment with its animal-referential, meaningful descriptors—remains unscathed by the effort of Gestalt theory to establish a single mode of discourse. How did this perplexing state of affairs arise? The answer, we believe (and as intimated earlier), is that Gestalt psychologists were concerned with keeping the descriptors commensurate at that scale of discourse that is *talk about mechanical or causal contact* between different phases of matter, but they were not concerned with keeping the descriptors commensurate at that scale of discourse that is *talk about epistemic contact* between an animal and its environment. In this section we have seen how the objects of reference (the geographical environment) and the objects experienced and known (the behavioral environment) were construed as logically separate and their descriptors, as incommensurate. In the preceding section we saw the acceptance as doctrine of a pronounced discontinuity between the descriptors of the energy media at receptor surfaces and the descriptors of the geographical environment. To summarize, Gestalt psychology sought to dispel unbridgeable gaps in the causal process defined over different phases of matter but *created* unbridgeable gaps in the epistemic act defined over the animal and its environment.

THE CLAIM THAT PERCEPTUAL ORGANIZATION IS AN ACHIEVEMENT OF THE NERVOUS SYSTEM: COUNTERPOINTS FROM A COMMITMENT TO REALISM

We have considered the historical perspective of phenomenalism that is the backdrop for a good deal of perceptual analysis. *Phenomenalism,* as we have used the term here (see Mundle, 1971, for a more discriminating account), holds that direct knowledge of one's environment is not possible and that what is known is constituted by the fact that it *is* known. The examination of Gestalt theory in the first section of this chapter underscored the theory's allegiance to phenomenalism and dualism—that is to say, the theory's continuity with epistemological positions that are contrary to perceptual realism.

Let us now proceed to identify more fully the set of interlocking themes that underly the central claim of Gestalt psychology—the claim that perceptual organization is an achievement of the nervous system. Our preceding analysis of Gestalt psychology was intended to set the stage for this discussion. First and foremost, we observe that these themes are not independent; indeed, they may be viewed as various instantiations of one of them—precisely, animal–environment dualism (Fitch & Turvey, 1978; Turvey & Shaw, 1979). Nevertheless, for purposes of argument, it is to our advantage to identify them separately even though independent discussion of them is strained.

Not unexpectedly, we treat these themes from the perspective of a commitment to realism. Gestalt psychology (see Köhler, 1947) warned against the *experience error*—that is, attributing the organization of perceptual experience to the proximal stimuli when in fact it should be attributed, they argued, to the organizing tendencies of the nervous system. Taking a leaf from Gestalt psychology but in the spirit of a commitment to realism, we label each of the to-be-identified themes as an *error*. We do so because each theme leads to attributing perceptual organization to the animal, more accurately, to its nervous system—a position consonant with phenomenalism; when in fact it should be attributed to a larger system, the (epistemic) ecosystem, of which the animal is a part—a position consonant (so we argue) with realism.

An Inventory of Errors

The major theses—or errors as we call them—may be identified as follows:

1. The error of choosing descriptors, or predicates, for the animal term, the environment term, and the energy-medium term of a statement about perception so as to introduce discontinuities or incompatibilities among the three terms.
2. The error of restricting to "inside the skin" the argument against reducing the predicates of psychology to those of a (putative) reducing science (say, physics or even physiology) but accepting, even promoting, reductionism "outside the skin."
3. The error of taking conventional physical descriptors as the most fundamental *or* the error of assigning to the basic variables of physics primary reality status.
4. The error of slipping between scales of discourse in the phrasing of explanation.
5. The error of confusing the causal support for perception with the epistemic act of perceiving.
6. The error of taking the Newtonian space and time as standard and attempting to force the facts of perception into their form.
7. The error of attributing to a part of a system responsibility for the properties of the system as a whole.
8. The error of holding animal and environment as logically independent.

Let us give due consideration to these errors, respecting the earlier caveat that they are not independent.

Metaphors for the Nervous System

In Gestalt theory a discontinuity of descriptors is expressed between the geographical environment and the energy media (proximal stimuli); the energy media and the behavioral environment (what the animal is conscious of); and the behavioral environment and the geographical environment. We cannot doubt that the inequity of descriptors theme places the burden of perceptual organization on the animal. For example, in identifying the proximal stimulus and the percept as end points of the perceptual process and in ascribing to these end points inequitable or incompatible description, Gestalt psychology equated the question of the mechanism of perception with the question of how the terminal description (the percept) is derived from, or arises from, the initial description (the proximal stimulus). That is to say, the question of mechanism was the question of how the activity of the nervous system converts from the vocabulary of stimulation, with its *impoverished* organizational predicates, to the vocabulary of perception, with its *rich* organizational predicates.

Let us be clear on why it is that the first thesis is an error from the perspective of a commitment to perceptual realism. In the first section we remarked on the phenomenalist consequence of inequitable descriptors, and we took note of a contrast between the traditional doctrine of intractable nonspecificity and the doctrine advocated by perceptual realism, a doctrine of necessary specificity. What requires highlighting at this juncture is the following understanding: A way of talking about the surrounding layout of surfaces and substances, the light as structured by that layout, and the layout as perceived and acted upon, such that the languages in all three cases were commensurate (with no queer discontinuity in descriptor type, number, grain, and variety) and would permit the (realist) claim that direct knowing of one's environment is possible and that what is known is constituted by the fact that it *exists*.

By the foregoing understanding, and presuming that it is defensible (see Shaw et al., 1981), the equation cannot be drawn between the question of the mechanism of perception and the question of how the nervous system converts, or translates, from one description to another, because the latter is a false question. With regard to the nervous system, the understanding just aired promotes a radically different and, to most, a curious interpretation of its role in perception. Clearly, terms such as *translation, conversion, organization* are ruled out as labels for what a nervous system can be said to do when an organism is said to perceive, or for what a nervous system can be said to evolve or acquire the capability of doing when a species of organism or an individual is said to become a more proficient perceiver. If X is a fact of an organism's reality and is perceived as such, then we should say that the tissue medium (the organism's nervous system), like the energy medium in which the organism is immersed (say light), is *functionally transparent* to those properties of the world upon which the organism's successful survival depends (Shaw & Bransford, 1977). We offer the tentative thesis that from the perspective of perceptual realism, the (selective, functional) transparency metaphor connotes the principle to be pursued in discerning the nature of neuroanatomical mechanisms supporting perception and the content to be ascribed to the neural events concomitant to perception.

Reductionism and Fundamentality in the Context of Animal-Environment Dualism

What determines the promotion of incompatible descriptors? The answer, we believe, rests specifically with the second and third errors already detailed but most fundamentally with the last error, that of animal-environment dualism. Let us elaborate on the second error and then show how Gestalt theory committed a variant of it. Psychology, it can be said, is a special science. It involves predicates of a special order, ones that differ in type from the predicates of what might be referred to as the reducing sciences, physics and (perhaps) physiology. A reasonable belief in the unity of science has led many to advocate that the descriptive predicates of psychology be reduced to the descriptive predicates of physics. Others, to the contrary, have felt that although a unitary science may be a reasonable goal, it is nevertheless unreasonable to reconceptualize the predicates of psychology (and of other unreduced sciences such as economics) in terms of the predicates of physics. To do so would be a denial of the very usefulness of the predicates that gave rise to the unreduced science and promoted interest in its study as a separate discipline.

Psychology, however, can and does receive a curiously unscientific treatment in the hands of those eager to establish its independence. The domain of the predicates of the science of psychology is conceived of as "inside" the body and separated from the rest of the universe by the skin (cf. Bentley, 1954). Hence, when arguments are made to counter or, at least, to hold at arm's length the reducing of psychology to physics, those arguments are solely *intradermal* in focus; *extradermally,* the predicates of physics reign unquestioned (e.g., Fodor, 1975). In short, implicit in opposition to reductionism is the claim that with regard to perceiving (or knowing), the perceiver (or knower) resides inside the skin and constitutes the object of psychological investigation with its special predicates, whereas that which is perceived (or known) lies outside the skin and is quite properly the domain of physical inquiry and reduced predicates. The assumed dualism of knower and known, of animal and environment, is obvious.

Consider now Gestalt theory. As we have taken care to point out, Gestalt theory saw that the predicates and laws of psychology in general and those of perception in particular were molar. They resisted, therefore, the reduction of psychological predicates, or descriptors, to the most molecular physical predicates. In order not to abandon the utility of the molar predicates of psychology—for as Koffka (1935) claimed, psychology should have something useful to say to the historian and the artist whose interests lie with molar behavior—Gestalt theory committed itself to molar physical, and hence molar physiological, predicates.

Recall the Gestalt argument that if the predicates of physiology are molar, then their molar properties will be identical to the conscious processes that they putatively underly (see, particularly, Köhler, 1947, pp. 37–40). But this concern of Gestalt psychology for molar predicates was bounded by the skin: It promoted a theoretical language of molar predicates inside the skin and denied such a language outside the skin. The predicates of the light to the eye were, after all, molecular (see quotes in first section). To be consistent, Gestalt theory should have argued that the physical medium of the light, no less than the physical medium of the nervous system, is describable by molar predicates, a subset of the molar properties of which are consonant with the predicates of perceptual experience. This commendable consistency, however, was denied Gestalt psychology by its rigid adherence to an entrenched dualism that detaches at the skin perceiver from world, knower from known—animal from environment.

What is at issue when one opposes reducing the predicates of a so-called special science to those of physics is the very notion of fundamentality and the imputed primacy of physics as such. There is an emerging orthodoxy (e.g., Fodor, 1975; Pattee, 1972; Putnam, 1973) that holds that it is legitimate to speak of alternative, autonomous grains or scales (or *levels*—but this is a misleading term) of description and that fundamentality, perhaps, is a functional matter.[1]

The third error detailed earlier dovetails with the second as follows: It is to assume that *extradermally*, the conventional descriptors of physics have a monopoly on describing what is real. To reiterate, whereas a theorist may be inclined to question the primacy and sufficiency of conventional physical descriptors "inside the skin," he or she would be less inclined to question their primacy and sufficiency "outside the skin." For observations that are relevant to physics, energy emitted by a source is an appropriate reality, and the descriptors, or predicates, of energy as such are the apposite descriptors of what is real. But to make a similar assumption for observations that are relevant to psychology is—from the perspective of a commitment to realism and, less generally, from the perspective of the emerging orthodoxy already voiced—an error. To ascribe primary reality status to the conventional physical description of an energy medium (or of the surrounding surfaces and substances) is to do two things: It is to assume that any other description must be, in some sense, unreal, and it is to assume that intradermal processes must register these basic descriptors logically prior to anything else they may happen to do (cf. Runeson, 1977). Consider, for instance, a conventional physical description of the light to an eye. A molecular description in terms of photons or, relatedly, in terms of rays of light that may vary in intensity and wavelength is a description of a complex aggregate—more

---

[1]Particularly important grist for the mill of the emerging orthodoxy is being provided by: (a) Bunge's arguments for a pluralism of distinct scales and a "moderate" reductionism that pursues an explanation in depth without a denial of novelty (Bunge, 1967; 1977); and (b) the arguments of Iberall and his colleagues for analyzing all systems, whatever their scale, in terms of *physical principles that are scale independent*—that is to say, a reduction to *physics* rather than the reduction traditionally sought, which is to *structures* such as molecules (Iberall, 1977; Yates, Marsh, & Iberall, 1972).

precisely, a complex *chaotic* aggregate when one takes animals into consideration, as Koffka (1935) and Köhler (1947) most vigorously underlined. The point
is that whereas a fine-grained scale of description may be exhaustive in terms of
the laws of particle physics, there is nothing at that scale of description that
explains how the light is information about the animal's environment and the
animal's relation to it (Fitch & Turvey, 1978; Turvey & Shaw, 1979). Echoing
the evolutionary concern voiced in the first section, if adaptive relations evolve
between the molecular scale of description and visual systems, then there would
be no accounting for the variety of visual capabilities exhibited across species.
For there is nothing in the molecular scale of description that accounts for why
any visual beast should limit itself to a restricted subset of the visual experiences
made possible by the terrestrial and aquatic configurations of surfaces and substances. In sum, with respect to light, there are reasonable grounds as well as a
commitment (to realism) for rejecting the fundamentality of a molecular scale of
description. The alternative, which a committed realist should abide, is that there
is an autonomous scale of description—a scale that is neither redundant nor
inconsistent with more molecular scales—the predicates of which are both
animal—referential and environment-referential (Fitch & Turvey, 1978; Gibson,
1977; Lee, 1974, 1976; Shaw et al., 1981).

What of the other feature of the third error currently under discussion—that an
animal must register the so-called fundamental predicates of physics *logically
prior* to registering anything else? If it can be agreed that what is basic to physics
need not be construed as monopolizing what is real, then there is no reason to
adhere to the claim that what is basic to physics has logical priority in perception.
Nevertheless, the student of perception who is drawn toward its supportive
neurophysiology may find this conclusion hard to swallow. For surely, is it not a
fact that the first intradermal step registers and represents the most molecular
physical predicates, with successive steps (or a single step, as the case probably
is for Gestalt psychology) yielding and representing the predicates of a higher
order?

The putative fact in question bears blatantly the stamp of animal–environment
dualism. It presupposes that a major task of the nervous system is to get the world
that is exterior to the skin (or some facsimile of it) represented *inside* the
skin—more specifically, *inside* the head. The following quote expresses this
presupposition with its phenomenalist consequences for neurophysiology
(Attneave, 1974b):

All of it [experiencing of the world], to the best of our knowledge, is mediated by
receptor activity and is relayed to the brain in the form of Morse code signals, as it
were, so that what we experience as the "real world," and locate outside ourselves
cannot possibly be anything better than a *representation* of the external world [p.
493]

The buying of this presupposition blinds one to an important distinction between the content of a neural signal to a neural device and the content that one assigns to the signal as an outside observer when one describes the signal and the devices that it goes between (Dennett, 1969). Thus, for example, with regard to the popular conception of feature detector, the scientist so blinded proclaims that a signal from a cell identified as such a detector to a cell with which it is linked is synonymous to the statement: ''There is a line of orientation such-and-such (say, 60° on some coordinate system) at a location of such-and-such (say, 30° NE of some origin in the coordinate system.'' The highly questionable belief is that the cell receiving the signal understands and uses information of the kind couched in the statement. To the contrary, and even here we are guilty of overpresumption: ''What it gets in the way of data are at best reports with uninterpreted predicates ('it is intensely F at location L again') and out of this it must confirm its own dummy hypotheses'' (Dennett, 1977, p. 274). The latter statement is overly presumptuous precisely because, like the statement it supplants, it presumes the format of neural signals and the nature of the neural tasks. Unfortunately, thorough examination of token signals will prescribe neither vocabulary nor task for us. As Dennett (1977) puts it: ''In fact is either way of talking appropriate? The vocabulary of the signals is not something that is to be settled by an examination of tokens . . . and when we turn to indirect evidence of 'psychological reality' any evidence we turn up will perforce be neutral between interpreted and uninterpreted predicates [p. 274].''

We would like to argue that there are two cognate points that follow from this line of reasoning. One is that neurophysiological ''facts'' *qua* statements about perception are suspect; they are what they are by virtue of the phenomenalist/dualist tradition guiding their perpetration. The other point is that any claim about what a given piece of the nervous system tells another piece should not be read as a claim about what a given piece of the nervous system tells the animal. Put succinctly, what the frog's eye tells the frog's brain is not the same as what the frog's eye tells the frog—if there is any telling to be done at all.

Newtonian Space and Time and Causal Interconnection as Allied to Animal–Environment Dualism

Let us proceed to make more precise how it is that animal–environment dualism taints the conventional interpretation of the nervous system's role in perception. In so doing, we will bring together the errors discussed so far and those merely noted in the inventory. In addition we will lay the groundwork for establishing a perspective in which to reevaluate the status of basic physical variables in a theory of perception. Ideally, the perspective sought and the reevaluation given will be consonant with perceptual realism.

In accord with animal/environment dualism is the assumed appropriateness of Newtonian space and time for matters of psychology and the causal-chain theory of perception. Given this dualism, which in its mind–body subtheme distinguishes the object of reference from the object of experience, and given the unchallenged authority (until this century) of the Newtonian formulation, it would have been a historical oddity if no attempt were made to fit the terms espoused by the one tradition to the terms of the other. The fit, however, was never technically secure. Although adherents to the Cartesian-Newtonian scheme of things felt that the reference object could be located with some conviction in Cartesian coordinates, the intentional object (or object of experience), being phenomenal rather than noumenal, could only be given a quasi location—a location that was "not definitely but indefinitely, 'in' or 'at' an organism" (Bentley, 1954), p. 215). The eventual fit, therefore, took the following form: The reference object located extradermally was separated by a distance in Newtonian space from a representation of it, the object of experience, which was located (roughly) intradermally. How, then, might the aforementioned distance be bridged and the two object kinds coordinated? The answer was looked for in Newtonian mechanics and given as thus: A causal sequence of energy propagations and neural signals covers the distance from the loci of the reference object to the loci of its representation. According to this causal analysis of perception, the reference object is the initial cause, and the representation, or intentional object, the final effect.

Consider two humans—one speaking, the other listening. We can presume that the speaker intends to say something meaningful to the listener. What we wish to note is that a causal chain analysis of this situation, which will unavoidably introduce discontinuities in descriptors—much like the descriptor discontinuity manifest in the analysis of vision by Gestalt psychology—raises two perplexing puzzles: how meaning is lost in transmission and how meaning is recovered. There is a familiar story (see MacKay, 1969) that tells how the speaker's intent, the speaker's speech plan (which is the reference object in this particular case), is meaningful but how the mechanical embodiment of the message, first by the efferent neural activity of the speaker's motor system and then by the acoustic signal generated by the speaker's vocal activity, is devoid of meaning. "Discussion at this level proceeds in exactly the same terms whether the air is handling the outpourings of a genius or the jabber of a monkey" (MacKay, 1969, p. 20). Thus the first puzzlement: How did something meaningful become meaningless? What is being assumed, of course, is that the proper theoretical language for describing the speaker's utterance-as-planned will contain predicates sufficiently rich to capture the utterance's meaning, but the proper theoretical language for describing the speaker's utterance-as-executed can contain no such predicates.

Because the listener experiences the message and not the properties of the media that mechanically embody it, it must be claimed that the afferent activity caused in the listener's nervous system by the speaker-produced sounds, although without meaning initially, acquires meaning eventually, at some later point in brain processing. Here lies the second puzzlement: How does a thing that is meaningless become meaningful, and where does it become so?

This story of human communication vividly expresses the errors discussed: a discontinuity in descriptors, the intradermal location of the special predicates of psychology (meaning is inside the head), and an acceptance of the physicist's description of an energy medium as the only and proper description. In addition the foregoing story gives due expression to the following. It provides a spurious causal analysis of speech perception by means of slipping between modes of discourse, or causally interconnecting distinct scales of description as if they were logically alike (cf. Fowler & Turvey, 1978). One mode of discourse in which the story is conducted is talk about communicating; the other mode of discourse is talk about the properties of media that mechanically support but are not identical with the act of communicating. We can appreciate that sound pressure-waves mechanically stimulate the eardrum. We can also appreciate that this stimulation is conveyed by a further mechanical process, that of nerve activity. And although the stages that follow may prove exceedingly more abstruse in their details, they remain, nevertheless, mechanical stages. Thus MacKay's (1969, p. 21) question: "Where to draw the line?"

The point is that talk about the energy states of a system is not talk about the information states of a system,[2] and to confuse or causally blend the two is to invite muddled thinking and misleading questions—such as inquiring of the stage at which the meaning of a message is acquired. A considerably more general point is the paramount importance of holding epistemic acts distinct from their causal support.

The muddled story of human communication that we have been considering was spawned primarily, so it can be argued, by the allied biases of animal-environment dualism, the Newtonian framework, and the causal-chain theory. What follows is a critical evaluation of each.

Scales of Description as a Temporal Sequence

Is it legitimate to assume that distinct scales of description can be temporally concatenated? Imagine a state of affairs such as a book sitting on a desk. At one scale of description, the book is describable in the molecular terms of quantum

---

[2]This requires some qualification. Given a more enlightened interpretation of dynamics (e.g., Glandsdorff & Prigogine, 1971; Iberall, 1977) and explicit recognition of an animal and its environment as logically dependent components of a single system, we might expect the notion of energy states of the system to approximate more closely the notion of information states of the system. Notable in this regard is Thom's (1975) description of information as form—as the geometric parameterization of a stationary regime of local dynamics—and the meaning of a "message" as the topological relation between the form of the message and the eigenforms of the receptor.

mechanics; at another and coarser scale of description, the descriptors are the dimensions of Newtonian mechanics; and at yet another scale of description, the terms are those depicting the properties of the object—the book—taken with reference to human activity. Without embroiling ourselves in debate on whether the different scales identify separate realities or, less ambitiously, distinct realms of inquiry, we can appreciate, by the preceding example, that a state of affairs may succumb to several analyses involving distinctively different scales of predicates, yielding distinctively different understandings. We can appreciate, further, that it would be nonsense to argue that the most fine grained scale of description temporally prefaces scales of a coarser grain. In short, there is no manner of talking that permits us to claim that events captured in the finest scale of description occur first, with the events captured in the language of the other scales occurring thereafter—as so many tumbling dominoes. There is a manner of talking, however, that permits us to say that the scales of description are coordinated; for we may presume that scales of description are alternative descriptions that, although not redundant, are also not inconsistent with one another (Pattee, 1973).

The Newtonian Framework as Standard

Is there any compelling reason why perceptual theory should assume the Newtonian formulation of space and time as *the* framework for its facts? The answer to this question is, we believe, a tart "no!" (see Gibson, 1966; Shaw & Pittenger, 1977, 1978). Newton's space for classical physics was absolute; it was a locus in which objects could be placed. Einstein, however, in pursuing an explanation for the facts of physics, followed Riemann's suggestion and rejected the Newtonian absolute space in favor of a conception of space as relative. On this latter conception, space itself has structure—a structure that is owing to, or induced by, the material that comprises it. In the Riemannian conception of space, there is, strictly speaking, a *single* object—precisely, the space structure as a whole—as a *single* system. The individual objects *in* the Newtonian space are local aspects *of* the structure in the Reimannian space.

We should not suppose that the success of Einstein's conception of space (and time) and of relativity physics requires the perceptual theorist to shift from a Newtonian view to an Einsteinian view. Rather, the import of Einstein's work is that psychological theory should not feel compelled (or seduced) to press its facts into the mold of Newtonian space and time. The lesson to be learned is that if physical theory could construct a space and time befitting the facts of research in physics, perceptual theory should pursue the construction of a space and time befitting the facts of research in perception. An argument of like kind was made by Bentley (1954). It was summarized by him as follows:

1. Psychology has always concerned itself with facts which do not tolerate technical description in technical Newtonian space and time.

2. These facts, nevertheless, have their own manifest extensions and durations.
3. Psychology is now at last free to describe them as it finds and observes them.
4. Such observation and description becomes practicable with the frame of a full naturalism for organic and environmental facts [p. 479].

The Dualism of Animal and Environment

Is it logical to treat the concepts of animal and environment as independent? It is readily agreed that no animal has been observed in the state of animal-alone or animal-by-itself. It can also be agreed—although it will take some argument to engender agreement—that no environment exists in the state of environment-alone or environment-by-itself. The very term *environment* implicates a thing environed, a thing surrounded; without a thing that is environed, the term *environment* makes no sense. If we take that which is environed to be living things— that is, life in general—then the term *environment* can reasonably be equated with the solids, liquids, and gases that compose life's terrestrial and aquatic support. This equation is useful to a point; but it is far too general—far too homogeneous a depiction of environment—for most purposes. In order that we can talk sensibly about adaptation, we must guarantee that *the definition of environment expresses approximately the same order of variety as the definition of species*. An increase in variety is obtained by recognizing that geographical distinctions represent different partitionings on the solids, liquids, and gases that make up the planet. Geographical distinctions stand in correspondence to distinctions among species in terms of *where* they live—their habitats. But the order of variety so gained is insufficient, as evidenced by the observation that many species can occupy the same geographical region; habitats are shared. What is needed is a further refinement in the conception of environment, a refinement that introduces distinctions that stand in correspondence to distinctions among species in terms of *how* they live (Gibson, 1977).

In other words, what is needed is a way of describing the substances and surfaces comprising the terrestrial or aquatic surroundings of an animal that is in reference to that animal's body, in reference to the kinds of activities in which it engages. A predicate or descriptor of this type has been referred to by Gibson (1977) as an *affordance* (see also Shaw et al., in press; Turvey & Shaw, 1979): a combination of surface and substance properties that is uniquely suited to a given animal—to its nutritive system or to its action system. Given this animal-referential descriptor, we can proceed to equate the environment for a given species with a set of affordances—or affordance structure—and to recognize the necessary reciprocity between animal and environment: An environment defined as an affordance structure implies a certain kind of animal, an animal that exhibits a particular set of capabilities, or effectivities, as we have called them (Shaw et al., 1981; Turvey & Shaw, 1979; Turvey et al., 1978); and an animal defined as an effectivity structure implies a certain kind of environment.

Affordance and the Geographical
Environment–Behavioral Environment Distinction

This is an especially good place at which to return the discussion's focus to Gestalt theory, particularly the predicament of the first section of this chapter— the distinction between geographical and behavioral environment. We can do so by considering why a notion such as affordance is necessary and unavoidable from the perspective of a commitment to realism.

The assumed dualism of animal and environment encourages the perceptual theorist to distinguish between what a thing *is* and what a thing *means;* a thing that simply *is* inhabits the physical domain, whereas a thing that *means* inhabits the mental domain. In this vein, as observed earlier, Koffka (1935) distinguished between the geographical world (noumena) and the behavioral world (phenomena) and proposed the latter as the framework for behavior. Thus, Koffka (1935) would say that a handle "invites" or "demands" grasping. But a physical description of the surface and substance properties that constitute the material nature of a handle contains no animal-referential or activity-relevant terms; the physical dimensions used to describe the handle are animal-indifferent. So what is the status of the characteristics of surfaces and substances that behavior is in reference to? As they are not characteristics or dimensions of the geographical or physical environment, they must be dimensions of the behavioral or phenomenal environment. The claim that Koffka was making is that the dimensions of surfaces and substances that behavior is in reference to *are not ordinary physical dimensions* and, therefore, *are not real dimensions.* These dimensions that invite behavior owe their very existence, in Koffka's (1935) reasoning, to an animal's needs. Here we have what has been referred to elsewhere (Shaw et al., 1981) as the incommensurability of natural kinds: The reference object, the mailbox as an object described in physical terms, is logically distinct from the intentional object, the mailbox as an object that invites a particular behavior. And whereas the reference object may have (for a phenomenalism of Koffka's kind) an existence independent of perception, the intentional object cannot.

From the perspective of a commitment to realism, the foregoing conclusions are anathema. They can be avoided, however, by taking the following as a fundamental precept for realism: The dimensions of configurations of surfaces and substances that behavior is with respect to may not be ordinary physical dimensions, in that conventional physical language fails to describe them; but they are, none the less, real dimensions. It would seem that conclusions opposed to realism arise from describing the reference object in a physical language that is committed to a reality but is noncommittal or neutral with regard to animals as epistemic agents, and describing the intentional object in a phenomenal language that is noncommittal on reality but *is* agent oriented. These distinct and irreducible languages are in the spirit of animal–environment dualism. What is needed is a *single* theoretical language—in the spirit of animal–environment synergy (Fitch & Turvey, 1978; Turvey & Shaw, 1979)—that manages to incorporate both the objectivity of the physical language and the agent orientation of the phenomenal language.

We see, in short, that a concept such as affordance is not optional; rather, it is mandated by a commitment to realism. That commitment also mandates that the affordance of a given thing is always there to be perceived. An affordance exists, we argue (and see Gibson, 1977), as *a real property of the ecosystem* and not by virtue of its being perceived. Defining environment as an affordance structure is to remove the problems that Koffka (1935) addressed and to obviate the distinction (geographical versus behavioral) that he felt compelled to make.

The steps we took toward a conception of environment that exhibits variety consonant with that of species may be characterized as a shift from a conception of environment relating to animals as physical and biological entities to a conception of environment that relates to animals as knowing agents; and, relatedly, a shift from seeking a definition of environment in absolute terms (along the lines of a Newtonian conception of space and time) to an attempt to define environment in relative and fuctional terms. In sum, the shift in definition is from an absolute and species-indifferent emphasis to a relative and species-specific emphasis.

One should not suppose that a relativistic account of environment, given here in terms of affordances, is just so much heterodoxy; on the contrary, it would seem to approximate the kind of definition that students of evolution are reaching for (see Lewontin, 1978). Waddington (1961) remarks: "The situation is that existing modes of behavior . . . combine with external circumstances to determine the nature of the effective environment [p. 91]." And moreover, one should not suppose that the claim for a synergy (as opposed to a dualism) of animal and environment with their respective definitions reciprocally linked is not without predecessors in biology. Comte (see Jacob, 1976), Needham, and Haldane (see Haraway, 1976) can be counted among those who often gave lip service, and sometimes more, to the critique of conceptually dissociating animal and environment.

From a Self-Actional to a Transactional Observation Base

We would do well at this juncture to collect our thoughts. Our intention in this section has been to identify those themes, which we take to be conceptual errors, that inspired Gestalt theory to an organocentric view of perceptual organization. In the process of identifying and discussing these errors, we have painted in broad strokes a partial view of the realist backdrop for perceptual theory. Central to that view—to which we have alluded here and argued elsewhere (Shaw et al., in press; Turvey & Shaw, 1979)—is the synergy of animal and environment, and it has received a brief hearing in the immediately preceding pages. By emphasizing the synergy, or reciprocity, of animal and environment, we intend to rule out other, historically more popular ways of viewing their relation. In the synergy perspective, an animal and its environment are not, in any act of knowing, rigid separables but, rather, complementary constituents of a system—an (epistemic) ecosystem (Turvey & Shaw, 1979). It may prove convenient and profitable for certain inquiries (those of physics and, perhaps, of physiology) to detach animal and environment. But we would agree with Dewey and Bentley (1949) that: "The student of the processes of knowings and knowns lacks this convenience. He can not successfully make such a separation at any time [p. 151]." And we can enjoy accord with Dewey and Bentley (1949) on further points—specifically, with regard to their analysis of styles of inquiry as they bear on the relation of animal and environment.

These authors identify two traditional forms of inquiry that would be consistent with animal–environment dualism. In one form, *self-action,* things are viewed as acting under their own powers. In earlier times it was commonplace to assign to gods or spirits sole responsibility for physical phenomena; in more recent times it has become commonplace to assign to mental or neural entities responsibility for behaviors and perceptions. Thus, for example, "mind" and a mental constituent such as a "faculty for music" are charged, respectively, with responsibility for behavior in the full and behavior of a restricted kind. Similarly, "brain" and a neural component such as "limbic system" are charged, respectively, with responsibility for behavior most generally and behavior more specifically. This custom has a long history—of regarding behavior and the like as initiated by the animal or, more precisely, by some actorlike entity resident in or at the animal.

Although not explicitly mentioned by Dewey and Bentley, there is a converse form of inquiry to the self-actional—what might be called the *other-actional.* In this view, the control of the behavior of a natural system is seen as lying in something beyond itself, such as in a deity that expresses its volition through animals or people. This view of the actions of a given system being based in an outside agent, shorn of its theistic trappings, is but a small step from the strict behaviorism of the 20th century, which attempted to locate the control of behavior in rewards, reinforcements, incentives, or triggering stimuli seated in the environment.

The second traditional style of inquiry identified by Dewey and Bentley is *interactional.* Here, rigidly separate things—that is, things that one assumes can be described as indifferent to any joint operation—are isolated and held to relate through causal interaction. This form of inquiry—essentially the model of scientific analysis handed down to us by Galileo and Newton—is manifest in the causal-chain theory of perception as depicted earlier. As a substitute for the older self-action form of inquiry, interaction—purely interpreted—would not suppose that perceiving is the responsibility of an animal-localized entity but rather results from the causal interconnection of animal and environment. Of course, in practice, the older (self-action of other-action) and newer (inter-action) styles of inquiry rarely occur in a pure form. More often than not in interaction analysis, the animal is given the spotlight, ascribed special powers (self-actional entities), and held superior over and against the environment to which is is causally interconnected; but not uncommonly, and as a backlash, some scholars adopt the other-actional stance by assigning to the environment superior reality status, with the animal being just a pawn to the environment's regularities and variations. Where the self- or other-actional scheme requires descriptors for monadic or single-variable states, the interactional form of inquiry requires descriptors that can handle dyadic, or two- variable, relations. In the two-place relationship most cited, the two terms stand to each another as cause to effect or stimulus to response.

There has been a most noticeable change in styles of scientific inquiry or observation bases, as Bentley (1954) and Dewey and Bentley (1949) point out: Physics, the oldest science, has transformed its observation base from one of initiating powers or forces—through one of things *solus,* organized by causal interconnection—to one where the focus is *system,* described in full. This contemporary trend in scientific inquiry is referred to as *transaction.*[3] In a transactional inquiry, it is impossible to study one component of a system as an element in isolation; rather, components necessarily co-implicate their complementary aspects. The transactional form of inquiry eschews the enterprise of decomposing whole systems into separate and distinct substructures that are then treated as if their isolated functions are simply linearly additive to express the functional capabilities of the whole. Dewey and Bentley (1949) oppose the "analytic" fallacy of attributing to any part of a system the responsibility for the whole system's properties (Turvey & Shaw, 1979); moreover, they intend that the concept of transaction, unlike self-action or interaction, should preserve the sense of reciprocity among complementary components that is essential to the integrity of any system. Clearly, the transactional form of inquiry is consistent with animal–environment synergy. The following quote from Dewey and Bentley (1949) expresses this consistency and may be taken as an appropriate summary of the present section and a departure point for the next.

---

[3]Dewey and Bentley's term *transaction* was made popular by the Ames group, who labeled their brand of psychology "transactionalism" or "transactional psychology" (Ittelson, 1952; Kilpatrick, 1961). It would be a mistake, however, to assume that the usage of the term by the Ames group was consistent with that intended by Dewey and Bentley. "Transactional psychology" was (is?) a phenomenalism in which the Helmholtzian concept of unconscious inference is taken to the extreme. Although Dewey and Bentley, on initial encounter, expressed enthusiasm for the work of the Ames group and sanctioned the labeling of it as "transactional," they were to become increasingly disturbed by the way in which the group misinterpreted and misused the concept. (See the correspondence between Dewey and Bentley in Dewey & Bentley [1964].)

Our position is simply that since man as an organism has evolved among other organisms in an evolution called "natural," we are willing under hypothesis to treat all his behavings, including his most advanced knowings, as activities not of himself alone, nor even as primarily his, but as processes of the full situation of organism–environment; and to take this full situation as one which is before us within the knowings, as well as being the situation in which the knowings themselves arise [p. 104].

ECOLOGICAL THEORY AS A PRAGMATIC REALISM

Let us return to a persuasive Lockean theme: Knowing in all its forms (perceiving, remembering, and so on) requires the interfacing of the knower to the objects and events known. Therefore, there must exist somewhere a medium of "between-things" (ideas, percepts, meanings, organizing principles, propositions, models, and the like) that carry the burden of the interaction of the agent with its world. Locke, in short, posited three ontological realms, and we may recognize that Hume's skepticism and Berkeley's subjective idealism were attempts to rid epistemology, and hence psychology, of the necessity of a third realm of mediating epistemic constructs. But Locke prevailed. Consequently, it has been commonplace for past and present perceptual theory to accept as an explanatory paradigm a three-realm relation, or "semantic triad": Hence, the so-called semantic triad of communication situations: sender $\rightarrow$ message $\rightarrow$ receiver; of logical theory world facts (or states of affairs: $\rightarrow$ proposition $\rightarrow$ statement (e.g., sentence or utterance); of abstract machine theory (computer science): data $\rightarrow$ program $\rightarrow$ output; and, of course, of various mediational accounts of stimulus–response theory: S $\rightarrow$ O $\rightarrow$ R. Each generation of psychological theory manages to rediscover this notion; and although the triad is clothed in new terms, no fundamental change in theory occurs.

The crux of the argument we wish to pursue in the present part of the chapter is that the transactional form of inquiry provides a means of avoiding the semantic triad, presumed by nearly all forms of scientific inquiry into matters pertaining to perception. Most pointedly, we attempt to show that the transactional style of inquiry, like its descendant, the ecological style of inquiry, circumvents the need for a third realm of entities interceding between animal and environment–knower and known.

Our hand, however, must not be overplayed in these matters. Let it be clearly understood that we recognize that many of the constructs used by us and our peers are meant to have no reality status beyond analytic or methodological usefulness: Their value is pragmatic rather than ontologic. On the other hand, where analytic concepts are involved in the perception literature, confusion often arises about whether the constructs are real. Such confusion presumably, in more cases than not, betrays real confusion in the minds of the investigators themselves. Such constructs are discussed as if they belong to a causal chain of events that begin with physical activities in the world and are conveyed by biological processes to a "sensorium" from which eventually psychological species are extracted and, perhaps, abstracted. Nowhere is there an admission or implied qualification that the causal chain supporting perception may not be wholly real or unbroken. Clearly, such an admission that some link was unsubstantial—say, the final one—would make a mockery of the argument. *Herein lies the uncritical acceptance of the Lockean metaphysics.* Its limitations and inconsistencies were recognized by both Berkeley and Hume. Time has in no way healed these defects of Locke's thesis but has, perhaps, allowed them to recede into the background, so that incautious theorists no longer see them and, therefore, countenance the thesis unwarily.

Given agreement with respect to the origins of the problems that bedevil current theorizing about perception, the question naturally arises as to an alternative approach that might avoid them: The transactional form of inquiry, updated to accommodate ecological concerns, offers one such alternative. As already intimated, the concept of animal–environment synergy is at least transactional.

Semantic Triads

It is difficult to grasp fully what is philosophically troublesome and scientifically misleading about too easy an acceptance of three-realm approaches. In a nutshell, however, it is the uncritical treatment of epistemic mediators (psychological constructs) as real objects rather than as analytic categories with no more than pragmatic convenience for scientific inquiry.

Ironically, the need for positing a third realm of existent entities so as to account for meaning is no better seen than in the attempt of traditional logicians to characterize one of the primary conceptual building blocks for logic—the proposition. The traditional conception of a logical proposition—in its rawest, most commonsense form—is any overt act, usually a spoken or written sentence, by which some state of affairs is affirmed or denied. What makes the issue of what really constitutes a proposition problematic is the notion that it might be an implicit rather than an overt act of affirmation or denial. More precisely, the problem reads: Is a proposition identical to the overt act or merely associated with it (say, as the idea that it expresses or entails)?

But such a move lands the issue in the semantic quagmire, a quandary regarding how one can have a theory of entailment logically prior to a theory of propositions, because propositions as formal objects, strictly speaking, may only formally entail other propositions. Hence to base the notion of a proposition on an intuitive conception of entailment—say, that the idea behind the act is somehow entailed by the act itself—is already to prejudge the nature of entailment and to remove it, as it were, from the realm of formal logic to that conceptually more vague realm of meanings hidden from the public eye. Similarly, any attempt to define a proposition as a judgment rather than an overt act pushes the foundations of logic into the psychology of judgments—a most unlikely place in which to find clarity or lucidity.

Dewey and Bentley, among others, have been justifiably unhappy with this turn of events, for one important ramification of the view that propositions are "mental" rather than "behavioral" in nature is to place a realm of mediating entities between thinking animals and their world; unlike overt actions that are, at the same time, animal-based as well as activities in the public domain of the environment, "mental" propositions become reified as a third realm of objects that mediate the epistemic relation holding between a knowing animal and a knowable environment. Dewey and Bentley's (1949) criticism of this traditional propinquity to confuse ontological status of a concept with its pragmatic value as an analytic category of inquiry was directed at many of the most noted philosophers of their day: Lewis (1943), Cohen and Nagel (1934), Ogden and Richards (1930), Carnap (1942), and Russell (1925). Dewey and Bentley (1949) assert: "[One must avoid treating] . . . a use, a function, and service rendered in conduct of inquiry as if it had ontological reference apart from inquiry [p. 320]."

The things typically given the status of existents by such traditional philosophers were (1) agents or actors, (2) things, and (3) an intervening interpretative activity, product, or medium—linguistic, symbolic, mental, rational, logical, or other (such as language, sign, sentence, proposition, meaning, truth, or thought). For instance, Ogden and Richards' (1930) semantic triangle included at its vertices "thought or reference," "symbol," and "referent or object [p. 14]." Similarly, in Cohen and Nagel (1934), we have the claim that "it seems impossible that there should be any confusion between a physical object, our 'idea' or image of it, and the word that denotes it [p. 16]." Carnap (1942) defines the meaning situation as comprising "the speaker, the expression uttered, and the designatum of the expression," or alternatively as "the speaker, the expression, and what is referred to [pp. 8–9]," where "what is referred to" is also spoken of as that to which the speaker "intends" to refer.

There can be little doubt about the fairness of Dewey's criticism of semantic theory in the first half of the 20th century; the philosophers identified earlier, like Brentano (1874–1925) early in his career (but he later repudiated the point), all tacitly agreed to reify a realm of immanently or intentionally specified objects— variously termed *ideas, propositions, concepts, images,* or whatnot—as the ghostly entities that mediate our perceivings, rememberings, actings, and knowing with respect to the world (see Shaw et al., 1981, for a fuller criticism of the role of Brentano's fallacy in contemporary psychology). And more contemporary theorists are scarcely less guilty of confusing concepts convenient to inquiry with those that denote things possessing some kind of an ephemeral existence.

Pierce (Mis)Interpreted as Advocating a Semantic Triad

Nowhere is this traditional attitude more elegantly stated than by Lewis (1943) in a vain attempt to echo the authority of Peirce (1940–1950) by claiming that "the essentials of the meaning-situation are found wherever there is anything which, for some mind, stands as sign of something else [p. 236]." Indeed, Peirce *can* be read (although, as we shall see, he should *not* be read) as championing such a view, for in his letters to Lady Welby, Peirce (1940/1950) attempts to explain his difficult concept of *Thirdness*, the name he used to denote his view of meaning as a triadic relation existing between a sign, its object, and the interpreting thought. In a different essay, Peirce (1940/1950) argues that "every genuine triadic relation involves meaning, as meaning is obviously a triadic relation [p. 91]."

Now on casual reading, it surely seems that Peirce would approve the interpretation of his semantic theory given by Lewis, but strong exception is taken to this fact by Dewey and Bentley (1949); their concept of the transactional is essentially a restatement of Peirce's more subtle and too often misunderstood notion of Thirdness. Indeed, as ecological psychologists and students of perception, our concern with this debate between Dewey and Bentley and their peers devolves upon this very important point of disagreement—namely, the question of whether semantics, and hence the meaning of perceptual experiences, necessarily requires a triad of realms among which relationsips must hold in any meaning transaction. If so, then it is difficult to see how Gibson and other ecological psychologists can continue to oppose so-called mediational accounts of perception that reflect an *in*direct realism—that is, where propositions, signs, or other forms of symbolic representation are required to stand between a knower and its world.

And if our earlier arguments are valid (e.g., Shaw et al., 1981; Turvey & Shaw, 1979), then it is also difficult to see how we can avoid not just a dualism but a tripartite pluralism where thoughts or experiences may be held as separate from those who think and experience, as are the objects to which they refer.

Semantic Relations Do Not Involve an Ontological Triad of Realms: Peirce Properly Interpreted

Let us proceed to buttress the claim that Peirce, as Dewey and Bentley (1949) correctly point out, has been misread as endorsing an ontological triad of realms over which semantic situations must be defined. Most pointedly, Dewey and Bentley (1949) were against unnecessarily reifying such things as relations or propositions, as this proves to be more of a hindrance than a help to theory. A telling remark by Dewey is the following (Dewey & Bentley, 1949): "I did not originate the main figures that play their parts in my theory of knowing. I tried the experiment of transferring the old well-known figures from the stage of ontology to the stage of inquiry [p. 328]." Bentley (Dewey & Bentley, 1964) also offers the following observations: "If one takes two 'things' and does not permit the use of a transactional view, then one adds a third 'thing' namely a 'relation.'. . . I have always been rabid against the use of the word 'relation' as a thing [p. 534]."

On first blush, the last remark may appear nominalistic, but we believe this is
to miss the main point; for given their presumed understanding and endorsement
of Peirce over and against traditional semanticists, Dewey and Bentley can
hardly be considered as nominalists. No, much more is at stake here. Consider
their sharp criticism of Lewis' claim cited earlier that Peirce (1940/1950) meant
to endorse the semantic triad when he admitted that "every genuine triadic
relation involves meaning, as meaning is obviously a triadic relation [p. 91]." To
the contrary, they argue, to view this as an endorsement of the ontologic triad is a
spurious reading fostered by taking Peirce's thought out of the context of his
whole system. Lewis' mistake was particularly ironic and irksome to them because Peirce's concept of Thirdness, which provided the basis for the transactional form of inquiry, was conceived primarily for the purpose of avoiding such
fallacies arising from wantonly ignoring the context dependence of concepts.
They express it this way (Dewey & Bentley, 1949): "Such words as Lewis takes
from Peirce *do not* mean that minds, signs and things should be established in
credal separations sharper than those of levers, fulcrums, and weights; Peirce
was probing a linguistic disorder and learning fifty years ago how to avoid the
type of chaos Lewis' development shows [p. 7]."

But is not a triad of terms involved in their analogy of levers, fulcrums, and
weights? How does this relational complex of three things differ significantly
from Lewis' and others' use of a triad of terms to capture the relational complex
needed to express semantic situations? After all, one might ponder, is not the
essence even of a transactional relationship also a triad consisting of two things
plus the relationship that "connects" them—as action and reaction connect the
opposite but equal forces of one piece of matter on another? Yet Dewey and
Bentley (1949) persist stubbornly to deny that Peirce's Thirdness and their transaction necessarily posit three ontological realms of distinct kinds of objects to be
studied by science, as is clearly shown by their view of a communication
paradigm—a particular kind of semantic situation: "It [transaction] will treat the
talking and talk-products of man (the namings, thinkings, arguings, reasonings,
etc.) as the men themselves in action, not as some third type of entity to be
inserted between the men and things they deal with. To *this extent* it will be not
three-realm but two-realm: men and things [p. 5–6]." They go on to point out
that in current logics, probably the commonest third-realm insertion between
men and things is "proposition," although among other insertions, "meaning"
and "thought" are at times most popular rivals for that position of epistemic
mediator.

Our own view as to who is correct in this debate, Dewey and Bentley as
Peirce's supporters or their opponents such as Lewis, should be transparent.
Dewey and Bentley seem to have not only the more accurate reading of Peirce's
intentions but also a more clear-eyed grasp of the fundamentals required for the
semantics and the logic of scientific inquiry. If they prevail, then a strong
historical continuity of principle will exist between the transactional form of

inquiry sired by American pragmatism and the ecological form of inquiry sired by Gibson and currently under development, study, and evaluation by the present authors and others.

It is now time to focus sharply on defense of the claim that the transactional approach, the concept of Thirdness, and ecological psychology are of two rather then three ontological realms and, therefore, to break sharply with traditional forms of scientific enquiry that assume the semantic triad to be equally *real* in each of its parts. To offer a plausible defense, we must show that there is some way to "de-ontologize" one member of the semantic triad—namely, that usually referred to as the proposition, thought, concept, or idea that is typically reified as a bond behind the symbolic or sign relationship imputed to hold between the object (or event) perceived or known and the agent who perceives or knows that object (or event).

The Concept of Thirdness as the Basis of Transactions

Let us then return to consider more carefully the quote from Peirce that was spuriously interpreted as support for Lewis and others' contention that Peirce was a three-realm theorist simply because he recognized a need for a triad of analytic categories. *Our purpose is to show that one might hold to a triad of terms in a language of descriptors for semantic situations, as Peirce did, while at the same time rationally disavowing that they necessarily refer to three ontologic realms.* Such a strategy provides the logical and philosophical foundations for establishing a direct rather than a mediated theory of perception—that is, a theory of perception that a committed realist would endorse.

The reader will recall the earlier quote from Peirce (1940–1950). We now present the quote in full with the passages missing in the earlier version in italics so as to emphasize their importance in establishing the full context of interpretation required to understand Peirce's intent: "Thirdness is the triadic relation existing between a sign, its object, and the interpreting thought, *itself a sign, considered as constituting the mode of being of a sign.* A sign mediates between the interpretant sign and its object [p. 11]."

The clue we seek is in the phrase asserting that the interpreting thought is "itself a sign, considered as constituting the *mode of being* of a sign." Two things are now apparent that have typically been overlooked by casual readers of Peirce who were attempting to force his conceptions into the context of traditional semantic theory: First, in the preceding quote, Peirce invokes only two realms of entities—signs and objects; thoughts belong not to a third realm but are themselves signs of some sort. Second, the sort of signs they are has to do with their "mode of being." Now a *mode* is but another word for *function;* thus, we have a thought or, better, thinking construed as a function of signs, or a sign-function. Clearly, if we agree with Bentley and Dewey, we no more want to reify a function than we would a relation. The trick of avoiding treating thoughts, propositions, or ideas as real "things" is to understand more about how sign-functions may specify the relationship that must exist between things in the world called signs and things in the world to which they refer. Thoughts, or thinking, will then be a functionally specified activity of people *in the world* rather than a vague entity with some immanent existence outside the world or outside the people who populate that world along with its usual furnishings.

Let us pursue an understanding of Thirdness as an analytic rather than ontological category. To do so and to get the full flavor of Peirce's argument, we must also understand his concepts of Firstness and Secondness. It is pedagogically useful to recognize that Peirce's concept of Firstness is the progenitor of the notion of self-action, although the latter is an abomination of the former. Similarly, interaction is akin to Peirce's notion of Secondness, but as a descendant, it has traits not possessed by the first. And, finally, one rightfully expects transaction to be an heir to both the conceptual richness and subtlety of Thirdness, so long as only a family resemblance is sought. But to understand any one of these concepts, one must place it in the context of an understanding of the others. Because our concern, however, is not to present Peirce's system completely but to borrow from it what we may use to understand the transactional view better, a few passing remarks must suffice.

Peirce argues that there are three modes of being that can be directly apprehended whenever we apprehend anything—say, as in perceiving, communicating, or carrying out other epistemic activities. Firstness is the mode of being that consists in the quality of something being exactly what it is without reference to anything else. It would be an animal in and of itself, conceptually isolated from its environment of other animals and things and therefore disengaged from all activities. Hence Firstness provides the explanatory basis of self-actional forms of inquiry. But because qualities of things are defined by inquiry through the activities in which they participate, no self-actional theories in science are possible and must remain in the realm of speculative metaphysics.

Secondness is the mode of being that comes about through the action of one thing upon another, such as when an animal behaves in accordance with the forces from its environment that constrain those activities of the animal that make manifest the animal's intrinsic qualities. Hence Secondness, by connecting a given thing to other things, brings Firsts into relationship with other Firsts. The relationship is one of causal interaction and thereby provides the explanatory basis of the interactional form of inquiry. Finally, Thirdness is the mode of being that brings interaction (a Second) into relationship with a third thing, a context of constraint (a Third). Peirce illustrates these three analytic categories with the example of a gift: John's giving of a present to Jane exemplifies Thirdness not simply because three things—the giver, the receiver, and the gift, all Firsts—are brought into some definitive relationship to one another, for this would only be Secondness (the relating of Firsts); rather, the giving of a gift exemplifies Thirdness because the interaction of John with Jane *vis à vis* a gift invokes the context of a rule, principle, or law. To give a gift is to relinquish one's rights to an object such that in future activities, a set of new interactions will now follow according to a predictive rule or constraint; namely, Jane may do whatever she pleases with the object John gave her as a gift without fear of moral or legal repercussions. Conversely, John has no right to interfere if the transaction was truly the giving of a gift. On the other hand, if John merely left the object in the care of Jane, she is constrained to act toward it both morally and, perhaps, legally in ways not permitted if it had been a gift. And of course if Jane takes the object without John's permission, it is called stealing rather than receiving of gifts. So here is the main characteristic of Thirdness, or transactions in general: Thirdness denotes the context of constraint (e.g., rule, principle, or law) that must be used to evaluate the meaning of interactions (e.g., giving and receiving of objects), or Seconds, which in turn define the relationships that are manifest among the objects, or Firsts, involved.

By this view, then, note that Thirdness does not have to do with a triad of realms of "things" (Firsts) with coordinate existences, as traditional theorists are wont to argue. Peirce's concept of Thirdness, as Dewey and Bentley point out, cuts vertically over "grains" of analyses or ordered scales of description, if you will, rather than horizontally over realms of coordinate existences. This point—where the triad of terms needed to capture semantic situations is not equated with a triad of ontological realms—defines a significant commonality between the ecological orientation and the American pragmatism movement. Consequently, it is here—in the full realization that Peirce's concept of Thirdness, Dewey and Bentley's transactional inquiry, and Gibson's ecological approach are philosophically of the same breed—that incisive questions might be usefully raised and significant methodological evaluations made.

THE CLAIM THAT PERCEPTUAL ORGANIZATION IS AN ACTIVITY OF THE ECOSYSTEM: POINTS IN SUPPORT OF COALITIONAL MODELS FOR PSYCHOLOGY

The Problem of Context for Transactional Theories

A major stumbling block in the path of all theory construction, regarding natural systems, the transactional not excluded, is how to treat them as "closed" with respect to the manifold and variety of influences from sources within the universe that are not numbered among the known variables of the system. Such uncontrolled sources of variability on systems under study are usually ascribed to a *context of constraints* in which the system is immersed and by whose influences the system is badgered. In such cases, then, we say the system is "open" rather than closed. An *open* system has the nasty habit of behaving in ways that appear scientifically capricious from the standpoint of explanation solely in terms of the closed set of variables deemed essential to its characterization. On the other hand, any attempt to expand the characterization of the system so as to explain its behavior better, leads to a regress that only ends when the universe as a whole is made the closed field of inquiry.

Laplace treated the whole universe as a kind of cosmic machine whose behavior was in principle totally explicable in terms of mechanical laws. Einstein, in his early stages of theorizing, based his theory of relativity on the assumption that the universe was a closed, steady-state system whose local behaviors were to be explained by its global space-time structure (although he later repudiated this view under the onslaught of evidence that the universe was expanding). Scarcely thirty years ago, the philosopher of science Phillip Frank (1946), in a highly acclaimed book, defended the need for theory on the grand scale by observations of the following sort (quoted by Dewey & Bentley, 1949): "The path of a light ray, without including the environment of the light ray in the description, is an incomplete expression and has no operational meaning. . . . Speaking exactly, a particle by itself without the description of the whole experimental setup is not a physical reality [p. 113]." And, of course, the *whole* experimental setup includes the local expression of variables of cosmic extension (such as gravity); finally, "The law [of causality] in its whole generality cannot be stated exactly if the state variables by which the world is described are not mentioned specifically [p. 113]."

The penchant for grand-scale theorizing that treats local phenomena as inexplicable unless opened up to the source of uncontrolled variability in its wider-world context is not a trait of physicists alone; biologists, psychologists, and social scientists in general have not shied from such expansive theorizing. Under the influence of Darwin's remarkable achievements in the last century, evolutionary factors have been given an indispensable role in attempts to explain the behavior of all kinds of systems—living ones as well as social and political ones. There is general recognition that no evolutionary system, however terrestrially based it may be, can be seriously entertained in a cosmological vacuum; theoretical presuppositions about the history of the universe are prerequisite for understanding the birth and support of any such evolutionary system. This acceptance of the causal regress is common to so many diverse fields as now to have the status of a metatheoretical truism and, therefore, scarcely needs expanding upon. We mention it only to force recognition of what must seem a much belabored and rather obvious point: The poet Donne observed that no man is an island; neither is any given natural system on which we focus scientific inquiry, for it is afloat in a cosmic sea of constraint.

The triteness of this observation, however, vanishes as soon as one raises the possibility that such grand-scale theorizing, which admits to scientific orthodoxy the regressive causal nexus of events, may be not only troublesome but quite unnecessary as a theory-making convention. Perhaps there is a way to close a system of of inquiry short of including all. The mere presumption of such a possibility is evidence enough in the minds of many theorists to brand its author as naive and uninformed regarding the futility of arbitrarily closing systems at boundaries short of cosmic proportions. Indeed, an unkind (and we think unfair) critic of Dewey and Bentley's conception of transactional theory (and Peirce's seminal concept of Thirdness) might smirk and raise a knowing eyebrow at their failure to recognize that transactional analysis, no less than the interactional analysis they criticize, offers no real help in the matter of setting boundaries on inquiry into the bases for explaining the behavior of a system. The critic might point out that Dewey and Bentley correctly expose the limits on interactional principles of inquiry but chastise them for failing to recognize that the absence of all limits is just as damning a fault—a fault that renders transactional inquiry a methodologically naive and unmitigated failure. Both of the foregoing faults were duly noted by Tarski (1944) in his attempt to provide a semantic theory of truth. If we are permitted to identify methods of inquiry—such as self-actional, interactional, and transactional—with attempts to provide a language of semantic descriptors for phenomena, then Tarksi's double-barreled criticism surely seems to apply to arbitrarily closed, self-actional languages and prematurely closed interactional systems, on one hand, and to open transactional languages of scientific description on the other. Briefly, Tarski (1944) gave a proof for a very general form of the incompleteness and inconsistency theorem of formal (semantic) languages, of which Gödel's more famous theorems are a special case. Put simply, Tarksi showed that any nontrivial language of descriptors that is arbitrarily closed necessarily is inconsistent, whereas any language that is left open to elaboration so as to handle all context effects will necessarily be incomplete. Consequently, we may ask if transactional languages can avoid the charge of necessary incompleteness and, hence, will fail to account for all aspects of the behavior of systems due to contextual influences. To avoid incompleteness by arbitrary truncation of the context of constraint on the system would not be a possible ploy, either, because it leads to necessary inconsistencies among descriptors.

The question arises, then, as to how a phenomenon can be understood as a closed system independently of its world context without introducing self-actional components to take up the slack left by denial of the contribution of contextual factors. Similarly, a contrasting question arises as to how a system, open to the effects of interaction with its immediate context, can not avoid the regress to ever more remote but equally significant contextual effects.

The Problem of Perceptual Mechanisms

The narrow 19th-century concept of mechanism was an assembly of moving parts performing a function usually as a part of a larger machine that acted as a linkage. The interactional theorists of the 20th century attempted to apply this concept of mechanism to perception by viewing perception as a causal biological linkage between the physical world and the psychological experiences or judgments of an animal or human—hence, the notions of sensory channels or receptor systems as a biological interface by which stimulation or sensory information "flowed" freely or, perhaps, was processed into a different form. However, given the earlier arguments, it now seems wiser to replace this interactional account of perceptual mechanism with, at the very least, a transactional one.

Prior to the philosophy of mechanical contrivance born during the industrial revolution, there was a deeper, more abstract conception of mechanism that we might do well to reintroduce—namely, that of mechanism merely as the agency or means by which an effect is produced or a purpose accomplished. Under this view, a perceptual mechanism is one that produces a designated effect, whereas an action mechanism is one that accomplishes a designated purpose. Any system, natural or contrived, that is capable of producing the designated effect would be properly termed a "perceiver," whereas one that accomplished a designated purpose would be properly termed an "actor." It is our goal, for the reasons stated earlier and elsewhere (Shaw et al., 1981; Turvey & Shaw, 1979), to avoid a three-realm ontological view that reifies psychological predicates as primitive structural realms—say, as some kind of percept, image, idea, proposition, or other immanent existent. Rather, we pursue a two-realm theory that treats psychological predicates functionally—say, as a functionally specified relationship between some semantic aspect of the perceiver's world and some purposive aspect of the perceiver's ability as an actor to accomplish ends in that world.

More specifically, we would argue that perception is the mechanism that functions to inform the actor of the means the environment *affords* for realizing the actor's goals. Correspondingly, we would argue that action is the mechanism that functions to select the means by which the goals of the actor may be effected.

When the mechanism of action successfully accomplishes its goals, then the mechanism of perception completes its functional cycle by moving from information about means to information about ends; in this way, the effect sought by action merges with the effect produced by perception. In seeing that the coffee cup affords grasping, one acts to grasp it; in grasping the cup, one perceives it grasped. In this way, perception and action merge as congruent functional effects determined by "dual"—that is, complementary—mechanisms.

Thus, an isomorphism is achieved between those aspects of the world acted upon and those perceived, just as an isomorphism is achieved between the states of the animal as actor and its states as perceiver. Isomorphisms of the first type are *affordances,* as defined earlier, whereas isomorphisms of the second type, following our earlier usage (Shaw et al., 1981; Turvey & Shaw, 1979), are called *effectivities.* It is important to note that Type 1 isomorphisms (affordances) are reciprocal to Type 2 isomorphisms (effectivities). Such reciprocal isomorphisms are typically called "dual" isomorphisms, or simply *dualities,* and are to be distinguished from other types of isomorphisms, such as identities and equalities (see following).

Advisedly, we can now speak of the epistemic transactions animals engage in with their worlds as being reciprocal isomorphisms, or dualities, between designated affordances and effectivities rather than as interactions between physical stimulation and biological states, or between stimuli and responses. More generally, the environment of an animal as perceiver can be considered an *affordance structure* that is reciprocally isomorphic, or dual, to the *effectivity structure* of the animal as an actor upon that environment. And most generally of all, the higher-order relational structure consisting of the dual affordance and effectivity structures, as defined for a specific type of animal, is the ecological system, or *ecosystem*, for the designated type of actor-perceiver. In this way, an environment (i.e., an affordance structure) is functionally defined for an animal as perceiver, and an animal as actor (i.e., an effectivity structure) is functionally defined for the stipulated environment as an econiche for that animal.

It should be clear from the foregoing discussion that an environment is not simply a partition of the physical world, as characterized by physicists, any more than an agent is simply a partition of the world of biological functions, as characterized by biologists. Something more has been added to each concept. Physics provides the necessary support to the functionally defined properties (affordances) of the environment, just as biology provides the necessary support for the functionally defined capabilities (effectivities) of the animal.

In other words, the theoretic language of descriptors provided by physics and biology will necessarily be included in the arsenal of analytic concepts for psychology but will be insufficient to capture all the descriptions required to characterize its mechanisms. For instance, a frown on the face of a parent has perceptual meaning for a child that affords constraining or redirecting its activities—say, the retracting of the hand from the cookie jar. The significance of a facial expression to a perceiver transcends any analysis that might be given solely in terms of physical motions of facial parts, or in terms of the muscle synergisms whose actions in concert determine the epidermal stresses that define the various facial expressions.

With this brief discussion of the "ecological" requirements for perceptual mechanism, let us return to address several important issues. If a perceptual mechanism is one that produces a designated effect, what is the nature of this effect, and how is it produced? In addition to answering these questions, we must show how the mechanism for perception to be described can also be used to characterize action; that is, it must function reciprocally as an action mechanism.

Furthermore, the mechanism should also suggest the categories of descriptors, or semantic concepts, and rules for relating them, such that all the significant aspects of perceptual knowing can be accounted for; namely, the mechanism should exhibit in explicit fashion the transactional character of perception and action at multiple grains of analysis that are closed to the context-regress problem.

And, finally, although perception (and action) must be *at least* transactional in order to avoid reifying a third and quite unnecessary ontological realm—one that ultimately invokes self-actional concepts—it must be something more than merely transactional if it is to avoid a context-regress problem arising from rampant proliferation of higher and higher grains of analysis. Another way of posing this problem is to point out that if transaction is a Third, then there must be the concept of a Fourth by which contexts are logically bound to some finite number; no Fifths, Sixths, or Nths grains of analysis should be needed.

Knowing as a Duality of Constraint
Between Animal and Environment

What kind of relationship exists between an agent and its environment when we are willing to say that the agent knows its environment (e.g., perceives it or acts purposively toward it)? The foregoing argument suggests two postulates that an ecological style of inquiry might be founded upon: First, the epistemic act mandates a duality, or reciprocal isomorphism, between an environment as an affordance structure and an animal as an effectivity structure.[4] Our suspicion, as already voiced, is that this reciprocal isomorphism is best captured by a duality (see Turvey & Shaw, 1979; Turvey et al., 1978). Second, this duality is of a special sort; it is a reciprocal relationship of mutual constraint that must exist between an animal and its environment if the environment is to be a source of perceptual information for an animal and the animal is to be capable of acting adaptively with respect to its environment. This mutual "fit" of animal and environment requires that each be a context for constraining variations in the other. Let us call these two postulates of the ecological style of scientific inquiry, respectively, the Postulate of Duality and the Postulate of Reciprocal Contexts.

Our main goal in this section is to offer an intuitive characterization of the mathematical structure that satisfies in a rudimentary way these two postulates. (In the next section, we present a more formal account.) Such mathematical structures are referred to as "coalitions," and we offer them as possible candidates for modeling the relationships of animal–environment synergies, or what we have termed an (epistemic) *ecosystem*. More importantly, in keeping with the claim that something more than the Thirds recognized by the transactional style of scientific inquiry are required to avoid the context-regress problem, we offer coalitions as *Fourths* upon which to establish the ecological style of scientific inquiry as means of avoiding this problem.

Let us now proceed to attempt to clarify these two postulates before using them to provide a more formal characterization of the concept of coalition in the next section.

---

[4]The argument that the conceptions of an animal and its environment are *logical duals* has been made independently by Patten, whose theoretical motivations are different from but not unrelated to ours.

The Postulate of Duality

A duality is a type of isomorphism that can be distinguished from an isomorphism such as equality because it lacks the property of transitivity, and from an isomorphism such as identity because it lacks the property of reflexivity. In other words, a duality is an isomorphism that has only one of the three properties needed to characterize an equality—namely, the property of symmetry, where x R z = z R x (hence, the alternative name of reciprocal isomorphism). However, it is not enough merely to distinguish a duality from other isomorphisms; it must also be sharply distinguished from all the other relations, nonisomorphic ones as well. Table 11.1 summarizes those distinctions.

From inspection of the table, it is apparent that all the isomorphic relations are formally distinguished from the nonisomorphic ones, on one hand, and that all the relations of each type are distinguished from one another. Roughly speaking, a duality relation between two structures X and Z is specified by any symmetrical rule, operation, transformation, or "mapping", T, where T applies to map X onto Z and Z onto X: that is, where $T(X) \rightarrow Z$ and $T(Z) \rightarrow X$ such that for any relation r_1 in X, there exists some relation r_2 in Z such that $T : r_1 \rightarrow r_2$ and $T : r_2 \rightarrow r_1$; hence, $X R Z = Z R X$ under the transformation T.

Duality relations are very general and occur at various grains of abstraction throughout the diverse categories of mathematics and logic. In the next section of this paper, however, we show why the number of grains of abstraction may be naturally restricted to only four in number—a fact that can be used to avoid the

TABLE 11.1
Table of Relations

Type of Relation	Properties[a]		
	Reflexive	Symmetrical	Transitive
Resemblance[b]	+	+	0
Similarity[c]	−	−	+
Identity	+	−	−
Equality	+	+	+
Duality	0	+	−

[a] A + marks the properties possessed by the relation in all cases where the relation is nontrivial. An 0 signifies that the property may hold under special cases of the relation. And finally, a − signifies the absence of the property as part of the definition of the relation in all its nontrivial forms.

[b] Resemblance as defined here is a *tolerance* relationship and should not be confused with other meanings the word might have colloquially. Given a mapping ϕ between two sets M, L, ϕ: M $\rightarrow$ L and elements $x, y \in$ M, then a relation x R y is said to be a tolerance relation if and only if the images of x and y in L share properties that intersect—that is, x R y if $\phi(x) \cap \phi(y) \neq \emptyset$. If identity refers to the perfect interchangeability of x with y, then their resemblance refers to their partial interchangeability (e.g., machine parts tooled to be within certain tolerances are functionally interchangeable).

[c] The geometric relationship that defines an equivalence class of objects having the same shape but not necessarily the same size. For instance, large and small equilateral triangles necessarily have the same shape (are similar) but not congruent.

context-regress problem. Consequently, it will be helpful to survey briefly the role that duality has played in logic and mathematics so as to grasp the power of this extremely abstract concept better. A fundamental aspect of this concept to be illustrated is that dualities may exist not only among the objects and functions within a given category of mathematics but also between alternative axiom systems for a given category (e.g., between projective geometries based on lines versus those based on points). In other words, as a general principle, the concept of duality has import for metamathematics as well as for mathematics. Ultimately, we draw upon this fact to suggest by formal analogy that the concept of duality will have import for metatheory in psychology as well as for specific theories of psychological phenomena (e.g., perception).

A very famous duality in symbolic logic, known as deMorgan's Law, relates two theorems so that proof of one theorem automatically entails proof of the other. It is instructive to examine the nature of the relation between the two theorems:

Theorem 1: $(p \vee q)' \rightarrow (p' \& q') \rightarrow (p \vee q)'$
Theorem 2: $(p \& q)' \rightarrow (p' \vee q') \rightarrow (p \& q)'$,

where "v" signifies the disjunction *or*, "→" the conditional *if* _____ *then*, "&" signifies the conjunction *and*, and the prime "'" signifies the negation *not*. The importance of these two theorems is not of interest at this time; rather, it is their duality that is of interest to us. The nature of the duality that relates them is obvious on inspection of their related syntactical forms. This becomes most clear when the two theorems are verbalized: Theorem 1 asserts that "the negation of a disjunction yields the conjunction of negations," whereas "the conjunction of negations yields the negation of a disjunction." Theorem 2 is, if you will, the vice versa of Theorem 1: "The negation of a conjunction yields the disjunction of negations," whereas "the disjuction of negations yields the negation of a conjunction."

The duality that relates these two theorems is the fact that a very simple rule (a duality operation) exists by which one theorem can be translated into the other: If in Theorem 1 we replace the word (or symbol) for *disjunction* by that for *conjunction* throughout, then (with but trivial changes to agree with acceptable grammatical form in English) we obtain Theorem 2, and vice versa. Let us call this simple translation rule T; then T(Theorem 1) → Theorem 2, and T(Theorem 2) → Theorem 1. The relationship between Theorems 1 and 2, as defined by T, clearly satisfies the symmetry property required of dualities.

Consider another example. One of the most beautiful applications of the duality principle is in projective geometry. In projective geometry, as in Euclidean geometry, it is true that any two (nonidentical) coplanar points determine, or lie on, one line. But it is also true that any two intersecting lines determine, or lie on, one point. Again we see that a duality relation holds between these two theorems because it is possible to translate one into the other by merely interchanging the words *point* and *line*. Thus we can build up two distinct geometries—one that takes points as primitives and derives lines, and one that takes lines as primitives and derives points. In the former case, more complex geometric forms will be defined as loci of points, whereas in the latter case, they will be defined as envelopes of tangent lines. These two geometries are metamathematically equivalent in the sense that any theorem proven in one has a "dual" theorem provable in the other. Hence a great economy of thought is introduced into geometry by this fact: One need only prove the theorems of one of the two geometries, because those of its "dual" geometry can be got by a simple rule that commutes the appropriate terms.

To see more precisely how the principle of duality applies in geometry, let us consider a famous theorem from projective geometry. At age 16, the precocious French mathematician and philosopher Blaise Pascal proved a major theorem of projective geometry. Pascal asserted that if the opposite sides of any hexagon inscribed in a circle are prolonged, the three points at which the extended pairs of lines meet will lie on a straight line. This theorem can be construed both in the terms of a point-geometry and its dual, a line-geometry (Kline, 1953). The point-dual of the theorem reads:

If we take six points, A, B, C, D, E and F, on the point circle, then the lines which join A and B and E join in a point P; the lines which join B and C and E and F join in a point Q; the lines which join C and D and F and A join in a point R. The three points P, Q and R lie on one line l [p. 116].

The line-dual reads:

If we take six lines, a, b, c, d, e, and f, on the line circle, then the points which join a and b and d and e are joined by the line p; the points which join b and c and e and f are joined by the line q; the points which join c and d and f and a are joined by the line r. The three lines p, q and r lie on one point L [pp. 116–117].

The latter theorem is known as Brianchon's theorem because it was discovered by Charles Brianchon, who derived it by applying the principle of duality to Pascal's theorem. Indeed, it is possible to show by a single proof that every rephrasing of a theorem of projective geometry in accordance with the principle of duality must lead to a new theorem (Kline, 1953).

The remarkable thing, however, is that the application of the duality principle to logic and geometry is not an exception, but the rule in that it belies a deep-seated truth of mathematics. For instance, similar dualities can be shown to exist in Boolean algebra between theorems based on addition $+$ and multiplication $\times$; in set theory between theorems based on union $\cup$ and intersection $\cap$ or between disjoint union $\subset$ and Cartesian products $\times$; in geometry between points and lines; in vector theory between bases of different fields; in graph theory between vertices and arrows; in the theory of formal grammars between generative and categorical grammars; in symmetry group theory between enantiomorphic groups; in topology between open and closed sets; and most probably in all other branches of mathematics as well.

Before proceeding to apply the concept of duality to the problem at hand, let us step back from the specifics of the foregoing examples and abstract the form of the duality principle as a conceptual scheme. This can best be seen when expressed in terms of the mathematically neutral device of a *diagram*. A diagram is "neutral" in the sense that it is a metamathematical scheme of relations and functions over sets of variables that belongs to no particular category of mathematic structure (e.g., group, ring, geometry) but can be applied to describe structures that belong to any such category.

Following MacLane and Birkhoff (1967) a "diagram" is defined informally as a set "of vertices p, q, . . . together with arrows from one vertex to another, where each vertex p labeled by a set S_p and each arrow $p \rightarrow q$ labeled by a function f on S_p to S_q. A 'path' in a diagram is a succession of arrows $p \overset{f}{\rightarrow} q \overset{g}{\rightarrow} r \overset{h}{\rightarrow} t$ such that each path determines the corresponding composite function $h \circ g \circ f$ from S_p to S_t. Finally, a diagram is commutative when any two paths from any one vertex p to another vertex s in the diagram which yield by composition the same function $S_p \rightarrow S_s$ [p. 32]." The "dual" of a diagram is simply one obtained by reversing all arrows.

Therefore, a concept defined by means of a diagram necessarily has a dual concept defined in terms of the same diagram if a rule, called a "contravariant functor," exists by which the arrows may be legitimately reversed. (For instance, a pair of dual concepts to be defined and used widely in the next section is that of product $\times$ and disjoint union $\cup$, whose diagrams are $S \rightarrow S \times T \leftarrow T$ and $S \leftarrow S \cup T \rightarrow T$, respectively.)

In short, the concept of duality is so general, pervasive, and profound that we should not be surprised to find its outcroppings in scientific areas whose theoretic languages incorporate any of the foregoing mathematical tools or whose concepts can be formulated in terms of diagrams.

Thus the gist of the preceding observations for science is that the principle of duality may prove as regulatory in guiding theory construction about natural phenomena as it has in guiding theory about mathematical ones. Indeed, if it should deserve the status of a metatheoretical principle in science, then a theory designed to characterize formally some natural phenomenon X would at the same time yield, free of charge, a theory mutatis mutandis for some dual phenomenon Z (i.e., after the appropriate changes are made in the diagrams for the first theory). This idea is not so speculative nor farfetched as might first be thought, for the search for dualities in physics has revealed a near-perfect symmetry between the so-called classical symmetries of Newtonian theory and the dynamic symmetries of quantum mechanics (Wigner, 1970). Likewise, in chemistry and crystallography, the principle of duality comes into play in the study of steroids and other enantiomorphic structures—the so-called "colored" symmetries (Shubnikov & Koptsik, 1974). Less heralded is the role the principle has played in computer science by constraining the design of programs and switching circuits through the theorems of duals implicit in formal grammars, automata theory, and Boolean algebra.

In spite of the ubiquitous nature of the duality concept in many branches of science, is there any prima facie evidence of it being at work in psychology, especially in perceptual psychology? We believe so and have argued to this effect elsewhere (Shaw & McIntyre, 1974; Shaw et al., 1981; Turvey, 1977; Turvey & Shaw, 1979; Turvey et al., 1978). Briefly, before returning to the use of the duality concept to help characterize perceptual mechanism, we would like to reiterate some of those arguments here.

Many examples of dual structures exist in perceptual psychology. For instance, the global invariants of the optical flow field determined by the locomotion of an observer toward a given object are *dual* with the local invariants of the optical flow field determined if the object should move toward the static observer. It can be shown in general that the *open* set of globally invariant vectors associated with observer movement is *dual* to the *closed* set of locally invariant vectors associated with the inverse motion of objects (e.g., when they are inverse rectilinear motions).

The duality relation between these two sets of velocity vectors as defined by some transformation T provides dual forms of perceptual information: Any invariant style of change in vectors in a local region of the perceiver's field of vision specifies that it is the object that is moving in such and such a manner, whereas, reciprocally, any invariant style of change in the velocity vectors defined globally over the perceiver's whole field of vision specifies that it is the perceiver moving in such and such a manner relative to the object fixated rather than the other way around. Similarly, the rotation of an object for a static observer determines perceptual information that is dual to the perceptual information determined by the observer who "orbits" around the fixed object. These examples illustrate how the principle of duality might apply in the area of "event" perception (Johansson, von Hofsten, & Jansson, 1979; Shaw & McIntyre, 1974).

In particular, the former example suggests that a duality relation might exist between information that specifies properties of the world (e.g., object motion) and information that specifies properties of animals as actors in the world (e.g., its locomotions). The information that specifies properties of the world corresponds to *perceptual* information, whereas its dual—information that specifies properties of the active self—corresponds to *action* information.

Most generally, as a regulatory metatheoretical principle, the principle of duality offers the hope that the conceptual economy alluded to earlier might be introduced into psychology by adopting the ecological style of scientific inquiry: Theorems that might be proven about the perception of the environment by an animal could be reformulated as dual theorems that assert truths about the actions the animal might perform on the environment and vice versa. Thus any degree of success that might be achieved in characterizing perceptual processes would ipso facto apply to derive true dual characterizations of action processes and vice versa at some appropriate level of abstraction.

The Postulate of Reciprocal Contexts

Assuming that a case has now been established for the possible validity and theoretic usefulness of the Postulate of Duality, we would like to argue in favor of the validity and usefulness of the other postulate of the ecological approach identified earlier—the Postulate of Reciprocal Contexts (of constraint). The main point to be made is the following: Not only do we wish to exploit the existence of a formal duality relation holding between animals and their environments but, more importantly, to emphasize that this dependency is a very special sort of duality (one that we have argued elsewhere [Turvey et al., 1978] is of great practical significance for theories of control and coordination). The additional claim that goes beyond that assented to in the first postulate is that perception and action are not only duals in the formal descriptive sense already discussed; rather, each process provides a necessary source of constraint on the other in that they act as dual contexts of mutual constraint. Where the first postulate asserts that a useful constraint on the descriptors used for characterizing animals as actors and perceivers is the descriptors selected for the environment that is perceived and acted upon and vice versa, the second postulate posits acausal constraints between an animal and its environment. To see what this means, consider a duality in the context of a linear functional (i.e., a linear transformation whose codomain is the field of scalars with which we are concerned). The duality to be exposed is that of buying groceries from the perspective of the seller and from the perspective of the buyer.

The customer's shopping list is constructed so as to guarantee a desired balance of carbohydrates, proteins, vitamins, and so forth. Let the shopping list be (a, b, c, . . .), and let the price list be [A, B, C, . . .], so that the cost of the groceries is given by $Aa + Bb + Cc$. . . . The customer sees the problem as that of choosing a shopping list that meets his or her purposes but that, at the same time, is minimal in cost. In short, with reference to dietary needs, the customer seeks a minimal value of $Aa + Bb + Cc$. . . . We can identify the customer's vector space as being that in which price lists are functionals and shopping lists are vectors. In contrast, the grocer's vector space identifies the shopping lists as functionals and the price lists as vectors, for the grocer is interested in maximizing profits. So his or her concern is with how the cost of a given shopping list depends on the price list. There is, therefore, a symmetrical relation between the customer's vector space and the grocer's vector space, and the two spaces are referred to as *dual spaces*.

Tentatively, we might regard the relationship between an animal that acts in an environment and an environment that is perceived as duals in formal analogy to the grocer's vector space and the customer's vector space: The actions of the grocer (in buying wholesale goods) are practically constrained by the perception of the changing state of the shelves of the store environment. Dually speaking, the actions of the customer (in buying retail goods) are practically constrained by the perceived availability of the items to be acted upon (i.e., bought) in the context of the store environment. The environment that is perceived by the customer (i.e., stock on the shelves) is grocer-referential and, therfore, constrained by the grocer's acts, whereas the environment that is perceived by the grocer (i.e., shelves to be restocked) is customer-referential and similarly constrained by the customer's acts. By generalization, this reciprocity of the mutually constraining contexts of actions and perceptions is seen to hold in other synergistic relations than the grocer–customer synergy.

The foregoing bilinear functional between dual vector spaces provides one way to model the duality of information made available to an animal about its environment as an affordance structure and to an animal about itself as an effectivity structure. At all events, using the formal concept of duality as expressed in the foregoing examples, it is now possible to make more precise this relationship between affordances specified by perception and the effectivities that specify the actions by which the agent realizes the goal-directed relations potentiated by its environment.

We say a cup X *affords* grasping Y (or, alternatively, has the property of *graspability*) for an agent Z (e.g., a baby) on the occasion O (say, on the occasion that Z is thirsty or playful) if and only if there exists a duality relation between X and Z on that occasion (i.e., the baby Z has matured normally to have both the strength and coordinative capabilities to grasp the cup X *and* that the cup is not too large, heavy, or ill shaped to be grasped by Z). In other words, somewhat tautologously, we say X affords Y for Z if and only if there exists a duality, $X \Diamond Z$ (to be read as "X and Z are compatible"), or reciprocal isomorphism between the properties of X and those of Z. We can represent this formally as the affordance schema (see Shaw et al., in press) whose argument has four variables: $(X,Z,O|X \Diamond Z) = Y$ (to be read as "X, Z, and O, given the compatibility of X and Z, equal Y").

Now if perceptually specified affordances are truly dual concepts of the effectivities for the actions potentiated by the affordances, then there should exist some duality operation T, a metatheoretic principle, by which the semantic descriptor for an affordance Y (as already depicted) might be translated into the semantic descriptor for some corresponding effectivity Y'. In other words, T (Y) → Y' and T (Y') → Y should be possible just as in the analogous case of deMorgan's Law in logic and the Pascal–Brianchon theorems in projective geometry. Indeed, we find this is so.

Let T be the following rule: $(X,Z)' \rightarrow (Z,X)$ and $(Z,X)' \rightarrow (X,Z)$. We apply the first part of this rule to our semantic descriptor for affordances; namely, $T(Y) = Y' = (X,Z,O|X \Diamond Z) = (Z,X,O|Z \Diamond X)$. By inspection, we see then that the schema that defines an affordance, $(X,Z,O|X \Diamond Z)$, is dual with the schema $(Z,X,O|Z \Diamond X)$ under application of the rule already stipulated. This resulting schema should correspond to an effectivity.

Again, we see most clearly the essence of the duality relation when stated in words: "An object X affords grasping Y by an animal Z if and only if the structure of X is isomorphic with the structure of Z"; and, dually, "An animal Z can effect grasping Y' if and only if the structure of Z is isomorphic with the structure of X."

The general form of this duality of perception and action, vis à vis affordances and effectivities, is by no means trivial; for it provides the basis for our original assumption that perception and action must be closely linked. Furthermore, it also provides a concrete way of interpreting the isomorphism between an animal and its environment that is neither an identity nor an equality.

Our task now is to use this duality relation as the fundamental building block from which to characterize in an abstract fashion the style of inquiry that we believe is needed to accommodate the mechanism of perception and its relation to action.

Coalitions: Treating Perceptual Mechanism as a Fourth

Recall that a transaction, as expressed in the writings of the American pragmatists, is a relational structure defined over three categories of entities—the so-called Firsts, Seconds, and Thirds. And recall further that once a transactional structure is adopted as the minimal structure for accommodating a natural phenomenon, there arises the unwelcome problem of a regress to further contexts. We want to show in the present section and those that immediately follow that there is a way of conceptualizing a relational structure qua style of inquiry that avoids the regress to further contexts. What follows should be read as a constructive definition—an "existence" proof, as it were—of the desired relational structure.

A coalition will be defined as a structure relating four categories of mathematical entities: B—an *underlying set of bases* consisting of all the disjoint subsets of distinguished variables over which relations might be defined; R—a set of *relations* defined in terms of the pairings of the distinguished disjoint subsets in B; O—a set of *orders* defined in terms of the pairings of distinguished disjoint relations; and finally, V—a set of *values* defined in terms of pairs of distinguished disjoint orders of relations.

Each descriptor category just identified designates a "grain" of analysis.[5] By a *grain of analysis*—g (α)—we mean to designate one of the descriptor categories in E = <B;R;O;V> such that $\alpha \rightarrow$ {B,R,O,V}. Moreover, we will call g(V) the "value-grain"; g(O), the "order-grain"; g(R), the "relation-grain"; and g(B), the "basis-grain." A requirement of the relational structure we seek is that each grain g(α) is ordered with respect to the others, so that g(B) > g(R) > g(O) > g(V) where the basis-grain is coarser than the relation-grain; the relation-grain coarser than the order-grain; and the order-grain coarser than the value-grain. (Read "finer-than" in reverse order.)

Necessarily, in order to avoid the regress problem in either direction, coarser grains than g(B) and finer grains than g(V) must be ruled out. In short, the lattice of grains must be bounded on either end. This requires that beyond g(B), there is only the universal set U—namely, U $\supseteq$ B; and below g(V), there is only the null set $\emptyset$—namely, V $\supseteq$ $\emptyset$; hence U > g(B) > g(R) > g(O) > g(V) > $\emptyset$.

A further requirement of the relational structure we seek is that each grain be exhaustively (although not exclusively) characterized as the disjoint union of dual subsets so as to close the whole lattice of grains under duality operations yielding a *closed duality structure*. This means that it must be the case that B = X $\cup$ Z, such that T(X) = Z and T(Z) = X; R = $\phi \cup \psi$, such that T(ϕ) = ψ and T(ψ) = ϕ; O = A $\cup$ E such that T(A) = E and T(E) = A; and V = S $\cup$ N such that T(S) = N and T(N) = S. To anticipate, a coalition will be a relational structure E = <B:X,Z; R: ϕ, ψ; O: A,E; V:S,N> that is closed under the duality operation T. And assuming that this relational structure can be captured in table form, we might try to anticipate how many entries are required to characterize even the simplest coalition. Including E, U, and $\emptyset$, there will be 15 distinct subsets of E—namely, U,E,B,R,O,V,X,Z,ϕ,ψ,A,E,S,N,$\emptyset$. The number of dualities, however, will be considerably greater being the Cartesian product of E × E—namely, (B × R × O × V) = (2 × 2^2 × 2^3 × 2^4) = 2 × 4 × 8 × 16 = 1024. Thus, it will require a 64 × 64 table with 1024 cells to describe any coalition, from the simplest with only two variables to the most complex having many variables. (In the latter case, however, the cells will have multiple entries.)

---

[5]The terms *scale, level,* and *grain* have appeared at various places in the present chapter. We can now consider them together. Scientific models of natural phenomena can be characterized according to scale, level, and grain. The scale of a model refers to the ordinal position it occupies along some extensive dimension of magnitude—for example, atomic, molecular, cellular, organismic, ecosystemic, terrestrial, and so on. The level (of abstraction) of a model refers to its degree of specificity or generality regarding semantic referent—that is, the degree to which it signifies the properties of the phenomenon modeled. The grain of a model at a given scale and a given level refers to its ordinal position with respect to contexts of constraint—for example, value, order, relations, bases. Scales are typically conceived of linearly; levels are typically conceived of hierarchically; grains, by the arguments presented here, are conceived of coalitionally.

With the foregoing stipulations in mind, let us proceed to construct a simple coalition: Let the universal set U consist of all the pairs of bases U = { (b_1, b_1'), (b_2, b_2'), . . . } that define the "polar" concepts of all dimensions of significant variation in nature where each (b_i, b_i') pair defines a unique dimension where each b_i is a variable and b_i' its dual covariate variable. For instance, a dimension of thermal variation might be some b_i; then b_i' would be the covariate dimension of radiant variation as represented in a light bulb; the hotter the filament (thermal increase), the more intense the illumination (radiant increase), and vice versa. The basis of our coalition, therefore, can be defined as B = {X,Z} where $(b_1, b_2, . . . b_k) = X$ and $(b_1', b_2', . . . b_k') = Z$. Hence, B = X ∪ Z such that for all $b_i \in X$ and $b_i' \in Z$, $T(b_i) \rightarrow b_i'$ and $T(b_i') \rightarrow b_i$. Consequently, X and Z will be called the *dual* bases of E (symbolized as X ◇ Z) and B, the underlying set of dimensions of E. Furthermore, we define this grain of analysis to be g(B) = X × Z where X and Z are duals. Therefore, g(B) is *closed* under the duality operation T; that is, g(B) is closed because if some $b_i \in X$ exists, then so does $b_i' \in Z$.

Next we proceed to define the grain of analysis of relations g(R) so as to be finer in structure than g(B). By "finer" in structure, we mean only that g(R) be defined over g(B), making g(B) more primitive and having fewer coarser-grain elements than g(R). We do this by defining the set of relations R over B in the usual way by using the Cartesian product: R = B × B = {X,Z} × {X,Z}. The product produces the set of all possible ordered pairs: R = { <X,X>, <X,Z>, <Z,X>, <Z,Z>} where <X,Z> ≠ <Z,X>.

For convenience, we designate the disjoint subsets of R to be ϕ and ψ where ϕ = {<X,X>, <X,Z>} and ψ = {<Z,Z>,<Z,X>}. Notice that R − ϕ = ψ and R − ψ = ϕ, which implies that ψ and ϕ are duals under complementation; namely, that $\phi' = \psi$ and $\psi' = \phi$ satisfy the dual operation $T(\phi) \rightarrow \psi$ and $T(\psi) \rightarrow \phi$, respectively. We define this new grain of analysis over relations, g(R) = ϕ × ψ. Because ϕ and ψ are duals, then g(R) must be closed under the duality operation. Moreover, g(R) must be finer grained than g(B); that is, g(B) > g(R) because ϕ and ψ are disjoint subsets in g(B).

The next finer grain of analysis is defined over the orders of relations O where O = R × R = {<X,X>, <X,Z>, <Z,X>, <Z,Z>} × {<X,X>, <X,Z>, <Z,X>, <Z,Z>} = {<<X,X>, <X,X>>, <<X,X>, <X,Z>>,. . . , <<Z,Z>, <Z,Z>>} where <<X,X>, <X,Z>> ≠ <<X,Z>, <X,X>>; <<X,X>, <Z,X>> ≠ <<Z,X>, <X,X>>,. . . , etc. For convenience, we designate the disjoint subsets of relations whose orders are defined by the relation schema <<X, >,< , >> as A, and those whose orders are defined by the relation schema <<Z, >,< , >> as E (e.g., compare <<X,X>, <X,Z>> and <<Z,X>,<X,X>>, respectively). Therefore A = {<<X,X>, <X,X>>, . . . , <<X,Z>, <Z,Z>>}, whereas E = {<<Z,X>, <X,X>>,. . . , <<Z,Z>, <Z,Z>>}, and O = {A,E} where O − E = A and O − A = E. Consequently, as before, this implies that A and E are not only disjoint subsets but are also complementary, so that $E' = A$ and $A' = E$. This also satisfies the requirements of a duality, operation T, such that $T(A) \rightarrow E$ and $T(E) \rightarrow A$; hence, the duality relation $E \Diamond A$ holds. Moreover, the order-grain is defined as $g(0) = A \Diamond E$. The construction runs as before: Given $R = B \times B$ and $O = R \times R$, $g(O)$ is finer grained than $g(R)$, so that $g(B) > g(R) > g(O)$ is now the case, along with the fact that $g(B)$, $g(R)$, and $g(O)$ are all closed under the duality operation of set complementation. It only remains to establish the finest grain of analysis as the value-grain $g(V)$.

The value-grain $g(V)$ is defined over V where V is the Cartesian product of $g(O)$ and a two-valued set $\{+,-\}$; that is, $V = A \times E \times \{+,-\} = 32 \times 32 = 1024$ items to be cross-compared so as to ascertain the dualities that hold. As already stated, this yields 1024 possible comparisons in the simplest coalition. A *value* is to be thought of as a designation of a relation in a sequence to be *selected* or *ignored*. In other words, within a given sequence of ordered relations, some of the relations may be "active," whereas others are "quiescent" in the use of the sequence to define the actual as opposed to the potential activities performed by the specified mechanism, or subsystem. Clearly, then, V is a set of relation sequences that are partitioned into two mutually exclusive subsets by the selection criterion: Those sequences in O that receive a positive selection value (+) versus those identical sequences that receive a negative selection value (−). For convenience, let $S = O \times \{+\}$ and $N = O \times \{-\}$ (standing for *selections* and *non*selections, respectively). This means, of course, that $N \cup S = V$ and a complementary relation again holds: $V - S = N$ and $V - N = S$, so that as $S' = N$ and $N' = S$, or $T(S) \rightarrow N$ and $T(N) \rightarrow S$, then the duality relation $N \Diamond S$ obtains. Thus $g(V) = N \times S$ and $g(V)$ is a grain closed under a duality operation T. Furthermore, because $V = O \times \{+,-\}$, it follows that $V \subset O$ and $g(O)$ must be more coarse grained than $g(V)$.

Thus, we have constructed a relational structure that meets two of the stipulations identified earlier; First, from the basis-grain $g(B)$, through the relation-grain $g(R)$, and from the order-grain, $g(O)$ through the value-grain $g(V)$, there is an increasing fineness of analysis such that $g(B) > g(R) > g(O) > g(V)$ holds. Second, each grain of analysis is a closed Cartesian product of duality relations because each set over which the grain is defined consists of dual subsets (i.e., is the disjoint union of complementary subsets).

To summarize: In descending order of coarseness of grain, or context of constraint, we have the inclusion relation among structures closed under duality operations.

$$g(B) = X \Diamond Z$$
$$g(R) = \phi \Diamond \psi$$
$$g(O) = A \Diamond E$$
$$g(V) = N \Diamond S$$

Let us now see whether the relational structure we have constructed meets the remaining stipulation identified earlier—namely, that the four grains of analysis are exclusive in the sense that the lattice of grains is bounded on either end.

Recall that the universe of covariate dimensions U, postulated as the underlying set for a coalition, contains all dimensions over which relations in E might be defined—that is, $U \supseteq B$. This means that the basis-grain g(B) is the *least upper bound* for the other grains; but there can be no coarser grain than this. Because U contains only dual partitions, one can augment any given basis-grain, but it will necessarily remain a closed Cartesian product of dual bases; namely, B = $(b_1,b_1') \times (b_2,b_2') \times \ldots = X \times Z$ where $X = (b_1,b_2,\ldots)$ and Z = $(b_1,'b_2',\ldots)$. Hence the set U is *open* to the number of pairs of dual subsets (i.e., can be an infinite list of pairs) while still being closed under duality because no member of a pair, $b_i \in X$, occurs without its dual, $b_i' \in Z$.

Similarly, the finest grain possible is the value-grain g(V). As V constitutes all the members of the set of relations that can be defined over B by Cartesian products, then g(V) is the greatest lower bound of the lattice of grains. Recall that each grain finer than g(B) was defined as the product of disjoint subsets defined at the grain immediately superior to it in coarseness. Hence g(B) $\cap$ g(R) $\cap$ g(O) $\cap$ g(V) = $\emptyset$. By adding new variables to the sets in B, we can increase the number of relations on each of the dual subsets of R, likewise increasing the number of dual orders in O, which increases the size of the dual subset in V. But none of these increments can add another finer grain to E, for there are no new subsets of V produced by such additions that may be joined by a product relation. Any attempt to fabricate arbitrary partitions under V, aside from those dual partitions specified by $\{+,-\}$, will fail to be closed under a duality operation. Hence it follows that the ordering of set products U > g(B) > g(R) > g(O) > g(V) > $\emptyset$ holds as claimed.

To summarize: A *coalition* is a superordinate system (relation structure) consisting of eight pairs of subsystems (with 1024 states) nested at four exclusive "grains" of analysis (bases, relations, orders, values) and *closed* at each grain under a (duality) operation.

It is important to note clearly what the foregoing constructive definition, or "existence" proof, does and does not do: What it does is provide an in principle example of a mathematical structure in which there is, by definition, no place for self-actional explanation; a mathematical structure in which the variety of forms, interactions, and transactions it might assume are duly stipulated; and finally, a mathematical structure that consists of a nesting of grains of reciprocal contexts closed under duality operations and that is thereby formally impervious to the context-regress problem.

On the other hand, this schematic definition of a coalition does not provide a complete specification of all the variables required to describe an actualized (i.e., natural) coalition. Most emphatically, it is not intended to be a dynamic model of natural systems, for these must include, in addition to the structural variables already stipulated, both time-dependent and energy-dependent processes. Rather, the preceding definition provides a formal description for how many grains of analysis are minimally required and maximally allowed over which variables must be selected (bases), related, ordered, and evaluated if the system under analysis is to qualify as a coalition. Thus there are two modeling senses in which the coalitional schema already described might be used—as an a priori formal "recipe" for guiding and evaluating the construction of artifactual coalitions such as machines, factories, or governments; or as a post hoc "blueprint" for describing existing natural coalitions such as evolving molecular systems, social groups, or ecosystems.

The Ecosystem as a Coalition

Let the coalition $E = <B;R;O;V>$ be an ecosystem where $B = \{X,Z\}$ is the set of dual bases for the ecosystem. The set X will be associated with all the environment-based variables (e.g., objects, events, media, energy), whereas the set Z will be associated with all the animal-based variables (e.g., CNS, events, muscle potentials, body size).

$R = \{\phi, \psi\}$ is defined to be the set of all possible *ecological* relations over B, where ϕ is the set of relations defining the environment as both perceived and acted upon, and ψ is the set of relations defining the animal as both perceiver and actor. Hence the environment corresponds to the set $\phi = \{<X,X>, <X,Z>\}$, whereas the animal corresponds to the set $\psi = \{<Z,X>, <Z,Z>\}$. But notice that under this conception, the environment is not merely *physical*, nor the animal merely *biological* (as these terms are conventionally used), for this would entail that each be defined over reflexive relations only; that is, to be purely physical, the environment concept would include only those relations $<X,X>$ based on X; and to be purely biological, the animal concept would include only those relations $<Z,Z>$ based on Z. On the contrary, at this grain of analysis, $g(R)$, the environment ϕ and the animal ψ include *ecological* relations as well—namely, $<X,Z>$ and $<Z,X>$ respectively. This means that $g(R)$ is an *ecological* grain where the environment concept is defined in reference to some associated animal concept, and conversely, the animal concept is defined in reference to some associated environment concept. Hence ϕ and ψ constitute dual components of a single ecosystem.

The set of ordered relations $0 = \{A,E\}$ is to be semantically interpreted as the descriptors for the *affordance structure* of the environment, $A = \{<<X,X>, <X,X>>, \ldots, <<X,Z>, <Z,Z>>\}$, and the descriptors for the *effectivity structure* of the animal, $E = \{<<Z,X>, <X,X>>, \ldots, <<Z,Z>, <Z,Z>>\}$. In other words, an affordance structure description of an environment consists of all those and only those properties of ϕ that can be related to properties of ψ (where by properties of ϕ or ψ, we mean a relation over variables in ϕ to variables in ψ, and vice versa), whereas an effectivity structure consists of all those and only those properties of ψ that can be related to properties of ϕ.

Earlier, we illustrated how an affordance structure might be considered a dual concept of an effectivity structure and proved that the schema for one could be simply translated into the schema for the other—namely, that $A' = (X,Z,O|X \Diamond Z) \Diamond (Z,X,O|X \Diamond Z) = E$.[6] The general proof for translations $T(A) \rightarrow E$ and $T(E) \rightarrow A$ consists in showing that for each ordered pair of relations in A, there exists a corresponding ordered pair in E under some duality specification rule T, and vice versa. We now show this to be the case: Let T be the rule whose defining schema is $T = <<a,b>, <c,d>>' = <<c,d>', <a,b>'> = <<c',d'>, <a',b'>>$ where if a, b, c, d take values in X or Z, then a',b',c',d' take values in X' or Z' where X' = Z and Z' = X. For instance, $<<X,Z>, <Z,Z>>' \rightarrow <<Z,Z>', <X,Z>'> \rightarrow <<Z',Z'>, <X',Z'>> \rightarrow <<X,X>, <Z,X>>$. Hence $A \Diamond E$. Table 11.2 gives all of the dualities of the order-grain of analysis g(O). This table requires considerable discussion to be fully appreciated. Consequently, only a few of the dualities at this grain of analysis are discussed at this time. A most important aspect of the order-grain are the other duals that relate affordances to effectivities (I, Table 11.2). By a *perception* we mean the specification of the effectivity-dual of an affordance (i.e., $T(A) \rightarrow E$); by an *action* we mean the specification of the affordance-dual of an effectivity (i.e., $T(E) \rightarrow A$). (For instance, the perception that the cup *affords* grasping by the hand *versus* the hand *effects* grasping the cup.) In this sense, perceiving and acting can be said to be dual such that theoretical truths about one necessarily imply corresponding theoretical truths about the other. If this is so, then considerable conceptual economy and explanatory power can be introduced into psychology by the stubborn pursuit of the coalitional (ecological) style of scientific inquiry.

A second important aspect is the order-reflexive duals that relate affordances to affordances and effectivities to effectivities (II, Table 11.2). The $A \Diamond A$ duals specify complementary affordance properties of objects, such as the fact that a knife can be sharpened or dulled by stoking its blade with a grinding stone; a brick picked up or dropped; a glass filled or emptied. By contrast, the $E \Diamond E$ duals specify complementary effectivity capabilities of an animal, such as the fact that a hand can be closed to grasp object or opened to release it; in walking, a leg may be involved at one moment in the support phase and at the next in the transport phase. The self-duals (III, Table 11.2) are those affordances or effectivities that specify themselves as duals. This is the case whenever an event or an act cycles through repetitions, as when a ball bounces or the hands are clapped. One might speculate that self-duals may prove important to understanding persistent patterns of activity often attributed to memorial processes.

---

[6]In the dual schemata for affordances (X,Z,O | X $\Diamond$ Z) and effectivities (Z,X,O | X $\Diamond$ Z) defined at the order-grain, the context of constraint or mutual compatibility condition |X $\Diamond$ Z receives its theoretic motivation and explication from the fact that both the basis-grain and relation grain are realized and elaborated at the order-grain.

TABLE 11.2
The Dualities at the Order-Grain Where $0 = \{A,E\}$

I. OTHER-DUALS: AFFORDANCES ⟷ EFFECTIVITIES

A	E	graph
≪X,X>, <X,X≫ ◊ ≪Z,Z>, <Z,Z≫		
≪X,X>, <X,Z≫ ◊ ≪Z,X>, <Z,Z≫		
≪X,Z>, <X,X≫ ◊ ≪Z,Z>, <Z,X≫		
≪X,Z>, <X,Z≫ ◊ ≪Z,X>, <Z,X≫		

II. ORDER-REFLEXIVE DUALS: AFFORDANCES ⟷ AFFORDANCES
EFFECTIVITIES ⟷ EFFECTIVITIES

a)   A   A

≪X,X>, <Z,X≫ ◊ ≪X,Z>, <Z,Z≫

b)   E   E

≪Z,Z>, <X,Z≫ ◊ ≪Z,X>, <X,X≫

III. SELF-DUALS

a)   A   A

≪X,X>, <Z,Z≫ ◊ ≪X,X>, <Z,Z≫
≪X,Z>, <Z,X≫ ◊ ≪X,Z>, <Z,X≫

b)   E   E

≪Z,Z>, <X,X≫ ◊ ≪Z,Z>, <X,X≫
≪Z,X>, <X,Z≫ ◊ ≪Z,X>, <X,Z≫

The set of values $V = \{N,S\}$ specifies which affordances among all those composing the affordance structure of a given environment are noticed, S, or ignored, N, on a given occasion or, alternately, which effectivities in the effectivity structure of an animal are active, S, or quiescent, N, on a given occasion. The role of the *occasion* variable defined at the value-grain of analysis g(V) can be seen in the dual schemata for defining affordances and effectivities discussed earlier—namely, $A = (X,Z,O|X \Diamond Z) \longleftrightarrow (Z,R,O|X \Diamond Z) = E$.

It is interesting to note that the foregoing definitions simultaneously invoke every grain of analysis: X,Z are dual bases at g(B); $X \Diamond Z$ implicates both ϕ and ψ, which are dual subsets of relations at g(R); (X,Z . . .) versus (Z,X . . .) are dual orders of relation at g(O); and the occasion variable O implicates the value-grain g(V).

From the specific evaluation of g(R) in the context of g(B), g(O) in the context of g(R), and g(V) in the context of g(O), a specific act of perceiving, with a co-implicated effectivity for acting, is not merely potentiated but is actualized. The interdependence of the various grains of analysis is complete: Without bases at g(B) over which relations might be defined, then no g(R); without relations to be ordered, then no g(O); and without different orders of relations to be evaluated, then no g(V). In this way, it is fair to think of a coalition as a structure that carries with it, as an integral part of its conception, all the contexts of constraint on it that can be meaningfully defined.[7] Each coarser grain provides a "ball park" of constraint for the next finer grain, whereas each finer grain provides the evaluation of variables at the next coarser grain. Thus, no regress is possible in either direction.

The Architectural Capability of Bees

For purposes of illustration, let us consider the beehive within its context of constraints—the honeybee ecosystem. The preservation of the life cycle of a colony of some forty to eighty thousand bees requires exact coordination among the queen, drones, and workers in carrying out their multifarious, intricate activities: The drones fertilize the queen for life, furnishing her with several million sperm cells; the queen lays hundreds of thousands of eggs, fertilizing many of them so as to produce the proper proportion of female workers to male drones; the workers secrete wax, build combs, gather resin (propolis) with which they patch defects in the comb, defend the hive, mummify small intruders with propolis, gather pollen and nectar, produce honey, feed and care for the brood (thirteen hundred meals a day!), clean evacuated cells to receive new larvae, keep the hive warm by fanning their wings, scout for sources of food or new sites to swarm to, dance to inform the other bees of these locations, and then swarm to a new site, where the cycle of life-sustaining work begins all over again.

A complete coalitional account of a honeybee ecosystem should include all such hive activities; however, for our present purposes, it suffices to consider only the architectural behavior of the workers in building combs. It is our intention to show that even such a limited ecosystem activity as comb construction cannot be scientifically explicated at less than all four grains of analysis over which a coalition is defined.

---

[7]This is essentially the definition of coalition that we have expressed previously (Turvey & Shaw, 1979; Turvey et al., 1978).

Details of a Comb's Design. A comb in a domesticated hive (of the Dadant design) consists of two vertical, back-to-back, parallel sheets of cells, or tessellations, the shapes of each cell being very nearly perfect hexagonal tubes, or prisms, ranging in diameter from 5.2 millimeters for a worker cell to 6.2 millimeters for a drone cell. These tubular hexagonal cells are packed in each sheet in a highly efficient manner, with cells of one row falling neatly between the cells of the rows above and below it—much the same way that hexagonal tiles may be packed to cover a bathroom floor. Furthermore, there is a savings in the wax used in the construction of the comb, because each flat wall of a hexagonal cell is shared by the adjoining cell and has a thickness of around 0.073 millimeter, with a tolerance of no more than 0.002 millimeter in most cases. Moreover, the hexagonal tubes of each opposing sheet are combined inwardly at approximately a 13-degree angle measured downward from the vertical—a slope sufficient to keep the viscous honey liquid from running out until the cell can be capped. An additional savings in wax accrues from the fact that the ends of the cellular tubes in the opposing parallel sheets not only abut but also share adjoining sides: Each end-wall of an opposing cell forms a tetrahedral pyramid consisting of three rhombic plates, each plate forming a common end-wall with a trio of cells in the opposing layer (von Frisch, 1974). Such a tight packing of hexagonal cells has been shown to provide a greater storage capacity than the packing of cells of any other shape.

It has been calculated that it takes approximately 37,000 nectar-gathering flights for a colony to produce just 1 pound of honey (Teale, 1940). However, it takes 5 pounds of honey as nourishment for the bees to secrete the 450,000 wax scales required to produce 1 pound of wax. But from just this 1 pound of wax, the bees can fashion a comb with 35,000 cells that will hold 22 pounds of honey. This means that the top cells of a fully loaded comb must support 1320 times their own weight (Ribbands, 1953).

How Is This Design Achieved? There are those, over the years, who have ascribed the design to the intrinsic "intelligence" of the bee. D'Arcy Thompson (1917/1942) tells us how the fourth-century mathematician Pappus of Alexandria remarked on the "geometric forethought" of the bee in selecting hexagonal cells rather than square or triangular cells, which would consume more wax. In the 18th century, Huber (cited in Thompson, 1917/1942, footnote, p. 541) took the manner in which bees fashioned the prismatic shape of the end-walls of the cellular tube, by pulling and pushing the soft wax from opposing sides of the comb, as unmistakable evidence of bee intelligence.

Patently, in the extreme, the latter views exemplify the self-actional approach to scientific explanation. But as we might suppose, the interactional approach has not, over the years, been unrepresented. The 17th-century Danish scholar Erasmus Bartholin was, by Thompson's (1917/1942) account, among the first to interpret the comb's design as arising from an appropriate ordering of causal forces. For Bartholin, the shape of the cell was due to the equal application of pressure from *each* bee striving to make circular cells as large as possible.

An approximation to a transactional account can also be noted. If Bartholin was to emphasize bee interactions, D'Arcy Thompson was to underscore the material context in which those interactions take place and by which they are constrained. Thompson drew the parallel between the close packing of soap bubbles and the close packing of hemispherical wax cups manufactured by the bees. In both cases, relatively uniform, spherical bodies contact at their boundaries, and as a general principle, symmetrical tensions of the semifluid films are sufficient to bring the system into an equilibrium state in which potential energy is mimimal. That state is one in which surface area is minimal; and surface area is minimal when the closely clustered bodies join at 120-degree angles—in short, when the pattern is hexagonal.

Though terribly elegant, the Thompson account is not without its detractors. Von Frisch (1974), for one, is of the opinion that the hexagonal tessellation does not arise gradually with the increasing tensions and general stresses that accompany the accumulation of cells. Rather, von Frisch (1974) is strongly of the opinion that the hexagonal shape is there *from the very beginning* of the comb. Each cell is constructed from rhomb-shaped modular units starting with the base section. Thus, a phenomenon that Thompson had sought to explain at the relation-grain and Bartholin at the order-grain is returned, by this claim of von Frisch's, to the value-grain. Unfortunately, to relinquish the explanation of an effect to the value-grain is to grant the effect a status sui generis. In the present example, this is tantamount to ascribing the hexagonal shape of the cell to a genetic program. To the question: Why is the comb hexagonally patterned? is given the answer: Because the bee is genetically programmed to build hexagonally shaped cells.

Not surprisingly, we would not consider the latter an acceptable answer. It would be mistaken, however, to assume that our displeasure would be due simply to the fact that a self-actional assumption is involved. The main result of raising an account of a phenomenon to higher grains of analysis is that self-actional assumptions become increasingly attenuated until, by the time the account attains a proper coalitional explication, the degree of reliance on self-actional assumptions, or variables at the value-grain, is no longer scientifically objectionable. (After all, the goal is not to demand that lower grains of analysis be rendered null, but to offer instead a more balanced account that places no disproportionate weight on any grain.)[8]

---

[8]This theme is eloquently expressed by Pronko, Ebert, and Greenberg (1966), who promote a style of inquiry in which "all variables share the burden and the organism is freed from its crushing and perplexing job of doing a theoretical solo [p. 77].

One misgiving we have about the von Frisch (1974) claim is that inspection of photographs and scientific illustrations that exhibit combs at various stages of construction suggests that cells befitting the label "hexagonal" do not appear to be available at the earliest stages. Nevertheless, assuming that they were, it is not necessarily the case that this fact enforces the extreme self-actional interpretation. There is a line of reasoning, owing to Darwin (1859/1959), that reduces the weightiness of self-actional assumptions (without eliminating them) by enriching the order-grain of analysis. Darwin (1859/1959) notes that the Mexican bee (which makes a nearly regular comb of cylindrical cells) is intermediate between the bumble bee (which makes very irregular, rounded cells) and the honey- or hive bee (which makes regular hexagons). The thrust of his argument is that only a slight modification in the "not very wonderful [p. 244]" instincts of the Mexican bee—such as turning on a fixed point to hollow out spherelike burrows, laying cells one upon another, standing at a certain distance from her neighbors—would be sufficient to produce a structure "as wonderfully perfect as that of the hive [p. 244]." Darwin's hypothesis is that with regard to comb construction, natural selection selectively tuned the individual action capabilities of the Mexican bee so as to produce the individual action capabilities of the honeybee. In neither case are the action capabilities especially fanciful, but in the latter case, the action capabilities interact to produce hexagonally shaped cells.

Of course, one is wont to ask about the origins of even the crude architectural capabilities of the Mexican bee upon which was forged *ex hypothesis* the honeybee's more stylish development. Origins aside, however, the instinctive capabilities ascribed to the individual bee by Darwin are many steps removed from the conception of a bee-mind containing a complete architectural blueprint of the comb. For Darwin, the exact shape of the cells in the comb derives from the order imposed on the work done by the individual bees.

At all events, the foregoing, though a rough and far from complete overview of theorizing on bee-produced hexagonal patterns, serves to highlight the inadequacy of an account that (1) fixates at a single grain of analysis and (2) fails to appreciate the reciprocity of animal and environment variables at any grain of analysis. Where analysis is at the order-grain, substantial self-actional assumptions must be made to take up the slack. With regard to cone architecture, the self-actional fallacy is not simply that of imparting a motive force to the bee or intentional direction to its behavior, for surely both of these are true. The fallacy inheres to the degree that a theory ignores the valid contribution made by ecosystem constraints that can only be adequately characterized at the higher grains of analysis. A fallacy of like kind inheres in Thompson's approach. Thompson sought an account of cone architecture in terms of a free interplay of forces and mutual interactions among components tending toward equilibrium where the forces and components were almost solely of the bee's econiche to the exclusion of the bee. We would say of Thompson's approach that it excludes the bee at the relational-grain of analysis and trivializes the order- and value-grains.

An Introduction to a Coalitional Analysis
of Comb Construction

Let us give a simple sketch of the kinds of questions and the types of resolution that the coalitional style of inquiry would entail. Ideally, this sketch should carry us a little way in the direction of an adequate and satisfactory picture of comb construction; but perhaps the most we should expect of it is that it prepares us for the very much harder things that coalitional inquiry demands.

What are the basic dimensions over which the bee ecosystem is defined? More particularly, what variables are pertinent to the problem of comb construction? A cursory examination reveals five prominent dimensions. (Our ''examination'' is based in very large part on the details provided by von Frisch, 1974.) Three of these dimensions can be defined simply and precisely. The other two dimensions, however, by their very nature resist concise identification. Nevertheless, they can be intuitively grasped, and if time and space permitted, they could be more properly articulated. Recall that in detailing the basis-grain, the task is to identify covariate dimensions over the animal and environment components of the ecosystem.[9]

Temperature and two forces, gravitational and magnetic, comprise the concisely defined environment-based dimensions. Their covariate animal-based dimensions are proximity to other bees, rotation in the vertical plane, and rotation in the horizontal plane, respectively. Let us elaborate on these three covariate dimensions in turn.

The wax secreted by the worker bee is optimally malleable by legs and mandible at 95 degrees Fahrenheit. Owing to the vagaries of ambient air temperature, the temperature in the hive cannot be expected to remain at the optimal level for wax as a building material. The optimal temperature is preserved by the activity of the bees; at lower ambient air temperatures, the bees are distributed compactly in the hive; at higher temperatures, they cluster more loosely. By varying the manner of their clustering—that is, their proximity to their neighbors—the bees vary the contribution of their body heat to the temperature of the wax. We may suppose that this contribution is ''inadvertent'' in the sense that the proximity of a bee to its neighbors is probably due to the individual bee moving on a local temperature gradient in response to its individual heat-balance requirements. Importantly, the density of bees in a cluster decreases from the middle outward. There is, in consequence, a temperature gradient or, reciprocally, a gradient in the production and malleability of the wax, so that inner bees, in principle, are able to build more in the same amount of time than their more peripherally located neighbors. Combs exhibit a rate of completion gradient that

---

[9]The task of detailing the basis-grain shares much in common with the task of applying dimensional analysis to problems in biology (Günther, 1975; Rosen, 1978; Stahl, 1961). We would expect both the specifics and the spirit of dimensional analysis to be significant to the coalitional style of inquiry.

follows the thermal gradient—inner cells of the comb are completed earlier than more peripheral cells.

Combs are constructed downward—with gravity, rather than against it. Bees orient in the vertical plane with respect to gravity. Curiously, successive combs built by the same bee colony are virtually identical in their horizontal alignment; and their common alignment can be offset by introducing a magnet into a hive in which bees must forge their comb without the benefit of light. Bees orient in the horizontal plane with respect to the earth's magnetic lines of force. (In contemplating the means by which a cluster of thousands of bees work in unison to produce such an intricate architectural structure, much help is provided, as von Frisch [1974] notes, by recognizing the shared orientation of all workers—building downward with gravity and in the magnetic direction of the original comb.)

The dimensions that resist concise identification might be termed chemical and geometric. By the former, we recognize an umbrella label for variables such as concentration, flux, viscosity, energy, and the like as they bear on the materials ingested and excreted and the metabolic processes that mediate them. By the latter, geometric, we recognize the very important fact that *space* precludes very many things and permits very few things, so that *nature* is not free to build any structure it desires in any way it desires (Stevens, 1974; Thom, 1975; Wheeler, 1962). If nature ''requires'' that the flow of material from a central point traverse the least distance in the most direct fashion, then it has no option but to introduce branching; if nature ''wishes'' to close pack in order to save space, it must use hexagons. (The significance of hexagonal tessellation for the bee is that the comb contains the maximum volume for storing honey while using the least amount of wax, which in turn requires less honey to be eaten by the workers in order to secrete the required wax; the fewest number of trips to flowers to retrieve nectar; and hence, in general, more honey for the brood to survive on with the least work invested.) If for simplicity (but not for accuracy) we speak of the environmental-based geometric dimensions as structural and the animal-based geometric dimensions as transformational, then we can intuit covariation. Moreover, this manner of speaking gives us a crude way of conceptualizing the geometric dimensions of the basis-grain that is helpful for present purposes: They constrain both the forms that structures can take and the formative processes that can be enacted. Let us focus on dimensions of geometric constraint to illustrate the kind of analysis that the coalitional style of inquiry motivates at the relation-grain.

Recall that the relation-grain $R = \{\phi, \psi\}$ consists of all possible ecological relations, with the environment $\phi = \{<X,X>, <X,Z>\}$ and animal $\psi = \{<Z,Z>, <Z,X>\}$ being defined in reference to one another rather than as logically independent systems. The aspects of the ecosystem of the bee that pertain to comb construction consists of all those ways in which the environment ϕ and the animal ψ mutually constrain one another. A mutual constraint is, by definition, a bidirectional relationship between two variables that restricts the number of degrees of freedom each might assume to something less than what each might assume if they were unrelated. But in order for constraints to exist between an animal (here, a bee) and some significant aspects of its surroundings (here, flowers, structural supports for combs, and so on), the two systems must be *mutually* compatible; that is, they must reciprocate along shared dimensions. This means they must not only share bases, but they must also be duals of one another. Suppose that one were to assume that bees, working independently of one another, share nothing but an instinctual propinquity to build hexagonal cells; then because of their ability to start building at different sites, under a common support, and to interchange work in the middle of constructing even a single cell, nothing should prevent them from creating a jumble of hexagons. To make such a self-actional thesis plausible, one must assume not only that each bee has *a* program for building hexagons but also that each must possess the same mental blueprint of the comb-to-be, with constant updating of how far the work has proceeded at each separate locale. This would require either careful, time-consuming, and detailed communication among workers or a strong overseer who sees everything at once and gives simultaneous directions to all personnel. The only plausible self-actional thesis is to assume that each bee has precognition or partakes of a single "mind" of the collective. Is there a more acceptable alternative?

In the long term, a better alternative will follow, we believe, from the assumption that a higher-order set of relations exists between the comb, at various stages of construction, and the anatomy of the bee such that those forms that result do so as a product of ecological constraints—that is, as a product of the ongoing interactions of the bee-collective with certain specific global chemical, thermal, geometrical (and the like) relations that either exist throughout, or gradually unfold during, the dynamic process of comb construction.

Traditionally, dynamics has been concerned with systems that are linear and conservative and, thus, with functions that are continuous. The newer dynamics (Glandsdorff & Prigogine, 1971; Prigogine, 1978), largely inspired by biology, is concerned with systems that are nonlinear, nonconservative, and, thus, with functions that are discontinuous. For nonlinear systems displaced far from equilibrium, fluctuation plays a central role. Fluctuations force the system to leave a given macroscopic state and lead it to a new state that has a different spatiotemporal structure. Prigogine (1976) gives a brief but illuminating application of the theory of "dissipative structures" to the construction of a termite nest. Nest building is initially uncoordinated and characterized by a random depositing of building material. In manipulating the construction material, the termites mix in a chemical attractor that diffuses over time, giving rise to a "scent" gradient. Equations can be written that express the relations among the concentration of insects carrying material, the density of the building material, and the density of the chemical attractor. Where the density of material in each location is low, the said equation has a stable solution—a uniform distribution of the termites over the region on which they are depositing material. However, when the uncoordinated activity of the termites raises the density of deposited material in a location or number of locations above a particular value, the uniform distribution ceases to be a stable solution. The new stable solution is one in which the termites cluster about the locations of higher density. At these loctions, the termites deposit more material, and if two such locations are close, an arch will form; on the other hand, if a location of high density is relatively isolated, then merely a pillar or wall will be formed. In brief, a new spatial structure arises from the dynamics of nest building—or, as Prigogine would express it, order arises from fluctuations. The immediately following shares the spirit but not the details of Prigogine's analysis. It is a first pass at identifying a geometric relation in the bee-ecosystem from which hexagonal tessellation might arise.

1. It can be shown that three-dimensional tessellations of cylindrical cells can be readily transformed into a tessellation of hexagonal prisms by any process that simply removes the excess material between cell walls so that the walls are thinned uniformly. Of course, the walls between cells may be made as thin as the material will allow under prevailing conditions of heat and stress (e.g., wax will allow walls of only 0.073 millimeters thickness, which will support 1320 times its own weight).

2. Bees have been observed to gnaw away excess way to make curved walls more rectilinear.

3. In order to gnaw down the walls shared by any two cylindrical cells to a minimal thickness, the bee must insert its head into the cell at an angle that will bring its mandibles into contact with the plane of the wall. This means that the main axis of the bee's body must fall on a line that is roughly the perpendicular bisector of the wall section shared by the two cells. (Typically, the opposite side of the wall is being gnawed in a similar manner at the same time by a co-worker.) Moreover, given the size of the worker bee's head, it is impossible for the bee to rotate its mandibles while in the hole of the cell by an angle of less than approximately 120 degrees (i.e., the interior angles of a hexagon).

The preceding constraints are sufficient to guarantee that the bee will ultimately produce combs whose cells are hexagonal prisms to the extent that, at some early stage of construction, the cells assume a cylindrical shape. Let us now try to give a more precise characterization of the geometric constraints that are implicit in the foregoing assumptions and that—for this limited analysis—guarantee closure of the comb construction activity of a bee-ecosystem at the relation-grain.

It is convenient to use what is known as Schläfli notation to represent regular tessellations (Coxeter, 1961). Let $\{p, q\}$ stand for the tessellation of regular p-sided polygons with q of them surrounding each vertex. In this notation, the symbol for a honeycomb is clearly $\{6, 3\}$ (see Fig. 11.2). The *dual* of a $\{p, q\}$ tesselation is that tessellation whose edges are perpendicular bisectors of the edges of $\{p, q\}$ and that has the Schläfli symbol $\{q, p\}$. Thus the dual of the hexagonal comb $\{6,3\}$ is a tessellation $\{3,6\}$ consisting of a packing of triangles ($p = 3$) in the plane such that exactly six ($q = 6$) meet at any given vertex. (For convenience, the dual tesselations $\{6, 3\} \diamondsuit \{3, 6\}$ are reproduced in Fig. 11.2 by superimposition.)

The importance of this duality is that it provides a means for explicating the relationship between the bee's activities in producing and reshaping cell walls and the total shape of the honeycombed tessellation that is finally created. Let us assume that the alignment of the bee's body that permits the mandibles to come into play falls on the perpendicular bisectors of the line separating the wall of adjoining cells into two equal halves. The gnawing of the bee that thins the wall to its minimal thickness, or that builds it in the first place, conserves wax to the extent that the cell wall approaches his imaginary line. As the wall does so, it approaches rectilinearity and thereby becomes a shared wall with an adjoining, incipient hexagonal cell. The lines of alignment, noted in Fig. 11.2 as broken lines, constitute a $\{3, 6\}$, whereas the comb pattern that results is its dual, a $\{6, 3\}$.

We represent this state of affairs at the relation-grain as follows:

$\phi = \{<c, t>, <t, b>\}$ and $\psi = \{<b, h>, <h, c>\}$ for

c = cylindrical walls

t = $\{3, 6\}$ axes of alignment for bee's body

b = bees

h = $\{6, 3\}$ tessellation of hexagonal cells

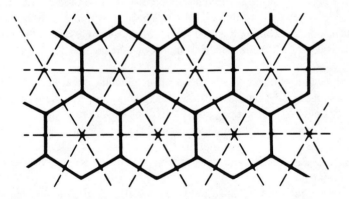

FIG. 11.2.   The hexagonal tessellation is a [6,3], whereas the triangular tessellation is its dual, a [3,6].

That is, ϕ equals the environmental constraints consisting of cylindrical walls to be gnawed by bees and the perpendicular bisectors of the walls that constitute the axes of alignment along which the bees must orient their bodies; and ψ equals the bee's behavior of gnawing the cylindrical walls of the cells and the hexagons that that behavior produces.[10] The following dualities hold to guarantee closure of the comb production activity of the bee-ecosystem:

(1) $c' = b$ and $b' = c$, (2) $t' = h$ and $h' = t$.

The duality $c \diamond b$ holds in the sense that the cylindrical walls are the object acted upon (gnawed) and the bee is the actor, whereas the duality $t \diamond h = \{3, 6\}\ \{6, 3\}$ holds for reasons already given. The test of closure is given as follows:

$$\phi = \{<c,t>, <t,b>\}' = \{<c,t>', <t,b>'\} = \{<c', t'>, <t', b'>\}$$
$$= \{<b, h>, <h, c>\} = \psi.$$

To articulate the duality schemata of the order-grain will require resolution to such problems as determining the nature of the perceptual information that allows bees to distribute themselves at the appropriate relative distances over the comb work-space; the perceptual information by which they determine exactly how much to excavate in wax foundations for cells; the perceptual information for exactly how high to construct a cell wall before moving on to another site, and so forth.

There is, however, one piece of information reported by von Frisch (1974) that sheds light on the very important perceptual process that guides the bee in determining how thin a wall might be gnawed. Von Frisch (1974) suggests that bees gauge the thickness of a wall by pressing their mandibles against the wall so as to produce a mechanical deflection. Upon removing its mandibles, the bee senses the degree of deflection and recovery through sensitive cells in its antennae. Under the prevailing conditions of consistency of wax and temperature, there is sufficient invariant information for walls of constant thickness to be produced. It is just such a reciprocal coordination of action (deflecting the wall) and perception (measuring its recovery) in the midst of dynamic, ongoing behavior that precludes the need for radical self-actional constructs. One might reasonably assume that the degree of mechanical deflection afforded by the wall is peculiar to the mass and biokinematic links of the bee's anatomy. The antennae might register no more than a simple "stop" or "go" singal for gnawing or, alternatively and perhaps more rarely, for depositing more wax. *The bee's body would*

---

[10]Implicit in this analysis is an appreciation of the dynamical nature of ecosystems: What is a Z term in an earlier phase is an X term at a later phase. Thus, in the present illustration, the hexagonal cell is a Z term; it is bee-referential in comparison to the cylindrical cell from which it arises in the same sense that wax is bee-referential in comparison to the nectar from which it is produced. At an even later phase of the ecosystem, where our concern might be the honey-storing activity of the bees, the hexagonal cell would assume the status of an X term.

itself be the standard for measurement as well as the means for creating the deflection to be measured. Hence no "mental" copy of the perceptual standard or the actional means need be stored as an "instinctual" program. This account exploits perceptual information and action goals as duals and shows how environmental properties may be defined in reference to body or action coordinates of the agent.

And finally, with respect to the value-grain, we should expect the particular features and specific dimensions of combs to be determined by a convergence of constraint from the other three grains plus adventitious aspects of the materials and site layout encountered. Notice, in particular, that the value-grain under a complete coalitional analysis would not be trivialized, but it would, nevertheless, be excised of deus ex machina.

Coalitions: A Step Beyond Transactional Structures

To end this section of the chapter, we underscore why it is that coalitions are more than transactional. The concept of the tranactional is a Third, a law or rule, that relates Seconds or interactions. Interactions, the reader will recall, are defined as relations among Firsts. But what are Firsts? Consider the example of the giving of gifts. In this example, the giver, the receiver, and the gift are all Firsts. A giver or receiver is necessarily a person; a person, however, is able to do many things other than just give or receive and, therefore, is a complex effectivity structure. In order to specify just those aspects of a person involved in giving or receiving, then certain effectivities must be selected and others ignored. Thus, as explained earlier, the value-grain, g(V), must be invoked when members of a set are selected, or activated, ignored, or left quiescent. A gift is only an object qua object at this grain and can not be ascribed as a role in the gift function.

Similar analysis must be carried out at the grain of order g(O) where perceptions (of the gift) and actions (realization of the intent to give it) are defined. This is the grain where the displacing of the object (the gift) from one person to another involves an interaction that is an ordered relation (i.e., X gives and Y receives). But the legal aspects of this gift-giving activity, as a voluntary transaction among responsible parties, require additional analysis at the grain of relation g(R), for it is here that the lawful aspects and significant meaning of the transaction are revealed. For instance, one's ability to give gifts is a social effectivity just as the affordance of an object to be a gift requires a social context (e.g., customs, laws, and so forth) of interpretation. In other words, the effectivity pertaining to the giving or receiving of gifts, like the affordance value legitimately ascribed to objects that qualify as gifts, exists not by virtue of the physical interaction alone but also by virtue of the cultural constraints (e.g., laws and customs) that define the social transaction. This requires analysis at the relation-grain g(R), where laws as Thirds can be defined. For these reasons, we see that a transactional analysis ranges over three grains: Firsts are specified at the value-grain (e.g., givers, receivers, gifts as objects); the interactions of Firsts as Seconds are specified at the order-grain (e.g., the activity of giving objects); the laws that constrain and interpret Seconds are Thirds (e.g., laws governing gift giving) and must be specified at the relation-grain. But Thirds or transactions as invoked by Peirce or Dewey and Bentley, respectively, cover only three of the four possible grains of analysis. What of the remaining grain, the basis-grain; what role does it play?

As we have argued, transactions, like interactions, may lead to a regress unless constrained by some higher context. This can be seen in the foregoing example with respect to the social relativity of gift laws: What counts as a binding transaction between people is dependent on the legal basis of the society to which they belong. Consequently, the abstract ground of the analogy holding among instances of gift giving across distinct societies can not reside at the transactional alone but must be defined at a higher, more inclusive level. What is required for a valid comparison to be made over different legal bases is a grain of analysis at which the commensurability of gift giving in different societies is defined. That such an analysis is possible presupposes the existence of minimal mutual compatibilities, or dualities. The concept of dual bases, or basis-grain, is that which constrains the transactional (relation-) grain. But if the transactional is a Third because it constrains an interaction, a Second, then the basis-grain—or what we shall call the coalitional—because it constrains a Third can be properly deemed a Fourth—a concept that transcends anything explicitly introduced by Peirce or Dewey and Bentley. In summary, let us sharpen the analogy between the foregoing example and perception. The analogy is straightforward: Perceiving logically corresponds to the act of giftgiving at the order-grain, whereas the ecosystem, or grain of ecological law, corresponds to the social law of gift giving at the relation-grain. The comparison of perceptual activities of different species depends on the existence of an abstract analogue over the distinct but commensurate (dual) bases of diverse ecosystems to which each species belongs. This of course must proceed at the basis-grain, as do comparisons of gift laws over different societies.

In sum, we have argued that the designated effect of a perceptual mechanism to establish a reciprocal isomorphism, or duality, between animal and environment is a relation that must be considered a Fourth to be coalitional, rather than a Third—transactional. Also we have argued that by treating perception as an activity of an ecosystem (a coalition), all regresses are avoided, and yet sufficient grains of analyses are defined to permit incorporation of all the defensible aspects of interactional and self-actional principles. In the final section of the chapter, we return to consider the contribution of Gestalt psychology in the light of these results.

THE FAILURE OF THE GESTALTIST VIEW
OF PERCEPTUAL ORGANIZATION

The Gestaltists' formula for perception was predicated on the proposition that distal objects look as they look because the perceptual experience is isomorphic to the field organization of the brain to which the proximal stimulus gives rise. Two factors are supposedly at work here—first, an interactional component by which the distal object interacts with the brain field vis à vis the proximal stimulus; and second, the self-actional component consisting of the autochthonous forces by which the percept is finally organized. Hence the Gestaltist theory offers no new principle of perceptual organization beyond that based on Firsts (self-actional) and Seconds (interactional). Because their view is merely interactional, the laws of perceptual organization that might otherwise have been truly transactional, as Bentley warned, necessarily must be construed as self-actional in order to account for the sources of variability not explicable in terms of interaction with the distal stimulus alone. In other words, the degrees of freedom for explaining perceptual phenomena are greater than the degrees of constraint offered by interactive principles; hence, to take up the slack in their theory, the Gestaltists were forced to postulate a power of "things solus," the self-acting biotonic forces.

Most theorists, however, have found such an explanation unrevealing and treat the so-called laws of Gestalt psychology as merely descriptive principles that summarize a common set of experiences over a widely diverse class of perceptual displays. Moreover, we can now recognize in Gestalt theory the reification of a relational term and the consequent endorsement of a rather crass semantic triad consisting of the distal stimulus, the experience of the proximal stimulus, and the laws of psychoneural isomorphism—a reification of a complex set of relationships.

The irony of it all is that the Gestalists who admonished others to be more molar than molecular in explanations were themselves apparently guilty of not being sufficiently molar. Had they understood Peirce's thesis—namely, that a Third is something that brings Firsts (the distal object; the proximal stimulus) into relation to a Second (the brain-field organization)—then they would not have mistakenly interpreted the brain-field forces as being self-actional; rather, they would have looked beyond the brain-field organization to a broader context of constraint lying beyond the perceiver. And, of course, what lies beyond the perceiver as a self-organizational entity is the transactions the perceiver-as-actor has with its environment.

Lest it be claimed that the Gestaltists did indeed mean to interpret the laws of organization as a Third and hence as transactional, consider the following quote from one of their chief spokesmen, Wolfgang Köhler (1958a):

Organization ought not to be interpreted as a mere formation of agglomerates [of Firsts]. In the first place, the characteristics of things are generally affected by their inclusion in larger organizations. In other words, organization involves *interaction*. Such interaction seems to explain colour and brightness contrast, most so-called optical illusions and also, several perceptual constancies. . . . According to the Gestalt psychologists, this constancy of object colour is brought about by *interaction* between the object and its brain-field environment. They claim that, under the circumstances given a case of constancy, this *interaction* operates against the effects of changed local stimulation, and thus exerts a compensating influence [p. 715] [authors' emphases and additions].

There can be little doubt from this authoritative text that the Gestaltists, perhaps unwittingly, were theoretically fixated in their language of descriptors for perception at the grain of interaction (what we called g(O) earlier).

However, to be fair, there is another aspect of Gestalt theory that recognizes the role of contexts of constraint on the interactions that take place within the field of cerebral forces and that must be invoked to explain contrast and constancy effects. There are also those structural properties, called variously Gestalt or Ehrenfel's qualities, that are produced by the dynamic constraints resident in the whole field and that act upon the phenomenal products of perceptual experience. Köhler (1958a) explains it this way in contrast to the first point made in the preceding quote: "In the second place, organization gives its products characteristics of their own, such as Ehrenfel's qualities. . . . Thus, a certain point in an object is a corner only within this larger unit, a line is a boundary only with reference to a segregated area, etc. [p. 715]."

Clearly, they do mean to propose some kind of context of constraints to help explain the perceived structure of objects. However, the shortcomings of their proposal do not lie in their inability to see the *need* for context effects but in their unfailing loyalty to an interactive interpretation of how contexts produce their constraining effects. The somewhat surprising point to be emphasized in this regard, given their otherwise high degree of sophistication in theory construction, is that the Gestalt program of inquiry failed primarily because of its failue to grasp the fundamental notion of context.

For Gestalt psychologists, at least those of them who agreed with Köhler, the principles of organization were the dynamic field properties of the electrical brain potentials. Most contemporary psychologists are willing to recognize such properties as a necessary but insufficient part of the causal nexus of support for perceptual experience but are not willing to impute to such field properties total responsibility as the efficient cause of organization. This amounts to an attempt to explain perception from below rather than from above, because causal support for a phenomenon is a finer grain of analysis than the context that constrains it. In terms of our earlier analysis, it is an attempt to reduce the order-grain g(O) (interactions) to the properties selected at the value-grain g(V) (specific causal chains) and ignores the true context of constraints on interactions that are provided from above by the relation-grain g(R) and the basis-grain g(B).

The truth of the matter is that the Gestalt theory, at least as interpreted by Köhler, was fundamentally inconsistent in the use of the concept of organization by which perceptual phenomena might be explained. On some occasions, it is argued that the essence of the Gestalt approach is an analysis "from the top" as opposed to the elementarism of the associationists that proceeded "from the bottom" (Köhler, 1958a).

In contrast, on other occasions, it was argued that the properties of perception were, if you will, induced from the dynamic relations of the supporting medium, the psychoneural basis, that in their own words was itself an "underlying process" (Köhler, 1958a). The Gestalt principle of isomorphism clearly shows that all perceptual organization was coordinate with this underlying causal nexus of relations that support, and from which structural properties are induced onto, the phenomenal field of experience.

To summarize: The Gestaltists' program went astray because, surprisingly, they confused the concept of context of constraint (which by definition must act from above) with the concept of causal support (which by definition must act from below); they confused a Third for a Second, a transaction for an interaction, and hence had to fall even further back to reliance on Firsts, self-actional unanalyzable "laws." This is clearly a reductionistic attempt to explain perception at a finer grain of analysis than can be adequate.

Perhaps they did this in order to avoid what they correctly saw was the ever-present danger of molar approaches to regress to ever-coarser grains of analysis. If so, we now see that like nearly every one of their predecessors, Gestalt theorists fall into a conservative stance of dualism in theorizing that attempts to avoid the dreaded regress by spuriously isolating the animal-as-perceiver from the environment on which the animal acts. But is there anything positive to be gained for future endeavors from this critical examination of Gestalt theory?

Indeed, the ecological approach can be viewed as an attempt to salvage to some extent this *one* aspect of the Gestalt program—namely, the notion that the properties of perceptual experience are not to be explained "from the bottom" alone, nor even "from the top" alone, but must be explained *simultaneously* at all grains of analysis. The four grains proposed should be considered to be a closed set of perspectives on the same underlying reality, rather than as different *levels* of analysis that are somehow in competition. All four grains, no fewer nor less, must be invoked in order to obtain an explanation of perception that avoids incompleteness or regress. This is the essence of the coalition style of inquiry.

In closing, let us venture to speculate where the coalitional or ecological style of inquiry might lead. To see these prospects most clearly, a brief recounting of the positive features of the ecological program that arose in contrast to the Gestalt program will prove helpful. In spite of our criticism, it should be emphasized that we feel that the Gestalt program may yet prove to have made an important contribution to scientific theory in psychology—that of suggesting a cure to the ills that have plagued perceptual psychology for over 2 millennia. It is with this belief and in great respect that the following concluding remarks were framed.

The Lesson to Be Learned From Gestalt Psychology

The fundamental insight upon which the ecological approach rests was offered by J. J. Gibson (1966): The language of description required for the object perceived should and can be the same language of description required for the perceptual experience (see Fowler & Turvey, in press). By contrast, the Gestalt program set up incompatible descriptors for the distal object and the proximal object of experience. This makes the avoidance of phenomenalism impossible. The ecological style of inquiry, because of its commitment to realism and rejection of phenomenalism, seeks a language of descriptors that treats the object of experience and the object of reference at the same grain or, better, grains. The treating of perception in terms of the duality structure outlined earlier offers the formal means for fulfilling this criterion.

The ecological approach, as most other approaches, nevertheless agrees with the fundamental Gestaltist claim that some kind of isomorphism exists between whatever is perceived and the perceptual experience. The two approaches differ radically, however, with respect to what counts as the object of experience: For the Gestaltist perceptual experience is isomorphic with the brain field, making the Gestalt theory a form of indirect realism with no clear way of avoiding phenomenalism and its entailed dualism; for the ecological theorist, the experience is of the functionally specified environment itself (not to be confused with the world as defined by conventional physics)—an affordance structure.

Because many contemporary theorists would still prefer the Gestaltist indirect view to the epistemically more direct ecological view, let us reiterate briefly where the two views may lead with respect to a broader perspective on scientific inquiry.

Even if a psychoneural isomorphism as proposed by the Gestaltists did exist, the organization of the field of brain events would require explanation in terms of a context of constraints that transcends an interactional account; otherwise, self-actional elements analogous to Gestalt ''laws'' would have to be invoked—such self-actional entities as homunculi, executors, egos, ''unconscious'' inferences, ''self-reading representations,'' and so on, as were noted as already being in the current literature. These views, to be harshly candid, are no more than species of scientistic animism and hold no real interest as sources of scientific explanation for perceptual mechanism for reasons given earlier.

Consequently, even if we admit to some form of brain–experience isomorphism, this is no theory of perceptual mechanism until some explanation is given for
the origin of the interactional properties registered on the brain that convey
pragmatic information about the environment to the agent who owns the brain.
But to what broader context of constraints might appeal be made to explain the
ultimate origin of animal–environment isomorphism?

We have already seen that such an appeal can not be simply "causal," as
causal interaction in no way can be identified with informational transactions.
Similarly, we have also seen that no rational appeal can be made to evolutionary
adaptation, because that same intractable nonspecificity that holds for visual
perception must hold likewise for all other perceptual processes as well. If one is
inadequate to evolve powers of induction to elaborate inadequate information
available from the world, then so are they all equally inadequate. This line of
reasoning, therefore, was found to lead ultimately to the *reductio ad absurdum*
of the interactional mode of inquiry—namely, that the cerebral system must
receive the content and organization from somewhere other than causal interaction. If the causal is the most molar context of constraint, then self-actional
entities must be invoked. But by what means, if not interactional, could such
self-actional entities have evolved? Such self-organizing principles must be part
of the design of the perceptual mechanism but could not have evolved by adaptive means.

Thus, the causal process approach (interactional) leaves the fundamental nature of perceptual mechanism a mystery to be puzzled over, perhaps by speculative metaphysics but in an area quite beyond the purview of science. Clearly, a
view that treats the isomorphism of animal experiences with the objects of
experience as a miraculous happenstance in the evolutionary design of the central
nervous system—one that just happens to coincide with the pragmatic goals of
the species in its struggle to sustain life and maintain health—is no theory at all.

The alternative program of inquiry offered by ecological psychology as a
legitimate extension of the pragmatist's program avoids the premature closing of
the context of constraints at an interactional grain of analysis. Such a program
renders unnecessary the postulation of self-actional entities, or magical contriv-
ances by evolution, to explain the reciprocal isomorphism that naturally exists
between the logically distinct but interdependent components of the ecosystem.

The ecological approach, by defining the environment in reference to the
animal and the animal in reference to the environment, avoids the troublesome
and unnecessary semantic independence of a phenomenal, or behavioral, environment from a geographical environment and, hence, of perceptual experience
of an object from the object experienced. It is this spurious semantic independence that renders the interactional approach a source of mystery rather than
enlightment, for there is no way that two semantically independent realms
could have coevolved so as to achieve the coordination required to define the
reciprocal isomorphism demanded for perceptual knolwedge.

The question of the origin of perceptual mechanism, when construed from the standpoint of ecological theory, can be dealt with as a problem rather than a mystery. *The problem framed under an ecological mode of inquiry is not how the animal's biological system evolved so as to explain the organizational properties of perceptual mechanism, but how the affordances and effectivities that define an ecosystem coevolved.* A study of affordances naturally entails the study of effectivities and vice versa for they are dually specified aspects of the same ecosystem. Put even more simply, the evolutionary question for an ecological theory of perceptual mechanism is not *how* the necessary biological support evolved but *what kind* of ecosystem evolved, because it is here that all four grains of analysis are to be found that provide an adequate explanation of perceptual mechanism. In other words, evolution of perceptual mechanism is to be understood as the constrained development of the ecosystem to which it belongs as a dual aspect—the action mechanism being its other coevolved partner.

But what of the still broader context of physical constraints in which ecosystems evolve? Before there were animals, there were necessarily no environments and vice versa, for these are functionally defined terms that co-implicate one another. Environments and animals coevolved, so that there was either no time in cosmological history when ecosystems did not exist, or they must have somehow emerged from a more primitive physical world. Whatever causal support might eventually have been required for explaining how ecosystems arose or how they function (e.g., support perceiving, acting, remembering, and so on) must reside in the descriptors for a primordial physical world. Does this mean, then, that ultimately even the ecological approach must regress to a more general, more primitive context of constraints? And, more pessimistically, does this mean that because all the grains of analysis available are specified within the ecological coalition, the regress to an all-embracing physical context takes us beyond the purview of the ecological style of inquiry?

These are serious questions and can not be lightly dismissed. Therefore, the final issue that must be addressed is the relationship of the physical world to the ecosystems that exist within its context of constraints.

Ecological Psychology and "Ecological" Physics

The relation existing between the physical world and an ecosystem is most probably a duality of an open set of constraints (termed the universal set earlier) with a relatively closed system (the ecosystem) that can be biased by the former, may even causally interact with it, but transacts no epistemic business with it.

The further speculative question regarding what, if anything, lies behind the scientific description of reality is an open question and can not be addressed by current scientific principles. Scientific views of cosmological development are limited by the singularity from which all matter was promulgated by the "big bang." Similarly, current attempts to grapple with the universe around us are limited by the fact that "black holes," also singularities, can not be peered into or through so as to discover what, if anything, might be on the "other side." The unanalyzability of such opaque windows to whatever might lie behind the impenetrable wall of mystery surrounding current conceptions of physical reality, a wall assured of its existence by modern physical theory itself, makes it less than reasonable to predicate the future of ecological style of inquiry on the physical style of inquiry. But is there any pragmatic alternative to this metaphysical impasse?

What the existence of these barriers to physical inquiry implicate is an open set of possibilities for ecological science. As the current language of descriptors for physical science changed dramatically in the passage from the Newtonian conception of the world to the Einsteinian conception, and from the view of Laplace to that of Heisenberg, so did our view of the nature of the physical constraints that shaped ecosystems. Science progressed from a view of an observer-free description of nature to an observer-dependent one. Contemporary physical conceptions of events in nature—as Wigner (1970), Wheeler (1974), von Neumann (1966), Schrödinger (1962), and Trimble (1977), among others, point out—co-implicate psychological variables in such a way as to render the equations of physics virtually uninterpretable without them (Shaw & McIntyre, 1974).

Hence the pragmatic rule that seems on the verge of emerging is that there can be no absolute physical conception of nature but only a total ecology for physics that includes the physicist as both perceiver and actor in the experiments run or the observations made. A direct consequence of a change in our conception of the psychological variables implicated in physics would necessarily alter our conceptions of physical reality. Does this tight fit of physics and psychology arise from the coalitional structure of nature? Perhaps there exists a duality between physical theory and ecological theory, a complementation of the physical world as the "environment" with those ecosystems as coarse-grained "organisms" surrounded by it. If so, we should look for this duality at the basis-grain—a grain only partially exploited by the ecological approach to terrestrial systems.

Just as a change in our *Weltanschauung* in psychology was precipitated by Darwin's providing biology with an evolutionary language of description, so might a change in the physicists' *Weltanschauung* be wrought by a successful theory of the evolution of psychological ecosystems. We see this possibility very clearly in the argument offered by the noted physicist Wheeler (1974)—that the fact of the existence of conscious, intelligent forms of life in nature logically (although not teleologically) preconditions our rational reconstruction of the conditions for the cosmological evolution of matter: Whatever primordial properties of matter-energy existed just prior to the "big bang," they must be conceived of as accommodating the ultimate outcome for intelligent life (see Turvey & Shaw, 1979).

Similarly, we see this need to accommodate psychological descriptors in the field of computer science, where physical devices are seriously described in terms borrowed directly from contemporary psychology—terms such as *memory, problem solving, pattern recognition, decision making*. Moreover, to the extent that robots, cyborgs, and bionic mechanisms in the future achieve a wedding of the psychology of natural systems to a psychology of artificial ones, to that extent will physics be forced to accommodate directly psychological descriptors without cushioning the blow by a layer of biological descriptors.

Therefore, it is not unreasonable to suppose that in the years to come, there should arise a scientific ecology that encompasses the science of the living and the nonliving, on one hand, and the intelligent and nonintelligent on the other (where perception and action are included among intelligent functions of matter). Psychologists no longer have the luxury of merely sitting back and letting the physicists and biologists work on the fundamental grains of analysis at which ultimate constraints on ecosystems emerge. Rather, the time may well be upon us when the language of description we develop as psychologists provides constraints on the doing of physics and biology. Thus, we seem to be at that point sometimes referred to as the "mind–matter meld" or, better, we think, the animal–world synergy.

ACKNOWLEDGMENTS

The writing of this chapter was supported, in part, by Grant 1 R01 DEO4990-01 from the National Institute of Dental Research awarded to the first author, and by Grant HD-01994 from the Institute of Child Health and Human Development and Grant RR-5596 from the National Institutes of Health, both awarded to the Haskins Laboratories. The authors wish to acknowledge the significant contribution of Peter Kugler to the ideas expressed herein.

Three Approaches to Perceptual Organization: Comments on Views of Hochberg, Shepard, and Shaw and Turvey[1]

Fred Attneave
University of Oregon

DISCUSSION ON HOCHBERG

I think it is evident that we don't all mean quite the same thing by Prägnanz. It can mean something quite different from the old classical Gestalt brain-field idea. Let me suggest an alternative formulation. On one hand, I believe in mental images. I believe that the system in which they exist may legitimately be called an analogue system. Roger Shepard presents some evidence to that effect in Chapter 10. I also believe that the nervous system *describes* the images—that is, that people who talk in terms of propositional representation are essentially right as well. In fact, I would like to hypothesize a Prägnanz principle that is based on a two-way communication between an analogue image system and a languagelike or propositional system to allow hill climbing toward simple representations. Suppose that what the system *likes* is short descriptions and that the

---

[1]Professor Attneave was an invited participant at the symposium from which this volume originated. We asked him to comment during the symposium on a few of the papers that were read there. This chapter represents an edited version of his remarks. Although the chapters he discusses have changed somewhat in their transition to the printed page, we believe that the intelligibility and interest of his comments are not impaired by these changes. The first set of remarks concerns the concept of Prägnanz and was directed at Professor Hochberg's presentation. The second set deals with issues raised in the papers read by Professor Shepard and by Professors Shaw and Turvey. In discussing the Shaw–Turvey presentation, reference is made to two problems that do not appear in their chapter (11) in this volume: (1) the solution of motor problems using a motor system that has a surfeit of degrees of freedom, (2) the polar planimeter analogy, and (3) the perception of age in faces. The interested reader will find this work summarized in the following papers: (1) Turvey, Shaw, and Mace (1978); (2) Runeson (1977); Pomerantz and Kubovy, Chapter 13; (3) Pittenger and Shaw (1975a, 1975b); Pittenger, Shaw, and Mark (1979); Shaw and Pittenger (1977, 1978).

image is progressively changed, within the constraints of the input, until its description is minimized. This way of looking at the matter, which is considerably different from the classical Gestalt point of view, has the advantage of taking into account not only intrinsic stimulus properties—that is, redundancy, uniformity, or homogeneity in the stimulus itself—but also schemata corresponding to familiar objects. If an input can be brought into conformity with a well-formed schema that is frequently used and to which a short symbol has been assigned, it might be described quite as economically as if it were intrinsically simple.

I have to say that Julian Hochberg's demonstrations give me trouble, even with this weaker or deviant version of a Prägnanz principle, and I have been trying to see if it can work. Look at Fig. 9.1E. Think of describing it in terms of schema and correction. If "transparent cube" is taken as the schema, one possible and adequate correction would be that the side on the right is opaque. Another possibility would be that one of the sticks or wires making up edges of the cube is broken at Point 2 and is incomplete. It is not obvious to me that one of these corrections is particularly better or worse than the other. One can at least argue that the descriptions are equally simple; the second seems perhaps more objectionable on Helmholtzian grounds of likelihood than on grounds of unncessary complexity. Maybe this is sophistry. I have to say, in fairness, that when I see the central left corner as convex, I'm not at all sure the edge looks like a broken stick; rather, it is as if the whole region on the right were unsettled and ill described.

The elongated Penrose figure, Hochberg's Fig. '9.1D, again raises the question of the visual system's capacity for dishonesty in ignoring peripheral information, but an alternative view deserves consideration. Hochberg found in one experiment that naive subjects could inspect a figure like this without ever realizing that it was impossible, and I find (trying to be similarly naive) that when I look back and forth from one end of the figure to the other, I perceive it as a perfectly reasonable rectangular frame that is merely *twisted*. When fixation is near either end, disconfirming this interpretation requires a precision in following lines across the figure that may be beyond the limits of visual acuity.

DISCUSSION ON SHEPARD
AND ON SHAW, AND TURVEY

Most of my comments have to do with the highly diverse ideas of *space* that are introduced in Chapters 10 and 11, but first let me make a few miscellaneous comments.

What Roger Shepard is doing is very pretty indeed, as his work always is, and my point of view is so close to his that I am hard put to stimulate any argument over his paper. The only quibble I have is with his notion of complementarity between representation and reality. He has not really convinced me that there is (in his thinking) a nontrivial distinction between complementarity and resemblance. This looks to me about like the complementarity of a photographic positive and its negative—which, you can also say, are very much alike. On the other hand, I think Shaw and Turvey may be using *complementarity* in a more serious sense, at least in some of their examples. In others, not: In the case of a simple tracking task, the behavior is not complementary to the stimulus; it's simply copying or following it. I like many aspects of what Shaw and Turvey say in Chapter 11. I find the notion of "affordances and effectivities" quite compatible; in a much less elegant way, I've played with an idea of "SRS connections" that I think is basically similar. And I'm grateful for the hill-climbing explanation of the way one degree of freedom in feedback enables the solution of a problem involving two degrees of freedom in action (Turvey, Shaw, and Mace, 1978) because the model of Prägnanz that I was suggesting earlier is essentially a hill-climbing machine involving feedback on a single variable from a descriptive system to a modeling system. Again, I think the polar planimeter analogy (described by Pomerzntz and Kubovy, Chapter 13) is rather nice in many respects. We need to know more about the polar planimeters that the nervous system may have evolved. It struck me forcibly a few years ago that we don't really know even how the nervous system measures the length of a line in the frontal plane. There are dozen of cases like this at seemingly simple levels in which we really don't know what the mechanism is that the organism is using.

Before mentioning the objections I have to this point of view, let me talk a little about Bob Shaw's work on the changes that occur with aging. It seems to me that this is probably a very nice description of an event space: I think he has been doing the sort of thing D'Arcy Thompson was trying to do quite well indeed. Where he loses me is in the step between this and perception, or psychophysics. However elegant this may be as a description of the biophysical changes that occur, I don't see that he has demonstrated in any compelling way that judgments of youth or age are dependent on these strain and shear variables per se. Within this domain, there is just no end of cues on which judgments of this sort might be based. Maybe it's the local radius of curvature of some part of the skull; maybe it's the distance between the eyes and the top of the head. I just don't see how you know. As long as the subject's variable has some substantial correlation with the age variable, you'll get good judgments, and highly correlated judgments can result from very diverse mechanisms. Any way you look at it, this is quite an important problem in psychophysics that has been frequently ignored—that the elegant way of describing the stimulus, the psychologist's way of describing the stimulus, may have little to do (at least in terms of mechanism) with the stimulus variables the subject is using. If you were just trying to *predict* people's judgments, this wouldn't matter, but if you're interested in mechanisms, it does. So I really wonder if Shaw's approach is the way of getting at these "polar planimeters"—to take this much trouble with the stimulus domain as opposed to trying to find out what the subject is actually doing.

Where I find myself most in disagreement with Shaw and Turvey (and squarely on the side of Roger Shepard) is on their belief that human behavior requires no internal model of the world. This provides an excuse for me to tell you about a recent experiment of mine in which the subject's task on each trial was to identify the object (out of a closely spaced set) at which the experimenter was pointing. One might think this task readily amenable to the Gibsonian sort of treatment that Turvey and Shaw favor; for example, the subjects might pick up from their optical array some higher-order variable such as collinearity that directly identifies the object with which the pointer is aligned. However, we compared the condition in which the target objects were all visible to the subjects with a closely matched condition in which the targets were all located behind them, and in which they knew their locations only from memory. The results were surprising, even to me: In terms of overall error, the subjects did just as well when the targets were behind them as when they were constantly visible in front. People seem to be very good at picking up collinearity in the field of the *mind's eye!*

Let's consider for a little bit the various concepts of *space* that have cropped up in these talks. Real space is the tridimensional medium in which we exist and move about. Ever since Descartes invented graph paper, scientists have delighted in the use of metaphorical spaces, which enable them to transfer their highly developed real-space skills to more abstract matters that would otherwise be harder to think about. A very simple example is the frequency-amplitude space in which pure tones can be represented as points. This is a physical space in the sense that it represents physical rather than subjective variables (although one can draw into it isophonic contours which do refer to the subjective). It is metaphorical in that the variables of interest are not real-space variables; they are merely represented *by* real-space variables—that is, the two dimensions of the graph paper. (Shaw's strain-shear space is such a physical-metaphorical space, but its variables, being more abstract, have more physical correlates that might alternatively serve as stimuli, as noted earlier). Such a physical space may have a more-or-less corresponding subjective-metaphorical space, but even when the variables of the latter are causally dependent on (and not merely correlated with) those of the former, the correspondence may be more complex; for example, loudness and pitch *both* depend on *both* amplitude and frequency, and none of the relationships are linear.

Rarely if ever do the scientist's metaphorical spaces have all the formal properties of real space. What is particularly distinctive about real space is its *isotropy:* The same yardstick can be used for measuring in all possible directions, whereas one metric applies to amplitude, another to frequency; and diagonal "distances" across both are of dubious meaning. People have devised various schemes for imposing a common metric on naturally incommensurate variables—z scores and $j.n.d.$'s are examples—but there is no need for artifices of this sort in measuring real space.

Over the past few years, Roger Shepard and his associates, along with miscellaneous other people including myself, have accrued a good deal of evidence that a functional *analog* of real space exists inside the head. My present point is that this subjective real space is absolutely unique among psychological "spaces": It reflects not only values on dimensions but also the relationship of isotropy among the three dimensions. Isotropy is of the essence of mental rotation, because without it, distances would not be preserved under rotation.

The conceptual status of the space in which Roger is trying to deal with apparent movement, in which he represents *rotation* with *distance*, is slightly mind-boggling. As nearly as I can figure out, it employs real space as a metaphor to represent a subjective space that is an analog representation of real space!

13 Perceptual Organization: An Overview

James R. Pomerantz
State University of New York at Buffalo

Michael Kubovy
Rutgers University

This concluding chapter provides an overview of some fundamental issues in perceptual organization. To this end, we have not summarized the preceding chapters, but instead we have focused on themes common to all of them. In analyzing these themes, we have found that the main problems facing us today are quite similar to those faced by the Gestalt psychologists in the first half of this century.

We have chosen to classify these problems into four categories. First is *phenomenology*. Gestalt psychology relied heavily on the phenomenological method, and although this method is fraught with difficulties, both logical and practical, it continues to be used today. Second is the issue of *isomorphism*. The correspondences between stimuli, brain, and perceptions were of major concern to Gestalt psychologists, and they made strong claims about them. Certain of these claims have been misinterpreted, and some have been shown to be false. But the question of possible isomorphic relationships remains at the forefront of debates about the nature of mental representations. Third is the matter of *Prägnanz*. One permanent contribution of the Gestalt psychologists is the wealth of demonstrations they provided purporting to show that percepts organize themselves in the simplest possible way. The demonstrations remain, but their interpretation is in question, particularly with regard to whether they imply a general principle of Prägnanz. Fourth and finally is the problem of *part–whole relationships*. We have today experimental (in addition to phenomenological) evidence for interactions between elements in the perceptual field, and so it is clear that wholes are different from the sum of their parts. But how are wholes treated in the perceptual process? Are wholes perceived directly without prior perception of their parts? This question has recently assumed a new significance, following proposals that the perceptual system employs "smart" mechanisms for the direct detection of complex stimuli.

423

THE PROBLEM OF PHENOMENOLOGY

The primary method of Gestalt psychology was phenomenological. This is not surprising given that for them, the core question in perception was "Why do things look as they do?" (Koffka, 1935/1963), rather than "What mechanisms may explain our perceptual systems' capabilities?" Modern experimental psychologists question any method that deals with events that are, in principle, private. Such distrust is justified with respect to phenomenology in its philosophical guise, as described by Turner (1967):

> In general terms, phenomenology is that empiricistic philosophy which asserts that the givens of experience are configurational entities having a unique integrity of their own and are, therefore, not reducible to sense contents or to any other elemental structure. Stress is placed on uniqueness of events. Formalized science is suspect because of its abstractive character. To name or to classify an object of experience is to deprive it of its phenomenological purity as a unique event [p. 60].

This quotation reflects the philosophical source of the phenomenological method used by Gestalt psychologists, but it fails to capture the special use to which they put it. This special use is best characterized as a method of demonstration. Gestalt phenomena were usually presented through a descriptive text laced with striking visual displays. The observer was asked to consider these displays in two frames of mind: the spontaneous and the metaperceptual. In the *spontaneous* mode, the observer simply views the display and witnesses the way in which it organizes itself. An example of grouping by similarity is shown in Panels (a) and (b) of Fig. 13.1. The observer is also asked to adopt a *metaperceptual* attitude and to compare Panels (a) and (b), to recognize that the spacing in the two arrays is exactly the same, and to infer that the grouping effect must be psychological in origin (because of so-called forces of attraction; Koffka, 1935/1963, p. 165).[1] A complementary formulation of this approach stresses *emergent properties* due to perceptual organization. (For an introductory analysis of the Doctrine of Emergence, see Nagel, 1961.) The realization that a stimulus possesses an unpredicted, emergent property is the essence of the metaperceptual experience. We are somehow convinced that if we were confronted with Panel (c) of Fig. 13.1 while still untainted with any familiarity with Gestalt perceptual demonstrations, we would not be able to predict the appearance of Panels (a) or (b).

---

[1]This spontaneous–metaperceptual distinction is similar to Gibson's (1950) contrast between attending to the perceptual world and attending to the perceptual field, and also to Garner's (1974b) contrast between primary and secondary perceptual processes (see also Garner, Chap. 5, this volume).

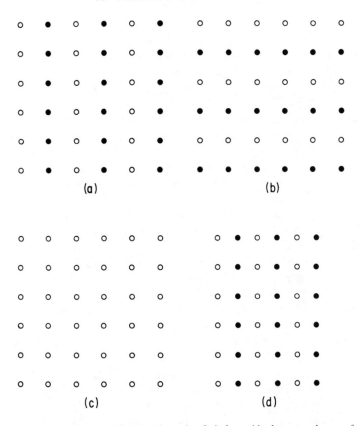

FIG. 13.1.   (a) An equally spaced matrix of circles, with alternate columns of circles darkened (favoring grouping by columns). (b) An equally spaced matrix of circles, with alternate rows of circles darkened (favoring grouping by rows). (c) An equally spaced matrix of circles, which alternates between an organization by rows and by columns. (d) A matrix of circles in which the intercolumn distances are smaller than the interrow distances (favoring grouping by rows), and in which alternate columns of circles are darkened (favoring grouping by columns).

Virtually all observers of Wertheimer's (1912/1961; 1923/1958) arrays of regularly spaced dots (Panel (c) in Fig. 13.1) see the dots spontaneously reorganize themselves from row groupings into column groupings and vice versa, with no need for instructions from the experimenter. When they realize that these changes are not occurring on the printed page but are generated internally, observers are *forced* into the metaperceptual mode. In this fashion they are made aware of the workings of their perceptual processes, of which they are usually unaware; processes that are normally "transparent." We believe that this is the essence of the Gestalt phenomenological method, and that it should not be judged solely on the basis of its philosophical ancestry as encapsulated in Turner's foregoing quote. As a didactic tool, Gestalt phenomenology has much in common with the Socratic method: By questioning, one can suggest where knowledge might be found, but knowledge cannot be imparted—it must be discovered.

Operationalization of Gestalt Concepts

One of the hallmarks of the phenomenological method is that the subjects' reports are based on private experiences and thus are generally irrefutable. Irrefutability, however, is less of a liability than may seem at first blush: It poses a problem mainly where there is disagreement between subjects' reports on what they experience in perceiving certain objects. Most Gestalt demonstrations are (at least to a first approximation) universally effective: Rarely does anyone disagree with the description offered by the Gestalt psychologists of these so-called private experiences. Nevertheless, the pragmatist streak in American psychology drives us to ask what role such experiences, however compelling their demonstration, play in the causal chain that ends in action. Thus we ask whether such phenomenology might not be a mere epiphenomenon, unrelated to behavior. But if we can set up situations in which we ask subjects questions about the stimulus that have a correct answer, and if organizational processes affect their judgments (and so their answers), then the experimentalists' skepticism about the importance of organizational phenomena should be dispelled. This book presents a wealth of organizational phenomena that can be demonstrated by both the phenomenological method and by objective experimental techniques. These techniques range from demonstrating that subjects can detect and correctly identify patterns that could be perceived only by way of complex organizational processes (see Bregman's, Julesz's, and Kubovy's chapters in this volume—4, 2, and 3, respectively) to measuring accuracy and reaction time in information-processing tasks (see the chapters of Biederman, Garner, Kahneman and Henik, Pomerantz, and Shepard—8, 5, 7, 6, and 10).

Returning to the grouping effect in Wertheimer's arrays, how might we demonstrate objectively the organizational process underlying the metaperceptual experience? There can be no single answer to this question until we operationalize what the supposed grouping effects are. What do we mean when we claim that certain elements group together? One interpretation of this claim yields the hypothesis that grouped elements appear to be closer together in space than elements that do not group. In Panels (a) and (b) of Fig. 13.1, grouping has been manipulated by varying element similarity. In Panel (a) the horizontal spacing between elements appears greater than the vertical spacing, and vice versa in Panel (b). The objective effects of grouping can be demonstrated by varying the physical vertical spacing, as in panel (d). The subject's task would be to decide whether the physical spacing is greater between rows or between columns. If an unequal physical spacing of rows or columns induces identical psychological spacing, the reaction times and error rates should be elevated. Thus a hypothesis suggested by the phenomenological method could be translated into operational terms and so become refutable by the most stringent objective standards.[2]

The role of the phenomenologist in guiding the research of the experimental psychologist is comparable to the role of the experimental psychologist in guiding the research of the physiological psychologist: Their relationship should be thought of not as antagonistic but rather as complementary.

THE PROBLEM OF ISOMORPHISM

The issue of isomorphism concerns the relationship between two systems and, in particular, the way in which one entity may serve as a representation of another. In the past, several types of isomorphism have been described. These include the possible isomorphism between the distal and the proximal stimulus, between the proximal stimulus and its corresponding neural representation, and between neural representations and experience.

Isomorphism in Gestalt Psychology

The Gestalt psychologists hypothesized that perceptual experience stood in an isomorphic relationship with brain processes. They did not claim that the relationship between perceptual experience and the perceived world was an isomorphic one (Köhler, 1947, 1969), although this claim has been erroneously attributed to them often enough to have become widely accepted as true (e.g., Zusne, 1970). On the contrary, they devoted much of their efforts to the explanation of nonveridicality, such as the tendency of perception and memory to make forms "better" and the distortion of perceived forms following prolonged inspection (i.e., figural aftereffects). Let us read Köhler's (1969) last statement on isomorphism from his Herbert Sidney Langfeld Memorial Lectures, given in 1966 at Princeton University. In his first lecture, he discussed some observations that motivated the theorizing of the Gestalt psychologists: stroboscopic motion, the geometric illusions, and the effects of context on perceived form. In the following passage, drawn from his second lecture, he refers to these phenomena as "curious interactions in perceptual fields."

---

[2]An experiment quite similar to this was reported by Hochberg and Silverstein (1956; see also Rush, 1937). They presented subjects with an array like that in Fig. 13.1 (c), in which the brightness difference was fixed but the spacing was adjustable. Subjects were asked to adjust this spacing to the "transition point" where the spacing adjustment just canceled out the grouping-by-similarity effect and perceived organization by rows or by columns was equally likely. The expected results were obtained. But in effect, subjects' adjustments were a form of phenomenal report of how they saw the organization of the array. Because subjects were not asked to judge the physical spacing, their responses could not be scored right or wrong, and so this procedure does not provide a *performance* measure of grouping. See also Coren and Girgus (1980).

The Gestalt psychologists had to assume that the unknown events responsible for such curious interactions in perceptual fields were processes in corresponding parts of the human brain. . . . Our main question is, of course, what physiological events occur in these places when human beings have experiences of one kind or another. Wilhelm Wundt gave this radical answer: "Brain processes and corresponding psychological facts differ entirely as to the nature of their elements and of the connections among their elements.". . . To be sure human perception contains many facts the like of which never occur in the physical world. Take the sensory qualities in vision, such as blue, gray, yellow, green, and red. In the physical world, the physicists find nothing that resembles these qualities, and nobody expects physiological processes in the visual cortex of the brain to have such characteristics. But we did not refer to sensory qualities when we began to suspect that certain properties of perceptual fields resemble properties of cortical processes to which they are related. The properties we had in mind were *structural* properties. If, for instance, under certain conditions, perceptual processes tend to assume particularly regular and simple forms, and if we suspect that, under the same conditions, corresponding processes in the brain show the same tendency, then we refer to what I call "structural" characteristics. It is only such structural characteristics which . . . perceptual facts and corresponding brain events have in common.*

The Fall of Gestalt Brain–Experience Isomorphism and the Rise of New Ones

In order to explain "curious interactions in perceptual fields," the Gestalt psychologists postulated a physiological model in which perceived form corresponded to the shape of electrical fields in the brain. Although the Gestalt psychologists performed few physiological experiments to test their models (but see Köhler & Held, 1949)—an observation that raises the question of how seriously they took their physiological speculations—they appear to have taken their conjectures literally. Koffka cites Köhler's (1923) rejection of the interpretation that the theory of isomorphism is "purely speculative, brain mythology" (Koffka, 1935/1963, p. 64). In any case, brain fields of the type hypothesized by the Gestalt psychologists were taken seriously enough by Lashley, Chow, and Semmes (1951), by Sperry, Miner, and Myers (1955), and by Sperry and Miner (1955), whose experiments, in the eyes of most, have put to rest forever any serious belief in these notions (Hochberg, 1974b; but see also Köhler, 1965/1971, for a rebuttal). Of course one can still adopt a "brain mythology" and so treat field theory as a model of the perceptual process, devoid of neurophysiological interpretation. Indeed, a number of models incorporating geometric or topological components have been proposed in recent years, such as Blum's (1973)

---

*From Wolfgang Köhler, The Task of Gestalt Psychology, with an Introduction by Carroll C. Pratt (Copyright 1969 by Princeton University Press; Princeton Paperback, 1972), pp. 64–66. Reprinted by permission of Princeton University Press.

"grassfire" model of shape coding, Julesz's (1971) spring-coupled dipole model of stereopsis, and Hoffman's (1966) Lie transformation-group approach to illusions. The physiological interpretation of the elements of all these models is left open.

It is unlikely that psychologists will prefer a brain-mythology approach over physiological explanations, if and when the latter become available. Indeed, experience shows that when a powerful physiological explanation is proposed to account for a pervasive psychological phenomenon, it is accepted with no qualms by the majority of the community of psychologists.[3] Take, for instance, the explanation of Mach bands first proposed by Mach (1868) and later formalized and confirmed by Ratliff and Hartline (1959). There are plenty of data to support a physiological basis for Mach bands. In this case, we are not aware of any objections to claims of brain–experience isomorphism. There are receptors that correspond to points in the perceptual field, and the firing rates of these receptors stand in direct relation to the brightnesses of the corresponding points. The pattern of activity in the retina is presumed to be isomorphic to the appearance of Mach bands. Thus, we believe that in general no philosophical objections are likely to be raised if well-founded physiological mechanisms are proposed to account for phenomena more complicated than Mach bands.

Indeed, a new such proposal has been recently published by Schwartz (1977a, 1977b). Although the details of Schwartz's model are complex, a brief overview will illustrate a new approach to brain–experience isomorphism. At the core of the model is the anatomical mapping of the retina onto the visual cortex. The mapping follows a conformal transformation; that is, any two curves on the retina are mapped by this transformation into curves on the cortex that make the same angle with each other as do original ones. Such a mapping has valuable properties. For instance, in conjunction with an asymmetric lateral inhibitory mechanism, it can account for Hubel and Wiesel's (1974) discovery that some microelectrode paths follow iso-orientation columns (i.e., columns consisting of elongated receptive fields whose major axes are parallel), whereas other paths, oriented orthogonally to the first, pass through an orderly succession of receptive fields whose major axes are systematically rotated with respect to the major axes of their neighbors. Furthermore, Schwartz shows that his model has a natural size-invariance property that is a basic requirement of preprocessors for pattern recognition.

According to this approach—which Schwartz (1977a) calls a Gestalt approach—"the relationship between structure and function in the cortex might be more aptly described in terms of 'computational geometry' rather than

---

[3]This acceptance does not imply that such explanations are thought to be complete in the sense of being sufficient, or even in the sense of being necessary. Rather, this acceptance implies that these explanations are thought to be *relevant* to the understanding of perceptual problems. For a dissenting view on this matter, see Chapter 11 by Shaw and Turvey.

'neuronal feature extraction' [p. 2].'' The model suggests two sorts of isomorphic relationships: between the proximal stimulus (on the retina) and the
corresponding cortical representation, and also between the cortical representation and experience. It is premature to assess the fruitfulness of this approach.
We present it as a modern version of the Gestalt program that seeks a physiological basis for experience, grounded in a spatial isomorphism.

As another modern example of appeal to brain-experience isomorphism, consider Richards' (1971) analysis of the ''fortification'' images experienced by
sufferers of migraine headaches. Often, such patients perceive a set of line
segments arranged in circular paths that spread slowly across the visual field.
Richards argues that the orientations and arrangements of these images are explainable by the geometric arrangement of line detectors in the visual cortex.

Where does this discussion leave us? It leaves us with the impression that the
notion of brain-experience isomorphism put forward by the Gestalt psychologists
has been maligned because it was identified with the Gestalt theory of cortical
fields. To equate the two and then to reject them both may be to throw out the
baby with the bath water. It is unproductive to rule out, a priori, all types of
isomorphism as explanatory devices.

PSYCHOPHYSICAL ISOMORPHISM

Up to this point, we have discussed the Gestalt conception of isomorphism—
namely, brain-experience isomorphism. What about psychophysical
isomorphism—that is, the relationship between the world and the corresponding
perceptual experiences? To argue in favor of psychophysical isomorphism as the
sole relation between the percept and the perceived is tantamount to claiming that
perception is always veridical. Nevertheless, even though perception is not always veridical, it is often so, and thus it is of some interest to inquire to what
extent (or under what conditions) psychophysical isomorphism may hold.

Shepard's Formulation

One psychologist who has investigated this question thoroughly is Roger
Shepard. Let us now turn our attention to his version of psychophysical
isomorphism, which he calls ''psychophysical complementarity.'' The essence
of Shepard's idea is shown in Fig. 13.2, taken from his chapter (10) in this
volume. Distal stimuli, labeled A, B, and C, are related to proximal stimuli A',
B', and C' by a physical transformation p, the optical projection onto the retina.
The proximal stimuli, A', B', and C' are related to internal representations A*,
B*, and C* by means of f*, a ''rule of formation.'' Objects may be transformed
into one another by means of a physical transformation t. In addition, internal
representations can be transformed into one another by ''rules of transforma-

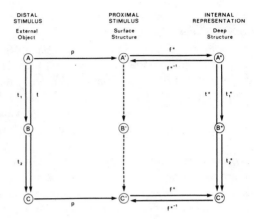

FIG. 13.2.   Shepard's representation of the relation between distal stimuli, proximal stimuli, and mental representations.

tion.'' For example, A* may be transformed into C* by means of t*, a rule of transformation.

To be concrete, imagine three objects, A, B, and C, that are the same irregular polygon at three different planar orientations—say 0°, 45°, and 90°. These objects can be transformed into one another by means of a physical transformation t, which in this case would be a rotation in the plane. Shepard now claims the following:

> This internal transformation t* is an analog of the corresponding external transformation t in the sense that in the course of the internal transformation t*, the representational process passes through intermediate states, such as B*, with a demonstrable one-to-one correspondence to what would be intermediate states B in the external world. Speaking abstractly, we say that the scheme depicted in Fig. 10.1 commutes: The sequence of transformations t, p, f* has the same internal result as the sequence of transformations p, f*, t*, . . . With respect to the rules of formation, our experiments have also established that the formational mapping f* is analogous to an inverse of the optical projection p. [pp. 294, 295, this volume].

Rephrasing this argument, Shepard is claiming that the same sequence of internal representations A*, B*, and C* may be generated either by perceiving a form undergoing a physical rotation or by ''rotating'' a mental representation of that same form. In either case, the transformation between two states is continuous and passes through the same intermediate states.

In an earlier paper, Shepard and Chipman (1970) distinguished between first- and second-order isomorphism. Let us compare these concepts to Shepard's analysis of mental representation as embodied in his concept of complementarity in the present volume. In first-order isomorphism, a square is represented by a square in the internal representation, and a green patch is internally represented by green. Shepard and Chipman rejected first-order isomorphism as foolish, because our neurons need not turn green when exposed to a green patch in order to represent the patch as green. The mention of neurons in Shepard and Chipman's rejection of first-order isomorphism shows that there is a difference between the domains related by first-order isomorphism and by the psychophysical complementarity proposed by Shepard in Chapter 10. Shepard and Chipman's first-order isomorphism is between the physical (green patch) and the physiological (green neurons), whereas Shepard's complementarity is between the physical and the *mental*.

Instead of first-order isomorphism, Shepard and Chipman (1970) proposed a second-order isomorphism, "between (a) the relations among alternative external objects, and (b) the relations among their corresponding internal representations [p. 2]." This formulation is potentially misleading, for it does not correspond well with the experiment Shepard and Chipman actually performed. They demonstrated that the similarity structure of *perceived* shapes of states on the map,[4] as derived by multidimensional scaling of judgments of the similarity of physically present maps of states, was close to the similarity structure of *remembered* shapes of states, as derived by the multidimensional scaling of judgments of the similarity of imagined maps of states. Thus, the only relations critical for second-order isomorphism are *similarity* relations. Because similarity is a psychological concept and not a physical one, similarities can only apply to mental representations, not to physical objects. Thus Shepard and Chipman's experimental result does not allow us to say anything about psychophysical isomorphism, because no observer-independent characterization of shapes of states is available to compare with the scaled judgments of the shapes of states. The two domains that Shepard and Chipman showed to be isomorphic are *percepts* and *images,* rather than physical objects and mental representations. It is not even about the relation between percepts and mental images, for what is demonstrated is an isomorphism between *relations* among percepts and *relations* among images. And if we want to be even more precise, this result allows us to claim only that a *model* of relations among percepts is isomorphic with a *model* of relations among images!

There is a need for two concepts—one to denote the relation between imaginal representations and perceptual representations, and the other to denote the relation between the world and mental representations, whether perceptual or imaginal. At the risk of further muddying some already murky waters, we propose to reserve "second-order isomorphism" for the former concept and "psychophysical complementarity" for the latter, for Shepard's concept of psychophysical complementarity has implications beyond those of Shepard and Chipman's concept of second-order isomorphism (as we have interpreted it). The mental rotation experiments and the apparent motion experiments allow Shepard to move

---

[4]From here to the end of this section, the word *state* will refer to a geographical region.

beyond second-order isomorphism because they allow him to *ascribe properties to a mental-representation-cum-mental-transformation* system. And as some of these mental properties (such as continuity) are also ascribed to the physical-object-*cum*-physical-transformation system, Shepard can legitimately claim to have moved beyond second-order isomorphism.

This sharing of properties does not, however, imply a return to a first-order isomorphism. For one thing, the terms that are being compared are different in first-order isomorphism and psychophysical complementarity: In the former, the isomorphism is between the physical and the physiological, whereas in the latter, the isomorphism is between the physical and the mental. Second, Shepard takes great pains to remind us that complementarity does not imply any similarity between mental representation and the physical world, in the manner that picture-in-the-head theories do. Shepard's metaphor for complementarity is the lock-and-key; a key does not resemble the lock it opens, and yet there is a clear relationship between the two. To be sure, some keys resemble the lock in the way a photographic negative resembles a positive; but the key–lock relation is more abstract. (But see Attneave's comments in Chap. 12, this volume). Consider, for example, the relation between the operations performed to open a combination lock and the internal structure of the lock: There is a complementary relation between them but no first-order isomorphism.

It should be clear that psychophysical complementarity (physical–mental correspondence) implies second-order isomorphism (imaginal–perceptual correspondence). Recall that the issue of second-order isomorphism is whether different and distinct internal representations underlie imaginal and perceptual representations. In Fig. 13.2, the internal representations A^*, B^*, and C^* are neither identified as being strictly imaginal nor as being strictly perceptual. If the distal stimulus C activates the internal representation C^*, then C^* would be considered a percept. If the internal representation A^* were transformed into C^* via t^*_1 and t^*_2, then C^* would be considered an image. Although it is possible that these two C^*s would differ in certain respects (images might be less intense or vivid than percepts), Shepard claims that the mental result is the same whether one perceives A being physically transformed into C or whether one mentally transforms A^* into C^*. Thus, psychophysical complementarity, as presented here, does imply second-order isomorphism.[5]

Palmer's Interpretation of Second-Order Isomorphism

We are aware of another analysis of second-order isomorphism, which has been presented by Palmer (1978). Palmer notes that there are two largely independent differences between first- and second-order ismorphism, as defined by Shepard and Chipman (1970). The first difference is that first-order isomorphism is con-

---

[5]We thank Irving Biederman for clarifying this point for us.

cerned with elements, whereas second-order isomorphism concerns relations between elements. The second difference is that in first-order isomorphism, representation is based on physical sameness (e.g., greenness represents greenness), whereas in second-order isomorphism, representation is based on functional sameness (e.g., squareness might represent greenness). Palmer (1978) describes a second-order isomorphism in which only the relational aspect and not the functional sameness holds:

> Consider the binary relation "greener than" in contrast to the unary relation "green.". . . If second-orderness is the essence of second-order isomorphism, then replacing "green" with "greener than" relationships should yield an example of second-order isomorphism. Thus, if object A is greener than object B, then the representation of A should be greener than the representation of B. The only constraint that has been lifted is that the properties of individual objects in the external and internal worlds need not be identical. That is, the representation of A need not be itself green (it might be blue-green or even blue), but it still must be greener than the representation of B [p. 292].

Palmer (1978, 1979) believes that this second-orderness or relational aspect of second-order isomorphism is not the critical one and will not help psychologists to construct more plausible theories of representation. His position suggests that both relational correspondence and functional (rather than physical) equivalence are necessary conditions for a plausible theory of psychological representation; neither one alone is sufficient. We concur that the system of representation described in the preceding quotation is hardly more plausible than first-order isomorphism, because if one neuron must be greener than another, then both neurons might as well be green in the first place! Thus we agree with Palmer that the functional equivalence aspect of second-order isomorphism is more critical than second-orderness per se. We also see representation based on relations and transformations between elements (as embodied in psychophysical complementarity) as being of central importance. We should note that to the Gestalt psychologists, isomorphism was always conceived of as relational (Hochberg, 1979). It seems equally clear to us that functional equivalence, in which greenness could be represented by (say) squareness, is an essential component of any plausible scheme of representation. Indeed, this notion is implicit in virtually all theories of stimulus coding: The relation "more quanta than" is coded by "more neural impulses per unit time than."

Second-Order Isomorphism, Psychophysical Complementarity, and Gestalt

In some ways Shepard's position on psychophysical complementarity resembles earlier formulations of Gestalt psychologists, such as Heider (1930/1959). Heider presents Fig. 13.3 and discusses it as follows:

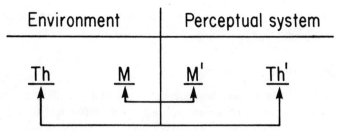

FIG. 13.3. *Th* represents the vitally relevant things in the environment; *M* represents the proximal stimulus; *M'* represents the processes in the organism caused by the proximal stimulus; *Th'* represents experiences that refer to things. (After Heider, 1930/1959, p. 43.)

The regions MM', the regions of mediation, do not exactly correspond to the two regions ThTh' which are correlated to each other and which, so to speak, hold hands across the mediation region. . . . Of course this correspondence between Th and Th' is perfect only when we assume an object-adequate perception, in which the relation M'–Th' is a mirror image of Th–M. . . . To a certain extent, the M regions can be considered as irrelevant. The essential invariance in the perceptual process concerns the relation of the regions Th and Th' [pp. 43–46].

But Shepard goes beyond this position in allowing us to talk meaningfully about the relationship between (1) the mental representation in the absence of *Th* (call it *Th''*), and (2) *Th'*, the experience that arises in the presence of *Th*. This is the relationship we have identified with second-order isomorphism. A further difference between Shepard's approach and Heider's is that Shepard remains neutral on the possibility of identifying mental representations with experiences (although some relation to experience is apparently assumed), and prefers to give it the status of a theoretical construct to be converged upon by multiple experimental operations.

The second Gestalt precursor of Shepard's formulation of psychophysical complementarity involves the notion that the representational processes pass through intermediate states that have a demonstrable one-to-one correspondence to what would be intermediate states in the physical transformation. For instance, Boring (1942) summarizes the Gestalt position on this matter as follows:

One system is said to be isomorphic with another in respect to their spatial relations if every point in the one corresponds to a point in the other and the topological relations or spatial orders of the points are the same in the two. . . . If perception and brain fields are both isomorphic with the stimulus field, they must be isomorphic with each other. It is to this solution of the mind–body problem that Köhler has applied the term *isomorphism*—meaning psychoneural isomorphism. The simplest test of such isomorphism is to see whether adjacencies and inbetweennesses are preserved from one system to the other [pp. 83–84].

Shepard has taken us several steps toward operationalizing these hard-to-define ideas in his experiments on mental rotation and apparent motion.

Philosophy and Isomorphism

We must confess that we have experienced considerable difficulty in trying to produce a philosophically consistent account of isomorphism. But we have not struggled alone. Along the way, we have found much solace in Turner's (1967) *Philosophy and the Science of Behavior*. Turner makes it clear how complex the problem really is. To realize the difficulty of the problem, it is sufficient to review the wealth of metaphors used by psychologists straining to capture this elusive idea: eidola, icon, resonance, mirroring, parallelism, internal representation, meshing, complementarity, lock and key, hand and cup, and so on. It is our impression that Shepard's presentation (on pages 291 and 292) says all that can be said about isomorphism at this time: These are theoretical statements whose meanings are unambiguous and that could in principle be refuted by empirical evidence.

Recent philosophical debates on issues such as the nature of the internal representation (e.g., Anderson, 1978; Kosslyn & Pomerantz, 1977) may be a symptom of a certain malaise afflicting contemporary cognitive psychology. Kuhn (1970) puts it very well:

> It is, I think, particularly in periods of acknowledged crisis that scientists have turned to philosophical analysis as a device for unlocking the riddles of their field. Scientists have not generally needed or wanted to be philosophers. Indeed, normal science usually holds creative philosophy at arm's length, and probably for good reason. To the extent that normal research work can be conducted by using the paradigm as a model, rules and assumptions need not be made explicit. . . . The search for assumptions [may be] an effective way to weaken the grip of a tradition upon the mind and to suggest the basis for a new one [p. 88].*

THE PROBLEM OF PRÄGNANZ

An important aspect of perceptual organization is the processing of relational information from the sensory input. This includes, at a minimum, the operations of grouping and figure–ground segregation. By grouping, we refer to the segmentation or parsing of the perceptual input into chunks or units, whereas by figure–ground segregation, we refer to the differential processing received by one (or more) of these chunks, called the ''figure.'' Perceptual organization also includes the representation of relationships among the various objects in the

---

*From Thomas Kuhn, The Structure of Scientific Revolutions, 1962, pp. 87–88. (Copyright 1962 by the University of Chicago Press. Reprinted by permission.)

perceptual world, including spatial relationships such as support, occlusion, and the like in the visual modality and analogous relationships in the other modalities. The principle of Prägnanz makes strong claims about how perception departs from veridicality. This principle holds that perception describes or models the world in the simplest, best, or briefest way it can. This claim has two implications. First, perception will capitalize on regularities and redundancies in the world and eliminate them from perceptual representations. Thus, when the system is presented with a symmetrical figure, it will (say) not represent both sides of the axis of symmetry in memory. When the system is presented with a figure similar to a frequent one, it may represent the figure as a "schema plus correction" (Woodworth, 1938). Second, the principle of Prägnanz holds that certain distortions will be introduced into the representation to simplify coding. As the Gestalt demonstrations have shown, perception will fill in "missing" information such as subjective contours or apparent motion so as to simplify representations. Similarly, it may ignore or distort stimulus information toward the same end. In one sense, Prägnanz is a matter of selecting the most parsimonious guess about the environment, and thus it may often be a useful heuristic. But sometimes the less parsimonious guess is correct. So, perceptual organization based on Prägnanz implies that perception will not always be veridical.

Some believe that Prägnanz, more than any other concept, serves as the cornerstone of the Gestalt approach. The principle of Prägnanz has a special, superordinate status in this approach, for it may serve as a summary statement of the function served by the other principles. The purpose of all the various principles of grouping and figure–ground segregation is to achieve the simplest, best, and most stable organization of the stimulus field.

More than any other principle, Prägnanz led the Gestalt approach to emphasize the global qualities of stimuli. Although other principles such as proximity or similarity could operate locally, Prägnanz could not, for the most minor local change in the sensory input could, it was claimed, precipitate a reorganization of the entire field.

The greatest difficulty for the concept of Prägnanz has been the absence of any general, clear, unambiguous, and noncircular definition of "best" or "simplest." Major inroads into the problem of perceptual goodness or simplicity were made by Attneave, Garner, and Hochberg in the 1950s and 1960s (and more recently by Leeuwenberg, 1978, and by Restle, 1979), but a universal definition has not been proposed.

This problem is so thorny because the properties that make a stimulus simple or complex do not reside entirely in that stimulus. As Garner (1962) made clear, the meaning of a stimulus resides not just in itself, a single instance, but in the set of alternatives to which it belongs. Good (i.e., perceptually simple) patterns, Garner (1970a) argues, are those with few alternatives. Therefore, goodness cannot be measured without a method for discovering the alternatives to any single stimulus as they are implicitly inferred by the observer. This method must be independent of the assessment of goodness.

Attneave (1954, p. 191; Chap. 12, this volume) has suggested that we interpret Prägnanz as a striving toward economy of description. This view was anticipated by Mach (1886/1897, pp. 96–97) in his discussion of the most parsimonious representation of a straight line (see also Kopfermann, 1930; Heider, 1930/1959, p. 57). That is, a stimulus will be encoded as compactly as possible. This interesting approach is unlikely to bear fruit until we know what coding schemes are used in perception. Changes in coding schemes can have enormous impact on the brevity of codes. For example, certain shapes are far easier to describe using Cartesian coordinates than polar coordinates (e.g., a square), whereas for others, the opposite is true (e.g., a circle).

To answer this question, it is necessary to distinguish, as we and others (e.g., Hochberg, Chap. 9, this volume) have, between two different forms of the Prägnanz principle, which can be called the *simplicity principle* and the *likelihood principle*. The first, which is linked closely with the classical Gestalt conception, holds that we organize our percepts so as to minimize their complexity. In information-processing terms, this principle would imply processing small elements of a scene first, then conjoining them into larger clusters, which are then combined into even larger groups until the process reaches a stopping point. Such procedures are known as "bottom-up" procedures (although "top-down" procedures could be at work as well; [6] see below). The second principle, that of likelihood, is definitely not part of the Gestalt heritage but instead may be attributed to Helmholtz. It holds that we organize our percepts so as to perceive the most likely distal stimulus that could have given rise to them. In more modern terms, the likelihood principle would operate via a learned "top-down" process (although evolution could have provided us with a bottom-up process to serve this function; see Shepard, Chap. 10, this volume).

Any outline shape drawn on paper could be the projection of an infinite number of three-dimensional objects. Yet we interpret such drawings consistently; the agreement among observers is remarkable. Prägnanz is supposed to give us the rules used by the perceptual system to yield few interpretations where many are possible. We briefly discuss three examples: the interpretation of a trapezoid drawn on paper, the Ames distorted room, and the interpretation of variants on Necker cube drawings.

A trapezoid drawn on paper is often seen as a rectangle tilted in depth, even though a trapezoid outline could just as easily be projected by a trapezoid parallel

---

[6]Wertheimer (1923/1955) believed in top-down processes of one sort or another: "The mind and the psychophysical reception of stimuli do *not* respond after the manner of a mirror photographic apparatus receiving individual 'stimuli' *qua* individual units and working them up 'from below' into the objects of experience. Instead response is made to articulation as a whole. . . . It follows that the apparatus of reception cannot be described in a piecewise sort of mechanism. It must be of such a nature as to be able *to grasp the inner necessity* of the articulated wholes. When we consider the problem in this light, it becomes apparent that pieces are not even experienced as such but that apprehension itself is characteristically from above [p. 88]."

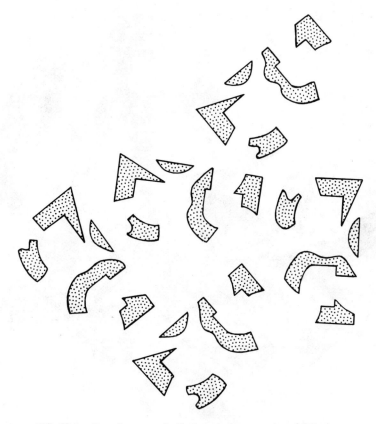

FIG. 13.4.   Form fragments for Bregman's demonstration of Prägnanz.

to the plane of the picture. According to Prägnanz, we perceive a rectangle (albeit a tilted one) because it is simpler than a trapezoid. This claim is attractive because a trapezoid has more degrees of freedom than a rectangle. Furthermore, in a carpentered environment, rectangles may be more likely than trapezoids, and right angles may be more likely than acute or obtuse ones. The problem for Prägnanz is that the benefit accruing from the simplification of form is obtained at the cost of tilting the form into the third dimension. To claim, in this case, that Prägnanz results in a net benefit in simplicity presupposes knowledge of the relative costs and benefits involved. Until a cost–benefit analysis is possible, such an appeal to Prägnanz will remain circular and vacuous.

A similar argument applies to the Ames distorted room. Is the cost of distorting the apparent size of people seen inside the room less than the cost of seeing the room as irregularly shaped? Without an answer to this question, the term *Prägnanz* adds nothing to Ames' observations.

As a third example, consider the Necker cube. Hochberg and McAlister (1953), and later Hochberg and Brooks (1960), showed that: (1) some variants of

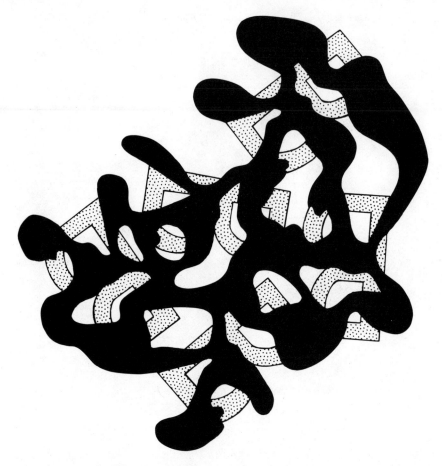

FIG. 13.5.   Bregman's demonstration of Prägnanz.

the Necker cube are more likely to be described as two-dimensional figures, and some are more likely to be described as three-dimensional; and (2) these differences could be predicted by an objective and plausible coding scheme. Within this scheme, the economy of description was assessed by (among other measures) the number of lines and angles contained within the coding. Thus, the costs and benefits of two- versus three-dimensional interpretations could be assessed. Figures that could be coded more simply under a depth interpretation were, in fact, seen in depth; those that could not be simplified in this way were seen to lie in the picture plane. This demonstration, unlike the preceding two examples, shows that within some limited stimulus domains, it may be possible to explain how Prägnanz could work. But we doubt that any general mechanism for Prägnanz exists.

Notwithstanding this conclusion, the concept of Prägnanz continues to guide our exploration of perceptual phenomena. Bregman, for instance, has provided

FIG. 13.6.   James' Prägnant Dalmatian.

us with a unique demonstration of Prägnanz. In Fig. 13.4, taken from his chapter in this volume (4), only fragments of forms are seen. When we look at Fig. 13.5, we experience a striking organization of these fragments. There exist other examples of sudden reorganization of a perceptual field following prolonged inspection (e.g., James' photograph of the Dalmatian in Fig. 13.6), or following verbal hints (e.g., Shepard's 1978d, p. 129, version of a "droodle" created by one of Arnheim's students). But we know of no other example where the cue that precipitates such a reorganization (here, an occlusion cue) is so clear.[7] The existence of an occlusion cue appears to trigger a search for links or interpolations. This search may be operating on the simplicity principle; the output of the search process could be monitored by another mechanism based on the likelihood principle, which would terminate the search when a familiar figure was detected (see following on top-down and bottom-up processes).

Bregman's demonstration constitutes support for Mahalaba's approach to pre-processing pictures before submitting them to scene-recognizing programs (described by Winston, 1970/1975, pp. 161–162). Mahalaba's program classifies and labels the vertices in a line drawing according to the number of converging lines and the angles between them. In addition, the program finds pairs of

[7]A somewhat less compelling version of the same demonstration may be found in Kennedy (1974), Figures 47 (p. 140) and 48 (p. 142). It first appeared in Kennedy (1971).

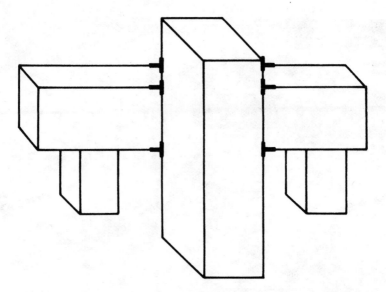

FIG. 13.7.   An example of matched Ts indicating that one object is partially occluding another.

T-vertices where the crossbars lie between collinear uprights (see Fig. 13.7). These pairs are called "matched Ts" and are interpreted as an indication that one object is partially occluding another. This program is an example of bottom-up processing in scene recognition.

Impossible Figures

As Hochberg has pointed out, one difficulty for the Prägnanz principle has been the existence of impossible figures. These are drawings that are interpreted perceptually as three-dimensional objects that could not in fact exist.[8] Take, for example, the Schuster (1964) impossible three-stick clevis, shown in Panel (a) of Fig. 13.8. Why, if Prägnanz were operating, would this figure be perceived as an impossible object when it could be viewed as a possible one—namely, a flat design drawn on paper?

First of all, the existence of impossible figures is not necessarily damaging to the simplicity aspect of Prägnanz, for simplicity is not incompatible with impossibility. For example, the four-dimensional cube, although quite simple to describe formally (Green, 1961; Noll, 1967), is nonetheless impossible to construct. Second, although the existence of impossible figures would seem fatal to

[8]As Gregory (1970) has pointed out, it is not the pictures that are impossible but our interpretations of them. Gregory constructed wooden objects that, when photographed from a particular angle, look impossible. Thus it is clear that an impossible figure is one whose description does not correspond to any possible object.

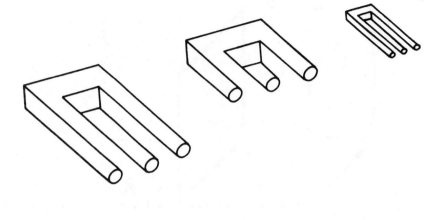

(a)   (b)   (c)

FIG. 13.8.   (a) The impossible three-stick clevis created by Schuster (1964). (b) The shortened three-stick clevis. (c) A smaller version of the three-stick clevis.

the likelihood aspect of Prägnanz (because impossible objects are completely improbable), the problem is not as severe as it might seem at first glance. Most impossible figures are possible at the local level. For example, the left portion and the right portion of the Schuster three-stick clevis are both physically possible and perceptually stable when considered separately. Moreover, even these partial views may be simplified when viewed as three-dimensional; for when they are considered three-dimensional, all angles are interpreted as projections of right angles, ellipses as projections of circles, and so forth. If we assume that viewers experience only that part of the figure upon which they are focusing their attention at any given moment, the problem of the impossible object disappears. Observers experience a paradox only when they realize that they are switching between two incompatible representations (cf. the notion of a "metaperceptual experience" developed earlier in this chapter). It is important to note, in this regard, that when the Schuster three-stick clevis is altered as Panel (b) of Fig. 13.8, it tends to go perceptually "flat" and is no longer seen as impossible (cf. Hochberg, 1978, p. 154).

When we refer to local regions of a figure, we do not mean this in absolute terms—that is, a region subtending some small visual angle—but in a relative sense. For example, making the Schuster three-stick clevis smaller, as in Panel (c) of Fig. 13.8, does not make the figure appear flat. Thus the parsing of the figure is determined by the relative or proportional spacing of the parts. This point has not been sufficiently emphasized in previous discussions of impossible figures.

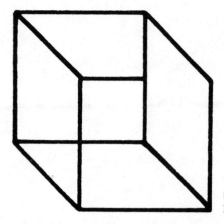

FIG. 13.9. Hochberg's incomplete Necker cube.

Hochberg's Modified Necker Cube

The alternations of a Necker cube are often taken to support a likelihood principle of Prägnanz (e.g., Gregory, 1974). As there are two or three objects that could reasonably be represented by this drawing, the perceptual system vacillates among them, as Attneave (1971) has described. But how can the likelihood principle explain these alternations? The Necker cube has a preferred orientation: It is more likely to be perceived as if viewed from above than from below. If this preference is due to the greater likelihood of seeing cubes (or any rigid body, for that matter) from above in our environment, there is no reason for the cube to depart from its preferred orientation. One explanation of the fluctuation involves satiation: The processes underlying one percept become fatigued over time until, eventually, the processes underlying the other percept become dominant (Attneave, 1971; Köhler, 1947). A more thoroughgoing likelihood explanation could argue that the perceptual system does not simply bet on the single most likely world, but hedges its bets by probability matching: Because it is not impossible to encounter cubes supported or suspended higher than our horizon, only less likely, we occasionally see the cube as if from below.[9]

Hochberg (1978; Chap. 9, this volume) has presented evidence against the principle of Prägnanz. His argument is based on the drawing shown in Fig. 13.9. This figure, like the conventional Necker cube, undergoes spontaneous reversals. It differs from the Necker cube in that in one of its appearances, it is held to represent an impossible (or at least an extremely unlikely) object. Thus, the observer sees the cube flip from a possible object seen in depth to an unlikely and complicated object seen in depth. That the perceptual system alternates with such impartiality between these two states provides more powerful evidence against any general Prägnanz than do the traditional impossible figures, Hochberg ar-

---

[9]Note that this explanation fails to account for the perception of impossible figures, for there is no reason to hedge one's bets against the occurrence of impossible objects.

gues, especially as the Necker cube is the very figure most often used to *support* the idea of Prägnanz.

It is not clear whether the less likely interpretation of Hochberg's cube, shown in Fig. 13.9, is impossible or just improbable. Many observers see the drawing representing a possible object by interpreting certain of the cube's surfaces as transparent and certain as opaque; alternatively, some see it as a possible wire cube in which one of the wires has been snipped in midair, only coincidentally at the exact point where it would intersect another wire in the drawing. If so, Hochberg's cube presents a case of perceptual alternation between two possible interpretations—one being less probable than the other. It might bolster his argument to create a figure that would alternate between an impossible interpretation and one that is both possible and probable. We offer in Fig. 13.10 a variation of Hochberg's cube that may meet this criterion; we call it the *ambiguous triptych*. As with Hochberg's figure, different parts of the triptych flip independently of others, and we have illustrated this independence in Panels (b) and (c) of Fig. 13.10. There are still other interpretations of the ambiguous triptych; they are difficult to capture on paper, but the patient observer will see them eventually. We believe that this example, taken together with Hochberg's, provides compelling phenomenological evidence against any notion of Prägnanz, of either the simplicity or the likelihood types, that would apply globally to entire figures rather than to local regions. Hochberg (Chap. 9, this volume) argues strongly that if Prägnanz doesn't operate globally—that is, across large portions of the visual field—then nothing remains of the original Gestalt idea of Prägnanz.

Subjective Contours

Another phenomenon bearing on the issue of Prägnanz is subjective contours (Coren, 1972; Kanizsa, 1976). Examples of this phenomenon are presented in Fig. 13.11. The most common explanation of subjective contours (e.g., Gregory, 1974) appeals to the likelihood principle of Prägnanz: Subjective contours are seen ("hypothesized," in Gregory's terminology) in order to account for an otherwise inexplicable set of irregularities present in the stimulus. Such an explanation would account for the appearance of the subjective triangle if it is granted that an equilateral triangle occluding portions of three disks is a more likely state of affairs than three well-aligned notches in otherwise complete disks. Consistent with this explanation is the observation (Coren, 1972) that when the disks are replaced by jagged patches (Panel (b) of Fig. 13.11) that still contain the same three notches, it becomes extremely difficult to see the subjective triangle.[10]

---

[10]Note that the possibility of seeing a triangle in this figure with some effort suggests that the situation is more complicated, and that some "top-down" processing may be required to explain subjective contours. We return to this issue later.

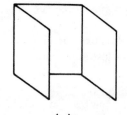

(a)

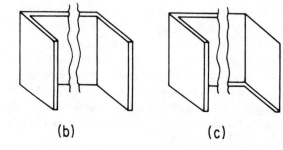

(b)   (c)

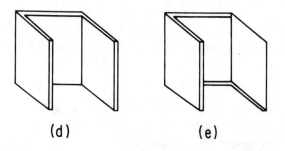

(d)   (e)

FIG. 13.10.   (a) the ambiguous triptych. It fluctuates between an interpretation that is both possible and probable, illustrated in Panels (b) and (d), and an impossible interpretation, illustrated in Panels (c) and (e). In Panels (b) and (c) we illustrate how the two leaves of the triptych can have compatible and incompatible orientations respectively. In Panels (d) and (e) we depict unified representations that may be experienced from the ambiguous triptych.

The Prägnanz explanation, as plausible as it may be, has several deficiencies. First, as Kanizsa (1976) has shown, subjective contours can define complex and unlikely figures (for example, Panel (c) of Fig. 13.11). In fact, as Hochberg has conjectured, one can create impossible figures using subjective contours. We present the Penrose and Penrose (1958) impossible triangle defined by subjective contours in Panel (d) of Fig. 13.11. Again, it is difficult to reconcile such figures with any sort of global Prägnanz principle.

Second, the Prägnanz explanation overlooks the cost-benefit issue we discussed earlier. The simplification of the visual field achieved by seeing subjective contours entails the cost of constructing discontinuities in apparent brightness and in depth that are inconsistent with sensory data. A satisfactory explanation must include independent evidence that the benefits outweigh the costs.

Local Versus Global Prägnanz

In the preceding discussion of Prägnanz, we have repeatedly made reference to the terms *global* and *local*, without always drawing a distinction between two different senses in which they may be used. First, by local we may refer to limited regions of the visual field. Let us call this sense *spatially local*. Subjective contours are not spatially local, because they are examples of perceptual interactions over broad distances. On the other hand, impossible figures do seem to be determined by processes that are spatially local, as we have already argued. Second, by local we may refer to low-level nodes in a hierarchical system. Let us call this sense *hierarchically local*. The subjective contour examples we have discussed to this point have been hierarchically local, because Fig. 13.11, for

(a)   (b)

(c)   (d)

FIG. 13.11.   (a) Standard subjective contour. (b) Reducing the strength of subjective contours by introducing features that could not be accounted for by the subjective contours. (c) An ill-defined and therefore unlikely figure outlined by subjective contours. (d) The Penrose and Penrose (1958) impossible triangle outlined by subjective contours.

example, shows how indifferent the subjective contour mechanism may be to the regularity and likelihood of the figure it creates. Impossible figures also seem to be local in this sense.

Top-Down Effects. There is strong evidence that subjective contours are influenced by cognitive factors (Banks and Coffin, 1974; Bradley, Dumais, & Petry, 1976). Consider, for example, Fig. 13.12. One may elect to perceive the Necker cube as floating above the page; in this case, the disks appear to lie on the page. Alternatively, the disks can be perceived as holes in the page through which the Necker cube is seen, floating behind the page against a black backdrop. In the former case, subjective contours are seen, but in the latter case they are not. As it is possible to choose which of these two organizations to perceive, and because the organization chosen dictates whether subjective contours will be perceived, the figure demonstrates the importance of top-down processes. A similar point is made in Fig. 13.13, which is adapted from Coren (1972); when the entire word *FEET* is presented, most skilled readers of English have no trouble identifying the component letters and seeing them in relief above the page, as brighter than the page, and as casting shadows on the page. But if the letter *T* is presented in isolation, and especially if it is rotated to an unusual orientation, few will recognize it as a *T* or perceive depth or brightness effects.

Apparent Motion

Prägnanz may seem a fitting way in which to explain apparent motion. When an object suddenly disappears at one location and reappears at another an instant later, it would seem reasonable for the perceptual system, using either a likelihood or a simplicity principle, to conclude that the object had moved from one

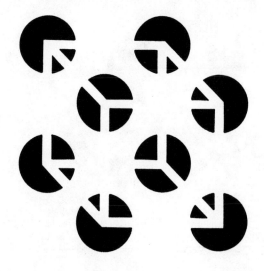

FIG. 13.12.   A Necker cube formed by subjective contours demonstrates effects of cognitive factors on subjective contours. (From Bradley, Dumais, & Petry, 1976).

(a)

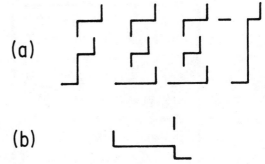

FIG. 13.13. A Second demonstration of cognitive effects on subjective contours. (Adapted from Coren, 1972.)

(b)

location to the other. But again, how could the perceptual system justify the construction of apparent motion over empty space? Alternatively, how would it rationalize the absence of sensory input during the interstimulus interval? There are at least two explanations for why the sensory data are missing: one, an eyeblink; and two, insufficient sensitivity. But consider the situation depicted in Fig. 13.14. In the upper panel of Fig. 13.14, a circle is put into apparent motion through empty space by flashing it alternately in the positions marked 1 and 2. In the lower panel of Fig. 13.14, a solid square "blocks" the circle's trajectory. As has been described elsewhere (Kolers, 1972), the circle moves into depth in this situation. There are, of course, two possible paths the circle could follow in depth—one in front of the square and one behind it. Following a Prägnanz principle, one might expect a preference for the latter trajectory, because the presence of the opaque square would readily explain the absence of the circle from the sensory input during motion. Despite the availability of this simple and likely interpretation of the sensory data, we have observed that the motion of the circle in front of the square is perceived just as readily as motion behind it.

THE PROBLEM OF PART–WHOLE RELATIONSHIPS

Gestalt psychologists may be best remembered for their association with the phrase: "The whole is more than the sum of its parts." In fact, however, we know of no instance where Wertheimer, Koffka, or Köhler ever made this claim. Pratt, in his introduction to Köhler's (1969, pp. 9–10) *Task of Gestalt Psychology* (the Langfeld Memorial Lectures referred to earlier), cites Köhler's dismay at being misquoted repeatedly on this crucial point. Their claim, more precisely, was that the whole was different from, or other than, the sum of its parts and, moreover, that the perception of the whole occurred *prior to* the parts. But what does it mean to say that the whole is "different from" the sum of its parts?

One of the major issues surrounding part–whole relationships is whether perceivers can attend to the parts of a stimulus configuration. Consider the

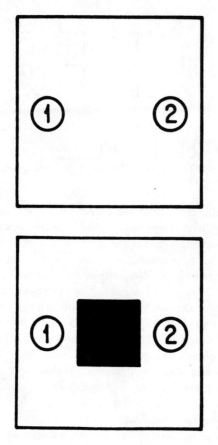

FIG. 13.14.   Two apparent motion experiments.

distinction between the perception of chords and of timbre (a tone and its harmonics). In both cases, the auditory system is presented with multiple frequencies concurrent in time. In the case of chords, listeners may attend either to the chord as a whole, as witnessed by their ability to name or classify it, or to component notes individually, as witnessed by the ability of many listeners to name these notes. In the case of timbre, listeners cannot (under all but the most contrived of circumstances; see Kubovy & Jordan, 1979) attend to the individual harmonics of a tone. Following Helmholtz (1877/1954), we may call a chord *analyzable* and a tone with its harmonics, *synthetic* (cf. the concepts of Garner, Lockhead, Shepard, and others relating to stimulus integrality and separability).

Consider once more the photograph of the Dalmatian (Fig. 13.6). The picture is analyzable in Helmholtz's sense: Individual spots are perceptible, and although at first they group themselves in various ways, they do not form an interpretable whole. After the figure snaps into a coherent organization, we are struck by the way in which the parts, which at first were barely related, form a meaningful picture. By experiencing this transition, we are made aware of the existence of parts that are not necessarily linked in perception.

Similarly, if we see an array of dots alternating between an organization by columns and an organization by rows, we become aware of the parts that remain unchanged when the organization changes. It is thus quite natural to think of organization as something "added" to the parts.

Direct Perception and "Smart" Perceptual Mechanisms

The part-whole problem, which was forcefully brought to our attention by the Gestalt psychologists, is at the center of a renewed debate concerning "direct perception." Gibson (1950, 1966, 1979) and Johansson (1950, 1964, 1974a, 1974b), in similar reactions to what they perceived as an atomistic streak in theories of perception, argued that even though parts can be perceived, they need not mediate the perception of a whole. Hence, it was quite natural for Gibson and his followers to speak of "direct" perception. Sensation is "transparent," Gibson argued, and one need not process sensory elements in order to perceive and interpret the world. More recently, Runeson (1977) has claimed that traditional perceptual theorists have been misled into thinking that "the basic variables of physics [should be] given primary reality status [p. 172]." By traditional thought, if an object has parts, the percept of the object must be constructed out of the perception of these same parts. Similarly, such a conception would imply that if speed is defined in physics as distance covered per unit time, then perceived speed must be mediated by perceived distance covered per perceived unit of time.

There are two reasons why this traditional viewpoint is false, according to Runeson. First, much more information is available in the optic array (about the speed of locomotion, for example; see Lee, 1974) than was suspected by the proponents of the traditional view. Furthermore, this "undiscovered" information is no less accessible than information previously assumed to be employed by the perceptual system (such as distance covered and elapsed time). This statement implies that it is no more difficult to construct a perceptual speedometer than it is to construct a perceptual odometer or a perceptual clock. Second, "smart" perceptual mechanisms can be designed to pick up this wealth of information without the mediation of the basic physical variables of distance and time.

In order to clarify this position, Runeson (1977) has used the example of the polar planimeter. This device measures area, but none of its parts can be identified with any standard or intuitive method of measuring area; it certainly does not divide the area to be measured into small areas in order to count them. Yet another example: The soap bubble's spherical construction solves some complex geometric problems in a manner that would be called "smart" because the solution lacks distinguishable, identifiable steps (Boys, 1912/1959).

Because of the relative obscurity of the ingenious polar planimeter, and the complexity of the physics of soap bubbles, we find it more convenient to use a speedometer as an example of a "smart" mechanism. It is illustrated in Fig. 13.15. The speedometer measures neither distance nor time in determining speed; for example, it contains no clock. Indeed, the odometer measures distance by integrating speed (counting revolutions of the speedometer's drive shaft). It is a "smart" instrument for two reasons. First, it is designed to perform a very specific function and to "capitalize on the peculiarities of the situation and the task, i.e. use shortcuts, etc." (Runeson, 1977, p. 174). Hence, it is efficient and economical. Second, it consists of only a few specialized components that are not readily interchangeable with other smart mechanisms.

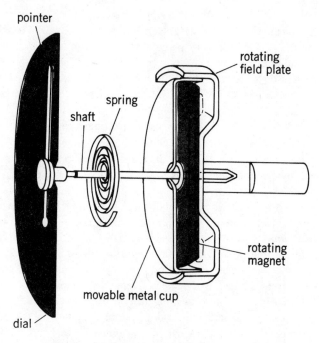

Mechanism of a circular dial speedometer.

FIG. 13.15.   Schematic drawing of a circular speedometer (Hustead, 1977, p. 736). The most important part of the speedometer is a permanent magnet, which rotates at an angular velocity proportional to the angular velocity of the wheels. The magnet rotates concentrically in an aluminum ring on which the rotating magnet exercises a torque proportional to its angular velocity. The ring is prevented from rotating along with the magnet by a calibrated spiral spring. The stronger the torque applied to the ring, the further it turns, carrying with it a needle that points to a graduated dial. From *The Encyclopedia of Science and Technology*, Vol. 12. Copyright 1976, McGraw-Hill. Used with permission.

Runeson contrasts smart mechanisms with "rote" mechanisms such as digital computers. Rote mechanisms contain large numbers of a few basic components, each of which performs a single, simple function. They can be made to perform complex tasks, either by being appropriately wired once and for all or by being programmed.

In line with Runeson's argument, Shepard (Chap. 10, this volume) has contrasted smart analog perceptual mechanisms with rote propositional systems:

> Being a "jack of all trades," it [a rote mechanism] necessarily is a master of none. In particular, such a general-purpose system will not be suited to the rapid prediction of and preparation for external developments in a three-dimensional, Euclidean world any more than a Turing machine will provide for the safe and efficient control of air traffic [p. 288].

Information-processing models of human perceptual and cognitive processes are structured after rote mechanisms, by and large. Flow diagrams that represent these processes are generally constructed from a few basic units (buffer stores, logical gates, comparators, and so on) that are interconnected via arrows in different configurations to different mental processes. Rarely, if ever, do information-processing models incorporate specialized, smart devices that are tailored uniquely to serve in one model only. Were such devices to be proposed, they would probably be criticized for being ad hoc.

Few who value the notion of direct perception as a heuristic would claim that it is as yet anything more than a heuristic. Would anyone wish to claim that *all* perception is direct? If not, direct perception can never be a universal perceptual theory.[11] One might claim that certain information about the world is picked up without processing intermediate types of information, but in support, one must produce the smart device itself and show the secret of its operation, as is done with the speedometer in Fig. 13.15. This type of analysis is still missing from the Gibsonian approach as represented by Shaw and Turvey in Chapter 11 in this volume. We believe that their call for a radical reconceptualization of perceptual psychology will not meet with much favorable reaction until the mechanism underlying some *perceptual* process is revealed.

---

[11]The following statement from Gibson's recent book, *The Ecological Approach to Visual Perception* (1979), is representative of the extent to which a proponent of direct perception is willing to concede the operation of intervening interpretative processes. Here, Gibson discusses the misperception of the Ames distorted room: "The explanation is that, in the absence of information, the observer has presupposed (assumed, expected, or whatever) the existence of rectangular surfaces causing the solid angles at the eye. That is reasonable, but it is then concluded that presuppositions are necessary for perception in general, since a visual solid angle cannot specify its object. . . . The main fallacy in this conclusion, as the reader will recognize, is the generalization from peephole observation to ordinary observation [pp. 167–168]." At the very least, Gibson is conceding that peephole perception is not entirely direct. We wonder whether the supporters of direct perception can contain the spread of indirect perceptual concepts once they have been admitted under conditions of impoverished stimulation.

In some areas of perception, we know much about mechanisms, which the proponents of direct perception might consider "smart," that have evolved to pick up information; they are found most often in peripheral transducers. The cochlea is a smart device that performs an approximate frequency analysis on the incoming pressure wave. It does this with a complex of well-matched physical and neural elements that form a unique mechanism, many parts of which work on principles that are not exploited anywhere else in the sensory domain, precisely because their function is extremely specialized.

Although we see merit in the concept of smart mechanisms, to contrast "smart" and "rote" is to imply that "rote" mechanisms are "dumb." This implication is misleading. Indeed, the contrast of "smart" versus "rote" is misleading. If one substitutes the more neutral terms "general-purpose" for "rote" and "special-purpose" for "smart," we will be free to discuss "smartness" of devices in an unbiased fashion.

Take, for example, the Hurvich–Jameson opponent process model for color vision. The process in question performs a highly sophisticated transformation of incoming sensory signals, in a manner few would describe as "dumb." It performs this task using standard and interchangeable components (e.g., neurons) and processes (e.g., inhibition and excitation). It is an example of a neural smart device created by smart programming on a general-purpose mechanism.

The implication that general-purpose mechanisms are "dumb" has been shown to be unfounded in the theory of computation as well. Many modern algorithms for the solution of numerical problems are quite nonintuitive, in the sense that it is not obvious at what point the program is dealing with which part of the problem space as we construe it (Kolata, 1978). Solving a problem "smartly" has little to do with the nature of the building blocks out of which the problem-solving device is built. To be sure, the building blocks constrain the domain of solutions, but the "smartness" of a solution must be evaluated relative to the costs and benefits of other solutions achievable with the tools at the disposal of the problem solver. Thus, some problems are better solved using general-purpose mechanisms, implementing "smart" solutions on a mechanism that could also solve the problem in a "dumb" way. The difference between a special-purpose device, like the speedometer or the polar planimeter, and a general-purpose device, like a digital computer, is not that the former is "smart" and the latter "dumb," but rather that the former cannot vary in its degree of "smartness," whereas the latter is a tool that can be used "smartly" or "dumbly." Thus the contrast should be between the "smart" and "dumb" use of a tool, on one hand, and between a special-purpose tool and a general-purpose tool on the other.

If general-purpose mechanisms can be "smart" in Runeson's sense, the direct-perceptionists' predilection for minimizing the role of information-processing models may be misguided. Thus although we agree that perceptual processes may employ information that we would intuitively call "higher-order,'' this fact implies nothing concerning perceptual mechanisms. In any case, it is unlikely that this issue will be resolved in the armchair. Experiments and simulations will give us the final answer on whether our models for perceptual software and hardware are adequate.

CONCLUSIONS

Gestalt psychology has now been with us well over half a century. Despite attacks upon it and periods of neglect, Gestalt thought continues to have an impact on theory and experimentation in perceptual psychology. Were outsiders to judge perceptual psychology by reviewing its treatment in introductory textbooks, they might get the impression that Gestalt phenomena, laws, and methods formed the very foundation for studying complex perceptual processes. Few who work in the field would agree with this impression, although few would claim that Gestalt psychology is dead. Where, then, does Gestalt psychology stand today?

First of all, many of the problems first pointed out by the Gestalt psychologists (apparent motion, grouping, figure–ground segregation, to mention just a few) remain today, even though the solutions offered by the Gestalt psychologists have not been widely accepted. We now have far better evidence that perception is organized, and we have a far more systematic picture of the varieties of organizational phenomena to be explained.

Second, there is the Gestalt commandment: ''Thou shalt take phenomenology seriously.'' To the extent that the Gestalt demonstrations preserve their interest, we are obeying that commandment. They represent a style of research that is still relatively rare in psychology: research by demonstration. It may turn out that certain of the Gestalt demonstrations mean little; they may be mere epiphenomena that play no role in the general scheme of perception. Alternatively, they may direct us toward solutions of the basic problems of perceptual organization. Either way, their further elucidation will certainly teach us much about perception.

Third, we have the commandment: ''Seek ye a principle of simplicity.'' In keeping with that injunction, the general concept of Prägnanz is a useful heuristic. Despite the concept's fuzziness, and despite the several counterexamples to this principle that have been offered, it remains a heuristic and a guide to research. We can only conclude by noting the irony that Prägnanz is not as simple as it seems. That is, although percepts may in fact be organized in the simplest way possible, the processes that yield this outcome may be diverse.

Fourth and finally, we have the commandment: ''Thou shalt not be overly atomistic.'' Many fascinating perceptual phenomena, which can be thought of as interactions among elements or processes, would escape our analysis if we did not develop special conceptual and experimental tools to deal with them. To some extent, the fashionable notion of top-down processes represents a way of obeying this commandment. But is is still unclear how such processes are related to the *experience* of perceptual organization.

What have we discarded from the original Gestalt view of perception? First, we have discarded the physiological model of electromagnetic fields in the brain. Second, experimental method has allowed us to transcend phenomenological observation—research by demonstration—and thus to merge the contributions of the Gestalt psychology into the mainstream of research in cognitive psychology.

ACKNOWLEDGMENTS

The work reported in this chapter was supported by USPHS Grant 1 RO3 28531 and NSF Grant BNS76-21018. We wish to thank I. Biederman, J. Hochberg, P. Podgorny, M. Sebrechts, E. Segal, and A. Wearing for their helpful comments.

Bibliographic Index

A

Abadi, R., see Kulikowski, Abadi, & King-Smith (1973).

Abel, L. A., & Quick, R. F. Weiner analysis of grating contrast judgements. *Vision Research,* 1978, *18,* 1031–1039. **12**

Abrams, M., see Sekuler & Abrams (1968).

Achim, A., see Bregman & Achim (1973).

Adrian, E. D. *The basis of sensation.* London: Christophers, 1928. **68**

Ahroon, W. A., Jr., & Pastore, R. E. *Selective attention II. Channel separation in two-channel frequency discriminations.* Unpublished manuscript, 1977. (Available from R. E. Pastore, Department of Psychology, State University of New York at Binghamton, Binghamton, New York 13901.) **92**

Aitkin, L. M. Tonotopic organization at higher levels of the auditory pathway. In R. Porter (Ed.), *Neurophysiology II* (Vol. 10). Baltimore, Md.: University Park Press, 1976. **83**

Allmeyer, D., see Estes, Allmeyer, & Reder (1976).

Alluisi, E. A., see Morgan & Alluisi (1967).

Ambler, B., see Beck & Ambler (1972).

Anderson, J. M. *The grammar of case: Towards a localistic theory.* Cambridge, England: Cambridge University Press, 1971. **336**

Anderson, J. R. *Language, memory, and thought.* Hillsdale, N.J.: Lawrence Erlbaum Associates, 1976. **293,295,314,322**

Anderson, J. R. Arguments concerning representations for mental imagery. *Psychological Review,* 1978, *85,* 249–277. **293,295,436**

Anderson, J. R., see King & Anderson (1976).

Andriessen, J. J., see Bouma & Andriessen (1970).

Anstis, S. M., see Mayhew & Anstis (1972).

Arend, L., & Lange, R. Bandwidth for frequency interaction at threshold and above threshold. *Investigative Ophthalmology and Visual Science,* 1978, *17* (supplement), 242. (Abstract) **12**

Asch, S. E., Ceraso, J., & Heimer, W. Perceptual conditions of association. *Psychological Monographs,* 1960, *74*(3, Whole No. 490). **83**

Atkinson, J., & Campbell, F. W. The effect of phase on the perception of compound gratings. *Vision Research,* 1974, *14,* 159–162. **13**

Attneave, F. Dimensions of similarity. *American Journal of Psychology,* 1950, *63,* 516–556. **143**

Attneave, F. Some informational aspects of visual perception. *Psychological Review,* 1954, *61,* 183–193. **127,263,438**

Attneave, F. Symmetry, information, and memory for patterns. *American Journal of Psychology,* 1955, *68,* 209–222. **286**

Attneave, F. *Applications of information theory to psychology.* New York: Holt, Rinehart & Winston, 1959. **263**

Attneave, F. Multistability in perception. *Scientific American,* 1971, *225,* 62–71. **151,444**

Attneave, F. Apparent movement and the what–where connection. *Psychologia,* 1974, *17,* 108–120. (a) **322,328**

Attneave, F. How do you know? *American Psychologist,* 1974, *29,* 493–499. (b) **333,340,358**

Attneave, F., & Block, G. Apparent movement in tridimensional space. *Perception & Psychophysics,* 1973, *13,* 301–307. **319,323**

Attneave, F., & Frost, R. The determination of perceived tridimensional orientation by minimum criteria. *Perception & Psychophysics,* 1969, *6,* 391–396. **263,286,305**

Attneave, F., & Olson, R. K. Pitch as a medium: A new approach to psychophysical scaling. *American Journal of Psychology,* 1971, *84,* 147–166. **78**

Attneave, F., see Olson & Attneave (1970).

Averbach, E., & Coriell, A. S. Short-term memory in vision. *Bell System Technical Journal,* 1961, *40,* 309–328. **89,136**

B

Bach, E. *Syntactic theory.* New York: Holt, Rinehart & Winston, 1974. **336**

Bachrach, K., see Banks, Bachrach, & Larson (1977).

Bagrash, F. M. Size-selective adaptation: Psychophysical evidence for size-tuning and the effects of stimulus contour and adapting flux. *Vision Research,* 1973, *13,* 575–598. **5**

Baird, J. C., see Szilagyi & Baird (1977).

Balzano, G. J. *The structural uniqueness of the diatonic order.* Paper presented in the symposium "Cognitive structure of musical pitch" at the annual meeting of the Western Psychological Association, San Francisco, April 20, 1978. **320,321**

Bamber, D. Reaction times and error rates for "same"–"different" judgments of multidimensional stimuli. *Perception & Psychophysics,* 1969, *6,* 169–174. **165**

Banks, W. P., Bachrach, K., & Larson, D. The asymmetry of lateral interference in visual letter identification. *Perception & Psychophysics,* 1977, *22,* 232–240. **198**

Banks, W. P., Bodinger, D., & Illige, M. Visual detection accuracy and target noise proximity. *Bulletin of the Psychonomic Society,* 1974, *2,* 411–414. **191**

Banks, W. P., & Coffin, S. Implicit depth cues do not create subjective contours. *Psychological Review,* 1974, *81,* 265. **448**

Banks, W. P., & Prinzmetal, W. Configurational effects in visual information processing. *Perception & Psychophysics,* 1976, *19,* 361–367. **153,160,191**

Banks, W. P., see Prinzmetal & Banks (1977a).

Banks, W. P., see Prinzmetal & Banks (1977b).

Barfield, L. P., see Tolhurst & Barfield (1978).

Barker, R. A., see Thomas & Barker (1977).

Bartlett, F. E. *Remembering: A study in experimental and social psychology.* Cambridge, England: The University Press, 1932. **215**

Bassman, E. *Mental processes in imagined and perceived cube folding.* Unpublished doctoral dissertation, Stanford University, 1979. **311**

Beck, J. Perceptual grouping produced by changes in orientation and shape. *Science*, 1966, *154*, 538–540. **154**

Beck, J. Perceptual grouping produced by line figures. *Perception & Psychophysics*, 1967, *2*, 491–495. **154,155**

Beck, J. Similarity grouping and peripheral discriminability under uncertainty. *American Journal of Psychology*, 1972, *85*, 1–20. **154,179**

Beck, J., & Ambler, B. Discriminability of differences in line slope and in line arrangement as a function of mask delay. *Perception & Psychophysics*, 1972, *12*, 33–38. **155**

Becklen, R., see Neisser & Becklen (1975).

von Békésy, G. Neural volleys and the similarity between some sensations produced by tones and by skin vibrations. *Journal of the Acoustical Society of America*, 1957, *29*, 1059–1069. **329**

Bell, H. H., & Handel, S. The role of pattern goodness in the reproduction of backward masked patterns. *Journal of Experimental Psychology: Human Perception and Performance*, 1976, *2*, 139–150. **162**

Bell, H. H., see Lappin, Bell, Harm, & Kottas (1975).

Bellugi, U., & Fischer, S. A comparison of sign language and spoken language. *Cognition*, 1972, *1*, 173–200. **335**

Bennett, D. C. *Spatial and temporal uses of English prepositions.* New York: Longmans, 1974. **337,338**

Bennett, J. *Kant's Analytic.* Cambridge, England: Cambridge University Press, 1966. **97**

Bentley, A. F. *Inquiry into inquiries: Essay in social theory* (S. Ratner, Ed.). Boston: Beacon Press, 1954. **356,360,362,367**

Bentley, A. F., see Dewey & Bentley (1949).

Bentley, A. F., see Dewey & Bentley (1964).

Berbaum, K., see Weisstein, Harris, Berbaum, Tangney, & Williams (1977).

Bergen, J., see Wilson & Bergen (1977).

Berglund, B., Berglund, U., & Lindvall, T. Psychological processing of odor mixtures. *Psychological Review*, 1976, *83*, 432–441. **77**

Berglund, U., see Berglund, Berglund, & Lindvall (1976).

Bergmann, G. *Realism: A critique of Brentano and Meinong.* Madison: University of Wisconsin Press, 1967. **97**

Biederman, I. Perceiving real-world scenes. *Science*, 1972, *177*, 77–80. **215,216,230**

Biederman, I. On processing information from a glance at a scene. Some implications for a syntax and semantics of visual processing. In S. Treu (Ed.), *User-oriented design of interactive graphics systems.* New York: ACM, 1977. **216**

Biederman, I., & Checkosky, S. F. Processing redundant information. *Journal of Experimental Psychology*, 1970, *83*, 486–490. **232**

Biederman, I., Glass, A. L., & Stacy, E. W., Jr. Scanning for objects in real world scenes. *Journal of Experimental Psychology*, 1973, *97*, 22–27. **216,243.**

Biederman, I., Rabinowitz, J. C., Glass, A. L., & Stacy, E. W., Jr. On the information extracted from a glance at a scene. *Journal of Experimental Psychology*, 1974, *103*, 597–600. **216,230**

Biederman, I., see Moore & Biederman (1979).

Birkhoff, G., see MacLane & Birkhoff (1967).

Bisaha, J., see Weisstein & Bisaha (1972).

Blake, F. R. A semantic analysis of case. In J. T. Hatfield, W. Leopold, & A. J. F. Zieglschmid (Eds.), *Curme volume of linguistic studies.* Baltimore, Md.: Waverly Press, 1930. (Reprint of Language Monograph No. 7 of the Linguistic Society of America, Philadelphia.) **336**

Blakemore, C., & Campbell, F. W. On the existence of neurones in the human visual system selectively sensitive to the orientation and size of retinal images. *Journal of Physiology*, 1969, *203*, 237–260. **4,5,23,45**

Blakemore, C., Carpenter, R. H. S., & Georgeson, M. A. Lateral inhibition between orientation detectors in the human visual system. *Nature*, 1970, *228*, 37–39. **18,23**

Blakemore, C., Muncey, J. P. J., & Ridley, R. M. The perceptual fading of a stabilized cortical image. *Nature,* 1971, *223,* 204-205. **5**

Blakemore, C., Muncey, J. P. J., & Ridley, R. M. Stimulus specificity in the human visual system. *Vision Research,* 1973, *13,* 1915-1931. **5,18**

Blakemore, C., & Nachmias, J. The orientation specificity of two visual after-effects. *Journal of Physiology,* 1971, *213,* 157-174. **18**

Blakemore, C., Nachmias, J., & Sutton, P. Perceived spatial frequency shift: Evidence of frequency-selective neurones in the human brain. *Journal of Physiology,* 1970, *210,* 727-750. **8**

Blakemore, C., & Sutton, P. Size adaptation: A new aftereffect. *Science,* 1969, *166,* 245-247. **8**

Block, G., see Attneave & Block (1969).

Blum, H. Biological shape and visual science (Part 1). *Journal of Theoretical Biology,* 1973, *38,* 205-287. **428**

Bobrow, D., see Norman & Bobrow (1975).

Bodinger, D., see Banks, Bodinger, & Illige (1974).

Bohr, N. *Atomic theory and the description of nature.* Cambridge, England: Cambridge University Press, 1934. **332**

Bohr, N. *Atomic physics and human knowledge.* New York: Wiley, 1958. **280,332**

Boring, E. G. *Sensation and perception in the history of experimental psychology.* New York: Appleton-Century-Crofts, 1942. **119,129,435**

Boring, E. G. *A history of experimental psychology* (2nd ed.). New York: Appleton-Century-Crofts, 1950. **332**

Bosserman, R. W., see Patten, Bosserman, Finn, & Cale (1976).

Bouma, H., & Andriessen, J. J. Induced changes in the perceived orientation of line segments. *Vision Research,* 1970, *10,* 333-349. **23**

Bouman, M. A., see Van Nes, Koenderink, Nas, & Bouman (1967).

Bower, G. H. A selective review of organizational factors in memory. In E. Tulving & W. Donaldson (Eds.), *Organization of memory.* New York: Academic Press, 1970. (a) **198**

Bower, G. H. Imagery as a relational organizer in associative learning. *Journal of Verbal Learning and Verbal Behavior,* 1970, *9,* 529-533. (b) **219**

Boys, Sir C. V. *Soap bubbles, their colours and the forces which mold them.* New York: Dover, 1959. (Originally published, 1912.) **451**

Bradley, D. R., Dumais, S. T., & Petry, H. M. Reply to Cavonius. *Nature,* 1976, *261* (May 6), 77-78. **271,448**

Bransford, J. D., see Franks & Bransford (1971).

Bransford, J. D., see Shaw & Bransford (1977).

Braunstein, M. L. *Depth perception through motion.* New York: Academic Press, 1976. **289,323**

Bregman, A. S. Perception and behavior as compositions of ideals. *Cognitive Psychology,* 1977, *9,* 250-292. **102**

Bregman, A. S. The formation of auditory streams. In J. Requin (Ed.), *Attention and performance VII.* Hillsdale, N.J.: Lawrence Erlbaum Associates, 1978. **59,82,110,203,206**

Bregman, A. S., & Achim, A. Visual stream segregation. *Perception & Psychophysics,* 1973, *13,* 451-454. **60**

Bregman, A. S., & Campbell, J. Primary auditory stream segregation and the perception of order in rapid sequences of tones. *Journal of Experimental Psychology,* 1971, *89,* 244-249. **59,101,110, 116,tape**

Bregman, A. S., & Dannenbring, G. L. The effect of continuity on auditory stream segregation. *Perception & Psychophysics,* 1973, *13,* 308-312. **59,110,tape**

Bregman, A. S., & Dannenbring, G. L. Auditory continuity and amplitude edges. *Canadian Journal of Psychology,* 1977, *31,* 151-159. **108,117**

Bregman, A. S., & Pinker, S. Auditory streaming and the building of timbre. *Canadian Journal of Psychology,* 1978, *32,* 19-31. **112,tape**

Caelli, T. M., & Julesz, B. On perceptual analyzers underlying visual texture discrimination: Part I. *Biological Cybernetics*, 1978, *28*, 167-175. **37,38,45,48,49**

Caelli, T. M., Julesz, B., & Gilbert, E. N. On perceptual analyzers underlying visual texture discrimination: Part II. *Biological Cybernetics*, 1978, *29*, 201-214. **34,35,39-44**

Cale, W., see Patten, Bosserman, Finn, & Cale (1976).

Campbell, F. W., & Howell, E. R. Monocular alternation: A method for the investigation of pattern vision. *Journal of Physiology*, 1972, *225*, 19-21. **13**

Campbell, F. W., & Kulikowski, J. J. Orientation selectivity of the human visual system. *Journal of Physiology*, 1966, *187*, 437-455. **18**

Campbell, F. W., & Robson, J. G. Application of Fourier analysis to the modulation response of the eye. *Journal of the Optical Society of America*, 1964, *54*, 518A. (Abstract) **4,10**

Campbell, F. W., & Robson, J. G. Application of Fourier analysis to the visibility of gratings. *Journal of Physiology*, 1968, *197*, 551-566. **4,10,45,82**

Campbell, F. W., see Atkinson & Campbell (1974).

Campbell, F. W., see Blakemore & Campbell (1969).

Campbell, F. W., see Furchner, Thomas, & Campbell (1977).

Campbell, J., see Bregman & Campbell (1971).

Carnap, R. *The logical structure of the world* (R. A. George, trans.). Berkeley & Los Angeles: University of California Press, 1967. (Originally published in German, 1928.) **97,280**

Carnap, R. *Introduction to semantics*. Cambridge, England: Cambridge University Press, 1942. **370**

Carpenter, P. A., see Just & Carpenter (1976).

Carpenter, R. H. S., see Blakemore, Carpenter, & Georgeson (1970).

Carroll, J. D., & Chang, J. J. Analysis of individual differences in multi-dimensional scaling via an N-way generalization of "Eckart-Young" decomposition. *Psychometrika*, 1970, *35*, 283-319. **325,328**

Carroll, J. D., see Wish & Carroll (1973).

Cassirer, E. The concept of group and the theory of perception. *Psychologia*, 1944, *5*, 1-35. **259,326**

Ceraso, J., see Asch, Ceraso, & Heimer (1960).

Cermak, G. W., see Shepard & Cermak (1973).

Chambers, S., see Morton & Chambers (1975).

Chambers, S., see Morton & Chambers (1976).

Chang, J. J., & Shepard, R. N. Meaningfulness in classification learning with pronounceable trigrams. *Journal of Verbal Learning and Verbal Behavior*, 1964, *3*, 85-90. **135**

Chang, J. J., see Carroll & Chang (1970).

Chang, J.J., see Julesz & Chang (1976).

Checkosky, S. F., & Whitlock, D. Effects of pattern goodness on recognition time in a memory search task. *Journal of Experimental Psychology*, 1973, *100*, 341-348. **162**

Checkosky, S. F., see Biederman & Checkosky (1970).

Chipman, S., see Shepard & Chipman (1970).

Chomsky, N. *Syntactic structures*. The Hague, Netherlands: Mouton, 1957. **328**

Chomsky, N. *Aspects of the theory of syntax*. Cambridge, Mass.: M.I.T. Press, 1965. **217**

Chomsky, N. *Language and mind*. New York: Harcourt, Brace & World, 1968. **289**

Chomsky, N. *Reflections on language*. New York: Pantheon Books, 1975. **289,340**

Chow, K. L., see Lashley, Chow, & Semmes (1951).

Clark, E. V. Locationals: Study of the relations between existential, locative, and possessive constructions. *Working Papers in Language Universals*, 1970, *3*, 11-36. **336,337**

Clark, E. V. Normal states and evaluative viewpoints. *Language*, 1974, *50*, 116-132. **336,337**

Clark, F. T., see Teft & Clark (1968).

Clark, H. H. Space, time, semantics, and the child. In T. E. Moore (Ed.), *Cognitive development and the acquisition of language*. New York: Academic Press, 1973. **336,338**

Clement, D. E., & Weiman, C. F. R. Instructions, strategies, and pattern uncertainty in a visual discrimination task. *Perception & Psychophysics*, 1970, *7*, 333-336. **137,165**

Clement, D. E., see Garner & Clement (1963).

Coffin, S., see Banks & Coffin (1974).

Cohen, M. R., & Nagel, E. *An introduction to logic and scientific method.* New York: Harcourt Brace, 1934. **370**

Cole, R. A., & Scott, B. Perception of temporal order in speech: The role of vowel transition. *Canadian Journal of Psychology,* 1973, *27,* 441-449. **110**

Collins, A. M., & Loftus, E. F. A spreading-activation theory of semantic processing. *Psychological Review,* 1975, *82,* 407-428. **322**

Coltheart, M. Visual information processing. In P. C. Dodwell (Ed.), *New horizons in psychology 2.* Baltimore, Md.: Penguin Books, 1972. **207**

Condon, W. S., & Sander, L. W. Neonate movement is synchronized with adult speech: Interactional participation and language acquisition. *Science,* 1974, *183,* 99-101. **335**

Conrad, C. Context effects in sentence comprehension: A study of the subjective lexicon. *Memory & Cognition,* 1974, *2,* 130-138. **184**

Cooper, L. A. Mental rotation of random two-dimensional shapes. *Cognitive Psychology,* 1975, *7,* 20-43. **288,293,310**

Cooper, L. A. Demonstration of a mental analog of an external rotation. *Perception & Psychophysics,* 1976, *19,* 296-302. **294,296,310**

Cooper, L. A., & Podgorny, P. Mental transformations and visual comparison processes: Effects of complexity and similarity. *Journal of Experimental Psychology: Human Perception and Performance,* 1976, *2,* 503-514. **288,310**

Cooper, L. A., & Shepard, R. N. Chronometric studies of the rotation of mental images. In W. G. Chase (Ed.), *Visual information processing.* New York: Academic Press, 1973. (a) **288,293,296,310**

Cooper, L. A., & Shepard, R. N. The time required to prepare for a rotated stimulus. *Memory & Cognition,* 1973, *1,* 246-250. (b) **310**

Cooper, L. A., & Shepard, R. N. Mental transformations in the identification of left and right hands. *Journal of Experimental Psychology: Human Perception and Performance,* 1975, *1,* 48-56. **293,311**

Cooper, L. A., & Shepard, R. N. Transformations on representations of objects in space. In E. C. Carterette & M. P. Friedman (Eds.), *Handbook of perception* (Vol. 8). New York: Academic Press, 1978. **293,294,310,311**

Cooper, L. A., see Shepard & Cooper (1975).

Corbin, H. H. The perception of grouping and apparent movement in visual depth. *Archives of Psychology,* 1942 (Whole No. 273). **323**

Coren, S. Subjective contours and apparent depth. *Psychological Review,* 1972, *79,* 359-367. **445,448,449**

Coren, S., & Girgus, J. S. Principles of perceptual organization and spatial distortion: The Gestalt illusions. *Journal of Experimental Psychology: Human Perception and Performance,* 1980, *6,* 404-412. **427**

Coriell, A. S., see Averbach & Coriell (1961).

Cornsweet, T. N. *Visual perception.* New York: Academic Press, 1970. **2**

Corteen, R. S., & Wood, B. Autonomic responses to shock-associated words in an unattended channel. *Journal of Experimental Psychology,* 1972, *94,* 308-313. **189**

Corwin, T., see Green, Corwin, & Zemon (1976).

Coxeter, H. S. M. *Introduction to geometry.* New York: Wiley, 1961. **403**

Cramer, E. M., & Huggins, W. H. Creation of pitch through binaural interaction. *Journal of the Acoustical Society of America,* 1958, *30,* 413-417. **58**

Crowder, R. G. Waiting for the stimulus suffix: Decay, delay, rhythm, and readout in immediate memory. *Quarterly Journal of Experimental Psychology,* 1971, *23,* 324-340. **201,202**

Crowder, R. G. Mechanisms of auditory backward masking in the stimulus suffix effect. *Psychological Review,* 1978, *85,* 502-524. (a) **201-203,205,208**

DeValois, K. K. Spatial frequency adaptation can enhance contrast sensitivity. *Vision Research,* 1977, *17,* 1057-1066. **5**

DeValois, K. K., & Switkes, E. Patterns of randomly positioned dot pairs produce spatial frequency specific adapation. *Investigative Ophthalmology and Visual Science,* 1978, *17,* 243. (Abstract) **5**

Dewey, J., & Bentley, A. F. *Knowing and the known.* Boston: Beacon, 1949. **366,367,370-372,376**

Dewey, J., & Bentley, A. F. *A philosophical correspondence, 1932-1951.* New Brunswick, N.J.: Rutgers University Press, 1964. **367,371**

Distelhorst, J., see Sansbury, Distelhorst, & Moore (1978).

Divenyi, P. L., & Hirsh, I. J. Identification of temporal order in three-tone sequences. *Journal of the Acoustical Society of America,* 1974, *56,* 144-151. **83**

Divenyi, P. L., & Hirsh, I. J. The effect of blanking on the identification of temporal order in three-tone sequences. *Perception & Psychophysics,* 1975, *17,* 246-252. **83**

Dixon, P. Numerical comparison processes. *Memory & Cognition,* 1978, *6,* 454-461. **329**

Dixon, P., & Just, M. A. Normalization of irrelevant dimensions in stimulus comparisons. *Journal of Experimental Psychology: Human Perception and Performance,* 1978, *4,* 36-46. **329,330**

Dorman, M. F., Cutting, J. E., & Raphael, L. J. Perception of temporal order in vowel sequences with and without formant transitions. *Journal of Experimental Psychology: Human Perception and Performance,* 1975, *4,* 121-129. **110**

Duifhuis, H. Audibility of high harmonics in a periodic pulse. *Journal of the Acoustical Society of America,* 1970, *48,* 888-893. **66**

Duifhuis, H. Audibility of high harmonics in a periodic pulse. II. Time effect. *Journal of the Acoustical Society of America,* 1971, *49,* 1155-1162. **66**

Dumais, S. T., see Bradley, Dumais & Petry (1976).

Durlach, N. I. Binaural signal detection: Equalization and cancellation theory. In J. V. Tobias (Ed.), *Foundations of modern auditory theory (Vol. 2).* New York: Academic Press, 1972. **58**

Dyer, F. N. The Stroop phenomenon and its use in the study of perceptual, cognitive, and response processes. *Memory & Cognition,* 1973, *1,* 106-120. (a) **184**

Dyer, F. N. Interference and facilitation for color naming for separate bilateral presentation of the word and the color. *Journal of Experimental Psychology,* 1973, *99,* 314-317. (b) **186**

E

Ebert, R., see Pronko, Ebert, & Greenberg (1966).

Eccles, J. C. *The understanding of the brain.* New York: McGraw-Hill, 1977. **50**

Eddington, A. S. *Space, time and gravitation.* Cambridge, England: Cambridge University Press, 1920. **340**

Egeth, H. E. Parallel versus serial processes in multidimensional stimulus discrimination. *Perception & Psychophysics,* 1966, *1,* 245-252. **165**

Egeth, H., Jonides, J., & Wall, S. Parallel processing of multi-element displays. *Cognitive Psychology,* 1972, *3,* 674-698. **193,239,240,242**

Egeth, H. E., see Gatti & Egeth (1978).

Ehrenfels, C. von Uber Gestaltqualitäten. *Vierteljahrschrift für Wissenschaftliche Philosophie,* 1890, *14,* 249-292. **78**

Eigen, M., & Winkler, R. Das Spiel. Munich: R. Piper, 1975. **50**

Eimas, P. D., see Riggs, White, & Eimas (1974).

Ellis, S. R. Orientation selectivity of the McCollough effect: Analysis by equivalent contrast transformation. *Perception & Psychophysics,* 1977, *22,* 539-545. **18**

Emery, D. A., see Köhler & Emery (1947).

Emlen, S. T. Celestial rotation: Its importance in the development of migratory orientation. *Science,* 1970, *170,* 1198-1201. **334**

Emlen, S. T. Celestial rotation and stellar orientation in migratory warblers. *Science,* 1971, *173,* 460-461. **334**

Emlen, S. T. Migration: Orientation and navigation. In D. S. Farner & J. R. King (Eds.), *Avian biology* (Vol. 5). New York: Academic Press, 1975. **334**

Engel, F. L., see Ritsma & Engel (1964).

Enroth-Cugell, C., & Robson, J. G. The contrast sensitivity of retinal ganglion cells of the cat. *Journal of Physiology*, 1966, *187*, 517-552. **4**

Erickson, R. P. Stimulus coding in topographic and nontopographic afferent modalities: On the significance of the activity of individual sensory neurons. *Psychological Review*, 1968, *75*, 447-465. **77**

Eriksen, B., & Eriksen, C. W. Effects of noise letters upon the identification of a target letter in a nonsearch task. *Perception & Psychophysics*, 1974, *16*, 143-149. **186**

Eriksen, C. W., & Hoffman, J. E. Temporal and spatial characteristics of selective coding from visual displays. *Perception & Psychophysics*, 1972, *12*, 201-204. **186**

Eriksen, C. W., & Hoffman, J. E. Selective attention: Noise suppression or signal enchancement? *Bulletin of the Psychonomic Society*, 1974, *4*, 587-589. **186**

Eriksen, C. W., see Eriksen & Eriksen (1974).

Eriksen, C. W., see Garner, Hake, & Eriksen (1956).

Estes, W. K. An associative basis for coding and organization in memory. In A. W. Melton & E. Martin (Eds.), *Coding processes in human memory*. Washington, D.C.: Winston, 1972. (a) **198**

Estes, W. K. Interaction of signal and background variables in visual processing. *Perception & Psychophysics*, 1972, *12*, 278-286. (b) **191,192,208**

Estes, W. K. Redundancy of noise elements and signals in the visual detection of letters. *Perception & Psychophysics*, 1974, *16*, 53-60. **191,192**

Estes, W. K., Allmeyer, D., & Reder, S. Serial position functions for letter identification at brief and extended exposure durations. *Perception & Psychophysics*, 1976, *19*, 1-15. **198,208**

Estes, W. K., & Wolford, G. L. Effects of spaces on report from tachistoscopically presented letter strings. *Psychonomic Science*, 1971, *25*, 77-80. **198**

Evans, N. J., see Lockhead, Gaylord, & Evans (1977).

F

Farber, J., & McConkie, A. Linkages between apparent depth and motion in linear flow fields. *Bulletin of the Psychonomic Society*, 1977, *10*, 250. (Abstract) **277**

Farmer, R. M., see Warren, Obusek, Farmer, & Warren (1969).

Farrell, J. E., & Shepard, R. N. Shape, orientation, and apparent rotational motion. *Journal of Experimental Psychology: Human Perception and Performance*, in press. **317,318**

Felfoldy, G. Repetition effects in choice reaction time to multidimensional stimuli. *Perception & Psychophysics*, 1974, *15*, 453-459. **148**

Feng, C., see Shepard & Feng (1972).

Fillmore, C. F. The case for case. In E. Bach & R. T. Harms (Eds.), *Universals in linguistic theory*. New York: Holt, Rinehart & Winston, 1968. **336-338**

Fillmore, C. F. *Lectures on deixis at the University of California at Santa Cruz, summer 1971*. Unpublished manuscript, Department of Linguistics, University of California at Berkeley, 1971. **335,336**

Finke, R. A., & Schmidt, M. J. Orientation-specific color after-effects following imagination. *Journal of Experimental Psychology: Human Perception and Performance*, 1977, *3*, 599-606. **9**

Finn, J. T., see Patten, Bosserman, Finn, & Cale (1976).

Fiorentini, S., Sireteanu, R., & Spinelli, D. Lines and gratings: Different interocular after-effects. *Vision Research*, 1976, *16*, 1303-1309. **5**

Fischer, S., see Bellugi & Fischer (1972).

Fitch, H., & Turvey, M. T. On the control of activity: Some remarks from an ecological view. In B. Landers & R. Christina (Eds.), *Psychology of motor behavior and sport*. Urbana, Ill.: Human Kinetics, 1978. **353,358,364**

Fodor, J. A. *The language of thought.* New York: Thomas Y. Crowell, 1975. **356,357**

Foster, D. H. Visual apparent motion and the calculus of variations. In E. L. J. Leeuwenberg, & H. F. J. M. Buffart (Eds.), *Formal theories of visual perception.* New York: Wiley, 1978. **312,313**

Fowler, C. A., & Turvey, M. T. The concept of "command neurons" in explanations of behavior. *Behavioral and Brain Sciences,* 1978, *1,* 20-22. **361**

Fowler, C. A., & Turvey, M. T. Observational perspective and descriptive level in perceiving and acting. In W. Weimer & D. Palermo (Eds.), *Cognition and the symbolic processes II.* Hillsdale, N.J.: Lawrence Erlbaum Associates, 1981. **349,411**

Fraisse, P., see Hirsh & Fraisse (1964).

Frank, P. *Foundations of physics.* Chicago: University of Chicago Press, 1946. **376**

Franks, J. J., & Bransford, J. D. Abstraction of visual patterns. *Journal of Experimental Psychology,* 1971, *90,* 65-74. **326**

Friedman, C., & Pastore, R. E. The effects of lateralization on selective and divided attention. *Journal of the Acoustical Society of America,* 1977, *62* (Suppl. 1: Program of the 94th Meeting of the Acoustical Society of America, Miami Beach, December 1977), S1. (Abstract) **92**

Frisch, H. L., see Julesz, Gilbert, Shepp, & Frisch (1973).

Frisch, K. von *Animal architecture.* New York: Harcourt Brace Jovanovich, 1974. **397-401,405**

Fromkin, V. A. Slips of the tongue. *Scientific American,* 1973, *229,* 110-117. **144**

Frost, R., see Attneave & Frost (1969).

Fryklund, I. Effects of cued-set spatial arrangement and target-background similarity in the partial-report paradigm. *Perception & Psychophysics,* 1975, *17,* 375-386. **189,190**

Furchner, C., Thomas, J., & Campbell, F. W. Detection and discrimination of simple and complex patterns at low spatial frequencies. *Vision Research,* 1977, *17,* 827-836. **13**

G

Galanter, E., see Miller, Galanter, & Pribram (1960).

Galie, A., see Hock, Romanski, Galie, & Williams (1978).

Gallistel, C. R. *The organization of action: A new synthesis.* Hillsdale, N.J.: Lawrence Erlbaum Associates, 1980. **334**

Ganz, L., see Breitmeyer & Ganz (1976).

Ganz, L., see Breitmeyer & Ganz (1977).

Ganz, L., see Kline, Stromeyer, & Ganz (1974).

Garner, W. R. *Uncertainty and structure as psychological concepts.* New York: Wiley, 1962. **263,437**

Garner, W. R. Good patterns have few alternatives. *American Scientist,* 1970, *58,* 34-42. (a) **263,437**

Garner, W. R. The stimulus in information processing. *American Psychologist,* 1970, *25,* 350-358. (b) **161**

Garner, W. R. Attention: The processing of multiple sources of information. In E. C. Carterette & M. P. Friedman (Eds.), *Handbook of perception* (Vol. 2). New York: Academic Press, 1974. (a) **89**

Garner, W. R. *The processing of informaion and structure.* Hillsdale, N.J.: Lawrence Erlbaum Associates, 1974. (b) **82,85,120,127,130,137,138,239,326,424**

Garner, W. R. Aspects of a stimulus: Features, dimensions, and configurations. In E. H. Rosch & B. B. Lloyd (Eds.), *Cognition and categorization.* Hillsdale, N.J.: Lawrence Erlbaum Associates, 1978. (a) **85,123**

Garner, W. R. Selective attention to attributes and to stimuli. *Journal of Experimental Psychology: General,* 1978, *107,* 287-308. (b) **124,132,133,154**

Garner, W. R., & Clement, D. E. Goodness of pattern and pattern uncertainty. *Journal of Verbal Learning and Verbal Behavior,* 1963, *2,* 446-452. **165**

Garner, W. R., Hake, H. W., & Eriksen, C. W. Operationism and the concept of perception. *Psychological Review,* 1956, *63,* 149-159. **127,281**

Garner, W. R., & Morton, J. Perceptual independence: Definitions, models, and experimental paradigms. *Psychological Bulletin*, 1969, *72*, 233-259. **125**

Garner, W. R., & Sutliff, D. The effects of goodness on encoding time. *Perception & Psychophyscis*, 1974, *16*, 426-430. **130,162**

Garner, W. R., see Gottwald & Garner (1975).

Garner, W. R., see Pomerantz & Garner (1973).

Garner, W. R., see Sebrechts & Garner (1980).

Gatti, S. V., & Egeth, H. E. Failure of spatial selectivity in vision. *Bulletin of the Psychonomic Society*, 1978, *11*, 181-184. **186**

Gauthier, R. *Metrics and models in form perception.* Unpublished doctoral dissertation, Stanford University, 1977. **299**

Gaylord, S. A., see Lockhead, Gaylord, & Evans (1977).

Gebhardt, J. W., & Mowbray, G. H. On discriminating the rate of visual flicker and auditory flutter. *American Journal of Psychology*, 1959, *72*, 521-528. **85**

Geffen, G., see Treisman & Geffen (1967).

Gelade, G., see Treisman & Gelade (1979).

Gellman, L., see Hochberg & Gellman (1977).

Gengel, R. W., & Hirsh, I. J. Temporal order: The effect of single versus repeated presentations, practice, and verbal feedback. *Perception & Psychophysics*, 1970, *7*, 209-211. **83**

Gentry, T., see Skowbo, Timney, Gentry, & Morant (1975).

Georgeson, M. A. Antagonism between channels for pattern and movement in human vision. *Nature*, 1976, *259*, 413-415. (a) **14**

Georgeson, M. A. Psychophysical hallucinations of orientation and spatial frequency. *Perception*, 1976, *5*, 99-111. (b) **14**

Georgeson, M. A., & Sullivan, G. D. Contrast consistency: Deblurring in human vision by spatial frequency channels. *Journal of Physiology*, 1975, *252*, 627-656. **5,23**

Georgeson, M. A., see Blakemore, Carpenter, & Georgeson (1970).

Georgeson, M. A., see Sullivan, Georgeson, & Oatley (1972).

Gervais, M. J., see Harvey & Gervais (1977).

Gibson, A. R., see Harris & Gibson (1968).

Gibson, E. J. *Principles of perceptual learning and development.* New York: Appleton-Century-Crofts, 1969. **127**

Gibson, E. J., Owsley, C. J., & Johnston, J. Perception of invariants by five-month-old infants: Differentiation of two types of motion. *Developmental Psychology*, 1978, *4*, 407-415. **312**

Gibson, J. J. *The perception of the visual world.* Boston: Houghton Mifflin, 1950. **260,424,451**

Gibson, J. J. Ecological optics. *Vision Research*, 1961, *1*, 253-262. **349**

Gibson, J. J. *The senses considered as perceptual systems.* Boston: Houghton Mifflin, 1966. **76,82,99,128,225,267,285,297,311, 326,344,349,362,411,451**

Gibson, J. J. The theory of affordances. In R. E. Shaw & J. D. Bransford (Eds.), *Perceiving, acting, and knowing.* Hillsdale, N.J.: Lawrence Erlbaum Associates, 1977. **326,358,363,364**

Gibson, J. J. *The ecological approach to visual perception.* Boston: Houghton Mifflin, 1979. **144,451,453**

Gibson, J. J., Olum, P., & Rosenblatt, F. Parallax and perspective during aircraft landings. *American Journal of Psychology*, 1955, *68*, 372-385. **266,268**

Giese, J., see Wilson & Giese (1977).

Gilbert, E. N., see Caelli, Julesz, & Gilbert (1975).

Gilbert, E. N., see Julesz, Gilbert, & Victor (1978).

Gilbert, E. N., see Julesz, Gilbert, Shepp, & Frisch (1973).

Gilchrist, A. L. Perceived lightness depends on perceived spatial arrangement. *Science*, 1977, *75*, 185-187. **108**

Ginsburg, A. *Psychological correlates of a model of the human visual system.* Unpublished master's thesis, Air Force Institute of Technology, 1971. **23**

Gregory, R. L., & Harris, J. P. Illusion-destruction by appropriate scaling. *Perception*, 1975, *4*, 203–220. **262,278**

Griffin, D. R. A possible window on the minds of animals. *American Scientist*, 1976, *64*, 530–535. **334**

Gruber, J. S. *Studies in lexical relations*. Unpublished doctoral dissertation, Massachusetts Institute of Technology, 1965. **336**

Gruber, J. S. Look and see. *Language*, 1967, *43*, 937–947. **336,338**

Günther, B. Dimensional analysis and theory of biological similarity. *Physiological Review*, 1975, *55*, 659–699. **400**

Guttman, N., see Julesz & Guttman (1965).

Guzman, A. *Computer recognition of three-dimensional objects in a visual scene* (Project MAC Tech. Rep. 59). Cambridge, Mass.: M.I.T., Artificial Intelligence Laboratory, December 1968. (a) **217,219,221–223**

Guzman, A. Decomposition of a visual scene into three-dimensional bodies. *AFJPS, Fall Joint Computer Conference*, 1968, *33*, 291–304. (b) **309**

H

Hake, H. W., see Garner, Hake, & Eriksen (1956).

Halper, F., see Rock, Schauer, & Halper (1976).

Halpern, Lynn. *The effect of harmonic ratio relationships on auditory stream segregation*. Undergraduate research report, Department of Psychology, McGill University, Montreal, Quebec, 1977. **113**

Hamerly, J. R., Quick, R. F., Jr., & Reichert, T. A. A study of grating contrast judgement. *Vision Research*, 1977, *17*, 201–207. **12**

Hamerly, J. R., see Quick, Hamerly, & Reichert (1976).

Handel, S., see Bell & Handel (1976).

Haraway, D. J. *Crystals, fabrics and fields: Metaphors of organicism in twentieth century developmental biology*. New Haven, Conn.: Yale University Press, 1976. **365**

Harm, O. J., see Lappin, Bell, Harm, & Kottas (1975).

Harmon, L. D., & Julesz, B. Masking in visual recognition: Effects of two-dimensional filtered noise. *Science*, 1973, *180*, 1194–1197. **13**

Harris, C. S. Effect of viewing distance on a color aftereffect specific to spatial frequency. *Psychonomic Science*, 1970, *21*, 350. **9**

Harris, C. S. Orientation-specific color after effects dependent on retinal spatial frequency, rather than on stripe width. *Journal of the Optical Society of America*, 1971, *61*, 689. (Abstract) **9**

Harris, C. S. Insight or out of sight?: Two examples of perceptual plasticity in the human adult. In C. S. Harris (Ed.), *Visual coding and adaptability*. Hillsdale, N.J.: Lawrence Erlbaum Associates, 1979. **10**

Harris, C. S., & Gibson, A. R. Is orientation-specific color adaptation in human vision due to edge detectors, afterimages or "dipoles"? *Science*, 1968, *162*, 1506–1507. **6**

Harris, C. S., see Weisstein & Harris (1974).

Harris, C. S., see Weisstein & Harris (1980).

Harris, C. S., see Weisstein, Harris, Berbaum, Tangney, & Williams (1977).

Harris, J. P., see Gregory & Harris (1975).

Hart, G., see Tolhurst, Sharpe, & Hart (1973).

Hartline, H. K., see Ratliff & Hartline (1959).

Harvey, L. O., & Gervais, M. J. Fourier analysis and the perceptual similarity of texture. *Investigative Ophthalmology and Visual Science*, 1977, *16*(supplement), 48. (Abstract) **14,22**

Hauske, G., see Lupp, Hauske, & Wolf (1976).

Hay, J. Optical motions and space perception: An extension of Gibson's analysis. *Psychological Review*, 1966, *73*, 550–565. **268**

Hochberg, J. Perception: Toward the recovery of a definition. *Psychological Review*, 1956, *63*, 400–405. **259**

Hochberg, J. Nativism and empiricism in perception. In L. Postman (Ed.), *Psychology in the making*. New York: Knopf, 1962. **274**

Hochberg, J. In the mind's eye. In R. N. Haber (Ed.), *Contemporary theory and research in visual perception*. New York: Holt, Rinehart & Winston, 1968. **258,265,271,272,276**

Hochberg, J. Attention, organization and consciousness. In D. L. Mostofsky (Ed.), *Attention: Contemporary theory and analysis*. New York: Appleton-Century-Crofts, 1970. **152,276**

Hochberg, J. Perception: I. Color and shape. In J. W. Kling & L. A. Riggs (Eds.), *Woodworth & Schlosberg's experimental psychology* (3rd ed.). New York: Holt, Rinehart & Winston, 1971. (a) **84,274,275**

Hochberg, J. Perception: II. Space and movement. In J. W. Kling & L. A. Riggs (Eds.), *Woodworth & Schlosberg's experimental psychology* (3rd ed.). New York: Holt, Rinehart & Winston, 1971. (b) **274,275**

Hochberg, J. Higher order stimuli and interresponse coupling in the perception of the visual world. In R. B. MacLeod & H. L. Pick (Eds.), *Perception: Essays in honor of James J. Gibson*. Ithaca: N.Y., Cornell University Press, 1974. (a) **259,274**

Hochberg, J. Organization and the Gestalt tradition. In E. C. Carterette & M. P. Friedman (Eds.), *Handbook of perception* (Vol. 1). New York: Academic Press, 1974. (b) **86,160,275,428**

Hochberg, J. Personal communication, November 9, 1977. **308**

Hochberg, J. *Perception* (2nd ed.). New York: Prentice-Hall, 1978. (a) **262,269,271,272,443,444**

Hochberg, J. *Motion pictures of mental structures*. Presidential address given at the meeting of the Eastern Psychological Association, Washington, D.C., March 29–April 1, 1978. (b) **273,274**

Hochberg, J. Sensation and perception. In E. Hearst (Ed.), *The first century of experimental psychology*. Hillsdale, N.J.: Lawrence Erlbaum Associates, 1979. **259,261**

Hochberg, J. Personal communication, August 1979. **434**

Hochberg, J., & Brooks, V. The psychophysics of form: Reversible perspective drawings of spatial objects. *American Journal of Psychology*, 1960, *73*, 337–354. **263,265,286,439**

Hochberg, J., & Brooks, V. The integration of successive cinematic views of simple scenes. *Bulletin of the Psychonomic Society*, 1974, *4*, 263. (Abstract) **268–270**

Hochberg, J., Brooks, V., & Roule, P. J. *Movies of mazes (and wallpaper)*. Paper presented at the meeting of the Eastern Psychological Association, Boston, April 13–16, 1977. **270**

Hochberg, J., & Gellman, L. The effect of landmark features on mental rotation times. *Memory & Cognition*, 1977, *5*, 23–26. **268**

Hochberg, J., Green, J., & Virostek, S. *Texture-occlusion as a foveal depth cue*. Paper presented at the meeting of the American Psychological Association, Toronto, August 28–September 1, 1978. **266,267**

Hochberg, J., & McAlister, E. A quantitative approach to figure "goodness." *Journal of Experimental Psychology*, 1953, *46*, 361–364. **263,286,307,439**

Hochberg, J., & Silverstein, A. A quantitative index of stimulus similarity: Proximity vs. differences in brightness. *American Journal of Psychology*, 1956, *69*, 456–458. **427**

Hock, H. S., Romanski, L., Galie, A., & Williams, C. S. Real-world schemata and scene recognition in adults and children. *Memory & Cognition*, 1978, *6*, 423–431. **218,221,230**

Høffding, H. *Outlines of psychology*. New York: Macmillan, 1891. **332**

Hoffman, J. E. Interaction between global and local levels of a form. *Journal of Experimental Psychology: Human Perception & Performance*, 1980, *6*, 222–234. **175**

Hoffman, J. E., see Eriksen & Hoffman (1974).

Hoffman, W. C. The Lie algebra of visual perception. *Journal of Mathematical Psychology*, 1966, *3*, 65–98. (Errata, *ibid.*, 1967, *4*, 348–349.) **329,429**

Hoffman, W. C., see Caelli, Hoffman, & Lindman (1978a).

Hoffman, W. C., see Caelli, Hoffman, & Lindman (1978b).

Holding, D. H., see Jones & Holding (1975).

Jansson, G., see Johansson, von Hofsten, & Jansson (1980).

Jeffress, L. A. Binaural signal detection: Vector theory. In J. V. Tobias (Ed.), *Foundations of modern auditory theory* (Vol. 2). New York: Academic Press, 1972. **58,75**

Jensen, A. R., & Rohwer, W. D. The Stroop color–word test: A review. *Acta Psychologica*, 1966, *25*, 36–93. **184**

Johansson, G. *Configurations in event perception.* Uppsala, Sweden: Almqvist & Wiksell, 1950. **258,326,451**

Johansson, G. Perception of motion and changing form. *Scandinavian Journal of Psychology*, 1964, *5*, 181–208. **113,451**

Johansson, G. Visual perception of biological motion and a model for its analysis. *Perception & Psychophysics*, 1973, *14*, 201–211. **113**

Johansson, G. Projective transformations as determining visual space perception. In R. B. MacLeod & H. L. Pick (Eds.), *Perception: Essays in honor of James J. Gibson*. Ithaca, N.Y.: Cornell University Press, 1974. (a) **451**

Johansson, G. Visual perception of rotary motion as transformations of conic sections. *Psychologia*, 1974, *17*, 226–237. (b) **451**

Johansson, G. Visual motion perception. *Scientific American*, 1975, *232*, 76–88. **142.**

Johansson, G. Spatio-temporal differentiation and integration in visual motion perception. *Psychological Research*, 1976, *38*, 379–393. **326**

Johansson, G. Spatial constancy and motion in visual perception. In W. Epstein (Ed.), *Stability and constancy in visual perception: Mechanisms and processes*. New York: Wiley, 1977. **258,267**

Johansson, G., von Hofsten, C., & Jansson, G. Event perception. *Annual Review of Psychology*, 1980, *31*, 27–63. **385**

Johnson, N. F. The role of chunking and organization in the process of recall. In G. H. Bower (Ed.), *The Psychology of Learning and Motivation* (Vol. 4). New York: Academic Press, 1970. **198**

Johnson, N. F. Organization and the concept of a memory code. In A. W. Melton & E. Martin (Eds.), *Coding processes in human memory*. Washington, D.C.: Winston, 1972. **198**

Johnston, J. C., & McClelland, J. L. Visual factors in word perception. *Perception & Psychophysics*, 1973, *14*, 365–370. **166**

Johnston, J. C., & McClelland, J. L. Perception of letters in words: Seek not and ye shall find. *Science*, 1974, *184*, 1192–1194. **166**

Jones, M. R. Time, our lost dimension: Toward a new theory of perception, attention, and memory. *Psychological Review*, 1976, *83*, 323–355. **60,319,324**

Jones, P. D., & Holding, D. H. Extremely long-term persistence of the McCollough effect. *Journal of Experimental Psychology: Human Perception and Performance*, 1975, *1*, 323–327. **9**

Jones, R., & Tulunay-Keesey, U. Local retinal adaptation and spatial frequency channels. *Vision Research*, 1975, *15*, 1239–1244. **6**

Jonides, J., & Gleitman, H. H. A conceptual category effect in visual search: O as letter or as digit. *Perception & Psychophysics*, 1972, *12*, 457–460. **183**

Jonides, J., see Egeth, Jonides, & Wall (1972).

Jonides, J., see Gleitman & Jonides (1978).

Jordan, R., see Kubovy & Jordan (1979).

Judd, S. A., see Shepard & Judd (1976).

Julesz, B. Binocular depth perception of computer-generated patterns. *Bell System Technical Journal*, 1960, *39*, 1125–1162. **46,47**

Julesz, B. Visual pattern discrimination. *IRE Transactions on Information Theory*, 1962, *IT-8*, 84–92. **27,29,31,34**

Julesz, B. Binocular depth perception without familiarity cues. *Science*, 1964, *145*, 356–362. **46,47**

Julesz, B. Texture and visual perception. *Scientific American*, 1965, *212*(2), 38–48. **34,53**

Julesz, B. *Foundations of cyclopean perception*. Chicago: University of Chicago Press, 1971. **27,46,55–57,77,86,429**

Julesz, B. Experiments in the visual perception of texture. *Scientific American*, 1975, *232*(4), 34–43. **28–30,34,155,156**

L

LaBerge, D. H. Identification of two compounds of the time to switch attention: A test of a serial and a parallel model of attention. In S. Kornblum (Ed.), *Attention and performance IV*. New York: Academic Press, 1973. **182,183**

LaBerge, D. Acquisition of automatic processing in perceptual and associative learning. In P. M. A. Rabbitt & S. Dornic (Eds.), *Attention and performance V*. New York: Academic Press, 1975. **182,184,189**

Lackner, F. R., & Goldstein, L. M. Primary auditory stream segregation of repeated consonant-vowel sequences. *Journal of the Acoustical Society of America*, 1974, 56, 1651-1652. **110**

Lange, R., Sigel, C., & Stecher, S. Adapted and unadapted spatial-frequency channels in human vision. *Vision Research*, 1973, *13*, 2139-2143. **10**

Lange, R., see Arend & Lange (1978).

Lange, R., see Stecher, Sigel, & Lange (1973).

Lappin, J. S., Bell, H. H., Harm, O. J., & Kottas, B. On the relation between time and space in the visual discrimination of velocity. *Journal of Experimental Psychology: Human Perception and Performance*, 1975, *1*, 383-394. **163**

Larkin, W. D., see Greenberg & Larkin (1968).

Larsen, A., & Bundesen, C. Size scaling in visual pattern recognition. *Journal of Experimental Psychology: Human Perception and Performance*, 1978, *4*, 1-20. **310,329**

Larsen, A., see Bundesen & Larsen (1975).

Larson, D., see Banks, Bachrach, & Larson (1977).

Lashley, K. S., Chow, K. L., & Semmes, J. An examination of the electrical field theory of cerebral integration. *Psychological Review*, 1951, *58*, 123-136. **428**

Lee, D. N. Visual information during locomotion. In R. B. MacLeod & H. L. Pick (Eds.), *Perception: Essays in honor of James J. Gibson*. Ithaca, N.Y.: Cornell University Press, 1974. **266,268,358,451**

Lee, D. N. The functions of vision. In H. L. Pick & E. Saltzman (Eds.), *Modes of perceiving and processing information*. Hillsdale, N.J.: Lawrence Erlbaum Associates, 1976. **358**

Leeuwenberg, E. L. J. A perceptual coding language for visual and auditory patterns. *American Journal of Psychology*, 1971, *84*, 307-349. **286**

Leeuwenberg, E. L. J. Quantification of certain visual pattern properties: Salience, transparency, similarity. In E. L. J. Leeuwenberg & H. F. J. M. Buffart (Eds.), *Formal theories of visual perception*. Chichester, England: Wiley, 1978. **437**

Legge, G. Adaptation to a spatial impulse: Implications for Fourier transform models of visual processing. *Vision Research*, 1976, *16*, 1407-1418. **5**

Legge, G. Sustained and transient mechanisms in human vision: Temporal and spatial properties. *Vision Research*, 1978, *18*, 69-81. **6,20**

Lenneberg, E. H. *Biological foundations of language*. New York: Wiley, 1967. **335**

Lettvin, J. Y., Maturana, H. R., McCulloch, W. S., & Pitts, W. H. What the frog's eye tells the frog's brain. *Proceedings of the Institute of Radio Engineers*, 1959, *47*, 1940-1951. **48**

Levinson, E., see Sekuler & Levinson (1977).

Levinson, G., see Sekuler, Pantle, & Levinson (1978).

Levitt, H., see Julesz & Levitt (1966).

Lewis, C. I. The modes of meaning. *Philosophy and Phenomenological Research*, 1943, *4*, 326-349. **370**

Lewontin, R. C. Adaptation. *Scientific American*, 1978, *239*, 212-230. **364**

Lichten, W., see Miller, Heise, & Lichten (1951).

Limb, J. O., & Rubinstein, C. B. A model of threshold vision incorporating inhomogeneity of the visual field. *Vision Research*, 1977, *17*, 571-584. **19**

Lindsay, P. H., & Norman, D. A. *Human information processing*. New York: Academic Press, 1977. **152,162**

Lindsay, R. K., & Lindsay, J. M. Reaction time and serial versus parallel information processing. *Journal of Experimental Psychology,* 1966, *71,* 294–303. **164**

Lindsay, J. M., see Lindsay & Lindsay (1966).

Lindvall, T., see Berglund, Berglund, & Lindvall (1976).

Lockhead, G. R., Gaylord, S. A., & Evans, N. J. *Priming with nonprototypical colors.* Paper presented at the annual meeting of the Psychonomic Society, Washington, D.C., November 11, 1977. **329**

Lockhead, G. R., & King, M. C. Classifying integral stimuli. *Journal of Experimental Psychology: Human Perception and Performance,* 1977, *3,* 436–443. **148**

Lockhead, G. R., see Hutchinson & Lockhead (1977).

Loeb, A. L. *Color and symmetry.* New York: Wiley, 1971. **87**

Loftus, E. F., see Collins & Loftus (1975).

Loftus, G. R., & Mackworth, N. H. Cognitive determinants of fixation location during picture viewing. *Journal of Experimental Psychology: Human Perception and Performance,* 1978, *4,* 565–576. **230**

Lopes Cardozo, B., see Schouten, Ritsma, & Lopes Cardozo (1962).

Lorber, C. M., see White & Lorber (1976).

Lovegrove, W. J., & Over, R. Color adaptation of spatial frequency detectors in the human visual system. *Science,* 1972, *176,* 541–543. **9**

Lucas, J. R. *A treatise on time and space.* London: Methuen, 1973. **96–98**

Lupp, U., Hauske, G., & Wolf, W. Perceptual latencies to sinusoidal gratings. *Vision Research,* 1976, *16,* 969–972. **20**

Lynch, K. *The image of the city.* Cambridge, Mass.: M.I.T. Press, 1960. **268**

M

Mace, W., see Shaw, Turvey, & Mace (1981).

Mace, W., see Turvey, Shaw, & Mace (1981).

Mach, E. Über die physiologische Wirkug räumliche verheilter Lichtreise. *Sitzungsberichte Mathematisch-naturwissenschaftlichen Classe der Kaiserlichen Akademie der Wissenschaften, Wien,* 1868, *57,* 11–19. **429**

Mach, E. *Contributions to the analysis of the sensations* (C. M. Williams, trans.). Chicago: Open Court, 1897. (Originally published in German, 1886.) **438**

Mach, E. *The analysis of sensations and the relation of the physical to the psychical* (C. M. Williams, trans.; S. Waterlow, rev. & suppl.). New York: Dover, 1959. (Originally published in German, 1906.) **77,78,308**

MacKay, D. M. The epistemological problem for automata. In C. E. Shannon & J. McCarthy (Eds.), *Automata studies.* Princeton, N.J.: Princeton University Press, 1955. **333**

MacKay, D. M. *Information, mechanism and meaning.* Boston: M.I.T. Press, 1969. **360,361**

MacKay, D. M., & MacKay, V. Antagonism between visual channels for pattern and movement? *Nature,* 1976, *263,* 312–314. **14**

MacKay, V., see MacKay & MacKay (1976).

Mackworth, N. H., & Morandi, A. J. The gaze selects informative details within pictures. *Perception & Psychophysics,* 1967, *2,* 547–552. **230**

Mackworth, N. H., see Loftus & Mackworth (1978).

MacLane, S., & Birkhoff, G. *Algebra.* New York: Macmillan, 1967. **384**

MacLeod, D. I. A. Visual sensitivity. *Annual Review of Psychology,* 1978, *29,* 613–645. **21**

Macmillan, N. A., & Schwartz, M. A probe signal investigation of uncertain-frequency detection. *Journal of the Acoustical Society of America,* 1975, *58,* 1051–1057. **12**

Maier, N. R. F. Reasoning in white rats. *Comparative Psychology Monographs,* 1929, *6* (No. 29). **334**

Mark, L. S., see Pittenger, Shaw, & Mark (1979).

Marks, L. E. *The unity of the senses.* New York: Academic Press, 1978. **76**

Marr, D. Early processing of visual information. *Philosophical Transactions of the Royal Society of London,* 1976, *275,* 483-534. **53**

Marsh, D. J., see Yates, Marsh, & Iberall (1972).

Martin, R. C., & Pomerantz, J. R. Visual discrimination of texture. *Perception & Psychophysics,* 1978, *24,* 420-428. **158,159**

Mason, W. A. Environmental models and mental modes: Representational processes in the great apes and man. *American Psychologist,* 1976, *31,* 284-293. **334**

Massaro, D. W. *Experimental psychology and information processing.* Chicago: Rand McNally, 1975. **166**

Mast, T. E. Study of single units of the cochlear nucleus of the chinchilla. *Journal of the Acoustical Society of America,* 1970, *48,* 505-512. **68**

Matteson, H. H., see May & Matteson (1976).

Maturana, H. R., see Lettvin, Maturana, McCulloch, & Pitts (1959).

May, J. G., & Matteson, H. H. Spatial frequency-contingent color aftereffects. *Science,* 1976, *192,* 145-147. **9**

Mayhew, J. E. W., & Anstis, S. M. Movement aftereffects contingent on color, intensity, and pattern. *Perception & Psychophysics,* 1972, *12,* 77-85. **9,10**

McAdams, S. E. *The effect of quality on auditory stream segregation.* Undergraduate honours thesis, Department of Psychology, McGill University, Montreal, Quebec, 1977. **113**

McAlister, E., see Hochberg & McAlister (1953).

McClelland, J. L. Perception and masking of wholes and parts. *Journal of Experimental Psychology: Human Perception and Performances,* 1978, *4,* 210-223. **179**

McClelland, J. L., see Johnston & McClelland (1973).

McClelland, J. L., see Johnston & McClelland (1974).

McCollough, C. Color adaptation of edge-detectors in the human visual system. *Science,* 1965, *149,* 1115-1116. **9**

McConkie, A., see Farber & McConkie (1977).

McCulloch, W. S., see Lettvin, Maturana, McCulloch, & Pitts (1959).

McGuire, R. M., see Kubovy, Cutting, & McGuire (1974).

McIntyre, M., see Shaw & McIntyre (1974).

Meltzoff, A. N., & Moore, M. K. Imitation of facial and manual gestures by human neonates. *Science,* 1977, *198,* 75-78. **335**

Melville, H. *Moby Dick, or the white whale.* Boston: L. C. Page, 1850. **340**

Menzel, E. W. Chimpanzee spatial memory organization. *Science,* 1973, *182,* 943-945. **334**

Metelli, F. The perception of transparency. *Scientific American,* 1974, *230*(4), 90-98. **80**

Metzler, J., & Shepard, R. N. Transformational studies of the internal representation of three-dimensional objects. In R. Solso (Ed.), *Theories in cognitive psychology: The Loyola Symposium.* Potomac, Md.: Lawrence Erlbaum Associates, 1974. **286,292,293,295,296,310**

Metzler, J., see Shepard & Metzler (1971).

Michotte, A. *The perception of causality.* London: Methuen, 1963. **211**

Miller, G. A. The magical number seven, plus or minus two: Some limits on our capacity for processing information. *Psychological Review,* 1956, *63,* 81-97. **100,198**

Miller, G. A., Galanter, E., & Pribram, K. H. *Plans and the structure of behavior.* New York: Holt, 1960. **215,333**

Miller, G. A., & Heise, G. A. The trill threshold. *Journal of the Acoustical Society of America,* 1950, *22,* 637-638. **110**

Miller, G. A., Heise, G. A., & Lichten, W. The intelligibility of speech as a function of the context of the test materials. *Journal of Experimental Psychology,* 1951, *41,* 329-335. **216**

Miller, G. A., & Taylor, W. G. Perception of repeated bursts of noise. *Journal of the Acoustical Society of America,* 1948, *20,* 171-182. **82**

Miller, G. A., see Heise & Miller (1951).

N

Nachmias, J. Effect of exposure duration on visual contrast sensitivity with square-wave gratings. *Journal of the Optical Society of America,* 1967, *57,* 421–427. **20**

Nachmias, J., & Sansbury, R. B. Grating contrast: Discrimination may be better than detection. *Vision Research,* 1974, *14,* 1039–1042. **7**

Nachmias, J., Sansbury, R. B., Vassilev, A., & Weber, A. Adaptation to square-wave gratings: In search of the elusive third harmonic. *Vision Research,* 1973, *13,* 1335–1342. **5**

Nachmias, J., & Weber, A. Discrimination of simple and complex gratings. *Vision Research,* 1975, *15,* 217–224. **13**

Nachmias, J., see Blakemore & Nachmias (1971).

Nachmias, J., see Blakemore, Nachmias, & Sutton (1970).

Nachmias, J., see Graham & Nachmias (1971).

Nachmias, J., see Graham, Robson, & Nachmias (1978).

Nachmias, J., see Sachs, Nachmias, & Robson (1971).

Nachmias, J., see Sigel & Nachmias (1975).

Nachmias, J., see Watson & Nachmias (1977).

Nagata, S., see Watanabe, Mori, Nagata, & Hiwatashi (1968).

Nagel, E. *The structure of science: Problems in the logic of scientific explanation.* New York: Harcourt, Brace & World, 1961. **424**

Nagel, E., see Cohen & Nagel (1934).

Nas, H., see Van Nes, Koenderink, Nas, & Bouman (1967).

Navon, D. Irrelevance of figural identity for resolving ambiguities in apparent motion. *Journal of Experimental Psychology: Human Perception and Performance,* 1976, *2,* 130–138. **268,270**

Navon, D. Forest before trees: The precedence of global features in visual perception. *Cognitive Psychology,* 1977, *9,* 353–383. (a) **174,177**

Navon, D. Personal communication, July 1977. (b) **174**

Navon, D. On a conceptual hierarchy of time, space, and other dimensions. *Cognition,* 1978, *6,* 223–228. **95**

Neill, W. T., see Keele & Neill (1979).

Neisser, U. Decision-time without reaction-time: Experiments in visual scanning. *American Journal of Psychology,* 1963, *76,* 376–385. **242**

Neisser, U. Visual search. *Scientific American,* 1964, *210* (June), 94–102. **276**

Neisser, U. *Cognitive psychology.* New York: Appleton-Century-Crofts, 1967. **28,125,150,164, 194,276**

Neisser, U. *Cognition and reality.* San Francisco: Freeman, 1976. **311,335,336**

Neisser, U., & Becklen, R. Selective looking: Attending to visually specified events. *Cognitive Psychology,* 1975, *7,* 480–494. **206**

von Neumann, J. *Theory of self-reproducing automata.* Urbana: University of Illinois Press, 1966. **414**

Newell, A., & Simon, H. A. *Human problem solving.* Englewood Cliffs, N.J.: Prentice-Hall, 1971. **333**

Nickerson, R. S. Response times for "same"–"different" judgments. *Perceptual and Motor Skills,* 1965, *20,* 15–18. **165**

Nickerson, R. S. "Same"–"different" response times with multiattribute stimulus differences. *Perceptual and Motor Skills,* 1967, *24,* 543–554. **165**

Nielsen, D. W., see Yost & Nielsen (1977).

Nielsen, G. D., & Smith, E. E. Imaginal and verbal representations in short-term recognition of visual forms. *Journal of Experimental Psychology,* 1973, *101,* 375–378. **288**

Ninio, A., & Kahneman, D. Reaction time in focused and in divided attention. *Journal of Experimental Psychology,* 1974, *103,* 393–399. **183**

Noll, A. M. Computer-generated three-dimensional movies. *Computers & Automation,* 1965, *14,* 20. **289**

Noll, A. M. A computer technique for displaying n-dimensional hyperobjects. *Communications of the ACM*, 1967, *10*, 469-473. **442**

van Noorden, L. P. A. S. *Temporal coherence in the perception of tone sequences.* Eindhoven, Netherlands: Institute for Perception Research, 1975. **59,60,82,110,111,tape**

Norman, D. A. Towards a theory of memory and attention. *Psychological Review*, 1968, *75*, 522-536. **183**

Norman, D. A., & Bobrow, D. On data-limited and resource-limited processes. *Cognitive Psychology*, 1975, *7*, 44-64. **201**

Norman, D. A., see Lindsay & Norman (1977).

O

Oatley, K., see Sullivan, Georgeson, & Oatley (1972).

Obusek, C. J., see Warren, Obusek, Farmer, & Warren (1969).

Ogasawara, J. Effect of apparent separation on apparent movement. *Japanese Journal of Psychology*, 1936, *11*, 109-122. **323**

Ogden, C. K., & Richards, I. A. *The meaning of meaning.* New York: Harcourt Brace, 1930. **370**

Ogle, K. N. Theory of stereoscopic vision. In S. Koch (Ed.), *Psychology: A study of science* (Vol. 1). New York: McGraw-Hill, 1959. **46**

O'Hara, W., see Keren, O'Hara, & Skelton (1977).

Olson, R. K., & Attneave, F. What variables produce similarity grouping? *American Journal of Psychology*, 1970, *83*, 1-21. **154,155,158,159,176**

Olson, R. K., see Attneave & Olson (1971).

Olum, P., see Gibson, Olum, & Rosenblatt (1955).

Orlansky, J. The effect of similarity and difference in form on apparent visual movement. *Archives of Psychology*, 1940 (Whole No. 246), 85. **268**

Osgood, C. E. *Method and theory in experimental psychology.* New York: Oxford University Press, 1953. **122**

Over, R., see Lovegrove & Over (1972).

Owsley, C. J., see Gibson, Owsley, & Johnston (1978).

Oyama, T. Feature analysers, optical illusions, and figural aftereffects. *Perception*, 1977, *6*, 401-406. **23**

Ozog, G., see Weisstein, Ozog, & Szoc (1975).

P

Palmer, S. E. Visual perception and world knowledge: Notes on a model of sensory-cognitive interaction. In D. A. Norman & D. E. Rumelhart (Eds.), *Explorations in cognition.* San Francisco: Freeman, 1975. **243**

Palmer, S. E. Fundamental aspects of cognitive representation. In E. Rosch & B. Lloyd (Eds.), *Cognition and categorization.* Hillsdale, N.J.: Lawrence Erlbaum Associates, 1978. **433,434**

Palmer, S. E. Personal communication, July 1979. **434**

Palmer, S. E., & Hemenway, K. Orientation and symmetry: Effects of multiple, rotational, and near symmetries. *Journal of Experimental Psychology: Human Perception and Performance*, 1978, *4*, 691-702. **313**

Pantle, A. Visual effects of sinusoidal components of complex gratings: Independent or additive? *Vision Research*, 1973, *13*, 2195-2204. **10**

Pantle, A. Simultaneous masking of one spatial sine wave by another. *Investigative Ophthalmology and Visual Science*, 1977, *16*(supplement), 47. (Abstract) **7**

Pantle, A., & Picciano, L. A multistable movement display: Evidence for two separate motion systems in human vision. *Science*, 1976, *193*, 500-502. **22**

Pantle, A., & Sekuler, R. Size-detecting mechanisms in human vision. *Science*, 1968, *162*, 1146-1148. **4,45**

Pantle, A., see Sekuler, Pantle, & Levinson (1978).

Papert, S., see Minsky & Papert (1969).

Parsons, T. W. Separation of speech from interfering speech by means of harmonic selection. *Journal of the Acoustical Society of America,* 1976, *60,* 911-918. **114**

Pastore, R. E., see Ahroon & Pastore (1977).

Pastore, R. E., see Friedman & Pastore (1977).

Pastore, R. E., see Puleo & Pastore (1978).

Pattee, H. H. Laws and constraints, symbols and languages. In C. H. Waddington (Ed.), *Towards a theoretical biology* (Vol. 4). Chicago: Aldine, 1972. **357**

Pattee, H. H. The physical basis and origin of hierarchical control. In H. H. Pattee (Ed.), *Hierarchy theory: The challenge of complex systems.* New York: Braziller, 1973. **362**

Patten, B. C., Bosserman, R. W., Finn, J. T., & Cale, W. Propagation of causes in ecosystems. In B. C. Patten (Ed.), *Systems analysis and simulation in ecology* (Vol. 4). New York: Academic Press, 1976. **380**

Patterson, R. D. The effects of relative phase and the number of components on residue pitch. *Journal of the Acoustical Society of America,* 1973, *53,* 1565-1572. **71**

Peirce, C. S. The principles of phenomenology. In J. Buchler (Ed.), *The philosophy of Peirce: Selected writings.* London: Routledge & Kegan Paul, 1950. (Originally published, 1940.) **370-373**

Penfield, W. Speech, perception and the uncommitted cortex. In J. C. Eccles (Ed.), *Brain and conscious experience.* New York: Springer-Verlag, 1966. **335**

Penrose, L., & Penrose, R. Impossible objects: A special type of visual illusion. *British Journal of Psychology,* 1958, *49,* 31-33. **446,447**

Penrose, R., see Penrose & Penrose (1958).

Perkins, D. N. *Geometry and the perception of pictures: Three studies.* (Project Zero, Tech. Rep. No. 5). Cambridge, Mass.: Harvard University, 1971. **303**

Perkins, D. N. Visual discrimination between rectangular and nonrectangular parallelopipeds. *Perception & Psychophysics,* 1972, *12,* 396-400. **286,303,305**

Peters, S. The projection problem: How is a grammar to be selected? In S. Peters (Ed.), *Goals of linguistic theory.* Englewood Cliffs, N.J.: Prentice-Hall, 1972. **336**

Petry, H. M., see Bradley, Dumais, & Petry (1976).

Pfeiffer, R. R. Classification of response patterns of spike discharges for units in the cochlear nucleus: Tone-burst stimulation. *Experimental Brain Research,* 1966, *1,* 220-235. **68**

Picciano, L., see Pantle & Picciano (1976).

Pierce, J. R. Some work on hearing. *American Scientist,* 1960, *48,* 40-45. **70**

Pinker, S., see Bregman & Pinker (1978).

Pirenne, M. H. *Optics, painting and photography.* Cambridge, England: Cambridge University Press, 1970. **302**

Pittenger, J. B., & Shaw, R. E. Aging faces as viscal-elastic events: Implications for a theory of nonrigid shape perception. *Journal of Experimental Psychology: Human Perception and Performance,* 1975, *1,* 374-382. (a) **417**

Pittenger, J. B., & Shaw, R. E. Perception of relative and absolute age in facial photographs. *Perception & Psychophysics,* 1975, *18,* 137-143. **417**

Pittenger, J. B., Shaw, R. E., & Mark, L. S. Perceptual information for the age-level of faces as a higher-order invariant of growth. *Journal of Experimental Psychology: Human Perception and Performance,* 1979, *5,* 478-493. **417**

Pittenger, J., see Shaw & Pittenger (1977).

Pittenger, J., see Shaw & Pittenger (1978).

Pitts, W. H., see Lettvin, Maturana, McCulloch, & Pitts (1959).

Podgorny, P., & Shepard, R. N. Functional representations common to visual perception and imagination. *Journal of Experimental Psychology: Human Perception and Performances,* 1978, *4,* 21-35. **305**

Podgorny, P., see Cooper & Podgorny (1976).

Podgorny, P., see Shepard & Podgorny (1978).

Polanyi, M. Knowing and being. In M. Grene (Ed.), *Essays by Michael Polanyi*. Chicago: University of Chicago Press, 1969. **51**

Polit, A., see Richards & Polit (1974).

Pollack, I. Continuation of auditory frequency gradients across temporal breaks: The auditory Pogendorff. *Perception & Psychophysics*, 1977, *21*, 563-568. **82**

Pomerantz, J. R. Pattern goodness and speed of encoding. *Memory & Cognition*, 1977, *5*, 235-241. **130,131,162**

Pomerantz, J. R. Are complex visual features derived from simple ones? In E. L. J. Leeuwenberg & H. F. J. M. Buffart (Eds.), *Formal theories of visual perception*. Chichester, England: Wiley, 1978. **171**

Pomerantz, J. R., & Garner, W. R. Stimulus configuration in selective attention tasks. *Perception & Psychophysics*, 1973, *14*, 565-569. **132,144,145,152,167**

Pomerantz, J. R., & Sager, L. C. Asymmetric integrality with dimensions of visual pattern. *Perception & Psychophysics*, 1975, *18*, 460-466. **137,173,177**

Pomerantz, J. R., & Sager, L. C. Line-slope vs. line-arrangement discrimination: A comment on Ambler and Finklea's paper. *Perception & Psychophysics*, 1976, *20*, 220. **156**

Pomerantz, J. R., Sager, L. C., & Stoever, R. J. Perception of wholes and of their component parts: Some configural superiority effects. *Journal of Experimental Psychology: Human Perception and Performance*, 1977, *3*, 422-435. **166,167,171,177,243**

Pomerantz, J. R., & Schwaitzberg, S. D. Grouping by proximity: Selective attention measures. *Perception & Psychophysics*, 1975, *18*, 355-361. **147,152,159,167**

Pomerantz, J. R., see Kolers & Pomerantz (1971).

Pomerantz, J. R., see Kosslyn & Pomerantz (1977).

Pomerantz, J. R., see Martin & Pomerantz (1978).

Popper, K. R. *The logic of scientific discovery* (K. R. Popper, trans.). London: Hutchinson, 1968. (Originally published in German, 1935.) **46,50**

Popper, K. R. *Conjectures and refutations: The growth of scientific knowledge*. London: Hutchinson, 1963. **27**

Popper, K. R. *Unended quest*. La Salle, Ill.: Open Court, 1976. **321**

Posner, M. I. Information reduction in the analysis of sequential tasks. *Psychological Review*, 1964, *71*, 491-504. **147**

Posner, M. I. *Chronometric explorations of mind*. Hillsdale, N.J.: Lawrence Erlbaum Associates, 1978. **182,184,189**

Posner, M. I., & Snyder, C. R. R. Attention and cognitive control. In R. L. Solso (Ed.), *Information processing and cognition: The Loyola symposium*. Hillsdale, N.J.: Lawrence Erlbaum Associates, 1975. (a) **182**

Posner, M. I., & Snyder, C. R. R. Facilitation and inhibition in the processing of signals. In P. M. A. Rabbitt & S. Dornič (Eds.), *Attention and performance V*. New York: Academic Press, 1975. (b) **182**

Powers, W. T. *Behavior: The control of perception*. Chicago: Aldine, 1973. **333**

Pratt, C. C. The spatial character of high and low tones. *Journal of Experimental Psychology*, 1930, *13*, 278-285. **78**

Pratt, C. C. Wolfgang Köhler: 1887-1967. Introduction to W. Köhler, *The task of Gestalt psychology*. Princeton, N.J.: Princeton University Press, 1969. **449**

Pribram, K. H., Nuwer, M., & Baron, R. J. The holographic hypothesis of memory structure in brain function and perception. In R. C. Atkinson, D. H. Krantz, R. C. Luce, & P. Suppes (Eds.), *Contemporary developments in mathematical psychology*. San Francisco: Freeman, 1974. **315**

Pribram, K. H., see Miller, Galanter, & Pribram (1960).

Prigogine, I. Order through fluctuation: Self-organization and social system. In E. Jantsch & C. H. Waddington (Eds.), *Evolution and consciousness: Human systems in transition*. Reading, Mass.: Addison-Wesley, 1976. **402**

Prigogine, I. Time, structure and fluctuations. *Science,* 1978, *201,* 777-785. **402**

Prigogine, I., see Glansdorff & Prigogine (1971).

Prinzmetal, W., & Banks, W. P. Good continuation affects visual detection. *Perception & Psychophysics,* 1977, *21,* 389-395. (a) **153**

Prinzmetal, W., & Banks, W. P. *Simultaneous vs. successive presentation of visual arrays revisited.* Paper presented at the annual meeting of the Psychonomic Society, Washington, D.C., November 10-12, 1977. (b) **191,208**

Prinzmetal, W., see Banks & Prinzmetal (1976).

Proffitt, D. R., see Cutting, Proffitt & Kozlowski (1978).

Pronko, N. H., Ebert, R., & Greenberg, G. A critical review of theories of perception. In A. L. Kidd & J. L. Riviore (Eds.), *Perceptual development in children.* New York: International Universities Press, 1966. **398**

Prussin, H. A., see Morton, Crowder, & Prussin (1971).

Puleo, J. S., & Pastore, R. E. Critical band effects in two-channel auditory signal detection. *Journal of Experimental Psychology: Human Perception and Performance,* 1978, *4,* 153-163. **92,93**

Purcell, D. G., Stanovich, K. E., & Spector, A. Visual angle and the word superiority effect. *Memory & Cognition,* 1978, *6,* 3-8. **136**

Purdy, W. C. *The hypothesis of psychophysical correspondence in space perception.* Unpublished doctoral dissertation, Cornell University, 1958. **266,268**

Putnam, H. Reductionism and the nature of psychology. *Cognition,* 1973, *2,* 131-146. **357**

Pylyshyn, Z. What the mind's eye tells the mind's brain: A critique of mental imagery. *Psychological Bulletin,* 1973, *80,* 1-24. **287,293**

Pylyshyn, Z. Imagery and artificial intelligence. In C. W. Savage (Ed.), *Perception and cognition: Issues in the foundations of psychology* (Minnesota studies in the philosophy of science, Vol. 9). Minneapolis: University of Minnesota Press, 1978. **287-289,296**

Q

Quick, R. F., Hamerly, J. R., & Reichert, T. A. The absence of a measurable "critical band" at low suprathreshold contrasts. *Vision Research,* 1976, *16,* 351-356. **12**

Quick, R. F., Mullins, W. W., & Reichert, T. A. Spatial summation effects on two-component grating thresholds. *Journal of the Optical Society of America,* 1978, *68,* 116-121. **11,18**

Quick, R. F., & Reichert, T. A. Spatial-frequency selectivity in contrast detection. *Vision Research,* 1975, *15,* 637-643. **10,17**

Quick, R. F., see Hamerly, Quick, & Reichert (1977).

Quick, R. F., see Abel & Quick (1978).

Quillian, M. R. *Semantic memory.* Unpublished doctoral dissertation, Carnegie Institute of Technolgoy, 1966. (Reprinted in part in M. Minsky (Ed.), *Semantic information processing.* Cambridge, Mass.: M.I.T. Press, 1968.) **322**

R

Rabinowitz, J. C., see Biederman, Rabinowitz, Glass, & Stacy (1974).

Raphael, L. J., see Dorman, Cutting, & Raphael (1975).

Rashbass, C. Spatio-temporal interaction in visual resolution. *Journal of Physiology,* 1968, *196,* 102-103. **22**

Ratliff, F. *Mach bands: Quantitative studies on neural networks in the retina.* San Francisco: Holden-Day, 1965. **203**

Ratliff, F., & Hartline, H. K. The responses of *Limulus* optic nerve fibers to patterns of illumination on the receptor mosaic. *Journal of General Physiology,* 1959, *42,* 1241-1255. **429**

Reder, S., see Estes, Allmeyer, & Reder (1976).

Regan, D., & Spekreijse, H. Auditory-visual interactions and the correspondence between perceived auditory space and perceived visual space. *Perception,* 1977, *6,* 133–138. **85**

Reicher, G. M. Perceptual recognition as a function of meaningfulness of stimulus materials. *Journal of Experimental Psychology,* 1969, *81,* 275–280. **166**

Reichert, T. A., see Hamerly, Quick, & Reichert (1977).

Reichert, T. A., see Quick & Reichert (1975).

Reichert, T. A., see Quick, Hamerly, & Reichert (1976).

Reichert, T. A., see Quick, Mullins, & Reichert (1978).

Restle, F. Coding theory of the perception of motion configurations. *Psychological Review,* 1979, *86,* 1–24. **437**

Ribbands, C. R. *The behaviour and social life of honeybees.* Hapeville, Ga.: Hale, 1953. **397**

Richards, I. A., see Ogden & Richards (1930).

Richards, W. The fortification illusions of migraines. *Scientific American,* 1971, *224* (May), 88–96. **430**

Richards, W., & Polit, A. Texture matching. *Kybernetic,* 1974, *16,* 155–162. **14,22**

Ridley, R. M., see Blakemore, Muncey, & Ridley (1971).

Ridley, R. M., see Blakemore, Muncey, & Ridley (1973).

Riggs, L. A., White, K. D., & Eimas, P. D. Establishment and decay of orientation-contingent aftereffects of color. *Perception & Psychophysics,* 1974, *16,* 535–542. **9**

Ritsma, R. J., & Engel, F. L. Pitch of frequency-modulated signals. *Journal of the Acoustical Society of America,* 1964, *36,* 1637–1644. **71**

Ritsma, R. J., see Schouten & Ritsma (1962).

Robins, C., & Shepard, R. N. Spatio-temporal probing of apparent rotational movement. *Perception & Psychophysics,* 1977, *22,* 12–18. **294,296,310,312,319**

Robson, J. G. Spatial and temporal contrast-sensitivity functions of the visual system. *Journal of the Optical Society of America,* 1966, *56,* 1141–1142. **20**

Robson, J. G., & Graham, N. Probability summation and regional variation in sensitivity across the visual field. *Investigative Ophthalmology and Visual Science,* 1978, *17*(supplement), 221. (Abstract) **11,19**

Robson, J. G., see Campbell & Robson (1964).

Robson, J. G., see Campbell & Robson (1968).

Robson, J. G., see Enroth-Cugell & Robson (1966).

Robson, J. G., see Graham, Robson, & Nachmias (1978).

Robson, J. G., see Sachs, Nachmias, & Robson (1971).

Rock, F., Schauer, R., & Halper, F. Form perception without attention. *Quarterly Journal of Experimental Psychology,* 1976, *28,* 429–440. **206**

Rock, I. In defense of unconscious inference. In W. Epstein (Ed.), *Stability and constancy in visual perception: Mechanisms and processes.* New York: Wiley, 1977. **277**

Rock, I., & Brosgole, L. Grouping based on phenomenal proximity. *Journal of Experimental Psychology,* 1964, *67,* 531–538. **153**

Rodgers, J., & Ruff, W. Kepler's harmony of the world: A realization for the ear. *American Scientist,* 1979, *67,* 286–292. **321**

Roffler, S. K., & Butler, R. A. Localization of tonal stimuli in the vertical plane. *Journal of the Acoustical Society of America,* 1968, 43, 1260–1266. **78**

Rogowitz, B. Backward masking with sinusoidal gratings: A look at spatial frequency and temporal response. *Investigative Ophthalmology and Visual Science,* 1977, *16*(supplement), 123. (Abstract) **7,20–22**

Rogowitz, B. *Spatial-temporal interactions in the processing of visual patterns.* Unpublished doctoral dissertation, Columbia University, 1978. **7,20–22**

Rogowitz, B., see Graham & Rogowitz (1976).

Rohwer, W. D., see Jensen & Rohwer (1966).

Romanski, L., see Hock, Romanski, Galie, & Williams (1978).

Rosen, R. Dynamical similarity and the theory of biological transformations. *Bulletin of Mathematical Biology*, 1978, *40*, 549–579. **400**

Rosenblatt, F., see Gibson, Olum, & Rosenblatt (1955).

Rosenblatt, M., & Slepian, D. Nth order Markov chains with every N variables independent. *Journal of the Society for Industrial and Applied Mathematics*, 1962, *10*, 537–549. **30**

Roule, P. J., see Hochberg, Brooks, & Roule (1977).

Rubinstein, C. B., see Limb & Rubinstein (1977).

Rudnicky, A. I., see Bregman & Rudnicky (1975).

Ruff, W., see Rodgers & Ruff (1979).

Rumelhart, D. E. *Introduction to human information processing*. New York: Wiley, 1977. **152,162,225**

Runeson, S. On the possibility of "smart" perceptual mechanisms. *Scandinavian Journal of Psychology*, 1977, *18*, 172–179. **357,417,451,452**

Rupert, A. L., see Moushegian & Rupert (1970).

Rush, G. P. Visual grouping in relation to age. *Archives of Psychology*, 1937, *217*, 5–95. **427**

Russell, B. *Mysticism and logic*. London: Longmans, Green, 1925. **370**

Ruth, D. S. *The effects of pattern goodness on automatic and strategy-dependent processes*. Unpublished doctoral dissertation, Yale University, 1976. **131**

Ryle, G. *The concept of mind*. London: Hutchinson, 1949. **351**

S

Sachs, M. B., Nachmias, J., & Robson, J. G. Spatial-frequency channels in human vision. *Journal of the Optical Society of America*, 1971, 61, 1176–1186. **10,17**

Sager, L. C. *Preattentive processing of visual pattern information*. Unpublished doctoral dissertation, Johns Hopkins University, 1978. **156**

Sager, L. C., see Pomerantz & Sager (1976).

Sager, L. C., see Pomerantz, Sager, & Stoever (1977).

Sakrison, O. J., see Mostafavi & Sakrison (1976).

Sander, L. W., see Condon & Sander (1974).

Sansbury, R. V. *Some properties of spatial channels revealed by pulsed simultaneous masking*. Unpublished doctoral dissertation, University of Pennsylvania, 1974. **7**

Sansbury, R. V., Distelhorst, J., & Moore, S. A phase-specific adaptation effect of the square-wave grating. *Investigative Ophthalmology and Visual Science*, 1978, *17*, 442–448. **7**

Sansbury, R. B., see Nachmias & Sansbury (1974).

Sansbury, R. B., see Nachmias, Sansbury, Vassilev, & Weber (1974).

Saucer, R. T. Processes of motion perception. *Science*, 1954, *120*, 806–807. **22**

Sauer, E. G. F. Celestial navigation by birds. *Scientific American*, 1958, *199*(2), 42–47. **334**

Sauer, E. G. F. Celestial rotation and stellar orientation in migratory warblers. *Science*, 1971, *173*, 459–460. **334**

Schatz, B. R. *The computation of immediate texture discrimination* (Memo. 426). Cambridge, Mass.: M.I.T., Artificial Intelligence Laboratory, 1977. **35**

Schauer, R., see Rock, Schauer, & Halper (1976).

Schendel, J. D., & Shaw, P. A test of the generality of the word-context effect. *Perception & Psychophysics*, 1976, *19*, 383–393. **166,177**

Schmidt, M. J., see Finke & Schmidt (1977).

Schneider, W., & Shiffrin, R. M. Controlled and automatic human information processing: I. Detection, search and attention. *Psychological Review*, 1977, *84*, 1–66. **182,183,188,194**

Schneider, W., see Shiffrin & Schneider (1977).

Schober, H. A. Q., & Hilz, R. Contrast sensitivity of the human eye for square-wave-gratings. *Journal of the Optical Society of America*, 1965, *55*, 1086–1091. **20**

Schouten, J. F. *Five articles on the perception of sound (1938-1940)*. Eindhoven, Netherlands: Institute for Perception, 1940. **71**

Schouten, J. F., Ritsma, R. J., & Lopes Cardozo, B. Pitch of the residue. *Journal of the Acoustical Society of America*, 1962, *34*, 1418-1424. **71**

Schrödinger, E. *What is life? The physical aspects of the living cell* (2nd ed.). Cambridge, England: Cambridge University Press, 1962. **414**

Schroeder, M. R. New results concerning monaural phase sensitivity. *Journal of the Acoustical Society of America*, 1959, *31*, 1579. (Abstract) **70**

Schuster, D. H. A new ambiguous figure: A three-stick clevis. *American Journal of Psychology*, 1964, *77*, 673. **442,443**

Schwaitzberg, S. D., see Pomerantz & Schwaitzberg (1975).

Schwartz, E. L. Afferent geometry in the primate visual cortex and the generation of neuronal trigger features. *Biological Cybernetics*, 1977, *28*, 1-14. (a) **429**

Schwartz, E. L. Spatial mapping in the primate sensory projection: Analytic structure and relevance to perception. *Biological Cybernetics*, 1977, *25*, 181-194. (b) **429**

Schwartz, M., see Macmillan & Schwartz (1975).

Scott, B., see Cole & Scott (1973).

Sebrechts, M. M., & Garner, W. R. Stimulus-specific processing consequences of pattern goodness. *Memory & Cognition*, 1980, in press. **131**

Sekuler, R., & Abrams, M. Visual sameness: A choice time analysis of pattern recognition processes. *Journal of Experimental Psychology*, 1968, *77*, 232-238. **164**

Sekuler, R., & Levinson, E. The perception of moving targets. *Scientific American*, 1977, *236*(1), 60-73. **21**

Sekuler, R., Pantle, A., & Levinson, G. Physiological basis of motion perception. In R. Held, H. Liebowitz, & H. L. Teuber (Eds.), *Handbook of sensory physiology* (Vol. 8). Berlin: Springer-Verlag, 1978. **21**

Sekuler, R., see Pantle & Sekuler (1968).

Sekuler, R., see Tynan & Sekuler (1974).

Semmes, J., see Lashley, Chow, & Semmes (1951).

Sharpe, C. R., see Tolhurst, Sharpe, & Hart (1973).

Shaw, P. Processing of tachistoscopic displays with controlled order of characters and spaces. *Perception & Psychophysics*, 1969, *6*, 257-266. **197**

Shaw, P., see Schendel & Shaw (1976).

Shaw, R. E. Personal communication, November 9, 1977. **293**

Shaw, R. E., & Bransford, J. D. Introduction: Psychological approaches to the problem of knowledge. In R. E. Shaw & J. Bransford (Eds.), *Perceiving, acting and knowing: Toward an ecological psychology*. Hillsdale, N.J.: Lawrence Erlbaum Associates, 1977. **344,355**

Shaw, R. E., & McIntyre, M. Algoristic foundations to cognitive psychology. In W. B. Weimer & D. S. Palermo (Eds.), *Cognition and the symbolic processes*. Hillsdale, N.J.: Lawrence Erlbaum Associates, 1974. **385,414**

Shaw, R. E., & Pittenger, J. Perceiving the face of change in changing faces: Implications for a theory of object perception. In R. E. Shaw & J. Bransford (Eds.), *Perceiving, acting and knowing: Toward an ecological psychology*. Hillsdale, N.J.: Lawrence Erlbaum Associates, 1977. **327,362,417**

Shaw, R. E., & Pittenger, J. Perceiving change. In H. Pick & E. Saltzman (Eds.), *Modes of perceiving and processing information*. Hillsdale, N.J.: Lawrence Erlbaum Associates, 1978. **362,417**

Shaw, R. E., Turvey, M. T., & Mace, W. Ecological psychology: The consequences of a commitment to realism. In W. Weimer & D. Palermo (Eds.), *Cognition and the symbolic processes II*. Hillsdale, N.J.: Lawrence Erlbaum Associates, 1981. **344,346,348,349,355,358,363–365,370, 371,378,385**

Shaw, R. E., see Pittenger & Shaw (1975).

Shaw, R. E., see Pittenger, Shaw, & Mark (1979).

Shaw, R. E., see Turvey & Shaw (1979).

Shaw, R. E., see Turvey, Shaw, & Mace (1978).

Shepard, R. N. *Stimulus and response generalization during paired-associates learning.* Unpublished doctoral dissertation, Yale University, 1955. **313**

Shepard, R. N. Stimulus and response generalization: Deduction of the generalization gradient from trace model. *Psychological Review,* 1958, *65,* 242–256. **314,322**

Shepard, R. N. Application of a trace model to the retention of information in a recognition task. *Psychometrika,* 1961, *26,* 185–203. **322**

Shepard, R. N. The analysis of proximities: Multidimensional scaling with an unknown distance function, I & II. *Psychometrika,* 1962, *27,* 125–140; 219–246. **313,335**

Shepard, R. N. Attention and the metric structure of the stimulus space. *Journal of Mathematical Psychology,* 1964, *1,* 54–87. (a) **290,325**

Shepard, R. N. Circularity in judgments of relative pitch. *Journal of the Acoustical Society of America,* 1964, *36,* 2346–2353. (b) **319**

Shepard, R. N. Representation of structure in similarity data: Problems and prospects. *Psychometrika,* 1974, *39,* 373–421. **313**

Shepard, R. N. Form, formation, and transformation of internal representations. In R. Solso (Ed.), *Information processing and cognition: The Loyola symposium.* Hillsdale, N.J.: Lawrence Erlbaum Associates, 1975. **288–291,293,294,296,311,326,335**

Shepard, R. N. *Trajectories of apparent transformations.* Paper presented at the annual meeting of the Psychonomic Society, Washington, D.C., November 10, 1977. **313,315**

Shepard, R. N. The circumplex and related topological manifolds in the study of perception. In S. Shye (Ed.), *Theory construction and data analysis in the behavioral sciences.* San Francisco: Jossey-Bass, 1978. (a) **294,313,328,329**

Shepard, R. N. *The double helix of musical pitch.* Paper presented in the symposium "Cognitive structure of musical pitch" at the annual meeting of the Western Psychological Association, San Francisco, April 20, 1978. (b) **320,325**

Sehpard, R. N. Externalization of mental images and the act of creation. In B. S. Randhawa & W. E. Coffman (Eds.), *Visual learning, thinking, and communication.* New York: Academic Press, 1978. (c) **328,338,339**

Shepard, R. N. The mental image. *American Psychologist,* 1978, *33,* 125–137. (d) **281,288,290, 296,305,310,339,441**

Shepard, R. N. On the status of "direct" psychophysical measurement. In C. W. Savage (Ed.), *Perception and cognition: Issues in the foundations of psychology* (Minnesota studies in the philosophy of science, Vol. 9). Minneapolis: University of Minnesota Press, 1978. (e) **287,293, 296**

Shepard, R. N. Reconstruction of witnesses' experiences of anomalous phenomena. In R. F. Haines (Ed.), *UFO phenomena and the behavioral scientist.* Metuchen, N.J.: Scarecrow Press, 1979. **299**

Shepard, R. N., & Cermak, G. W. Perceptual-cognitive explorations of a toroidal set of free-form stimuli. *Cognitive Psychology,* 1973, *4,* 351–377. **299,305,325**

Shepard, R. N., & Chipman, S. Second-order isomorphism of internal representations: Shapes of states. *Cognitive Psychology,* 1970, *1,* 1–17. **291,336,431–433**

Shepard, R. N., & Cooper, L. A. *Representation of colors in normal, blind, and color blind subjects.* Paper presented at the joint meeting of the American Psychological Association and the Psychometric Society, Chicago, September 2, 1975. **325**

Shepard, R. N., & Feng, C. A chronometric study of mental paper folding. *Cognitive Psychology,* 1972, *3,* 228–243. **311**

Shepard, R. N., & Judd, S. A. Perceptual illusion of rotation of three-dimensional objects. *Science,* 1976, *191,* 952–954. **294,310,312,318,319,323**

Shepard, R. N., Kilpatric, D. W., & Cunningham, J. P. The internal representation of numbers. *Cognitive Psychology*, 1975, *7*, 82-138. **291**

Shepard, R. N., & Metzler, J. Mental rotation of three-dimensional objects. *Science*, 1971, *171*, 701-703. **293,310-312,323**

Shepard, R. N., & Podgorny, P. Cognitive processes that resemble perceptual processes. In W. K. Estes (Ed.), *Handbook of learning and cognitive processes*. Hillsdale, N.J.: Lawrence Erlbaum Associates, 1978. **287,291,293**

Shepard, R. N., see Cooper & Shepard (1973a).

Shepard, R. N., see Cooper & Shepard (1973b).

Shepard, R. N., see Cooper & Shepard (1975).

Shepard, R. N., see Cooper & Shepard (1978).

Shepard, R. N., see Cunningham & Shepard (1974).

Shepard, R. N., see Farrell & Shepard (in press).

Shepard, R. N., see Krumhansl & Shepard (1979).

Shepard, R. N., see Metzler & Shepard (1974).

Shepard, R. N., see Podgorny & Shepard (1978).

Shepard, R. N., see Robbins & Shepard (1977).

Shepp, L. A., see Julesz, Gilbert, Shepp, & Frisch (1973).

Shiffrin, R. M., & Schneider, W. Controlled and automatic human information processing: II. Perceptual learning, automatic attending, and a general theory. *Psychological Review*, 1977, *84*, 127-190. **183,189,309**

Shiffrin, R. M., see Schneider & Shiffrin (1977).

Shimamura, K. K., see Thomas & Shimamura (1975).

Siegel, C., see Lange, Siegel, & Stecher (1973).

Shipley, T. Auditory flutter-driving of visual flicker. *Science*, 1964, *145*, 1328-1330. **85**

Shubnikov, A. V., & Koptsik, V. A. *Symmetry in science and art*. New York: Plenum Press, 1974. **385**

Sigel, C., & Nachmias, J. A re-evaluation of curvature-specific chromatic aftereffects. *Vision Research*, 1975, *15*, 829-836. **9**

Sigel, C., see Stecher, Sigel, & Lange (1973).

Silverman, W. P. Can "words" be processed as integrated units? *Perception & Psychophysics*, 1976, *20*, 143-152. **135**

Silverstein, A., see Hochberg & Silverstein (1956).

Simon, H. A. How big is a chunk? *Science*, 1975, *183*, 482-488. **198**

Simon, H. A., see Newell & Simon (1971).

Simmons, F. B. Monaural processing. In J. V. Tobias (Ed.), *Foundations of modern auditory theory* (Vol. 1). New York: Academic Press, 1970. **68**

Sireteanu, R., see Fiorentini, Sireteanu, & Spinelli (1976).

Skelton, J., see Keren, O'Hara, & Skelton (1977).

Skinner, B. F. Behaviorism at fifty. *Science*, 1963, *140*, 951-958. **284,290**

Skowbo, D., Timney, B., Gentry, T., & Morant, R. B. The McCollough effects: Experimental findings and theoretical accounts. *Psychological Bulletin*, 1975, *82*, 497-510. **10**

Slepian, D., see Rosenblatt & Slepian (1962).

Smith, E. E., see Nielsen & Smith (1973).

Smith, R. L., & Zwislocki, J. J. Responses of some neurons of the cochlear nucleus to tone-intensity increments. *Journal of the Acoustical Society of America*, 1971, *50*, 1520-1525. **68**

Snyder, C. R. R., see Posner & Snyder (1975a).

Snyder, C. R. R., see Posner & Snyder (1975b).

Sober, W. *Simplicity*. Oxford: Clarendon Press, 1975. **307**

Spector, A., see Purcell, Stanovich, & Spector (1978).

Spekreijse, H., see Regan & Spekreijse (1977).

Spence, K. W. The postulates and methods of "behaviorism." *Psychological Review*, 1948, *55*, 67-78. **119**

Sperling, G. The information available in brief visual presentations. *Psychological Monographs*, 1960, *74*(11, Whole No. 498). **89,136**

Sperling, G. A model for visual memory tasks. *Human Factors*, 1963, *5*, 19-31. **207**

Sperling, G. Successive approximations to a model for short-term memory. *Acta Psychologica*, 1967, *27*, 285-292. **207**

Sperry, R. W., & Miner, N. Pattern perception following insertion of mica plates into visual cortex. *Journal of Comparative and Physiological Psychology*, 1955, *48*, 463-469. **428**

Sperry, R. W., Miner, N., & Myers, R. E. Visual pattern perception following subpial slicing and tantalum wire implantation in the visual cortex. *Journal of Comparative and Physiological Psychology*, 1955, *48*, 50-58. **428**

Spinelli, D., see Fiorentini, Sireteanu, & Spinelli (1976).

Stacy, E. W., Jr., see Biederman, Glass, & Stacy (1973).

Stacy, E. W., Jr., see Biederman, Rabinowitz, Glass, & Stacy (1973).

Stahl, W. R. Dimensional analysis in mathematical biology. I. General discussion. *Bulletin of Mathematical Biophysics*, 1961, *23*, 355-376. **400**

Stanovich, K. E., see Purcell, Stanovich, & Spector (1978).

Stecher, S., Sigel, C., & Lange, R. Composite adaptation and spatial frequency interactions. *Vision Research*, 1973, *13*, 2527-2531. **5**

Stecher, S., see Lange, Sigel, & Stecher (1973).

Stevens, P. S. *Patterns in nature*. Boston, Mass.: Little, Brown, 1974. **401**

Stevens, W. *The man with the blue guitar*. New York: Knopf, 1945. **288**

Stiles, W. S. The directional sensitivity of the retina and the spectral sensitivities of the rods and cones. *Proceedings of the Royal Society of London*, 1939, *127*, 64-105. **45**

Stoever, R. J., see Pomerantz, Sager, & Stoever (1977).

Strawson, P. F. *Individuals*. London: Methuen, 1959. **97**

Stromeyer, C. F. Edge-contingent color aftereffects: Spatial frequency specificity. *Vision Research*, 1972, *12*, 717-733. **9**

Stromeyer, C. F., & Julesz, B. Spatial-frequency masking in vision: Critical bands and spread of masking. *Journal of the Optical Society of America*, 1972, *62*, 1221-1232. **7**

Stromeyer, C. F., & Klein, S. Spatial frequency channels in human vision as asymmetric (edge) mechanisms. *Vision Research*, 1974, *14*, 1409-1420. **7**

Stromeyer, C. F., see Klein, Stromeyer, & Ganz (1974).

Stroop, J. R. Studies of interference in serial verbal reactions. *Journal of Experimental Psychology*, 1935, *18*, 643-662. **185**

Sullivan, G. D., Georgeson, M. A., & Oatley, K. Channels for spatial frequency selection and the detection of single bars by the human visual system. *Vision Research*, 1972, *12*, 383-394. **5**

Sullivan, G. D., see Georgeson & Sullivan (1975).

Sutliff, D., see Garner & Sutliff (1974).

Sutton, P., see Blakemore & Sutton (1969).

Sutton, P., see Blakemore, Nachmias, & Sutton (1970).

Swets, J. A., see Green & Swets (1966).

Switkes, E., see DeValois & Switkes (1978).

Szilagyi, P. G., & Baird, J. C. A quantitative approach to the study of visual symmetry. *Perception & Psychophysics*, 1977, *22*, 287-292. **84**

Szog, R., see Weisstein, Ozog, & Szog (1975).

T

Tangney, J., see Weisstein, Harris, Berbaum, Tangney, & Williams (1977).

Tarski, A. The semantic conception of truth and the foundations of semantics. *Philosophical and Phenomenological Research*, 1944, *4*, 341-376. **377**

Treisman, A., & Gelade, G. A feature-integration theory of attention. *Cognitive Psychology*, 1980, *12*, 97–136. **188,194**

Trimble, V. Cosmology: Man's place in the universe. *American Scientist*, 1977, *65*, 76–87. **414**

Tulunay-Keesey, U., see Jones & Tulunay-Keesey (1975).

Turner, M. B. *Philosophy and the science of behavior*. New York: Appleton-Century-Crofts, 1967. **424,436**

Turner, M. B. *Psychology and the philosophy of science*. New York: Appleton-Century-Crofts, 1968. **122**

Turvey, M. T. Contrasting orientations to the theory of visual information processing. *Psychological Review*, 1977, *84*, 67–88. **267,344,385**

Turvey, M. T., & Shaw, R. E. The primacy of perceiving: An ecological reformulation of perception for understanding memory. In L. G. Nilsson (Ed.), *Perspectives on memory research: Essays in honor of Uppsala University's 500th anniversary*. Hillsdale, N.J.: Lawrence Erlbaum Associates, 1979. **344,348,349,353,358,363–367,371,378,380,385,396,414**

Turvey, M. T., Shaw, R. E., & Mace, W. Issues in the theory of action: Degrees of freedom, coordinative structures and coalitions. In J. Requin (Ed.), *Attention and performance VII*. Hillsdale, N.J.: Lawrence Erlbaum Associates, 1978. **344,363,380,385,386,396,417,419**

Turvey, M. T., see Fitch & Turvey (1978).

Turvey, M. T., see Fowler & Turvey (1978).

Turvey, M. T., see Shaw, Turvey & Mace (1981).

Tversky, A. Personal communication, 1978. **292**

Tynan, P., & Sekuler, R. Perceived spatial frequency varies with stimulus duration. *Journal of the Optical Society of America*, 1974, *64*, 1251–1255. **20**

U

Ullman, S. Transformability and object identity. *Perception & Psychophysics*, 1977, *22*, 414–415. **268**

Uttal, W. R. *Autocorrelation theory of form detection*. Hillsdale, N.J.: Lawrence Erlbaum Associates, 1975. **315**

V

Van Nes, F. L., Koenderink, J. J., Nas, H., & Bouman, M. A. Spatiotemporal modulation transfer in the human eye. *Journal of the Optical Society of America*, 1967, *57*, 1082–1088. **20,22**

Vassilev, A., & Mitov, D. Perception time and spatial frequency. *Vision Research*, 1976, *16*, 89–92. **20**

Vassilev, A., see Nachmias, Sansbury, Vassilev, & Weber (1973).

Victor, J. D., see Julesz, Gilbert, & Victor (1978).

Virostek, S., see Hochberg, Green & Virostek (1978).

von Hofsten, C., see Johansson, von Hofsten, & Hansson (1980).

Vurpillot, E. *The visual world of the child*. New York: International Universities Press, 1976. **128**

W

Waddington, C. H. *The nature of life*. New York: Harper & Row, 1961. **364**

Walker, D. P. Kepler's celestial music. *Journal of the Warburg and Courtauld Institutes*, 1967, *30*, 228–250. **321**

Wall, S., see Egeth, Jonides, & Wall (1972).

Wallace, G. F. The critical distance of interaction in the Zöllner illusion. *Perception & Psychophysics*, 1969, *5*, 261–264. **23**

Wallach, H., see Köhler & Wallach (1944).

Warren, R. E. Stimulus encoding and memory. *Journal of Experimental Psychology*, 1972, *94*, 90-100. **184**

Warren, R. E. Association, directionality, and stimulus encoding. *Journal of Experimental Psychology*, 1974, *102*, 151-158. **184**

Warren, R. M., Obusek, C. J., & Ackroff, J. M. Auditory induction: Perceptual synthesis of absent sounds. *Science*, 1972, *176*, 1149-1151. **107**

Warren, R. M., Obusek, C. J., Farmer, R. M., & Warren, R. P. Auditory sequence: Confusion of patterns other than speech or music. *Science*, 1969, *164*, 586-587. **101,tape**

Warren, R. P., see Warren, Obusek, Farmer, & Warren (1969).

Warren, W. H. Visual information for object identity in apparent movement. *Perception & Psychophysics*, 1977, *22*, 264-268. **268**

Watanabe, A., Mori, T., Nagata, S., & Hiwatashi, K. Spatial sine-wave responses of the human visual system. *Vision Research*, 1968, *8*, 1245-1263. **20,22**

Watson, A. B. *The visibility of temporal modulations of a spatial pattern*. Unpublished doctoral dissertation, University of New Jersey, 1977. **21**

Watson, A. B. Summation of temporal modulations of a spatial pattern. *Investigative Ophthalmology and Visual Science*, 1978, *17*(supplement), 223. (Abstract) **21**

Watson, A. B., & Nachmias, J. Patterns of temporal interaction in the detection of gratings. *Vision Research*, 1977, *17*, 893-902. **20,22**

Wiener, N. *Cybernetics*. New York: Wiley, 1948. **333**

Weber, A., see Nachmias & Weber (1975).

Weber, A., see Nachmias, Sansbury, Vassilev, & Weber (1973).

Weiman, C. F. R., see Clement & Weiman (1970).

Weisstein, N., & Bisaha, J. Gratings mask bars and bars mask gratings: Visual frequency response to aperiodic stimuli. *Science*, 1972, *176*, 1047-1049. **7**

Weisstein, N., & Harris, C. S. Visual detection of line segments: An object superiority effect. *Science*, 1974, *186*, 752-755. **166,177,179,298**

Weisstein, N., & Harris, C. S. Masking and unmasking of distributed representations in the visual system. In C. S. Harris (Ed.), *Visual coding and adaptability*. Hillsdale, N.J.: Lawrence Erlbaum Associates, 1980. **2,7,23**

Weisstein, N., Harris, C. S., Berbaum, K., Tangney, J., & Williams, A. Contrast reduction by small localized stimuli: Extensive spatial spread of above-threshold orientation-selective masking. *Vision Research*, 1977, *17*, 341-350. **7**

Weisstein, N., Ozog, G., & Szoc, R. A comparison and elaboration of two models of metacontrast. *Psychological Review*, 1975, *82*, 325-343. **7**

Weisstein, N., see Williams & Weisstein (1978).

Wertheimer, M. Experimentelle Studien über das Sehen von Bewegung. *Zeitschrift für Psychologie*, 1912, *61*, 161-265. (Translated in part in T. Shipley [Ed.], *Classics in psychology*. New York: Philosophical Library, 1961.) **311,425**

Wertheimer, M. Laws of organization in perceptual forms. In W. D. Ellis (Ed.), *A source book of Gestalt psychology*. London: Routledge & Kegan Paul, 1955. (First published in German, 1923.) **438**

Wertheimer, M. Principles of perceptual organization. In D. C. Beardslee & M. Wertheimer (Eds.), *Readings in perception*. Princeton, N.J.: Van Nostrand-Reinhold, 1958. (Originally published in German, 1923.) **425**

Wheeler, D. D. Processes in word recognition. *Cognitive Psychology*, 1970, *1*, 59-85. **166**

Wheeler, J. A. *Geometrodynamics*. New York: Academic Press, 1962. **401**

Wheeler, J. A. The universe as home for man. *American Scientist*, 1974, *62*, 683-691. **414**

White, C. W., & Lorber, C. M. Spatial-frequency specificity in visual masking. *Perception & Psychophysics*, 1976, *19*, 281-284. **7**

White, K. D., see Riggs, White, & Eimas (1974).

Whitlock, D., see Checkosky & Whitlock (1973).

Wiesel, T. N., see Hubel & Wiesel (1962).
Wiesel, T. N., see Hubel & Wiesel (1965).
Wiesel, T. N., see Hubel & Wiesel (1968).
Wiesel, T. N., see Hubel & Wiesel (1974).
Wightman, F. L. The pattern-transformation model of pitch. *Journal of the Acoustical Society of America*, 1973, *54*, 407–416. (a) **70,71**
Wightman, F. L. Pitch and stimulus fine structure. *Journal of the Acoustical Society of America*, 1973, *54*, 397–406. (b) **70,71**
Wightman, F. L., & Green, D. M. The perception of pitch. *American Scientist*, 1974, *62*, 208–215. **70**
Wigner, E. P. *Symmetries and reflections: Scientific essays of Eugene P. Wigner.* Cambridge, Mass.: M.I.T. Press, 1970. **384,414**
Williams, A., see Weisstein, Harris, Berbaum, Tangney, & Williams (1977).
Williams C. S., see Hock, Romanski, Galie, & Williams (1978).
Williams, D. W., & Wilson, H. R. Localized effects of spatial frequency adaptation. *Investigative Ophthalmology and Visual Science*, 1978, *17*(supplement), 243. (Abstract) **5**
Williams, M., & Weisstein, N. Line segments are perceived better in a coherent context than alone: An object-line effect in visual perception. *Memory & Cognition*, 1978, *6*, 85–90. **166,179**
Wilson, H. R. A synaptic model for spatial frequency adaptation. *Journal of Theoretical Biology*, 1975, *50*, 327–352. **6**
Wilson, H. R. Quantitative characterization of two types of line spread functions near the fovea. *Vision Research*, 1978, *18*, 971–982. **21**
Wilson, H. R., & Bergen, J. A four mechanism model for spatial vision. *Investigative Ophthalmology and Visual Science*, 1977, *16*(supplement), 46. (Abstract) **11,19,21,22**
Wilson, H. R., & Giese, J. Threshold visibility of frequency gradient patterns. *Vision Research*, 1977, *17*, 1177–1190. **19**
Wilson, H. R., see Williams & Wilson (1978).
Windelband, W. *A history of philosophy* (Vol. 1). New York: Harper Torchbooks, 1958. (Originally published, 1901.) **97**
Winkler, R., see Eigen & Winkler (1975).
Winston, P. H. Learning structural descriptions from examples. In P. H. Winston (Ed.), *The psychology of computer vision*. New York: McGraw-Hill, 1975. (Originally published, 1970.) **219,220,225,441**
Winston, P. H. (Ed.). *The psychology of computer vision.* New York: McGraw-Hill, 1975. **99,103, 309**
Wish, M., & Carroll, J. D. Applications of "INDSCAL" to studies of human perception and judgment. In E. C. Carterette & M. P. Friedman (Eds.), *Handbook of perception* (Vol. 2). New York: Academic Press, 1973. **325**
Wolf, W., see Lupp, Hauske, & Wolf (1976).
Wolfe, J. M., see Kinchla & Wolfe (1979).
Wolford, G. L. Perturbation model for letter identification. *Psychological Review*, 1975, *82*, 184–199. **198,208**
Wolford, G. L., & Hollingsworth, S. Evidence that short-term memory is not the limiting factor in the tachistoscopic full-report procedure. *Memory & Cognition*, 1974, *2*, 796–800. (a) **208**
Wolford, G. L., & Hollingsworth, S. Lateral masking in visual information processing. *Perception & Psychophysics*, 1974, *16*, 315–320. (b) **198**
Wolford, G. L., see Estes & Wolford (1971).
Wood, B., see Corteen & Wood (1972).
Woodworth, R. S. *Experimental psychology.* New York: Holt, 1938. **437**
von Wright, J. M. Selection in visual immediate memory. *Quarterly Journal of Experimental Psychology*, 1968, *20*, 62–68. **89,189**

von Wright, J. M. On selection in visual immediate memory. *Acta Psychologica*, 1970, *33*, 280–292. **189**

Wyatt, H. J. Singly and doubly contingent aftereffects involving color, orientation and spatial frequency. *Vision Research*, 1974, *14*, 1185–1193. **9**

Y

Yates, F. E., Marsh, D. J., & Iberall, A. S. Integration of the whole organism: A foundation for a theoretical biology. In J. A. Behnke (Ed.), *Challenging biological problems: Directions toward their solution*. New York: Oxford University Press, 1972. **357**

Yost, W. A., & Nielsen, D. W. *Fundamentals of hearing: An introduction*. New York: Holt, Rinehart & Winston, 1977. **67**

Young, J. Z. Why do we have two brains? In V. B. Mountcastle (Ed.), *Inter-hemispheric relations and cerebral dominance*. Baltimore, Md.: The Johns Hopkins University Press, 1962. **330,335**

Z

Zemon, V., see Green, Corwin, & Zemon (1976).

Zucker, S. W. Relaxation labelling and the reduction of local ambiguities. *Proceedings of the Third International Joint Conference on Pattern Recognition*. Long Beach, Ca.: IEEE Computer Society, 1976. **108**

Zuckerkandl, V. *Sound and symbol: Music and the external world*. Princeton, N.J.: Princeton University Press and Bollingen Foundation, 1969. (Originally published, 1956.) **77**

Zusne, L. *Visual perception of form*. New York: Academic Press, 1970. **427**

Zwislocki, J. J., see Smith & Zwislocki (1971).

Subject Index

499